Java™

Annotated Archives

ABOUT THE AUTHOR ...

Naba Barkakati, Ph.D., is an expert programmer and successful computer book author with experience in a wide variety of systems, from MS-DOS and Windows to UNIX, and in several programming languages, including C, C++, and Java. He bought his first personal computer—an IBM PC-AT—in 1984 after graduating with a Ph.D. in electrical engineering from the University of Maryland at College Park, Maryland. While pursuing a full-time career in engineering, Naba dreamed of writing software for the emerging PC software market. As luck would have it, instead of building a software empire like Microsoft, in 1987 he ended up writing *The Waite Group's Microsoft C Bible*—a tutorial-reference book that started a new trend in computer book publishing.

Over the past twelve years, Naba has written 23 computer books on a number of topics ranging from object-oriented programming in C++ to Linux. He has authored several best-selling titles, such as *The Waite Group's Turbo C++ Bible*, *Object-Oriented Programming in C++*, *X Window System Programming*, *Visual C++ Developer's Guide*, and *Borland C++ 4 Developer's Guide*. Naba's books have been translated into many languages, including Spanish, French, Dutch, Polish, Greek, Italian, Russian, Chinese, Japanese, and Korean. His most recent book is *Red Hat Linux SECRETS, Second Edition*, published by IDG Books.

Naba lives in North Potomac, Maryland, with his wife, Leha, and their children, Ivy, Emily, and Ashley.

Java™

Annotated Archives

Naba Barkakati, Ph.D.

Osborne **McGraw-Hill**

Berkeley   New York   St. Louis   San Francisco   Auckland   Bogotá
Hamburg   London   Madrid   Mexico City   Milan   Montreal   New Delhi
Panama City   Paris   São Paulo   Singapore   Sydney   Tokyo   Toronto

Osborne/McGraw-Hill
2600 Tenth Street
Berkeley, California 94710
U.S.A.

For information on translations or book distributors outside the U.S.A., or to arrange bulk purchase discounts for sales promotions, premiums, or fund-raisers, please contact Osborne/**McGraw-Hill** at the above address.

Java™ Annotated Archives

1234567890 AGM AGM 90198765432109

ISBN 0-07-211902-0

Publisher	**Copy Editor**
Brandon A. Nordin	Rebecca Pepper
Associate Publisher and Editor-in-Chief	**Proofreader**
Scott Rogers	Paul Tyler
Acquisitions Editor	**Indexer**
Wendy Rinaldi	Valerie Robbins
Project Editor	**Computer Designer**
Madhu Prasher	Roberta Steele
	Gary Corrigan
Editorial Assistant	**Illustrators**
Monika Faltiss	Beth Young
Technical Editor	Brian Wells
Greg Guntle	**Series Design**
	Roberta Steele
	Peter F. Hancik

To my wife, Leha, and our daughters, Ivy, Emily, and Ashley

Contents at a Glance

PART 4
Servlets

Contents

PART 1
Applets

PART 2

JavaBeans

PART 3

Java Applications

Acknowledgments

I am grateful to Wendy Rinaldi for providing me the opportunity to write a book that presents practical Java programming tips through annotated source code. Thanks to Scott Rogers for initiating the Annotated Archives series and for trusting me to write the Java title for the series.

Monika Faltiss kept everything moving in the manuscript submission process. As the Project Editor, Madhu Prasher coordinated the copyediting and proofreading and guided the book through production. I appreciate the support both of you have given me during this project.

Thanks to everyone at Osborne/McGraw-Hill who worked behind the scenes to transform my raw manuscript into this well-edited and beautifully packaged book. In particular, thanks to Rebecca Pepper for the thorough copyediting, George Anderson for making the necessary arrangements for the companion CD-ROM, and Ann Sellers and Jean Butterfield for taking care of the book's production.

I would like to thank Greg Guntle for reviewing the manuscript for technical accuracy and for testing the programs included on the CD-ROM. Greg provided many useful suggestions for improving the book's content.

Finally, I am most thankful to my wife, Leha, and our daughters, Ivy, Emily, and Ashley—it is their love and support that keeps me going.

Introduction

In the short time since version 1.0 was released in January 1995, Java has captured the hearts and minds of millions of programmers. Java is an object-oriented programming language that began life as a language for embedded systems—small computers that control electronic devices. As such, Java was designed to be portable; Java programs are compiled into bytecodes that can be executed by a Java Virtual Machine (JVM). This means that a Java program can be executed anywhere a JVM is available.

The world got its first taste of Java in 1996, when Netscape incorporated a JVM into its Web browser, thereby enabling Web pages with executable content—small Java application programs called *applets* that are downloaded and executed on the user's system where the Web browser runs. To be more precise, these applets are transmitted as sequences of bytes that are executed by the JVM embedded in the Web browser.

Java applets are popular because they allow Web sites to provide information in a unique way. Programmers can write an applet that downloads data from the Web server and plots the data in various ways based on the user's selection. The key is that the Web server sends the applet's code and the applet then downloads the data once. After that, all data manipulation and display is handled by the applet running inside the Java-capable Web browser.

Java's use has extended beyond applets (which are embedded in the HTML code of a Web page) to general-purpose applications that do not have to run inside a Web browser. Many organizations now use Java for developing mission-critical applications, including three-tiered Web applications that provide access to the corporate databases that often reside on older mainframe systems.

The popularity of Java has spawned a huge market for Java books. According to a recent count, there are several hundred books on Java. There is no shortage of Java tutorials that teach Java programming or reference guides that provide detailed information about Java classes. However, programmers often look for sample code to perform a specific programming task—anything from displaying a ticker tape in a

Web page to accessing a database. The existing crop of books does not focus on this need. The only option for developers is to search on the Internet, but that takes time, and often the code samples are not easy to understand. What Java developers need is a collection of practical code samples with expert advice on how to use the code.

Java Annotated Archives is a source code archive designed to address these needs. A companion CD-ROM includes all of the source code presented in the book. In keeping with the *Annotated Archives* series, this book provides detailed commentary on how the code works and how to use the code.

What makes *Java Annotated Archives* unique are the tips, techniques, and shortcuts for using sample Java source code in various real-world tasks that range from animating an advertisement banner on a Web page to three-tiered Web applications for your business.

By reading *Java Annotated Archives*, you get the following benefits:

◆ Receive a CD-ROM containing all source code from the book and ready-to-run Java programs

◆ Find sample code to perform a specific task

◆ Learn how the sample code works

◆ Learn how to customize and use the sample code for various tasks

◆ Learn about Java resources that can serve as continuing sources for information in the ever-changing world of Java

Organization of the Book

Java Annotated Archives has 14 chapters organized into four parts, and an appendix:

◆ **Part 1: Applets** focuses on applets—small programs that run inside a Java-capable Web browser and often interact with other servers on a network. Part 1 is organized into six chapters, each of which is devoted to a specific category of applets. These categories are Web page enhancements, business and finance, network and communications, multimedia, games, and tools and utilities.

◆ **Part 2: JavaBeans** provides code samples showing JavaBeans—reusable components that developers can plug together to make Java applications. There are two chapters in this part of the book: one covers components with visible beans that display some output, and the other focuses on invisible beans that perform some computation.

◆ **Part 3: Java Applications** has six chapters that cover both stand-alone and client/server applications. These chapters show how Java is used to develop many different types of applications as a general-purpose programming language like C++. This part includes examples of applications with a graphical user interface (GUI) that does not need a Web browser to run. One of the chapters focuses on Java database applications that use Java Database Connectivity (JDBC) to access databases.

◆ **Part 4: Servlets** presents Java programs that execute in a Web server in response to requests from a Web browser. Servlets are considered more powerful than the CGI programs commonly used as gateways between Web servers and other services such as databases. This part has two chapters that illustrate several applications that use servlets.

◆ **Appendix: Java Resources** lists resources on the Internet where the user can obtain the latest information about Java (including more source code samples).

You will typically look up a chapter based on the chapter title, which reflects the category of programming task. The chapter cover page shows the names of the programs presented in the chapter. You can then browse through the program most likely to fit the programming task at hand. You may also use the index to locate specific sample code, using keywords such as *JDBC* to find programs that use the Java Database Connectivity API (application programming interface).

Conventions Used in This Book

Java Annotated Archives uses a simple notational style. All listings are typeset in a monospace font for ease of reading. Because this book's focus is on code with commentary, the listings include line numbers and the annotations refer to specific lines by line number.

All file names, function names, variable names, and keywords appearing in text are shown in **boldface**. The first occurrence of new terms and concepts is in *italic*. In listings, the text you are directed to type is in *italic*.

Following the conventions of the Osborne/McGraw-Hill *Annotated Archives* series, I have used a few notes and icons to help you pinpoint useful information quickly:

This icon highlights a feature of Java 2, the latest version of Java.

Java 2

PROGRAMMER'S NOTE *These notes sit apart from the rest of the text and provide some helpful information or tip to the programmer.*

Applets

Web Page Enhancements

Business and Finance

Networking and Communications

Multimedia

Games

Tools and Utilities

Web Page Enhancements

An Animated Text Banner (AnimateText)

A Fading Text Banner (FadeText)

A Rainbow-Colored Animated Ruler (RainbowRuler)

An Image Button (ImageButton)

A Drop-Down Menu (DropDownMenu)

A Scrolling LED Ticker (LEDTicker)

Java first became popular as a programming language for writing *applets*—small application programs that can be embedded in a Web page. When a user views a Web page on a Web browser, any embedded applets are downloaded and executed on the user's system. To be more precise, these Java programs are transmitted as sequences of bytes that can be executed by a Java Virtual Machine (JVM) embedded in the Web browser. To run Java applets, all a user needs is a Java-capable Web browser such as Netscape Navigator 2.0 or later or Microsoft Internet Explorer 3.0 or later.

Java applets are often used to add special effects that enhance the appearance of a Web page. For example, you may have seen Web sites with messages that scroll across the screen similar to stock tickers. Or you may have noticed Web pages with multicolored text that jumps around in a frame. Most of these special effects include some animation—some feature that changes over time—and serve as a link to other Web pages. For example, when the user clicks on an animated banner, the browser displays a new Web page.

This chapter shows you several Java applets that add different types of special effects to a Web page. You can study these applets and then write your own, or you can adapt them for your own use. You will find the following applets in this chapter:

- ◆ **AnimateText**—Multicolored animated text messages
- ◆ **FadeText**—Text banners that fade into the background
- ◆ **RainbowRuler**—An animated rainbow-colored horizontal ruler
- ◆ **ImageButton**—A button that displays an image and acts as a link
- ◆ **DropDownMenu**—A drop-down list of links
- ◆ **LEDTicker**—A scrolling ticker message on an electronic message board

An Animated Text Banner

Sometimes you want to draw attention to a message displayed in a Web page. You could use features of Hypertext Markup Language (HTML)—the language used to lay out Web pages—and display the text in different fonts or colors. However, that still leaves you with a static rendering of the message. You can capture the user's attention better by animating the message—displaying it in colors that change over time and moving the letters around so that the message seems to come alive on the browser's screen. The **AnimateText** applet does just that.

Using AnimateText

Before you learn the programming details of the **AnimateText** applet, you should see how it works. You should also understand how to configure the applet through parameters specified in the HTML file that embeds the applet. The **ch01\AnimText** directory of the companion CD-ROM includes all the files you need to try out the **AnimateText** applet.

To see the **AnimateText** applet in action, follow these steps:

1. Insert this book's companion CD-ROM into your system's CD-ROM drive. On UNIX systems, you also have to mount the CD-ROM with the **mount** command.

2. Start a Java-capable Web browser.

3. Using the browser's File | Open command, open the HTML file **AnimTest.html** in the **ch01\AnimText** directory of the CD-ROM.

As the **AnimateText** applet runs, it animates a text message (specified through a <param> tag, as you will see in the next section). A typical frame of animated text looks like this:

If you have the Java Development Kit installed on your system, you can also test the **AnimateText** applet using the **appletviewer** tool (**appletviewer** is a utility program that can load an HTML file and execute any applet embedded in that file), as follows:

```
appletviewer AnimTest.html
```

When you use **AnimateText** in an HTML document, you can configure several of its parameters. This is done through <param> tags that appear within the <applet> tag. For example, here is the **AnimTest.html** file that you used when trying out the **AnimateText** applet:

```
<html>
<body>
```

```
<applet code="AnimateText.class" width=350 height=60>
<param name=text value="Animated Text">
<param name=delay value=250>
</applet>

</body>
</html>
```

This minimal HTML file embeds the **AnimateText** applet, using the **<applet>** tag. The body of this tag includes everything between the **<applet>** and **</applet>** tags. Note that HTML tags are not case-sensitive, so you can write the tags in uppercase, lowercase, and even mixed case. I am used to the lazy programmer's style of typing everything in lowercase.

In this example, the **<applet>** tag has three attributes:

- **code="AnimateText.class"** specifies the name of the Java applet's class.
- **width=350** specifies the applet's display width as 350 pixels.
- **height=60** specifies the applet's display height as 60 pixels.

In addition to these three attributes, the **<applet>** tag accepts several other attributes, but these three are the minimum necessary to embed the applet in the HTML document.

Between the opening **<applet>** tag and the closing **</applet>** tag appears one or more **<param>** tags. These tags allow users to specify various parameters that essentially configure the applet. For example, the **AnimateText** applet accepts two parameters:

- **text**—the text to be animated
- **delay**—the number of milliseconds between successive animation steps

In the **AnimTest.html** file, these parameters are specified by the following **<param>** tags:

```
<param name=text value="Animated Text">
<param name=delay value=250>
```

Nearly all useful applets, including **AnimateText**, are designed to accept parameters through the **<param>** tag. After all, if the text message were hard-coded into the **AnimateText** applet's source code, you would have to edit the source code and recompile whenever the message changed.

AnimateText

Understanding AnimateText

Now that you have seen the **AnimateText** applet in action and learned how to configure it through parameters, let's turn to the Java program **AnimateText.java**, which implements this applet. The following listing shows the **AnimateText.java** program in its entirety.

```
1  //----------------------------------------------------------------
2  // File: AnimateText.java
3  //
4  // Animates a text message by displaying the letters in
5  // random colors and by making the letters jump around.
6  //
7  // Compile with: javac AnimateText.java
8  //
9  // Author: Naba Barkakati
10 //----------------------------------------------------------------
11 // Imports for this applet
12 import java.awt.*;
13 import java.applet.*;
14
15 // Documentation for javadoc
16 /**
17  * The AnimateText class is a Java applet that animates a text
18  * message, using random colors for the letters. The applet uses
19  * a thread to repeatedly redraw the message after a
20  * specified delay.
21  * <p>
22  * Use the &#60;applet&#62; tag to embed the animated text in an
23  * HTML file. Parameters accepted by the AnimateText applet:
24  * <ul>
25  *    <li> text      - string with message to be animated
26  *    <li> delay     - integer denoting delay in milliseconds
27  * </ul>
28  *
29  * @author Naba Barkakati
30  * @version 1.1 August 16, 1998
31  */
32 public class AnimateText extends java.applet.Applet
33                                         implements Runnable
34 {
```

```
35     String message = null;// Text being animated
36     int delay = 200;        // Delay between successive redrawing
37     Dimension size;         // Size of applet's display area
38     Image oIm;              // Off-screen image
                               //   for double buffering
39     Graphics oGC;           // Graphics context to draw off-screen
40     Font font;              // Font used to display text
41     FontMetrics fm;         // Various dimensions of the font
42     int textHeight;         // Height of the characters
43     int baseline;           // Baseline for the characters
44     Color colors[] = new Color[10]; // Colors for characters
45     Thread animThread = null;       // Thread to animate text
46 //-----------------------------------------------------------------
47     /** Class initialization method */
48     public void init()
49     {
50 // Get the size of applet's display area
51        size = size(); // use getSize() in Java 1.1.6 or later
52
53 // Get the parameters from the <applet> tag
54        message = getParameter("text");
55        if(message == null) message = "Animated Text";
56
57        String p = getParameter("delay");
58        if(p != null) delay = Integer.valueOf(p).intValue();
59        if(delay < 10) delay = 100;
60
61 // Select text height such that the message fits in the
62 // width specified in the <applet> tag.
63        Graphics g = getGraphics();
64        textHeight = size.height - 8;
65        int maxWidth = size.width - (message.length() +1)*4 - 8;
66
67        int width = maxWidth+1;
68        while(width > maxWidth)
69        {
70          font = new Font("Helvetica", Font.BOLD, textHeight);
71          g.setFont(font);
72          fm = g.getFontMetrics();
73          width = fm.stringWidth(message);
74          if(width > maxWidth) textHeight--;
75        }
```

```
76          baseline = size.height - fm.getMaxDescent();
77  // Initialize an array of colors using the predefined colors
78          colors[0] = Color.blue;
79          colors[1] = Color.cyan;
80          colors[2] = Color.gray;
81          colors[3] = Color.green;
82          colors[4] = Color.magenta;
83          colors[5] = Color.orange;
84          colors[6] = Color.pink;
85          colors[7] = Color.red;
86          colors[8] = Color.white;
87          colors[9] = Color.yellow;
88  // Set up the off-screen image and Graphics context
89          oIm = createImage(size.width, size.height);
90          oGC = oIm.getGraphics();
91
92      }
93  //-------------------------------------------------------------
94      /** Starts applet by creating the animation thread */
95      public void start()
96      {
97          if(animThread == null)
98          {
99  // Create a thread to animate the text and start the thread
100             animThread = new Thread(this);
101             animThread.start();
102         }
103     }
104 //-------------------------------------------------------------
105     /** Stops the applet by stopping the animation thread */
106     public void stop()
107     {
108 // Stop the animation thread
109         if(animThread != null)
110         {
111             animThread.stop();
112             animThread = null;
113         }
114     }
115 //-------------------------------------------------------------
116     /** Updates the display (calls paint() immediately) */
117     public void update(Graphics g) { paint(g); }
```

```
118  //------------------------------------------------------------------
119      /** Displays the text in the applet */
120      public void paint(Graphics g)
121      {
122          Color bgColor = getBackground();
123          oGC.setColor(bgColor);
124          oGC.setFont(font);
125  // Clear the display area
126          oGC.fillRect(0, 0, size.width, size.height);
127  // Display each letter using a random color and a
128  // random position (near its normal position)
129          int x = 0, y;
130          for(int i = 0; i < message.length(); i++)
131          {
132  // Set the location of the letter
133              x += (int)(Math.random()*8);
134              y = baseline - (int)(Math.random()*8);
135  // Randomly pick color for this letter (but make
136  // sure color is not same as background)
137              Color color;
138              do
139              {
140                  int j = (int)((Math.random()+0.1)*9);
141                  color = colors[j];
142              }while(bgColor.equals(color));
143              oGC.setColor(color);
144  // Pick a substring consisting of a single letter
145              String s = message.substring(i, i+1);
146  // Now print this letter to the offscreen image
147              oGC.drawString(s, x, y);
148              x += fm.stringWidth(s);
149          }
150          g.drawImage(oIm, 0, 0, this);
151      }
152  //------------------------------------------------------------------
153      /** Runs the animation thread. */
154      public void run()
155      {
156          while(true)
157          {
158              try
159              {
```

```
160        repaint();
161        Thread.sleep(delay);
162      }
163    catch(InterruptedException e) {stop();}
164  }
165 }
166 }
```

ANNOTATIONS

The **AnimateText** applet is designed to accept two user-provided parameters: the text message to animate and the delay between successive steps of animation. The user specifies these parameters through **<param>** tags. The applet reads these parameters in its **init()** method by calling **getParameter()**.

AnimateText uses a thread to perform animation. By design, an applet is loaded and executed by another program such as a Web browser or **appletviewer**. The applet simply provides methods that are invoked by the browser when needed. For example, the browser calls the applet's **paint()** method when the applet's display area has to be redrawn. The basic idea of the animation is to draw something different each time **paint()** is called and to make sure that **paint()** is called frequently enough to give the appearance of movement. To accomplish this, the applet has to create a new thread of execution. The **AnimateText** applet creates the **animThread** thread and starts running it in the **start()** method. Also, the applet implements the **Runnable** interface by defining the **run()** method. When the thread starts, it calls the **run()** method. The **run()** method then repaints the applet's display, sleeps for a specified number of milliseconds, and repeats this process until the thread is stopped.

AnimateText also uses an off-screen image to make the animation appear smooth. The applet's **paint()** method first draws each frame of the animation on the off-screen image and then copies the off-screen image to the applet's display area. This animation technique is also known as *double buffering*. Without double buffering, the animation would appear to flicker because the applet's display area has to be cleared and redrawn for each frame.

STRUCTURE OF ANIMATETEXT.JAVA   When you want to understand how an applet (or any other program) is implemented, it's helpful to look at the skeletal structure of the applet before studying the details of each of the methods within the applet's body. You can get the skeletal view of an applet by retaining key statements such as class and method declarations but discarding detailed code in the body of methods. Using this approach, I created the following skeleton of

AnimateText.java, showing the key elements (and some comments in italics to help you understand each element):

```
11  // Imports for this applet
12  import java.awt.*;
13  import java.applet.*;
... List of classes and packages used by this applet
15  // Documentation for javadoc
16  /**
... Comments used by the automatic documentation tool
31   */
32  public class AnimateText extends java.applet.Applet
33                                          implements Runnable
34  {
35      String message = null;// Text being animated
36      int delay = 200;      // Delay between successive redrawing
...
48      public void init()
49      {
...        body of init() method
92      }
95      public void start()
96      {
...        body of start() method
103     }
106     public void stop()
107     {
...        body of stop() method
114     }
117     public void update(Graphics g) { paint(g); }
120     public void paint(Graphics g)
121     {
...        body of paint() method
151     }
154     public void run()
155     {
...        body of run() method
165     }
166 }
```

As this skeletal view shows, the **AnimateText** applet has essentially the same structure as any other Java applet. **AnimateText** is a subclass of the **Applet** class in the **java.applet** package (the full name of the class is **java.applet.Applet**). Inside the class body (lines 34 through 166), you see a number of methods such as **init()**, **start()**,

stop(), **update()**, and **paint()**. Because this applet performs animation using a thread, it also includes a **run()** method. The next few sections further describe these methods and how they display and animate text.

The **import** statements on lines 12 and 13 specify the Java packages this applet needs. This applet imports classes from the **java.applet** and the **java.awt** packages. The **java.applet** package defines the **Applet** class from which the **AnimateText** class is derived. The **java.awt** package includes the classes constituting Java's Abstract Windowing Toolkit (AWT)—everything you need to create user interfaces and display images and text in a Java program.

When an applet needs several classes from a package, it is common practice to append an asterisk to the package name. For example, the following statement imports all classes in the **java.awt** package:

```
12  import java.awt.*;
```

ANIMATETEXT CLASS DECLARATION   Lines 32 and 33 declare the **AnimateText** class as follows:

```
32  public class AnimateText extends java.applet.Applet
33                                          implements Runnable
```

Because **AnimateText** is an applet, it has to be a subclass of **java.applet.Applet**. **AnimateText** also uses a thread for animation, and to construct the thread it needs a class that implements the **Runnable** interface. In this case, the **AnimateText** class itself implements the **Runnable** interface, which involves defining the **run()** method that will be called by the thread.

Lines 34 through 166 constitute the body of the **AnimateText** class. This is where the class variables and methods are defined.

VARIABLES   Lines 35 through 45 declare the variables used in the **AnimateText** class. The user-defined parameters—the text message and the delay between animation frames—are stored in the following variables:

```
35      String message = null;// Text being animated
36      int delay = 200;       // Delay between successive redrawing
```

The text is stored in a **String** object, and the delay (in milliseconds) is stored as an integer.

The applet also needs other variables, such as the dimensions of the applet's display area, the off-screen image, the graphics context for drawing on the off-screen image, information about the font used to display the text, and the colors used to animate the letters of the message. These variables are declared as follows:

```
37      Dimension size;        // Size of applet's display area
38      Image oIm;             // Off-screen image for double buffering
39      Graphics oGC;          // Graphics context to draw off-screen
```

```
40    Font font;              // Font used to display text
41    FontMetrics fm;         // Various dimensions of the font
42    int textHeight;         // Height of the characters
43    int baseline;           // Baseline for the characters
44    Color colors[] = new Color[10]; // Colors for characters
```

Finally, the **animThread** variable represents the thread that performs the animation:

```
45    Thread animThread = null;        // Thread to animate text
```

APPLET INITIALIZATION   The applet's **init()** method is called when the applet is first loaded by the Web browser or **appletviewer**. In **AnimateText**, the **init()** method first gets the size of the applet's window by calling the **size()** method (this method is defined in the **Component** class, which is the superclass of **Applet**):

```
50  // Get the size of applet's display area
51        size = size(); // use getSize() in Java 1.1.6 or later
```

Java 2

The **size()** method is *deprecated* in Java 1.1.6; this means that the **size()** method is replaced by a newer method, called **getSize()**. Unfortunately, most Web browsers do not yet support Java 1.1.6 or later versions, and attempting to run the applet in such a browser generates a **java.lang.NoSuchMethodError** exception. That's why the **AnimateText** applet uses the **size()** method instead of the recommended **getSize()** method.

After getting the size of the applet's display area, the **init()** method gets the values of the user-provided parameters from the HTML file's **<param>** tags. Each parameter value is obtained by calling the **getParameter()** method of the **Applet** class. The **getParameter()** method is called with the name of the parameter as an argument, and it returns the parameter's value as a **String**. The **message** variable is a **String**, so the value returned by **getParameter("text")** is assigned to **message**, as shown in line 54:

```
54        message = getParameter("text");
55        if(message == null) message = "Animated Text";
```

You do, however, have to check for the condition that the returned value is **null**. The **getParameter()** method returns **null** if none of the **<param>** tags in the HTML file define the requested parameter's value. In this case, line 55 sets the **message** variable to a default value.

When reading an integer value with the **getParam()** method, you have to first store the **String** and then convert it to an integer. Lines 57 and 58 show how this is done:

```
57        String p = getParameter("delay");
58        if(p != null) delay = Integer.valueOf(p).intValue();
```

Typically, after reading an integer parameter, you should check whether the value is acceptable. For example, if the value of **delay** is less than 10 milliseconds, line 59 sets **delay** to 100 milliseconds:

```
59          if(delay < 10) delay = 100;
```

After reading in the parameters from the HTML file, the **init()** method selects the largest font size that can be used to display the message. The code in lines 63 through 75 performs this task:

```
63          Graphics g = getGraphics();
64          textHeight = size.height - 8;
65          int maxWidth = size.width - (message.length() +1)*4 - 8;
66
67          int width = maxWidth+1;
68          while(width > maxWidth)
69          {
70             font = new Font("Helvetica", Font.BOLD, textHeight);
71             g.setFont(font);
72             fm = g.getFontMetrics();
73             width = fm.stringWidth(message);
74             if(width > maxWidth) textHeight--;
75          }
```

Line 63 initializes the variable **g** with the graphics context of the applet; this is needed to create and try out fonts. Line 64 sets the **textHeight** variable, denoting the font size, to a value slightly less than the height, **size.height**, of the applet's display area, leaving some room for a border. The **maxWidth** variable (line 65) is set to the maximum number of pixels available for the horizontal extent of the message.

The **while** loop in lines 68 through 75 iterates through different font sizes until the entire message can be displayed within **maxWidth** pixels. In each iteration of the loop, a new font is created (line 70), the font is set in the graphics context (line 71), the font dimensions are obtained (line 72), and the message width in pixels is obtained (line 73). Then, in line 74, if the width exceeds **maxWidth**, the font size is reduced by 1.

After exiting the **while** loop, the applet computes the location of the baseline of the text message on line 76:

```
76          baseline = size.height - fm.getMaxDescent();
```

The **fm.getMaxDescent()** method (of the **FontMetrics** class) returns the maximum descent—the amount by which any character of this font extends below the baseline.

Next, lines 78 through 87 of the **init()** method initialize the **colors[]** array, which is an array of ten **Color** objects. The color values, such as **Color.white** and **Color.yellow**, are defined as static variables of the **Color** class in the **java.awt** package.

Finally, lines 89 and 90 set up the off-screen image for animation and a graphics context used to draw in the off-screen image:

```
89      oIm = createImage(size.width, size.height);
90      oGC = oIm.getGraphics();
```

Here **oIm** is an **Image** object and **oGC** is a **Graphics** object.

APPLET STARTUP AND SHUTDOWN   The Web browser calls the **start()** method (lines 95 through 103) to start executing the applet. Because **AnimateText** uses the thread **animThread** for animation, the body of the **start()** method creates and starts the thread, as follows:

```
97      if(animThread == null)
98      {
99 // Create a thread to animate the text and start the thread
100         animThread = new Thread(this);
101         animThread.start();
102     }
```

The **Thread** object **animThread** is created by calling its constructor and providing a **Runnable** object as an argument. In this case, the **AnimateText** class itself implements the **Runnable** interface, so the keyword **this** is used as the argument to the **Thread()** constructor in line 100. The **this** keyword refers to the current object, which, in this case, is the **AnimateText** applet.

As soon as **animThread.start()** is called on line 101, the Java Virtual Machine calls the **run()** method of the **Runnable** object that was used to create **animThread**. In this case, the thread was created using the **AnimateText** applet, so the **run()** method of the **AnimateText** object is called. From this point on, there are two concurrent threads of execution: one is the current thread that returns from the **start()** method, and the other is the body of the **run()** method. In other words, after **animThread.start()** is called, the **run()** method begins to execute as a separate thread of execution.

When the Web browser wants to stop the applet (for example, when the user clicks on a link and goes to another Web page), the browser calls the **stop()** method (lines 106 through 114) of the applet. The **stop()** method calls the **animThread** object's **stop()** method and sets **animThread** to **null**, as shown in lines 109 through 113:

```
109     if(animThread != null)
110     {
111         animThread.stop();
112         animThread = null;
113     }
```

ANIMATION THREAD EXECUTION   The **run()** method, shown in lines 154 through 165, is the body of the thread of execution that constitutes the **animThread** object.

You can essentially think of everything inside the **run()** method as a separate program that shares the variables and methods that are defined within the **AnimateText** class. The body of the **run()** method is simple:

```
158            try
159            {
160                repaint();
161                Thread.sleep(delay);
162            }
163            catch(InterruptedException e) {stop();}
```

A **try** block (lines 159 and 162) encloses the main steps of animation. The code first calls the applet's **repaint()** method to request a redrawing of the applet. The **repaint()** method causes a call to the applet's **update()** method as soon as possible. Then the **Thread.sleep()** method is called to cause this thread to suspend execution for the number of milliseconds specified by the **delay** variable.

If the thread is interrupted, the **catch()** block on line 163 calls the **stop()** method to stop the applet.

TEXT ANIMATION   When the **repaint()** method is called, the Web browser (or **appletviewer**) schedules a call to the **update()** method as soon as possible. In **AnimateText**, the **update()** method (line 117) immediately calls the **paint()** method to redraw the text in the applet's display area.

The **paint()** method (lines 120 through 151) is where each animation frame is composed and displayed. The frame is composed by drawing on the off-screen image, and the current frame is displayed by copying the off-screen image to the applet's display area.

The first step in drawing on the off-screen image is to clear the image by filling it with the background color. This is accomplished in lines 122 through 126:

```
122            Color bgColor = getBackground();
123            oGC.setColor(bgColor);
124            oGC.setFont(font);
125    // Clear the display area
126                oGC.fillRect(0, 0, size.width, size.height);
```

Line 122 gets the current background color. That color and the current font are set in the graphics context for the off-screen image (lines 123 and 124). Then the entire off-screen image is filled in with that color (line 126).

Lines 129 through 149 draw the text message, one letter at a time. The **for** loop (lines 130 through 149) goes through the letters one by one.

```
130            for(int i = 0; i < message.length(); i++)
131                {
...    body of for loop
149                }
```

For each letter, a random x and y position are computed:

```
133                  x += (int)(Math.random()*8);
134                  y = baseline - (int)(Math.random()*8);
```

Both of these coordinates are just slightly offset from the normal position of the letter. The **Math.random()** method returns a random number between 0.0 and 1.0. Line 133 multiplies this random number by 8 and casts it as an integer to get a value between 0 and 8. This random offset is then added to the nominal x coordinate of the letter. Line 134 applies a similar random offset to the y coordinate.

Next, lines 137 through 142 select a random color for the letter. The **do-while** loop in lines 138 through 142 performs this task:

```
138                  do
139                  {
140                      int j = (int)((Math.random()+0.1)*9);
141                      color = colors[j];
142                  }while(bgColor.equals(color));
```

Line 140 computes an index between 0 and 9 and then picks the color from the **colors[]** array. However, line 142 repeats the **do** loop if the selected color is the same as the background color, which is stored in the **bgColor** object. Line 142 uses the **equals()** method of the **Color** object to determine whether the selected color is equal to the background color.

After a color has been selected, line 143 sets that color in the off-screen image's graphics context:

```
143                  oGC.setColor(color);
```

The current letter is then assigned to a **String**, as shown in line 145:

```
145                  String s = message.substring(i, i+1);
```

The **substring()** method of the **String** class is used to extract the single letter into the **String s**.

Line 147 calls the **drawString()** method of the off-screen graphics context (**oGC**) to draw the **String s** at the previously computed x and y coordinates:

```
147                  oGC.drawString(s, x, y);
```

Line 148 then advances the x coordinate to the next character's nominal position:

```
148                  x += fm.stringWidth(s);
```

Finally, the **for** loop is repeated with the next letter until all of the letters are displayed.

After the off-screen image is ready, line 150 performs the final step of copying the off-screen image to the applet's display area:

```
150         g.drawImage(oIm, 0, 0, this);
```

EMBEDDED DOCUMENTATION   You should also take note of another useful item in the **AnimateText.java** file. The file includes embedded comments that can be extracted with the **javadoc** tool that comes with the Java Development Kit. For example, consider lines 16 through 31, which appear immediately before the **AnimateText** class declaration. These comment lines have the following structure (my comments are in italic):

```
16  /**
... comment lines that begin with * and may include HTML tags
28  *     (a blank line precedes the @author and @version lines)
29  * @author Naba Barkakati
30  * @version 1.1 August 16, 1998
31  */
... class declaration follows end of comment block
```

These documentation comment blocks must begin with /** (note the two asterisks) and end with */. Each line within the block may begin with an asterisk that **javadoc** ignores. After a brief description of the class, there must be a blank line of comment. Then you can place the **@author** and **@version** tags with author and version information.

You can also embed documentation for each public method in the class. Just place the /** ... */ comment block immediately before each method declaration.

To generate the class documentation from the **AnimateText.java** file, run **javadoc** with the following command:

```
javadoc AnimateText.java
```

You'll see the following output from **javadoc**:

```
Generating package.html
Generating documentation for class AnimateText
Generating index
Sorting 7 items...done
Generating tree
```

To view the documentation generated by **javadoc**, open the **AnimateText.html** file (created by **javadoc**) in a Web browser. Figure 1-1 shows the documentation generated by **javadoc** after it processes the **AnimateText.java** file.

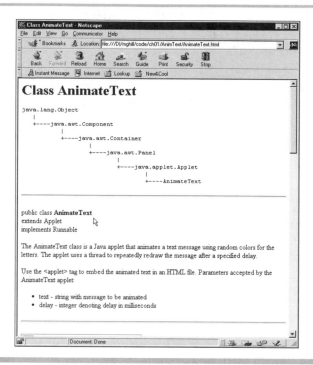

FIGURE 1-1.   Documentation for the **AnimateText** class, generated by the
javadoc tool.

A Fading Text Banner

As the previous section's **AnimateText** applet shows, rendering a message in
multicolored letters and animating the letters is one way to attract users' attention.
Another way is with a fading text banner, in which the message gradually fades into
the background. The **FadeText** applet lets you specify several messages, choose the
text color, and choose the background color through the **<param>** tags in the HTML
file. **FadeText** then cycles through the messages, fading each one from full
brightness into the background.

Using FadeText

The **ch01\FadeText** directory of the companion CD-ROM includes all of the files you
need to try out the **FadeText** applet. You should first see the applet in action and then
study the HTML file to learn how to specify parameter values for the applet. Then you
can go through the **FadeText.java** file and learn how the applet works.

To try out the **FadeText** applet, follow these steps:

1. Insert this book's companion CD-ROM into your system's CD-ROM drive. On UNIX systems, you also have to mount the CD-ROM with the **mount** command.

2. Start a Java-capable Web browser.

3. Using the browser's File | Open command, open the HTML file **TestFade.html** from the **ch01\FadeText** directory of the CD-ROM.

As the **FadeText** applet runs, it animates a text message (specified through a **<param>** tag, as you will see in the next section).

If you have the Java Development Kit installed on your system, you can also test the **FadeText** applet using the **appletviewer** tool, which can load an HTML file and execute any applet embedded in that file. The command line for loading the **TestFade.html** file into **appletviewer** is as follows:

```
appletviewer TestFade.html
```

When you use the **FadeText** applet in an HTML document, you can configure its parameters through **<param>** tags that appear within the **<applet>** tag. For example, here is the **TestFade.html** file that you used when trying out the **FadeText** applet:

```
<html>
<body>

<applet code="FadeText.class" width=350 height=40>
<param name=messages value="FadeText applet|by Naba Barkakati|One
message|fades into the next...">
<param name=textcolor value="ffffff">
<param name=bgcolor value="0000ff">
<param name=delay value=75>
</applet>

</body>
</html>
```

This HTML file embeds the **FadeText** applet, using the **<applet>** tag. In this example, the **<applet>** tag has three attributes:

◆   **code="FadeText.class"** specifies the name of the Java applet's class.

◆   **width=350** specifies the applet's display width as 350 pixels.

◆   **height=40** specifies the applet's display height as 40 pixels.

The **<param>** tags are placed between the opening **<applet>** tag and the closing **</applet>** tag. Through the **<param>** tags you can specify various parameters that configure the **FadeText** applet. The **FadeText** applet accepts four parameters:

◆ **messages**—the text messages, separated by |

◆ **textcolor**—the color for the text in hexadecimal format

◆ **bgcolor**—the background color in hexadecimal format

◆ **delay**—the number of milliseconds between successive fade steps

In the **TestFade.html** file, these parameters are specified by the following **<param>** tags:

```
<param name=messages value="FadeText applet|by Naba Barkakati|One
message|fades into the next...">
<param name=textcolor value="ffffff">
<param name=bgcolor value="0000ff">
<param name=delay value=75>
```

The parameter named **messages** specifies the text messages that **FadeText** should loop through and fade. A vertical bar (|) separates the messages from one another.

The **textcolor** parameter specifies the initial color of the text, and the **bgcolor** parameter specifies the background color into which each message fades. Note that each of these colors is specified as six hexadecimal digits that are treated as three pairs of hexadecimal digits denoting the intensity of the red (R), green (G), and blue (B) components of the color. Thus, each color component, R, G, and B, can have values between **00** and **ff**, with **00** denoting no intensity and **ff** denoting full intensity. For example, **ffffff** denotes white color and **0000ff** denotes blue. This notation for colors is often referred to as *hexadecimal RGB value*.

FadeText

Understanding FadeText

You have seen the **FadeText** applet in action and learned how to specify **<param>** tags to configure it when it is placed in an HTML document. Now let's turn to the Java program, **FadeText.java**, that implements this applet. The following listing shows the **FadeText.java** program in its entirety. Subsequent sections discuss the program in detail.

```
1  //-------------------------------------------------------------
2  // FadeText.java
3  // Fades any color text into background.
4  //-------------------------------------------------------------
5  // Java imports
6  import java.applet.*;
```

```
 7  import java.awt.*;
 8  import java.util.StringTokenizer;
 9  // Documentation for javadoc
10  /**
11   * FadeText displays text messages that fade into the background.
12   * The messages can be in any color.
13   * <p>
14   * Applet parameters are:
15   * <ul>
16   *    <li> messages - a string with the messages separated from
17   *                     each other by a |
18   *    <li> textcolor - color of text messages (specified as 6
19   *                        hexadecimal digits denoting RGB value)
20   *    <li> bgcolor - background color (such as "ffffff" for white)
21   *    <li> delay - number of milliseconds between fades
22   * </ul>
23   *
24   * @author Naba Barkakati
25   * @version 1.00 September 3, 1998
26   */
27  public class FadeText extends Applet implements Runnable
28  {
29      Thread fader = null;
30      Graphics oGC;
31      Image oIm;
32      Font font;
33      int delay = 100;
34      Color textColor;
35      Color bgColor;
36      String messages;
37      String currentMsg = "";
38      Color currentColor;
39      Dimension size;
40      FontMetrics fm;
41      private final int FADE_STEP = 50;
42      private int redStep, blueStep, greenStep;
43      private int red, green, blue;
44      private int initRed, initGreen, initBlue;
45  //-------------------------------------------------------------------
46      /** Gets the parameters from the "param" tag */
47      public void init()
48      {
```

```
49          font = new Font("Helvetica", Font.BOLD, 28);
50
51      messages= getParameter("messages");
52      if (messages == null) messages = "Testing...|FadeText";
53
54      size = size(); // Call getSize() in Java 1.1.6 or later
55      oIm = createImage(size.width, size.height);
56      oGC =  oIm.getGraphics();
57      fm = oGC.getFontMetrics();
58
59      String param = getParameter("delay");
60      if (param != null)
61          delay = Integer.valueOf(param).intValue();
62
63      param=getParameter("textcolor");
64      if(param != null) textColor=parseColorString(param);
65      else textColor=Color.white;
66      currentColor = textColor;
67
68      param=getParameter("bgcolor");
69      if(param != null) bgColor=parseColorString(param);
70      else bgColor=Color.black;
71
72      initRed = textColor.getRed();
73      initGreen = textColor.getGreen();
74      initBlue = textColor.getBlue();
75
76      red = initRed;
77      green = initGreen;
78      blue = initBlue;
79
80      redStep = (red - bgColor.getRed()) / FADE_STEP;
81      greenStep = (green - bgColor.getGreen()) / FADE_STEP;
82      blueStep = (blue - bgColor.getBlue()) / FADE_STEP;
83   }
84 //----------------------------------------------------------------
85   /** Updates the display by calling paint(). */
86   public void update(Graphics g) { paint(g);}
87 //----------------------------------------------------------------
88   /** Paints the current message in the applet */
89   public void paint(Graphics g)
90   {
91      FontMetrics fm = oGC.getFontMetrics();
92
```

```
93        oGC.setColor(bgColor);
94        oGC.fillRect(0,0,size.width,size.height);
95        oGC.setColor(currentColor);
96        oGC.setFont(font);
97        oGC.drawString(currentMsg,
98                  (size.width - fm.stringWidth(currentMsg))/2,
99                  size.height - fm.getMaxDescent());
100
101       if (oIm != null)
102           g.drawImage(oIm, 0, 0, this);
103
104    }
105 //------------------------------------------------------------
106    /** Starts the thread that fades text. */
107    public void start()
108    {
109        if (fader == null)
110        {
111            fader = new Thread(this);
112            fader.start();
113        }
114    }
115 //------------------------------------------------------------
116    /** Stops the thread that fades text. */
117    public void stop()
118    {
119        if (fader != null)
120        {
121            fader.stop();
122            fader = null;
123        }
124
125    }
126 //------------------------------------------------------------
127    /** Runs the thread that fades the text into background. */
128    public void run()
129    {
130        StringTokenizer t = new StringTokenizer(messages, "|");
131        currentMsg = t.nextToken();
132
133        while (true)
134        {
```

```
135            try
136            {
137                if((red - bgColor.getRed()) <= redStep &&
138                   (green - bgColor.getGreen()) <= greenStep &&
139                   (blue -  bgColor.getBlue()) <= blueStep)
140                {
141                    currentColor = textColor;
142                    red = initRed;
143                    green = initGreen;
144                    blue = initBlue;
145
146                    if(t.hasMoreTokens())
147                    {
148                        currentMsg = t.nextToken();
149                    }
150                    else
151                    {
152                        t = new StringTokenizer(messages, "|");
153                        currentMsg = t.nextToken();
154                    }
155                }
156                else
157                {
158 // Fade the color to background
159                    red -= redStep;
160                    green -= greenStep;
161                    blue -= blueStep;
162                    currentColor = new Color(red, green, blue);
163                }
164
165                repaint();
166                Thread.sleep(delay);
167            }
168            catch(InterruptedException e)
169            {
170                stop();
171            }
172        }
173    }
174 //------------------------------------------------------------------
175    /** Parses a color specified as a 6-digit hexadecimal value*/
176    public Color parseColorString(String cs)
177    {
```

```
178          int R = 127, G = 127, B = 127;
179          if(cs.length()==6)
180          {
181              R = Integer.valueOf(cs.substring(0,2),16).intValue();
182              G = Integer.valueOf(cs.substring(2,4),16).intValue();
183              B = Integer.valueOf(cs.substring(4,6),16).intValue();
184
185          }
186          return new Color(R,G,B);
187      }
188 }
```

ANNOTATIONS

The design of the **FadeText** applet is similar to that of the **AnimateText** applet described earlier in this chapter. **FadeText** accepts four user-provided parameters: the text messages to animate, the text color, the background color, and the delay between successive steps of fading. The user specifies these parameters through **<param>** tags. The applet reads these parameters in its **init()** method by calling **getParameter()**.

FadeText uses a thread to perform the fading, which is a type of animation. The applet needs a separate thread of execution so that it can repeatedly paint the text with changing color, allowing the text to gradually fade into the background. The **FadeText** applet creates a **Thread** object named **fader** in its **start()** method.

Because **FadeText** needs an object with a **Runnable** interface to create a **Thread** object, it also implements the **Runnable** interface by defining the **run()** method. When the **fader** thread starts, it calls the **run()** method in the **FadeText** class. The **run()** method selects the current message, picks a color (gradually changing the color so that it fades into the background), and then calls the **repaint()** method to update the applet's display. After repainting the display, the **run()** method calls the **Thread.sleep()** method to stop execution for a specified number of milliseconds, and then repeats the process until the thread is stopped.

FadeText also uses an off-screen image to make the fading appear smooth. The applet's **paint()** method first draws each frame of the text message on the off-screen image and then copies the off-screen image to the applet's display area.

FADETEXT CLASS DECLARATION   Lines 6 through 8 of the **FadeText.java** file list the classes imported into the **FadeText** class:

```
6 import java.applet.*;
7 import java.awt.*;
8 import java.util.StringTokenizer;
```

As these **import** statements indicate, the **FadeText** class uses classes from the **java.applet** and **java.awt** packages. Additionally, **FadeText** uses the **StringTokenizer** class from the **java.util** package to parse the messages, which are separated from one another by vertical bars (|).

Line 27 declares the **FadeText** class as follows:

```
27 public class FadeText extends Applet implements Runnable
```

As an applet, **FadeText** has to be a subclass of **java.applet.Applet**. Because **FadeText** uses a thread for animation, it also implements the **Runnable** interface by providing a **run()** method that can be called by the thread.

Lines 28 through 188 constitute the body of the **FadeText** class, where the class variables and methods are defined.

VARIABLES   Lines 29 through 44 declare the variables used in the **FadeText** class. Line 29 declares a **Thread** object named **fader** used to perform the animations:

```
29     Thread fader = null;
```

The variables named **delay**, **textColor**, **bgColor**, and **messages** are used to store the user-defined parameters—the delay between animation frames, the text color, the background color, and the text messages, respectively:

```
33     int delay = 100;
34     Color textColor;
35     Color bgColor;
36     String messages;
```

The **delay** variable is an integer that holds the number of milliseconds between successive frames of animation. Both **textColor** and **bgColor** are **Color** objects that are initialized from user-specified values in the **init()** method. The **messages** variable is a **String** that holds the text messages, as specified by the user through the **<param>** tag.

The applet also needs an off-screen image, a graphics context for drawing on the off-screen image, and a **Font** object. These variables are declared as follows:

```
30     Graphics oGC;
31     Image oIm;
32     Font font;
```

Because the user-specified text contains multiple messages separated by vertical bars, **FadeText** uses a **String** object called **currentMsg** to store the current message being faded:

```
37     String currentMsg = "";
```

FadeText declares the **currentColor** variable to store the current color value (which changes as the color is faded to the background), the **size** variable to store the dimensions of the applet's display area, and the **fm** variable to store font information:

```
38      Color currentColor;
39      Dimension size;
40      FontMetrics fm;
```

Finally, **FadeText** uses several private variables for intermediate calculations:

```
41      private final int FADE_STEP = 50;
42      private int redStep, blueStep, greenStep;
43      private int red, green, blue;
44      private int initRed, initGreen, initBlue;
```

The **FADE_STEP** variable stores the number of steps in which a color fades into the background. The **final** qualifier means that the value of this variable won't change. The **redStep**, **blueStep**, and **greenStep** variables store the amount by which the red, green, and blue components of color must change at each step. The **initRed**, **initGreen**, and **initBlue** variables store the red, green, and blue components of the initial text color, whereas the **red**, **green**, and **blue** variables store the red, green, and blue components of the current text color.

FADETEXT INITIALIZATION   The Web browser or **appletviewer** calls the applet's **init()** method when the applet is first loaded. In **FadeText**, the **init()** method first sets up a font on line 49:

```
49          font = new Font("Helvetica", Font.BOLD, 28);
```

To keep it simple, I specified the font that the applet should use, but you could allow users to choose a font through a <**param**> tag. The **init()** method then calls **getParameter()**, gets the user-specified text messages, and stores the value in the **String** object named **messages**:

```
51          messages= getParameter("messages");
52          if (messages == null) messages = "Testing...|FadeText";
```

Next the **init()** method gets the size of the applet's window by calling the **size()** method (this method is defined in the **Component** class, which is the superclass of **Applet**):

```
54          size = size(); // Call getSize() in Java 1.1.6 or later
```

Java 2

In Java 1.1.6 and later, the **size()** method has been replaced by the newer **getSize()** method. I used **size()** here because most Web browsers do not yet support newer versions of Java.

After getting the size of the applet's display area, the **init()** method initializes the off-screen image (**oIm**), the graphics context (**oGC**), and the font metrics (**fm**):

```
55        oIm = createImage(size.width, size.height);
56        oGC =  oIm.getGraphics();
57        fm = oGC.getFontMetrics();
```

In lines 59 through 61, **init()** calls **getParameter()** to get the value of the delay (in milliseconds) between animation frames:

```
59        String param = getParameter("delay");
60        if (param != null)
61            delay = Integer.valueOf(param).intValue();
```

To convert the **String** value **param** into an integer, line 61 calls methods of the **Integer** class.

Lines 63 through 70 get the values of the remaining user-specified parameters: the text color and the background color. As in the **AnimateText** applet (described earlier in this chapter), these color values are specified as six hexadecimal digits that are treated as three pairs of hexadecimal values, denoting the red (R), green (G), and blue (B) intensities of the color. A method called **parseColorString()** is used to convert the hexadecimal RGB color value into a **Color** object. For example, here is how the text color is initialized:

```
63        param=getParameter("textcolor");
64        if(param != null) textColor=parseColorString(param);
65        else textColor=Color.white;
```

Similarly, lines 68 through 70 initialize the background color, **bgColor**.

Lines 72 through 82 set up for the fading of a color into the background. The basic algorithm is to change each component—red (R), green (G), and blue (B)—of the **textColor** object, a step at a time, into the corresponding component of the **bgColor** object. The red component is changed in steps of **redStep** units, green in **greenStep** units, and blue in **blueStep** units. These fading steps are computed in lines 80 through 82.

FADETEXT STARTUP AND SHUTDOWN   The Web browser calls the **start()** method (lines 107 through 114) to start executing the applet. In **FadeText**, the **start()** method creates the **Thread** named **fader** and starts the thread, as follows:

```
109       if (fader == null)
110       {
111           fader = new Thread(this);
112           fader.start();
113       }
```

When creating the **Thread fader**, the **start()** method calls the **Thread()** constructor with the **this** keyword, which refers to the **FadeText** applet. **Thread()** expects as an argument an object that implements the **Runnable** interface. **FadeText** implements the **Runnable** interface by defining a **run()** method. When **fader.start()** is called on line 112, the Java Virtual Machine calls the **run()** method of the **FadeText** class to get the thread running. At this point, the **run()** method begins to execute as a separate thread of execution.

When the user clicks on a link and the browser jumps to another Web page, the browser calls the applet's **stop()** method (lines 117 through 125). The **stop()** method stops the execution of the **fader** thread by calling the **fader.stop()** method and then setting **fader** to **null**, as shown in lines 119 through 123:

```
119        if (fader != null)
120        {
121            fader.stop();
122            fader = null;
123        }
```

THE THREAD THAT FADES TEXT   The **run()** method, shown in lines 128 through 173, is the code that the **fader** thread executes. The **run()** method first extracts the current message from the **messages** string:

```
130        StringTokenizer t = new StringTokenizer(messages, "|");
131        currentMsg = t.nextToken();
```

Line 130 initializes a **StringTokenizer** object named **t** with the **messages** string as the string to be parsed and the token separator string ("|"). Then line 131 extracts the first token by using the **nextToken()** method of the **StringTokenizer** and saves the token in the **currentMsg** string. You can keep getting tokens by repeating the call to **nextToken()**. This is a typical way of extracting tokens from a string.

The **run()** method then uses a **while** loop (lines 133 through 172) to repeatedly perform the following steps:

1. If the current red, green, and blue components are close to the corresponding components of the background color, the color is reset back to **textColor** (lines 137 through 144).

2. In lines 146 through 154, the next token, if any, is obtained from the **messages** string and saved in the **currentMsg** string. Otherwise, the token extraction process is reinitialized.

3. The current color's red, green, and blue components are adjusted and the **currentColor** object initialized so that the color fades to the background (lines 159 through 162).

4. The applet's display is redrawn by calling the **repaint()** method (line 165). This causes the browser or **appletviewer** to call the applet's **update()** method, which in turn calls the **paint()** method.

5. In line 166 the **Thread.sleep()** method is called, with the user-specified delay (in milliseconds) as its argument. This suspends the thread of execution for the specified interval.

A **try-catch** pair encloses the steps performed inside the **while** loop. If the thread is interrupted, the **catch()** block on lines 168 through 171 calls the **stop()** method to stop the applet.

TEXT DISPLAY   When the **repaint()** method is called (line 165), the Web browser (or **appletviewer**) schedules a call to the applet's **update()** method as soon as possible. In **FadeText**, the **update()** method (line 86) immediately calls the **paint()** method to draw the text in the applet's display area.

The **paint()** method (lines 89 through 104) displays the **currentMsg** string, using the current color stored in the **currentColor** object. However, instead of simply drawing the string directly in the applet's display area, the **paint()** method first draws the text in the off-screen image, **oIm**, as follows:

```
91          FontMetrics fm = oGC.getFontMetrics();
92
93          oGC.setColor(bgColor);
94          oGC.fillRect(0,0,size.width,size.height);
95          oGC.setColor(currentColor);
96          oGC.setFont(font);
97          oGC.drawString(currentMsg,
98                  (size.width - fm.stringWidth(currentMsg))/2,
99                  size.height - fm.getMaxDescent());
```

Line 91 obtains the dimensions of the font; these are needed to position the text in the off-screen image. Lines 93 and 94 fill the image with the background color. Line 96 sets the font, and line 97 draws the current string in the off-screen image.

After the off-screen image is prepared, lines 101 and 102 copy the image onto the applet's display area:

```
101         if (oIm != null)
102             g.drawImage(oIm, 0, 0, this);
```

A Rainbow-Colored Animated Ruler

The **RainbowRuler** applet doesn't do much—it fills its display area with rainbow colors and then animates the ruler by gradually shifting the colors in a specified direction. You can use the **RainbowRuler** applet as an interesting horizontal ruler on a Web page.

Using RainbowRuler

You will find the files for the **RainbowRuler** applet in the **ch01\HRuler** directory of the companion CD-ROM. First, you should try out the applet with a Web browser or **appletviewer** to see how it works. Next, study the HTML file to see how to specify parameter values for the applet. Then you can go through the **RainbowRuler.java** file to learn how the applet works.

To see the **RainbowRuler** applet in action, follow these steps:

1. Insert this book's companion CD-ROM into your system's CD-ROM drive.

2. Start a Java-capable Web browser.

3. Using the browser's File | Open command, open the HTML file **TestRuler.html** from the **ch01\HRuler** directory of the CD-ROM.

As the **RainbowRuler** applet runs, it animates the rainbow colors in its display area.

If you want to view the **TestRuler.html** file with the **appletviewer** program that comes with the Java Development Kit, use the following command line:

```
appletviewer TestRuler.html
```

You can provide three parameters to the **RainbowRuler** applet through **<param>** tags that appear within the **<applet>** tag in an HTML file. For example, here is the **TestRuler.html** file that you used when trying out the **RainbowRuler** applet:

```
<html>
<body>
<applet code="RainbowRuler.class" width=500 height=5>
<param name=direction value=right>
<param name=delay value=100>
<param name=shift value=5>
</applet>
</body>
</html>
```

This HTML file incorporates the **RainbowRuler** applet with the **<applet>** tag. In this example, the **<applet>** tag has three attributes:

- ◆ **code="RainbowRuler.class"** specifies the file with the applet's compiled code.
- ◆ **width=500** specifies the applet's display width as 500 pixels.
- ◆ **height=5** specifies the applet's display height as 5 pixels.

Because **RainbowRuler** is used as a horizontal ruler, the height should be much smaller than the width.

Between the **<applet>** and **</applet>** tags are the **<param>** tags, through which you can specify various parameters that configure the **RainbowRuler** applet. The **RainbowRuler** applet accepts three parameters:

- ◆ **delay**—the number of milliseconds between successive color shifts
- ◆ **shift**—the number of pixels by which colors are shifted during each step
- ◆ **direction**—the direction in which the colors are shifted

In the **TestRuler.html** file, these parameters are specified by the following **<param>** tags:

```
<param name=direction value=right>
<param name=delay value=100>
<param name=shift value=5>
```

The **direction** parameter can have the values **right**, **left**, or **none**. When you set **direction** to **none**, the rainbow ruler is not animated.

RainbowRuler

Understanding RainbowRuler

The following listing shows the **RainbowRuler.java** program in its entirety. Subsequent sections explain the program in detail.

```
1  //------------------------------------------------------------------
2  // RainbowRuler.java
3  // An animated rainbow-colored horizontal ruler.
4  //------------------------------------------------------------------
5  // Java imports
6  import java.awt.*;
7  import java.applet.Applet;
8  // Documentation for javadoc
9  /**
```

```
10   * RainbowRuler fills its display area with animated rainbow
11   * colors. Use it in an applet with a long rectangular area
12   * (for example, width=500, width=5)
13   * <p>
14   * Parameters accepted by RainbowRuler:
15   * <ul>
16   *    <li> delay - milliseconds between animation frames (integer)
17   *    <li> shift - pixels to shift between frames (integer)
18   *    <li> direction - direction in which colors move
19   *                        ("right", "left", or "none")
20   * </ul>
21   *
22   * @author Naba Barkakati
23   * @version 1.00 Sept. 7, 1998
24   */
25  public class RainbowRuler extends Applet implements Runnable
26  {
27      int delay;
28      int shift;
29      boolean moveRight, moveLeft;
30      Dimension appletSize;
31      int appletWidth, appletHeight;
32      Thread colorShiftThread;
33      Image oIm = null;
34      Graphics oGC;
35      int offset;
36      //------------------------------------------------------------
37      /** Initializes the RainbowRuler class */
38      public void init()
39      {
40          String param;
41          moveLeft = false;
42          moveRight = true;
43          appletSize = size(); // use getSize() in Java 1.1.6 and later
44          appletWidth = appletSize.width;
45          appletHeight = appletSize.height;
46
47          // delay = milliseconds between successive frames
48          param = getParameter("delay");
49          if(param != null)
50              delay = Integer.valueOf(param).intValue();
51          if(delay <10) delay = 100;
```

```
52
53          // shift = number of pixels to shift between frames.
54          param = getParameter("shift");
55          if(param != null)
56              shift = Integer.valueOf(param).intValue();
57          if(shift < 0 || shift > appletWidth)
58              shift = appletWidth/100;
59
60          // direction = which way should the colors move
61          param = getParameter("direction");
62          if (param != null)
63          {
64              if(param.equalsIgnoreCase("right")) moveRight = true;
65              else if(param.equalsIgnoreCase("left")) moveLeft = true;
66              else if(param.equalsIgnoreCase("none"))
67                      { moveLeft = false; moveRight=false;}
68          }
69
70          if (oIm == null)
71              oIm=createImage(appletWidth, appletHeight);
72          oGC=oIm.getGraphics();
73
74          int xpos;
75          for (xpos = 0; xpos < appletWidth; xpos++)
76          {
77              oGC.setColor(computeColor(xpos));
78              oGC.drawLine(xpos, 0, xpos, appletHeight);
79          }
80      }
81      //-------------------------------------------------------------
82      /** Returns a rainbow color for a specified x position */
83      private Color computeColor(int x)
84      {
85          if (x >= appletWidth) x %= appletWidth;
86          double f = (double)x * 6. / (double)(appletWidth);
87          double r, g, b;
88
89          if(f < 1)      { r = 1;     g = 0;     b = 1.0-f;}
90          else if(f < 2) { r = 2.0-f; g = 0;     b = 1;}
91          else if(f < 3) { r = 0;     g = f-2.0; b = 1;}
92          else if(f < 4) { r = 0;     g = 1;     b = 4.0-f;}
93          else if(f < 5) { r = f-4.0; g = 1;     b = 0;}
94          else           { r = 1;     g = 6.0-f; b = 0;}
```

```
95
96          return new Color((float)r, (float)g, (float)b);
97      }
98      //-------------------------------------------------------------
99      /** Starts the applet by starting the animation thread */
100     public void start()
101     {
102         if (colorShiftThread == null)
103         {
104             colorShiftThread = new Thread(this);
105             colorShiftThread.start();
106         }
107     }
108
109     //-------------------------------------------------------------
110     /** Stops the applet by stopping the animation thread */
111     public void stop()
112     {
113         if(colorShiftThread != null)
114         {
115             colorShiftThread.stop();
116             colorShiftThread = null;
117         }
118     }
119     //-------------------------------------------------------------
120     /** Updates applet by calling paint() method */
121     public void update(Graphics g) { paint(g);}
122     //-------------------------------------------------------------
123     /** Copies appropriate parts of off-screen image to applet */
124     public void paint(Graphics g)
125     {
126         if (oIm != null)
127         {
128             g.drawImage(oIm, -offset, 0, this);
129             g.drawImage(oIm, appletWidth-offset, 0, this);
130         }
131     }
132     //-------------------------------------------------------------
133     /** Animate the ruler by repainting at regular intervals */
134     public void run()
135     {
136         // If no animation needed, just paint the ruler and return
137         if(!moveLeft && !moveRight)
138         {
```

```
139          offset = 0;
140          repaint();
141          return;
142      }
143
144      while(colorShiftThread != null)
145      {
146          repaint();
147          if(moveRight)
148          {
149              offset -= shift;
150              if(offset < 0) offset = appletWidth;
151          }
152          else
153          {
154              if(moveLeft)
155              {
156                  offset += shift;
157                  if (offset >= appletWidth) offset = 0;
158              }
159          }
160          // Sleep until it's time for next frame
161          try
162          {
163              Thread.sleep(delay);
164          }
165          catch(InterruptedException e)
166          {
167              break;
168          }
169      }
170  }
171  //------------------------------------------------------------
172  /** Returns a summary description of the applet */
173  public String getAppletInfo()
174  {
175      return "RainbowRuler applet by Naba Barkakati, 1998";
176  }
177  //------------------------------------------------------------
178  /** Returns information about this applet's parameters */
179  public String[][] getParameterInfo()
180  {
181      String[][] info =
182      {
```

```
183        // Parameter Name    Type         Description
184            {"delay",      "Integer", "delay between frames"},
185            {"shift",      "Integer", "pixels to shift per frame"},
186            {"direction", "String",  "direction: left or right"}
187        };
188        return info;
189    }
190 }
```

ANNOTATIONS

The **RainbowRuler** applet uses an off-screen image to prepare the rainbow-colored bar. It fills the off-screen image with a series of vertical lines, each drawn in a different color. The color changes gradually as the lines are drawn from the left edge (where the x coordinate is zero) to the right (as the x coordinate gradually increases). A method called **computeColor()** computes the color to be used for a line drawn at a specific x coordinate.

RainbowRuler performs the animation using a thread called **colorShiftThread** that calls **repaint()** periodically. Calling **repaint()** causes the applet's **update()** method to be invoked, which in turn calls **paint()**. The **paint()** method copies the off-screen image of the ruler to the applet's display, each time shifting the image horizontally in a direction specified by a user-provided parameter. That's how the colors in the ruler appear to move along the bar.

RAINBOWRULER CLASS DECLARATION   The **RainbowRuler.java** file imports the standard packages into the class.

```
6 import java.awt.*;
7 import java.applet.Applet;
```

The **RainbowRuler** class is a subclass of the **java.applet.Applet** class, and **RainbowRuler** uses various classes from the **java.awt** package for graphics.
Line 25 declares the **RainbowRuler** class as follows:

```
25 public class RainbowRuler extends Applet implements Runnable
```

RainbowRuler is declared as a subclass of the **Applet** class because it's an applet. **RainbowRuler** also implements the **Runnable** interface by providing a **run()** method that can be called by the thread that animates the ruler.
The body of the **RainbowRuler** class encompasses lines 26 through 190.

VARIABLES IN RAINBOWRULER   RainbowRuler uses a dozen or so variables that are declared in lines 27 through 35. The first few variables are for storing values obtained from the **<param>** tags in the HTML file:

```
27      int delay;
28      int shift;
29      boolean moveRight, moveLeft;
```

The **delay** variable is the number of milliseconds between successive shifts in the colors, and **shift** is the number of pixels to shift in each frame of the animation. The **boolean** variables **moveRight** and **moveLeft** are used to control the direction of shift. All of these variables are initialized in the **init()** method based on user-provided parameters in the HTML file.

RainbowRuler also needs the dimensions of the applet's display area. Lines 30 and 31 declare variables that store the applet's display dimensions:

```
30      Dimension appletSize;
31      int appletWidth, appletHeight;
```

Line 32 declares a **Thread** object named **colorShiftThread** that **RainbowRuler** uses for its animation thread. The off-screen image is stored in an **Image** object named **oIm** (line 33). Line 34 declares the **Graphics** object **oGC**, used to draw the off-screen image.

Finally, line 35 declares an integer variable, **offset**, that denotes the current number of pixels by which to shift during each step.

RAINBOWRULER INITIALIZATION   When the Web browser or **appletviewer** first loads the applet, the applet's **init()** method is invoked. In **RainbowRuler**, the **init()** method first initializes some of the variables to default values. It then gets the size of the applet's display area and initializes the **appletWidth** and **appletHeight** variables:

```
43         appletSize = size(); // use getSize() in Java 1.1.6 and later
44         appletWidth = appletSize.width;
45         appletHeight = appletSize.height;
```

Java 2

The call to **size()** should be replaced with **getSize()**, which supersedes **size()** beginning in Java 1.1.6. Unfortunately, many browsers still do not support 1.1.6, so the **RainbowRuler** class continues to call **size()**.

In lines 48 through 51, the **init()** method calls **getParameter()** to retrieve the value of the **delay** parameter. It then converts the value to an integer. If **delay** is less than 10 milliseconds, it's reset to 100 milliseconds.

Lines 54 through 58 initialize the value of the **shift** variable by getting the value from the **<param>** tag and converting the value to an integer.

Line 61 gets the value of the parameter called **direction**:

```
param = getParameter("direction");
```

Lines 62 through 68 then set the values of the variables **moveRight** and **moveLeft** based on the value of the **direction** parameter. If **direction** is specified as **"right"**, the **moveRight** variable is set to **true**; if **direction** is **"left"**, **moveLeft** is set to **true**. If **direction** is **"none"**, both **moveRight** and **moveLeft** are set to **false**. When comparing the parameter value in **param** to a string such as **"right"**, the **equalsIgnoreCase()** method of the **String** class is used, as follows:

```
64              if(param.equalsIgnoreCase("right")) moveRight = true;
```

Lines 70 and 71 create the off-screen image **oIm** by calling the **createImage()** method:

```
70          if (oIm == null)
71              oIm=createImage(appletWidth, appletHeight);
```

This off-screen image has the same dimensions as the applet. Line 72 initializes the **Graphics** object **oGC** that will be used to draw in the off-screen image.

Next, the **for** loop in lines 75 through 79 prepares the off-screen image of the rainbow-colored ruler by drawing a vertical line at each x coordinate:

```
74          int xpos;
75          for (xpos = 0; xpos < appletWidth; xpos++)
76          {
77              oGC.setColor(computeColor(xpos));
78              oGC.drawLine(xpos, 0, xpos, appletHeight);
79          }
```

Note that on line 77, the color for a specific x position is obtained by calling the private **computeColor()** method.

The **computeColor()** method, shown in lines 83 through 97, divides the x coordinate by **appletWidth** to restrict the value to between 0.0 and 1.0 (because the x coordinate can be at most equal to **appletWidth**). Then it computes a factor **f** with values between 0.0 and 6.0 by multiplying the normalized value by 6:

```
86          double f = (double)x * 6. / (double)(appletWidth);
```

Next the red (**r**), green (**g**), and blue (**b**) components of the color are computed based on the value of **f**. The color assignments are made in lines 89 through 94 for six ranges of **f** values:

```
89          if(f < 1)      { r = 1;     g = 0;     b = 1.0-f;}
90          else if(f < 2) { r = 2.0-f; g = 0;     b = 1;}
91          else if(f < 3) { r = 0;     g = f-2.0; b = 1;}
92          else if(f < 4) { r = 0;     g = 1;     b = 4.0-f;}
93          else if(f < 5) { r = f-4.0; g = 1;     b = 0;}
94          else           { r = 1;     g = 6.0-f; b = 0;}
```

The **r**, **g**, and **b** values must be between 0.0 and 1.0. Also, care is taken to ensure that each color component, **r**, **g**, and **b**, changes smoothly as **f** goes from one range to the next.

Once the **r**, **g**, and **b** values are computed, line 96 creates a new **Color** object from these components and returns that object:

```
96        return new Color((float)r, (float)g, (float)b);
```

RAINBOWRULER STARTUP AND SHUTDOWN   The Web browser calls the **start()** method (lines 100 through 107) to start executing the **RainbowRuler** applet. As in other applets that use threads for animation, the **start()** method creates a thread and then starts the thread:

```
102        if (colorShiftThread == null)
103        {
104            colorShiftThread = new Thread(this);
105            colorShiftThread.start();
106        }
```

On line 104 the **Thread()** constructor is called with the **RainbowRuler** class as argument (that's what the **this** keyword means). This is possible because **RainbowRuler** implements the **Runnable** interface, which means that **RainbowRuler** implements the **run()** method. When the thread's **start()** method is called (line 105), the Java Virtual Machine calls the **run()** method of the **RainbowRuler** class to get the thread running. At that point, the **run()** method starts as a separate thread of execution.

When appropriate, the browser calls the applet's **stop()** method (lines 111 through 118) to stop the applet. The **stop()** method stops the execution of the thread:

```
113        if(colorShiftThread != null)
114        {
115            colorShiftThread.stop();
116            colorShiftThread = null;
117        }
```

THE THREAD THAT SHIFTS THE COLORS   RainbowRuler's **run()** method, shown in lines 134 through 170, is the code that runs when the **colorShiftThread** executes. The **run()** method sets up the value of **offset** and then calls **repaint()** to update the applet's display area.

If the user specifies the **direction** parameter as **none**, the **run()** method simply paints the applet and returns (lines 137 through 142). Otherwise, a **while** loop (lines 144 through 169) repeatedly calls **repaint()**, changes the value of the **offset** variable, and sleeps for a specified number of milliseconds.

When **repaint()** is called, the browser or **appletviewer** (wherever the applet is running) calls the **update()** method. As shown in line 121, **update()** immediately calls **paint()** to redraw the applet. The **paint()** method simply copies the off-screen image onto the display. The copying is performed in two steps:

```
128          g.drawImage(oIm, -offset, 0, this);
129          g.drawImage(oIm, appletWidth-offset, 0, this);
```

First, the image is copied with a horizontal shift of **-offset**. Then the image is copied again with a horizontal shift of **appletWidth-offset**. The net effect is to move the colors in one direction. As the colors move out of one end, they reappear at the other end, essentially cycling through in a horizontal direction.

RAINBOWRULER APPLET INFORMATION   You can override two other methods of the **Applet** class—**getAppletInfo()** and **getParameterInfo()**—to provide information about the **RainbowRuler** applet and the parameters it accepts.

In **RainbowRuler.java**, lines 173 through 176 implement the **getAppletInfo()** method. The method simply returns a string with information about the applet, such as name, author, and version number, if any.

Lines 179 through 189 implement the **getParameterInfo()** method, which returns a two-dimensional array of **String** objects named **info** with information about the parameters accepted by the **RainbowRuler** applet.

Although today's browsers do not actually use this information, someday browsers may use these methods to display this information to users.

An Image Button

Often Web pages display images that act as links to other Web pages. When the user clicks on the image, the Web browser loads the document linked to that image. When you use HTML tags to make an image a link, the image does not look like a button. You can do a better job with a Java applet. With an applet, you can display a button that actually appears to depress when the user clicks on it. You can display an image on the button and make that button a link to another Web page. When the user clicks on the button, the applet can load the other Web page. The **ImageButton** applet implements such an image button.

Using ImageButton

The **ch01\ImgBtn** directory of the companion CD-ROM contains the files for the **ImageButton** applet. To see how the **ImageButton** applet works, run a Java-capable Web browser and open the **Buttons.html** file. Figure 1-2 shows the browser after that file has been loaded.

The HTML file **Buttons.html** includes three **ImageButton** applets with images of a wolf, a cat, and a horse to display links to Web sites devoted to these animals. When you move the mouse over an image button, the name of the link appears in

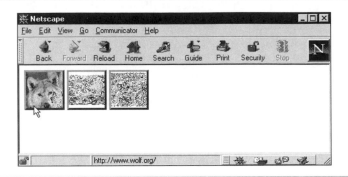

FIGURE 1-2.   An HTML file with three **ImageButton** applets.

the browser's status window. If you click on a button, the button appears to depress. As soon as you finish clicking, the Web browser jumps to the link associated with that image button.

To see how the **ImageButton** applet is used in the HTML file, let's study the **Buttons.html** file:

```
<html>
<body>

<applet code=ImageButton.class width=64 height=64>
    <param name=image value="wolf2s.jpg">
    <param name=bkgray value="100">
    <param name=url value="http://www.wolf.org/">
</applet>

<applet code=ImageButton.class width=64 height=64>
    <param name=image value="cat1.jpg">
    <param name=bkgray value="100">
    <param name=url value="http://www.catlovers.com/">
    <param name=target value="_top">
</applet>

<applet code=ImageButton.class width=64 height=64>
    <param name=image value="horse1.jpg">
    <param name=bkgray value="100">
    <param name=url value="http://www.horses.org/">
</applet>

</body>
</html>
```

As you can see, there are three separate **<applet>** tags, each with an **ImageButton** applet, but with different parameters in the **<param>** tags. In this case, the display areas of all three applets are 64 by 64 pixels in size. The images assigned to the buttons should also be approximately 64 by 64 pixels.

You specify the image file's name as the value for the **image** parameter, and you give the link associated with the button as the **url** parameter. (URL stands for Uniform Resource Locator, the full name of a Web page.) You can also use the **bkgray** parameter to specify a gray level (between 0 and 255) for the three-dimensional shading around the image button. Another optional parameter is **target**, through which you can specify the name of the HTML frame where the Web browser is to display the Web page referenced by the **url** parameter. You can use one of the following predefined frame names as the **target** parameter's value:

- **_self** means the frame where the applet is displayed.

- **_parent** means the applet's parent frame (if there is no parent, it's the same as **_self**).

- **_top** means the top-level frame of the applet's window (if the applet's frame is the top-level one, this is the same as **_self**).

- **_blank** means a new top-level window.

You can also use the name of a frame that appears in your Web page (the frame name appears as an attribute in the **<frame>** tag).

ImageButton

Understanding ImageButton

The **ImageButton.java** file, in the **ch01\ImgBtn** directory of the companion CD-ROM, implements the **ImageButton** applet. The following listing shows the **ImageButton.java** file. The next few sections describe the key methods of this Java applet. I don't discuss some of the routine methods, such as **start()**, **stop()**, and the ones that return applet information such as **getAppletInformation()** and **getParameterInformation()**, because you can understand them just by looking at the source listing.

```
1  //-----------------------------------------------------------------
2  // ImageButton.java
3  // Displays a button with an image and an associated link (URL).
4  // Jumps to the URL when the user clicks on the button.
5  //-----------------------------------------------------------------
6  // Java imports
7  import java.applet.*;
8  import java.awt.*;
9  import java.net.*;
```

```
10   // Documentation for javadoc
11   /**
12    * A button with an image; the button is a link to a URL.
13    * The Web browser jumps to the URL when user clicks on the
14    * button.
15    * <p>
16    * Parameters for applet:
17    * <ul>
18    *    <li> image - name of image file (such as "icon1.gif")
19    *    <li> url - destination URL (such as "http://java.sun.com")
20    *    <li> target - frame where document is loaded ("_self")
21    *    <li> bkgray - background gray level (integer between 0
22    *                  and 255)
23    * </ul>
24    *
25    * @author Naba Barkakati
26    * @version 1.00 August 10, 1998
27    */
28   public class ImageButton extends java.applet.Applet
29   {
30       String urlString = null;
31       String target = "_parent";
32       Color bgColor = Color.lightGray;;
33       URL url;
34       Image imgOffscreenNormal = null;
35       Image imgOffscreenBtnPressed = null;
36       Image imgButton = null;
37       Graphics gcOffscreen = null;
38       boolean mouseOnBtn = false;
39       boolean btnPressed = false;
40       int imageWidth, imageHeight;
41       Dimension appletSize;
42       int appletWidth, appletHeight;
43       //-------------------------------------------------------------
44       /** Initializes applet by creating off-screen images */
45       public void init()
46       {
47           String param;
48           // Start loading the image for the button
49           MediaTracker  tracker = new MediaTracker(this);
50           param = getParameter("image");
51           if(param != null)
52           {
```

```
53          imgButton =  getImage(getCodeBase(), param);
54          tracker.addImage(imgButton, 0);
55      }
56      try
57      {
58          tracker.waitForAll();
59      } catch(InterruptedException e) {}
60
61      param = getParameter("bkgray");
62      int graylevel = 127;
63      if(param != null)
64          graylevel = Integer.valueOf(param).intValue();
65      if(graylevel >= 0 && graylevel <= 255)
66          bgColor = new Color(graylevel, graylevel, graylevel);
67
68      imageWidth  = imgButton.getWidth(this) ;
69      imageHeight = imgButton.getHeight(this);
70      appletSize = size(); // call getSize() in Java 1.1.6 or later
71      appletWidth = appletSize.width;
72      appletHeight = appletSize.height;
73
74      imgOffscreenNormal = createImage(appletWidth,
75                                          appletHeight);
        imgOffscreenBtnPressed = createImage(appletWidth,
                                            appletHeight);
76
77      int x = 0, y = 0;
78      if(appletWidth > imageWidth)
79          x = (appletWidth - imageWidth)/2;
80      if(appletHeight > imageHeight)
81          y = (appletHeight - imageHeight)/2;
82
83      // Button image in its normal (unpressed) state
84      gcOffscreen = imgOffscreenNormal.getGraphics();
85      gcOffscreen.drawImage(imgButton,x,y,this);
86      gcOffscreen.setColor(bgColor);
87      gcOffscreen.draw3DRect(2, 2,
88                              appletWidth-5,
                                appletHeight-5, true);
89      gcOffscreen.draw3DRect(1, 1,
90                              appletWidth-3,
                                appletHeight-3, true);
```

```
91        gcOffscreen.draw3DRect(0, 0,
92                              appletWidth-1,
                               appletHeight-1, true);
93        gcOffscreen.dispose();
94
95        // Button image in its pressed state
96        gcOffscreen = imgOffscreenBtnPressed.getGraphics ();
97        gcOffscreen.drawImage(imgButton, x+2, y+2,this);
98        gcOffscreen.setColor(bgColor);
99        gcOffscreen.draw3DRect(2, 2,
100                             appletWidth-5,
                               appletHeight-5, false);
101       gcOffscreen.draw3DRect(1, 1,
102                             appletWidth-3,
                               appletHeight-3, false);
103       gcOffscreen.draw3DRect(0, 0,
104                             appletWidth-1,
                               appletHeight-1, false);
105       gcOffscreen.dispose();
106
107       // target - where browser loads page referenced by URL
108       param = getParameter("target");
109       if(param != null) target = param;
110
111       // URL associated with the button
112       urlString = getParameter("url");
113   }
114   //--------------------------------------------------------------
115   /** Starts applet by repainting the display area */
116   public void start()
117   {
118       repaint();
119   }
120   //--------------------------------------------------------------
121   /** Handles mouse buttonpress event. Note that event handling
122    *  has changed in Java 1.1.6 and later. You are supposed
123    *   to use MouseListener and MouseMotionListener classes.
124    */
125   public boolean mouseDown(Event e, int x, int y)
126   {
127       btnPressed = true;
128       repaint();
```

```
129        return(true);
130    }
131    //-------------------------------------------------------------
132    /** Called when user releases mouse button. (This is
133     *     deprecated in Java 1.1.6 or later. You are supposed
134     *     to use MouseListener and MouseMotionListener classes.
135     */
136    public boolean mouseUp(Event evt, int x, int y)
137    {
138        if(btnPressed && mouseOnBtn)
139        {
140            btnPressed = false;
141            repaint();
142            try
143            {
144                URL url = new URL(urlString);
145                getAppletContext().showDocument(url, target);
146            }
147            catch(MalformedURLException e)
148            {
149                getAppletContext().showStatus("ImageButton: Bad
                                                    URL");
150            }
151        }
152        else
153        {
154            btnPressed = false;
155            repaint();
156        }
157        return(true);
158    }
159    //-------------------------------------------------------------
160    /** Called when mouse enters the applet */
161    public boolean mouseEnter(Event e, int x, int y)
162    {
163        mouseOnBtn = true;
164        getAppletContext().showStatus(urlString);
165        repaint();
166        return(true);
167    }
168    //-------------------------------------------------------------
169    /** Called when mouse pointer leaves applet */
170    public boolean mouseExit(Event e, int x, int y)
```

```
171      {
172          mouseOnBtn = false;
173          getAppletContext().showStatus("");
174          repaint();
175          return(true);
176      }
177      //-----------------------------------------------------------
178      /** Updates display by calling paint() immediately */
179      public void update(Graphics g) { paint(g);}
180      //-----------------------------------------------------------
181      /** Paints the applet's display area */
182      public void paint(Graphics g)
183      {
184          if(mouseOnBtn && btnPressed)
185          {
186              g.drawImage(imgOffscreenBtnPressed,0,0,this);
187          }
188          else
189          {
190              g.drawImage(imgOffscreenNormal,0,0,this);
191          }
192      }
193      //-----------------------------------------------------------
194      /** Returns information about this applet */
195      public String getAppletInfo()
196      {
197          return "ImageButton v1.00 by Naba Barkakati";
198      }
199      //-----------------------------------------------------------
200      /** Returns information about this applet's parameters */
201      public String[][] getParameterInfo()
202      {
203          String[][] info =
204          {
205              {"image",   "String",            "image file name"},
206              {"bgcolor", "Hexadecimal color", "background color"},
207              {"url",     "String",            "destination URL"},
208              {"target",  "String",            "target frame"},
209          };
210          return info;
211      }
212  }
```

ANNOTATIONS

The **ImageButton** applet is simple in that it does not involve any animation, as do some of the other applets presented in this chapter. Nevertheless, **ImageButton** uses off-screen images to render the button before drawing it onto the applet's display area. To give the visual feedback of a button press—that is, to make the button appear to be pressed in—**ImageButton** uses two off-screen images: one for the button in its normal state and the other showing the button in its pressed state. The off-screen images are initialized in the **init()** method. The **paint()** method then displays the appropriate image of the button, depending on whether the user has clicked on it or not.

The applet uses two **boolean** variables to track whether the user has clicked on the button. The **mouseOnBtn** variable is set to **true** whenever the mouse enters the applet area, and the **btnPressed** variable is **true** when the user holds down the mouse button. These **boolean** variables are set in various mouse event handlers—the methods that get called when the user does something with the mouse, such as move the pointer into the applet area or click the mouse button. The "Mouse Event Handlers" section covers the details of the **ImageButton** applet's event-handling methods.

IMAGEBUTTON INITIALIZATION   After loading the **ImageButton** applet, the Web browser calls the applet's **init()** method. The **init()** method gets the parameters specified through the **<param>** tags and initializes two off-screen images—one showing the image button in its normal state and the other showing the button as if it were pressed.

On line 49, the **init()** method creates a **MediaTracker** object to track the image to be drawn on the applet. **MediaTracker** is a utility class that can track one or more media objects, such as image or audio files. After creating the **MediaTracker**, all you need to do is add images to it and assign an integer ID.

Next, on line 50, **init()** calls **getParameter()** to read the value of the **image** parameter from the HTML file. The value, stored in the **String** variable named **param**, is an image filename (such as **"wolf.jpg"**). Lines 51 through 55 take care of downloading the image (from the same URL—Web site—from which the applet itself was downloaded) and adding it to the **MediaTracker** object named **tracker**:

```
51        if(param != null)
52        {
53            imgButton =  getImage(getCodeBase(), param);
54            tracker.addImage(imgButton, 0);
55        }
```

Line 53 calls the **getImage()** method of the **Applet** class to download the image and assign it to an **Image** object named **imgButton**. The **getImage()** method requires two arguments: an absolute URL (this should be the same location as that from which the applet's code was loaded) and the name of the image file. Typically, as line 53 shows, the **getCodeBase()** method is used as the first argument to **getImage()**. The **getCodeBase()** method returns the URL of the applet's code. This approach works regardless of whether the applet is loaded from the local disk or from an Internet host.

The **getImage()** method returns immediately (without waiting for the image to be loaded). The next step is to call the **addImage()** method of the **MediaTracker** object to keep track of the image, as shown in line 54. The first argument of the **addImage()** method is the **Image** object to track; the second argument is an integer ID for that image. Although in this applet the **MediaTracker** object tracks only one image, you can use **MediaTracker** to track multiple images.

Even at this point, the image may not yet be fully downloaded from its file. The **try** and **catch** blocks of lines 56 through 59 wait for the image to finish loading:

```
56          try
57          {
58              tracker.waitForAll();
59          } catch(InterruptedException e) {}
```

The **tracker.waitForAll()** method starts loading all of the images being tracked by the **MediaTracker** object named **tracker**. The **waitForAll()** method waits until all images have finished loading. If this method is interrupted by another thread, it throws an exception of type **InterruptedException**. The **catch** block in line 59 handles the **InterruptedException**.

After the image is loaded, lines 61 through 66 get the gray level for the background from the **bkgray** parameter and initialize the **Color** object named **bgColor**. Later on, this **Color** is used to draw the 3-D rectangles around the image button.

The next major initialization step is to prepare the off-screen images of the button in its normal state and in its "pressed" state. To do this, the **init()** method first obtains the width and height of both the image and the applet:

```
68          imageWidth  = imgButton.getWidth(this) ;
69          imageHeight = imgButton.getHeight(this);
70          appletSize = size(); // call getSize() in Java 1.1.6 or later
71          appletWidth = appletSize.width;
72          appletHeight = appletSize.height;
```

Lines 68 and 69 obtain the image width and height by calling the **getWidth()** and **getHeight()** methods of the **imgButton** object (this object is of the **Image** class). Line 70 calls the deprecated method **size()** to get the applet's display size; call the newer **getSize()** method in Java 1.1.6 or later versions. The **size()** method returns a **Dimension** object from which the applet's width and height are obtained in lines 71 and 72. The applet's width and height are needed to create the off-screen images (because these images have the same dimension as the applet). The image width and height are used to center the image within the applet, if the image is smaller than the applet.

After the applet's dimensions are available, lines 74 and 75 call the **createImage()** method to initialize the off-screen images:

```
74          imgOffscreenNormal = createImage(appletWidth,
                                             appletHeight);
75          imgOffscreenBtnPressed = createImage(appletWidth,
                                                 appletHeight);
```

The next two steps involve preparing these two off-screen images. If the image is smaller than the applet, lines 78 through 81 compute the x and y coordinates of the location where the image should be drawn. Then lines 84 through 92 draw the off-screen image for the button in its normal state. This involves first getting a **Graphics** object for the off-screen image and then drawing the image (the one that's supposed to appear on the button):

```
84          gcOffscreen = imgOffscreenNormal.getGraphics();
85          gcOffscreen.drawImage(imgButton,x,y,this);
```

Here **gcOffScreen** is the **Graphics** object, initialized by calling the **getGraphics()** method of the **imgOffscreenNormal** object. Line 85 draws the button image by calling the **drawImage()** method. The last step is to draw a 3-D border around the button. Line 86 sets the color to the gray level indicated in the user-specified **bkgray** parameter:

```
86          gcOffscreen.setColor(bgColor);
```

Lines 87 through 92 call the **draw3DRect()** method three times to draw a thick 3-D border around the applet. The **draw3DRect()** method has the following signature (the signature of a method is its calling sequence, which shows the argument types and the type of return value):

```
public void draw3DRect(int x, int y, int width, int height,
                       boolean raised)
```

Here **x** and **y** denote the location of the upper-left corner of the rectangle, and **width** and **height** are the dimensions of the rectangle. Figure 1-3 illustrates the resulting 3-D rectangle. Because of the way the Java Abstract Windowing Toolkit draws, the resulting rectangle covers an area that's **width** + 1 pixels wide and **height** + 1 pixels tall. If the **raised** argument is **true**, the rectangle has a raised appearance (the top and left edges have a lighter shading than the bottom and right edges). The shading depends on the current color; you should use gray for the best 3-D effect. Because the border that **draw3DRect()** draws is only one pixel wide, the **init()** method calls the **draw3DRect()** method three times to get a thick 3-D border. Study lines 87 through 92 and notice that each time the 3-D rectangle is shifted to the right and down by one pixel.

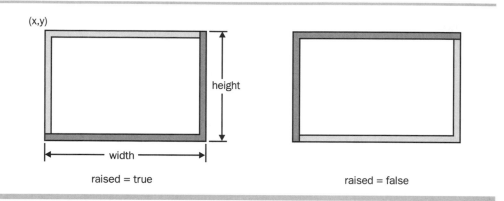

FIGURE 1-3. Three-dimensional rectangle drawn by the **draw3DRect()** method.

Lines 96 through 104 repeat the same process to draw the off-screen image representing the button in its "pressed" state. The key differences are that the button's image is drawn with a two-pixel shift to the right and down. Also, the 3-D borders are drawn sunk into the surface (see Figure 1-3).

The only remaining initialization steps are to get the **url** and **target** parameters. Lines 108 through 112 accomplish these steps. As explained in the "Using ImageButton" section, the **url** parameter denotes the link associated with the button, and **target** is the HTML frame where the document referenced by **url** is loaded.

MOUSE EVENT HANDLERS   The **ImageButton** applet reacts to mouse events—what the user does with the mouse. The applet responds to four mouse events, each handled by a separate method:

- Mouse enters applet: The **mouseEnter()** method is called.

- Mouse exits applet: The **mouseExit()** method is called.

- Mouse button pressed: The **mouseDown()** method is called.

- Mouse button released: The **mouseUp()** method is called.

Lines 161 through 167 implement the **mouseEnter()** method. It sets the **mouseOnBtn** variable to **true**, displays the URL on the status line, and calls **repaint()**. The **mouseExit()** method, shown in lines 170 through 176, does the reverse. It sets **mouseOnBtn** to **false**, displays a blank line on the Web browser's status line, and repaints the applet. To display a string on the browser's status line, these methods call **getAppletContext()** to get the applet's context and then call the **showStatus()** method. Line 164 illustrates how this is done:

```
getAppletContext().showStatus(urlString);
```

The **mouseDown()** method, in lines 125 through 130, sets **btnPressed** to **true** and repaints the applet. When a user clicks on the applet, the last action is the mouse button being released. That's when the **mouseUp()** method (lines 136 through 158) is called. This is where the actual job of jumping to the new URL is performed. First, line 138 makes sure that the mouse has been clicked on the applet:

```
138        if(btnPressed && mouseOnBtn)
```

If this condition is true, line 140 sets **btnPressed** to false and calls **repaint()** to redraw the button (although the applet jumps off to a new URL soon). Then lines 142 through 146 create a new URL object from the specified link and load that document in the Web browser. These two steps occur in lines 144 and 145:

```
144            URL url = new URL(urlString);
145            getAppletContext().showDocument(url, target);
```

These lines are enclosed in a **try** block because the URL constructor may throw a **MalformedURLException**. The **catch** block in lines 147 through 150 catches this exception.

The **ImageButton** class uses old Java 1.0–style event-handling methods. These

Java 2

methods are now deprecated, replaced by a new approach to event handling. In Java 1.1.6 or later, you have to create listener objects to handle these events. To convert the event handling to the new approach, add to **ImageButton** a new class that implements the **MouseListener** interface. For example, here's a skeleton listener class:

```
class ImageButtonMouseListener implements MouseListener
{
    public void mouseEntered(MouseEvent ev){ ... }
    public void mouseExited(MouseEvent ev) { ... }
    public void mousePressed(MouseEvent ev) { ... }
    public void mouseReleased(MouseEvent ev) { ... }
    public void mouseClicked(MouseEvent ev) { ... }
}
```

The method names reflect the mouse event that's handled by the method. For example, **mouseEntered()** is called when the user moves the mouse pointer over the applet. Implement these methods as follows:

◆ **mouseEntered()**: Copy the body of the old **mouseEnter()** method into this method, but get rid of the **return** statement (because the new methods are declared as void—they do not return any value).

◆ **mouseExited()**: Copy the body of the old **mouseExit()** method and omit the **return** statement.

◆ **mousePressed()**: Copy the body of the old **mouseDown()** method and omit the **return** statement.

◆ **mouseReleased()**: Copy the body of the old **mouseUp()** method and omit the **return** statement.

◆ **mouseClicked()**: Leave the body empty (just the opening and closing braces { }).

Next, add the following line of code to the **init()** method of the **ImageButton** class:

```
addMouseListener(new ImageButtonMouseListener());
```

Finally, add the following line to the **import** statements at the beginning of **ImageButton.java**:

```
import java.awt.event.*;
```

While you're at it, change the call to **size()** in line 70 to **getSize()**. Now you have a Java 2–compatible **ImageButton** class. If you want to try out this version of the applet (provided you have a browser that supports Java 1.1.6 or later), the files are in the **ch01\ImgBtn\java2** directory of the companion CD-ROM.

IMAGEBUTTON DISPLAY　　The **paint()** method, shown in lines 182 through 192, takes care of displaying the correct off-screen image on the applet's display area. The following **if-else** statement takes care of painting the applet:

```
184        if(mouseOnBtn && btnPressed)
185        {
186             g.drawImage(imgOffscreenBtnPressed,0,0,this);
187        }
188        else
189        {
190             g.drawImage(imgOffscreenNormal,0,0,this);
191        }
```

When the mouse pointer is over the applet and the button is pressed, line 186 displays the image of the button in its "pressed" state. Otherwise, line 190 displays the button in its normal state.

A Drop-Down Menu

The **DropDownMenu** applet uses the **Choice** class from the Java Abstract Windowing Toolkit to display a list of links in a drop-down menu. You can embed this applet on a Web page to show many links in a limited amount of space. When the user selects a link from the drop-down menu, the applet loads the document corresponding to that link.

Using DropDownMenu

You will find the files for **DropDownMenu** in the **ch01\DDMenu** directory of the companion CD-ROM. Use a Java-capable Web browser to open the **TestMenu.html** file from the **ch01\DDMenu** directory of the CD-ROM. Figure 1-4 shows the resulting display in the browser. Now click the downward arrow next to the text in the box. A list drops down. You can scroll up and down on this list and select a link. Figure 1-5 shows the drop-down menu after you click on the arrow and move the mouse to an item on the list.

Now that you have seen how the **DropDownMenu** applet works, let's look at the **TestMenu.html** file showing how the applet is used in an HTML file:

```html
<html>
<body>
Select a destination:<br>
<applet code="DropDownMenu.class" height=30 width=300>
  <param name= "target" value = "_parent">
  <param name = "bgColor" value = "ffffff">
  <param name = "url1" value = "Java Home Page|http://java.sun.com/">
  <param name = "url2" value = "IBM jCentral Basic
Search|http://www.ibm.com/java/jcentral/basic-search.html">
  <param name = "url3" value = "Java World|http://www.javaworld.com">
  <param name = "url4" value = "Java Review
  Service|http://www.jars.com">
  <param name = "url5" value = "Gamelan Java
Directory|http://www.developer.com/directories/pages/dir.java.html">
  <param name = "url6" value = "Java
  Lobby|http://www.javalobby.org/">
  <param name = "url7" value = "Java Developer's
  Journal|http://www.sys-con.com/java/index2.html">
  <param name = "url8" value = "Java
  Report|http://www.javareport.com/">
  <param name = "url9" value = "Java Developer
  Connection|http://developer.java.sun.com/">
</applet>
</body>
</html>
```

FIGURE 1-4.   The initial drop-down menu in the Web browser.

As you can see, the **DropDownMenu** applet accepts a large number of parameters. The **target** parameter denotes the HTML frame where the documents referenced by the URLs are loaded. The **bgcolor** parameter defines the background color for the applet. The rest of the parameters are the links to be displayed in the drop-down menu. These parameters are named sequentially: **url1**, **url2**, **ur3**, and so on. The value of each of these parameters has a specific format:

```
"Descriptive text|http://www.xyz.com"
```

It's a string with two parts separated by a vertical bar (|). The first part is a description of the link, and the second part is the complete URL for the Web page.

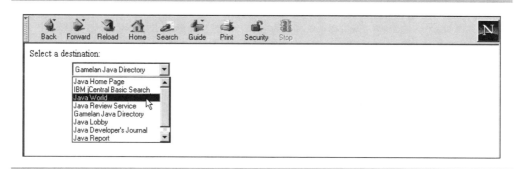

FIGURE 1-5.   The drop-down menu after a click on the down arrow.

DropDownMenu

Understanding DropDownMenu

The following listing shows the **DropDownMenu.java** file that implements the **DropDownMenu** applet. You'll find this file in the **ch01\DDMenu** subdirectory of the companion CD-ROM. The next few sections describe the source code.

```
1  //------------------------------------------------------------------
2  // DropDownMenu.java
3  // Displays a drop-down menu of links.
4  //------------------------------------------------------------------
5  // Java imports
6  import java.applet.*;
7  import java.awt.*;
8  import java.util.*;
9  import java.net.*;
10 // Documentation for javadoc
11 /**
12  * DropDownMenu displays a list of links in a drop-down menu.
13  * It uses Java's Choice component.
14  * <p>
15  * <ul>
16  *    <li> bgcolor - background color in hexadecimal RGB
17  *                     format ("ffffff" means white)
18  *    <li> target - where the document referenced by a URL is
19  *                     loaded ("_self", "_parent", or "_top")
20  *    <li> url1 - first label and link with | as separator
21  *                     (example: "Java World|http://www.javaworld.com")
22  *    <li> url2 - second label and URL
23  *    <li> ... and so on.
24  * </ul>
25  *
26  * @author Naba Barkakati
27  * @version 1.00 August 1997
28  */
```

```java
29  public class DropDownMenu extends Applet
30  {
31      public int number;
32      public Vector urlArray = new Vector(10);
33      public Vector labelArray = new Vector(10);
34      public URL url = null;
35      String frame;
36      Color bgColor = Color.lightGray;
37      //------------------------------------------------------------
38      /** Initializes this applet */
39      public void init()
40      {
41          String param;
42          param = getParameter("bgcolor");
43          if(param != null)
44                  bgColor = new Color(Integer.parseInt(param, 16));
45          else bgColor = Color.lightGray;
46  
47          param = getParameter("target");
48          if(param != null)
49              frame = param;
50          else
51              frame = "_parent";
52  
53          StringTokenizer st;
54          number = 1;
55          Choice Entries = new Choice();
56          String text, urlString;
57  
58          while(true)
59          {
60              param = getParameter("url" + number);
61              if(param == null)
62              {
63                  number--; // so we have correct total
64                  break;
65              }
66  
67              st = new StringTokenizer(param, "|");
68              text = new String(st.nextToken());
69              labelArray.addElement(text);
```

```
70          urlString = new String(st.nextToken());
71          urlArray.addElement(urlString);
72          Entries.addItem(text);
73          number++;
74      }
75      add(Entries);
76      setBackground(bgColor);
77  }
78  //-------------------------------------------------------------
79  /**  Handles event that occurs when user selects an item.
80   *   In Java 1.1.6 or later, use ItemListener (see the
81   *   DropDownMenu.java file in the java2 subdirectory).
82   */
83  public boolean action(Event event, Object obj)
84  {
85      if(event.target instanceof Choice)
86      {
87          String item = (String)obj;
88          for(int n = 0; n <= number-1; n++)
89          {
90              if(item.equals((String)labelArray.elementAt(n)))
91              {
92                  try
93                  {
94                      url = new
95                              URL((String)urlArray.elementAt(n));
                        getAppletContext()
                         .showDocument(url,frame);
96                  }
97                  catch(MalformedURLException e)
98                  {
99                      getAppletContext().showStatus("Bad URL");
100                 }
101             }
102         }
103     }
104     return true;
105 }
106 }
```

ANNOTATIONS

The **DropDownMenu** applet has a simpler design than typical applets because **DropDownMenu** uses the **Choice** component from the Java Abstract Windowing Toolkit (AWT). The Java AWT includes several predefined graphical user interface (GUI) components, one of which is **Choice**. **Choice** displays what is commonly known as a drop-down menu or option menu, in which only the current selection is visible but the entire list of choices appears when the user clicks on the component.

Because it uses the **Choice** component, the **DropDownMenu** applet needs only to provide the **action()** method to handle mouse clicks on the **Choice**. None of the other methods, such as **start()**, **stop()**, **update()**, and **paint()**, are required, because the **Choice** component handles the painting chores.

The basic design then boils down to getting the parameters, such as **url1**, **url2**, and so on, from the **<param>** tags and keeping track of them. Because each parameter has two parts—a description of the link and the associated URL—two **Vector** objects are used to track these items (a **Vector** is an array that grows as elements are added to it). Each description is also added to the **Choice** component; these descriptions appear as items in the drop-down menu displayed by **Choice**.

The **Choice** component's event handler—the **action()** method in the **DropDownMenu** class—finds the selected item in the array of descriptions, gets the corresponding URL string, and loads the document referenced by that URL.

DROPDOWNMENU INITIALIZATION   Lines 39 through 77 constitute the **init()** method that initializes the **DropDownMenu** applet. The primary initialization steps involve getting the parameters by calling the **getParameter()** method and then appropriately processing the parameters.

Lines 42 through 45 retrieve the **bgcolor** parameter, denoting a six-digit hexadecimal value (such as **"ffffff"** for white) for the background color and initializing a **Color** object named **bgColor**:

```
42        param = getParameter("bgcolor");
43        if(param != null)
44                bgColor = new Color(Integer.parseInt(param, 16));
45        else bgColor = Color.lightGray;
```

Line 42 gets the parameter value by calling **getParameter()** and stores that value in the **String** named **param**. If **param** is not **null** (this is the case if the **bgcolor** parameter is found in a **<param>** tag), line 44 sets **bgColor** to a new **Color** object created using the specified color value. Notice that line 44 uses the **Integer.parseInt()** method (a static method of the **Integer** class) to convert the hexadecimal color into a value that can be used with the **Color()** constructor. If the **bgcolor** parameter is not specified, line 45 sets the **bgColor** variable to **Color.lightGray**.

The next initialization step, in lines 47 through 51, retrieves the **target** parameter and saves the value in a **String** variable called **frame**. Recall that **target** is the name of an HTML frame in which the documents referenced by the URLs are to be loaded.

The next step is to get and process all of the remaining parameters: **url1**, **url2**, **url3**, and so on. Lines 53 through 74 take care of this step. Lines 53 through 56 declare the variables used to perform this step:

```
53      StringTokenizer st;
54      number = 1;
55      Choice Entries = new Choice();
56      String text, urlString;
```

Line 53 declares a **StringTokenizer** object to be used to separate each parameter into two parts: a description text and the URL string, separated by a vertical bar (|). Line 54 sets the **number** variable to 1; **number** is used to count the total number of parameters of the form **url1**, **url2**, and so on. Line 55 creates a **Choice** component named **Entries** to which all drop-down menu entries will be added. Line 56 declares two **String** variables for temporary storage: **text** is used for the description of a link (such as **"Java Home Page"**), and **urlString** is used for the URL (such as **"http://java.sun.com/"**).

The **while** loop (lines 58 through 74) retrieves and processes each of the parameters **url1**, **url2**, **url3**, and so on. Line 60 calls **getParameter()** to retrieve a parameter value:

```
60          param = getParameter("url" + number);
```

The argument for the **getParameter()** method is supposed to be a string with the name of the parameter. In this case, the parameter name is constructed by appending a number to the string **"url"**. For example, when **number** is 2, the argument will be **"url2"**. This convention of adding a number to a string is a common trick used to construct parameter names that increase sequentially.

Lines 61 through 65 break the **while** loop when the parameter value is **null**.

```
61          if(param == null)
62          {
63              number--; // so we have correct total
64              break;
65          }
```

Line 63 adjusts the **number** variable by subtracting 1, so we have the correct number of URL parameters. To see how this works, suppose that the current value of **number** is 6. The argument to **getParameter()** would then be **"url6"**. If **getParameter()** returns **null**, the **url6** parameter does not appear in any of the

<param> tags in the HTML file. This means that there must be only five parameters: **url1**, **url2**, **url3**, **url4**, and **url5**. That's why line 63 decrements the **number** variable by 1. Line 64 uses the **break** statement to end the **while** loop.

Lines 67 through 73 process a single parameter value of the form **"Java Home Page | http://java.sun.com/"** that is in the **String** named **param**:

```
67          st = new StringTokenizer(param, "|");
68          text = new String(st.nextToken());
69          labelArray.addElement(text);
70          urlString = new String(st.nextToken());
71          urlArray.addElement(urlString);
72          Entries.addItem(text);
73          number++;
```

Line 67 initializes the **StringTokenizer st** with the **String param** and the vertical bar as a token separator. Line 68 extracts the first token by calling the **nextToken()** method of the **StringTokenizer st**. This token is the text description (such as **"Java Home Page"**); it is stored in the **text** variable. Line 69 adds **text** to the **Vector** variable **labelArray**. Similarly, in lines 70 and 71 the URL string is extracted and added to the **urlArray Vector**. Finally, line 72 adds the text description to the **Choice** component named **Entries**, and line 73 increments the **number** variable by 1.

After the **while** loop ends, line 75 calls the **add()** method to add the **Choice** component named **Entries** to the applet's display area. Line 76 then sets the background color of the applet.

```
75          add(Entries);
76          setBackground(bgColor);
```

EVENT HANDLER The only other method in the **DropDownMenu** applet is the **action()** method, called when the user selects items from the drop-down menu. Lines 83 through 105 implement the **action()** method.

Line 87 gets the item that the user has selected:

```
87          String item = (String)obj;
```

Next, the **for** loop in lines 88 through 102 searches through the **labelArray** to see which of the entries matches the selected item. Line 90 performs the **String** comparison:

```
90          if(item.equals((String)labelArray.elementAt(n)))
```

Here, **labelArray.elementAt(n)** is the nth element of the **labelArray Vector**. This element is returned as an **Object** (the generic object in Java). It is then cast as a **String** and compared with the **String** named **item**.

When a matching element of **labelArray** is found, the **try** block of lines 92 through 96 is executed.

```
94          url = new
                    URL((String)urlArray.elementAt(n));
95          getAppletContext().
              .showDocument(url,frame);
```

Here, line 94 creates a **URL** object from the corresponding element of **urlArray**.
Notice how the returned value from **urlArray.elementAt(n)** is cast as a **String** before
it is used as an argument to the **URL()** constructor. Next, line 95 calls
getAppletContext() to obtain the applet's context and then calls **showDocument()** to
display the new URL in the user-specified frame. At this point, the Web browser
should display the document in the appropriate HTML frame.

A Scrolling LED Ticker

A popular Java applet is a scrolling ticker that displays one or more scrolling
messages. You may have seen variants of the scrolling ticker applet at various Web
sites. This section presents the **LEDTicker** applet, a representative sample of typical
scrolling ticker applets. **LEDTicker** has the following key characteristics:

- It displays the messages on an electronic message board with an array of
  simulated light-emitting diodes (LEDs).

- Each message can be associated with a URL of a Web page (when the user
  clicks on the ticker, the applet loads that Web page).

- It allows the user to specify the messages, colors, fonts, and URL associated
  with each message.

- The user can select the direction of scroll: left to right or right to left.

The remainder of this chapter shows how the **LEDTicker** applet works and how
it is programmed. First you'll try out the **LEDTicker** applet, then learn its overall
design, and finally study the Java source code.

Using LEDTicker

The companion CD-ROM's **ch01\Ticker** directory contains all of the files you need
to try out the **LEDTicker** applet. From a Java-capable Web browser, open the HTML
file **TickerTest.html**. After loading the file, the browser's window should display
the **LEDTicker** applet. Figure 1-6 shows a typical frame of the ticker. If you watch
the ticker for a while, you will see it scroll through several messages. If you move
the mouse pointer onto the ticker, the status area at the bottom of the screen
displays the URL associated with the message. For example, the status area in
Figure 1-6 shows the URL associated with the message scrolling in the ticker.

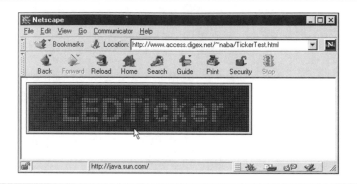

FIGURE 1-6.   The **LEDTicker** applet displays a scrolling message.

To see how you can use and configure the **LEDTicker** applet, you should study
the **TickerTest.html** file:

```
<html>
<body>
<applet code="LEDTicker.class" width="400" height="100">
  <param name="url" value="http://java.sun.com/">
  <param name="target" value="_top">
  <param name="borderoutline" value="true">
  <param name="ledsize" value="4">
  <param name="delay" value="100">
  <param name="message1" value="LEDTicker">
  <param name="font1"     value="Helvetica,Bold,14">
  <param name="message2" value="a Java Applet">
  <param name="color2"    value="00ffff">
  <param name="message3" value="by  Naba Barkakati">
  <param name="font3"     value="TimesRoman,Plain,12">
  <param name="color3"    value="ffff00">
  <param name="url3"      value="http://www.access.digex.net/~naba/">
  <param name="message4" value="from Java Annotated Archives">
  <param name="font4"     value="Helvetica,Plain,12">
  <param name="color4"    value="ff00ff">
  <param name="url4"      value="http://www.osborne.com">
  <param name="message5" value="Osborne/McGraw-Hill">
  <param name="font5"     value="Helvetica,Plain,12">
  <param name="color5"    value="ccb0b0">
  <param name="url5"      value="http://www.osborne.com">
</applet>
</body>
</html>
```

The **<applet>** tag specifies the class file for the **LEDTicker** applet (**LEDTicker.class**), as well as the width and height. In this case, the ticker is 400 pixels wide by 100 pixels tall. Next comes a long sequence of **<param>** tags, each specifying a parameter name and a value. These parameters let you configure the **LEDTicker** applet to suit your needs. This applet accepts the following basic set of parameters:

- **url**—indicates the default URL associated with all messages
- **target**—specifies the default frame where documents are loaded when the user clicks on the ticker
- **borderoutline**—draws an extra border outline when this parameter is **true**
- **direction**—scrolls left to right if this parameter's value is **"left-to-right"**
- **ledsize**—specifies the size of the LEDs in pixels
- **ledshape**—draws oval-shaped LEDs when set to **"oval"** (the default is square LEDs)
- **borderwidth**—specifies the width of the border in pixels
- **bgcolor**—specifies the background color for the LED array
- **bordercolor**—specifies the color of the border around the LED panel
- **textcolor**—specifies the default color of LEDs that are on
- **ledoff-color**—indicates the color of the LEDs when they are turned off
- **delay**—gives the number of milliseconds between successive scrolling steps
- **message**N—gives the text of the Nth message, where $N = 1, 2, 3, \ldots$
- **font**N—specifies the font, style, and size to be used for the Nth message, separated by commas (such as **"Helvetica,Plain,12"** and **"TimesRoman,Bold,14"**)
- **color**N—gives the hexadecimal RGB color for the Nth message (such as **"00ff00"** for green)
- **url**N—specifies the URL associated with the Nth message (such as **"http://java.sun.com"**)
- **target**N—indicates the HTML frame where **URL**N is loaded (such as **"_top"** or **"_blank"**)

For each message parameter, **message1**, **message2**, **message3**, and so on, you can optionally specify corresponding font (**font1**, **font2**, . . .), color (**color1**, **color2**, . . .), URL (**url1**, **url2**, . . .), and target (**target1**, **target2**, . . .) parameters.

You might want to experiment with the HTML file. Change some of the parameters and see the effect on the applet.

LEDTicker

Understanding LEDTicker

The **LEDTicker** applet is the most complex applet in this chapter. Even though this ticker applet does not have all the bells and whistles of many other tickers (such as flashing messages), it still takes a lot of Java code to do the job. As you can see, the source file, **LEDTicker.java**, is rather long. However, you will be able to understand the code because the applet has the same set of methods as other applets that perform animations. I will describe the applet's design to help you understand the tricks used in the applet's code. Then you can learn about specific details of the variables and methods in the **LEDTicker.java** file.

```
1  //----------------------------------------------------------------
2  // File: LEDTicker.java
3  // Compile with: javac LEDTicker.java
4  // Generate documentation with: javadoc LEDTicker.java
5  // Author: Naba Barkakati, 1998
6  //----------------------------------------------------------------
7  // Standard imports
8  import java.applet.*;
9  import java.awt.*;
10 import java.awt.image.*;
11 import java.net.*;
12 import java.util.*;
13 //----------------------------------------------------------------
14 // Documentation to be extracted by javadoc
15 /**
16  * A ticker applet that displays scrolling messages on an
17  * electronic message board that appears to use light-emitting
18  * diodes (LED) to display the characters.
19  * <P>
20  * Parameters specified through the &#60;param&#62; tag:
21  * <ul>
22  *    <li> bgcolor      - background color
23  *    <li> ledoff-color - color of LEDs when they are off
24  *    <li> textcolor    - default color of LEDs that are on
25  *    <li> bordercolor  - color of the border around LED panel
26  *    <li> borderwidth  - width of border in pixels
27  *    <li> borderoutline- specify "true" to outline the border
28  *                        in black (default is "false")
29  *    <li> direction    - direction of scrolling (specify
30  *                        "left-to-right" as value to override
31  *                        the default right-to-left direction)
```

```
32   *     <li> delay         - Delay in milliseconds between
33   *                          successive movements of ticker
34   *     <li> font          - default font specified as a string
35   *                          (e.g. "Courier,Plain,12" means 12-point
36   *                          Courier font in plain style)
37   *     <li> url           - URL to jump to when user clicks mouse
38   *                          button on the message
39   *     <li> target        - frame where the URL is loaded
40   *     <li> <b>Add the following set for each message</b>
41   *     <ul>
42   *       <li> messageN      - first message
43   *       <li> fontN         - (optional) font for Nth message
44   *       <li> urlN          - (optional) URL for Nth message
45   *       <li> targetN       - (optional) target frame for URL
46   *       <li> colorN        - (optional) color of lit LEDs for
47   *                            Nth message
48   *     </ul>
49   *     <li> repeat with N=1, 2, ... for as many messages as
50   *          you want to scroll on the LED ticker.
51   * </ul>
52   *
53   * @author    Naba Barkakati
54   * @version   1.00 June 1998
55   *
56   */
57  public class LEDTicker extends Applet implements Runnable
58  {
59      /**
60       * TickerMessage class holds information about each
61       * message to be scrolled.
62       */
63      final class TickerMessage extends Object
64      {
65          public boolean isInitialized;
66          public int delay;
67          public int msgWidth;
68          public int msgHeight;
69          public int imgWidth;
70          public int imgHeight;
71          public Color color;
72          public Font font;
```

```
73      public Image imgMsg;
74      public String message;
75      public String urlString;
76      public String target;
77
78      protected TickerMessage()
79      {
80          isInitialized = false;
81          msgWidth = 0;
82          msgHeight = 0;
83          imgWidth = 0;
84          imgHeight = 0;
85          color=null;
86          font = null;
87          imgMsg = null;
88          message = null;
89          urlString = null;
90          target = null;
91      }
92  }
93
94  static final int BEGIN_SCROLL_IN  = 1;
95  static final int SCROLL_IN        = 2;
96  static final int BEGIN_SCROLL_OUT = 3;
97  static final int SCROLL_OUT       = 4;
98  static final int END_SCROLL       = 5;
99
100 Thread tickerThread = null;
101
102 Vector MessageList = new Vector(10);
103 int msgNum;
104 TickerMessage curMsg;
105 boolean mouseEnter;
106 int delay;
107 boolean scrollright;
108 Font font;
109 String urlString;
110 String target;
111 boolean ovalLED;
112 int bwidth;
113 boolean borderoutline;
114 int LEDsize;
```

```
115        Color bgColor, LEDonColor, borderColor, LEDoffColor;
116        Image imgDisp, imgLEDoff;
117        //-------------------------------------------------------------
118        /** Initializes the applet and gets the parameters. */
119        public void init()
120        {
121            msgNum = 0;
122            curMsg = null;
123            mouseEnter = false;
124            delay = 100;
125            scrollright = false;
126            font = parseFontParam("Helvetica,PLAIN,12");
127            urlString = null;
128            target = "_top";
129            ovalLED = false;
130            bwidth = 6;
131            borderoutline = false;
132            LEDsize = 4;
133            bgColor = Color.black;
134            LEDonColor = Color.red;
135            borderColor = Color.lightGray;
136            LEDoffColor = Color.darkGray;
137            imgDisp = null;
138            imgLEDoff = null;
139 // Get the parameters from the <param> tags
140            String param;
141            param = getParameter("bgcolor");
142            if(param != null) bgColor = parseColorParam(param);
143            param = getParameter("textcolor");
144            if(param != null) LEDonColor = parseColorParam(param);
145            param = getParameter("ledoff-color");
146            if(param != null) LEDoffColor = parseColorParam(param);
147            param = getParameter("bordercolor");
148            if(param != null) borderColor = parseColorParam(param);
149            param = getParameter("borderwidth");
150            if (param != null)
151                bwidth = Integer.valueOf(param).intValue();
152            param = getParameter("ledsize");
153            if (param != null)
154            {
```

```
155              LEDsize = Integer.valueOf(param).intValue();
156              if (LEDsize <= 1) LEDsize = 4;
157          }
158          param = getParameter("ledshape");
159          if(param != null && param.equalsIgnoreCase("oval"))
160              ovalLED = true;
161          param = getParameter("borderoutline");
162          if(param != null && param.equalsIgnoreCase("true"))
163              borderoutline = true;
164          param = getParameter("delay");
165          if (param != null)
166              delay = Integer.valueOf(param).intValue();
167          param = getParameter("direction");
168          if(param != null && param.equalsIgnoreCase("left-to-right"))
169              scrollright = true;
170          param = getParameter("url");
171          if (param != null)urlString = new String(param);
172          param = getParameter("target");
173          if (param != null)target = new String(param);
174          param = getParameter("font");
175          font = parseFontParam(param);
176
177          // Retrieve the messages to be
                 displayed from the <param> tags
178          int i;
179          for (i = 1; ; i++)
180          {
181              param = getParameter("message"+i);
182              if (param == null) break;
183
184              TickerMessage msg = new TickerMessage();
185              msg.delay = delay;
186              msg.color = LEDonColor;
187              msg.font = font;
188              msg.urlString = urlString;
189              msg.target = target;
190              msg.message = param;
191              // Override font, color, URL,
                     and target, if specified
192              param = getParameter("font"+i);
193              if(param != null) msg.font = parseFontParam(param);
194              param = getParameter("color"+i);
```

```
195          if(param != null) msg.color = parseColorParam(param);
196          param = getParameter("url"+i);
197          if(param != null) msg.urlString = param;
198          param = getParameter("target"+i);
199          if(param != null) msg.target = param;
200          MessageList.addElement(msg);
201      }
202    }
203    //-------------------------------------------------------------
204    /** Parses a color value passed in as a string.
205      *
206      * @param cs A 6-digit RGB color in hexadecimal ("ff0000")
207      * @return Color object based on input specifications
208      */
209    public Color parseColorParam(String cs)
210    {
211        int R = 127, G = 127, B = 127;
212        if(cs.length()==6)
213        {
214            R = Integer.valueOf(cs.substring(0,2),16).intValue();
215            G = Integer.valueOf(cs.substring(2,4),16).intValue();
216            B = Integer.valueOf(cs.substring(4,6),16).intValue();
217        }
218        return new Color(R,G,B);
219    }
220    //-------------------------------------------------------------
221    /** Creates a Font using parameters specified in a string.
222      *
223      * @param fs String with font info ("Courier,Bold,12")
224      * @return Font object created from the specifications
225      */
226    public Font parseFontParam(String fs)
227    {
228        String fontface = "Dialog";
229        int fontstyle = Font.PLAIN, fontsize = 12;
230
231        if (fs != null)
232        {
233            StringTokenizer st = new StringTokenizer(fs, ",");
234            try
235            {
```

```
236                   fontface = st.nextToken();
237                   StringTokenizer stStyle = new
238                                   StringTokenizer(st.nextToken());
239                   fontstyle = Font.PLAIN;
240                   while (stStyle.hasMoreTokens())
241                   {
242                       String style = stStyle.nextToken();
243                       if (style.equalsIgnoreCase("plain"))
244                           fontstyle |= Font.PLAIN;
245                       else if (style.equalsIgnoreCase("bold"))
246                           fontstyle |= Font.BOLD;
247                       else if (style.equalsIgnoreCase("italic"))
248                           fontstyle |= Font.ITALIC;
249                   }
250                   fontsize =
251                       Integer.valueOf(st.nextToken()).intValue();
252               }
253           catch(Exception e)
254           {
255               fontface = "Dialog";
256               fontstyle = Font.PLAIN;
257               fontsize = 12;
258           }
259       }
260       return(new Font(fontface, fontstyle, fontsize));
261   }
262   //------------------------------------------------------------
263   /** Handles mouse-down events and jump to a URL (if any).
264    *  Use a MouseListener in Java 1.1.6 or later.
265    */
266   public boolean mouseDown(Event evt, int x, int y)
267   {
268       if(curMsg != null && curMsg.isInitialized &&
269           curMsg.urlString != null)
270       {
271           try
272           {
273               URL url = new URL(curMsg.urlString);
274               if (curMsg.target == null)
275                   getAppletContext().showDocument(url);
276               else
```

```
277                    getAppletContext()
                         .showDocument(url, curMsg.target);
278              getAppletContext().showStatus("");
279          }
280          catch(MalformedURLException e)
281          {
282              getAppletContext()
                 .showStatus("LEDTicker: Bad URL");
283          }
284      }
285      return(true);
286  }
287  //------------------------------------------------------------
288  /** When mouse enters applet, displays URL in status area.
289   *  Use a MouseListener in Java 1.1.6 or later.
290   */
291  public boolean mouseEnter(Event evt, int x, int y)
292  {
293      if (curMsg != null && curMsg.isInitialized &&
294          curMsg.urlString != null)
295              getAppletContext().showStatus(curMsg.urlString);
296      mouseEnter = true;
297      return(true);
298  }
299  //------------------------------------------------------------
300  /** Handles mouse exit events
301   *  Use MouseListener in Java 1.1.6 or later.
302   */
303  public boolean mouseExit(Event evt, int x, int y)
304  {
305      if (curMsg != null && curMsg.isInitialized &&
306          curMsg.urlString != null)
307              getAppletContext().showStatus("");
308      mouseEnter = false;
309      return(true);
310  }
311  //------------------------------------------------------------
312  /** Runs the thread that scrolls the messages. */
313  public void run()
314  {
315      Rectangle rec = bounds();
       // Use getBounds in Java 1.1.6 or later
```

```
316     int x, y;
317     Graphics gcLEDoff;
318     imgDisp = createImage(rec.width, rec.height);
319     rec.width -= bwidth * 2;
320     rec.height -= bwidth * 2;
321     imgLEDoff = createImage(rec.width, rec.height);
322     gcLEDoff = imgLEDoff.getGraphics();
323     gcLEDoff.setColor(bgColor);
324     gcLEDoff.fillRect(0, 0, rec.width, rec.height);
325     gcLEDoff.setColor(LEDoffColor);
326
327     // Draw an array of unlit "light emitting diodes" (LED)
328     for (y = 0; y < rec.height; y += LEDsize)
329     {
330         for (x = 0; x < rec.width; x += LEDsize)
331         {
332             if(ovalLED)
333                 gcLEDoff.fillOval(x, y,
334                                     LEDsize - 1, LEDsize - 1);
335             else
336                 gcLEDoff.fillRect(x, y,
337                                     LEDsize - 1, LEDsize - 1);
338         }
339     }
340     gcLEDoff.dispose();
341
342     Graphics gcDisp;
343     int dispWidth, dispHeight;
344     x = 0;
345     y = 0;
346     gcDisp = imgDisp.getGraphics();
347     // Draw the 3-D border and outline (if specified)
348     if(bwidth != 0)
349     {
350         int bLine = 0;
351         if(borderoutline) bLine = 1;
352         gcDisp.setColor(borderColor);
353         gcDisp.fillRect(0, 0, rec.width, rec.height);
354         if (bwidth > 1)
355             gcDisp.draw3DRect(bLine, bLine,
356                     rec.width - 2*bLine - 1,
```

```
357                        rec.height - 2*bLine -1, true);
358        if (bwidth > 2)
359            gcDisp.draw3DRect(bwidth - bLine - 1,
360                bwidth - bLine - 1,
361                rec.width - 2*bwidth + 2*bLine + 1,
362                rec.height - 2*bwidth + 2*bLine + 1, false);
363        if(borderoutline)
364        {
365            gcDisp.setColor(Color.black);
366            gcDisp.drawRect(0, 0, rec.width-1, rec.height-1);
367            gcDisp.drawRect(bwidth - 1,
368                            bwidth - 1,
369                            rec.width - 2*bwidth + 1,
370                            rec.height - 2*bwidth + 1);
371        }
372    }
373    gcDisp.setColor(bgColor);
374    gcDisp.fillRect(bwidth, bwidth, rec.width - 2*bwidth,
375                                    rec.height - 2*bwidth);
376
377    dispWidth = rec.width - 2*bwidth;
378    dispHeight = rec.height - 2*bwidth;
379    gcDisp.clipRect(bwidth, bwidth, dispWidth, dispHeight);
380    gcDisp.translate(bwidth + 1, bwidth + 1);
381    gcDisp.drawImage(imgLEDoff, 0, 0, this);
382    gcDisp.dispose();
383    repaint(10);   // Paint the blank LED display panel
384
385    // Prepare offscreen images of messages and scroll them
386    int action = BEGIN_SCROLL_IN;
387    int xFinal = 0;
388    int yFinal = 0;
389
390    while((msgNum < MessageList.size()) && tickerThread != null)
391    {
392        curMsg = (TickerMessage) MessageList.elementAt(msgNum);
393        // Create an offscreen image of a message only once
394        if(curMsg.message != null &&
395           action == BEGIN_SCROLL_IN &&
396           !curMsg.isInitialized)
397        {
```

```
398              Graphics gcMsg;
399              FontMetrics fm;
400              int baseline;
401
402              Image imgTemp = createImage(1, 1);
403              Graphics gcTemp = imgTemp.getGraphics();
404              // Use a temporary image to figure out dimensions
405              gcTemp.setFont(curMsg.font);
406              fm = gcTemp.getFontMetrics();
407              curMsg.msgWidth = fm.stringWidth(curMsg.message);
408              curMsg.msgHeight = fm.getHeight();
409              baseline = fm.getMaxDescent();
410              curMsg.imgWidth = curMsg.msgWidth * LEDsize;
411              curMsg.imgHeight = curMsg.msgHeight * LEDsize;
412              gcTemp.dispose();
413              // Now create image with appropriate sizes
414              imgTemp = createImage(curMsg.msgWidth,
415                                           curMsg.msgHeight);
416              gcTemp = imgTemp.getGraphics();
417              gcTemp.setFont(curMsg.font);
418              curMsg.imgWidth = curMsg.msgWidth * LEDsize;
419              curMsg.imgHeight = curMsg.msgHeight * LEDsize;
420              gcTemp.setColor(Color.black);
421              gcTemp.fillRect(0, 0,
422                         curMsg.msgWidth,
                           curMsg.msgHeight);
423              gcTemp.setColor(Color.white);
424              gcTemp.drawString(curMsg.message, 0,
425                         curMsg.msgHeight - baseline);
426              gcTemp.dispose();
427
428              curMsg.imgMsg = createImage(curMsg.imgWidth,
429                                           curMsg.imgHeight);
430              gcMsg = curMsg.imgMsg.getGraphics();
431              gcMsg.setColor(bgColor);
432              gcMsg.fillRect(0, 0, curMsg.imgWidth,
433                         curMsg.imgHeight);
434
435              int [] pixels = new int[curMsg.msgWidth *
436                                           curMsg.msgHeight];
```

```
437        PixelGrabber pg = new PixelGrabber(imgTemp, 0, 0,
438            curMsg.msgWidth, curMsg.msgHeight, pixels, 0,
439                                    curMsg.msgWidth);
440        boolean grabbedPixels = false;
441        try
442        {
443            grabbedPixels = pg.grabPixels();
444        }
445        catch(InterruptedException e)
446        {
447            grabbedPixels = false;
448        }
449        if(grabbedPixels)
450        {
451            Color pixColor;
452            for (y = 0; y < curMsg.msgHeight; y++)
453            {
454                for (x = 0; x < curMsg.msgWidth; x++)
455                {
456                    if(pixels[y * curMsg.msgWidth + x] ==
457                                    Color.black.getRGB())
458                        pixColor = LEDoffColor;
459                    else
460                        pixColor = curMsg.color;
461                    gcMsg.setColor(pixColor);
462                    if(ovalLED)
463                    {
464                        gcMsg.fillOval(x*LEDsize, y*LEDsize,
465                                LEDsize - 1, LEDsize - 1);
466                    }
467                    else
468                    {
469                        gcMsg.fillRect(x*LEDsize, y*LEDsize,
470                                LEDsize - 1, LEDsize - 1);
471                    }
472                }
473            }
474        }
475        gcMsg.dispose();
476        curMsg.isInitialized = true;
477    }
```

```
478             // Get ready to scroll off-screen image of message
479             gcDisp = imgDisp.getGraphics();
480             gcDisp.clipRect(bwidth, bwidth,
481                           dispWidth, dispHeight);
482             gcDisp.translate(bwidth + 1, bwidth + 1);
483
484             if(action == BEGIN_SCROLL_IN)
485             {
486                 if(mouseEnter)
487                 {
488                     if(curMsg.urlString != null)
489                         getAppletContext().showStatus(
490                                         curMsg.urlString);
491                     else
492                         getAppletContext().showStatus("");
493                 }
494                 xFinal = (dispWidth - curMsg.imgWidth)/2 /
495                                         LEDsize*LEDsize;
496                 yFinal = (dispHeight - curMsg.imgHeight) / 2 /
497                                         LEDsize*LEDsize;
498             if(scrollright)
499                     x = -curMsg.imgWidth + LEDsize;
500             else
501                     x = dispWidth / LEDsize * LEDsize - LEDsize;
502             action = SCROLL_IN;
503             }
504             // Scroll current message into the LED panel
505             if(action == SCROLL_IN)
506             {
507                 if(scrollright)
508                 {
509                     gcDisp.drawImage(curMsg.imgMsg, x,
510                                         yFinal, this);
511                     if (x > 0)
512                     {
513                         gcDisp.clipRect(0, 0, x, dispHeight);
514                         gcDisp.drawImage(imgLEDoff, 0, 0, this);
515                     }
516                     x += LEDsize;
517                     if (x > xFinal)
518                         action = BEGIN_SCROLL_OUT;
519                 }
```

```
520              else
521              {
522                  gcDisp.drawImage(curMsg.imgMsg,
523                                   x, yFinal, this);
524                  if (x + curMsg.imgWidth <
525                          dispWidth / LEDsize * LEDsize)
526                  {
527                      gcDisp.clipRect(x + curMsg.imgWidth, 0,
528                                   dispWidth - x, dispHeight);
529                      gcDisp.drawImage(imgLEDoff, 0, 0, this);
530                  }
531                  x -= LEDsize;
532                  if (x < xFinal)
533                      action = BEGIN_SCROLL_OUT;
534              }
535          }
536          // Prepare to scroll out current message
537          if(action == BEGIN_SCROLL_OUT)
538          {
539              x = xFinal;
540              y = yFinal;
541              if(scrollright)
542              {
543                  x += LEDsize;
544                  xFinal = dispWidth / LEDsize * LEDsize;
545              }
546              else
547              {
548                  x -= LEDsize;
549                  xFinal = -curMsg.imgWidth;
550              }
551              action = SCROLL_OUT;
552          }
553          // Scroll the message out of the LED panel
554          if(action == SCROLL_OUT)
555          {
556              if(scrollright)
557              {
558                  gcDisp.drawImage(curMsg.imgMsg,
559                                   x, yFinal, this);
560                  if (x > 0)
561                  {
```

```
562                      gcDisp.clipRect(0, 0, x, dispHeight);
563                      gcDisp.drawImage(imgLEDoff, 0, 0, this);
564                  }
565              x += LEDsize;
566              if (x >= xFinal)
567                  action = END_SCROLL;
568          }
569          else
570          {
571              gcDisp.drawImage(curMsg.imgMsg,
572                              x, yFinal, this);
573              if(x + curMsg.imgWidth <
574                      dispWidth / LEDsize * LEDsize)
575              {
576                  gcDisp.clipRect(x + curMsg.imgWidth,
577                          0, dispWidth - x, dispHeight);
578                  gcDisp.drawImage(imgLEDoff, 0, 0, this);
579              }
580              x -= LEDsize;
581              if (x <= xFinal)
582                  action = END_SCROLL;
583          }
584      }
585      // Finish scrolling
586      if(action == END_SCROLL)
587      {
588          gcDisp.dispose();
589          gcDisp = imgDisp.getGraphics();
590          gcDisp.clipRect(bwidth, bwidth,
591                      dispWidth, dispHeight);
592          gcDisp.translate(bwidth + 1, bwidth + 1);
593          gcDisp.drawImage(imgLEDoff, 0, 0, this);
594          msgNum++; // Move on to next message
595          if(msgNum == MessageList.size()) msgNum = 0;
596          action = BEGIN_SCROLL_IN;
597      }
598      gcDisp.dispose();
599      repaint(curMsg.delay/5);
600      try
601      {
```

```
602                    Thread.sleep(curMsg.delay);
603              }
604          catch(InterruptedException e)
605          {
606              break;
607          }
608      }
609  }
610  //------------------------------------------------------------
611  /** Repaints the image when necessary. */
612  public boolean imageUpdate(Image img, int flags,
613                             int x, int y, int w, int h)
614  {
615      if((flags & ALLBITS) != 0)repaint();
616      return(true);
617  }
618  //------------------------------------------------------------
619  /** Updates the display by calling paint() */
620  public void update(Graphics g)
621  {
622      paint(g);
623  }
624  //------------------------------------------------------------
625  /** Displays off-screen image in the applet */
626  public void paint(Graphics g)
627  {
628      if(imgDisp != null) g.drawImage(imgDisp, 0, 0, this);
629  }
630  //------------------------------------------------------------
631  /** Starts the thread that scrolls the messages */
632  public void start()
633  {
634      if (tickerThread == null)
635      {
636          tickerThread = new Thread(this);
637          tickerThread.start();
638      }
639  }
640  //------------------------------------------------------------
641  /** Stops the applet by stopping the thread */
642  public void stop()
643  {
644      if (tickerThread != null)
645      {
```

```
646                    tickerThread.stop();
647                    tickerThread = null;
648            }
649        }
650 }
```

ANNOTATIONS

The **LEDTicker** class defines and uses a class named **TickerMessage** to store the information about each message that the ticker has to scroll. Among the information specific to a message is an off-screen image that stores the message as it would appear when rendered in its entirety on an LED message board. Note that this image is only as tall as the message text and only as wide as necessary to hold the entire message. Typically, the **LEDTicker** applet's display area will be taller than but not as wide as the off-screen image of the message.

The **LEDTicker** applet also uses an off-screen image of the applet's display area where everything is composed before actually drawing the applet on the screen. A thread repeatedly copies the off-screen image of the message onto the off-screen image of the applet's display area. Then the off-screen display is copied to the screen whenever the screen is repainted. Figure 1-7 illustrates this approach to scrolling the messages.

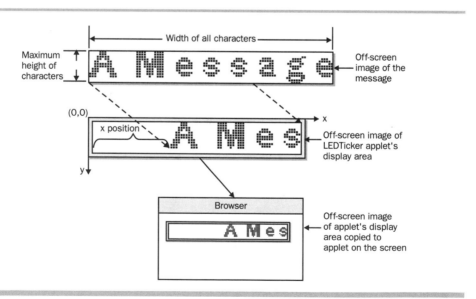

FIGURE 1-7.   The **LEDTicker** applet scrolls a message by repeatedly copying from the off-screen image while changing the x position.

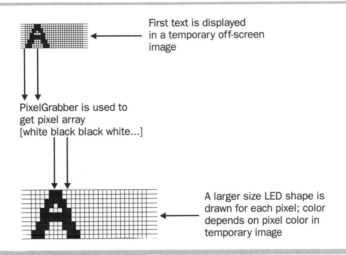

First text is displayed in a temporary off-screen image

PixelGrabber is used to get pixel array [white black black white...]

A larger size LED shape is drawn for each pixel; color depends on pixel color in temporary image

FIGURE 1-8. Preparing the array of LEDs in the **LEDTicker** applet.

The other tricky part of the design is to create the off-screen image of an array of LEDs that displays the message in a given font face, style, and size. Figure 1-8 illustrates how this off-screen image is prepared. As the figure shows, the message is first drawn on a temporary off-screen image, using the specified font face, style, and font size. The message is drawn on this temporary off-screen image in white on a black background. Then a **PixelGrabber** object is used to get all of the pixels from this temporary off-screen image. Next, a blank image is prepared with enough room to hold all of the LEDs required to display the message in its entirety.

The code then scans through the pixels and does one of the following:

◆ If a black pixel is found, it draws an LED using the unlit LED color.

◆ If a white pixel is found, it draws an LED in the current message color.

The end result is an off-screen image that has an array of LEDs (of a given shape, square or oval) with the message text.

These are the key aspects of the **LEDTicker** applet design. The rest of the work involves implementing the **run()** method to copy the message from the off-screen image to the applet (as illustrated in Figure 1-7).

THE TICKERMESSAGE CLASS   The **LEDTicker** class defines a **TickerMessage** class to store attributes of each message specified in the HTML file. Lines 63 through 92 define the **TickerMessage** class. The **isInitialized** variable (line 80) indicates whether the **TickerMessage** object is initialized or not. That variable is initially set to **false**. Later on, the **run()** method initializes the **TickerMessage** object and sets the **isInitialized** variable to **true**.

Another important variable in **TickerMessage** is **Image imgMsg**. This is the off-screen image of the message rendered on an array of LEDs, as discussed at the beginning of the "Annotations" section.

LEDTICKER INITIALIZATION   Lines 119 through 202 implement the **init()** method that initializes the **LEDTicker** applet. The bulk of the initialization work is to read all of the default parameter values and create a **TickerMessage** object for each message specified in the HTML file. These **TickerMessage** objects are then stored in the **MessageList** array declared in line 102.

Lines 121 through 138 of the **init()** method initialize various variables to a known initial state. Next, lines 140 through 175 get a number of parameter values. Each parameter value is obtained by calling **getParameter()**, and then the value is saved in an appropriate internal variable. I will not discuss each parameter in detail because the approach is similar to the ones used in the other applets in this chapter.

Color parameters are processed by calling the **parseColorParam()** method, defined in lines 209 through 219. Font parameters are processed using the **parseFontParam()** method, defined in lines 226 through 261. Each font parameter has a value in a specific format, such as **"Helvetica,Plain,12"**, where **Helvetica** is the font face, **Plain** is the style, and **12** is the font size. The **parseFontParam()** method parses this string and returns a **Font** object.

Lines 178 through 201 get and process individual message parameters (the ones with names **message1**, **message2**, **message3**, and so on). However, even after the **init()** method is finished, the actual off-screen images of the messages are not initialized. This step is done as each message is first scrolled in the **run()** method.

LEDTICKER STARTUP AND SHUTDOWN   After loading the **LEDTicker** applet, the Web browser (or **appletviewer**) calls the applet's **start()** method. Lines 632 through 639 implement the **start()** method, which gets everything going by creating the **tickerThread** object and calling its **start()** method, as follows:

```
634        if (tickerThread == null)
635        {
636            tickerThread = new Thread(this);
637            tickerThread.start();
638        }
```

To create the **tickerThread** object, line 636 calls the **Thread()** constructor with the **LEDTicker** class as its argument (the **this** keyword means the current class). This means that the new thread of execution will call the **run()** method in the **LEDTicker** class. Line 637 calls the new thread's **start()** method. At this point, the new thread of execution begins and the **run()** method is called.

To stop the applet, the Web browser (or **appletviewer**, wherever the applet is running) calls the **stop()** method, shown in lines 642 through 649. The **stop()** method simply calls the **stop()** method of the **tickerThread** object and then sets the **tickerThread** variable to **null**. This stops the scrolling message.

TICKER IMAGE INITIALIZATIONS   The **run()** method, in lines 313 through 609, performs all of the key steps of scrolling the ticker messages. Before displaying any messages, the **run()** method gets the dimensions of the applet's display area (line 315) and prepares two off-screen images:

◆   Line 318 creates the **Image imgDisp**, which serves as the off-screen image working area where every frame of the scrolling message is prepared before it is copied to the on-screen applet by the **paint()** method. The off-screen image **imgDisp** has the same size as the applet.

◆   Lines 319 through 340 prepare the **Image imgLEDoff**, which has the same size as the applet and depicts an array of unlit LEDs. Note that the rows of LEDs are drawn by two **for** loops (see lines 328 and 330). The **ovalLED** variable controls the shape of the LEDs. If **ovalLED** is **true**, line 333 calls the **fillOval()** method to draw oval-shaped LEDs; otherwise, line 336 calls **fillRect()** to draw square LEDs.

Lines 342 through 372 draw a 3-D border around the **imgDisp**, the off-screen image of the applet. Line 374 calls **fillRect()** to fill this image with the background color. Line 381 copies the unlit LED array from **imgLEDoff** to **imgDisp**. Then line 383 calls **repaint()** to update the applet's display. This way, the applet starts to show the empty LED message board right away.

There is still one more image initialization remaining. Line 390 starts the **while** loop that goes through the messages one by one and scrolls them in the applet. The **msgNum** variable keeps track of the current message number, while the **curMsg** variable is the **TickerMessage** object for the current message. The **if** statement on line 394 checks whether the current message has been initialized. If not, lines 398 through 477 prepare the off-screen image of the message as it appears when displayed on the LED message board (see the beginning of the "Annotations" section and Figure 1-8 for a description of this approach).

Lines 402 through 426 prepare a temporary **Image** called **imgTemp** that holds an image of the message as it is drawn with the specified font and color. Line 428 creates the off-screen image of the image **curMsg.imgMsg**, which is meant to hold the message as it appears on an array of LEDs.

Lines 435 through 448 get the pixels from the **imgTemp** image into the **pixels[]** array:

```
435        int [] pixels = new int[curMsg.msgWidth *
436                              curMsg.msgHeight];
437        PixelGrabber pg = new PixelGrabber(imgTemp, 0, 0,
438          curMsg.msgWidth, curMsg.msgHeight, pixels, 0,
439                              curMsg.msgWidth);
440        boolean grabbedPixels = false;
441        try
442        {
```

```
443                    grabbedPixels = pg.grabPixels();
444              }
445              catch(InterruptedException e)
446              {
447                    grabbedPixels = false;
448              }
```

Lines 437 through 439 create a **PixelGrabber** object named **pg** to hold the pixels of the **imgTemp** image. Line 443, inside the **try** block, calls the **grabPixels()** method to get the pixels. After **grabPixels()** returns, the pixels from the **imgTemp** image should be in the **pixels[]** array.

Lines 449 through 474 loop through the **pixels[]** array and for each pixel draw an LED in the **curMsg.imgMsg** image. If a pixel in the **pixels[]** array is black, an unlit LED is drawn; otherwise an LED in the current message color is drawn. As lines 462 through 471 show, the shape of the LED depends on the **ovalLED** variable:

```
462                    if(ovalLED)
463                    {
464                          gcMsg.fillOval(x*LEDsize, y*LEDsize,
465                                      LEDsize - 1, LEDsize - 1);
466                    }
467                    else
468                    {
469                          gcMsg.fillRect(x*LEDsize, y*LEDsize,
470                                      LEDsize - 1, LEDsize - 1);
471                    }
```

If **ovalLED** is true, line 464 calls **fillOval()** to draw an oval-shaped LED; otherwise line 469 calls **fillRect()** to draw a square LED.

TICKER SCROLLING   Apart from the lengthy image initializations, the **run()** method also scrolls each message. The scrolling is controlled by a variable named **action** that can take the following values:

◆ **BEGIN_SCROLL_IN** gets ready to start the scrolling. Lines 484 through 503 handle this case, where various variables are initialized in preparation for the scrolling to start. After initializing variables, this step sets **action** to **SCROLL_IN** (see line 502).

◆ **SCROLL_IN** continues to scroll. Lines 505 through 535 handle this case. Each time, the **curMsg.imgMsg** is copied to a new location of the applet's off-screen image, **imgDisp**, and the x coordinate is adjusted. When the message is completely in the applet, line 518 or line 533 sets the **action** to **BEGIN_SCROLL_OUT**.

◆ **BEGIN_SCROLL_OUT** gets ready to scroll the message out of the applet. Lines 537 through 552 handle this case. As in **BEGIN_SCROLL_IN**, this step initializes some variables so that the message properly scrolls out of the applet. Line 551 sets **action** to **SCROLL_OUT**.

◆ **SCROLL_OUT** continues to move the message out of the applet. Lines 554 through 584 handle the scrolling-out phase. In each step, the image from **curMsg.imgMsg** is copied to **imgDisp** and the x coordinate is adjusted. When the message is all out of the applet, line 567 or line 582 sets the **action** variable to **END_SCROLL**.

◆ **END_SCROLL** resets everything after scrolling is done so that scrolling can begin again. Lines 586 through 597 handle this phase. Line 596 sets **action** back to **BEGIN_SCROLL_IN**.

After every step, line 599 calls **repaint()** to update the applet. Then, lines 600 through 607 call the **sleep()** method to stop the thread of execution for a number of milliseconds (specified by the **delay** parameter in the HTML file).

The **paint()** method handles the actual painting of the applet. Lines 625 through 629 implement the **paint()** method, which simply copies the off-screen image of the applet onto the screen:

```
628    if(imgDisp != null) g.drawImage(imgDisp, 0, 0, this);
```

MOUSE EVENT HANDLERS   The **LEDTicker** class also includes three methods for handling mouse events:

◆ The **mouseDown()** method (lines 266 through 286) is called when the user clicks on the applet. This method creates a **URL** object for the current message's associated URL string (line 273) and then calls the **showDocument()** method (lines 275 and 277). This causes the Web browser to jump to the new URL.

◆ The **mouseEnter()** method (lines 291 through 298) is called when the user moves the mouse pointer into the applet. This applet displays the URL string in the status area (line 295) and sets the **mouseEnter** variable to **true** (line 296).

◆ The **mouseExit()** method (lines 303 through 310) is called when the user moves the mouse pointer out of the applet. This method displays a blank string in the status area (line 307) and sets the **mouseEnter** variable to **false** (line 308).

Java 2

These event handlers are deprecated in Java 1.1.6 and later. Instead, you should use a **MouseListener** object, as explained in the "Understanding ImageButton" section earlier in this chapter. In the **ch01\ticker\java2** directory of the CD-ROM, you will find a version of **LEDTicker.java** file, modified to use the new event-handling method.

Business and Finance

Billboard

Calculator

USMortgage

CurrencyConvert

Calendar

BusinessChart

J ava applets introduced the concept of *executable content* in the form of applets that execute in the browser. With executable content came the ability to do much more than simply display text and images in a Web page. Applets allow you to present information in a unique way. You can write an applet that downloads data from your Web server and plots the data in various ways based on the user's selection. The key is that the Web server sends the applet's code, and the applet then downloads the data once. After that, all data manipulation and display is handled by the applet running inside your Java-capable Web browser (a Java-capable Web browser includes a Java Virtual Machine that can execute Java code).

You can use Java applets for a variety of business and finance needs, such as advertising, scheduling, displaying business charts, calculating mortgage payments, converting from one currency to another, and so on. This chapter walks you through the source code for a few typical business and finance applets. You can use these applets as is or adapt them for your own use. You will find the following applets in this chapter:

◆ **Billboard**—An applet for displaying multiple advertisement banners, each of which is a link to a Web site

◆ **Calculator**—A simple calculator

◆ **USMortgage**—A mortgage calculator for U.S. mortgages

◆ **CurrencyConvert**—A currency conversion applet

◆ **Calendar**—A calendar applet

◆ **BusinessChart**—A charting applet that can display data in a pie chart or bar chart

An Advertisement Banner

Web sites are essentially storefronts on the Internet, and as such each Web site promotes an organization's products and services. The promotion is typically through advertisement banners—small strips of images that act as links to a Web page that further describes the advertised products or services. Sometimes companies pay for the privilege of displaying advertisement banners at popular Web sites such as a search engine that users visit often.

One way to display an advertisement banner is to use HTML's **<img>** and **<a>** tags with an animated GIF (CompuServe Graphics Interchange Format) image so that the Web browser jumps to a new page when the user clicks on the image. The animated GIF image is a single image with multiple animation frames that the browser can cycle through. This HTML-based approach is a quick and easy way to display advertisement banners. However, the HTML-only solution is somewhat limiting. You can have only one image with one associated link denoted by a URL

(Uniform Resource Locator) or address. Also, you need an animated GIF file for special effects. A more flexible solution would be to design a Java applet that displayed any number of images, each with a different URL. The applet could also display some special effects as it moved from one image to the next. The **Billboard** applet, presented in the new few sections, does just that—it displays advertisement banners.

Using Billboard

Before you learn the programming details of the **Billboard** applet, you should see what the applet does and how you can configure it through parameters in an HTML file. The companion CD-ROM's **ch02\billbrd** directory contains all of the files (including sample images for the advertisements) that you need to try out **Billboard**.

To see the **Billboard** applet in action, follow these steps:

1. Insert this book's companion CD-ROM into your system's CD-ROM drive. On UNIX systems, you also have to mount the CD-ROM with the **mount** command.

2. Start a Java-capable Web browser.

3. Using the browser's File | Open menu, open the HTML file **TestBB.html** from the **ch02\billbrd** directory of the CD-ROM.

As the **Billboard** applet runs, it displays advertisement banners (specified through **<param>** tags, as you will see in the next section) one after another, with a long pause in between. During each transition from one image to another, the applet uses one of several special effects. Figure 2-1 shows a typical advertisement banner displayed by **Billboard**. If you move the mouse pointer over the applet, the URL associated with that advertisement appears in the status area of the browser. If you click on the applet, the browser loads and displays the Web page referenced by the URL.

FIGURE 2-1. An advertisement banner displayed by the **Billboard** applet.

To use the **Billboard** applet in an HTML file, you have to configure it through **<param>** tags. These tags specify parameters such as the images to be displayed and the URL associated with each image. For example, here is the **TestBB.html** file that you used when you tried out the **Billboard** applet:

```
<html>
<body>
<applet code="Billboard.class" width = 400 height = 60>
   <param name=url value="http://jump.altavista.com/amazon.go?%2bbarkakati">
   <param name=image1 value = "javaaa.gif">
   <param name=url1 value = "http://www.osborne.com/program/index.htm">
   <param name=image2 value = "1xsimage.gif">
   <param name=url2 value =
"http://www.amazon.com/exec/obidos/ASIN/0764531751/o/qid=907982280/
sr=2-1/002-9577124-3582461">
   <param name=image3 value ="dpimage.gif">
   <param name=url3 value =
"http://www.amazon.com/exec/obidos/ASIN/0764530763/qid=907982363/
sr=1-1/002-9577124-3582461">
   <param name=image4 value = "uwbimage.gif">
   <param name=url4 value =
"http://www.amazon.com/exec/obidos/ASIN/076453016X/o/qid=907982363/
sr=2-1/002-9577124-3582461">
   <param name=image5 value = "nbbooks.gif">
   <param name=url5 value =
"http://www.amazon.com/exec/obidos/Author=Barkakati%2C%20Nabajyoti/
002-9577124-3582461">
</applet>
</body>
</html>
```

This HTML file is configured to display advertisement banners about some of my books. For each book, I used a URL that takes the user to an appropriate page on the online bookseller **www.amazon.com**.

The **TestBB.html** file embeds the **Billboard** applet with the following **<applet>** tag:

```
<applet code="Billboard.class" width = 400 height = 60>
```

In this example, the **<applet>** tag has three attributes:

◆ **code="Billboard.class"** specifies the name of the Java applet's class.

◆ **width = 400** specifies the applet's display width as 400 pixels.

◆ **height = 60** specifies the applet's display height as 60 pixels.

Next comes a set of **<param>** tags that are placed between the opening **<applet>** tag and the closing **</applet>** tag. Through these **<param>** tags you can specify various parameters that configure the **Billboard** applet:

◆ **delay**—the number of milliseconds between successive advertisement transitions

◆ **url**—the default URL, used for images without any specific URL

◆ **target**—the HTML frame in which the Web page referenced by a URL is loaded

◆ **image*N***—the filename for the *N*th image (such as **"javaaa.gif"**), where *N* = 1, 2, 3, . . .

◆ **delay*N***—the number of milliseconds for which the *N*th image is displayed

◆ **url*N***—the URL associated with the *N*th image (such as **"http://java.sun.com"**)

◆ **target*N***—the HTML frame in which **url*N*** is loaded (such as **"_top"** or **"_blank"**)

You do not have to override the delay, URL, and HTML target frame for each advertisement banner. Typically, you would specify only the image filename and the URL associated with the image. For example, in the **TestBB.html** file, the first image and URL are specified as follows:

```
<param name=image1 value = "javaaa.gif">
<param name=url1 value = "http://www.osborne.com/program/index.htm">
```

The value of each of the image parameters (**image1**, **image2**, **image3**, and so on) is the filename of the image to be used for that advertisement banner. The applet loads the image from the location in which the Web page (that references the applet's class) is stored. In other words, if you refer to the applet in an HTML file located in a specific directory on the Web server, place the image files in the same directory. The value of each URL parameter (**url1**, **url2**, **url3**, and so on) is a complete URL of the form **"http://www.osborne.com"**.

To learn more about the effect of these parameters on the behavior of the **Billboard** applet, you might want to experiment with them. Try changing some of the parameters in the HTML file, loading the applet in a Web browser or **appletviewer**, and seeing what happens.

It's easy to use the **Billboard** applet in a Web page to cycle through advertisement banners. Follow these steps to use **Billboard** at your Web site:

1. Copy the class files, **Billboard.class** and **Billboard$Advertisement.class**, from the CD-ROM's **ch02\billbrd** directory to your Web server. If you have a Web page from an Internet service provider (ISP), follow the ISP's instructions for uploading files to the Web server. Typically, you would use FTP (File Transfer Protocol) to send the class files to a specific directory on the Web server. When using FTP, remember to set the file type to Binary.

2. Using a paint program such as Paint Shop Pro 5, prepare the images for advertisement banners (make each image about 400 pixels wide by 60 pixels tall).

3. Upload these images to your Web server as well.

4. Edit your home page's HTML file on the Web server and add an **<applet>** tag to embed the **Billboard** applet. Using information from earlier parts of this section, add **<param>** tags with your image filenames and associated URLs.

5. Reload your home page on a Java-capable Web browser to see the results.

I used the **Billboard** applet on my home page at **www.psn.net/~naba/** to display some advertisement banners. I inserted the **<applet>** tag from the **TestBB.html** file into my home page and uploaded the class files and the image files to a directory on my ISP's Web server. Figure 2-2 shows my home page with the **Billboard** applet

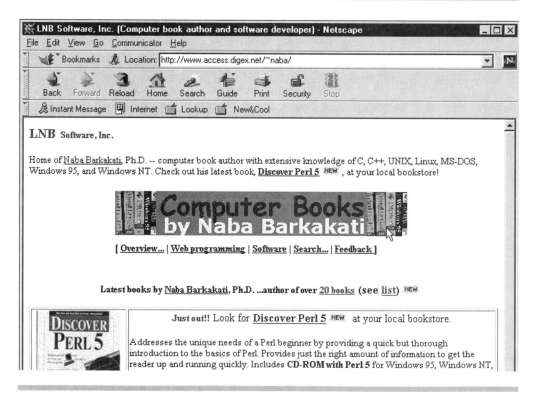

FIGURE 2-2.   The **Billboard** applet used in a Web page to display an advertisement banner.

displaying the advertisements. Note the URL in the status area at the bottom of the browser window.

Billboard

Understanding Billboard

Now that you have seen how the **Billboard** applet works and how you can configure and use it, let's study the **Billboard.java** file to understand how the applet is implemented. The following listing shows the **Billboard.java** program in its entirety. I describe the program in detail in the subsequent sections.

```
1  //------------------------------------------------------------------
2  // Billboard.java
3  //
4  // Implements a billboard that cycles through images that act
5  // as advertisements. When a user clicks on an image, the applet
6  // loads the Web page referenced by the associated URL.
7  //------------------------------------------------------------------
8  import java.applet.*;
9  import java.net.*;
10 import java.util.*;
11 import java.awt.*;
12 import java.awt.image.*;
13 // Javadoc comments
14 /**
15  * Billboard cycles through advertisements (each one is an image).
16  * When a user clicks on an advertisement, the applet loads the
17  * document corresponding to the URL associated with the image.
18  * <p>
19  * The Billboard applet accepts the following parameters:
20  * <ul>
21  *    <li> delay - default delay in milliseconds
22  *    <li> url   - default URL for all advertisements
23  *    <li> target - default HTML frame for all advertisements
24  *    <li> <b>Add the following set for each advertisement</b>
25  *    <ul>
26  *       <li> imageN - image for Nth (N=1, 2, 3, ...) advertisement
27  *       <li> delayN - (optional) delay for Nth advertisement
28  *       <li> urlN - (optional) URL for Nth advertisement
29  *       <li> targetN - (optional) HTML frame for Nth advertisement
30  *    </ul>
31  * </ul>
32  *
33  */
```

```
34  public class Billboard extends Applet implements Runnable
35  {
36      // Class used to store information about each advertisement
37      final class Advertisement
38      {
39          public String urlString;
40          public String target;
41          public Image image;
42          public int delay;
43          public Advertisement()
44          {
45              image = null;
46              delay = 0;
47              urlString = null;
48              target = null;
49          }
50      }
51      String urlString;
52      String target;
53      int delay;
54      Vector allAds = new Vector(8);
55      Advertisement curAd;
56      int curAdIndex;
57      Dimension appletSize;
58      int appletWidth, appletHeight;
59      int xStep, yStep;
60      public Thread animThread = null;
61      Image curImage = null;
62      Frame parentFrame = null;
63      // Various visual effects
64      static int L2R = 0;          // Left to right
65      static int R2L = 1;          // Right to left
66      static int T2B = 2;          // Top to bottom
67      static int B2T = 3;          // Bottom to top
68      static int C2O = 4;          // Center to out
69      static int CVO = 5;          // Center to vertically out
70      static int CHO = 6;          // Center to horizontally out
71      static int LTO = 7;          // Left top to out
72      static int LBO = 8;          // Left bottom to out
73      static int RTO = 9;          // Right top to out
74      static int RBO = 10;         // Right bottom to out
75      static int NUMEFFECTS = 11;  // Total number of effects
76      static long E_DELAY = 75;    // Effect animation delay (ms)
```

```
77   /** Initializes the Billboard class */
78   public void init()
79   {
80       appletSize = size();   // Call getSize() in Java 1.1.6 or later
81       appletWidth = appletSize.width;
82       appletHeight = appletSize.height;
83       xStep = appletWidth/10;
84       yStep = appletHeight/10;
85       delay = 10000;   // default delay = 10000 ms = 10 seconds
86       target = "_self";
87       curAdIndex = 0;
88       // Get the parameters from the <param> tags
89       String param;
90       param = getParameter("delay");
91       if (param != null)
92           delay = Integer.valueOf(param).intValue();
93       param = getParameter("url");
94       if (param != null) urlString = param;
95       param = getParameter("url");
96       if (param != null) target = param;
97       // Retrieve the advertisements from the <param> tags
98       int i;
99       for (i = 1; ; i++)
100      {
101          param = getParameter("image"+i);
102          if (param == null) break;
103
104          Advertisement ad = new Advertisement();
105          ad.delay = delay;
106          ad.urlString = urlString;
107          ad.target = target;
108          ad.image = getImage(getDocumentBase(), param);
109          // Override delay, URL, and target, if specified
110          param = getParameter("delay"+i);
111          if(param != null)
112              ad.delay = Integer.valueOf(param).intValue();
113          param = getParameter("url"+i);
114          if(param != null) ad.urlString = param;
115          param = getParameter("target"+i);
116          if(param != null) ad.target = param;
117          allAds.addElement(ad);
118      }
119      curAd = (Advertisement)allAds.elementAt(curAdIndex);
```

```
120         Component p=this;
121         while(((p=p.getParent())!=null) && !(p instanceof Frame));
122         parentFrame = (Frame)p;
123     }
124     /** Displays the current image */
125     public void paint(Graphics g)
126     {
127         g.drawImage(curAd.image, 0, 0, appletWidth, appletHeight,
128                    this);
129     }
130     /** Updates the applet by calling paint(). */
131     public void update(Graphics g) { paint(g);}
132     /** Returns information about applet */
133     public String getAppletInfo()
134     {
135         return "Billboard by Naba Barkakati, 1998";
136     }
137     /** Gradually transitions to the next image. Draws the
138      * image at (x,y) with a starting width and height. Then
139      * gradually changes (x,y) and the width and height (with
140      * a specified amount of delay in between) until the image
141      * fills the applet.
142      */
143     void transitionAd(int x, int y, int width, int height,
144                     int xDelta, int yDelta,
145                     int wDelta, int hDelta, long delay)
146     {
147         Graphics g = getGraphics();
148         int maxWidth = appletWidth;
149         int maxHeight = appletHeight;
150         while(width <= maxWidth && width >= 0 &&
151             height <= maxHeight && height >= && animThread != null)
152         {
153             g.drawImage(curAd.image, x, y, width, height, this);
154             getToolkit().sync();
155             x = x + xDelta;
156             y = y + yDelta;
157             width = width + wDelta;
158             height = height + hDelta;
159             try
160             {
161                 Thread.sleep(delay);
162             }
```

```
163         catch(InterruptedException e){};
164         if(width > maxWidth || height > maxHeight)
165         {
166             g.drawImage(curAd.image, 0, 0, appletWidth,
167                         appletHeight, this);
168             getToolkit().sync();
169         }
170     }
171 }
172 /** Rotates through the images one by one. */
173 public void run()
174 {
175     while((curAdIndex < allAds.size()) && animThread != null)
176     {
177         curAd = (Advertisement) allAds.elementAt(curAdIndex);
178         // Pick a random effect and apply it
179         int Effect = (int)(Math.random() * (NUMEFFECTS-1));
180         if(Effect == L2R)
181             transitionAd(0, 0, 0, appletHeight, 0, 0, xStep,
182                         0, E_DELAY);
183         else if(Effect == R2L)
184             transitionAd(appletWidth, 0, 0, appletHeight,
185                         -xStep, 0, xStep, 0, E_DELAY);
186         else if(Effect == T2B)
187             transitionAd(0, 0, appletWidth, 0, 0, 0, 0,
188                         yStep, E_DELAY);
189         else if(Effect == B2T)
190             transitionAd(0, appletHeight, appletWidth, 0, 0,
191                         -yStep, 0, yStep, E_DELAY);
192         else if(Effect == C2O)
193             transitionAd(appletWidth/2 - xStep/2,
194                         appletHeight/2 - yStep/2,
195                         xStep, yStep, -xStep/2, -yStep/2,
196                         xStep, yStep, E_DELAY);
197         else if(Effect == CVO)
198             transitionAd(0, appletHeight/2, appletWidth, 0,
199                         appletHeight, -yStep/2, 0, yStep,
200                         E_DELAY);
201         else if(Effect == CHO)
202             transitionAd(appletWidth/2, 0, 0, appletHeight,
203                         -xStep/2, 0, xStep, 0, E_DELAY);
204         else if(Effect == LTO)
205             transitionAd(0, 0, 0, 0, 0, 0, xStep, yStep,
```

```
206                                    E_DELAY);
207             else if(Effect == LBO)
208                 transitionAd(0, appletHeight, 0, 0, 0, -yStep,
209                                 xStep, yStep, E_DELAY);
210             else if(Effect == RTO)
211                 transitionAd(appletWidth, 0, 0, 0, -xStep, 0,
212                                 xStep, yStep, E_DELAY);
213             else if(Effect == RBO)
214                 transitionAd(appletWidth, appletHeight, 0, 0,
215                                 -xStep, -yStep, xStep, yStep,
216                                 E_DELAY);
217             try
218             {
219                 Thread.sleep(curAd.delay);
220             }
221             catch(InterruptedException e){};
222             curAdIndex++;
223             if(curAdIndex == allAds.size()) curAdIndex = 0;
224         }
225     }
226
227     /** Starts the applet by creating the animation thread */
228     public void start()
229     {
230         if(animThread == null)
231         {
232             animThread = new Thread(this);
233             animThread.start();
234         }
235     }
236     /** Stops the applet by stopping the thread. */
237     public void stop()
238     {
239         if(animThread != null)
240         {
241             animThread.stop();
242             animThread = null;
243         }
244     }
245     /** Loads new document when user releases mouse button. */
246     public boolean mouseUp( Event evt, int x, int Y )
```

```
247     {
248         URL url = null;
249         try
250         {
251             url = new URL(curAd.urlString);
252         }
253         catch(MalformedURLException e)
254         {
255             showStatus("Bad URL!");
256             return true;
257         }
258         getAppletContext().showDocument(url, curAd.target);
259         return true;
260     }
261     /** Displays URL when mouse enters applet. */
262     public boolean mouseEnter(Event evt, int x, int y)
263     {
264         if(parentFrame != null)
265             parentFrame.setCursor(Frame.HAND_CURSOR);
266
267         showStatus(curAd.urlString);
268         return true;
269     }
270     /** Stops showing URL when mouse exits the applet. */
271     public boolean mouseExit(Event evt, int x, int y)
272     {
273         if(parentFrame != null)
274             parentFrame.setCursor(Frame.DEFAULT_CURSOR);
275         showStatus("");
276         return true;
277     }
278 }
```

ANNOTATIONS

The **Billboard** applet is designed to animate a sequence of images, each representing an advertisement banner. The animation involves changing from one image to another after a specified delay. Also, each transition from one image to the next is done in a number of steps.

Billboard.java defines and uses an **Advertisement** class to store information about each advertisement banner. Each **Advertisement** object stores an off-screen image for that advertisement banner as well as the URL of the Web page associated with that advertisement.

During initialization, the **init()** method creates an **Advertisement** object for each advertisement banner and loads the image from the file (specified by a **<param>** tag in the HTML file) into the **Advertisement** object. The applet stores the **Advertisement** objects in an array.

Billboard performs the animations using a separate thread of execution. The applet's **start()** method creates a **Thread** object named **animThread** and calls that thread's **start()** method to get the animation started.

The applet's **run()** method constitutes the code that the **animThread** thread executes. The **run()** method selects a random transition effect and calls the **transitionAd()** method with appropriate arguments to perform the gradual transition from one image to the next.

The transition effects involve drawing the image in a series of rectangles that gradually grow in size to fill the applet's display area. The **transitionAd()** method accomplishes this by first drawing the image in a specified rectangle. Then it gradually changes the location and size of the rectangle until the image fills the applet's display area. By varying the starting rectangle and the increments, **transitionAd()** can provide a variety of transition effects.

BILLBOARD CLASSES   The **Billboard** applet has two classes, the **Billboard** class that implements the applet and the **Advertisement** class that stores information about each advertisement banner. Line 34 declares the **Billboard** class:

```
34  public class Billboard extends Applet implements Runnable
```

Because **Billboard** is an applet, it's a subclass of **Applet** (defined in the **java.applet** package). Billboard also implements the **Runnable** interface by providing a **run()** method that is used by the thread responsible for animating the advertisement banners.

Lines 37 through 50 define the **Advertisement** class used to store information about each advertisement banner. **Billboard** uses **Advertisement** as a simple data structure, like a **struct** in C or C++. There are four **public** member variables:

```
39          public String urlString;
40          public String target;
41          public Image image;
42          public int delay;
```

The **urlString** variable holds the URL associated with an advertisement banner; **image** is the off-screen image for that banner; **delay** is the number of milliseconds to display this banner; and **target** identifies the HTML frame where the URL is loaded. These variables are declared **public** to avoid having to write access methods for the **Advertisement** class. Any method in **Billboard** can access these variables simply by referring to the variable name.

Lines 43 through 49 implement the **Advertisement()** constructor, which initializes all member variables to default values.

BILLBOARD INITIALIZATION   Lines 78 through 123 implement the **init()** method that initializes the **Billboard** applet. The Web browser's Java Virtual Machine calls the **init()** method after loading the applet.

Line 80 calls **size()** and gets the dimensions of the applet's display area. The **size()** method is deprecated, meaning that it has been superseded by a newer method called **getSize()** that does the same job. Lines 81 and 82 initialize the **appletWidth** and **appletHeight** variables with the applet's width and height, respectively.

Two more variables, **xStep** and **yStep**, are initialized in lines 83 and 84. These variables are set to one-tenth the applet's width and height, respectively. The **xStep** and **yStep** variables are used in image transitions in the **run()** method.

The **init()** method then initializes a number of other variables and gets the parameters from the HTML file. For example, lines 89 through 92 get the **delay** parameter and initialize an internal integer variable named **delay**:

```
89        String param;
90        param = getParameter("delay");
91        if (param != null)
92            delay = Integer.valueOf(param).intValue();
```

Here line 90 reads the value of the **delay** parameter into the **String param**. If the parameter is specified, **param** is not **null**. Line 92 then converts the **param** string into an integer value that's stored in an integer variable, also named **delay**.

Lines 99 through 118 use a **for** loop to load all parameters named **image1**, image2, image3, and so on. The body of the **for** loop starts on line 101 with a call to the **getParameter()** method to read the value of the ith parameter. Line 102 breaks the loop if the ith parameter is not specified:

```
101           param = getParameter("image"+i);
102           if (param == null) break;
```

The **init()** method continues to read in image parameters sequentially (**image1**, **image2**, **image3**, and so on) until **getParameter()** fails to return a requested parameter value. This is a flexible way to handle parameters because it avoids having to ask the user to specify the actual number of image parameters.

After an image parameter has been read, line 104 creates an **Advertisement** object, and lines 105 through 108 initialize that object:

```
104           Advertisement ad = new Advertisement();
105           ad.delay = delay;
106           ad.urlString = urlString;
107           ad.target = target;
108           ad.image = getImage(getDocumentBase(), param);
```

Lines 105 through 107 set the **delay, urlString,** and **target** variables of the **Advertisement** object to default values. Line 108 performs the most important function—it calls the **getImage()** method to load the image for this advertisement banner. The first argument to **getImage()** is the absolute URL where the image is located. In this case, **getDocumentBase()** is used as the first argument. This means that the base URL for the image files is the same as that for the Web page. The second argument to **getImage()** is the location of the image file relative to the URL specified in the first argument. Thus, if the URL of the Web page is **"http://www.xyz.com"** and the second argument is **"images/anImage.gif"**, then **getImage()** concatenates these two strings and uses **"http://www.xyz.com/images/anImage.gif"** as the absolute URL of the image file. Hence, if you decided to place all of your images in a subdirectory named **images**, and you wanted to use an image file named **myImage.gif**, you would specify **"images/myImage.gif"** as the value of the image parameter in the HTML file.

After the **Advertisement** object has been initialized, lines 110 through 116 read and initialize image-specific URL, delay, and target parameters. Finally, line 117 adds the new **Advertisement** object to the array called **allAds** (**allAds** is initialized on line 54):

```
117            allAds.addElement(ad);
```

Line 119 initializes the current advertisement, stored in the variable named **curAd**:

```
119        curAd = (Advertisement)allAds.elementAt(curAdIndex);
```

Here **curAdIndex** is the index of the current advertisement; it's initialized to zero on line 87.

Lines 120 through 122 determine the parent frame of the applet and store the answer in the **parentFrame** variable. If the parent frame is known, the cursor can be changed when the mouse moves into the applet.

BILLBOARD STARTUP AND SHUTDOWN   After the applet is initialized, the browser's Java Virtual Machine calls the **Billboard** applet's **start()** method (lines 228 through 235) to start the applet. The **start()** method creates a new **Thread** object called **animThread** and calls that thread's **start()** method to get everything going:

```
230        if(animThread == null)
231        {
232            animThread = new Thread(this);
233            animThread.start();
234        }
```

Notice that line 232 initializes **animThread** by calling the **Thread()** constructor with **this** as its argument, where **this** refers to the **Billboard** applet. This means that the **animThread** thread will execute the **run()** method in the **Billboard** applet.

The **Billboard** applet's **stop()** method is called whenever the Web browser needs to stop the applet (because the user has jumped to a new page or the applet is no longer visible). The applet's **stop()** method (lines 237 through 244) calls the **stop()**

method of the **animThread** thread and sets the **animThread** variable to **null**. This stops the animation.

THE ANIMATION THREAD IN BILLBOARD The applet's **run()** method (lines 173 through 225) constitutes the body of code that the **animThread** thread executes in order to perform the animation. The **run()** method uses a **while** loop to rotate through the advertisements:

```
175              while((curAdIndex < allAds.size()) && animThread != null)
176              {
...  body of while loop
224              }
```

Line 177 of the **while** loop initializes the **curAd** variable to the current advertisement. Line 179 then selects a random transition effect:

```
179              int Effect = (int)(Math.random() * NUMEFFECTS);
```

The transition effects are numbered from 0 to 10 and are identified by static integer variables in lines 64 through 74. The variable **NUMEFFECTS** is set to 11, the number of transition effects. The **Math.random()** method returns a random floating-point value between 0.0 and 1.0. That floating-point value is then multiplied by **NUMEFFECTS-1** and cast to an integer to get a random number between 0 and 10.

Lines 180 through 216 call the **transitionAd()** method with different arguments to apply the transition effect. For example, here is how lines 181 and 182 call the **transitionAd()** method for a left-to-right transition (designated by variable **L2R**):

```
181              transitionAd(0, 0, 0, appletHeight, 0, 0, xStep,
182                              0, E_DELAY);
```

Now look at the transitionAd() method (lines 143 through 171). Note that lines 143 through 145 declare the method as follows:

```
143       void transitionAd(int x, int y, int width, int height,
144                          int xDelta, int yDelta,
145                          int wDelta, int hDelta, long delay)
```

where the arguments have the following meanings:

- ◆ **x, y**—initial coordinates of upper-left corner of rectangle
- ◆ **width, height**—initial size of the rectangle
- ◆ **xDelta, yDelta**—amounts by which the x and y coordinates of the rectangle's upper-left corner are incremented
- ◆ **wDelta, hDelta**—amounts by which the rectangle's width and height are incremented
- ◆ **delay**—milliseconds between successive changes in the rectangles

For the left-to-right effect, lines 181 and 182 call **transitionAd()** with the following arguments:

- ◆ **(x, y)** = (0,0), which is the upper-left corner of the applet
- ◆ **width** = 0 (the initial width is zero)
- ◆ **height** = **appletHeight** (the same height as the applet)
- ◆ **xDelta** = 0 (no change in the upper-left corner's x coordinate)
- ◆ **yDelta** = 0 (no change in the upper-left corner's y coordinate)
- ◆ **wDelta** = **xStep** (the width is incremented by one-tenth the applet's width at each step)
- ◆ **hDelta** = 0 (no change in height)
- ◆ **delay** = **E_DELAY** (defined to be 75 milliseconds on line 76)

This means that **transitionAd()** starts with an initial rectangle along the left edge of the applet with the same height as the applet. Because **xDelta** and **yDelta** are both zero, the rectangle's upper-left corner is always at the applet's upper-left corner. Because **hDelta** is zero, the rectangle's height is also fixed at the applet's height. In each step, **transitionAd()** draws the image into the rectangle, increases the rectangle's width by **xStep**, and then waits for 75 milliseconds before repeating the process. The drawing stops when the rectangle has grown to the size of the applet's display area. The end result is that the image appears to gradually grow from left to right until it finally fills the applet.

As you can see from this example of left-to-right transition effect, many different transition effects can be displayed by calling the **transitionAd()** method with different sets of arguments.

After performing the transition, the remainder of the **while** loop (lines 217 through 223) sleeps for a specified delay period and then advances to the next image before repeating the loop again.

BILLBOARD EVENT HANDLERS   When the user clicks on an advertisement banner, the **Billboard** applet jumps to the URL associated with that advertisement. In addition, when the mouse pointer moves into the applet's display area, **Billboard** displays the URL in the browser's status area. These tasks are performed by the methods that handle the mouse events. For the sake of compatibility with older browsers, **Billboard** uses the following Java 1.0–style event-handling functions:

- ◆ **mouseUp()**—called when the mouse button is released (lines 246 through 260)
- ◆ **mouseEnter()**—called when the mouse pointer enters the applet (lines 262 through 269)
- ◆ **mouseExit()**—called when the mouse pointer exits the applet (lines 271 through 277)

The **mouseUp()** method creates a URL, using the current **Advertisement** object's **urlString** variable:

251
```
url = new URL(curAd.urlString);
```

It then calls the **showDocument()** method of the applet's context to load that URL:

258
```
getAppletContext().showDocument(url, curAd.target);
```

The **mouseEnter()** method changes the cursor to a hand and displays the URL string in the browser's status area. The **mouseExit()** method does the opposite; it resets the cursor back to its default and displays an empty string in the status area.

DEPRECATED METHODS IN BILLBOARD   If you were to compile **Billboard.java** with the **javac** compiler, you would see the following warning message:

```
javac Billboard.java
Note: Billboard.java uses a deprecated API.  Recompile with "-deprecation"
for details.
1 warning
```

The term *deprecated API* refers to methods that have been replaced by newer ones. (API stands for application programming interface; APIs are the methods of the various Java classes.) If you follow the suggestion of that warning message and recompile the program with the following command:

```
javac -deprecation Billboard.java
```

you'll get a number of messages pointing out that the following methods are deprecated:

- **size()**, which gets the dimensions of the applet
- **mouseUp()**, **mouseEnter()**, and **mouseExit()**, which handle mouse events
- **setCursor()**, which sets the cursor

Of course, the **Billboard** applet continues to use these deprecated methods because many users run old Web browsers that do not support the new methods. If you want to modify the program to use the newer methods, you can do the following:

- Replace **size()** with **getSize()**.
- Replace **mouseUp()**, **mouseEnter()**, and **mouseExit()** with a class derived from **MouseListener** and override the methods **mouseClicked()**, **mouseEntered()**, and **mouseExited()**.
- Instead of calling the **setCursor()** method of the **Frame** class, call the **setCursor()** method of the **Component** class, with different arguments.

You will find the complete changes in a revised version of **Billboard.java** in the **ch02\billbrd\Java2** directory of the companion CD-ROM. If you have a newer Web browser that supports Java 1.1.5 or later, you can try out the revised applet by loading the **TestBB.html** file from the **ch02\billbrd\Java2** directory of the CD-ROM.

A Calculator

A calculator is an example of a typical business application that can be implemented easily as a Java applet. This section presents the **Calculator** applet, which demonstrates how to implement a typical Java calculator.

Using Calculator

You will find all of the files for the **Calculator** applet in the **ch02\calc** directory of the companion CD-ROM. To try out the **Calculator** applet, open the **Calc.html** file from that directory. Figure 2-3 shows a typical view of the **Calculator** applet after performing some simple calculations.

Try using the **Calculator** applet just as you would a normal pocket calculator. Click on a number button to enter a number, click one of the operation keys, such as + for addition or - for subtraction, enter another number, and finally click the = key to see the result. Of course, just like a normal calculator, the **Calculator** applet lets you keep adding or subtracting numbers one after another and finally press the =

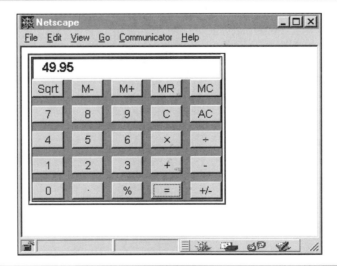

FIGURE 2-3.   The **Calculator** applet showing the result of some calculations.

key to see the result. As with a real calculator, you can then continue to add or subtract more numbers to the answer.

Unlike many of the applets you have seen so far, the **Calculator** applet does not accept any parameters from the **<param>** tags. All you need to do is include it with an **<applet>** tag. Here is the listing of the **Calc.html** file that you used to try out the **Calculator** applet in the previous section:

```
<html>
<body>
<applet code="Calculator.class" width=250 height=190>
</applet>
</body>
</html>
```

As you can see, an **<applet>** tag embeds the **Calculator** applet in the HTML file. The attributes of the **<applet>** tag are as follows:

◆ **code="Calculator.class"** specifies the name of the applet's class.

◆ **width=250** sets the applet's display width as 250 pixels.

◆ **height=190** sets the applet's display height as 190 pixels.

You can use other values for width and height; the applet's buttons and text field will resize automatically. If you want to experiment with the width and height, run the **Calculator** in **appletviewer** (which comes with the Java Development Kit) with the following command:

```
appletviewer Calc.html
```

Then resize the **appletviewer** window and see how the **Calculator** applet resizes the buttons.

Calculator

Understanding Calculator

The following listing shows the **Calculator.java** file, the Java program that implements the **Calculator** applet. Subsequent sections present the key programming features of the **Calculator.java** program.

```
1  //------------------------------------------------------------------
2  // Calculator.java
3  // A simple Java calculator
4  //------------------------------------------------------------------
5  import java.applet.*;
6  import java.awt.*;
7  /**
```

```
 8    * The Calculator applet implements a simple calculator.
 9    * It does not accept any parameters. For a good appearance,
10    * use an applet tag with width = 250 and height = 190.
11    */
12   public class Calculator extends Applet
13   {
14       // CalculatorButton represents a button on the calculator
15       class CalculatorButton extends Button
16       {
17          int operation;
18          int value;
19          CalculatorButton(String label, int operation, int value)
20          {
21             super(label);
22             this.value = value;
23             this.operation = operation;
24          }
25          public boolean action(Event evt, Object arg)
26           {
27             Panel p = (Panel)getParent();
28             Calculator parent = (Calculator)p.getParent();
29             if(operation == parent.NOOP)
30                parent.append(value);
31             else
32                parent.compute(operation);
33             return true;
34          }
35       }
36       // Operation codes associated with the buttons
37       static final int NOOP = 0;
38       static final int ADD = 1;
39       static final int SUBTRACT = 2;
40       static final int MULTIPLY = 3;
41       static final int DIVIDE = 4;
42       static final int CHANGE_SIGN = 5;
43       static final int SQUARE_ROOT = 6;
44       static final int EQUALS = 7;
45       static final int CLEAR = 8;
46       static final int ALL_CLEAR = 9;
47       static final int MEMORY_CLEAR = 10;
48       static final int MEMORY_RECALL = 11;
49       static final int MEMORY_MINUS = 12;
50       static final int MEMORY_PLUS = 13;
```

```
51    static final int PERCENT = 14;
52    static final int DECIMAL_POINT = -1;
53    // Other variables of the applet
54    boolean isNewNumber;
55    boolean hasDecimal;
56    boolean registerEmpty;
57    int lastBinOp;
58    String decimalPoint;
59    double registerValue;
60    double memoryValue;
61    TextField textDisplay;
62    /** Initializes the calculator's user interface */
63    public void init()
64    {
65        // Array of buttons for the calculator
66        CalculatorButton [] buttons =
67        {
68            new CalculatorButton("Sqrt", SQUARE_ROOT, 0),
69            new CalculatorButton("M-", MEMORY_MINUS, 0),
70            new CalculatorButton("M+", MEMORY_PLUS, 0),
71            new CalculatorButton("MR", MEMORY_RECALL, 0),
72            new CalculatorButton("MC", MEMORY_CLEAR, 0),
73
74            new CalculatorButton("7", NOOP, 7),
75            new CalculatorButton("8", NOOP, 8),
76            new CalculatorButton("9", NOOP, 9),
77            new CalculatorButton("C", CLEAR, 0),
78            new CalculatorButton("AC", ALL_CLEAR, 0),
79
80            new CalculatorButton("4", NOOP, 4),
81            new CalculatorButton("5", NOOP, 5),
82            new CalculatorButton("6", NOOP, 6),
83            new CalculatorButton("x", MULTIPLY, 0),
84            new CalculatorButton("÷", DIVIDE, 0),
85
86            new CalculatorButton("1", NOOP, 1),
87            new CalculatorButton("2", NOOP, 2),
88            new CalculatorButton("3", NOOP, 3),
89            new CalculatorButton("+", ADD, 0),
90            new CalculatorButton("-", SUBTRACT, 0),
91
92            new CalculatorButton("0", NOOP, 0),
93            new CalculatorButton(".", NOOP, DECIMAL_POINT),
```

```
 94            new CalculatorButton("%", PERCENT, 0),
 95            new CalculatorButton("=", EQUALS, 0),
 96            new CalculatorButton("+/-", CHANGE_SIGN, 0)
 97        };
 98        isNewNumber = true;
 99        lastBinOp = NOOP;
100        hasDecimal = false;
101        registerValue = 0.0;
102        memoryValue = 0.0;
103        registerEmpty = true;
104        decimalPoint = "."; // Decimal point representation
105        setLayout(new BorderLayout());
106        textDisplay = new TextField("0", 80);
107        textDisplay.setEditable(false);
108        textDisplay.setFont(new Font("Helvetica", Font.BOLD, 16));
109        textDisplay.setBackground(Color.white);
110        add("North", textDisplay);
111
112        Panel p = new Panel();
113        p.setLayout(new GridLayout(5, 5, 10, 10));
114        p.setFont(new Font("Helvetica", Font.PLAIN, 14));
115        p.setBackground(new Color(0xefefef));
116        for(int i=0; i < buttons.length; i++)
117            p.add(buttons[i]);
118        add("Center", p);
119        validate();
120    }
121    /** Appends digits to what's already in the calculator */
122    public void append(int value)
123    {
124        String digitString;
125        if(hasDecimal && value == DECIMAL_POINT) return;
126        if(value == DECIMAL_POINT)
127        {
128            if(isNewNumber)
129            {
130                textDisplay.setText("0");
131                isNewNumber = false;
132            }
133            hasDecimal = true;
134            digitString = decimalPoint;
135        }
136        else
```

```
137                 digitString = (new Integer(value)).toString();
138         if(isNewNumber)
139         {
140             textDisplay.setText(digitString);
141             if(value != 0)
142                 isNewNumber = false;
143         }
144         else
145             textDisplay.setText(textDisplay.getText() + digitString);
146         repaint();
147     }
148     /** Performs the required computation */
149     public void compute(int operation)
150     {
151         double currentValue =
152                 (new Double(textDisplay.getText())).doubleValue();
153         // OK to start a new number after an operation
154         isNewNumber = true;
155         hasDecimal = false;
156         // Process the unary operators (these apply to the value
157         // currently being displayed)
158         switch(operation)
159         {
160             case CHANGE_SIGN:
161                 currentValue = -currentValue;
162                 textDisplay.setText((new
163                                 Double(currentValue)).toString());
164                 break;
165             case SQUARE_ROOT:
166                 if(currentValue >= 0.0)
167                 {
168                     currentValue = Math.sqrt(currentValue);
169                     textDisplay.setText((new
170                                 Double(currentValue)).toString());
171                 }
172                 break;
173             case PERCENT:
174                 currentValue /= 100.0;
175                 textDisplay.setText((new
176                                 Double(currentValue)).toString());
177                 break;
178         }
179         if(operation == CHANGE_SIGN || operation == SQUARE_ROOT ||
```

```
180            operation == PERCENT)
181        {
182            registerValue = 0.0;
183            registerEmpty = true;
184            return;
185        }
186        // The remainder of this method handles binary operators
187        // and special keys such as =, C, AC, M+, M-, etc.
188        if(registerEmpty)
189        {
190            registerValue = currentValue;
191            registerEmpty = false;
192        }
193        else
194        {
195            switch(lastBinOp)
196            {
197                // Next comes binary operators that work with register
198                case ADD:
199                    registerValue += currentValue;
200                    currentValue = registerValue;
201                    textDisplay.setText((new
202                                Double(currentValue)).toString());
203                    break;
204                case SUBTRACT:
205                    registerValue -= currentValue;
206                    currentValue = registerValue;
207                    textDisplay.setText((new
208                                Double(currentValue)).toString());
209                    break;
210                case MULTIPLY:
211                    registerValue *= currentValue;
212                    currentValue = registerValue;
213                    textDisplay.setText((new
214                                Double(currentValue)).toString());
215                    break;
216                case DIVIDE:
217                    registerValue /= currentValue;
218                    currentValue = registerValue;
219                    textDisplay.setText((new
220                                Double(currentValue)).toString());
221                    break;
```

```
222                }
223            }
224            // Now the special keys such as M+, M-, C, AC, =, etc.
225            switch(operation)
226            {
227                case EQUALS:
228                    if(!registerEmpty)
229                    {
230                        currentValue = registerValue;
231                        textDisplay.setText((new
232                                        Double(currentValue)) .toString());
233                        registerValue = 0.0;
234                        registerEmpty = true;
235                    }
236                    break;
237                case MEMORY_PLUS:
238                    memoryValue += currentValue;
239                    break;
240                case MEMORY_MINUS:
241                    memoryValue -= currentValue;
242                    break;
243                case MEMORY_CLEAR:
244                    memoryValue = 0.0;
245                    break;
246                case MEMORY_RECALL:
247                    currentValue = memoryValue;
248                    textDisplay.setText((new
249                                        Double(currentValue)) .toString());
250                    registerValue = memoryValue;
251                    registerEmpty = false;
252                    break;
253                case ALL_CLEAR:
254                    registerValue = 0.0;
255                    registerEmpty = true;
256                    lastBinOp = NOOP;
257                case CLEAR:
258                    textDisplay.setText("0");
259                    isNewNumber = true;
260                    hasDecimal = false;
261                    break;
262            }
263            if(operation == ADD || operation == SUBTRACT ||
```

```
264              operation == MULTIPLY || operation == DIVIDE)
265          {
266              lastBinOp = operation;
267          }
268          else
269              lastBinOp = NOOP;
270      }
271      /** Updates applet by calling paint() */
272      public void update(Graphics g) { paint(g);}
273      /** Paints a 3-D border around the calculator.
274       *  The paint() method is there just for the border.
275       *  Otherwise, we won't need a paint() method.
276       */
277      public void paint(Graphics g)
278      {
279          // First, get the current size of the applet
280          Dimension appletSize = size(); // call getSize() in Java 2
281          int appletWidth = appletSize.width;
282          int appletHeight = appletSize.height;
283          g.setColor(Color.lightGray);
284          g.draw3DRect(1, 1, appletWidth-3, appletHeight-3,true);
285          g.draw3DRect(1, 1, appletWidth-7, appletHeight-7,false);
286          g.setColor(Color.black);
287          g.drawRect(0, 0, appletWidth-1, appletHeight-1);
288          g.drawRect(4, 4, appletWidth-9, appletHeight-9);
289      }
290      /** Overrides getInsets to make room for a border.
291       *  For example, returning Insets(50,5,10,5) reserves
292       *  50 pixels at the top, 5 at the sides, and 10 at the
293       *  bottom. We need the space to draw the border around
294       *  the applet.
295       */
296      public Insets getInsets()
297      {
298          return new Insets (5, 5, 5, 5);
299      }
300      /** Returns information about the Calculator applet */
301      public String getAppletInfo()
302      {
303          return "Calculator by Naba Barkakati, 1998";
304      }
305  }
```

ANNOTATIONS

As you can see from Figure 2-3, the **Calculator** applet uses a large number of buttons in the user interface. Each button has an associated operation; some are for entering numbers, and others perform an operation such as addition. To manage the buttons, the **Calculator** applet uses a **CalculatorButton** class that extends the **Button** class in the Java Abstract Windowing Toolkit (AWT). The applet creates an array of **CalculatorButton** objects, one for each button on the calculator, and stores them in an array. The **CalculatorButton** class overrides the **action()** method that handles mouse clicks on the button. The **action()** method calls an appropriate method of the **Calculator** class to accept numbers entered by the user and to perform computations.

The other important element of the **Calculator** applet is the graphical user interface (GUI) through which the user accesses the calculator. To construct a GUI using various GUI components, the Java AWT provides several layout managers. Each layout manager acts as a container for GUI components, and each has a specific way of arranging—resizing and positioning—the components.

You can use the layout managers to arrange GUI components in the applet's display area. When you have many components, a better way is to first arrange the GUI components in different **Panel** objects. A **Panel** is a GUI component capable of holding other components, including other **Panel** objects. After grouping GUI components in **Panel** objects, you can then arrange the panels inside the applet.

The **Calculator** applet uses two types of layout managers:

♦ **BorderLayout**—This layout manager lets a programmer place GUI components along the four borders and in the center of the available space. These locations are named **"North"**, **"South"**, **"East"**, **"West"**, and **"Center"**. The idea is to place menu bars, status bars, and other toolbars along the edges. The center is typically used for the main work area of the GUI.

♦ **GridLayout**—This layout manager divides the available space into a grid with a specified number of rows and columns. It then places each GUI component into its own cell in the grid.

Figure 2-4 illustrates the overall layout of the GUI components in the **Calculator** applet. As the figure shows, the **CalculatorButton** components are arranged in a panel, using a **GridLayout,** and a **BorderLayout** is then used to place the panel in the applet at the **"Center"** position. The calculator's **TextField** component (where the user enters numbers and views the results) is placed in the **"North"** position of the applet's **BorderLayout**.

To draw a border around the **Calculator** applet, some space has to be reserved around the border. This is done by overriding the **getInsets()** method, which returns the number of pixels by which the other GUI components should be inset from the applet's border.

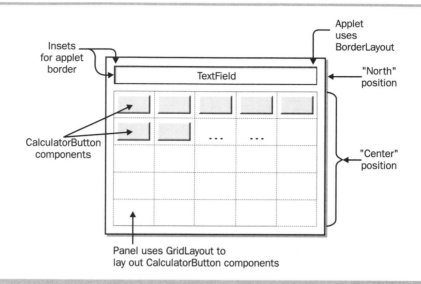

FIGURE 2-4.   Layout of the **Calculator** applet's GUI.

CALCULATOR CLASSES   The **Calculator** applet itself is a subclass of the Java **Applet** class (defined in the **java.applet** package) and is declared as such on line 12:

```
12 public class Calculator extends Applet
```

Calculator also uses an internal class, **CalculatorButton**, that extends the **Button** component of Java AWT. As the name implies, **Button** is a predefined GUI component that displays a label on a button (with a text label) that users can click with the mouse. **CalculatorButton** extends **Button** by storing additional information useful for the **Calculator** applet. As defined in lines 15 through 35, the **CalculatorButton** class includes two variables:

```
17         int operation;
18         int value;
```

Here **operation** is an integer code that indicates what operation is performed by a button, and **value** is used to store a number (used for those buttons that represent a digit such as 1, 2, 3, and so on).

Lines 19 through 24 define the **CalculatorButton()** constructor, which accepts a label and two integers—the operation and value—as arguments:

```
19         CalculatorButton(String label, int operation, int value)
20         {
21             super(label);
22             this.value = value;
```

```
23          this.operation = operation;
24      }
```

Line 21 calls the constructor of the superclass—**Button**—with the **label** as argument. This creates the **Button** GUI component with the specified label. Lines 22 and 23 simply copy the **operation** and **value** arguments into corresponding variables of the **ConstructorButton** class.

The **ConstructorButton** class also overrides the **action()** method of the **Button** class. The **action()** method is called when the user clicks on the button. Lines 25 through 34 implement the **action()** method:

```
25      public boolean action(Event evt, Object arg)
26        {
27          Panel p = (Panel)getParent();
28          Calculator parent = (Calculator)p.getParent();
29          if(operation == parent.NOOP)
30              parent.append(value);
31          else
32              parent.compute(operation);
33          return true;
34        }
```

Lines 27 and 28 get the **Calculator** applet that contains this **CalculatorButton**. Then lines 29 through 32 call an appropriate method of the **Calculator** class to handle the mouse click. If the **operation** is **NOOP** (meaning the button represents a digit and does not perform an operation such as addition or subtraction), line 30 calls the **append()** method of the **Calculator** class. Otherwise, line 32 calls the **compute()** method to perform the operation corresponding to the button.

Note that **action()** is a deprecated method for handling button click events. You should use an **ActionListener** interface for the newer approach to handling button clicks. See the "Deprecated Methods in Calculator" section for information on how to replace the deprecated methods with the newer methods.

CALCULATOR INITIALIZATION   The **Calculator** applet's **init()** method initializes and lays out the GUI components to create the calculator's on-screen appearance. Lines 66 through 97 of the **init()** method initialize the **buttons[]** array of **CalculatorButton** objects. Lines 98 through 104 initialize a number of internal variables of the **Calculator** applet.

Line 105 specifies a **BorderLayout** for the applet by calling the **setLayout()** method:

```
105      setLayout(new BorderLayout());
```

This is a typical way of setting a layout manager: A new manager is constructed by calling the constructor, and this new manager is provided as an argument to **setLayout()**.

Lines 106 through 110 create a **TextField** component (for text entry and result display) and place it at the **"North"** position of the applet:

```
106        textDisplay = new TextField("0", 80);
107        textDisplay.setEditable(false);
108        textDisplay.setFont(new Font("Helvetica", Font.BOLD, 16));
109        textDisplay.setBackground(Color.white);
110        add("North", textDisplay);
```

Line 106 creates the **TextField**. Line 107 makes sure that the user cannot edit the text field—it's used only by the applet to display numbers and results. Line 108 specifies the font, and line 109 sets the background color for the **TextField**. Finally, line 110 places the **TextField** along the applet's upper edge.

Lines 112 through 117 insert the **CalculatorButton** objects into a panel, using a **GridLayout**:

```
112        Panel p = new Panel();
113        p.setLayout(new GridLayout(5, 5, 10, 10));
114        p.setFont(new Font("Helvetica", Font.PLAIN, 14));
115        p.setBackground(new Color(0xefefef));
116        for(int i=0; i < buttons.length; i++)
117            p.add(buttons[i]);
```

Line 112 creates an empty **Panel** object. Line 113 specifies a **GridLayout** for the panel. The layout is a 5 by 5 grid with 10-pixel spacing between successive rows and columns. Line 115 sets the background color for the panel. The **for** loop in lines 116 and 117 adds all of the **CalculatorButton** objects from the **buttons[]** array into the panel.

Line 118 adds the panel to the **"Center"** position of the applet's layout:

```
118        add("Center", p);
```

Finally, line 119 calls the **validate()** method to ensure that the applet has a valid layout. The layout manager completes the layout when **validate()** is called.

COMPUTATIONAL METHODS IN CALCULATOR   The **CalculatorButton** class handles button clicks by calling one of two methods of **Calculator** class:

◆ **append()** to append digits to the text field
◆ **compute()** to perform the computation associated with a button

These two methods take care of all computations in the **Calculator** applet. The **append()** method, implemented in lines 122 through 147, handles clicks on the digit buttons. Whenever the **isNewNumber** variable is **true**, the user is entering a number. In this case, as the user clicks on each digit, the **append()** method keeps appending the digit to what's already in the text display. For example, if the text display currently shows **12**, a click on the button labeled **3** will change the text display to **123**. The **append()** method sets the **hasDecimal** variable when the user enters a decimal point and uses this variable to ignore any further decimal points. The **getText()** and **setText()** methods of the **TextDisplay** object are used to retrieve and set the text display.

The **compute()** method, in lines 149 through 270, contains all of the computational logic of the **Calculator** applet. This rather long method consists of three **switch** statements that handle many different cases of computation.

The **Calculator** applet performs its computations between a register variable and what's currently on the text display. When the user enters a number and then clicks a calculation button such as **+**, the number is stored in the register variable. The next number then appears in the text display. Next, when the user clicks another calculation button or the = button, the **switch** statement in lines 195 through 222 performs the computation between the register variable and the current text display and then updates the text display to show the result.

CALCULATOR BORDER   The **Calculator** applet includes the **update()** and **paint()** methods to draw a nice three-dimensional border around the applet. If it were not for the border, there would be no need for a **paint()** method in the **Calculator** class, because the text display and the buttons are drawn by the **paint()** methods of the **TextField** and **Button** classes.

Lines 277 through 289 show the **paint()** method that draws a 3-D border around the applet's display area. Essentially, **paint()** gets the current size of the applet and calls the **draw3DRect()** and **drawRect()** methods with appropriate arguments to draw the border.

In order to draw a border, the layout manager has to be forced to leave room for the border. This is accomplished by overriding the **getInsets()** method. The layout manager calls **getInsets()** to determine whether all of the items should be inset a certain amount from the borders of the applet. Lines 296 through 299 override the **getInsets()** method as follows:

```
296     public Insets getInsets()
297     {
298         return new Insets (5, 5, 5, 5);
299     }
```

Here line 298 returns an **Insets** object that specifies a five-pixel inset from each of the four borders of the applet. This ensures that there is room to draw a border that is five pixels wide around the boundaries of the **Calculator** applet.

DEPRECATED METHODS IN CALCULATOR   The **Calculator** applet uses two deprecated methods:

◆   Line 280 calls the deprecated method **size()** to get the applet's size.

◆ Lines 25 through 34 in the **CalculatorButton** class overload the **action()** method, which is also deprecated.

To avoid using these deprecated methods, you can replace the call to **size()** with **getSize()**—they both work the same way.

To replace the **action()** method, first insert the following **import** statement near the other **import** statements after line 6:

```
import java.awt.event.*;
```

Change the **CalculatorButton** class declaration on line 19 as follows:

```
class CalculatorButton extends Button implements ActionListener
```

Change the **action()** method declaration on line 25 to:

```
public void actionPerformed(ActionEvent evt)
```

and delete the **return** statement on line 33. That's it. Now the **Calculator.java** program should be free of any deprecated methods.

Note that the **ch02\calc\Java2** directory contains a revised version of the Calculator applet that does not use any deprecated methods.

A Mortgage Calculator

A mortgage calculator is another common financial applet. It's essentially a specialized version of a calculator that computes mortgage payments for a given loan amount, interest rate, and duration of loan. This section presents the **USMortgage** applet, designed to compute monthly loan payments for U.S.–style mortgages in which interest is compounded monthly (as opposed to mortgages found in other countries such as Canada in which interest is compounded semiannually).

Using USMortgage

You will find the files for the **USMortgage** applet in the **ch02\mortgage** directory of the companion CD-ROM. To try out **USMortgage**, open the file **Mortgage.html** from a Java-capable Web browser (or the **appletviewer** program that comes with the Java Development Kit). Figure 2-5 shows the applet after it has computed the monthly payments for a $225,000 loan to be paid over 30 years at an annual rate of

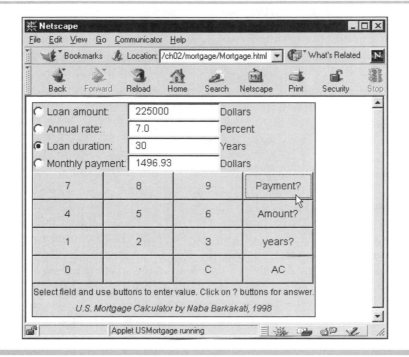

FIGURE 2-5. Computing mortgage payments with the **USMortgage** applet.

7.0 percent. As you can see, the monthly payment is $1,496.93. To perform this calculation, you would go through the following steps:

1. Click on the **Loan amount** checkbox, and then click the number buttons to enter the loan amount of **225000**.

2. Click on the **Annual rate** checkbox, and use the buttons to enter the interest rate of 7.0 (as a percentage).

3. Click on the **Loan duration** checkbox, then click on the number buttons to enter the loan duration of 30 (in years).

4. Click on the **Payment?** button to calculate the monthly payment. The answer appears in the **Monthly payment** field.

You can do much more than just calculate monthly mortgage payments with the **USMortgage** applet. You can change the monthly payment amount and then see how much you can afford to borrow at the specified rate. For example, if you can afford to pay only $1,000 per month, click on the **Monthly payment** checkbox and then click the **C** button to clear the value. Next use the buttons to enter **1000** in that field. Then click on the **Amount?** button to calculate the loan amount corresponding to the current payment ($1,000), rate (7 percent), and duration (30 years). In this case, **USMortgage** displays **150307.57** in the **Loan amount** field, indicating that you can afford a 30-year loan in the amount of $150,307.57 at 7 percent for a monthly payment of $1,000.

Similarly, you can also specify the loan amount, rate, and monthly payment and calculate the number of years. Typically, for a given loan amount and interest rate, you would enter the monthly payment you can afford and then click the **Years?** button to calculate the number of years it would take to pay off the loan. For example, for the $225,000 loan at a 7 percent annual interest rate, suppose that you can afford to pay $2,100 per month. After entering these values in the appropriate fields, click the **Years?** button. **USMortgage** displays 14.05 in the **Loan duration** field. This means that at that payment level, you can pay off the loan in approximately 14 years. Because 15-year loans have lower interest rates, you can then enter a 15-year loan rate in the **Annual rate** field and find the exact monthly payments for a 15-year loan.

These are some of the ways you can use the **USMortgage** applet to assess a mortgage loan.

The **USMortgage** applet does not accept any parameters. To use it on a Web page, simply embed it with an **<applet>** tag with an appropriate width and height. Although the user interface components in the applet will resize to fit the available space, you should make the applet's display area large enough so that all labels, buttons, and text fields have enough room. For the layout shown in Figure 2-5, the **Mortgage.html** file uses the following **<applet>** tag:

```
<applet code="USMortgage.class" width = 400 height = 300>
```

This specifies an applet size of 400 pixels wide by 300 pixels tall.

USMortgage

Understanding USMortgage

The following listing shows the file **USMortgage.java**, which implements the **USMortgage** applet. I discuss the applet's design and its implementation details in the subsequent sections.

```
1  //-----------------------------------------------------------------
2  // USMortgage.java
3  // U.S. mortgage calculator that computes monthly mortgage
4  // payments for specified loan amount, annual interest rate
5  // (in percentage), and loan duration (in years).
6  //-----------------------------------------------------------------
```

```java
import java.lang.*;
import java.awt.*;
import java.applet.*;
/**
 * USMortgage computes monthly payments for U.S. mortgages.
 *
 * @author Naba Barkakati
 * @version 1.0 October 1998
 */
public class USMortgage extends Applet
{
    // Class to accept numbers and display results
    class MortgageTextField extends TextField
    {
        boolean isNewNumber;
        boolean hasDecimal;
        MortgageTextField(String text, int nchar)
        {
            super(text, nchar);
            isNewNumber = true;
            hasDecimal = false;
            setEditable(false);
        }
        /** Displays a value with specified number of decimal points */
        public void displayValue(double v, int ndec)
        {
            double factor = 1;
            for(int i = 0; i < ndec; i++)
            {
                factor *= 10;
            }
            long l = (long)(Math.round(v*factor));
            v = (double)l / factor;
            setText(new Double(v).toString());
        }
        public void reset()
        {
            isNewNumber = true;
            hasDecimal = false;
            setText("0");
        }
        public void append(int value)
        {
```

```
50              String digitString;
51              if(hasDecimal && value == DECIMAL_POINT) return;
52              if(value == DECIMAL_POINT)
53              {
54                  if(isNewNumber)
55                  {
56                      setText("0");
57                      isNewNumber = false;
58                  }
59                  hasDecimal = true;
60                  digitString = decimalPoint;
61              }
62              else
63                  digitString = (new Integer(value)).toString();
64              if(isNewNumber)
65              {
66                  setText(digitString);
67                  if(value != 0)
68                      isNewNumber = false;
69              }
70              else
71                  setText(getText() + digitString);
72          }
73      }
74      // Represents the buttons through which user uses calculator
75      class MortgageCalcButton extends Button
76      {
77          int operation;
78          int value;
79          MortgageCalcButton(String label, int operation, int value)
80          {
81              super(label);
82              this.value = value;
83              this.operation = operation;
84          }
85          public boolean action(Event evt, Object arg)
86          {
87              Panel p = (Panel)getParent();
88              USMortgage parent = (USMortgage)p.getParent();
89              if(operation == parent.CALC_PAYMENT)
90                  parent.calculate(CALC_PAYMENT);
91              else if(operation == parent.CALC_PRINCIPAL)
92                  parent.calculate(CALC_PRINCIPAL);
```

```
93      else if(operation == parent.CALC_YEARS)
94          parent.calculate(CALC_YEARS);
95      else if(operation == parent.ALL_CLEAR)
96      {
97          parent.principalText.reset();
98          parent.rateText.reset();
99          parent.yearsText.reset();
100         parent.paymentText.reset();
101         return true;
102     }
103     // Call getSelectedCheckbox() in JDK 1.1.6 or later
104     Checkbox c = parent.textfieldGroup.getCurrent();
105     String label = c.getLabel();
106     if(label.equals(parent.principalLabel))
107     {
108         if(operation == NOOP)
109             parent.principalText.append(value);
110         else if(operation == CLEAR)
111             parent.principalText.reset();
112     }
113     else if(label.equals(parent.rateLabel))
114     {
115         if(operation == NOOP)
116             parent.rateText.append(value);
117         else if(operation == CLEAR)
118             parent.rateText.reset();
119     }
120     else if(label.equals(parent.yearsLabel))
121     {
122         if(operation == NOOP)
123             parent.yearsText.append(value);
124         else if(operation == CLEAR)
125             parent.yearsText.reset();
126     }
127     else if(label.equals(parent.paymentLabel))
128     {
129         if(operation == NOOP)
130             parent.paymentText.append(value);
131         else if(operation == CLEAR)
132             parent.paymentText.reset();
133     }
134     return true;
135 }
```

```
136        }
137
138        static final int NOOP = 0;
139        static final int CALCULATE = 1;
140        static final int CLEAR = 2;
141        static final int ALL_CLEAR = 3;
142        static final int CALC_PRINCIPAL = 4;
143        static final int CALC_YEARS = 5;
144        static final int CALC_PAYMENT = 6;
145        static final int DECIMAL_POINT = -1;
146
147        MortgageTextField principalText;
148        MortgageTextField yearsText;
149        MortgageTextField rateText;
150        MortgageTextField paymentText;
151        String principalLabel = "Loan amount:";
152        String yearsLabel = "Loan duration:";
153        String rateLabel = "Annual rate:";
154        String paymentLabel = "Monthly payment:";
155        CheckboxGroup textfieldGroup = new CheckboxGroup();
156
157        String decimalPoint = ".";
158        /** Lays out the user interface for the applet */
159        public void init()
160        {
161            MortgageCalcButton [] buttons =
162            {
163                new MortgageCalcButton("7", NOOP, 7),
164                new MortgageCalcButton("8", NOOP, 8),
165                new MortgageCalcButton("9", NOOP, 9),
166                new MortgageCalcButton("Payment?", CALC_PAYMENT, 0),
167
168                new MortgageCalcButton("4", NOOP, 4),
169                new MortgageCalcButton("5", NOOP, 5),
170                new MortgageCalcButton("6", NOOP, 6),
171                new MortgageCalcButton("Amount?", CALC_PRINCIPAL, 0),
172
173                new MortgageCalcButton("1", NOOP, 1),
174                new MortgageCalcButton("2", NOOP, 2),
175                new MortgageCalcButton("3", NOOP, 3),
176                new MortgageCalcButton("years?", CALC_YEARS, 0),
177
178                new MortgageCalcButton("0", NOOP, 0),
```

```
179             new MortgageCalcButton(".", NOOP, DECIMAL_POINT),
180             new MortgageCalcButton("C", CLEAR, 0),
181             new MortgageCalcButton("AC", ALL_CLEAR, 0),
182         };
183
184         Font fHelv14 = new Font("Helvetica", Font.PLAIN, 14);
185         setFont(fHelv14);
186         setBackground(Color.lightGray);
187
188         principalText = new MortgageTextField("0", 16);
189         yearsText = new MortgageTextField("0", 16);
190         rateText = new MortgageTextField("0", 16);
191         paymentText = new MortgageTextField("0", 16);
192         principalText.setBackground(Color.white);
193         rateText.setBackground(Color.white);
194         yearsText.setBackground(Color.white);
195         paymentText.setBackground(Color.white);
196
197         Panel p1 = new Panel();
198         p1.setFont(fHelv14);
199         p1.setLayout(new GridLayout(1,3));
200         p1.add(new Checkbox(principalLabel, textfieldGroup,
201                             true));
202         p1.add(principalText);
203         p1.add(new Label("Dollars"));
204
205         Panel p2 = new Panel();
206         p2.setFont(fHelv14);
207         p2.setLayout(new GridLayout(1,3));
208         p2.add(new Checkbox(rateLabel, textfieldGroup, false));
209         p2.add(rateText);
210         p3.add(new Label("Percent"));
211
212         Panel p3 = new Panel();
213         p3.setFont(fHelv14);
214         p3.setLayout(new GridLayout(1,3));
215         p3.add(new Checkbox(yearsLabel, textfieldGroup, false));
216         p3.add(yearsText);
217         p3.add(new Label("Years"));
218
219         Panel p4 = new Panel();
220         p4.setFont(fHelv14);
221         p4.setLayout(new GridLayout(1,3));
```

```
222        p4.add(new Checkbox(paymentLabel, textfieldGroup, false));
223        p4.add(paymentText);
224        p4.add(new Label("Dollars"));
225
226        Panel pBig = new Panel();
227        pBig.setLayout(new GridLayout(4,1));
228        pBig.add(p1);
229        pBig.add(p2);
230        pBig.add(p3);
231        pBig.add(p4);
232        setLayout(new BorderLayout());
233        add("North", pBig);
234
235        Panel pButtons = new Panel();
236        pButtons.setLayout(new GridLayout(4,4));
237        for(int i=0; i < buttons.length; i++)
238            pButtons.add(buttons[i]);
239        add("Center", pButtons);
240
241        Panel pBottom = new Panel();
242        pBottom.setLayout(new GridLayout(2,1));
243        Label l1 = new Label("Select field and use buttons to
               enter value. Click on ? buttons for answer.", Label.CENTER);
244        Label l2 = new Label("U.S. Mortgage Calculator
              by Naba Barkakati, 1998",
245                              Label.CENTER);
246        l1.setFont(new Font("Helvetica", Font.PLAIN, 12));
247        l2.setFont(new Font("Helvetica", Font.ITALIC, 12));
248        l2.setBackground(Color.lightGray);
249        pBottom.add(l1);
250        pBottom.add(l2);
251        add("South", pBottom);
252        validate();
253    }
254    /** Calculates the requested item */
255    public void calculate(int calculateWhat)
256    {
257        // Get current values from the fields
258        double principal =
259            (new Double(principalText.getText())).doubleValue();
260        double rate =
261            (new Double(rateText.getText())).doubleValue();
262        double years =
263            (new Double(yearsText.getText())).doubleValue();
```

```
264        double payment =
265            (new Double(paymentText.getText())).doubleValue();
266        // Computes selected item using other 3 values
267        double months = years * 12;
268        double monthlyRate = rate/12/100;
269        if(calculateWhat == CALC_PRINCIPAL)
270        {
271            principal = payment *
272                        (1 - Math.pow(1+monthlyRate, -months)) /
273                                                    monthlyRate;
274            principalText.displayValue(principal, 2);
275        }
276        else if(calculateWhat == CALC_YEARS)
277        {
278            months = Math.log(payment /
279                        (payment-principal*monthlyRate)) /
280                            Math.log(1 + monthlyRate);
281            yearsText.displayValue(months/12, 2);
282        }
283        else if(calculateWhat == CALC_PAYMENT)
284        {
285            payment = principal * (monthlyRate /
286               (1 - Math.pow(1+monthlyRate, -months)));
287            paymentText.displayValue(payment, 2);
288        }
289    }
290    /** Saves 1-pixel space around the applet for border */
291    public Insets getInsets()
292    {
293        return new Insets(1,1,1,1);
294    }
295    /** Draws a border around the applet */
296    public void paint(Graphics g)
297    {
298        Dimension appletSize = size(); // call getSize() in Java 2
299        g.setColor(Color.black);
300        g.drawRect(0, 0, appletSize.width-1, appletSize.height-1);
301    }
302    /** Returns information about the USMortgage applet */
303    public String getAppletInfo()
304    {
305        return "USMortgage calculator by Naba Barkakati, 1998";
306    }
307 }
```

ANNOTATIONS

The **USMortgage** applet's design is similar to that of the **Calculator** applet discussed earlier in this chapter. The applet uses two internal classes to manage the user interface:

- **MortgageTextField** to display values and results
- **MortgageCalcButton** to represent each button in the user interface (the user enters values and performs calculations through the buttons)

The user interface is laid out using an approach similar to that of the **Calculator** applet. The applet uses a **BorderLayout** layout manager with a **Panel** object holding four text fields at the **"North"** position (the top edge of the applet). Another panel with a **GridLayout** manager is used to arrange the buttons through which the user enters numbers and performs specific calculations. That panel is added to the **"Center"** position of the **BorderLayout**. Finally, a panel with two more labels is added to the **"South"** position (the bottom edge of the applet).

The U.S. mortgage calculation is done using the following formula:

$$M = P * R / [1 - (1+R)^{-N}]$$

where

- **M** is the monthly payment
- **P** is the principal amount
- **R** is the monthly interest rate (if the annual rate is **A** percent, then **R = A/12/100**)
- **N** is the number of months over which the loan has to be repaid (if the loan duration is **Y** years, then **N = 12 * Y**)

This same formula is used to compute **P** in terms of **M**, **R**, and **N** as well as **N** in terms of **M**, **P**, and **R**.

USMORTGAGE CLASSES   **USMortgage** uses the **MortgageTextField** class to display numbers as the user enters them and to display the results of calculations. Lines 19 through 73 implement the **MortgageTextField** class, which is a subclass of the **TextField** GUI component. **MortgageTextField** has two variables, declared on lines 21 and 22:

```
21        boolean isNewNumber;
22        boolean hasDecimal;
```

The **isNewNumber** variable is **true** whenever the user is entering a new number in that text field. The **hasDecimal** variable is set to **true** after the user has entered a decimal point; this is used to prevent the user from entering more than one decimal point in a number.

The **MortgageTextField** class has the following methods:

◆ **MortgageTextField(String text, int nchar)**, implemented in lines 23 through 29, calls the constructor of the superclass (**TextField**) to initialize the text field. It also calls **setEditable(false)** to prevent the user from editing the text field.

◆ **public void append(int value)** in lines 48 through 72 appends the value (which is a digit entered by the user through the buttons) to whatever is currently in the text field.

◆ **public void displayValue(double v, int ndec)** in lines 31 through 41 displays the floating-point number **v** with **ndec** digits after the decimal point.

◆ **public void reset()** in lines 42 through 47 resets the internal variables of **MortgageTextField** and displays a **0** in the text field.

The **USMortgage** applet also uses another class—**MortgageCalcButton**—to represent the buttons that appear in its user interface. Lines 75 through 136 implement the **MortgageCalcButton** class. This class is a subclass of the **Button** GUI component. As such, it displays a label on a button that the user can push with the mouse. However, **MortgageCalcButton** also stores a value and an operation associated with the button. The value represents the digit that the user may enter by clicking the button.

MortgageCalcButton also overrides the **action()** method of the **Button** class. Lines 85 through 135 implement the **action()** method, which supports old-fashioned Java event handling that has been superseded by newer methods. **USMortgage** continues to use the older event-handling approach to allow users with old Web browsers to use the applet.

The **action()** method is called when the user clicks on a button. The method performs whatever action is appropriate for that button. If the button represents a digit being entered by the user, the **action()** method appends that digit to the current contents of the text field. Of the four text fields in the **USMortgage** applet (see Figure 2-5), the digit is appended to the one that's currently checked. Line 104 gets the label of the checkbox that's currently checked and uses it in the code that follows.

USMORTGAGE INITIALIZATION   The **init()** method, in lines 159 through 253, initializes the internal variables and creates the user interface for the **USMortgage** applet.

Lines 161 through 182 initialize the **buttons[]** array of **MortgageCalcButton** objects, each representing a button in the applet's user interface. Lines 184 through 186 set the font and the background color of the applet. Lines 188 through 195 create and initialize four **MortgageTextField** objects. These are the text fields that display the loan principal, interest rate, loan duration, and monthly payment.

Lines 197 through 231 prepare four **Panel** components, named **p1** through **p4**, each holding a **Checkbox**, a **MortgageTextField**, and a **Label** component. For example, the panel **p1** is set up as follows:

```
197        Panel p1 = new Panel();
198        p1.setFont(fHelv14);
199        p1.setLayout(new GridLayout(1,3));
200        p1.add(new Checkbox(principalLabel, textfieldGroup,
201                                    true));
202        p1.add(principalText);
203        p1.add(new Label("Dollars"));
```

Line 197 creates an empty **Panel** component. Line 198 sets the font, and line 199 sets the layout manager to a **GridLayout** with a single row with three columns. Line 200 adds the **Checkbox**, line 202 adds the **MortgageTextField principalText**, and line 203 adds a **Label** to panel **p1**. The other three panels—**p2**, **p3**, and **p4**—are prepared in a similar manner.

When all four panels are done, lines 226 through 231 create another panel called **pBig** and add the previous panels into it, as follows:

```
226        Panel pBig = new Panel();
227        pBig.setLayout(new GridLayout(4,1));
228        pBig.add(p1);
229        pBig.add(p2);
230        pBig.add(p3);
231        pBig.add(p4);
```

Lines 232 and 233 then set the applet's layout manager to a **BorderLayout** and place the **pBig** panel at the "**North**" location of the applet:

```
232        setLayout(new BorderLayout());
233        add("North", pBig);
```

Next come the buttons. Lines 235 through 238 initialize a panel with the buttons that have already been initialized in the **buttons[]** array:

```
235        Panel pButtons = new Panel();
236        pButtons.setLayout(new GridLayout(4,4));
237        for(int i=0; i < buttons.length; i++)
238            pButtons.add(buttons[i]);
```

The **for** loop in lines 237 and 238 goes through the **buttons[]** array and adds each button to the **pButtons** panel.

Next, line 239 adds the **pButtons** panel to the **"Center"** position of the applet:

```
239          add("Center", pButtons);
```

The remainder of the **init()** method, from line 241 to line 252, creates another panel with two **Label** components and places that panel in the **"South"** position of the applet.

USMORTGAGE CALCULATION   The **calculate()** method, shown in lines 255 through 289, performs the mortgage calculations, using the U.S. mortgage formula shown in the beginning of the "Annotations" section. This method first gets the current values of all four parameters from the four **MortgageTextField** objects: **principalText**, **rateText**, **yearsText**, and **paymentText**. For example, lines 258 and 259 get the value of the principal, as follows:

```
258          double principal =
259                  (new Double(principalText.getText())).doubleValue();
```

The expression **principalText.getText()** returns a **String** representation of the value currently displayed in the **principalText** object (this is a **MortgageTextField**). This **String** is used to construct a **Double** object, whose floating-point value is then extracted by calling the **doubleValue()** method.

After getting the values, lines 267 and 268 convert the loan duration to months and the annual loan rate to a monthly rate (also changed from a percentage to a fraction):

```
267          double months = years * 12;
268          double monthlyRate = rate/12/100;
```

Lines 269 through 288 then perform the appropriate calculation, depending on what button the user has clicked. After calculating the specific variable, the code updates the appropriate text field to display the result. For example, lines 283 through 288 compute the monthly payment as follows:

```
283          else if(calculateWhat == CALC_PAYMENT)
284          {
285              payment = principal * (monthlyRate /
286                  (1 - Math.pow(1+monthlyRate, -months)));
287              paymentText.displayValue(payment, 2);
288          }
```

Line 283 checks whether the **calculateWhat** argument requests payment calculation. If so, lines 285 and 286 compute the monthly payment value. Line 287 then calls the **displayValue()** method of the **paymentText** text field to display the result using two decimal places.

A Currency Converter

An important financial utility is a currency conversion program that converts amounts from one currency to another. You can find quite a few currency conversion applets on the Internet. The basic calculations of currency conversion are simple; the main problem is in getting the latest foreign exchange rates and using those rates to perform the calculations. This section presents the **CurrencyConvert** applet, which downloads exchange rates from a text file on the Web server and lets users convert amounts from one currency to another. As you will learn in the following sections, **CurrencyConvert** accepts foreign exchange rates from a file in exactly the same format as the exchange rates posted at the Federal Reserve Bank of New York's Web site.

Using CurrencyConvert

You will find the files for the **CurrencyConvert** applet in the **ch02\cconvert** directory of the companion CD-ROM. To try out **CurrencyConvert**, open the **Convert.html** file from a Java-capable Web browser. The applet lets you select a currency to convert from, a currency to convert to, and an amount to convert. Initially, the applet shows 1 U.S. dollar converted to itself. To convert 1 U.S. dollar to another country's currency, click on the drop-down menu and select that country, as shown in Figure 2-6. When you click on a country and let go of the mouse button, **CurrencyConvert** will display the converted value, as shown in Figure 2-7. If you enter another value in the text field on the left and click on the result text field (on the right), the applet will convert the new value and show the result.

The **CurrencyConvert** applet is designed to work with currency rates in the same format as that used for the Federal Reserve Bank of New York's 12 Noon Foreign Exchange Rates, available at **http://www.ny.frb.org/pihome/mktrates/forex12.shtml**. As such, these exchange rates are read from a text file that should be on the same Web server from which the applet was originally loaded.

```
<applet code="CurrencyConvert.class" width=400 height=200>
  <param name="ratefile" value="rates.txt">
</applet>
```

This **<applet>** tag specifies a display area 400 pixels wide by 200 pixels tall. As you can see from Figure 2-7, this provides adequate space for the applet's simple user interface. The **ratefile** parameter specifies **rates.txt** as the file that contains the exchange rates.

If you want to provide the currency conversion service at your Web site, copy the Java class files from the **ch02\cconvert** directory of the CD-ROM to your Web

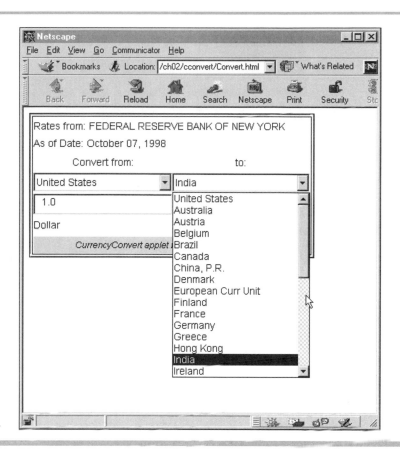

FIGURE 2-6. Selecting a country in **CurrencyConvert**.

server. Place the **<applet>** tag from the **Convert.html** file in your Web page. Next, you have to prepare a text file named **rates.txt** with the foreign exchange rates.

To prepare the rates file, open the URL **http://www.ny.frb.org/pihome/mktrates/ forex12.shtml** in a Web browser, cut and paste the latest rate table into a word processor, and save that as a text file named **rates.txt**. You can then upload that text file to your Web server and place it in the location where the applet's class files are located.

The applet would certainly be more useful if it could get the latest exchange rates directly from the Federal Reserve Bank of New York's Web site. However, the default security model of Web browsers does not allow applets to access any other Internet site besides the one from which the applet was loaded. This forces you to place the rate file on the same Web server as the applet, meaning that you end up having to update the rate file manually every day.

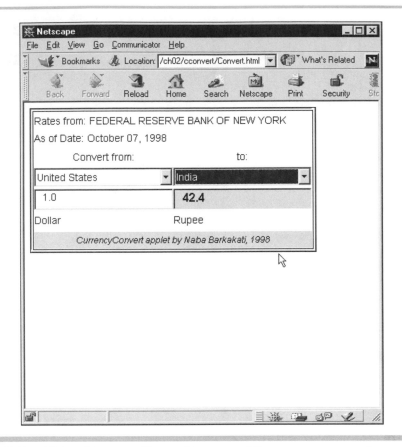

FIGURE 2-7.   Using **CurrencyConvert** to convert from one currency to another.

Understanding CurrencyConvert

The following listing shows the **CurrencyConvert.java** program that implements the
CurrencyConvert applet. The subsequent sections discuss various programming
details.

```
1  //-----------------------------------------------------------------
2  // CurrencyConvert.java
3  //
4  // Converts from one currency to another. Accepts exchange rates
5  // in the format reported by the New York Federal Reserve Bank
6  // at the following URL:
7  //    http://www.ny.frb.org/pihome/mktrates/forex12.shtml
8  // You should cut and paste the rate tables from this page into
```

CurrencyConvert

```
 9  // a text file that should be on the same server where this
10  // applet is located. Then specify that file's URL as the
11  // "ratefile" parameter for this applet.
12  //
13  /* The rate file format is as follows (exactly as shown below):
14                      Date: October 07, 1998
15
16                  FEDERAL RESERVE BANK OF NEW YORK
17
18                  Value of Foreign Currencies
19
20
21                                        Noon Buying Rates for Cable
22                                        Transfer in N.Y. Value in
23          Country            Monetary Unit    Foreign Currency Units
24
25      * Australia           Dollar             0.6178
26        Austria             Schilling         11.3500
27        Canada              Dollar             1.5288
28        China, P.R.         Yuan               8.2778
29      * European Curr Unit  ECU                1.2176
30        France              Franc              5.4080
31        Germany             Mark               1.6137
32        Greece              Drachma          279.6300
33        India               Rupee             42.4000
34      * Ireland             Pound              1.5478
35
36      An asterisk means the value is in U.S. Dollars (other values
37      are in the country's currency).
38  */
39  // Author: Naba Barkakati, October 7, 1998
40  //-----------------------------------------------------------
41  import java.applet.*;
42  import java.awt.*;
43  import java.net.*;
44  import java.io.*;
45  import java.util.*;
46  /** Converts one country's currency to another.
47   * Uses exchange rates from a text file on the
48   * server.
49   * <p>
```

```
50   *   Accepts one parameter:
51   *   <ul>
52   *     <li> ratefile - name of file with exchange rates (get
53   *           from New York Federal Reserve Bank's Web page at
54   *         http://www.ny.frb.org/pihome/mktrates/forex12.shtml
55   *           and paste the table into a text file)
56   *   </ul>
57   *
58   *   @author Naba Barkakati
59   *   @version 1.0 Oct 7, 1998
60   */
61   public class CurrencyConvert extends Applet
62   {
63       // Class to store exchange rate for a country
64       class CountryRateInfo extends Object
65       {
66           public String countryName;
67           public String currencyName;
68           public boolean valueIsUSD;
69           public double value;
70           CountryRateInfo(String countryName, String currencyName,
71                           double value, boolean valueIsUSD)
72           {
73               this.countryName = countryName;
74               this.currencyName = currencyName;
75               this.value = value;
76               this.valueIsUSD = valueIsUSD;
77           }
78       }
79       // Class to manage all exchange rates
80       class ExchangeRate extends Object
81       {
82           Vector rates;
83           ExchangeRate()
84           {
85               rates = new Vector(40);
86           }
87           public void addElement(CountryRateInfo rate)
88           {
89               rates.addElement(rate);
90           }
91           public CountryRateInfo elementAt(int i)
92           {
```

```
 93              return (CountryRateInfo)rates.elementAt(i);
 94          }
 95      public int size() { return rates.size();}
 96      public CountryRateInfo getInfo(String cname)
 97      {
 98          for(int i = 0; i < size(); i++)
 99          {
100              if(elementAt(i).countryName.equals(cname))
101                  return elementAt(i);
102          }
103          return null;
104      }
105  }
106
107  String dateString;
108  String sourceString;
109  String rateFileName;
110  ExchangeRate rates;
111
112  Choice fromCurrencyChoice, toCurrencyChoice;
113  TextField fromValueField, toValueField;
114  Label fromCurrency, toCurrency;
115  Font helvP14 = new Font("Helvetica", Font.PLAIN, 14);
116  boolean fromValueChanged;
117  CountryRateInfo currentFrom, currentTo;
118  /** Initializes the applet by laying out the user interface */
119  public void init()
120  {
121      rates = new ExchangeRate();
122      // Read rate file and set up internal data structures
123      rateFileName = getParameter("ratefile");
124      try
125      {
126          URL url = new URL(getCodeBase()+rateFileName);
127
128          // Open the rate file and process it line by line
129          try
130          {
131              // Add an entry for USA
132              rates.addElement(new CountryRateInfo("United States",
133                          "Dollar", 1.000, true));
134              DataInputStream in = new
135                  DataInputStream(url.openStream());
136              // In Java 2, use:
```

```
137              // BufferedReader in = new BufferedReader
138              //     new InputStreamReader(url.openStream()));
139
140          String line = in.readLine();
141          dateString = line.substring(28, 50);
142          line = in.readLine(); // skip blank line
143          line = in.readLine();
144          sourceString = line.substring(24, 56);
145          // Skip until we reach "Country"
146          while(true)
147          {
148              line = in.readLine();
149              if(line.length() > 13 &&
150                  line.substring(6, 13).equals("Country"))
151                      break;
152          }
153      // Skip one blank line
154          line = in.readLine();
155          line = null;
156          while(true)
157          {
158              line = in.readLine();
159              if(line == null) break;
160              String country = line.substring(6, 30);
161              boolean valueIsUSD = false;
162              if(line.substring(4,5).equals("*"))
163                  valueIsUSD = true;
164              // Get currency name and value
165              String currency = line.substring(30, 49);
166              String valueString = line.substring(50);
167              String NA = valueString.substring(3, 6);
168              if(!NA.equals("N/A"))
169              {
170                  try
171                  {
172                      StringTokenizer st = new StringTokenizer(
173                                              valueString);
174                      double value = Double.valueOf(
175                              st.nextToken()).doubleValue();
176                      rates.addElement(new CountryRateInfo(country,
177                              currency, value, valueIsUSD));
178                  }
179              catch(NumberFormatException e)
```

```
180                         {
181                             System.out.println("Error converting:"+
182                                 valueString);
183                         }
184                     }
185                 }
186             }
187         catch(IOException e)
188         {
189             System.out.println("IO error");
190         }
191     }
192     catch(MalformedURLException e)
193     {
194         System.out.println("Bad URL");
195     }
196     // Create and arrange the user interface elements
197     setLayout(new BorderLayout());
198     setFont(helvP14);
199     Panel pTop = new Panel();
200     pTop.setLayout(new GridLayout(2,1));
201     pTop.add(new Label("Rates from: "+sourceString));
202     pTop.add(new Label("As of "+dateString));
203     add("North", pTop);
204     Panel pMid = new Panel();
205     pMid.setLayout(new GridLayout(4,2));
206     pMid.add(new Label("Convert from:", Label.CENTER));
207     pMid.add(new Label("to:", Label.CENTER));
208     fromCurrencyChoice = new Choice();
209     toCurrencyChoice = new Choice();
210     for(int i=0; i < rates.size(); i++)
211     {
212         fromCurrencyChoice.addItem(rates.elementAt(i).countryName);
213         toCurrencyChoice.addItem(rates.elementAt(i).countryName);
214     }
215     currentFrom = rates.elementAt(0);
216     currentTo = rates.elementAt(0);
217     pMid.add(fromCurrencyChoice);
218     pMid.add(toCurrencyChoice);
219     fromValueChanged = false;
220     fromValueField = new TextField("1.0", 16);
221     toValueField = new TextField("1.0", 16);
222     toValueField.setBackground(Color.lightGray);
```

```
223        toValueField.setEditable(false);
224        toValueField.setFont(new Font("Helvetica", Font.BOLD, 16));
225        pMid.add(fromValueField);
226        pMid.add(toValueField);
227        fromCurrency = new Label("Dollar");
228        toCurrency = new Label("Dollar");
229        pMid.add(fromCurrency);
230        pMid.add(toCurrency);
231        add("Center", pMid);
232        Label info = new Label("CurrencyConvert applet
                                   by Naba Barkakati, 1998",
233                                  Label.CENTER);
234        info.setBackground(Color.lightGray);
235        info.setFont(new Font("Helvetica", Font.ITALIC, 12));
236        add("South", info);
237    }
238    /** Handles button clicks on the drop-down menus.
239     * In Java 1.1, use an ItemListener interface to
240     * handle mouse button clicks.
241     */
242    public boolean action(Event ev, Object obj)
243    {
244        if(ev.target == fromCurrencyChoice)
245        {
246            String from = fromCurrencyChoice.getSelectedItem();
247            if(!currentFrom.countryName.equals(from))
248            {
249                currentFrom = rates.getInfo(from);
250                fromCurrency.setText(currentFrom.currencyName);
251                computeValue();
252            }
253        }
254        else if(ev.target == toCurrencyChoice)
255        {
256            String to = toCurrencyChoice.getSelectedItem();
257            if(!currentTo.countryName.equals(to))
258            {
259                currentTo = rates.getInfo(to);
260                toCurrency.setText(currentTo.currencyName);
261                computeValue();
262            }
263        }
264        return super.action(ev, obj);
```

```
265        }
266        /** Handles mouse clicks on the text fields */
267        public boolean handleEvent(Event ev)
268        {
269            if(ev.target == fromValueField &&
270                ev.id == Event.LOST_FOCUS)
271            {
272                computeValue();
273            }
274            return super.handleEvent(ev);
275        }
276        /** Converts given amount from one currency to another */
277        public void computeValue()
278        {
279            String fromString = fromValueField.getText();
280            try
281            {
282                // Get the value to convert, convert it to
283                // U.S. Dollars, then to target currency
284                double fromValue = Double.valueOf(fromString).doubleValue();
285                double valueUSD = toDollars(fromValue, currentFrom);
286                double result = toCurrency(valueUSD, currentTo);
287                toValueField.setText((new Double(result)).toString());
288            }
289            catch(Exception e)
290            {
291                toValueField.setText("Error! Reenter a number");
292            }
293            repaint();
294        }
295        /** Converts any currency to U.S. Dollars */
296        double toDollars(double value, CountryRateInfo ci)
297        {
298            if(ci.valueIsUSD)
299                return value*ci.value;
300            else
301                return value/ci.value;
302        }
303        /** Converts from U.S. Dollars to any other currency */
304        double toCurrency(double usd, CountryRateInfo ci)
305        {
306            if(ci.valueIsUSD)
```

```
307          return usd/ci.value;
308      else
309          return usd*ci.value;
310  }
311  /** Sets 6-pixel inset for border */
312  public Insets getInsets()
313  {
314      return new Insets(6,6,6,6);
315  }
316  /** Paints a 1-pixel border around the applet */
317  public void paint(Graphics g)
318  {
319      Dimension aSize = size(); // Call getSize() in Java 2
320      g.setColor(Color.lightGray);
321      g.draw3DRect(1, 1, aSize.width-3, aSize.height-3,true);
322      g.draw3DRect(1, 1, aSize.width-7, aSize.height-7,false);
323      g.setColor(Color.black);
324      g.drawRect(0, 0, aSize.width-1, aSize.height-1);
325      g.drawRect(4, 4, aSize.width-9, aSize.height-9);
326  }
327  /** Returns information about the CurrencyConvert applet */
328  public String getAppletInfo()
329  {
330      return "CurrencyConvert 1.0 by Naba Barkakati, 1998";
331  }
332  /** Returns information about this applet's parameters */
333  public String[][] getParameterInfo()
334  {
335      String[][] info =
336      {
337      // Parameter Name Type      Description
338          {"ratefile",  "String", "Text file with exchange rates"}
339      };
340      return info;
341  }
342 }
```

ANNOTATIONS

CurrencyConvert is designed to accept the daily foreign exchange rates for a selected list of countries from the Federal Reserve Bank of New York's Web site (**http://www.ny.frb.org/pihome/mktrates/forex12.shtml**). During initialization, the **init()** method reads the rate information from a rate file and stores the country name, currency name, and exchange rate in a **CountryRateInfo** class. The exchange rates for all of the countries are managed as an array of **CountryRateInfo** objects in another class, **ExchangeRate**.

PROGRAMMER'S NOTE   *If you want CurrencyConvert to handle many more currencies, you may want to modify the applet so that it can accept the foreign exchange rates table provided by the International Monetary Fund on the Internet at* **http://www.imf.org/external/np/tre/sdr/drates/8101.htm.**

For most countries, the exchange rate is specified as the value of a U.S. dollar in that country's currency. For example, the rate for India might be given as 42.4 rupees, meaning that 1 U.S. dollar is equivalent to 42.4 Indian rupees. However, for some countries, marked by an asterisk, the rate is in fact the amount of U.S. dollars corresponding to one unit of the country's currency. For example, the exchange rate for the United Kingdom is given as 1.6968 U.S. dollars, which means 1 pound is equivalent to 1.6968 U.S. dollars. The **CurrencyConvert** applet accounts for this difference in exchange rate specification when reading the rates and when performing the currency conversions.

The actual currency conversion is done in a straightforward manner: Any currency is first converted to U.S. dollars, which are then converted to the target currency.

Aside from the currency conversion algorithm, the other important detail of **CurrencyConvert** is its user interface. As Figure 2-7 shows, **CurrencyConvert** uses a very simple layout. Two labels show the source of the rates and the current date. Then two drop-down menus list the countries between which you can convert currencies. Finally, there are two text fields, one to enter the amount to convert and the other to show the converted results. The currency names appear underneath these text fields. Arranging various GUI components inside panels and then placing these panels in the applet using a **BorderLayout** layout manager completes the layout.

CURRENCYCONVERT CLASSES   **CurrencyConvert** uses two internal classes:

♦ The **CountryRateInfo** class (lines 64 through 78) stores the country name, currency name, and exchange value for a specific currency. It also has a **boolean** variable named **valueIsUSD** (see line 68) that is set to **true** when the exchange value is in U.S. dollars.

♦ The **ExchangeRate** class (lines 80 through 105) simply stores **CountryRateInfo** objects in a **Vector** and provides a number of **public** methods to access these objects.

CURRENCYCONVERT INITIALIZATION   The **init()** method, in lines 119 through 237, reads the exchange rate information and sets up the user interface for the

CurrencyConvert applet. Line 121 creates an **ExchangeRate** object named **rates** where all of the rate information will be stored:

```
121        rates = new ExchangeRate();
```

Line 123 gets the name of the exchange rate file from the **ratefile** parameter:

```
123        rateFileName = getParameter("ratefile");
```

The **try** block in lines 124 through 186 reads from the rate file and processes its contents. Line 126 creates a URL from the rate filename:

```
126        URL url = new URL(getCodeBase()+rateFileName);
```

Lines 134 and 135 create a **DataInputStream** to read from that URL:

```
134        DataInputStream in = new
135                DataInputStream(url.openStream());
```

Line 140 shows how a line is read from the file:

```
140        String line = in.readLine();
```

Java 2

The **readLine()** method of the **DataInputStream** class returns a line of text as a **String**. This method returns a **null** when the file ends. In Java 1.1 and Java 2, the **readLine()** method of the **DataInputStream** class is deprecated. The **CurrencyConvert** applet uses this deprecated method to ensure that the applet will work with older Web browsers. To avoid using the deprecated **DataInputStream.readLine()** method, simply replace lines 134 and 135 with the following lines:

```
BufferedReader in = new BufferedReader(
        new InputStreamReader(url.openStream()));
```

The **substring()** method of the **String** class is used to extract specific parts of a line. For example, the date (on which the rates are valid) happens to be between character positions 28 and 50 of the first line in the rate file. Line 141 extracts this substring as follows:

```
141        dateString = line.substring(28, 50);
```

The **while** loop in lines 156 through 185 gets the exchange rates one country at a time and stores the values in the **rates** array.

After the **init()** method finishes reading the exchange rates from the file, it prepares the user interface in lines 197 through 237.

CURRENCYCONVERT CALCULATIONS   **CurrencyConvert** performs calculations when the user selects a country from one of the drop-down menus or enters an amount to convert. When the user selects from either drop-down menu, the **action()**

method is called. That method, shown in lines 242 through 265, determines which drop-down menu was clicked and then calls the **computeValue()** method to perform the currency conversion. For example, lines 244 through 253 handle any selections made from the "Convert From" drop-down menu:

```
244         if(ev.target == fromCurrencyChoice)
245         {
246             String from = fromCurrencyChoice.getSelectedItem();
247             if(!currentFrom.countryName.equals(from))
248             {
249                 currentFrom = rates.getInfo(from);
250                 fromCurrency.setText(currentFrom.currencyName);
251                 computeValue();
252             }
253         }
```

The **Event ev** is an argument to **action()**, and **ev.target** is the object on which the user clicked. Line 244 checks whether the user has clicked on the drop-down menu called **fromCurrencyChoice**. If so, line 246 gets the selected country's name. Line 247 ensures that the user has selected a new country (otherwise there is no need to recompute the value). Line 249 gets the rate information into a **CountryRateInfo** object named **currentFrom**. Line 250 displays the new currency name in the label underneath the drop-down menu. Finally, line 251 calls **computeValue()** to perform the currency conversion and display the results.

Java 2

The **action()** method is deprecated in Java 1.1 and 2. You should use an **ItemListener** interface instead. To see how to use the **ItemListener** interface, consult the revised version of **CurrencyConvert.java** file in the **ch02\cconvert\Java2** directory of the CD-ROM.

The other trigger for calculation is a mouse click on the text field where the user can enter a value to convert. Lines 267 through 275 implement the **handleEvent()** method that processes these events. If the event is a loss of focus (meaning that the mouse has been clicked elsewhere and further keystrokes are not meant for the text field), **handleEvent()** calls **computeValue()** to perform the currency conversion:

```
269         if(ev.target == fromValueField &&
270             ev.id == Event.LOST_FOCUS)
271         {
272             computeValue();
273         }
```

Java 2

Note that **handleEvent()** is also deprecated in Java 1.1 and 2. You should use a **FocusListener** interface with a **focusLost()** method instead. The updated **CurrencyConvert.java** file in the **ch02\cconvert\Java2** directory shows how to use the **FocusListener** interface.

The **computeValue()** method, in lines 277 through 294, performs the currency conversion. That method takes a two-step approach. First it calls the **toDollars()** method (lines 296 through 302) to convert a currency into U.S. dollars. Then it calls the **toCurrency()** method (lines 304 to 310) to convert from U.S. dollars to the target currency.

A Calendar

Calendars are fairly common Java applets. This particular **Calendar** applet basically displays a calendar for any selected month of a year. Although this specific feature is not implemented here, the **Calendar** applet is meant to serve as a shared community calendar where anyone can add an event for a specific date and everyone can access the calendar to look at the current list of events. To implement this feature, there has to be a database or some CGI program on the Web server. You will see examples of Java database programming in Chapter 12. For now, the applet demonstrates how to lay out the user interface using buttons (with the idea that users will later be able to click on them to view events for that day) and how to compute the weekday for any date.

Using Calendar

You will find all of the files for the **Calendar** applet in the **ch02\calendar** directory of the companion CD-ROM. To try out the **Calendar** applet, open the **Caltest.html** file in a Java-capable Web browser. Once the applet is loaded, you can select a month from the drop-down menu of months and change the year by typing a year in the text field. Figure 2-8 shows the calendar for the month of January 2000.

Notice that the **Calendar** applet shows two text areas below the monthly calendar. These areas are meant for future enhancements. The idea is that users will use **Calendar** as a community event calendar, clicking on a date to view that day's events. Also, anyone could enter a new event for a specific date and click on the **Insert Event** button to add that event to the calendar. As it stands now, the applet does not include any code to support these features.

You can incorporate the **Calendar** applet into an HTML file with an **\<applet\>** tag. For example, the file **Caltest.html** uses the following **\<applet\>** tag:

```
<applet code="Calendar.class" width=400 height=400>
</applet>
```

This **\<applet\>** tag causes the **Calendar** applet to display the calendar in an area 400 pixels wide by 400 pixels tall.

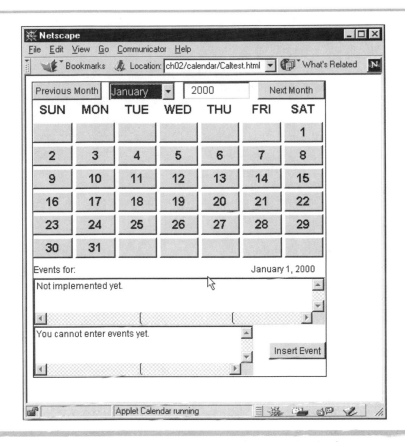

FIGURE 2-8.   The **Calendar** applet displaying the calendar for January 2000.

Calendar

Understanding Calendar

The following listing shows **Calendar.java**, the Java program that implements the **Calendar** applet. I explain the program in the subsequent sections.

```
1 //-----------------------------------------------------------------
2 // Calendar.java
3 // Displays a calendar for any month and any year (up to 9999).
4 //
5 // Can be expanded to allow user to enter events (this requires
6 // a CGI program at the Web server). When the ability to enter
7 // events is implemented, this applet can be used as a shared
8 // community event calendar.
9 //-----------------------------------------------------------------
```

```
10  import java.applet.*;
11  import java.awt.*;
12  import java.util.*;
13  /**
14   *  The Calendar applet displays a perpetual calendar and can be
15   *  enhanced to allow users to enter community events (which have
16   *  to be stored by a database or a script at the Web server).
17   *  This version shows the user interface for event display and
18   *  event entry, but does not actually implement these features.
19   *
20   *  @author Naba Barkakati
21   *  @version 0.9 October 1998
22   */
23  public class Calendar extends Applet
24  {
25      Choice      monthChoice;
26      TextField   year;
27      Button      previousButton;
28      Button      nextButton;
29      Date        today;
30      int         currentDate = 1;
31      int         currentMonth;
32      int         currentYear;
33      Label       currentDateLabel;
34      TextArea    eventsText;
35      TextArea    entryText;
36      Button      addEntry;
37      int         appletWidth;
38      int         appletHeight;
39      // Create some fonts
40      Font helvP12 = new Font("Helvetica", Font.PLAIN, 12);
41      Font helvP14 = new Font("Helvetica", Font.PLAIN, 14);
42      Font helvB16 = new Font("Helvetica", Font.BOLD, 16);
43      String days[] = {"SUN", "MON", "TUE", "WED", "THU",
44                      "FRI", "SAT"};
45      String months[] = {"January", "February", "March", "April",
46                          "May", "June", "July", "August", "September",
47                          "October", "November", "December"};
48      int daysInMonth[] = {31, 28, 31, 30, 31, 30, 31, 31, 30, 31,
49                          30, 31};
50      Button [][] monthButtons = new Button [6][7];
51      /** Initializes the Calendar's user interface */
52      public void init()
```

```
53        {
54            Dimension appletSize = size(); // call getSize() in Java 2
55            appletWidth = appletSize.width;
56            appletHeight = appletSize.height;
57            today = new Date();
58            currentMonth = today.getMonth();
59            currentYear = today.getYear(); // years since 1900
60            currentYear += 1900;
61            setLayout(new BorderLayout());
62
63            Panel pTop = new Panel();
64            pTop.setLayout(new GridLayout(1, 4, 10, 10));
65            previousButton = new Button("Previous Month");
66            pTop.add(previousButton);
67            monthChoice = new Choice();
68            monthChoice.setFont(helvP14);
69            for(int i = 0; i < months.length; i++)
70                monthChoice.addItem(months[i]);
71            monthChoice.select(currentMonth);
72            pTop.add(monthChoice);
73            year = new TextField("" + currentYear, 4);
74            year.setFont(helvP14);
75            pTop.add(year);
76            nextButton = new Button("Next Month");
77            pTop.add(nextButton);
78            add("North", pTop);
79
80            Panel pButtons = new Panel();
81            pButtons.setLayout(new GridLayout(7,7,4,4));
82            pButtons.setFont(helvB16);
83            for(int i=0; i < days.length; i++)
84                pButtons.add(new Label(days[i], Label.CENTER));
85            for(int i=0; i < 6; i++)
86                for(int j=0; j < 7; j++)
87                {
88                    monthButtons[i][j] = new Button("    ");
89                    pButtons.add(monthButtons[i][j]);
90                }
91            add("Center", pButtons);
92
93            Panel pBottom = new Panel();
94            pBottom.setLayout(new BorderLayout());
95            pBottom.setFont(helvP12);
```

```
96          Panel p = new Panel();
97          p.setLayout(new BorderLayout());
98          p.add("West", new Label("Events for:"));
99          currentDateLabel = new Label(months[currentMonth]+" "+
100                             currentDate+", "+currentYear);
101         p.add("East", currentDateLabel);
102         pBottom.add("North", p);
103         eventsText = new TextArea("Not implemented yet.",3,80);
104         pBottom.add("Center", eventsText);
105         entryText = new TextArea("You cannot enter events yet.",2,40);
106         p = new Panel();
107         p.setLayout(new BorderLayout());
108         p.add("West", entryText);
109         addEntry = new Button("Insert Event");
110         Panel pTemp = new Panel();
111         pTemp.setLayout(new GridLayout(3,1));
112         pTemp.add(new Label(" "));
113         pTemp.add(addEntry);
114         pTemp.add(new Label(" "));
115         p.add("East", pTemp);
116         pBottom.add("South", p);
117         add("South", pBottom);
118         validate();
119         repaint(75);
120     }
121     /** Returns true if the year is a leap year. */
122     public boolean isLeapYear(int year)
123     {
124         if((year % 400) == 0) return(true);
125         if((year > 1582) && ((year % 100) == 0)) return(false);
126         if((year % 4) == 0) return(true);
127         return(false);
128     }
129     /** Displays the calendar for a specific month of a year */
130     public void displayMonth(int month, int year)
131     {
132         int day = 1; // first of the month
133         int monthNum = month - 1; // month number, 1=Mar, 2=Apr, etc.
134         if(monthNum <= 0) monthNum += 12; // Jan = 11, Feb = 12
135         int tempYear = year;
136         if(monthNum > 10) tempYear = year - 1;
137         int century = tempYear / 100;
138         int yy = tempYear - 100 * century;
```

```
139        int factor = (int)(day +
140              (int)(2.6*(double)monthNum - 0.2) -
141              2*century + yy + yy/4 + century/4.0);
142        int firstWeekday = factor % 7; // 0=Sun, 1=Mon, 2=Tue, ...
143
144        // Now draw the dates on the buttons in the calendar
145        int maxDate = daysInMonth[month];
146        if(month == 1 && isLeapYear(year)) maxDate += 1;
147        int dateNow = 1;
148        for(int i=0; i < 6; i++)
149        {
150            for(int j=0; j < 7; j++)
151            {
152                if(dateNow == 1 && j < firstWeekday)
153                    monthButtons[i][j].setLabel("    ");
154                else if(dateNow > maxDate)
155                    monthButtons[i][j].setLabel("    ");
156                else
157                {
158                    monthButtons[i][j].setLabel(""+dateNow);
159                    dateNow++;
160                }
161            }
162        }
163    }
164    /** Processes the year entered by the user */
165    public int processYear(String yearString)
166    {
167        if((yearString.length() == 4))
168        {
169            try
170            {
171                int year = Integer.parseInt(yearString);
172                return year;
173            }
174            catch(NumberFormatException e)
175            {
176                return currentYear;
177            }
178        }
179        return -1;
180    }
181    /** Updates applet by calling paint(). */
```

```
182     public void update(Graphics g) { paint(g);}
183     /** Calls displayMonth() to display the calendar */
184     public void paint(Graphics g)
185     {
186         displayMonth(currentMonth, currentYear);
187         g.setColor(Color.black);
188         g.drawRect(0, 0, appletWidth-1, appletHeight-1);
189     }
190     /** Handles mouse clicks in the buttons and drop-down menus*/
191     public boolean action(Event ev, Object obj)
192     {
193         boolean eventHandled = false;
194         if(ev.target == previousButton)  // go to next month
195         {
196             if((currentYear > 1) || (currentMonth > 0))
197             {
198                 currentMonth--;
199                 if(currentMonth < 0)
200                 {
201                     currentMonth = 11;
202                     currentYear--;
203                 }
204                 monthChoice.select(currentMonth);
205                 year.setText(""+currentYear);
206                 currentDateLabel.setText(months[currentMonth]+" "+
207                                 currentDate+", "+currentYear);
208                 repaint();
209             }
210             eventHandled = true;
211         }
212         else if(ev.target == nextButton)
213         {
214             if((currentYear < 9999) || (currentMonth < 11))
215             {
216                 currentMonth++;
217                 if(currentMonth > 11)
218                 {
219                     currentMonth = 0;
220                     currentYear++;
221                 }
222                 monthChoice.select(currentMonth);
223                 year.setText(""+currentYear);
224                 currentDateLabel.setText(months[currentMonth]+" "+
```

```
225                                  currentDate+", "+currentYear);
226                 repaint();
227             }
228             eventHandled = true;
229         }
230         else if(ev.target == monthChoice)
231         {
232             int m = monthChoice.getSelectedIndex();
233             year.setText(""+currentYear);
234             if(m != currentMonth)
235             {
236                 currentMonth = monthChoice.getSelectedIndex();
237                 currentDateLabel.setText(months[currentMonth]+" "+
238                                 currentDate+", "+currentYear);
239                 repaint();
240             }
241             eventHandled = true;
242         }
243         else if(ev.target == year)
244         {
245             int y = processYear(year.getText());
246             if((y > 0) && (y != currentYear))
247             {
248                 currentYear = y;
249                 currentDateLabel.setText(
250                             months[currentMonth]+" "+
251                             currentDate+", "+currentYear);
252                 repaint();
253             }
254             eventHandled = true;
255         }
256         return(eventHandled);
257     }
258     /** Handles text entry by user. */
259     public boolean handleEvent(Event ev)
260     {
261         if(ev.target == year)
262         {
263             int yNow = processYear(year.getText());
264             if((yNow > 0) && (yNow != currentYear))
265             {
266                 currentYear = yNow;
267                 repaint();
```

```
268              }
269           }
270           return super.handleEvent(ev);
271       }
272       /** Makes room for a 1-pixel border. */
273       public Insets getInsets()
274       {
275           return new Insets(1,1,1,1); // 1-pixel border
276       }
277   }
```

ANNOTATIONS

The **Calendar** applet has two key design elements:

◆ A user interface to show the calendar and let the user interact with the calendar

◆ A formula used to calculate the day of the week for a date

The user interface is organized using **Panel** objects, where each panel holds other components such as **Label**, **Choice**, and **Button** objects. Typically, each panel uses a **GridLayout** layout manager to arrange its components into rows and columns. The **Panel** objects, in turn, are placed in the applet using a **BorderLayout** layout manager. The key elements of the **Calendar** applet's user interface are as follows:

◆ Clicking on the drop-down menu (implemented using a **Choice** component) displays a list of months from which the user can select a specific month. That month's calendar is then displayed.

◆ The user may type in a year (such as 2000) in the text field next to the drop-down menu for selecting a month. This updates the monthly calendar to reflect the change in year.

◆ Clicking on the **Previous Month** and **Next Month** buttons changes the month accordingly.

◆ The month's calendar appears as labels on an array of buttons. Although the feature is not yet implemented, the idea is that by clicking on a button the user can view that day's events in the text field under the calendar. Also, the user can enter a new event and click the **Insert Event** button to add an event to that day's list of events. These features require appropriate scripts or database support in the Web server.

To display the **Calendar**, the applet needs the day of the week for the first day of any month. The applet uses a formula described in the **sci.math** newsgroup's

Frequently Asked Questions (FAQ): Day of Week, at **http://www.faqs.org/faqs/ sci-math-faq/dayWeek/**. The formula gives the day of the week as follows:

W = (D + floor(2.6*M - 0.2) - 2C + Y + floor(Y/4) + floor(C/4)) modulo 7

where the various variables and functions have the following meaning:

♦ **W** is the day of the week (0 = Sunday, 1= Monday, . . . , 6 = Saturday).

♦ **floor()** denotes a function that returns the largest integer that is not greater than the floating-point argument passed to the function (for example, **floor(2.6)** returns 2).

♦ **D** is a day of the month between 1 and 31.

♦ **M** is the month, with 1 = March, 2 = April, . . . , 10 = December, 11 = January, 12 = February. You have to treat January and February as months of the preceding year.

♦ **C** is the century—that is, the first two digits of the year (for 1999, **C** = 19; for 2000, **C** = 20).

♦ **Y** is the year, excluding the century—that is, the last two digits of the year or, for January and February, of the previous year (for March through December 1999, **Y** = 99; for January and February 1999, **Y** = 98).

♦ **modulo 7** refers to the remainder after dividing by 7.

The leap year, including the fact that any year divisible by 400 is a leap year, is already built into the formula.

Java 2
In Java 1.1 and 2, you do not have to use this formula to find the day of the week corresponding to a specific date. You can use the **GregorianCalendar** class to create and use a Gregorian calendar. In particular, you can call the **get(Calendar.DAY_OF_WEEK)** method of the **GregorianCalendar** object to get the day of the week for a specific date. You can then use that information to display the calendar for a month.

CALENDAR VARIABLES   The **Calendar** applet's implementation begins on line 23 with the declaration of the **Calendar** class:

```
23 public class Calendar extends Applet
```

Inside the class declaration, lines 25 through 50 declare all of the variables used in the **Calendar** class. Many of the variables are used to create and manage the user interface. Here are some key variables and their descriptions:

♦ **Choice monthChoice** (line 25) is the drop-down menu for selecting a month.

♦ **TextField year** (line 26) is the text field where users can type in the year.

♦ **Button previousButton** and **nextButton** (lines 27 and 28) are used as the buttons labeled **Previous Month** and **Next Month** in the user interface.

♦ **Date today** (line 29) is used to store today's date (the day when the applet is run).

♦ **int currentDate**, **currentMonth**, and **currentYear** (lines 30 through 32) are the current day (1 through 31), month (0 through 11, with 0 representing January), and year (1998, 1999, and so on).

♦ **Font helvP12**, **helvP14**, and **helvB16** (lines 40 through 42) are fonts used in various parts of the user interface.

♦ **String days[]** and **months[]** (lines 43 through 47) are arrays with names of weekdays and months, respectively.

♦ **int daysInMonth[]** (lines 48 and 49) is an array with the number of days for each month (with January at index 0, February at index 1, and so on).

♦ **Button [][] monthButtons** (line 50) is a grid of buttons, six rows tall by seven columns wide, used to display the calendar for the current month.

CALENDAR INITIALIZATION   The **Calendar** applet's **init()** method initializes the variables and prepares the user interface. Lines 57 through 60 get the current date and initialize the variables **currentMonth** and **currentYear**.

```
57          today = new Date();
58          currentMonth = today.getMonth();
59          currentYear = today.getYear(); // years since 1900
60          currentYear += 1900;
```

Line 57 creates a **Date** object, which is automatically initialized with the current date. Line 58 gets the current month, which is a number between 0 and 11, with 0 denoting January and 11 representing December. Line 59 gets the current year as the number of years since 1900. Line 60 adds 1900 to convert the year to a four-digit value.

Java 2   Note that the **getMonth()** and **getYear()** methods of the **Date** class are deprecated in Java 1.1 and 2. You should call **calendar.get(Calendar.MONTH)** and **calendar.get(Calendar.YEAR)** instead (where **calendar** represents a **GregorianCalendar** object).

Lines 61 through 118 of the **init()** method lays out various user interface components to create the user interface of the applet. Line 61 specifies a **BorderLayout** layout manager for the applet:

```
61          setLayout(new BorderLayout());
```

Lines 63 through 77 create a panel named **pTop** that includes the buttons labeled **Previous Month** and **Next Month**, the drop-down menu for the months, and the **year** text field. Line 78 places the **pTop** panel along the top edge of the applet:

```
78          add("North", pTop);
```

Lines 80 through 90 initialize the panel named **pButtons**. Lines 80 and 81 initialize the panel and set a **GridLayout** for the panel:

```
80          Panel pButtons = new Panel();
81          pButtons.setLayout(new GridLayout(7,7,4,4));
```

Notice that this panel is expected to have seven rows and seven columns. The columns correspond to the seven days of the week. Lines 83 and 84 create the first row with the days of the week:

```
83          for(int i=0; i < days.length; i++)
84              pButtons.add(new Label(days[i], Label.CENTER));
```

Lines 85 through 90 create the next six rows with buttons that will be used to display the days of a month for a monthly calendar:

```
85          for(int i=0; i < 6; i++)
86              for(int j=0; j < 7; j++)
87              {
88                  monthButtons[i][j] = new Button("   ");
89                  pButtons.add(monthButtons[i][j]);
90              }
```

As line 88 shows, each button initially has a blank string as its label. Line 89 adds each button to the **pButtons** panel. After the panel is ready, line 91 places that panel in the **"Center"** position of the applet:

```
91          add("Center", pButtons);
```

Finally, lines 93 through 116 create another panel named **pBottom** with the text display areas that appear below the calendar. Line 117 places that panel along the bottom edge of the applet:

```
117         add("South", pBottom);
```

CALENDAR CALCULATIONS AND DISPLAY   The following methods in the **Calendar** applet perform calculations and display the calendar:

◆ **public boolean isLeapYear(int year)** in lines 122 through 128 returns **true** if the year is a leap year.

◆ **public void displayMonth(int month, int year)** in lines 130 through 163 computes the day of the week for the first day of the specified month and year. Lines 132 through 142 compute the day of the week, using the formula presented earlier. Then lines 145 through 162 display the days of the month on the **button[]** array in the applet. The **paint()** method calls **displayMonth()** to display the calendar for the current month.

◆ **public int processYear(String yearString)** processes a year entered by the user. It returns -1 if the year is invalid.

◆ **public void paint(Graphics g)** calls **displayMonth()** to display the monthly calendar. It also draws a one-pixel border around the applet.

◆ **public boolean action(Event ev, Object obj)** handles mouse clicks on the buttons labeled **Previous Month** and **Next Month** as well as the drop-down menu with month choices. Note that this method is deprecated in Java 1.1 and 2; you should use a different event-handling model that relies on objects that implement **ActionListener** and **ItemListener** interfaces.

◆ **public boolean handleEvent(Event ev)** handles text entry in the **year** field. It calls **processYear()** to process the text entered by the user. Note that **handleEvent()** is also deprecated in Java 1.1 and 2. Nowadays, you should implement an object with a **TextListener** interface to handle text-entry events.

A Business Chart Maker

Plotting data is an ideal application for a Java applet. You can write an applet that downloads data from a file on the Web server and then plots it in different ways in the Web browser. Once the data has been read by the applet, all the manipulation happens in the applet running on the Web browser. You have a lot of flexibility in what you do with the data. You can display it in a table, plot it in a pie chart, or draw a bar chart.

The **BusinessChart** applet is an example of a typical business charting applet. **BusinessChart** reads data from a text file and then renders it either as a pie chart or as a bar chart. The user can switch between the pie chart and the bar chart. If you were to search on the Web, you would find other business charting applets that are much more elaborate than **BusinessChart**. However, **BusinessChart** embodies the basic idea of reading the data from the Web server and rendering it in various ways on the Web browser. You can learn how to write a typical charting applet by studying how **BusinessChart** works and how it is implemented.

Using BusinessChart

You will find the files for the **BusinessChart** applet in the **ch02\chart** directory of the companion CD-ROM. To see how the applet works, open the **TestPlot.html** file from a Java-capable Web browser. Figure 2-9 shows the applet displaying some data in a pie chart. As the figure shows, **BusinessChart** has a very simple user interface. The title appears at the top, followed by the plot in the middle of the applet. Along the bottom of the applet, there are two checkboxes labeled **Pie Chart** and **Bar Chart**. Initially, the **Pie Chart** checkbox is selected and the applet displays a pie chart. If you click on the **Bar Chart** checkbox, the applet will switch to a bar chart. Figure 2-10 shows the applet displaying a bar chart using the same data as the pie chart in Figure 2-9.

The contents of the **TestPlot.html** file illustrate how to configure the **BusinessChart** applet:

```
<html>
<body>
<applet code="BusinessChart.class" width=400 height=300>
  <param name="title" value="Sales by region">
  <param name="datafile" value="sales.txt">
</applet>
</body>
</html>
```

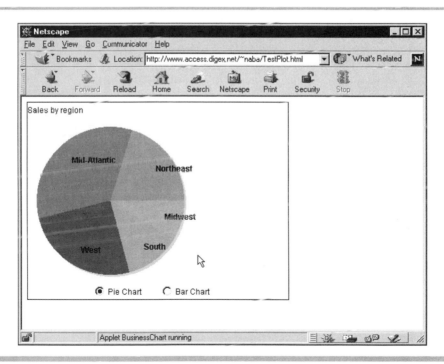

FIGURE 2-9. The **BusinessChart** applet plots data in a pie chart.

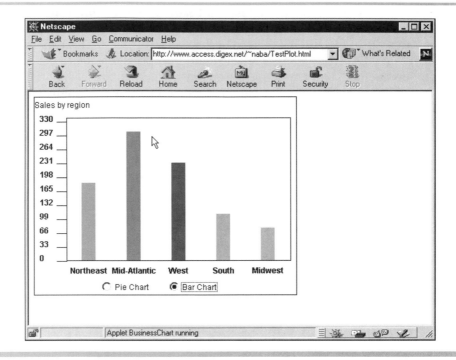

FIGURE 2-10. The **BusinessChart** applet displaying a bar chart.

The **<applet>** tag has the following attributes:

◆ **code="BusinessChart.class"** specifies the name of the file containing the compiled Java code for the applet.

◆ **width=400** specifies that the applet's display area is 400 pixels wide.

◆ **height=300** specifies that the applet's display area is 300 pixels tall.

◆ **BusinessChart** accepts two parameters through the following **<param>** tags:

    ◆ **title**—the text that appears at the top of the applet

    ◆ **datafile**—the name of the text file containing the data

In this case, the **datafile** parameter specifies **sales.txt** as the file containing the data to be plotted. Here the **sales.txt** file contains the following lines of text:

```
Northeast       200
Mid-Atlantic    330
West            250
South           120
Midwest         85
```

You may want to look at these lines and then look back at Figures 2-9 and 2-10 to see how the **BusinessChart** applet plots this data in a pie chart and in a bar chart.

To use **BusinessChart** at your Web site, copy the class file and the data file to a directory on the Web server. You should edit the data file to plot other data than what is shown in Figures 2-9 and 2-10. To embed the **BusinessChart** applet in your own HTML file, copy the **<applet>** tag from the **TestPlot.html** file. Edit the **title** and **datafile <param>** tags to suit your needs. In particular, make sure that the **datafile** parameter gives the name of the file where you have placed the data to be plotted.

BusinessChart

Understanding BusinessChart

Now that you have seen how the **BusinessChart** applet works and how you can use it at your Web site, let's study the applet's source code to see how it is implemented. The following listing shows the **BusinessChart.java** file that implements the applet. The subsequent sections describe key aspects of this program to help you understand it and enhance it to suit your needs.

```
1  //-------------------------------------------------------------
2  // BusinessChart.java
3  // Plots data in pie chart or bar chart. Data is downloaded from
4  // a specified file on the server and users can choose to plot
5  // data as a pie chart or bar chart.
6  //-------------------------------------------------------------
7  import java.awt.*;
8  import java.applet.*;
9  import java.net.*;
10 import java.io.*;
11 import java.util.*;
12 // Class to store each data item
13 class DataItem extends Object
14 {
15     public double value;  // value of this data item
16     public String label;  // label for this data item
17
18     DataItem (String s) // constructor
19     {
20         label = "NONE";
21         value = 0.0;
22         // s is of the form "Label     100.5"
23         StringTokenizer t = new StringTokenizer(s);
24         try
25         {
26             label = t.nextToken();
27             value = Double.valueOf(t.nextToken()).doubleValue();
```

```
28              }
29          catch(NoSuchElementException e) {}
30      }
31 }
32 // Class to store array of PlotData objects
33 class PlotData extends Object
34 {
35      Vector dataItems;
36      double total;
37      double min;
38      double max;
39      PlotData()
40      {
41          dataItems = new Vector(10);
42          total = 0.0;
43          min = Double.MAX_VALUE;
44          max = Double.MIN_VALUE;
45      }
46      public void addElement(DataItem item)
47      {
48          dataItems.addElement(item);
49          total += item.value;
50          if(item.value < min) min = item.value;
51          if(item.value > max) max = item.value;
52      }
53      public DataItem elementAt(int n)
54      {
55          return (DataItem)dataItems.elementAt(n);
56      }
57      public int size() { return dataItems.size();}
58      public double total() { return total;}
59      public double maxValue() { return max;}
60      public double minValue() { return min;}
61 }
62 // Class to atore attributes of the charts
63 class ChartAttributes extends Object
64 {
65      Vector colors;
66      Color bgColor;
67      Color txtColor;
68      Font  font;
69      static int index;
70      boolean defaultColors;
```

```java
71      ChartAttributes()
72      {
73          this.bgColor = Color.white;
74          this.txtColor = Color.black;
75          this.font = new Font("Helvetica",Font.BOLD,12);
76          colors = new Vector(10);
77          addElement(Color.cyan);
78          addElement(Color.green);
79          addElement(Color.magenta);
80          addElement(Color.orange);
81          addElement(Color.pink);
82          addElement(Color.red);
83          addElement(Color.yellow);
84          defaultColors = true;
85      }
86      ChartAttributes(Color bgColor, Color txtColor, Font font)
87      {
88          colors = new Vector(10);
89          defaultColors = false;
90          this.bgColor = bgColor;
91          this.txtColor = txtColor;
92          this.font = font;
93          index = 0;
94      }
95      public void addElement(Color color)
96      {
97          if(defaultColors)
98          {
99              colors.removeAllElements();
100             defaultColors = false;
101         }
102         colors.addElement(color);
103     }
104     public Color getBackgroundColor() { return bgColor;}
105     public Color getTextColor() { return txtColor;}
106     public Font getFont() { return font;}
107     public void resetColor() { index = 0; }
108     public Color getNextColor()
109     {
110         int n = index;
111         index++;
112         if(index >= colors.size()) index = 0;
113         return (Color)colors.elementAt(n);
```

```
114
115         }
116         public int size() { return colors.size();}
117         public void setBackgroundColor(Color bgColor)
118         {
119             this.bgColor = bgColor;
120         }
121         public void setTextColor(Color txtColor)
122         {
123             this.txtColor = txtColor;
124         }
125         public void setFont(Font font)
126         {
127             this.font = font;
128         }
129 }
130 // Plots data in a pie chart
131 class PieChartCanvas extends Canvas
132 {
133     PlotData data;
134     ChartAttributes attrib;
135     static final int pieBorderWidth = 10;
136     public PieChartCanvas(PlotData data, ChartAttributes attrib)
137     {
138         this.data = data;
139         this.attrib = attrib;
140         setFont(attrib.getFont());
141         setBackground(attrib.getBackgroundColor());
142     }
143     public void paint(Graphics g)
144     {
145         Dimension aSize = size(); //call getSize() in Java 2
146         int xSize = aSize.width, ySize = aSize.height;
147         int PieChartCanvasSize = Math.min(xSize, ySize);
148         int pieDiameter = PieChartCanvasSize-2*pieBorderWidth;
149         int pieRadius = pieDiameter/2;
150         int pieCenterPos = pieBorderWidth+pieRadius;
151         int startDegrees = 0;
152         int arcDegrees;
153         // Draw a shadow around the pie shape
154         g.setColor(Color.lightGray);
155         g.fillOval(pieBorderWidth+3, pieBorderWidth+3,
156                             pieDiameter, pieDiameter);
```

```
157         g.setColor(Color.gray);
158         g.fillOval(pieBorderWidth, pieBorderWidth,
159                             pieDiameter, pieDiameter);
160     // Draw the pie wedges
161     attrib.resetColor();
162     for(int i = 0; i < data.size(); i++)
163     {
164         arcDegrees = (int)(Math.round((
165                         data.elementAt(i).value /
166                             data.total()) * 360));
167         g.setColor(attrib.getNextColor());
168         g.fillArc(pieBorderWidth,pieBorderWidth,pieDiameter,
169                     pieDiameter, startDegrees, arcDegrees);
170         startDegrees += arcDegrees;
171     }
172     startDegrees = 0; // Draw labels on top of the wedges.
173     int x, y;
174     double angleRadians;
175     for(int i = 0; i < data.size(); i++)
176     {
177         arcDegrees = (int)(Math.round((
178                         data.elementAt(i).value /
179                             data.total()) * 360));
180         if (arcDegrees > 3)  // Label larger wedges only
181         {
182             g.setColor(attrib.getTextColor());
183             angleRadians = (float) (startDegrees+
184                         arcDegrees/2)* Math.PI / 180.0;
185             x = pieCenterPos + (int)((pieRadius/1.3)*
186                             Math.cos(angleRadians));
187             y = pieCenterPos - (int)((pieRadius/1.3)*
188                         Math.sin(angleRadians)) + 6;
189             g.drawString(data.elementAt(i).label, x, y);
190         }
191         startDegrees += arcDegrees;
192     }
193     }
194 }
195 // Plots data in a bar graph
196 class BarChartCanvas extends Canvas
197 {
198     PlotData data;
199     ChartAttributes attrib;
```

```
200   static final int borderWidth = 4;
201   BarChartCanvas(PlotData data, ChartAttributes attrib)
202   {
203       this.data = data;
204       this.attrib = attrib;
205       setBackground(attrib.getBackgroundColor());
206       setFont(attrib.getFont());
207   }
208   public void paint(Graphics g)
209   {
210       Dimension aSize = size(); //call getSize() in Java 2
211       int xSize = aSize.width, ySize = aSize.height;
212       double maxValue = data.maxValue();
213       double minValue = data.minValue();
214       if(minValue > 0.0) minValue = 0.0;
215       maxValue = Math.ceil(maxValue*1.1);
216       minValue = Math.floor(minValue*1.1);
217       long lMax = (long)maxValue;
218       long lMin = (long)minValue;
219       FontMetrics fm = g.getFontMetrics();
220       int fontHeight = fm.getHeight();
221       int tickSize = fontHeight;
222       int padding = 5;
223       int yLabelHeight = fontHeight + padding;
224       int labelWidth1 = fm.stringWidth(""+lMax);
225       int labelWidth2 = fm.stringWidth(""+lMin);
226       int xLabelWidth = Math.max(labelWidth1, labelWidth2) +
227                         tickSize + padding;
228       int chartWidth = xSize - 2*borderWidth - xLabelWidth;
229       int chartHeight = ySize - 2*borderWidth - yLabelHeight;
230       int numYTicks = 11;
231       if(chartHeight/(numYTicks-1) < fontHeight+padding)
232           numYTicks = chartHeight/(fontHeight+padding) + 1;
233       long lVStep = (lMax-lMin)/numYTicks;
234       int yStep = chartHeight / (numYTicks-1);
235       g.setColor(Color.black);
236       g.drawRect(xLabelWidth+borderWidth, borderWidth,
237                         chartWidth-1, chartHeight-1);
238       int xSlice = chartWidth / data.size();
239       int barWidth = xSlice / 3;
240       int xStart = xLabelWidth + borderWidth;
241       int x, y, barHeight;
242       // Draw the bars
```

```
243          attrib.resetColor();
244          for(int i = 0; i < data.size(); i++)
245          {
246              barHeight = (int)(data.elementAt(i).value/
247                          (maxValue-minValue)*chartHeight);
248              y = borderWidth + chartHeight - barHeight;
249              x = xStart + xSlice/2 - barWidth/2;
250              g.setColor(attrib.getNextColor());
251              g.fillRect(x, y, barWidth-1, barHeight-1);
252              // Add the x-axis label
253              y = ySize - yLabelHeight + fontHeight;
254              g.setColor(attrib.getTextColor());
255              int w = fm.stringWidth(data.elementAt(i).label);
256              x = xStart + xSlice/2 - w/2;
257              if(x < xStart) x = xStart;
258              g.drawString(data.elementAt(i).label, x, y);
259              xStart += xSlice;
260          }
261          // Draw the y-axis tick-marks and labels
262          x = borderWidth;
263          y = ySize - borderWidth - yLabelHeight;
264          long longValue = lMin;
265          for(int i = 0; i < numYTicks; i++)
266          {
267              g.setColor(Color.black);
268              g.drawLine(xLabelWidth+borderWidth-tickSize, y,
269                          xLabelWidth+borderWidth, y);
270              g.setColor(attrib.getTextColor());
271              g.drawString(""+longValue, x, y);
272              y -= yStep;
273              longValue += lVStep;
274          }
275      }
276 }
277 /**
278  * BusinessChart applet displays data in pie chart or bar graph.
279  * User can select plot type by clicking on a check box.
280  * <p>
281  * Applet accepts the following parameters:
282  * <ul>
283  *   <li> datafile - name of file with the data
284  *   <li> title - title of the plot
285  * </ul>
```

```
286    *
287    */
288    public class BusinessChart extends Applet
289    {
290        PieChartCanvas pieChart = null;
291        BarChartCanvas barChart = null;
292        Panel chartPanel = null;
293        String pieLabel = "Pie Chart", barLabel = "Bar Chart";
294        CheckboxGroup chartGroup = new CheckboxGroup();
295        CardLayout chartSelection = new CardLayout(4,4);
296        String dataFileName = null;
297        PlotData data = null;
298        ChartAttributes attrib = null;
299        /** Reads the data file and sets up the user interface */
300        public void init ()
301        {
302            // Read the applet arguments
303            data = new PlotData();
304            attrib = new ChartAttributes();
305
306            dataFileName = getParameter("datafile");
307            if(dataFileName == null)
308            {
309                getAppletContext().showStatus(
310                    "Must specify data file name through
311                        datafile parameter");
311                return;
312            }
313            // Open the data file and initialize the data items
314            try
315            {
316                URL url = new URL(getCodeBase()+dataFileName);
317                try
318                {
319                    DataInputStream in = new
320                        DataInputStream(url.openStream());
321                    // In Java 2, use:
322                    // BufferedReader in = new BufferedReader
323                    //      new InputStreamReader(url.openStream()));
324                    String line = null;
325                    while(true)
326                    {
327                        line = in.readLine();
```

```
328                          if(line == null) break;
329                          DataItem d = new DataItem(line);
330                          data.addElement(d);
331                     }
332                }
333           catch(IOException e) {}
334      }
335      catch(MalformedURLException e) {}
336
337      String chartTitle = "Business Chart Applet";
338      String param = getParameter("title");
339      if(param != null) chartTitle = param;
340
341      setLayout(new BorderLayout());
342      setBackground(Color.white);
343      setFont(new Font("Helvetica",Font.PLAIN,12));
344      add("North", new Label(chartTitle));
345      chartPanel = new Panel();
346      chartPanel.setLayout(chartSelection);
347      pieChart = new PieChartCanvas(data, attrib);
348      chartPanel.add(pieLabel, pieChart);
349      barChart = new BarChartCanvas(data, attrib);
350      chartPanel.add(barLabel, barChart);
351      add("Center", chartPanel);
352
353      Panel p = new Panel();
354      p.setLayout(new GridLayout(1,4,10,10));
355      p.add(new Label("       "));
356      p.add(new Checkbox(pieLabel, chartGroup, true));
357      p.add(new Checkbox(barLabel, chartGroup, false));
358      p.add(new Label("       "));
359      add("South", p);
360 }
361 /** Handles mouse clicks on the check boxes */
362 public boolean action(Event ev, Object obj)
363 {
364      if(!(ev.target instanceof Checkbox))
365           return false;
366      Checkbox c = chartGroup.getCurrent();
367      chartSelection.next(chartPanel);
368      return true;
369 }
```

```
370     /** Sets aside room for a 1-pixel border. */
371     public Insets getInsets()
372     {
373         return new Insets (1,1,1,1);
374     }
375     /** Draws a thin black border around the applet */
376     public void paint(Graphics g)
377     {
378         Dimension aSize = size(); //call getSize() in Java 2
379         g.setColor(Color.black);
380         g.drawRect(0, 0, aSize.width-1, aSize.height-1);
381     }
382 }
```

ANNOTATIONS

The **BusinessChart** applet uses two specialized **Canvas** objects to plot the data:

- ◆ **PieChartCanvas** renders the data in a pie chart.
- ◆ **BarChartCanvas** renders the data in a bar chart.

Both of these classes are subclasses of the **Canvas** class. The **paint()** method of each **Canvas** class handles the actual plotting of the data. During initialization the applet reads the data and creates instances of **PieChartCanvas** and **BarChartCanvas**. The rest of the work is then handled by these **Canvas** classes.

BusinessChart lays out the user interface components using a **BorderLayout** layout manager, as follows:

- ◆ The chart title is placed in a **Label** component at the **"North"** position, along the top edge of the applet's display area.

- ◆ Both the **PieChartCanvas** and the **BarChartCanvas** components occupy the large **"Center"** position of the applet.

- ◆ Two **Checkbox** components, used to switch between different chart types, are placed inside a panel, and that panel is located at the **"South"** position of the applet.

One key design element is the layout of the **PieChartCanvas** and **BarChartCanvas** components. Because only one of these has to be displayed at any time, these two components are arranged in a panel using a **CardLayout** layout manager. The **CardLayout** manager places its contents one on top of another. **CardLayout** also includes a method that can be called to bring a component to the top. Figure 2-11 illustrates the layout of the user interface components in the **BusinessChart** applet. When the user clicks on a checkbox along the bottom edge of the applet, the program calls the **next()** method of the **CardLayout** layout manager to bring the appropriate canvas to the top. The canvas then draws the selected chart.

BUSINESSCHART CLASSES   In addition to the **BusinessChart** class, which represents the applet, the program defines and uses the following classes to manage the data, keep track of various chart attributes, and plot the data:

◆ The **DataItem** class (lines 13 through 31) stores a single data item, provided in a line of text that specifies a label followed by a numeric value (for example, "Mid-Atlantic 330").

◆ The **PlotData** class (lines 33 through 61) stores one or more **DataItem** objects in a **Vector** and provides methods for adding and getting these objects. **PlotData** also keeps track of the maximum and minimum values as well as the sum of all **DataItem** values currently in **PlotData**.

◆ The **ChartAttributes** class (lines 63 through 129) stores various attributes of a chart, such as the background color, the text color, the text font, and a **Vector**

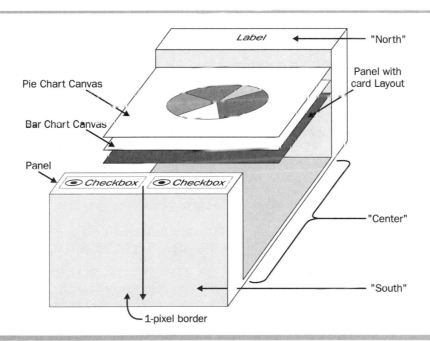

FIGURE 2-11.   Layout of the user interface components in the **BusinessChart** applet.

of colors to be used for the pie wedges or bars in the charts. This class also includes methods for setting and retrieving the various chart attributes.

◆ The **PieChartCanvas** class (lines 131 through 194) accepts a **PlotData** object and a **ChartAttributes** object and renders the data in a pie chart. The **paint()** method (lines 143 through 193) performs the necessary calculations, draws the pie wedges, and labels them.

◆ The **BarChartCanvas** class (lines 196 through 276) is similar to the **PieChartCanvas** class: it stores a **PlotData** object and a **ChartAttributes** object. Its **paint()** method (lines 208 through 275) then plots the data from the **PlotData** object in a bar chart, using the attributes from the **ChartAttributes** object.

BUSINESSCHART INITIALIZATION   The **init()** method in lines 300 through 360 reads the data from a specified file, creates the user interface components, and arranges them to create the applet's user interface. Lines 303 and 304 create new **PlotData** and **ChartAttributes** objects:

```
303        data = new PlotData();
304        attrib = new ChartAttributes();
```

The **PlotData** object will be used to store **DataItem** objects that will be created as each line of data is read from the data file. The **ChartAttributes** object is initialized with default values of colors and fonts.

Line 306 gets the **datafile** parameter that specifies the name of the file from which data will be read. Lines 314 through 335 open the specified file and read the data. Line 316 creates a **URL** object using the filename:

```
316        URL url = new URL(getCodeBase()+dataFileName);
```

Note that the filename is prefixed with the **String** returned by the **getCodeBase()** method. This means that the data file is expected to be in the same directory as this applet's class file.

Lines 319 and 320 open a **DataInputStream**, used to read lines from the data file:

```
319        DataInputStream in = new
320            DataInputStream(url.openStream());
```

Java 2   Note that in Java 1.1 and 2, you should use a **BufferedReader** object in place of the **DataInputStream**. To use a **BufferedReader**, simply replace lines 319 and 320 with the following lines:

```
BufferedReader in = new BufferedReader
    new InputStreamReader(url.openStream()));
```

Lines 324 through 331 read and process lines of text from the data file:

```
324              String line = null;
325              while(true)
326              {
327                  line = in.readLine();
328                  if(line == null) break;
329                  DataItem d = new DataItem(line);
330                  data.addElement(d);
331              }
```

Line 327 calls the **readLine()** method to read a line of text. If **readLine()** returns **null**, line 328 breaks the **while** loop. Line 329 creates a **DataItem** for a line of data. Line 330 then adds the **DataItem** to the **PlotData** object named **data**.

After the data has been read in, lines 337 through 339 set up the chart title from the **title** parameter:

```
337          String chartTitle = "Business Chart Applet";
338          String param = getParameter("title");
339          if(param != null) chartTitle = param;
```

The remainder of the **init()** method, from line 341 to line 359, prepares the user interface of the **BusinessChart** applet. Line 341 sets up a **BorderLayout** as layout manager for the applet:

```
341          setLayout(new BorderLayout());
```

Line 344 adds the chart title as a **Label** placed at the **"North"** position of the applet's **BorderLayout** layout manager:

```
344          add("North", new Label(chartTitle));
```

Lines 345 through 350 create the panel named **chartPanel**, which holds the **PieChartCanvas** and **BarChartCanvas** objects:

```
345          chartPanel = new Panel();
346          chartPanel.setLayout(chartSelection);
347          pieChart = new PieChartCanvas(data, attrib);
348          chartPanel.add(pieLabel, pieChart);
349          barChart = new BarChartCanvas(data, attrib);
350          chartPanel.add(barLabel, barChart);
```

Line 345 creates the **chartPanel**, and line 346 sets the **chartSelection** object as the layout manager for the **chartPanel**. If you look at line 295, you'll see that the

chartSelection object is a **CardLayout** manager. Line 347 creates a **PieChartCanvas** with the **PlotData** object named **data** and the **ChartAttributes** object named **attrib**. Next, line 348 adds the **PieChartCanvas** to the **chartPanel**. Lines 349 and 350 do the same with a **BarChartCanvas** object. Once the **chartPanel** is ready, line 351 places that panel at the **"Center"** position of the applet:

```
351         add("Center", chartPanel);
```

Lines 353 through 359 create a panel with two checkboxes, labeled **Pie Chart** and **Bar Chart**, respectively, and places this panel at the **"South"** position of the applet.

USER SELECTION OF CHARTS   Initially, the **BusinessChart** applet displays a pie chart and the **Pie Chart** checkbox is checked. When the user clicks on the **Bar Chart** checkbox, the **action()** method (lines 362 through 369) is called. This method calls the **next()** method of the **chartSelection** object (which is a **CardLayout** manager) to switch to the next plot:

```
367         chartSelection.next(chartPanel);
```

This brings the next component in the **chartPanel** to the top. That component happens to be a **BarChartCanvas** whose **paint()** method then renders the data in a bar chart.

PIE CHART PLOT   The **paint()** method of the **PieChartCanvas** class, in lines 143 through 193, draws the pie chart. This method first determines the size of the canvas and sets up several parameters such as the center and the diameter of the circle representing the pie chart. Then lines 154 through 159 draw two gray circles, one slightly offset from the other, to give a three-dimensional appearance to the chart.
    The **for** loop in lines 162 through 171 draws filled arcs representing the pie wedges:

```
162         for(int i = 0; i < data.size(); i++)
163         {
164             arcDegrees = (int)(Math.round((
165                             data.elementAt(i).value /
166                                 data.total()) * 360));
167             g.setColor(attrib.getNextColor());
168             g.fillArc(pieBorderWidth,pieBorderWidth,pieDiameter,
169                     pieDiameter, startDegrees, arcDegrees);
170             startDegrees += arcDegrees;
171         }
```

Lines 164 through 166 calculate the angular extent of a specific pie wedge. Note that the data item's value is obtained by calling the **elementAt()** method of the **PlotData** object named **data**. Line 167 sets the color for the pie wedge. Lines 168 and 169 then draw the filled arc for that pie wedge. Line 170 advances the **startDegrees** variable to the value needed for the next pie wedge.

Another **for** loop, in lines 175 through 192, draws the text labels on the pie wedges. A label is drawn on a wedge only if the extent of that wedge is larger than 3 degrees.

BAR CHART PLOT   The **paint()** method of the **BarChartCanvas** class (lines 208 through 275) draws the bar chart plot. This **paint()** method first determines the extent of the canvas and then initializes various variables used to draw the bar chart. In particular, lines 219 and 220 get the height of the characters displayed in the current font. The font height is used to estimate how much space should be left over for the labels along the horizontal axis of the bar chart. Similarly, the horizontal extents of the maximum and minimum values determine the space needed for the labels along the vertical axis. The **paint()** method also computes other parameters, such as the height and width of the chart itself and the number of ticks to draw along the vertical axis.

The **for** loop in lines 244 through 260 loops through the data items and draws a bar for each value and a label for that value underneath the horizontal axis:

```
244          for(int i = 0; i < data.size(); i++)
245          {
246              barHeight = (int)(data.elementAt(i).value/
247                              (maxValue-minValue)*chartHeight);
248              y = borderWidth + chartHeight - barHeight;
249              x = xStart + xSlice/2 - barWidth/2;
250              g.setColor(attrib.getNextColor());
251              g.fillRect(x, y, barWidth-1, barHeight-1);
252              // Add the x-axis label
253              y = ySize - yLabelHeight + fontHeight;
254              g.setColor(attrib.getTextColor());
255              int w = fm.stringWidth(data.elementAt(i).label);
256              x = xStart + xSlice/2 - w/2;
257              if(x < xStart) x = xStart;
258              g.drawString(data.elementAt(i).label, x, y);
259              xStart += xSlice;
260          }
```

Because the code is easier to understand if you can visualize the various items, Figure 2-12 illustrates the variables used in drawing the bar chart and shows what they mean. Line 246 computes the height of the bar for a specific data item. Line 248

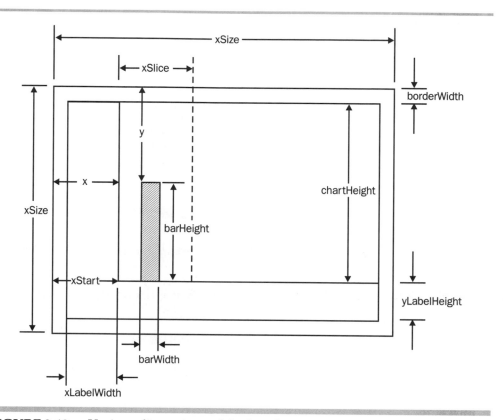

FIGURE 2-12. Various dimensions of the bar chart.

converts that to the y coordinate of the upper-left corner of the bar. Line 249 calculates the x coordinate of the bar's upper-left corner. Line 250 selects a color, and line 251 calls the **fillRect()** method to draw the bar. Lines 253 through 258 draw the label for that bar. When drawing the label, line 255 computes the extent of the label, using the font metrics, and line 256 positions the label to center it under the bar. Finally, line 259 advances the **xStart** variable to the next bar, corresponding to the next data item.

After the bars and x-axis labels have been drawn, lines 262 through 274 draw the tick marks and labels along the vertical axis of the chart.

Networking and Communications

J ava applets, running in a Web browser, can access Internet services such as file transfer using the File Transfer Protocol (FTP) and electronic mail through the Simple Mail Transfer Protocol (SMTP). These Internet services are provided by servers—computer programs running on machines (often referred to as hosts) that are connected by a data communications network such as the Internet or a company's private intranet.

Each type of Internet server (such as FTP or Web) provides a service, using the client/server model. A user who wants to access information uses a client (for example, a Web browser) to connect to a server and download information (for example, Web pages from a Web server). The client application establishes a network connection to the server and sends commands to the server, causing it to perform specific tasks.

Java includes networking classes that allow you to write client/server applications in Java. Chapter 11 describes such Java client/server applications, where both the server and the client are written in Java. This chapter focuses on Java applets that can communicate with various Internet services such as FTP and mail. In other words, these applets act as clients to specific Internet servers.

This chapter shows you several Java applets that illustrate how to establish a connection and exchange information with different Internet services. By studying these applets, you can write your own or you can adapt these samples for your own use. You will find the following applets in this chapter:

- **GetHostName**—An applet that displays a welcome message with the name of the local host

- **SMTPmail**—A simple mail applet that lets anyone visiting your Web page send mail through your SMTP mail server

- **FTPapplet**—An applet that downloads and uploads a file using FTP

- **Telnet**—An applet that provides a terminal for logging on to an Internet host

The chapter first takes you through a brief tutorial of various Internet services and a specific security restriction that applies to any Java applet that connects to an Internet server. After the tutorial, the chapter presents the applets in the usual Annotated Archives style, with the code followed by detailed explanations.

Internet Services and Applets

The applets in this chapter are designed to communicate with servers that provide specific Internet services, such as mail, file transfer, and terminal login. You will find it easier to understand the applets if you learn the common characteristics of these Internet services: how to connect to a service and how clients exchange data using specific Internet protocols. The next few sections summarize some common features of Java applets that communicate with Internet servers over a network such as the Internet or a company's private intranet.

Security Restrictions on Applets

When a Web page includes a Java applet, the Web browser (assuming that it supports Java) downloads that applet's code from the Web server and executes the code in the browser's Java Virtual Machine (JVM). The applet, in turn, can use Java networking classes to establish connections with other servers. However, the applet's networking and communication capabilities are severely restricted by the security features of Web browsers such as Netscape Navigator or Communicator and Microsoft Internet Explorer.

To ensure that a rogue applet does not cause any damage to the client machine, Java-capable Web browsers do not let applets access the local file system. Nor do they allow an applet to open network connections to any other computer on the Internet, except for the host from which the applet's class file was loaded. Figure 3-1 illustrates this networking restriction imposed on Java applets.

Because of the security restrictions imposed by Web browsers, an applet can access only Internet services such as FTP and SMTP mail that are on the same Internet host as the Web server from which the applet's code was loaded.

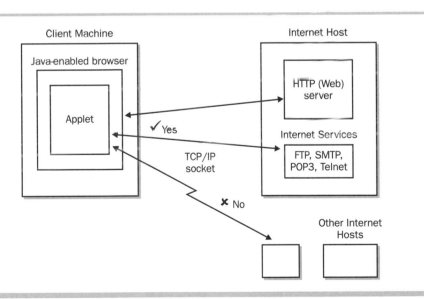

FIGURE 3-1.   An applet can open a connection only to the host from which it was loaded.

Client/Server Communications

Internet services rely on the client/server architecture, which requires clients to communicate with the servers. That's where TCP/IP comes in. TCP/IP provides a standard way for clients and servers to exchange packets of data.

IP stands for Internet Protocol; it provides an addressing scheme for identifying hosts and specifies how packets of data are sent from one host to another across multiple interconnected networks. TCP stands for Transmission Control Protocol; it uses IP to provide a reliable, bidirectional data transfer between applications running on different hosts. IP does not guarantee delivery of packets, nor does it deliver packets in any particular sequence. What IP does well is deliver a packet from one network to another in an efficient manner. It's TCP's responsibility to arrange the packets in the proper sequence, detect whether errors have occurred, and request retransmission of packets in the case of an error. TCP is useful for applications that plan to exchange large amounts of data at a time. Also, applications that need reliable data exchange use TCP. For example, the File Transfer Protocol (FTP) uses TCP to transfer files.

Because multiple applications can run on the same host, TCP uses the concept of a port number for data transfers between two applications. There is nothing physical about a port—it's simply a numeric identifier used to maintain separate data streams between two hosts. The ports are numbered from 0 to 65,536.

In addition to TCP, there is another protocol called UDP (User Datagram Protocol) that can also transfer data between applications running on different hosts on the network. Unlike TCP, UDP is a connectionless protocol. A connectionless data exchange protocol does not require the sender and receiver to explicitly establish a connection. It's like shouting to your friend in a crowded room—you can never be sure whether your friend has actually heard you. Unlike TCP, UDP does not guarantee that datagrams ever reached their intended destination. Nor does UDP ensure that datagrams are delivered in the order they were sent. UDP is used by applications that exchange small amounts of data at a time, or by applications that do not need the reliability and sequencing of data delivery. For example, SNMP (Simple Network Management Protocol) uses UDP to transfer data.

The term *socket* is used to characterize the endpoint of a bidirectional connection between a client and a server. There are two sockets in each client/server connection—one at the client and the other at the server. Because a socket is bidirectional, data can be sent as well as received through a socket. A socket has three attributes:

◆ The network address (the IP address) of the host

◆ The port number identifying the process (a *process* is a computer program running on a computer) that exchanges data through the socket

◆ The type of socket identifying the protocol (TCP or UDP) for data exchange

A socket that uses TCP is referred to as a *stream socket,* whereas a socket that uses UDP is referred to as a *datagram socket.*

Java provides the **java.net.Socket** class to create and use sockets in Java programs (including applets). One of the **Socket()** constructors creates a stream socket for a given host IP address and port number.

Well-Known Ports

When a client wants to establish communication with a server, it has to somehow identify the server. The IP address identifies the host where the server is running, and the port number identifies a specific service on that server. To make it easy for clients to access specific Internet services, Internet standards define well-known port numbers for various services. Internet users and programmers often refer to these standard port numbers in statements such as "the SMTP server listens on port 25." This means that a client application can connect to port 25 of an Internet host to establish communication with the Internet server that allows mail transfer using SMTP.

The TCP/IP protocol suite has become the lingua franca of the Internet, because many standard services are available on all systems that support TCP/IP. These services make the Internet work by enabling the transfer of mail, news, and Web pages. These services go by well-known names such as the following:

◆ FTP (File Transfer Protocol) allows transfer of files between computers on the Internet. FTP uses two ports: control information is exchanged on port 21, while data is transferred on another port (the default is port 20, but the client can request that the server listen on another port).

◆ HTTP (Hypertext Transfer Protocol) is a recent protocol for sending HTML documents from one system to another. HTTP is the underlying protocol of the Web. By default, the Web server and client communicate on port 80.

◆ SMTP (Simple Mail Transfer Protocol) is used for exchanging e-mail messages between systems. SMTP uses port 25 for information exchange.

◆ NNTP (Network News Transfer Protocol) allows distribution of news articles in a store-and-forward fashion across the Internet. NNTP uses port 119.

◆ TELNET allows a user on one system to log on to another system on the Internet (the user must provide a valid user ID and password to successfully log on to the remote system). TELNET uses port 23 by default. However, the TELNET client can connect to any specified port.

◆ SNMP (Simple Network Management Protocol) is used for managing all types of network devices on the Internet. Like FTP, SNMP uses two ports: 161 and 162.

◆ TFTP (Trivial File Transfer Protocol) is for transferring files from one system to another. (It is typically used by X terminals and diskless workstations to download boot files from another host on the network.) TFTP data transfer takes place on port 69.

◆ NFS (Network File System) is for sharing files among computers. NFS uses Sun's Remote Procedure Call (RPC) facility, which exchanges information through port 111.

A well-known port is associated with each of these services. The TCP protocol uses this port to locate a service on any system. (Each service is implemented by a server process—a computer program running on a system.)

Client/Server Protocols

After the client and server have established a socket connection, they exchange information using a well-defined protocol. Each Internet service has its own protocol. Typically, these client/server protocols are in the form of simple text commands. Consider, for example, SMTP, which allows a client to send a mail message to an SMTP server. The SMTP client and server use the same protocol as TELNET to exchange information. In fact, you can use the **Telnet** application provided later in this chapter to connect to an SMTP server and send a message. The following example shows how I use SMTP commands to send a mail message to myself from a **telnet** session on another system (the lines shown in italic are the commands I typed):

```
telnet your.hostname.net 25
Trying 192.168.10.11...
Connected to your.hostname.net.
Escape character is '^]'.
220 your.hostname.net ESMTP Sendmail 8.8.8/8.8.8; Sat, 31 Oct 1998
15:33:53-0500 (EST)
HELO yourpc.your.hostname.net
250 your.hostname.net Hello yourpc.your.hostname.net [192.168.10.240],
pleased to meet you
MAIL FROM: naba
250 naba... Sender ok
RCPT TO: naba@somewhere.net
250 naba@somewhere.net... Recipient ok
DATA
354 Enter mail, end with "." on a line by itself
Testing... 1 2 3
Sending mail by telnet to port 25
.
```

```
250 PAA23782 Message accepted for delivery
QUIT
221 your.hostname.net closing connection
```

In this example, I have changed the host names and IP addresses to fake ones. You should use the host name of your mail server when trying out these commands. Here, the **telnet** command opens a TELNET session to port 25—the port where a server called **sendmail** expects SMTP commands. The **sendmail** process on the host **your.hostname.net** immediately replies with an announcement.

I type **HELO yourpc.your.hostname.net** to indicate the host from which I am sending mail. The **sendmail** process replies with a greeting. To send the mail message, I start with the **MAIL FROM:** command, which specifies the sender of the message (I enter the user name on the system from which I am sending the message).

Next, I use the **RCPT TO:** command to specify the recipient of the message. If I want to send the message to several recipients, all I have to do is provide each recipient's address with the **RCPT TO:** command.

To enter the mail message, I use the **DATA** command. In response to the **DATA** command, **sendmail** displays an instruction that I should end the message with a period on a line by itself. I enter the message and end it with a single period on a separate line. The **sendmail** process displays a message indicating that the message has been accepted for delivery. Finally, I quit the **sendmail** session with the **QUIT** command.

Afterward, I log on to my system and check mail. The following is what I see when I display the mail message that I sent through the sample SMTP session with **sendmail**:

```
Message  2:
From naba Sat Oct 31 15:35:38 1998
Date: Sat, 31 Oct 1998 15:34:56 -0500 (EST)
From: Naba Barkakati <naba>

Testing... 1 2 3
Sending mail by telnet to port 25
```

As this example shows, the SMTP commands are simple to understand. This example should help you understand how the **SMTPmail** applet (described in the section "Sending Mail from a Web Page") uses SMTP to send mail.

RFCs

The details of each TCP/IP protocol (including TCP and IP as well as specific service protocols such as SMTP and FTP) are described in documents known as Requests for Comments (RFCs). These documents are freely distributed on the Internet. You can get RFCs from **http://www.cis.ohio-state.edu/hypertext/information/rfc.html** or **ftp://venera.isi.edu/in-notes/**.

In fact, this notation used to name Internet resources in a uniform manner is itself documented in an RFC. The notation, known as the Uniform Resource Locator (URL), is described in RFC 1738, "Uniform Resource Locators (URL)," written by, among others, T. Berners-Lee, the originator of the World Wide Web (WWW).

You can think of RFCs as the working papers of the Internet research-and-development community. All Internet standards are published as RFCs. Many RFCs do not specify any standards, however; they are informational documents only.

The following are some RFCs that you may find interesting:

- RFC 768, "User Datagram Protocol (UDP)"
- RFC 791, "Internet Protocol (IP)"
- RFC 792, "Internet Control Message Protocol (ICMP)"
- RFC 793, "Transmission Control Protocol (TCP)"
- RFC 821, "Simple Mail Transfer Protocol (SMTP)"
- RFC 822, "Format for Electronic Mail Messages"
- RFC 854, "TELNET Protocol Specification"
- RFC 950, "IP Subnet Extension"
- RFC 959, "File Transfer Protocol (FTP)"
- RFC 1034, "Domain Names: Concepts and Facilities"
- RFC 1058, "Routing Information Protocol (RIP)"
- RFC 1112, "Host Extensions for IP Multicasting"
- RFC 1155, "Structure of Management Information (SMI)"
- RFC 1157, "Simple Network Management Protocol (SNMP)"
- RFC 1310, "The Internet Standards Process"
- RFC 1519, "Classless Inter-Domain Routing (CIDR) Assignment and Aggregation Strategy"
- RFC 1521, "Multipurpose Internet Mail Extensions (MIME)"
- RFC 1583, "Open Shortest Path First Routing V2 (OSPF2)"
- RFC 1625, "WAIS over Z39.50-1988"
- RFC 1661, "Point-to-Point Protocol (PPP)"
- RFC 1725, "Post Office Protocol, Version 3 (POP3)"

- RFC 1738, "Uniform Resource Locators (URL)"
- RFC 1739, "A Primer on Internet and TCP/IP Tools"
- RFC 1796, "Not All RFCs Are Standards"
- RFC 1855, "Netiquette Guidelines"
- RFC 1866, "Hypertext Markup Language - 2.0"
- RFC 1883, "Internet Protocol, Version 6 (IPv6) Specification"
- RFC 1886, "DNS Extensions to Support IP Version 6"
- RFC 1918, "Address Allocation for Private Internets"
- RFC 2028, "The Organizations Involved in the IETF Standards Process"
- RFC 2060, "Internet Message Access Protocol - Version 4rev1 (IMAP4)"
- RFC 2305, "A Simple Mode of Facsimile Using Internet Mail"
- RFC 2368, "The mailto URL scheme"
- RFC 2373, "IP Version 6 Addressing Architecture"
- RFC 2396, "Uniform Resource Identifiers (URI): Generic Syntax"
- RFC 2400, "Internet Official Protocol Standards"

Displaying the Host Name in a Welcome Message

Suppose that you want to display a welcome message on your Web page showing the name of the host from which a user is visiting your site. You can use the **GetHostName** applet to get the host name of the client machine and display the host name in a welcome message.

Using GetHostName

You will find the files for the **GetHostName** applet in the **ch03\GetHost** directory of the companion CD-ROM. To try out the **GetHostName** applet, open the **GetHost.html** file from a Java-capable Web browser. Figure 3-2 shows a typical welcome message displayed by the **GetHostName** applet. In the welcome message shown in Figure 3-2, everything after the colon (:) is the name of the host where the Web browser is running.

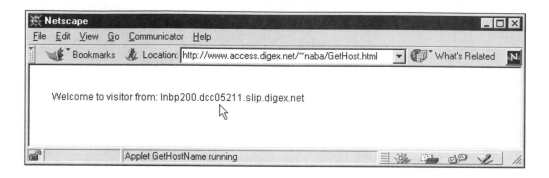

FIGURE 3-2.   The **GetHostName** applet displays a welcome message with the host name.

If you want to use **GetHostName** on a Web page, copy the applet's class file (**GetHostName.class**) to the Web server. Then include this class file in the HTML file with an **<applet>** tag. For example, here is the **<applet>** tag from the **GetHost.html** file that results in the display shown in Figure 3-2:

```
<applet code=GetHostName.class width=350 height=60>

</applet>
```

Understanding GetHostName

GetHostName

The following listing shows the **GetHostName.java** file with the source code for the **GetHostName** applet. You will learn more about the applet in the section that follows this listing.

```
1  //-----------------------------------------------------------------
2  // GetHostName.java
3  // Displays a welcome message with the name of the host from
4  // which the Web browser is accessing the applet.
5  //-----------------------------------------------------------------
6  import java.applet.*;
7  import java.awt.*;
8  import java.net.*;
9  /**
10  * Displays a welcome message with the name of the local host.
11  */
12  public class GetHostName extends Applet
```

```
13  {
14      String hostName;
15      public void init()
16      {
17          try
18          {
19              InetAddress localAddress = InetAddress.getLocalHost();
20              hostName = localAddress.getHostName();
21          }catch(UnknownHostException e)
22          {
23              hostName = "Unknown";
24          }
25      }
26      /** Displays the host name in a welcome message. */
27      public void paint(Graphics g)
28      {
29          String message = "Welcome to visitor from: "+hostName;
30          g.setFont(new Font("Helvetica", Font.PLAIN, 12));
31          FontMetrics fm = g.getFontMetrics ();
32          int fontAscent = fm.getAscent();
33          int fontDescent = fm.getDescent();
34          int messageWidth = fm.stringWidth(message);
35          Dimension aSize = size(); // call getSize() in Java 2
36          int x = aSize.width/2 - messageWidth/2;
37          int y = aSize.height/2 - fontDescent/2 + fontAscent/2;
38          // Display the message
39          g.drawString (message, x, y);
40      }
41
42  }
```

ANNOTATIONS

As you can see from the listing, the **GetHostName** applet is simple. All it does is get the name of the local host—the computer where the Web browser is running—and display a welcome message that includes the host name. The applet's code does demonstrate how to create an Internet address and how to get a host name. As you will see in the other applets in this chapter, these are steps you must perform in any program that connects to an Internet server.

Line 14 defines the **String** used to store the host name:

```
14      String hostName;
```

The **init()** method takes care of getting the host name. Lines 15 through 25 accomplish this task. The **try** block in lines 17 through 21 encloses the key lines of code for getting the host name:

```
19          InetAddress localAddress = InetAddress.getLocalHost();
20          hostName = localAddress.getHostName();
```

Line 19 gets the IP address of the local host (this is the machine where the Web browser is running) by calling the **getLocalHost()** method. Line 20 then calls **getHostName** to get the full host name (such as **www.altavista.com**) of the local host.

Applications should always use one of the methods **getLocalHost()**, **getByName()**, or **getAllByName()** to create a new **InetAddress** instance. In this case, line 19 calls **getLocalHost()** to create an instance of **InetAddress** representing the local host's IP address. The **getLocalHost()** method throws an **UnknownHostException** if the IP address of the local host cannot be found. The **catch** block that starts on line 21 handles this error condition by setting the **hostName** variable to **"Unknown"** if the local host's IP address cannot be found.

The **GetHostName** applet's **paint()** method simply constructs a welcome message that includes the host name (obtained earlier) and displays that message in the applet's display area. Line 29 creates the message by appending the host name to a message:

```
29          String message = "Welcome to visitor from: "+hostName;
```

Lines 30 through 34 set the font and compute the height and width of the message text when displayed with the selected font. Lines 35 through 37 figure out the point where the message should be drawn:

```
35          Dimension aSize = size(); // call getSize() in Java 2
36          int x = aSize.width/2 - messageWidth/2;
37          int y = aSize.height/2 - fontDescent/2 + fontAscent/2;
```

Java 2

Line 35 calls **size()** to get the applet's dimensions. This method is deprecated in Java 2; you should call the newer **getSize()** method.

Finally, line 39 displays the welcome message, centered in the applet's display area:

```
39          g.drawString (message, x, y);
```

Sending Mail from a Web Page

As I explained in the "Internet Services and Applets" section, SMTP is used to exchange mail between hosts. The **SMTPmail** applet connects to an SMTP server and allows users to send mail from a Web page. Because of Java's security restrictions, the applet can only establish connection to an SMTP server that's running on the same host as the Web server from which the applet was downloaded.

Using SMTPmail

The files for the **SMTPmail** applet are in the **ch03\SMTPmail** directory of the companion CD-ROM. To try out **SMTPmail**, you need an Internet host that runs your Web server as well as the SMTP mail server. Additionally, the SMTP server must accept mail sent from a user's host (some SMTP servers are configured to reject mail that did not originate in a specific Internet domain).

Copy the files **MailMe.html**, **SMTPmail.class**, and **SMTP.class** to the Web server. Then open the **MailMe.html** file from a Java-capable Web browser. You will see a simple form to type a mail message. Figure 3-3 shows the mail form after I edited the sender's address, typed a message (with a shameless plug for this book), and clicked the **Send** button.

To verify that the message was actually sent, I used TELNET to log on to the host where the mail should arrive. Figure 3-4 shows the message I saw when I used a mail reader to view the message.

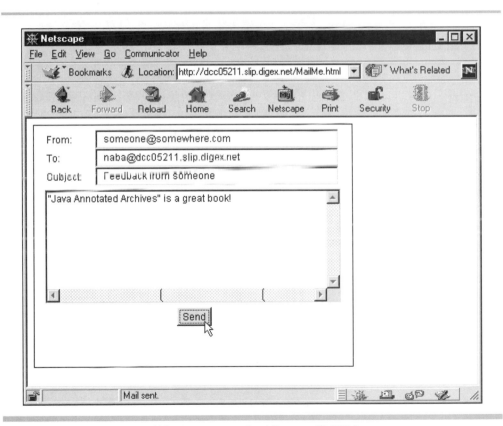

FIGURE 3-3. **SMTPmail** lets users send mail to an SMTP host.

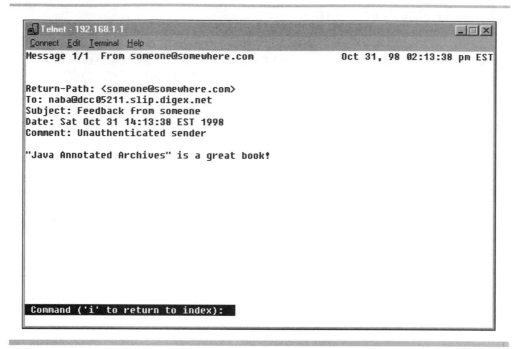

FIGURE 3-4. Verifying that **SMTPmail** successfully sent the mail message.

To learn how to embed **SMTPmail** in an HTML file, examine the contents of the **MailMe.html** file that produces the output shown in Figure 3-3. Here is what the file contains:

```
<html>
<body>
<applet code="SMTPmail.class" WIDTH=400 HEIGHT=300>
<param name="to" value="naba@dcc05211.slip.digex.net">
<param name="from" value="naba@dcc05211.slip.digex.net">
<param name="smtphost" value="dcc05211.slip.digex.net">
</applet>
</body>
</html>
```

As you can see, the **<applet>** tag has three attributes:

- **code="SMTPmail.class"** specifies the file containing the Java code for the applet.
- **WIDTH=400** specifies a 400-pixel-wide display area for the applet.
- **HEIGHT=300** specifies a 300-pixel-tall display area for the applet.

The **SMTPmail** applet accepts three parameters:

◆ **to** is the address of the recipient (it cannot be edited by the user).

◆ **from** is the sender's address (the user may edit this in the applet).

◆ **smtphost** is the fully qualified host name of the SMTP server (it must be the same as the host name of the Web server).

SMTPmail is ideal for a Web page that solicits feedback from users. With **SMTPmail**, visitors to your Web site can send you feedback through e-mail messages. Simply copy the **<applet>** tag (as in the **MailMe.html** file) and edit the **from, to,** and **smtphost** parameters.

Understanding SMTPmail

SMTPmail

The following listing shows the **SMTPmail.java** file that implements the **SMTPmail** applet. Subsequent sections explain how the code works.

```
1  //------------------------------------------------------------------
2  // SMTPmail.java
3  // Applet that sends mail through an SMTP (Simple Mail Transfer
4  // Protocol) server. Allows user to send feedback via e-mail to
5  // an address (specified via a parameter in the HTML file).
6  //------------------------------------------------------------------
7  import java.applet.*;
8  import java.net.*;
9  import java.awt.*;
10 import java.io.*;
11 import java.util.*;
12 /**
13  * SMTPmail allows user to send e-mail through an SMTP server.
14  * The SMTP server must be running on the same host as the
15  * Web server from which the applet was downloaded.
16  * <p>
17  * This applet accepts the following parameters:
18  * <ul>
19  *    <li> from - sender's e-mail address (may be entered
20  *             in the text field)
21  *    <li> to  - recipient's e-mail address (set through
22  *             param tag and cannot be altered)
23  *    <li> smtphost - full host name of the SMTP server
24  * </ul>
```

```
25   *
26   * @author Naba Barkakati
27   * @version 1.0 October 26, 1998
28   */
29  public class SMTPmail extends Applet
30  {
31      String from, to, subject, message, SMTPhost;
32      Button sendButton;
33      Label fromLabel, toLabel, subjectLabel;
34      TextField fromText, toText, subjectText;
35      TextArea messageText;
36      /** Creates a mail form and opens connection to SMTP server */
37      public void init()
38      {
39          from = getParameter("from");
40          if(from == null) from = "someone@somewhere.net";
41          to = getParameter("to");
42          if(to == null) to = "Please provide an address!!";
43          SMTPhost = getParameter("smtphost");
44          if(SMTPhost == null) SMTPhost = "Need mail host address.";
45          setLayout(new BorderLayout());
46          Panel pBig = new Panel();
47          pBig.setLayout(new BorderLayout());
48          fromLabel = new Label("From:      ");
49          fromText = new TextField(from,40);
50          toLabel = new Label("To:        ");
51          toText = new TextField(to,40);
52          toText.setEditable(false);
53          subjectLabel = new Label("Subject: ");
54          subjectText = new TextField("Feedback", 40);
55          Panel p1 = new Panel();
56          p1.setLayout(new GridLayout(3,1));
57          p1.add(fromLabel);
58          p1.add(toLabel);
59          p1.add(subjectLabel);
60          Panel p2 = new Panel();
61          p2.setLayout(new GridLayout(3,1));
62          p2.add(fromText);
63          p2.add(toText);
64          p2.add(subjectText);
65          pBig.add("West", p1);
66          pBig.add("Center", p2);
```

```
 67        add("North", pBig);
 68        messageText = new TextArea("",8,50);
 69        add("Center", messageText);
 70        Panel pBottom = new Panel();
 71        pBottom.setLayout(new GridLayout(1,3));
 72        sendButton = new Button("Send");
 73        Label l1 = new Label("    ");
 74        Label l2 = new Label("    ");
 75        pBottom.add(l1);
 76        pBottom.add(sendButton);
 77        pBottom.add(l2);
 78        add("South", pBottom);
 79    }
 80    /** Handles mouse click events (old style). Use appropriate
 81        Listener interface in Java 1.1.x or later. */
 82    public boolean action(Event ev, Object obj)
 83    {
 84        if(ev.target instanceof Button)
 85        {
 86            if (((String)obj).equals("Send"))
 87            {
 88                try
 89                {
 90                    showStatus("Connecting to SMTPhost " + SMTPhost);
 91                    SMTP connection = new SMTP(SMTPhost);
 92                    showStatus("Connected to "+SMTPhost);
 93                    subject = subjectText.getText();
 94                    message = messageText.getText();
 95                    from = fromText.getText();
 96                    showStatus("Sending mail...");
 97                    connection.sendmsg(from,to,subject,message);
 98                    connection.close();
 99                    showStatus("Mail sent.");
100                }
101                catch (UnknownHostException e)
102                {
103                    showStatus("Unknown host - " + SMTPhost);
104                    System.out.println(e.getMessage());
105                }
106                catch (ProtocolException e)
107                {
108                    showStatus("Unknown protocol");
```

```
109                         System.out.println(e.getMessage());
110                     }
111                 catch (IOException e)
112                 {
113                         showStatus(SMTPhost+" - Socket I/O error");
114                         System.out.println(e.getMessage());
115                 }
116                 return true;
117             }
118         }
119     return super.action(ev, obj);
120     }
121     /** Sets aside a 2-pixel border around the applet */
122     public Insets getInsets()
123     {
124         return new Insets(2,2,2,2);
125     }
126     /** Draws a border around the mail form */
127     public void paint(Graphics g)
128     {
129         g.setColor(Color.black);
130         g.drawRect(0, 0, size().width-1, size().height-1);
131     }
132     /** Returns the list of parameters for this applet */
133     public String[][] getParameterInfo()
134     {
135         String[][] info =
136         {
137             // Name        Type         Description
138             //-----        --------     ----------------------
139             {"to",         "String", "Recipient's address"},
140             {"from",       "String", "Sender's address"},
141             {"smtphost","String", "Name of SMTP mail host"}
142         };
143         return info;
144     }
145     /** Returns information about this applet */
146     public String getAppletInfo()
147     {
148         return "SMTPmail applet (sends mail through SMTP server)";
149     }
150 }
```

```java
151  /** SMTP class represents a connection to an SMTP server */
152  class SMTP extends Object
153  {
154      static final int SMTP_PORT = 25;
155      private BufferedReader input = null;
156      private PrintWriter output = null;
157      private Socket socket = null;
158
159      /** Create a SMTP connection to the specified host */
160      public SMTP(String hostid, int port)
161        throws UnknownHostException, IOException, ProtocolException
162      {
163          socket = new Socket(hostid, port);
164          input = new BufferedReader(new
165                        InputStreamReader(socket.getInputStream()));
166          output = new PrintWriter( socket.getOutputStream() );
167          String responseString = input.readLine();
168          if(!responseString.startsWith("220"))
169                        throw new ProtocolException(responseString);
170          while(responseString.indexOf('-') == 3)
171          {
172              responseString = input.readLine();
173              if(!responseString.startsWith("220"))
174                  throw new ProtocolException(responseString);
175          }
176      }
177      /** Creates SMTP connection to default port (25) */
178      public SMTP(String hostid) throws UnknownHostException,
179                              IOException, ProtocolException
180      {
181          this(hostid, SMTP_PORT);
182      }
183      /** Sends a mail message using SMTP protocol */
184      public void sendmsg(String fromAddress, String toAddress,
185                        String subjectText, String messageText)
186                        throws IOException, ProtocolException
187      {
188          InetAddress localAddress;
189          try
190          {
191            localAddress = InetAddress.getLocalHost();
192          }
```

```
193        catch (UnknownHostException e)
194        {
195            System.err.println("Unknown host-cannot send mail!");
196            throw(e);
197        }
198        String localHost = localAddress.getHostName();
199        output.print("HELO "+localHost+"\n");
200        output.flush();
201        String responseString = input.readLine();
202        if(!responseString.startsWith("250"))
203            throw new ProtocolException(responseString);
204        output.print("MAIL FROM: "+fromAddress+"\n");
205        output.flush();
206        responseString = input.readLine();
207        if(!responseString.startsWith("250"))
208            throw new ProtocolException(responseString);
209        output.print("RCPT TO: "+toAddress+"\n");
210        output.flush();
211        responseString = input.readLine();
212        if(!responseString.startsWith("250"))
213            throw new ProtocolException(responseString);
214        output.print("DATA\n");
215        output.flush();
216        responseString = input.readLine();
217        if(!responseString.startsWith("354"))
218            throw new ProtocolException(responseString);
219        output.print("From: " + fromAddress+"\n");
220        output.print("To: " + toAddress+"\n");
221        output.print("Subject: " + subjectText+"\n");
222        Date currentDate = new Date();
223        output.print("Date: " + currentDate.toString()+"\n");
224        output.print("Comment: Unauthenticated sender\n");
225        output.print("X-Mailer: SMTPmail applet\n");
226        output.print("\n");
227        output.print(messageText);
228        output.print("\n.\n");
229        output.flush();
230        responseString = input.readLine();
231        if(!responseString.startsWith("250"))
232            throw new ProtocolException(responseString);
233    }
234    /** Closes the socket connection to SMTP server */
```

```
235    public void close()
236    {
237        try
238        {
239            output.println("QUIT");
240            socket.close();
241        }
242        catch(IOException e){}
243    }
244 }
```

ANNOTATIONS

The **SMTPmail** applet uses a class named **SMTP** to implement an SMTP client that can send protocol messages to an SMTP host. Figure 3-5 shows how an SMTP client interacts with the SMTP server using the Simple Mail Transfer protocol. (SMTP is documented in RFC 821, "Simple Mail Transfer Protocol," Jonathan Postel, 1982, available on the Web at **http://www.cis.ohio-state.edu/htbin/rfc/rfc821.html.**) As Figure 3-5 shows, the client/server interactions for SMTP proceed as follows:

1. The client opens a socket to the SMTP host as port number 25 (the default SMTP port).

2. The SMTP server responds with a string that begins with the status code 220.

3. The client sends a **HELO** command followed by the client's domain name.

4. If the server accepts mail messages from the client, the server responds with a status message that begins with **250**.

5. The client sends the text **MAIL FROM:** followed by the sender's address.

6. The server responds with a 250 code, indicating that the sender's address is accepted.

7. The client sends the text **RCPT TO:** followed by the recipient's address.

8. The server acknowledges with a 250 status code, indicating that the recipient's address is accepted.

9. The client sends the **DATA** command.

10. The server responds with a 354 code and a message stating that the client should keep sending lines of text and indicate the end of the message by sending a single period on a line by itself.

11. The client sends the mail message followed by a period on a line by itself.

12. The server responds with a 250 status code, indicating that the message has been accepted.

13. The client sends the **QUIT** command to indicate that it's done.

14. The server sends a 221 status code and closes the connection.

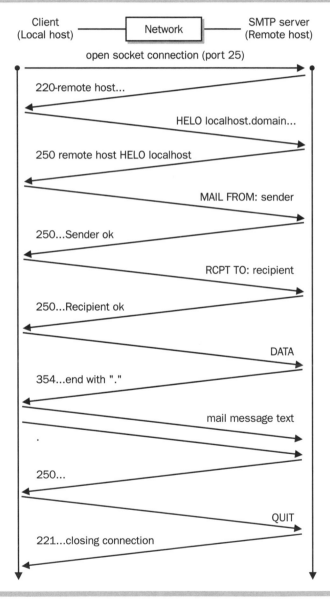

FIGURE 3-5. Client/server exchanges in a typical SMTP session.

As you will see in the next section, the **SMTP** class provides methods that implement various parts of this protocol message sequence.

THE SMTP CLASS   Lines 152 through 244 implement the **SMTP** class that can connect to an SMTP host and send a mail message. In other words, the **SMTP** class represents the client side of the SMTP exchange, as illustrated in Figure 3-5. Lines 154 through 157 define the variables of the **SMTP** class:

```
154    static final int SMTP_PORT = 25;
155    private BufferedReader input = null;
156    private PrintWriter output = null;
157    private Socket socket = null;
```

Line 154 defines **SMTP_PORT** as 25, which is the well-known port number for the SMTP service. Lines 155 and 156 define the input and output data streams. These are initialized later in the **SMTP()** constructor after a connection to the SMTP host has been established. Line 157 defines a **Socket** object that denotes the socket on the client side of the connection to the SMTP server.

Lines 160 through 176 show the **SMTP(String hostid, int port)** constructor, which takes an SMTP host name and the port number and establishes a socket connection to that address. The constructor first creates the socket connection in line 163 and then sets up the input and output data streams for that socket in lines 164 through 166:

```
163        socket = new Socket(hostid, port);
164        input = new BufferedReader(new
165                        InputStreamReader(socket.getInputStream()));
166        output = new PrintWriter( socket.getOutputStream() );
```

After the input and output data streams have been created, line 167 reads the response from the SMTP host:

```
167        String responseString = input.readLine();
```

As Figure 3-5 shows, this response text should begin with **220**. Line 168 and 169 make sure that the response does indeed begin with **220**. If it does not, line 169 throws a **ProtocolException** error condition, indicating an unknown protocol response:

```
168        if(!responseString.startsWith("220"))
169                        throw new ProtocolException(responseString);
```

After that, a **while** loop in lines 170 through 175 reads any other initial response lines from the SMTP server.

Lines 178 through 182 define the **SMTP(String hostid)** that calls the **SMTP(String hostid, int port)** constructor with the port set to **SMTP_PORT**.

The **sendmsg()** method of the **SMTP** class takes care of the protocol exchange involved in sending a message to the SMTP server (see Figure 3-5). Lines 184 through 233 implement the **sendmsg()** method, which accepts a from address, a to address, the subject, and the message text as arguments.

Lines 188 through 198 of the **sendmsg()** method get the host name of the local host (where the Web browser is running):

```
188        InetAddress localAddress;
189        try
190        {
191          localAddress = InetAddress.getLocalHost();
192        }
193        catch (UnknownHostException e)
194        {
195            System.err.println("Unknown host-cannot send mail!");
196            throw(e);
197        }
198        String localHost = localAddress.getHostName();
```

Line 191 gets the IP address of the local host. This line is enclosed in a **try** block because the **getLocalHost()** method may throw an **UnknownHostException**. If that error occurs, the catch block of lines 193 through 197 prints an error message and essentially ends the method. If all goes well, line 198 calls the **getHostName()** method to get the local host's fully qualified domain name (for example, **www.osborne.com**).

After the local host name has been retrieved, lines 199 and 200 send out a **HELO** message to the SMTP server:

```
199        output.print("HELO "+localHost+"\n");
200        output.flush();
```

Line 199 calls the **print()** method of the output stream and sends the line of text that constitutes the **HELO** protocol message. Then line 200 calls the **flush()** method to ensure that the text is actually sent out to the SMTP host (and not held in a buffer for later transmittal).

After the **HELO** message has been sent out, line 201 reads the response sent back by the SMTP host:

```
201        String responseString = input.readLine();
```

If the response does not begin with the expected response code (250, in this case), lines 202 and 203 throw a **ProtocolException**, indicating that the server is probably using some other protocol:

```
202        if(!responseString.startsWith("250"))
203            throw new ProtocolException(responseString);
```

Lines 204 through 232 continue with the rest of the SMTP protocol exchange (as shown in Figure 3-5).

The only other method of the **SMTP** class is **close()**, implemented in lines 235 through 243. Line 239 of the **close()** method sends the **QUIT** message to the SMTP host, and then line 240 closes the socket connection:

```
239             output.println("QUIT");
240             socket.close();
```

SMTPMAIL INITIALIZATION   Lines 37 through 79 implement the **SMTPmail** applet's **init()** method, which performs the following tasks:

◆ Lines 39 through 44 get the **from**, **to**, and **smtphost** parameters from the HTML file. The **from** and **to** parameters are the e-mail addresses of the sender and recipient, respectively. The **smtphost** parameter is the full host name of the SMTP server.

◆ Lines 45 through 78 display a form (as shown in Figure 3-3) by laying out a number of user interface components.

The **init()** method does not try to establish a connection with the SMTP server. That happens in the **action()** method, called when the user clicks on the **Send** button.

SMTPMAIL EVENT HANDLER   Whenever the user clicks the **Send** button in the **SMTPmail** applet's user interface (see Figure 3-3), the **action()** method (lines 82 through 120) is called. In lines 84 through 87, the **action()** method checks to make sure that the mouse click is indeed on the **Send** button; then it performs all of the steps needed to send the mail message to the SMTP server.

The important steps of the **action()** method occur within the **try** block in lines 88 through 100. Specifically, line 91 establishes a connection to the SMTP host by creating a new instance of the **SMTP** class:

```
91              SMTP connection = new SMTP(SMTPhost);
```

Lines 93 through 95 retrieve the subject, the message text, and the from address from the appropriate text fields:

```
93              subject = subjectText.getText();
94              message = messageText.getText();
95              from = fromText.getText();
```

The to address is read from the HTML file and cannot be edited by the user.

Line 97 calls the **sendmsg()** method of the SMTP class to send the message:

```
97              connection.sendmsg(from,to,subject,message);
```

Finally, line 98 calls the **close()** method to end the session with the SMTP server:

```
98              connection.close();
```

DEPRECATED METHODS IN SMTPMAIL   SMTPmail uses two features that are now deprecated, meaning that Java 2 includes newer features that supersede these old ones. In the **ch03\SMTPmail\Java2** directory of the CD-ROM, you will find a revised version of the **SMTPmail.java** file that does not use the deprecated features. The rest of this section summarizes the changes necessary to get rid of the deprecated features.

The two deprecated features in the **SMTPmail** applet are as follows:

◆ Line 130 calls the **size()** method, which has been superseded by the **getSize()** method. To fix this problem, replace the calls to **size()** with **getSize()**.

◆ The **action()** method (lines 82 through 120) is no longer the recommended way to handle mouse clicks on a button. Instead, you have to use the **ActionListener** interface, as explained later in this section.

To use the newer event-handling model, start by adding the following import statement to the **SMTPmail.java** file after line 11:

```
import java.awt.event.*;
```

This is needed to use the new **ActionListener** interface. The **ActionListener** interface class is defined in the **java.awt.event** package.

Modify line 29 to read as follows:

```
public class SMTPmail extends Applet implements ActionListener
```

This change indicates that the **SMTPmail** class will implement the **ActionListener** interface, which requires the **actionPerformed()** method.

Add the following statement after line 72:

```
sendButton.addActionListener(this);
```

This indicates that the **SMTPmail** class (indicated by the **this** keyword) provides the **ActionListener** interface used to process mouse clicks on the **Send** button.

Finally, you have to modify the **action()** method. Replace lines 82 through 120 with the following method:

```
/** Handles mouse clicks on the Button (new style) */
public void actionPerformed(ActionEvent ev)
{
    try
    {
        showStatus("Connecting to SMTPhost " + SMTPhost);
        SMTP connection = new SMTP(SMTPhost);
        showStatus("Connected to "+SMTPhost);
        subject = subjectText.getText();
        message = messageText.getText();
```

```
            from = fromText.getText();
            showStatus("Sending mail...");
            connection.sendmsg(from,to,subject,message);
            connection.close();
            showStatus("Mail sent.");
        }
        catch (UnknownHostException e)
        {
            showStatus("Unknown host - " + SMTPhost);
            System.out.println(e.getMessage());
        }
        catch (ProtocolException e)
        {
            showStatus("Unknown protocol");
            System.out.println(e.getMessage());
        }
        catch (IOException e)
        {
            showStatus(SMTPhost+" - Socket I/O error");
            System.out.println(e.getMessage());
        }
    }
```

This changes the method's name to **actionPerformed** and declares it as a **void** function (one that does not return anything). The argument list also changes—**actionPerformed()** takes a single **ActionEvent** argument. Also, some of the lines in the old **action()** method are no longer needed.

Using FTP to Download and Upload Files

File Transfer Protocol, or FTP for short, is another popular Internet service. As you might guess from its name, FTP allows file transfers between two Internet hosts. **FTPapplet** is an applet that uses the well-known **Linlyn** class (available from **http://www.afu.com**) to download and upload a file using FTP. The **Linlyn** class is copyright 1998 by Robert Lynch and Peter van der Linden and is distributed under GNU General Public License, version 2.

Using FTPapplet

You will find the source file and a sample HTML file (called **ToDo.html**) for **FTPapplet** in the **ch03\FTPapp** directory of the companion CD-ROM. As provided, the applet will not work; you have to first edit the applet and compile it (this means you will need a Java compiler such as **javac** that comes with Sun's Java Development Kit, available from **http://java.sun.com/products/jdk/**).

Before I explain why you have to edit the source code for **FTPapplet** and what changes you have to make, there is another important constraint for trying out this applet. You will need access to a system that runs both a Web server and an FTP server. Due to the security restrictions imposed on the applet (by the Web browser), the applet can connect only to an FTP server on the same Internet host as the one from which the applet's class file was downloaded. The applet's code is still worth studying because it shows you how to interact with an FTP server from a Java program.

The changes to the applet's source code also have a security implication. To make **FTPapplet** work, you have to fill in the host name, user name, and password to be used when connecting to the FTP server. Even after you compile the code, anyone with access to the applet's class file can easily retrieve the user name and password. As you can imagine, this is a security violation and will not be allowed by any Internet service provider. Your only option might be to try the applet in a private local area network (LAN) with a server. For example, I tested the applet on my home LAN with the Web server and FTP server running on a PC that runs Red Hat Linux as its operating system.

Now that you know the risks of using **FTPapplet**, here are the steps to edit the file (line numbers refer to the listing shown in the "Understanding FTPapplet" section):

1. Copy the **FTPapplet.java** file from the **ch03\FTPapp** directory of this book's companion CD-ROM to a directory on your hard disk.

2. Open the **FTPapplet.java** file in a text editor.

3. On line 32, set the **String FTP_SERVER** to the name of the host on which the Web server and FTP server are running.

4. On line 33, set the **String USERNAME** to the user name you want to use when logging on to the FTP server.

5. On line 34, set the **String PASSWORD** to the password for the user name you specified in step 4.

6. Save the **FTPapplet.java** file.

Next, compile the **FTPapplet.java** file with a Java compiler. For example, if you are using Sun's JDK, type the following command:

```
javac FTPapplet.java
```

This creates the class file **FTPapplet.class** with the applet's executable code.

Copy the **FTPapplet.class** and **ToDo.html** files to the Web server. Then open the **ToDo.html** file from a Java-capable Web browser. Figure 3-6 shows the resulting output. As you can see from Figure 3-6, **FTPapplet** downloads a text file and displays the contents in a text area. In this case, the file happens to be a "to do"

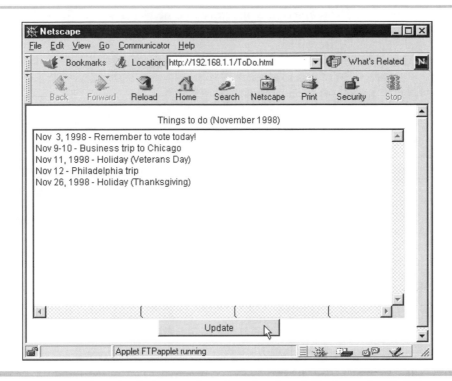

FIGURE 3-6. **FTPapplet** being used to download and display a "to do" list.

list. You can edit the text and upload any changed text by clicking on the **Update** button. This causes **FTPapplet** to upload the current contents of the text area to the FTP server.

Here is the listing of the **ToDo.html** file that results in Figure 3-6:

```
<html>
<body>
<applet code="FTPapplet.class" width=500 height=300>
  <param name=title value="Things to do (November 1998)">
  <param name=directory value=todo>
  <param name=file value=todo.nov>
</applet>
</body>
</html>
```

As this listing shows, **FTPapplet** accepts three parameters:

◆ **title** is a string displayed at the top of the applet's display area.

◆ **directory** is the name of the directory (on the FTP server) where the file is located.

◆ **file** is the name of the file to be downloaded (and uploaded).

FTPapplet

Understanding FTPapplet

The following listing shows the file **FTPapplet.java**. The listing includes the **Linlyn** class that implements the FTP client. Subsequent sections explain how this applet and the **Linlyn** class work.

```
 1 //----------------------------------------------------------------
 2 // FTPapplet.java
 3 //
 4 // Applet that uses the Linlyn class to download and upload file
 5 // using FTP.
 6
 7 // The Linlyn code (which appears later in this program) comes
 8 // with the following copyright notice:
 9 //
10 //     Copyright 1998 Robert Lynch, Peter van der Linden
11 //     This work is distributed under the GNU GPL, version 2.
12 //
13 // That code as well as this program are distributed under GNU
14 // General Public License, version 2.
15 //
16 //     !!! WARNING !!!  !!! WARNING !!!  !!! WARNING !!!
17 // CAUTION: To use this program, you have to include your user
18 // name and password in String variables. Anyone with access to
19 // the applet's class file can retrieve the password and log into
20 // your system. Ask your network administrator or Internet
21 // Service Provider (ISP) for guidance before using the program.
22 //
23 // If you still want to proceed, use the program at your own risk.
24 //----------------------------------------------------------------
25 import java.awt.*;    // The first two are for the applet
26 import java.applet.*;
27 import java.io.*;   // The rest are needed by the Linlyn class
28 import java.net.*;
29 import java.util.*;
30
31 public class FTPapplet extends Applet {
32     String FTP_SERVER = <<Fill in Host Name or IP address>>
33     String USERNAME = <<Fill in user name>>
34     String PASSWORD = <<Fill in password for FTP login>>
35     String dirname, filename, title;
36     TextArea content;
```

```
37    /** Downloads file and displays in a text entry area */
38    public void init() {
39        filename = getParameter("file");
40        if(filename == null){
41            TextArea ta = new TextArea(
42                "You must provide a file name!", 1, 40);
43            return;
44        }
45        dirname = getParameter("directory");
46        if(dirname == null) dirname = ".";
47        title = getParameter("title");
48        if(title == null)
49            title = "Contents of: "+dirname+"/"+filename;
50        try {
51            Linlyn d = new Linlyn(FTP_SERVER, USERNAME, PASSWORD);
52            String s = d.download(dirname, filename);
53            setLayout(new BorderLayout());
54            Label tlabel = new Label(title, Label.CENTER);
55            add("North", tlabel);
56            content = new TextArea( s, 10, 60);
57            add("Center", content);
58            Panel p = new Panel();
59            p.setLayout(new GridLayout(1,3));
60            Label pad1 = new Label("        ");
61            p.add(pad1);
62            Button ubutton = new Button("Update");
63            p.add(ubutton);
64            Label pad2 = new Label("        ");
65            p.add(pad2);
66            add("South", p);
67        } catch(java.io.IOException ioe) {ioe.printStackTrace();}
68    }
69    /** Handles mouse clicks on the "Update" button */
70    public boolean action(Event ev, Object obj) {
71        if(ev.target instanceof Button)  {
72            if (((String)obj).equals("Update")) {
73                try {
74                    showStatus("Updating file...");
75                    Linlyn u = new Linlyn(FTP_SERVER, USERNAME,
76                                                    PASSWORD);
77                    String s = content.getText();
78                    u.upload(dirname, filename, s);
79                    showStatus("File updated.");
80                } catch (IOException ioe) {
81                    showStatus("Error updating file");
82                    System.out.println(ioe.getMessage());
83                }
84                return true;
```

```
 85                   }
 86               }
 87               return super.action(ev, obj);
 88          }
 89  }
 90  /////////////////////////////////////////////
 91  /// split here for Linlyn.java //
 92  //  At last!  Java code to read/write files on the server from an applet!
 93  //  This is the famous Linlyn code.
 94  //
 95  //  Use:
 96  //    compile this file, and have your applet call it as below.
 97  //
 98  //    to upload a file:
 99  //          Linlyn ftp = new Linlyn( <servername>, <user>, <password> );
100  //          ftp.upload( <directory>, <filename>, <contents of file> );
101  //
102  //    to download a file:
103  //          Linlyn ftp = new Linlyn( <servername>, <user>, <password> );
104  //          String contents = ftp.download( <directory>, <filename> );
105  //
106  //          the default is ASCII transfer, an overloaded method does bin.
107  //
108  //    All parameters and return values are Strings. E.g.
109  //          Linlyn ftp = new Linlyn( "rtfm.mit.edu", "anonymous", "linden@" );
110  //          String contents = ftp.download(
111  //                          "/pub/usenet-by-group/omp.lang.java.programmer"
112  //                          "Java_Programmers_FAQ" );
113  //
114  //          [the actual values above are not generally valid, substitute
115  //           your own server for your first attempt, see note 1.]
116  //
117  //    Notes:
118  //      1.  Usual applet security rules apply: you can only get a file
119  //          from the server that served the applet.
120  //      2.  The applet server must also be an FTP server.  This is NOT true
121  //          for some ISPs, such as best.com.  They have separate FTP and
122  //          http machines.  This code may work on such a setup if you put
123  //          the classfiles into the ftp area, and in the HTML file, say:
124  //          <applet  codebase="ftp:///home/linden/ftp"  code="t.class"
125  //      3.  This code does not break Java security.
126  //          It uses FTP to transfer files.  If the author of the applet
127  //          has FTP disabled you are out of luck.
128  //          It breaks regular system security however, as it publishes
129  //          (effectively) your ftp password.  Only use on an Intranet and
130  //          with authorization.
131  //      4.  Compiling this causes some deprecation warnings.  We wanted to
132  //          stick with code that would work in JDK 1.0 browsers.
```

```
133 //        5.  Each upload or download creates, uses, and terminates a new
134 //            ftp session.  This is intended for low volume transfer, such
135 //            as the ever popular high-score files.
136 //        6.  Look at the source for the methods for binary transfers.
137 //
138 //    Version 1.0    May 6 1998.
139 //    Version 1.1    May 20 1998. -- added a debugging flag.
140 //    Version 1.1a   May 26 1998. -- fixed the ASCII/BIN flag inversion.
141 //    Version 1.1b   May 29 1998. -- added the security warning.
142 //    Version 2.0    Jul 1, 1998. -- Updated to parse multi-string responses
143 //                                   a la RFC 959.
144 //    Version 2.1    Aug 5, 1998. -- Updated to work with VMS ftp servers.
145 //                                   VMS does not send either a ")" OR a ")."
146 //                                   terminating the IP number, port sequence
147 //                                   in response to PASV.
148 //    Version 2.1a   Aug 6, 1998  -- more than one line as a "hello" message.
149 //                                   (tvalesky@patriot.net)
150 //    Version 2.2    Sep 22 1998  -- added a flush() in ftpSendCmd.
151 //
152 //    Authors:
153 //          Robert Lynch
154 //          Peter van der Linden  (Author of "Just Java 1.1" book).
155 //
156 //    Support:
157 //          Unsupported: That's why we give you the source.
158 //          Help may be available on time & materials basis only.
159 //           You can get copious debug information by changing to
160 //           DEBUG=true     below and recompiling.
161 //
162 //    Copyright 1998 Robert Lynch, Peter van der Linden
163 //    This work is distributed under the GNU GPL, version 2.
164 //
165 //    Those using the code do so at their own risk and the authors
166 //    are not responsible for any costs, loss, or damage which may
167 //    thereby be incurred.
168
169 // import java.io.*;
170 // import java.net.*;
171 // import java.util.*;
172
173 class Linlyn {
174
175     // FOR INITIAL DEBUGGING: set the variable to "true"
176     private boolean DEBUG = false;
177
178     // constructor needs servername, username and passwd
179     public Linlyn(String server, String user, String pass) {
180         try {
```

```
181              ftpConnect(server);
182              ftpLogin(user, pass);
183          } catch(IOException ioe) {ioe.printStackTrace();}
184      }
185
186      public String download(String dir, String file)
187          throws IOException { return download(dir, file, true); }
188
189      public String download(String dir, String file, boolean asc)
190          throws IOException {
191          ftpSetDir(dir);
192          ftpSetTransferType(asc);
193          dsock = ftpGetDataSock();
194          InputStream is = dsock.getInputStream();
195          ftpSendCmd("RETR "+file);
196
197          String contents = getAsString(is);
198          ftpLogout();
199          return contents;
200      }
201
202      public void upload(String dir, String file, String what)
203          throws IOException { upload(dir, file, what, true); }
204
205      public void upload(String dir, String file, String what, boolean asc)
206          throws IOException {
207          ftpSetDir(dir);
208          ftpSetTransferType(asc);
209          dsock = ftpGetDataSock();
210          OutputStream os = dsock.getOutputStream();
211          DataOutputStream dos = new DataOutputStream(os);
212          ftpSendCmd("STOR "+file);
213          dos.writeBytes(what);
214          dos.flush();
215          ftpLogout();
216      }
217
218      /////////////// private fields ///////////////////
219      private String getAsString(InputStream is) {
220          int c=0;
221          char lineBuffer[]=new char[128], buf[]=lineBuffer;
222          int room= buf.length, offset=0;
223          try {
224            loop: while (true) {
225                // read chars into a buffer which grows as needed
226                    switch (c = is.read() ) {
227                        case -1: break loop;
228
```

```
229                      default: if (--room < 0) {
230                                   buf = new char[offset + 128];
231                                   room = buf.length - offset - 1;
232                                   System.arraycopy(lineBuffer, 0,
233                                              buf, 0, offset);
234                                   lineBuffer = buf;
235                               }
236                               buf[offset++] = (char) c;
237                               break;
238                  }
239          }
240      } catch(IOException ioe) {ioe.printStackTrace();}
241      if ((c == -1) && (offset == 0)) {
242          return null;
243      }
244      return String.copyValueOf(buf, 0, offset);
245  }
246
247  private void ftpConnect(String server)
248      throws IOException {
249      // Set up socket, control streams, connect to ftp server
250      // Open socket to server control port 21
251      csock = new Socket(server, CNTRL_PORT);
252      // Open control streams
253      InputStream cis = csock.getInputStream();
254      dcis =  new BufferedReader(new InputStreamReader(cis));
255      OutputStream cos = csock.getOutputStream();
256      pos = new PrintWriter(cos, true); // set auto flush true.
257
258      // handle more than one line returned
259      String reply = dcis.readLine();
260          String numerals = reply.substring(0, 3);
261      String hyph_test = reply.substring(3, 4);
262      String next = null;
263      if(hyph_test.equals("-")) {
264          boolean done = false;
265          while(!done) { // read lines til find "" -> last line
266              next = dcis.readLine();
267              if(next.substring(0,3).equals(numerals) &&
268                  next.substring(3, 4).equals(" "))
269                  done = true;
270          }
271      }
272
273      if(numerals.substring(0,3).equals("220")) // ftp server alive
274          ; // System.out.println("Connected to ftp server");
275      else System.err.println("Error connecting to ftp server.");
276  }
```

```
277
278    private void ftpLogin(String user, String pass)
279        throws IOException {
280        ftpSendCmd("USER "+user);
281        ftpSendCmd("PASS "+pass);
282    }
283
284    private void ftpSetDir(String dir)
285        throws IOException {
286        // cwd to dir
287        ftpSendCmd("CWD "+dir);
288    }
289
290    private void ftpSetTransferType(boolean asc)
291        throws IOException {
292        // set file transfer type
293        String ftype = (asc? "A" : "I");
294        ftpSendCmd("TYPE "+ftype);
295    }
296
297    private Socket ftpGetDataSock()
298        throws IOException {
299         // Go to PASV mode, capture server reply, parse for socket setup
300         // V2.1: generalized port parsing, allows more server variations
301        String reply = ftpSendCmd("PASV");
302
303         // New technique: just find numbers before and after ","!
304        StringTokenizer st = new StringTokenizer(reply, ",");
305        String[] parts = new String[6]; // parts, incl. some garbage
306        int i = 0; // put tokens into String array
307        while(st.hasMoreElements()) {
308            // stick pieces of host, port in String array
309            try {
310                parts[i] = st.nextToken();
311                I++;
312            } catch(NoSuchElementException nope){nope.printStackTrace();}
313        } // end getting parts of host, port
314
315        // Get rid of everything before first "," except digits
316        String[] diggies = new String[3];
317        for(int j = 0; j < 3; j++) {
318            // Get 3 characters, inverse order, check if digit/character
319            diggies[j] = parts[0].substring(parts[0].length() - (j + 1),
320                parts[0].length() - j); // next: digit or character?
321            if(!Character.isDigit(diggies[j].charAt(0)))
322                diggies[j] = "";
323        }
324        parts[0] = diggies[2] + diggies[1] + diggies[0];
```

```
325        // Get only the digits after the last ","
326        String[] porties = new String[3];
327        for(int k = 0; k < 3; k++) {
328            // Get 3 characters, in order, check if digit/character
329            // May be less than 3 characters
330            if((k + 1) <= parts[5].length())
331                porties[k] = parts[5].substring(k, k + 1);
332            else porties[k] = "FOOBAR"; // definitely not a digit!
333            // next: digit or character?
334            if(!Character.isDigit(porties[k].charAt(0)))
335                    porties[k] = "";
336        } // Have to do this one in order, not inverse order
337        parts[5] = porties[0] + porties[1] + porties[2];
338        // Get dotted quad IP number first
339        String ip = parts[0]+"."+parts[1]+"."+parts[2]+"."+parts[3];
340
341        // Determine port
342        int port = -1;
343        try { // Get first part of port, shift by 8 bits.
344            int big = Integer.parseInt(parts[4]) << 8;
345            int small = Integer.parseInt(parts[5]);
346            port = big + small; // port number
347        } catch(NumberFormatException nfe) {nfe.printStackTrace();}
348        if((ip != null) && (port != -1))
349            dsock = new Socket(ip, port);
350        else throw new IOException();
351        return dsock;
352    }
353
354    private String ftpSendCmd(String cmd)
355        throws IOException
356    { // This sends a dialog string to the server, returns reply
357      // V2.0 Updated to parse multi-string responses a la RFC 959
358      // Prints out only last response string of the lot.
359    pos.print(cmd + "\r\n" );
360    pos.flush();
361    String reply = dcis.readLine();
362    String numerals = reply.substring(0, 3);
363    String hyph_test = reply.substring(3, 4);
364    String next = null;
365    if(hyph_test.equals("-")) {
366        boolean done = false;
367        while(!done) { // read lines til find "" -> last line
368            next = dcis.readLine();
369            if(next.substring(0,3).equals(numerals) &&
```

```
370                 next.substring(3, 4).equals(" "))
371                 done = true;
372         }
373         if(DEBUG)
374             System.out.println("Response to: "+cmd+" was: "+next);
375         return next;
376     } else
377         if(DEBUG)
378             System.out.println("Response to: "+cmd+" was: "+reply);
379         return reply;
380     }
381
382     private void ftpLogout() {// logout, close streams
383         try {
384             if(DEBUG) System.out.println("sending BYE");
385             pos.print("BYE" + "\r\n" );
386             pos.flush();
387             pos.close();
388             dcis.close();
389             csock.close();
390             dsock.close();
391         } catch(IOException ioe) {ioe.printStackTrace();}
392     }
393
394     private static final int CNTRL_PORT = 21;
395     private Socket csock = null;
396     private Socket dsock = null;
397     private BufferedReader dcis;
398     private PrintWriter pos;
399 }
```

ANNOTATIONS

FTPapplet relies on the **Linlyn** class to upload and download files using the File
Transfer Protocol. (FTP is documented in RFC 959, "File Transfer Protocol," J. Postel
and J. Reynolds, 1985, available on the Web at **http://www.cis.ohio-state.edu/
htbin/rfc/rfc959.html.**) The **Linlyn** class, described in the next section, embodies an
FTP client. Figure 3-7 illustrates how an FTP client interacts with the FTP server.
Like other Internet services, the FTP client communicates with the FTP server over a
socket connection at a well-known port. For the FTP server, the well-known port is
port number 21. The FTP client establishes what is known as a *control connection* at
port 21. The client sends all FTP commands over the control connection. These
commands take the form of short text strings, and they deal with file operations
such as storing a file, retrieving a file, changing the directory, and so on.

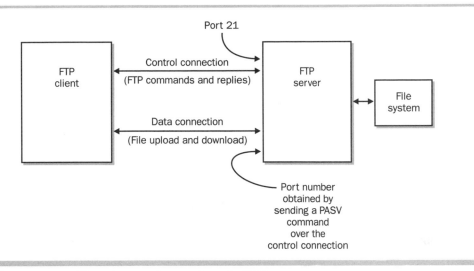

FIGURE 3-7. Client/server interactions in FTP.

The file transfer (which is the purpose of FTP) does not happen over the control connection. Instead, when it's time to transfer a file, the client sends a special command (**PASV**) over the control connection. The server replies with an IP address and port number. The client then establishes another socket connection, called a *data connection*, to that IP address and port number and sends or receives the file over that connection. After the file transfer is done, the data connection is closed. Thus, the data connection does not exist at all times.

LINLYN CLASS   The **Linlyn** class is at the heart of **FTPapplet**. Lines 90 through 399 of the listing represent the **Linlyn** class. First, note the contents of lines 162 and 163:

```
162 //     Copyright 1998 Robert Lynch, Peter van der Linden
163 //     This work is distributed under the GNU GPL, version 2.
```

As the notice indicates, this class is copyrighted by Robert Lynch and Peter van der Linden (author of *Just Java 1.1* and the Java FAQ available at **http://www.afu.com**). By concatenating the first three letters of the authors' names (Linden and Lynch), you get the class name, **Linlyn**. Line 163 tells you that the code is distributed under GNU GPL, version 2. GPL stands for General Public License, a licensing agreement that requires software to be distributed in source-code form and stipulates that any user can copy and distribute the software to anyone else in source-code form. Additionally, the agreement states that the software comes with absolutely no warranty. You'll find the text of the GPL in a file named **COPYING** in the top-level directory of the companion CD-ROM.

Lines 173 through 399 constitute the actual code of the **Linlyn** class. The class uses five **private** variables that are declared at the very end of the file, in lines 394 through 398:

```
394    private static final int CNTRL_PORT = 21;
395    private Socket csock = null;
396    private Socket dsock = null;
397    private BufferedReader dcis;
398    private PrintWriter pos;
```

Here, **CNTRL_PORT** is the well-known port number (21) for the FTP server. The **csock** and **dsock** variables are used for the **Socket** connections representing the control connection and data connection, respectively. The **BufferedReader dcis** is used to read responses from the FTP server. The **Printwriter pos** is used to send commands to the FTP server.

When you use the **Linlyn** class in a Java applet or program, you access its capabilities through the following five public methods:

♦ **Linlyn(String server, String user, String pass)**, shown in lines 179 through 184, is a **Linlyn** class constructor that requires a server name, user name, and password as argument. This constructor calls a private method, **ftpConnect()**, to open a socket connection to the FTP server. It then calls another private method, **ftpLogin()**, to log on to the FTP server with the specified user name and password.

♦ **String download(String dir, String file)**, in lines 186 and 187, downloads a text file from a specified directory and returns the file's contents in a **String** object. This method calls another overloaded **download()** method to the job.

♦ **public String download(String dir, String file, boolean asc)**, listed in lines 189 through 200, sends FTP protocol commands to the FTP server to download a file and return the file's contents in a **String**. The **boolean** argument **asc** controls whether the file is transferred as binary or ASCII (which essentially means text). If **asc** is **true**, the file transfer mode is ASCII; otherwise the transfer mode is binary. Line 191 sends a command to change the directory. Line 192 sets the transfer mode. Line 193 gets a socket for data connection by calling the private method **ftpGetDataSock()**. Line 194 opens an input stream on the data connection socket. Line 195 sends the FTP protocol command **RETR** to retrieve the file. Line 197 retrieves the file's contents in a **String**. Line 198 logs out of the FTP server, and line 199 returns the **String** that holds the file's contents.

♦ **public void upload(String dir, String file, String what)**, in lines 202 and 203, uploads the contents of the **String what** to a file in a specified directory. This method calls another **upload()** method to actually do its job.

- **public void upload(String dir, String file, String what, boolean asc)**, shown in lines 205 through 216, sends the contents of the **String what** to a file in a specific directory of the FTP server. The **boolean asc** argument controls the file transfer mode, which can be binary or ASCII (used to upload text files). When **asc** is **true**, the file transfer mode is ASCII; otherwise the mode is binary. Lines 207 and 208 set the directory and the file transfer mode. Line 209 calls **ftpGetDataSock()** to get a socket for data connection. Lines 210 and 211 set up an output stream for data transfer. Line 212 sends the FTP protocol command **STOR** to request that the FTP server store whatever is sent over the data connection in a file on the FTP server. Then lines 213 and 214 send the **String what** over the data connection. Finally, line 215 calls the **ftpLogout()** method to log out of the FTP server.

When you use the **Linlyn** class, you will call the public methods only. However, the public methods rely on a number of private methods to do their job. Here are the private methods in the **Linlyn** class:

- **String getAsString(InputStream is)**, in lines 219 through 245, reads a byte at a time from the input stream until the end of the stream is reached. A **switch** statement on line 226 calls the **read()** method to read bytes. If the byte is -1, that means the stream has ended. The bytes are accumulated into a **char[]** array. When the stream ends, line 244 returns the **char[]** array as a **String** object.

- **void ftpConnect(String server)**, shown in lines 247 through 276, opens a connection to the FTP server and initializes the private variables **csock**, **dcis**, and **pos**. Line 251 opens a control connection to the FTP server at port 21 (that number is stored in the private variable **CNTRL_PORT**) and saves the **Socket** in the **csock** variable. Line 253 opens an input stream, and line 254 initializes the **BufferedReader** object **dcis** (this is used later on to read responses sent by the FTP server). Line 255 and 256 create an output stream and then initialize the **PrintWriter** object **pos** through which commands are sent to the FTP server. Lines 259 through 270 read the responses returned by the FTP server after the socket connection has been established. Often an FTP server sends a series of lines as response, but all lines begin with three numerals that indicate a response code. A response code of 220 means that the connection is successful. Line 273 checks for a response code of 220 and prints an error message if it is not 220.

- **void ftpLogin(String user, String pass)**, in lines 278 through 282, logs on to the FTP server by sending the **USER** command with a user name followed by the **PASS** command with the password. This method calls the **ftpSendCmd()** method to send the commands to the FTP server.

- **void ftpSetDir(String dir)**, shown in lines 284 through 288, changes the directory at the FTP server by sending the **CWD** command with the new directory name (specified through the **dir** argument).

◆ **void ftpSetTransferType(boolean asc)**, listed in lines 290 through 295, sets the file transfer type by sending the **TYPE** command to the server. A single letter, **I** for binary or **A** for ASCII, follows the **TYPE** command. Line 293 sets that letter based on the value of the **boolean** argument **asc**. If **asc** is **true**, the transfer type is set to **A**; otherwise the transfer type is **I**. Line 294 sends the command by calling the **ftpSendCmd()** method.

◆ **Socket ftpGetDataSock()**, in lines 297 through 352, sends a **PASV** command to the FTP server. The server, in return, responds with a string of the form **227 Entering Passive Mode (192,168,1,1,16,82)**. The first part of the response is a status code followed by test message. The interesting part is the six comma-separated numbers enclosed in parentheses. The first four of these numbers denote an IP address, and the last two denote a port number where the client should establish a data connection to transfer a file. For the sample response string shown, the IP address is 192.168.1.1 and the port number is 16*256+82 = 4178 (that's how the port number is computed from the two separate numbers). As you can see, the **PASV** command causes the server to tell the client where to establish a connection to exchange data. Line 301 sends the **PASV** command by calling **ftpSendCmd()**. Next, lines 304 through 347 read and parse the server's response. In particular, the IP address and the port number are obtained. Then line 349 opens the new socket connection representing the data connection. Finally, line 351 returns the new socket.

◆ **String ftpSendCmd(String cmd)**, in lines 354 through 380, sends a command to the FTP server by printing it to the **pos PrintWriter** object (which sends the text to the server over the control connection). Lines 359 and 360 send the command. The rest of the method reads the responses from the server. Line 379 returns the last line of response text received from the server.

◆ **void ftpLogout()**, shown in lines 382 through 391, sends the **BYE** command to the server and then closes all sockets and streams. This essentially ends the session with the FTP server.

FTPAPPLET INITIALIZATION   Because **Linlyn** does all of the work, the rest of **FTPapplet** is quite simple. Lines 38 through 68 implement the **init()** method that initializes the applet. Lines 39 through 49 get the parameters (**directory**, **file**, and **title**) from the HTML file. Line 51 then creates an instance of the **Linlyn** class:

```
51          Linlyn d = new Linlyn(FTP_SERVER, USERNAME, PASSWORD);
```

This statement assumes that the **String** variables **FTP_SERVER**, **USERNAME**, and **PASSWORD** respectively hold the name (or IP address) of the FTP server, the user name, and the password. These variables are defined in lines 32 through 34 of the listing.

After a **Linlyn** instance has been created, line 52 calls the **download()** method to get the contents of the specified file:

```
52              String s = d.download(dirname, filename);
```

Lines 53 through 66 create a user interface using various Java AWT components. In particular, line 56 creates a **TextArea** component that displays the contents of the file (now in the **String s**):

```
56              content = new TextArea( s, 10, 60);
```

The user interface displays the title at the top, followed by the **TextArea** with the file contents. Then it shows a button labeled **Update**. After making any changes to the text in the **TextArea**, the user can click the **Update** button to upload the text to the server. The exact sequence of processing involves a call to the **action()** method, described in the next section.

THE FTPAPPLET EVENT HANDLER   When the user clicks on the **Update** button, the **action()** method is called. Lines 70 through 88 implement the **action()** method. Lines 71 and 72 make sure that the mouse click is on a **Button** object and that the label on the button is **Update**. Lines 75 through 78 then create an instance of **Linlyn** and upload the text to the FTP server:

```
75              Linlyn u = new Linlyn(FTP_SERVER, USERNAME,
76                                              PASSWORD);
77              String s = content.getText();
78              u.upload(dirname, filename, s);
```

Lines 75 and 76 create the **Linlyn** instance just as was done when downloading the file in line 51. Line 77 calls the **getText()** method of the **TextArea** class to get the current contents of the **TextArea** into **String s**. Finally, line 78 calls the **upload()** method of the **Linlyn** instance to upload **String s** to the FTP server and store it in the same file from which text was downloaded earlier in line 52.

Creating a TELNET Terminal Emulation

TELNET is a bidirectional communications protocol used by a terminal emulation application to provide access to an Internet host. The terminal emulation application uses the TELNET protocol to transmit data to the host interspersed with TELNET control information. (TELNET is documented in RFC 854, "TELNET Protocol Specification," J. Postel and J. Reynolds, 1983, available on the Web at **http://www.cis.ohio-state.edu/htbin/rfc/rfc854.html**.)

A TELNET-based terminal emulation application acts like a physical terminal connected to the host. You can use a TELNET terminal application to log on to a host (you'll need a valid user name and password for that host). Such a terminal application is useful for remote access to a host. For example, you will find a TELNET application in Windows 95 (look for the **TELNET.EXE** file in the **Windows** directory).

A Java applet with TELNET and terminal emulation capabilities can be a handy way for users to access a host and run text-based applications that are designed to run on a terminal. The remainder of this chapter presents such an applet, authored by Matthias L. Jugel and Marcus Meißner and distributed under the terms of the GNU General Public License (see the file **COPYING** in the **ch03\Telnet** directory of the companion CD-ROM). If you want to make use of the Java classes, they are distributed under the terms of the GNU Library General Public License (see the file **COPYING.LIB** in the **ch03\Telnet** directory of the CD-ROM).

The Java **Telnet** applet is a large software package with many source modules. I will describe the most relevant ones in the following sections. However, in the **ch03\Telnet** directory of the CD-ROM you will find the entire Java **Telnet** package, as distributed by the authors.

Using Telnet

You will find all of the files for the **Telnet** applet in the **ch03\Telnet** directory of the companion CD-ROM. To try out **Telnet**, you need a host that runs a Web server and also allows login through TELNET. Due to security restrictions imposed by the Web browser, the **Telnet** applet can establish a connection only back to the host from which it was downloaded.

If you want to view the online documentation for the **Telnet** applet, start your Web browser and open the **index.html** file from the **ch03\Telnet** directory of the CD-ROM. You will see an introductory Web page for the **Telnet** applet, as shown in Figure 3-8. To access more information about **Telnet**, click on the **Help** button (the one with a question mark on it) from the row of buttons along the bottom edge of the Web page shown in Figure 3-8. This takes you to the **index.html** file in the **ch03/Telnet/ Documentation** directory of the CD-ROM. If you scroll down in that Web page, you'll find information on how to set up the **Telnet** applet, as shown in Figure 3-9. The Web page tells you which files to install in the Web server and in which directories. I will briefly describe these steps next.

PROGRAMMER'S NOTE   *If you have a UNIX system, copy the **telnet.tgz** file from the **ch03\Telnet** directory of the CD-ROM. Then use the command **tar zxvf telnet.tgz** to extract the files from the compressed **tar** archive.*

To try the **Telnet** applet, follow these steps:

1. From the **ch03\Telnet** directory of the CD-ROM, upload (or copy) the **classes.zip** file to your Web server in the same directory in which you place HTML files. This file contains the compiled code of all Java classes in the **Telnet** package. It is referenced through the **archive** attribute in the **<applet>** tag. The applet loads faster with the **classes.zip** file.

2. Create a directory named **Telnet** in the same location on the Web server where you have placed the **classes.zip** file.

3. From the **ch03\Telnet** directory of the CD-ROM, upload the files **index.test.html**, **telnet.class**, and **appWrapper.class** to the **Telnet** directory on the Web server.

4. Create three directories named **display**, **socket**, and **modules** in the **Telnet** directory of the Web server.

5. From the **ch03\Telnet\display** directory of the CD-ROM, upload the files **SoftFont.class**, **CharDisplay.class**, **Terminal.class**, **TerminalHost.class**, and **vt320.class** to the **Telnet\display** directory on the Web server.

6. From the **ch03\Telnet\socket** directory of the CD-ROM, upload the files **StatusPeer.class** and **TelnetIO.class** to the **Telnet\socket** directory on the Web server.

7. From the **ch03\Telnet\modules** directory of the CD-ROM, upload the files **Module.class**, **Script.class**, **ButtonBar.class**, and **MudConnector.class** to the **Telnet\modules** directory on the Web server.

FIGURE 3-8. Introductory Web page for the **Telnet** applet.

FIGURE 3-9.   Web page with information on how to set up the **Telnet** applet.

That takes care of installing the minimal set of files needed to use the **Telnet** applet on a Web site. Next, use a text editor to edit the **index.test.html** file in the **Telnet** directory of the Web server. Find the following lines of code:

```
<!-- Here begins the applet code -->
<APPLET ARCHIVE="../classes.zip" CODE="appWrapper.class" WIDTH=590
HEIGHT=430>
  <PARAM NAME=applet        VALUE="telnet">
```

Continue down the list of **<PARAM>** tags and locate the following lines:

```
<!-- applet initialization: address and port -->
  <PARAM NAME=address       VALUE="www.first.gmd.de">
```

On that **<PARAM>** tag, change the **VALUE** attribute from **"www.first.gmd.de"** to your Web server's host name (or IP address). For example, if you have a private network with the Web server at IP address 192.168.1.1, use the string **"192.168.1.1"**.

After making the change, save **index.test.html** and exit the editor. Then start a Java-capable Web browser and access the **index.test.html** file from the **Telnet** directory of the Web server. For example, if the Web server's IP address is 192.168.1.1, the URL for that Web page will be **http://192.168.1.1/Telnet/index.test.html**. In the middle of the Web page, the **Telnet** applet displays a terminal window and presents a login prompt for the host. Using your user name and password, you can log on to the host and type commands (the commands depend on the operating system of the host). Figure 3-10 shows a typical session with the host using the **Telnet** applet.

An interesting feature of the **Telnet** applet is its ability to detach the applet from the Web page and display itself in a stand-alone window. Click on the **Detach/Delete Window** button above the terminal window. Figure 3-11 shows the result.

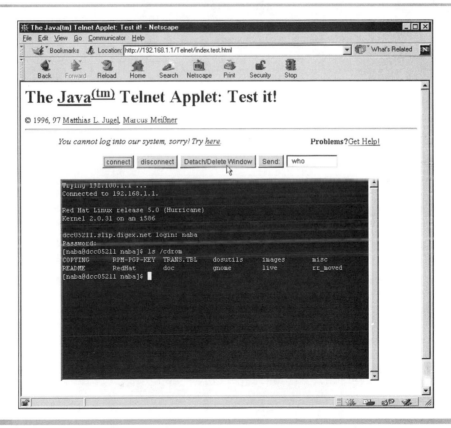

FIGURE 3-10. The **Telnet** applet provides a terminal window to log on to the host.

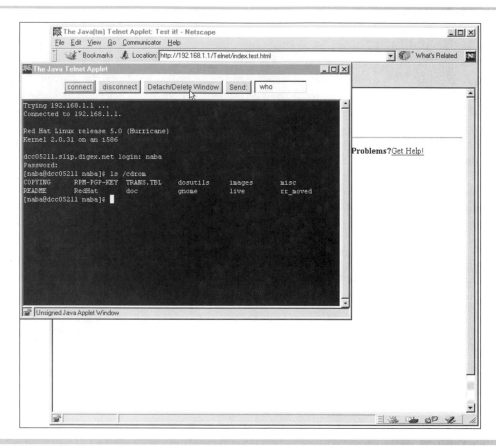

FIGURE 3-11. The **Telnet** applet can detach itself from the Web page.

As you can see, the **Telnet** applet now appears in a separate window. Click on the **Detach/Delete Window** button again and the **Telnet** applet will attach itself to the Web page in the Web browser's window. Later on you'll learn how the **appWrapper** class in the Java Telnet package implements this feature.

The final step in learning how to use the **Telnet** applet is to go through the **<applet>** tag and the **<param>** tags that you can use with this applet. Here is the **<applet>** tag from the **index.test.html** file that results in the display shown in Figure 3-10 (I have not shown the commented-out tags):

```
<APPLET ARCHIVE="../classes.zip" CODE="appWrapper.class" WIDTH=590
HEIGHT=430>
   <PARAM NAME=applet        VALUE="telnet">
   <!-- applet initialization: address and port -->
   <PARAM NAME=address       VALUE="www.first.gmd.de">
```

```
<PARAM NAME=port          VALUE="23">
<PARAM NAME=emulation     VALUE="vt320">
<!-- terminal emulation -->
<PARAM NAME=VTscrollbar VALUE="right">
<PARAM NAME=VTresize      VALUE="font">
<PARAM NAME=VTfont        VALUE="Courier">
<PARAM NAME=VTfontsize    VALUE="13">
<PARAM NAME=VTid          VALUE="vt220">
<!-- modules: #1 is a buttonbar -->
<PARAM NAME=module#1      VALUE="ButtonBar@North">
<PARAM NAME=1#Button      VALUE="connect|\$connect()">
<PARAM NAME=2#Button      VALUE="disconnect|\$disconnect()">
<PARAM NAME=3#Button      VALUE="Detach/Delete Window|\$detach()">
<PARAM NAME=4#Button      VALUE="Send:|\@send@\r\n">
<PARAM NAME=5#Input       VALUE="send#10|who|\@send@\r\n">
<!-- make sure, non-java-capable browser get a message: -->
<B>
Your Browser seems to have no <A
    HREF="http://java.sun.com/">Java</A>
    support. Please get a new browser or enable Java to see this
    applet!
</B>
</APPLET>
```

The **<APPLET>** tag on the first line has the following form:

```
<APPLET ARCHIVE="../classes.zip" CODE="appWrapper.class" WIDTH=590
HEIGHT=430>
```

This tag has the following attributes:

- **ARCHIVE="../classes.zip"** specifies that all of the applet's classes are in a compressed archive file named **classes.zip**, located in the parent directory of the HTML file. The browser downloads the file and loads the classes. Using an archive of classes speeds up the loading of the applet.

- **CODE="appWrapper.class"** specifies the name of the class file for the applet. As you will learn soon, there is a **telnet** class that represents the TELNET terminal applet; **appWrapper** is a class that actually loads the **Telnet** applet and that provides the ability to detach that applet from the browser, as shown in Figure 3-11.

- **WIDTH=590** specifies that the applet's display area is 590 pixels wide.

- **HEIGHT=430** specifies that the applet's display area is 430 pixels tall.

The **<APPLET>** tag is followed by a large number of **<PARAM>** tags that provide parameters to **appWrapper**, **telnet**, and other classes that implement the TELNET terminal. Table 3-1 summarizes the key parameters, grouped by the classes that use them.

Telnet

Understanding Telnet

The **Telnet** applet works by using quite a few classes, and the source code is in several files. The following sections present the source code for most of the classes and describe the general design of the applet. First you should go over Table 3-2,

Parameter	Class That Uses This Parameter	Description
applet	**appWrapper**	Name of the applet to be loaded by **appWrapper**.
address	**telnet**	Host name or IP address to which the TELNET connection is established.
port	**telnet**	Port number of TELNET connection (the well-known port number is 23).
emulation	**telnet**	The type of terminal to be emulated (for example, **vt320**).
module#1	**telnet**	Name of the first module to be loaded by **telnet**.
module#2	**telnet**	Name of the second module. Specify other modules through parameters named **module#3**, **module#4**, and so on.
VTscrollbar	**vt320**	Location of scroll bar in terminal window.
VTresize	**vt320**	When set to **font**, the font changes if the window is resized.
VTfont	**vt320**	Name of the font to be used for terminal emulation.
VTfontsize	**vt320**	Size of the font used in the terminal.
VTid	**vt320**	Terminal identifier string (can be **vt100**, **vt220**, or **vt320**).
1#Button	**ButtonBar**	Label and action for the first button (value is of the form **"Label | Action"**).
2#Button	**ButtonBar**	Label and action for the second button. Specify other buttons through parameters named **3#Button**, **4#Button**, and so on.
N#Input	**ButtonBar**	A text input field where the user can enter text.

TABLE 3-1.   Key Parameters Used by the **Telnet** Applet.

Directory	Relevant Java Files	Description
Top level (ch03\Telnet)	**appWrapper.java frame.java telnet.java**	The main Java source files. Also includes several useful HTML files (such as **index.test.html**) and the GNU licenses.
Documentation	None	HTML documentation for the applet and its support classes (see the **Source** subdirectory).
display	**CharDisplay.java SoftFont.java Terminal.java TerminalHost.java vt320.java**	Classes that display text in the terminal window and provide terminal emulation (for a VT 320 terminal).
examples	None	HTML files showing various ways to use the **telnet** and supporting classes.
modules	**ButtonBar.java Module.java Script.java**	Classes that can be dynamically loaded by the **Telnet** applet. Each module has to implement a predefined set of methods. The button bar above the terminal window (see Figure 3-10) is implemented by the **ButtonBar** module.
socket	**StatusPeer.java TelnetIO.java**	Classes that implement the TELNET protocol exchanges (as specified by RFC 854).
tools	**proxy.java**	A Java proxy server class to redirect TELNET access to another host.

TABLE 3-2. Java Source Files for the **Telnet** Applet in Various Directories

which summarizes the contents of various subdirectories of the **ch03\Telnet** directory. In particular, the table points out the relevant Java source files in each directory.

The following listing shows **telnet.java**, the main Java source file for the **Telnet** applet. As I explain this file in subsequent sections, I will show the relevant sections of code for a few more supporting classes used by the **Telnet** applet. Due to space limitations, this chapter does not include the listing of each and every Java file the applet requires. However, you will find all of the files in the **ch03\Telnet** directory of the CD-ROM.

PROGRAMMER'S NOTE *The Java source files and HTML files in the **ch03\Telnet** directory of the CD-ROM are UNIX text files. This means that each line ends with a line feed character (as opposed to a carriage return–line feed pair in Windows). However, you should be able to open and edit these files with Windows applications such as Notepad, Wordpad, or Microsoft Word.*

```
1  /**
2   * telnet -- implements a simple telnet
3   * --
4   * $Id: telnet.java,v 1.19 1998/02/09 10:22:15 leo Exp $
5   * $timestamp: Mon Aug  4 13:11:14 1997 by Matthias L. Jugel :$
6   *
7   * This file is part of "The Java Telnet Applet".
8   *
9   * This is free software; you can redistribute it and/or modify
10  * it under the terms of the GNU General Public License as published by
11  * the Free Software Foundation; either version 2, or (at your option)
12  * any later version.
13  *
14  * "The Java Telnet Applet" is distributed in the hope that it will be
15  * useful, but WITHOUT ANY WARRANTY; without even the implied warranty of
16  * MERCHANTABILITY or FITNESS FOR A PARTICULAR PURPOSE.  See the
17  * GNU General Public License for more details.
18  *
19  * You should have received a copy of the GNU General Public License
20  * along with this software; see the file COPYING.  If not, write to the
21  * Free Software Foundation, Inc., 59 Temple Place - Suite 330,
22  * Boston, MA 02111-1307, USA.
23  */
24
25 import java.applet.Applet;
26 import java.awt.Frame;
27 import java.awt.Component;
28 import java.awt.Container;
29 import java.awt.BorderLayout;
30 import java.awt.Dimension;
31 import java.awt.Panel;
32 import java.awt.Event;
33 import java.util.Vector;
34 import java.util.Hashtable;
35 import java.util.Enumeration;
36 import java.io.IOException;
37
38 import socket.TelnetIO;
39 import socket.StatusPeer;
40
41 import display.Terminal;
42 import display.TerminalHost;
43
44 import modules.Module;
45
46 /**
47  * A telnet implementation that supports different terminal emulations.
```

```
48   * @version $Id: telnet.java,v 1.19 1998/02/09 10:22:15 leo Exp $
49   * @author  Matthias L. Jugel, Marcus Meißner
50   */
51  public class telnet extends Applet implements Runnable, TerminalHost, StatusPeer
52  {
53    /**
54     * The telnet io methods.
55     * @see socket.TelnetIO
56     */
57    protected TelnetIO tio;
58
59    /**
60     * The terminal emulation (dynamically loaded).
61     * @see emulation
62     * @see display.Terminal
63     * @see display.TerminalHost
64     */
65    protected Terminal term;
66
67    /**
68     * The host address to connect to. This is retrieved from the PARAM tag
69     * "address".
70     */
71    protected String address;
72
73    /**
74     * The port number (default is 23). This can be specified as the PARAM tag
75     * "port".
76     */
77    protected int port = 23;
78
79    /**
80     * The proxy ip address. If this variable is set telnet will try to connect
81     * to this address and then send a string to tell the relay where the
82     * target host is.
83     * @see address
84     */
85    protected String proxy = null;
86    /**
87     * The proxy port number. This is the port where the relay is expected to
88     * listen for incoming connections.
89     * @see proxy
90     * @see port
91     */
92    protected int proxyport;
93
94    /**
```

```
 95    * Emulation type (default is vt320). This can be specified as the PARAM
 96    * tag "emulation".
 97    * @see term
 98    * @see display.Terminal
 99    * @see display.TerminalHost
100    */
101   protected String emulation = "vt320";
102
103   /**
104    * Dynamically loaded modules are stored here.
105    */
106   protected Vector modules = null;
107
108   // some state variables;
109   private boolean localecho = true;
110   private boolean connected = false;
111
112   private Thread t;
113   private Container parent;
114
115   /**
116    * This Hashtable contains information retrievable by getParameter() in case
117    * the program is run as an application and the AppletStub is missing.
118    */
119   public Hashtable params;
120
121   /**
122    * Retrieve the current version of the applet.
123    * @return String a string with the version information.
124    */
125   public String getAppletInfo()
126   {
127     String info = "The Java(tm) Telnet Applet\n$Id: telnet.java,v 1.19
        1998/02/09 10:22:15 leo Exp $\n";
128     info += "Terminal emulation: "+term.getTerminalType()+
129       " ["+term.toString()+"]\n";
130     info += "Terminal IO version: "+tio.toString()+"\n";
131     if(modules != null && modules.size() > 0) {
132       info += "Resident modules loaded: ("+modules.size()+")";
133       for(int i = 0; i < modules.size(); i++)
134         info += "    + "+(modules.elementAt(i)).toString()+"\n";
135     }
136
137     return info;
138   }
139
140   /**
141    * Retrieve parameter tag information. This includes the tag information from
```

```
142    * terminal and loaded modules.
143    * @return String an array of array of string with tag information
144    * @see java.applet.Applet#getParameterInfo
145    */
146   public String[][] getParameterInfo()
147   {
148     String pinfo[][];
149     String info[][] = {
150       {"address",  "String",   "IP address"},
151       {"port",     "Integer",  "Port number"},
152       {"proxy",    "String",   "IP address of relay"},
153       {"proxyport","Integer",  "Port number of relay"},
154       {"emulation","String",   "Emulation to be used (standard is vt320)"},
155     };
156     String tinfo[][] = (term != null ? term.getParameterInfo() : null);
157     if(tinfo != null) pinfo = new String[tinfo.length + 3][3];
158     else pinfo = new String[3][3];
159     System.arraycopy(info, 0, pinfo, 0, 3);
160     System.arraycopy(tinfo, 0, pinfo, 3, tinfo.length);
161     return pinfo;
162   }

163
164   /**
165    * We override the Applet method getParameter() to be able to handle
166    * parameters even as application.
167    * @param name The name of the queried parameter.
168    * @return the value of the parameter
169    * @see java.applet.Applet#getParameter
170    */
171   public String getParameter(String name)
172   {
173     if(params == null) return super.getParameter(name);
174     return (String)params.get(name);
175   }

176
177   /**
178    * The main function is called on startup of the application.
179    */
180   public static void main(String args[])
181   {
182     // an application has to create a new instance of itself.
183     telnet applet = new telnet();
184
185     // create params from command line arguments
186     applet.params = new Hashtable();
187     switch(args.length)
188     {
189     case 2: applet.params.put("port", args[1]);
```

```
190    case 1: applet.params.put("address", args[0]);
191      break;
192    default:
193      System.out.println("Usage: java telnet host [port]");
194      System.exit(0);
195    }
196    applet.params.put("VTscrollbar", "true");
197    applet.params.put("module#1", "ButtonBar");
198    applet.params.put("1#Button", "Exit|\\$exit()");
199    applet.params.put("2#Button", "Connect|\\$connect(\\@address@,\\@port@)");
200    applet.params.put("3#Input", "address#30|"
201        +(args.length > 0 ? args[0] : "localhost"));
202    applet.params.put("4#Input", "port#4|23");
203    applet.params.put("5#Button", "Disconnect|\\$disconnect()");
204
205    // we put the applet in its own frame
206    Frame frame = new Frame("The Java Telnet Application ["+args[0]+"]");
207    frame.setLayout(new BorderLayout());
208    frame.add("Center", applet);
209    frame.resize(380, 590);
210
211    applet.init();
212
213    frame.pack();
214    frame.show();
215
216    applet.start();
217  }
218
219  /**
220   * Initialize applet. This method reads the PARAM tags "address",
221   * "port" and "emulation". The emulation class is loaded dynamically.
222   * It also loads modules given as parameter "module#<nr>".
223   */
224  public void init()
225  {
226    String tmp;
227
228    // save the current parent for future use
229    parent = getParent();
230
231    // get the address we want to connect to
232    address = getParameter("address");
233
234    if((tmp = getParameter("port")) == null)
235      port = 23;
236    else
237      port = Integer.parseInt(tmp);
```

```
238
239     if((proxy = getParameter("proxy")) != null)
240       if((tmp = getParameter("proxyport")) == null)
241         proxyport = 31415;
242       else
243         proxyport = Integer.parseInt(tmp);
244
245     if((emulation = getParameter("emulation")) == null)
246       emulation = "vt320";
247
248     // load the terminal emulation
249     try {
250       term = (Terminal)Class.forName("display."+emulation).newInstance();
251       System.out.println("telnet: load terminal emulation: "+emulation);
252     } catch(Exception e) {
253       System.err.println("telnet: cannot load terminal emulation "+emulation);
254       e.printStackTrace();
255     }
256     setLayout(new BorderLayout());
257
258     // load modules, position is determined by the @<position> modifier
259     modules = new Vector();
260     int nr = 1;
261     while((tmp = getParameter("module#"+nr++)) != null) try {
262       Panel north = null, south = null, west = null, east = null;
263       String position = "North", initFile = null;
264
265       // try to get the initialization file name
266       if(tmp.indexOf(',') != -1) {
267         initFile = tmp.substring(tmp.indexOf(','+1));
268         tmp = tmp.substring(0, tmp.indexOf(','));
269         initFile = tmp.substring(tmp.indexOf(','+1));
270       }
271
272       // find the desired location
273       if(tmp.indexOf('@') != -1) {
274         position = tmp.substring(tmp.indexOf('@')+1);
275         tmp = tmp.substring(0, tmp.indexOf('@'));
276       }
277       Object obj = (Object)Class.forName("modules."+tmp).newInstance();
278
279       // probe for module (implementing modules.Module)
280       try {
281         ((Module)obj).setLoader(this);
282         modules.addElement((Module)obj);
283         System.out.println("telnet: module "+tmp+" detected");
284       } catch(ClassCastException e) {
285         System.out.println("telnet: warning: "+tmp+" may not be a "+
```

```
286                          "valid module");
287        }
288
289        // probe for visible component (java.awt.Component and descendants)
290        try {
291    Component component = (Component)obj;
292    if(position.equals("North")) {
293            if(north == null) { north = new Panel(); add("North", north); }
294            north.add(component);
295        } else if(position.equals("South")) {
296            if(south == null) { south = new Panel(); add("South", south); }
297            south.add(component);
298        } else if(position.equals("East")) {
299            if(east == null) { east = new Panel(); add("East", east); }
300            east.add(component);
301        } else if(position.equals("West")) {
302            if(west == null) { west = new Panel(); add("West", west); }
303            west.add(component);
304        }
305        System.err.println("telnet: module "+tmp+" is a visible component");
306      } catch(ClassCastException e) {}
307
308    } catch(Exception e) {
309      System.err.println("telnet: cannot load module "+tmp);
310      e.printStackTrace();
311    }
312    if(modules.isEmpty()) modules = null;
313    add("Center", term);
314 }
315
316 /**
317  * Upon start of the applet try to create a new connection.
318  */
319 public void start()
320 {
321    if(!connect(address, port) && params == null)
322      showStatus("telnet: connection to "+address+" "+port+" failed");
323 }
324
325 /**
326  * Disconnect when the applet is stopped.
327  */
328 public final void stop()
329 {
330    disconnect();
```

```
331    }
332
333    /**
334     * Try to read data from the sockets and put it on the terminal.
335     * This is done until the thread dies or an error occurs.
336     */
337    public void run()
338    {
339      while(t != null)
340        try {
341          String tmp = new String(tio.receive(), 0);
342
343          // cycle through the list of modules
344          if(modules != null) {
345            Enumeration modlist = modules.elements();
346            while(modlist.hasMoreElements()) {
347              Module m = (Module)modlist.nextElement();
348              String modified = m.receive(tmp);
349              // call the receive() method and if it returns null
350              // remove the module from the list
351              if(modified == null) modules.removeElement(m);
352              else tmp = modified;
353            }
354          }
355          // put the modified string to the terminal
356          term.putString(tmp);
357      } catch(IOException e) {
358        disconnect();
359      }
360    }
361
362    /**
363     * Connect to the specified host and port but don't break existing
364     * connections. Connects to the host and port specified in the tags.
365     * @return false if connection was unsuccessful
366     */
367    public boolean connect()
368    {
369      return connect(address, port);
370    }
371
372    /**
373     * Connect to the specified host and port but don't break existing
374     * connections. Uses the port specified in the tags or 23.
375     * @param host destination host address
376     */
377    public boolean connect(String host)
378    {
```

```
379      return connect(host, port);
380    }
381
382    /**
383     * Connect to the specified host and port but don't break existing
384     * connections.
385     * @param host destination host address
386     * @param prt destination hosts port
387     */
388    public boolean connect(String host, int prt)
389    {
390      address = host; port = prt;
391
392      if(address == null || address.length() == 0) return false;
393
394      // There should be no thread when we try to connect
395      if(t != null && connected) {
396        System.err.println("telnet: connect: existing connection preserved");
397        return false;
398      } else t = null;
399
400      try {
401        // In any case try to disconnect if tio is still active
402        // if there was no tio create a new one.
403        if(tio != null) try { tio.disconnect(); } catch(IOException e) {}
404        else (tio = new TelnetIO()).setPeer(this);
405
406        term.putString("Trying "+address+(port==23?"":" "+port)+" ...\n\r");
407        try {
408          // connect to to our destination at the given port
409          if(proxy != null) {
410            tio.connect(proxy, proxyport);
411            String str = "relay "+address+" "+port+"\n";
412            byte[] bytes = new byte[str.length()];
413            str.getBytes(0, str.length(), bytes, 0);
414            tio.send(bytes);
415          } else
416            tio.connect(address, port);
417          term.putString("Connected to "+address+".\n\r");
418          // initial conditions are connected and localecho
419          connected = true;
420          localecho = true;
421
422          // cycle through the list of modules and notify connection
423          if(modules != null) {
424            Enumeration modlist = modules.elements();
425            while(modlist.hasMoreElements())
426              // call the connect() method
```

```
427              ((Module)modlist.nextElement()).connect(address, port);
428          }
429        } catch(IOException e) {
430          term.putString("Failed to connect.\n\r");
431          // to be sure, we remove the TelnetIO instance
432          tio = null;
433          System.err.println("telnet: failed to connect to "+address+" "+port);
434          e.printStackTrace();
435          return false;
436        }
437        // if our connection was successful, create a new thread and start it
438        t = new Thread(this);
439        t.setPriority(Thread.MIN_PRIORITY);
440        t.start();
441      } catch(Exception e) {
442        // hmm, what happened?
443        System.err.println("telnet: an error occured:");
444        e.printStackTrace();
445        return false;
446      }
447      return true;
448    }
449
450    /**
451     * Disconnect from the remote host.
452     * @return false if there was a problem disconnecting.
453     */
454    public boolean disconnect()
455    {
456      if(tio == null) {
457        System.err.println("telnet: no connection");
458        return false;
459      }
460      try {
461        connected = false; t = null;
462        // cycle through the list of modules and notify connection
463        if(modules != null) {
464          Enumeration modlist = modules.elements();
465          while(modlist.hasMoreElements())
466            // call the disconnect() method
467            ((Module)modlist.nextElement()).disconnect();
468        }
469        term.putString("\n\rConnection closed.\n\r");
470        tio.disconnect();
471      } catch(Exception e) {
472        System.err.println("telnet: disconnection problem");
473        e.printStackTrace();
474        tio = null; t = null;
```

```
475        return false;
476      }
477      return true;
478  }
479
480  /**
481   * Send a String to the remote host. Implements display.TerminalHost
482   * @param s String to be sent
483   * @return true if we are connected
484   * @see display.TerminalHost
485   */
486  public boolean send(String str)
487  {
488    if(connected) try {
489      byte[] bytes = new byte[str.length()];
490      str.getBytes(0, str.length(), bytes, 0);
491      tio.send(bytes);
492      if(localecho) {
493        if ((str.length()==2) && (str.charAt(0)=='\r') && (str.charAt(1)==0))
494          term.putString("\r\n");
495        else
496          term.putString(str);
497      }
498    } catch(Exception e) {
499      System.err.println("telnet.send(): disconnected");
500      disconnect();
501      return false;
502    }
503    else return false;
504    return true;
505  }
506
507  /**
508   * Send a String to the remote Host.
509   * @param str String to be sent
510   * @return true if we are connected
511   * @see modules.BSXModule
512   */
513  public boolean writeToSocket(String str)
514    {
515      if (connected) try {
516    byte[] bytes = new byte[str.length()];
517    str.getBytes(0, str.length(), bytes, 0);
518    tio.send(bytes);
519      } catch(Exception e) {
520    System.err.println("telnet.send(): disconnected");
```

```
521     disconnect();
522     return false;
523       }
524      else return false;
525      return true;
526    }
527  /**
528   * Send a String to the users terminal
529   * @param str String to be displayed
530   * @return void
531   * @see modules.BSXModule
532   */
533  public void writeToUser(String str)
534  {
535    if (term!=null)
536       term.putString(str);
537  }
538
539  /**
540   * This method is called when telnet needs to be notified of status changes.
541   * @param status Vector of status information.
542   * @return an object of the information requested.
543   * @see socket.StatusPeer
544   */
545  public Object notifyStatus(Vector status)
546  {
547    String what = (String)status.elementAt(0);
548    if(what.equals("NAWS"))
549       return term.getSize();
550    if(what.equals("TTYPE"))
551       if(term.getTerminalType() == null)
552         return emulation;
553       else return term.getTerminalType();
554    if(what.equals("LOCALECHO"))
555       localecho = true;
556    if(what.equals("NOLOCALECHO"))
557       localecho = false;
558    return null;
559  }
560 }
```

ANNOTATIONS

The **telnet** class does its job with the help of several supporting classes. The first sign of these supporting classes is in the **import** statements in lines 25 through 44. After classes from the standard Java packages have been imported, lines 38 and 39 import the **TelnetIO** and **StatusPeer** classes from the socket package:

```
38 import socket.TelnetIO;
39 import socket.StatusPeer;
```

TelnetIO performs the TELNET protocol exchanges with the host. The **StatusPeer** class provides an interface (a method) that the **telnet** class implements. Other objects use this interface to inform the **telnet** class of any status changes.

PROGRAMMER'S NOTE *The package name for a class is specified with a **package** statement in the source file. For example, you'll see a **package socket;** statement in the **TelnetIO.java** file in the **ch03\Telnet\ socket** directory. Additionally, the package name also specifies the directory where the class file can be found. In other words, the **TelnetIO.class** file will be in the **socket** subdirectory of the current directory.*

Lines 41 and 42 import the **Terminal** and **TerminalHost** classes from the display package:

```
41 import display.Terminal;
42 import display.TerminalHost;
```

The **Terminal** class extends the **Panel** user interface component, and it represents the terminal window that you see in the **Telnet** applet. **Terminal** is an abstract class (it defines abstract methods that must be implemented by a subclass). **TerminalHost** defines an interface that any **Terminal** class must implement. The **Telnet** applet loads the actual terminal class, such as the **vt320** class, in its **init()** method. The **vt320** class is a subclass of **Terminal**; it implements the abstract methods that **Terminal** specifies.

Line 44 imports the **Module** class from the **modules** package:

```
44 import modules.Module;
```

The **Module** class is another abstract class representing the classes that can be loaded by the **telnet** class as it executes. The **ButtonBar** class is an example of a **Module** class that **telnet** typically loads.

Line 51 declares the **telnet** class as follows:

```
51 public class telnet extends Applet implements Runnable, TerminalHost,
       StatusPeer
```

As this declaration shows, the **telnet** class is a subclass of **Applet**, and it implements three interfaces:

◆ **Runnable** so that **telnet** can use a thread to read data from a socket connection and display it in the terminal window. The **telnet** class implements this interface by defining a **run()** method.

◆ **TerminalHost** so that the **Terminal** class (such as **vt320**) can send text to the host. To implement this interface, the **telnet** class provides a **send()** method.

◆ **StatusPeer** so that the **TelnetIO** class can notify the **telnet** class when any status changes occur. The **telnet** class defines the **notifyStatus()** method to implement the **StatusPeer** interface.

Although **telnet** and its supporting classes appear to be somewhat complex, the basic relationship of the classes is easy to understand. Figure 3-12 illustrates the relationship among various classes that make up the Telnet applet. The figure shows the **appWrapper** class that is used to load **Telnet** and run it. You'll learn about **appWrapper** in a later section. The **Telnet** applet uses a **TelnetIO** object to establish a socket connection to the host and conduct the TELNET protocol exchanges. The applet also uses a **Terminal** class (actually a subclass of **Terminal**) to emulate a terminal by displaying text in a panel and accepting keyboard input from the user.

The operation of the **Telnet** applet is also simple enough. Here are the basic steps that the applet goes through:

1. During initialization, the **Telnet** applet's **init()** method loads the **Terminal** class specified through the emulation parameter and any **Module** classes specified through the **module#N** (where $N = 1, 2, 3, \ldots$) parameters.

2. When the **Telnet** applet starts, its **start()** method calls the **connect()** method, which in turn uses a **TelnetIO** object name **tio** to establish a socket

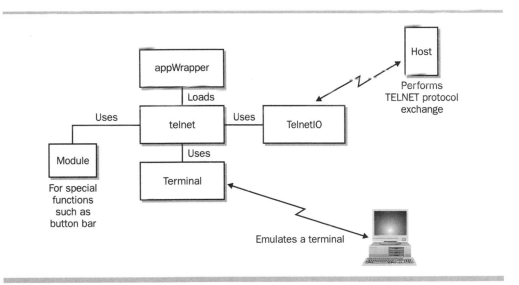

FIGURE 3-12. The relationships among classes that make up the **Telnet** applet.

connection to the host at a specified port number. The **connect()** method also creates a **Thread** and gets it going.

3. The thread calls the **Telnet** applet's **run()** method, which repeatedly receives characters from the **TelnetIO** object named **tio**. (The **TelnetIO** object reads these characters from the socket connection to the host.) The **run()** method sends the characters to the **Terminal** class and also to each of the **Module** classes loaded by **Telnet**.

4. When the user types any character on the keyboard, the **Terminal** class processes the keyboard event and sends the character to the host by calling the **Telnet** applet's **send()** method (which in turn calls the **send()** method of the **TelnetIO** class to perform that task).

5. When the **Telnet** applet's **stop()** method is called (by the Web browser or the **appWrapper**), the **stop()** method calls the **disconnect()** method to end the connection to the host and stop the thread.

The next few sections elaborate further on these steps.

INITIALIZATION OF TELNET   Lines 224 through 314 define the **init()** method that initializes the **Telnet** applet. Lines 232 through 246 retrieve the parameters from the HTML file by calling the **getParameter()** method. For example, lines 245 and 246 get the value of the **emulation** parameter, which specifies the name of the **Terminal** class to be used (this is the class that provides the terminal emulation):

```
245     if((emulation = getParameter("emulation")) == null)
246       emulation = "vt320";
```

If the HTML file does not have an **emulation** parameter, the **Telnet** applet uses the **vt320** class.

The next step, in lines 249 through 255, is to load the class specified by the **emulation** parameter. This section of code illustrates how to load a class in a Java program. Line 250, embedded in the **try** block (lines 249 through 252), performs the key step:

```
250       term = (Terminal)Class.forName("display."+emulation).newInstance();
```

This line calls the **Class.forName()** method with the class name as its argument. For example, when the **emulation** parameter is **vt320**, the class name is **display.vt320** (meaning that the **vt320** class is in the **display** package). **Class.forName()** returns the **Class** object for the specified class name. The same statement then calls the **newInstance()** method to create a new instance of that class. Finally, the returned object is cast as a **Terminal** (remember that all terminal emulation classes are subclasses of **Terminal**) and stored in the **term** variable.

After the **Terminal** object has been created, the rest of the **init()** method, in lines 259 through 311, gets the module names from the HTML file, creates the module instances, and positions the module's user interface components in specified positions in a **BorderLayout**. For example, note that the **module#1** parameter in the **index.test.html** file has the value **"ButtonBar@North"**. The **@North** part specifies that the **ButtonBar** should be positioned along the top edge of the applet.

Although modules are an important feature of the **Telnet** applet, they are incidental to the applet's core function—TELNET-based terminal emulation. Therefore, I am not going to describe modules in detail. A key feature of modules is the creation of a class instance at run time, but you have already seen this in line 250, which creates an instance of the terminal emulation class. Line 277 performs the same task: it creates an instance of a module class by using the **Class.forName()** method followed by the **newInstance()** method:

```
277     Object obj =     (Object)Class.forName("modules."+tmp).newInstance();
```

THE SOCKET I/O CLASS   The **Telnet** applet uses an instance of the **TelnetIO** class for the TELNET protocol exchanges with the host:

```
57   protected TelnetIO tio;
```

The **TelnetIO** class is part of the **socket** package, whose files are in the **ch03\ Telnet\socket** directory of the companion CD-ROM.

On line 321, the **Telnet** applet's **start()** method calls the **connect()** method. The **connect()** method, in lines 388 through 448, uses the **TelnetIO** instance **tio** to establish a socket connection to the host. Specifically, line 416 calls the **connect()** method of the **TelnetIO** class to establish a connection to the host (specified by the **address** argument):

```
416             tio.connect(address, port);
```

In the **TelnetIO.java** file in the CD-ROM's **ch03\Telnet\socket** directory, the **connect()** method is defined as follows:

```
/**
 * Connect to the remote host at the specified port.
 * @param address the symbolic host address
 * @param port the numeric port
 * @see #disconnect
 */
public void connect(String address, int port) throws IOException {
    if(debug > 0)
System.out.println("Telnet.connect("+address+","+port+")");
    socket = new Socket(address, port);
```

```
        is = new BufferedInputStream(socket.getInputStream());
        os = new BufferedOutputStream(socket.getOutputStream());
        neg_state = 0;
        receivedDX = new byte[256];
        sentDX = new byte[256];
        receivedWX = new byte[256];
        sentWX = new byte[256];
    }
```

The comment block has Javadoc-style comments. (These are comments that can be extracted by the **javadoc** utility and converted into HTML documentation about the class.) The **connect()** method creates a socket and initializes a number of variables used by the **TelnetIO** class. Note that the **neg_state** variable denotes the state variable that the **TelnetIO** class uses to keep track of its state during TELNET protocol negotiations with the host.

After the **connect()** method of the **TelnetIO** class has been called, lines 438 through 440 of the **Telnet** applet's **connect()** method create and start a thread:

```
438        t = new Thread(this);
439        t.setPriority(Thread.MIN_PRIORITY);
440        t.start();
```

Line 438 creates the thread **t** that is responsible for reading characters sent by the host over the socket connection. Line 439 sets the thread's priority to the lowest possible value.

The thread **t** executes the **Telnet** applet's **run()** method, shown in lines 337 through 360. The **run()** method consists of a **while** loop that repeatedly reads characters from the host, lets any installed modules process the characters, and displays the characters in the terminal window. Line 341 calls the **receive()** method of the **TelnetIO** class to get any characters sent by the host:

```
341        String tmp = new String(tio.receive(), 0);
```

In the **TelnetIO.java** file (in the CD-ROM's **ch03\Telnet\socket** directory), the **receive()** method is defined as follows:

```
    /**
     * Read data from the remote host. Blocks until data is available.
     * Returns an array of bytes.
     * @see #send
     */
    public byte[] receive() throws IOException {
        int count = is.available();
        byte buf[] = new byte[count];
```

```
count = is.read(buf);
if(count < 0) throw new IOException("Connection closed.");
if(debug > 1) System.out.println("TelnetIO.receive(): read
                              bytes: "+count);
buf = negotiate(buf, count);
return buf;
}
```

On the surface, this method seems simple. It first checks whether any data is available on the input stream named **is** (which reads from the socket connection to the host). Then the method calls **is.read()** to read the available data. However, after reading the data into the **buf[]** array, the **receive()** method calls the **negotiate()** method. This happens to be a crucial step because the **negotiate()** method handles any TELNET protocol commands embedded in the data sent by the host. TELNET protocol works by embedding special bytes within the stream of bytes that constitute normal text characters being sent back and forth between the terminal and the host. The **negotiate()** method goes through the received bytes and processes any characters that have special meanings in the TELNET protocol.

The **negotiate()** method is a private method of the **TelnetIO** class and is defined in the **TelnetIO.java** file in the **ch03\Telnet\socket** directory. According to RFC 854, "TELNET Protocol Specification," each TELNET command is 2 bytes long and starts with a special character known as an "Interpret as Command" (IAC) character, followed by the code for the command. If a command deals with the negotiation of some options (such as the character set or whether to echo characters), it has a third byte that denotes the option being negotiated. The **negotiate()** method defines a private variable **IAC** to denote the IAC character:

```
private final static byte IAC  = (byte)255;
```

As you can see, the IAC character is a byte with all eight bits set to 1, for an unsigned byte that amounts to a numerical value of 255.

The **negotiate()** method uses the **neg_state** variable to keep track of the specific stage of processing a TELNET command it has received from the host. It uses a number of **switch** statements to handle the variety of conditions that may occur. For example, initially the state is denoted by the variable **STATE_DATA**. When in that state, an IAC character causes the state to change to **STATE_IAC**, as follows:

```
switch (neg_state) {
case STATE_DATA:
    if (b==IAC) {
        neg_state = STATE_IAC;
    } else {
        nbuf[noffset++]=b;
    }
    break;
```

In this fragment of a **switch** statement, **b** denotes the current byte. When **b** is equal to **IAC**, the **neg_state** variable is set to **STATE_IAC**. Any other character is stored in the **nbuf[]** array that's eventually returned by the **negotiate()** method. Subsequently, that returned array of characters is returned by the **receive()** method back to line 341 of the **Telnet** applet's **run()** method.

Line 356 in the **Telnet** applet's **run()** method sends the received characters to the terminal window by calling the **putString()** method of the **Terminal** class:

```
356        term.putString(tmp);
```

Recall that **term** refers to the terminal emulation class (a subclass of **Terminal**), which is described in the next section.

THE TERMINAL EMULATION CLASS   The **Telnet** applet uses a terminal emulation object to display the terminal window and accept keyboard input from the user. You will find the terminal emulation classes in the **ch03\Telnet\display** directory of the CD-ROM. All terminal emulation classes must be subclasses of an abstract class named **Terminal**, which is defined in the **Terminal.java** file as follows:

```
package display;

import java.awt.Panel;
import java.awt.Dimension;

/**
 * Terminal is an abstract emulation class.
 * It contains a character display.
 *
 * @version $Id: Terminal.java,v 1.1.1.1 1997/03/05 13:35:16 leo Exp $
 * @author  Matthias L. Jugel, Marcus Meißner
 */
public abstract class Terminal extends Panel
{
    /**
     * Get the specific parameter info for the emulation.
     * @see java.applet.Applet
     */
    public abstract String[][] getParameterInfo();

    /**
     * Put a character on the screen. The method has to see if it is
     * a special character that needs special handling.
     * @param c the character
     * @see #putString
     */
```

```
public abstract void putChar(char c);

/**
 * Put a character on the screen. The method has to parse the string
 * may handle special characters.
 * @param s the string
 * @see #putString
 */
public abstract void putString(String s);

/**
 * Return the current size of the terminal in characters.
 */
public abstract Dimension getSize();

/**
 * Return actual terminal type identifier.
 */
public abstract String getTerminalType();
}
```

The **Terminal** class is a subclass of **Panel**, and it defines the following abstract methods:

- **String[][] getParameterInfo()** returns information about parameters of the terminal.

- **public abstract void putChar(char c)** displays a character on the terminal panel (and interprets any special characters meant for terminal control).

- **public abstract void putString(String s)** displays a string on the terminal after interpreting any special characters that are meant for terminal control (for example, a special sequence of characters might erase a line of text).

- **public abstract Dimension getSize()** returns the size of the terminal panel in terms of the number of characters that can fit in a line and the number of lines that fit vertically (for example, 80 characters wide and 24 lines tall).

- **public abstract String getTerminalType()** returns a string identifying the terminal type (for example, **"vt320"**).

The **vt320** class happens to be the only concrete terminal emulation class that comes with the **Telnet** applet. In the CD-ROM's **ch03\Telnet\display** directory, you'll find the **vt320.java** file that implements the **vt320** class. The **vt320** class relies on two other classes—**CharDisplay** and **SoftFont**; the source files for these classes are also in the **ch03\Telnet\display** directory of the CD-ROM.

The source file of the **vt320** class, **vt320.java**, is rather long (it would take more than 50 pages to show the listing in its entirety) and complicated because it takes lots of code to display all possible characters and handle any key that the user presses on the keyboard. The **CharDisplay** class, defined in the **CharDisplay.java** file, handles the character display. That class, in turn, uses the **SoftFont** class to draw the font bitmaps on the terminal panel.

Thankfully, you don't really need to know the details of the terminal emulation and display classes to understand how the **Telnet** applet works. However, you can always browse through the source files—**vt320.java**, **CharDisplay.java**, and **SoftFont.java**—if you want to learn the details of how characters are displayed on the terminal emulation panel.

THE APPWRAPPER CLASS   One remaining aspect of the **Telnet** applet is the **appWrapper** class that appears in the **CODE** attribute of the **<APPLET>** tag in the **index.test.html** file. Normally, you would expect the applet class to be the one specified in the **CODE** attribute. The **appWrapper** class happens to be a general-purpose class that loads and starts an applet just as the Web browser would have done. The added benefit of using **appWrapper** is that it allows you to display the applet in its own window, instead of being confined to the display area assigned to the applet inside a Web page. Note that the code that actually detaches the applet is in the **ButtonBar.java** file in the **ch03\Telnet\modules** directory of the CD-ROM.

In the **ch03\Telnet** directory of the CD-ROM you'll find the **appWrapper.java** file that implements the **appWrapper** class. The following listing is an excerpt from that file showing the **appWrapper** class declaration and a few key methods:

```java
public class appWrapper extends Applet implements AppletStub, Runnable
{
  Thread loader = null;
  String appletName = null;
  Applet applet = null;
  Button startButton = null;
  String startLabel, stopLabel, frameTitle;
  frame f;
  /**
   * Applet initialization. We load the class giving in parameter "applet"
   * and set the stub corresponding to ours. Thus we are able to give
   * it access to the parameters and any applet specific context.
   */
  public void init() {
    // get the applet parameter
    if((appletName = getParameter("applet")) == null) {
      showStatus("appWrapper: missing applet parameter, nothing loaded");
      System.err.println("appWrapper: missing applet parameter");
```

```
      return;
    }
    setLayout(new BorderLayout());
    // get the button and title parameters
    if((startLabel = getParameter("startButton")) == null)
      run();
    else {
      startButton = new Button(getParameter("startButton"));
      add("Center", startButton);
      if((stopLabel = getParameter("stopButton")) == null)
        stopLabel = "STOP!";
      if((frameTitle = getParameter("frameTitle")) == null)
        frameTitle = "The Java Telnet Applet";
    }
  }
  /**
   * Load the applet finally. When using a button this creates a new frame
   * to put the applet in.
   */
  public void run() {
    if(applet == null) try {
      applet = (Applet)Class.forName(getParameter("applet")).newInstance();
      applet.setStub(this);
    } catch(Exception e) {
      System.err.println("appWrapper: could not load "+appletName);
      e.printStackTrace();
      return;
    } else {
      System.err.println("appWrapper: applet already loaded");
      return;
    }
    if(startButton == null) {
      add("Center", applet);
      applet.init();
    } else {
      f = new frame(frameTitle);
      f.setLayout(new BorderLayout());
      f.add("Center", applet);
      applet.init();
      f.resize(applet.minimumSize());
      f.pack();
      f.show();
    }
```

```
    applet.start();
    if(startButton != null)
      startButton.setLabel(stopLabel);
    // stop loader thread
    while(loader != null) {
      if(f == null || !f.isVisible()) {
        startButton.setLabel(startLabel);
        loader.stop();
        loader = null;
      }
      try { loader.sleep(5000); }
      catch(InterruptedException e) {
        e.printStackTrace();
      }
    }
  }
}
// ... Other methods not shown...
}
```

The **appWrapper** class is itself an applet, and it implements the **AppletStub** and **Runnable** interfaces. The **AppletStub** interface allows **appWrapper** to load the applet; the **Runnable** interface is necessary because **appWrapper** uses a thread to run the applet.

In its **init()** method the **appWrapper** applet gets the **applet** parameter that specifies the name of the applet that **appWrapper** is expected to load and run. The **applet** parameter's value is the name of the applet's class file (without the **.class** extension). The **init()** method also looks for a parameter named **startButton** that specifies the label for a button to be displayed by **appWrapper**. When the user clicks on this button, **appWrapper** loads and runs the specified applet. Other optional parameters are **stopButton** for the label of a stop button and **frameTitle**, which specifies the text that **appWrapper** displays in the title bar of the window where the applet runs.

The **run()** method actually loads and runs the applet. The following line of code performs the loading:

```
    applet = (Applet)Class.forName(getParameter("applet")).newInstance();
```

The actual detaching of the applet is done by code in the **ButtonBar** module (see **ButtonBar.java** in the CD-ROM's **ch03\Telnet\modules** directory). Here is the code from **ButtonBar.java** that detaches the applet from the browser and displays it in its own window:

```
    System.out.println("ButtonBar: detaching applet...");
    toplevel = parent.getParent();
    frame top = new frame("The Java Telnet Applet");
```

```
Dimension s = parent.size();
top.reshape(0, 0, s.width, s.height);
top.setLayout(new BorderLayout());
top.add("Center", parent);
top.pack();
top.show();
```

When the user clicks on the button to reattach the applet to the browser window, the following code takes care of this task:

```
System.out.println("ButtonBar: reattaching applet...");
toplevel.setLayout(new BorderLayout());
toplevel.add("Center", parent);
toplevel.validate();
toplevel.layout();
toplevel = null;
```

Multimedia

Taken literally, multimedia means the use of multiple communications media such as sound (including music and sound effects), text, images, and video. Simple multimedia presentations include sound, text, and animated images. More sophisticated multimedia includes video—sequences of moving images with synchronized sound. Multimedia can also refer to other complex interactive presentations of information such as a three-dimensional view of an object which the user can grab and rotate using the mouse. Even interactive two-dimensional images can be thought of as examples of multimedia.

With the help of appropriate classes, Java applets can handle multimedia presentations. Typically, an applet with multimedia capability reads and processes a file containing the data for a specific medium—sound, image, or video. The processing involves displaying an image, playing digitized sound, or playing a video clip.

Java's Abstract Windowing Toolkit (AWT) includes classes that can display images and play sound. By using threads, an applet can rapidly display a sequence of images, thereby giving the appearance of animation. In Chapter 1, you saw examples of applets that perform animations. If you were to add some sound to those applets, they could be examples of simple multimedia applets. This chapter shows you some multimedia applets that demonstrate how to animate sprites (small images) over a background image, play sound files, play an MPEG video, and display three-dimensional models of objects. You will find the following applets in this chapter:

◆   **SndPlay**—An applet that plays a sound clip when a Web page is loaded

◆   **AnimateSprites**—An applet that animates small images (sprites) over a background and illustrates how to directly manipulate the pixels of an image

◆   **Viewer3D**—An applet that displays a 3-D wireframe model

◆   **MPEG_Play**—An applet that can play a video stored in the Motion Picture Experts Group (MPEG) format

Playing a Sound Clip When a Web Page Loads

Sound plays an important role in any multimedia application. In the digital world of computers, sound is usually stored as a bunch of numbers in a file. The numbers in these files are in binary form (meaning that you cannot open the file in a text editor and expect to read the numbers). Files containing information about sound or music are typically referred to as *sound files* or *audio files*. There are several different formats for sound files, such as the Microsoft Windows Wave format (**.wav** files), the Sun Audio format (**.au** files), the Audio Interchange File Format (AIFF), and the Musical Instrument Digital Interface (MIDI).

Typically, audio files contain digitized (also known as sampled) sound obtained by taking samples of continuously varying sound waveforms. Digitized waveform sound can represent any type of sound, no matter how complex. All you have to do is generate the sound waveform and take samples at a fast enough rate. A sound card that plugs into a PC can convert *analog* (continuously varying) sound waves into 8-bit or 16-bit numbers, sampling the wave at rates from 4 kHz to 44 kHz (44,000 times a second). Higher sampling rates and a higher number of bits (16 bits) provide better quality, but you need more disk space to store high-quality sound.

If your PC has a sound card, you can use a Windows program called **Sound Recorder** (**Start->Programs->Accessories->Multimedia->Sound Recorder** in Windows 95 and **Start->Programs->Accessories->Entertainment->Sound Recorder** in Windows 98) to create a **.wav** file with a microphone hooked up to the sound card. On a Sun workstation, you can use the **soundtool** to record audio in Sun **.au** files. Shareware programs are available that can convert audio files from **.wav** format to **.au** format.

Java 2

Before version 2, Java supported only the Sun audio format (**.au** files) through the **AudioClip** interface in the **Applet** class. This meant that you could play only Sun **.au** files, and you could do so only in an applet. Java 2 extends the **AudioClip** interface so that you can play audio from both applets and applications. Also, the audio clips can be in any of the following audio file formats:

- ◆ Audio Interchange File Format (AIFF)
- ◆ Musical Instrument Digital Interface (MIDI) Type 0 and Type 1
- ◆ Microsoft Windows Wave format (WAV)
- ◆ Sun Audio format (AU)
- ◆ Rich Music Format (RMF)

Java 2 plays audio files at a sample rate of 22 kHz in 16-bit stereo. If the computer's sound hardware doesn't support 16-bit data or stereo playback, Java 2 produces 8-bit mono audio.

This section presents **SndPlay**, a simple applet that plays a specified audio file as the applet is loaded.

Using SndPlay

The files for the **SndPlay** applet are in the **ch04\SndPlay** directory of the companion CD-ROM. The directory also includes a sample Sun AU-format audio file and an HTML file to try out the applet.

To see the **SndPlay** applet in action, open the **PlaySound.html** file (in the CD-ROM's **ch04\SndPlay** directory) from a Java-capable Web browser or from the **appletviewer** program that comes with the Java Development Kit (JDK). Make sure you try this on a computer with good sound capabilities (for a PC, this means one with a sound card and speakers). As the Web page loads, you will hear a welcome message. That's all the applet does—it plays the welcome message from the audio file whenever the applet starts; it does not display anything.

To see how the **SndPlay** applet can be used in a Web page, here is the complete
<applet> tag from the **PlaySound.html** file:

```
<APPLET CODE=SndPlay.class WIDTH=1 HEIGHT=1>
   <PARAM NAME=sound VALUE="Welcome.au">
This is a Java applet that plays a sound clip :-)
</APPLET>
```

As you can see, the **CODE** attribute of the **<APPLET>** tag specifies the name of the
class file. The **WIDTH** and **HEIGHT** attributes specify a display area 1 pixel wide
by 1 pixel tall because this applet does not display anything. The applet accepts a
single **<PARAM>** tag that specifies the name of an audio file. In this case, the audio
file, **Welcome.au**, happens to be in Sun AU format. If you run this applet in a
browser that supports Java 2, you can specify other files in other audio formats, such
as WAV, RMF, AIFF, or MIDI.

Understanding SndPlay

The following listing shows the **SndPlay.java** file that implements the **SndPlay**
applet. The subsequent sections explain the code.

SndPlay

```
1  //------------------------------------------------------------
2  // File: SndPlay.java
3  // Java applet that plays a sound clip when the Web page is
4  // loaded.
5  //------------------------------------------------------------
6  import java.applet.*;
7  /** SndPlay loads a audio clip and plays it.
8   *  The applet expects the name of the audio clip in a
9   *  parameter named sound.
10  *
11  *  @author Naba Barkakati
12  *  @version 1.0 Nov 17, 1998
13  */
14 public class SndPlay extends Applet
15 {
16     AudioClip sound = null;
17     /** Gets the name of sound clip and downloads the sound
18      */
19     public void init()
20     {
21         String soundName;
22         soundName = getParameter("sound");
23         if(soundName == null) return;
```

```
24            sound = getAudioClip(getCodeBase(), soundName);
25        }
26      /** Plays the sound clip
27       */
28      public void start()
29      {
30          if(sound != null) sound.play();
31      }
32      /** Stops playing the sound clip
33       */
34      public void stop()
35      {
36          if(sound != null) sound.stop();
37      }
38 }
```

ANNOTATIONS

The **SndPlay** applet is simple to understand because all it does is play an audio clip. Line 16 declares an **AudioClip** named **sound** that will hold the audio to be played by the applet. The **init()** method, shown in lines 19 through 25, loads the audio clip from the file specified through a parameter in the HTML file.

Lines 21 and 22 get the value of the **sound** parameter from the HTML file:

```
21        String soundName;
22        soundName = getParameter("sound");
```

If the **sound** parameter is not found, line 23 causes the **init()** method to return. When this happens, the applet does not play anything. Otherwise, line 24 calls the **getAudioClip()** method of the **Applet** class to load the audio file:

```
24        sound = getAudioClip(getCodeBase(), soundName);
```

The **getAudioClip()** method downloads the audio clip from the file indicated in **soundName** (specified through the HTML file). The file must be in the same location as the applet's class. Note that **getAudioClip()** returns only after the entire audio file has been loaded from the specified URL. This is in sharp contrast to the way the **getImage()** method works—**getImage()** returns immediately, without loading the image; the image is loaded only when the image is first used.

PROGRAMMER'S NOTE   *If you are downloading a large audio clip, create a separate thread and call the getAudioClip() method in that thread's run() method. This will allow users to begin interacting with the applet before the sound is fully loaded.*

Once the audio clip is loaded into the **AudioClip** named **sound**, you can call the **AudioClip** methods—**play()**, **loop()**, and **stop()**—to control the playback of the audio. As you might have guessed, **play()** plays the audio clip, **stop()** stops the playback, and **loop()** keeps playing the clip over and over again.

In this applet, the **start()** method, shown in lines 28 through 31, calls the **play()** method to start playing the audio clip. Specifically, line 30 performs this task:

```
30        if(sound != null) sound.play();
```

If the **AudioClip** named **sound** is not **null**, this line of code starts the playback by calling the **play()** method.

PROGRAMMER'S NOTE   *If you want to keep looping through the same audio clip, call the* **loop()** *method of the* **AudioClip** *instead of calling* **play()**.

When the applet stops (for example, when the user moves on to another Web page), line 36 of the **stop()** method calls **sound.stop()** to turn off the playback:

```
36        if(sound != null) sound.stop();
```

Java 2   You can also play an audio file by calling the **play()** method of the **Applet** class. The mechanism for playing sounds from an applet is unchanged in Java 2. You still call the **getAudioClip()** method to load an audio file and control the playback through the **AudioClip**'s **play()**, **loop()**, and **stop()** methods. The only difference is that in Java 2 you can load audio clips in several other formats, such as WAV, MIDI, RMF, and AIFF, besides the Sun AU format.

Animating Sprites over a Background

Animation is the process of bringing an image to life. We usually associate animation with movement of images. Some good examples of animation are the popular animated movies pioneered by the Walt Disney Company. The Disney movies use a traditional approach to animation, in which each frame of the movie has to be prepared individually. This style of animation is commonly known as *frame animation* or *cel animation.* (Cel refers to the sheets of celluloid on which the images are drawn). Cel animation is a discipline unto itself, and I will not cover the subject in this book. Instead, this section focuses on a technique called *sprite animation* that lets you move one or more overlapping images (called sprites) over a background without any flickering.

The term *sprite* refers to an image, usually a small one. Sprites are used in interactive video games to represent characters and fixtures that are part of the game. When the player moves an input device such as a joystick, a trackball, or a mouse, the sprite moves over the background. Essentially, the player plays the video game by manipulating the sprites. Video game machines usually have graphics hardware with built-in support for sprites. In a typical desktop computer, the display hardware does not support sprites, so you have to rely on software techniques.

An obvious way to move an image is to erase it at the old location and redraw it at the new location. In a Java program, you can use the **drawImage()** method of the **Graphics** class to accomplish this. If you erase and redraw repeatedly, the image will appear to move across the screen. However, a major drawback of this approach is that the display flickers as the image is erased and redrawn.

The reason for the screen flicker with erase-and-redraw animation is that all screen-drawing operations are visible. As an image is erased, you see it vanish from the screen. Then the image appears again at a new location. You can avoid the flicker by preparing the images off-screen and redrawing the updated screen quickly. Java supports drawing on an off-screen image, which can serve as an ideal canvas for preparing the display screen. Then a single call to **drawImage()** can quickly transfer the updated images to the display screen. Of course, you have to attend to myriad details to prepare the image properly in the off-screen image, but, as you will soon see, this basic idea works remarkably well for image animation in Java applets.

This section presents the **AnimateSprites** applet, which demonstrates how to use an off-screen image to animate a number of overlapping sprites across a background image. You will learn how to manipulate the pixels of the images and combine them to make the sprites move smoothly over the background.

Using AnimateSprites

To see how well sprite animation works, all you need to do is use a Java-capable Web browser to open the **SprAnim.html** file from the ch04**SprAnim** directory of this book's companion CD-ROM. That directory contains all of the sprite and background images needed to demonstrate the **AnimateSprites** applet.

After the Web browser loads the **SprAnim.html** file, you will see a number of sprites, including one with a text message, moving on a complex background image. Figure 4-1 shows a sample image.

To understand how the **AnimateSprites** applet is used in the **SprAnim.html** file, let's look at the **<applet>** tag from that file:

```
<APPLET CODE="AnimateSprites.class" WIDTH=640 HEIGHT=480>
   <PARAM NAME=background VALUE="Animbg.gif">
   <PARAM NAME=delay value=60>
   <PARAM NAME=sprite1 VALUE="Strange.gif,Strangem.gif,100,100,1,1,1">
   <PARAM NAME=sprite2 VALUE="Car.gif,Carm.gif,10,200,-1,-1,2">
   <PARAM NAME=sprite3 VALUE="Ring.gif,Ringm.gif,200,10,-3,2,5">
   <PARAM NAME=sprite4 VALUE="Face1.gif,Face1m.gif,10,10,3,2,4">
   <PARAM NAME=sprite5 VALUE="Msg.gif,Msgm.gif,100,50,1,0,99">
</APPLET>
```

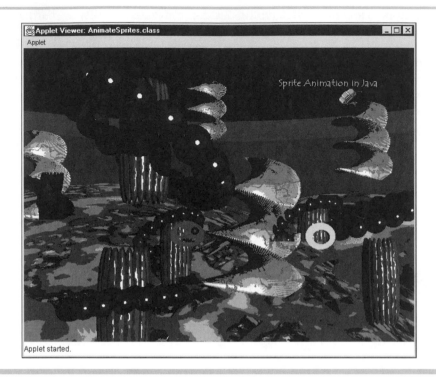

FIGURE 4-1. Sprites being animated over a complex background image.

The first line shows the **CODE** attribute, which specifies the name of the applet class file, as well as the **WIDTH** and **HEIGHT** attributes, which specify a display area 640 pixels wide by 480 pixels tall. The dimensions you specify should match the size of the background image.

As this **<applet>** tag shows, the **AnimateSprites** applet accepts several parameters through the **<param>** tags. The **background** parameter specifies the name of the background image (in this case, **Animbg.gif**). Through the **delay** parameter, you can set the number of milliseconds to delay after displaying each frame of the animation (how many milliseconds to wait before moving the sprites). The information about the sprites is provided through the parameters named **sprite1**, **sprite2**, **sprite3**, and so on. The applet's code keeps reading these parameters one after another until it does not find any more sprite parameters. To understand the format of the sprite parameter's value, consider **sprite3**, which is specified as follows:

```
<PARAM NAME=sprite3 VALUE="Ring.gif,Ringm.gif,200,10,-3,2,5">
```

The value is a set of comma-separated items without any embedded spaces. Here is what these items mean:

- **Ring.gif** is the name of the sprite's image file.
- **Ringm.gif** is the name of the file containing the sprite's mask (this will be explained later).
- **200,10** denote the x and y coordinates of the sprite's initial position.
- **-3,2** denote the sprite's velocity along the x and y axes (in this case the sprite moves 3 units backward on the x axis and 2 units forward on the y axis in each animation step).
- **5** is the sprite's display priority (when sprites overlap one another, the ones with a higher priority are drawn on top of sprites with a lower priority).

This should give you an idea of how to use the **AnimateSprites** applet with your own set of images. You have to read the description of the code to understand what it means to provide a mask for a sprite.

Understanding AnimateSprites

The listing in this section shows the **AnimateSprites.java** file containing the applet's source code. In the "Annotations" section, I first explain the overall design of the applet and describe how it uses **SpriteAnimation** and **Sprite** objects. I then provide the complete source code for the **Sprite** and **SpriteAnimation** classes. These two key classes provide all of the functionality needed to implement sprite animation using off-screen manipulation of pixels. When discussing the source code of the **SpriteAnimation** class, I also explain the basic principles behind the sprite animation. After you've gone through the descriptions of these classes, you should be able to use them in your own Java applets or applications.

When you use the **SpriteAnimation** class, you should consult the **AnimateSprites.java** file because it shows how to use the **SpriteAnimation** class to animate sprites over a background.

```
1  //-------------------------------------------------------------
2  // File: AnimateSprites.java
3  // An applet that demonstrates how to use the SpriteAnimation
4  // class to animate sprites (small images) over a background.
5  //-------------------------------------------------------------
6  import java.applet.*;
7  import java.awt.*;
8  import java.net.*;
```

nimateSprites

```
 9 import java.util.*;
10 /** Animates sprites on a background image.
11  *  Uses the SpriteAnimation and Sprite classes.
12  *  <p>
13  *  Parameters:
14  *  <ul>
15  *  <li> delay - milliseconds between animation steps
16  *  <li> background - name of background image file
17  *  <li> spriteN, where N = 1, 2, 3, ... are the sprites,
18  *        each of the form: "image,mask,x,y,xv,yv,prio" where
19  *        image and mask are names of image and mask files,
20  *        x and y are numbers denoting initial position of sprite,
21  *        xv, yv are the x- and y-velocities of the sprite,
22  *        prio is a number denoting the sprite's priority.
23  *  </ul>
24  *
25  *  @author Naba Barkakati
26  *  @version 1.0 April 1998
27  */
28 public class AnimateSprites extends Applet implements Runnable
29 {
30     class SpriteInfo
31     {
32         String image_source;
33         String mask_source;
34         int xpos, ypos;
35         int xvel, yvel;
36         int priority;
37         Sprite sprite;
38         /** Stores information about a sprite
39          */
40         SpriteInfo(String imagefname, String maskfname,
41                    int x, int y, int xv, int yv, int p)
42         {
43             image_source = imagefname;
44             mask_source = maskfname;
45             xpos = x;
46             ypos = y;
47             xvel = xv;
48             yvel = yv;
49             sprite = null;
50         }
```

```
51    }
52    Vector sprite_array = new Vector(16);
53    SpriteAnimation anim = null;
54    int  width, height;
55    Thread t_anim = null;
56    int delay = 50; // 50 milliseconds between steps
57    /** Initializes the applet by creating the SpriteAnimation
58     */
59    public void init()
60    {
61        showStatus("Loading background image...");
62        // Read parameters from HTML file
63        // First the background image
64        String param;
65        Image img = null;
66        param = getParameter("background");
67        if(param != null)
68        {
69            img = getImage(getCodeBase(), param);
70            MediaTracker mt = new MediaTracker(this);
71            mt.addImage(img, 0);
72            try
73            {
74                mt.waitForID(0);
75            }
76            catch(InterruptedException e) {}
77            width = img.getWidth(this);
78            height = img.getHeight(this);
79        }
80        else
81        {
82            // Read width and height from HTML file
83            param = getParameter("width");
84            if(param != null)
85                width = Integer.valueOf(param).intValue();
86            else
87                width = 400;
88            param = getParameter("height");
89            if(param != null)
90                height = Integer.valueOf(param).intValue();
91            else
92                height = 300;
```

```java
93          }
94          anim = new SpriteAnimation(width, height, img);
95          if((param = getParameter("delay")) != null)
96              delay = Integer.valueOf(param).intValue();
97          // Read the sprite information and add sprites
98          showStatus("Loading sprites ...");
99          int n=0;
100         while(true)
101         {
102             n++;
103             param = getParameter("sprite"+n);
104             if(param == null) break;
105             StringTokenizer st = new StringTokenizer(param, ",");
106             String nimage = st.nextToken();
107             String nmask = st.nextToken();
108             int x=0, y=0, xv=0, yv=0, p=0;
109             if(st.hasMoreTokens())
110             {
111                 String s = st.nextToken();
112                 x = Integer.valueOf(s).intValue();
113             }
114             if(st.hasMoreTokens())
115             {
116                 String s = st.nextToken();
117                 y = Integer.valueOf(s).intValue();
118             }
119             if(st.hasMoreTokens())
120             {
121                 String s = st.nextToken();
122                 xv = Integer.valueOf(s).intValue();
123             }
124             if(st.hasMoreTokens())
125             {
126                 String s = st.nextToken();
127                 yv = Integer.valueOf(s).intValue();
128             }
129             if(st.hasMoreTokens())
130             {
131                 String s = st.nextToken();
132                 p = Integer.valueOf(s).intValue();
133             }
134             SpriteInfo si = new SpriteInfo(nimage, nmask, x, y,
```

```
135                                            xv, yv, p);
136            sprite_array.addElement(si);
137            Image image = getImage(getCodeBase(), nimage);
138            Image mask = getImage(getCodeBase(), nmask);
139            MediaTracker mt = new MediaTracker(this);
140            mt.addImage(image, n);
141            mt.addImage(mask, 10*n);
142            try
143            {
144                mt.waitForID(n);
145                mt.waitForID(10*n);
146            }
147            catch(InterruptedException e){}
148            int w = image.getWidth(this);
149            int h = image.getHeight(this);
150            si.sprite = new Sprite(image, mask, w, h, p);
151            si.sprite.newpos(x, y);
152            anim.add(si.sprite);
153        }
154        add(anim);
155    }
156    /** Starts the animation by creating the animation thread
157     */
158    public void start()
159    {
160        if (t_anim == null)
161        {
162            t_anim = new Thread(this);
163            t_anim.start();
164        }
165    }
166    /** Stops the animation thread
167     */
168    public void stop()
169    {
170        if (t_anim != null)
171        {
172            t_anim.stop();
173            t_anim = null;
174        }
175
176    }
```

```
177    /** Body of the animation thread
178     */
179    public void run()
180    {
181        while(t_anim != null)
182        {
183            for(int i=0; i < sprite_array.size(); i++)
184            {
185                SpriteInfo si =
186                        (SpriteInfo)sprite_array.elementAt(i);
187                if(si.sprite.xpos() <= 0 ||
188                    si.sprite.xpos() >= width)
189                            si.xvel = -si.xvel;
190                if(si.sprite.ypos() <= 0 ||
191                    si.sprite.ypos() >= height)
192                            si.yvel = -si.yvel;
193                // Move the sprites
194                si.sprite.move(si.xvel, si.yvel);
195            }
196            // Display the sprites
197            Graphics g = getGraphics();
198            anim.animate(g, 0, 0);
199            // Sleep for specified amount of delay
200            try { Thread.sleep(delay);}
201            catch(InterruptedException e){}
202        }
203    }
204    /** Paints everything by setting the refresh variable to true
205     */
206    public void paint(Graphics g)
207    {
208        anim.refresh = true;
209    }
210    /** Returns information about the AnimateSprites applet
211     */
212    public String getAppletInfo()
213    {
214        return "AnimateSprites, Copyright (C) 1998 Naba Barkakati";
215
216    }
217    /** Returns information about the parameters
218     */
```

```
219    public String[][] getParameterInfo()
220    {
221        String[][] info =
222        {
223           //Parameter       Type        Description
224           {"delay",         "Integer",  "milliseconds between frames"},
225           {"background",    "String",   "name of background image"},
226           {"sprite1",       "String",   "image1,mask1,x,y,xv,yv,prio"},
227           {"sprite2",       "String",   "image2,mask2,x,y,xv,yv,prio"},
228           {"spriteN",       "String",   "imageN,maskN,x,y,xv,yv,prio"}
229        };
230        return info;
231    }
232 }
```

ANNOTATIONS

AnimateSprites makes use of the **Sprite** and **SpriteAnimation** classes to animate a number of sprites on a background image. Like any Java applet, **AnimateSprites** is a subclass of **Applet**. It also uses a thread to move the sprites at periodic intervals. For this, the **AnimateSprites** class implements the **Runnable** interface, which means that it defines the **run()** method. Line 28 declares the class as follows:

```
28 public class AnimateSprites extends Applet implements Runnable
```

To hold the information needed to create the **Sprite** objects, **AnimateSprites** uses the **SpriteInfo** class, defined in lines 30 through 51. This class essentially represents all of the data, such as the image, mask, position, velocity, and priority, needed to create a single **Sprite**. (See the section "The Sprite Class" for more information about **Sprite**.)

Line 52 defines a **Vector** named **sprite_array** that will hold **SpriteInfo** objects:

```
52    Vector sprite_array = new Vector(16);
```

Line 53 defines a **SpriteAnimation** object named **anim** that will take care of displaying the sprites over a background:

```
53    SpriteAnimation anim = null;
```

This **SpriteAnimation** object is initialized later in the **init()** method. The **init()** method also loads all of the images—for the background as well as the sprites—and creates the **Sprite** objects and adds them to the **SpriteAnimation** object named **anim**.

ANIMATESPRITES INITIALIZATION   The **init()** method, shown in lines 59 through 155, starts by loading the background image. Lines 64 through 66 get the name of the background image file from the HTML file. Lines 67 through 79 then load the background image. Specifically, lines 69 through 71 call the **getImage()** method of the **Applet** class to load the image and add the image to a **MediaTracker** object:

```
69              img = getImage(getCodeBase(), param);
70              MediaTracker mt = new MediaTracker(this);
71              mt.addImage(img, 0);
```

The **getImage()** method returns immediately without actually loading the image (the image is loaded only when it's first used). By adding the image to a **MediaTracker** (line 71), you force the loading of the image. However, this may take a bit of time (especially if it is large). To ensure that the image is fully loaded before attempting to get its width and height, lines 72 through 76 use a **try** and **catch** pair:

```
72              try
73              {
74                  mt.waitForID(0);
75              }
76              catch(InterruptedException e) {}
```

Notice that the **waitForID()** method uses an image ID as argument. In this case the argument is zero, the same value used when the background image was added to the **MediaTracker** on line 74.

If the background image is not specified, lines 80 through 93 attempt to read the width and height of the background from the HTML file.

After the background has loaded, line 94 creates the **SpriteAnimation** object **anim** as follows:

```
94          anim = new SpriteAnimation(width, height, img);
```

Lines 95 and 96 read the **delay** parameter, which specifies how many milliseconds to wait between successive steps of the animation. Then a **while** loop, shown in lines 100 through 153, reads the information about sprites, creates the sprites, and adds them to the **SpriteAnimation**. First, line 103 gets the value of the nth sprite parameter:

```
103             param = getParameter("sprite"+n);
104             if(param == null) break;
```

Note that the parameter's name is constructed by appending a number to the **String "sprite"**. For example, if **n** is 3, line 103 gets the value of the parameter named **"sprite3"**. Line 104 ends the **while** loop if the parameter is not found in the HTML file.

After the value has been obtained, lines 105 through 133 extract the comma-separated items that specify the sprite's image, mask, position, velocity, and priority. Lines 134 and 135 store these values in a **SpriteInfo** object:

```
134        SpriteInfo si = new SpriteInfo(nimage, nmask, x, y,
135                                        xv, yv, p);
```

Line 136 stores that **SpriteInfo** object in the **Vector** named **sprite_array**:

```
136        sprite_array.addElement(si);
```

Next, lines 137 through 147 load the image and mask of the sprite by using a **MediaTracker**, just as the background image was loaded earlier. Lines 150 through 152 create the **Sprite** and add it to the **SpriteAnimation** named **anim**:

```
150        si.sprite = new Sprite(image, mask, w, h, p);
151        si.sprite.newpos(x, y);
152        anim.add(si.sprite);
```

SpriteAnimation is a subclass of **Canvas**, a Java AWT component. Line 154 completes the initialization step by adding the **SpriteAnimation anim** to the applet's display area:

```
154        add(anim);
```

THE ANIMATION THREAD   AnimateSprites uses a thread, t_anim, to move the sprites every so often. The **start()** method, in lines 158 through 165, creates the **t_anim** thread and starts it by calling the thread's **start()** method. When the applet has to stop, the **stop()** method (lines 168 through 176) calls the thread's **stop()** method to stop the animation.

As long as the **t_anim** thread runs, it executes the code in the **run()** method, shown in lines 179 through 203. The **while** loop in lines 181 through 202 repeatedly moves the sprites and animates them. In each iteration through the **while** loop, lines 183 through 195 go through all of the sprites and move each one by calling the **move()** method of the **Sprite** class. Lines 197 and 198 then perform the animation by calling the **animate()** method of the **SpriteAnimation** class:

```
197        Graphics g = getGraphics();
198        anim.animate(g, 0, 0);
```

After each animation step, lines 200 and 201 sleep for a specified delay interval:

```
200        try { Thread.sleep(delay);}
201        catch(InterruptedException e){}
```

You can set this delay interval through the **delay** parameter in the HTML file. Try experimenting with different intervals to see how the animation appears on your system.

THE SPRITE CLASS   The **AnimateSprites** applet uses the **Sprite** class to model a sprite and the **SpriteAnimation** class to maintain the sprites and the background image. Because **Sprite** is a public class, it has to be defined in its own file, named **Sprite.java**. The following listing shows the **Sprite.java** file (shown with line numbers so that I can refer to the lines as I describe the code).

```
1  //--------------------------------------------------------------
2  // File: Sprite.java
3  // Defines the abstract class Sprite that represents a small
4  // image. Each sprite has an image and a mask (that shows the
5  // actual shape of the sprite in black over a white background).
6  //--------------------------------------------------------------
7  import java.applet.*;
8  import java.awt.*;
9  import java.awt.image.*;
10 /** Represents a sprite -- a small image.
11  *
12  *   @author Naba Barkakati
13  *   @version 1.0 April 1998
14  */
15 public class Sprite extends Object
16 {
17     Image      image;    // The sprite's image
18     Image      mask;     // The mask: a silhouette of image
19     int        w, h;     // Width and height of sprite
20     int[]      ipix;
21     int[]      mpix;
22     int        disp_priority; // Sprite's priority (higher priority
23                            // sprites lie over lower priority ones)
24     Point      current;
25     Point      last;
26     int        xdelta;
27     int        ydelta;
28     int        status;
29     Sprite     next_sprite;
30     Sprite     previous_sprite;
31     boolean    sprite_active;
32     boolean    sprite_update;
```

```
33      boolean  sprite_overlap;
34      boolean  sprite_erase;
35      public Sprite()
36      {
37          image = null;
38          mask = null;
39          disp_priority = 1;
40          sprite_active = false;
41          sprite_update = false;
42          sprite_overlap = false;
43          sprite_erase = false;
44          current = new Point(0,0);
45          last = new Point(0,0);
46          next_sprite = null;
47          previous_sprite = null;
48          ipix = null;
49          mpix = null;
50      }
51      /** Constructs a Sprite with a given image, a mask,
52       *  and the display priority
53       */
54      public Sprite(Image img, Image msk, int w, int h, int priority)
55      {
56          // Initialize class variables
57          image = img;
58          mask = msk;
59          this.w = w;
60          this.h = h;
61          disp_priority = priority;
62          current = new Point(0,0);
63          last = new Point(0,0);
64          sprite_active = true;
65          sprite_update = true;
66          next_sprite = null;
67          previous_sprite = null;
68          // Get the pixels for the image
69          ipix = new int[w*h];
70          PixelGrabber pg = new PixelGrabber(image, 0, 0,
71                              w, h, ipix, 0, w);
72          try
73          {
74              pg.grabPixels();
```

```
 75          }
 76      catch(InterruptedException e){ipix = null;}
 77      // Get the pixels for the mask
 78      mpix = new int[w*h];
 79      pg = new PixelGrabber(mask, 0, 0,
 80                              w, h, mpix, 0, w);
 81      try
 82      {
 83          pg.grabPixels();
 84      }
 85      catch(InterruptedException e){mpix = null;}
 86  }
 87  public Point curpos() { return current;}
 88  public Point lastpos() { return last;}
 89  public int xpos() { return current.x;}
 90  public int ypos() { return current.y;}
 91  public int priority() { return disp_priority;}
 92  public void priority(int dp) { disp_priority = dp; }
 93  public int width() { return w;}
 94  public int height() { return h;}
 95  public void width(int w) { this.w = w;}
 96  public void height(int h) { this.h = h;}
 97  public void xpos(int x)
 98  {
 99      last.x = current.x;
100      current.x = x;
101  }
102  public void ypos(int y)
103  {
104      last.y = current.y;
105      current.y = y;
106  }
107  public void newpos(int x, int y)
108  {
109      last.x = current.x;
110      last.y = current.y;
111      current.x = x;
112      current.y = y;
113      reset_moves();
114  }
115  public int lastxpos() { return last.x;}
116  public int lastypos() { return last.y;}
```

```
117    public void reset_moves() { xdelta = ydelta = 0;}
118    public int xmove() { return xdelta;}
119    public int ymove() { return ydelta;}
120    public void move(int x, int y)
121    {
122        xdelta += x;
123        ydelta += y;
124        sprite_update = true;
125    }
126    public boolean is_active() { return sprite_active;}
127    public boolean needs_update() { return sprite_update;}
128    public boolean is_overlapping() { return sprite_overlap;}
129    public boolean to_be_erased() { return sprite_erase;}
130    public void active()
131    {
132        sprite_active = true;
133        sprite_update = true;
134    }
135    public void update() { sprite_update = true;}
136    public void erase() { sprite_erase = true;}
137    public void overlaps(){ sprite_overlap = true;}
138    public void update_done(){ sprite_update = false;}
139    public void unerase() { sprite_erase = false;}
140    public void inactive() { sprite_active = false;}
141    public void no_overlap() { sprite_overlap = false;}
142    public Image sprite_image() { return image;}
143    public Image sprite_mask() { return mask;}
144    public int[] image_pixels(){ return ipix;}
145    public int[] mask_pixels() { return mpix;}
146    public void next(Sprite s) { next_sprite = s;}
147    public Sprite next() { return next_sprite;}
148    public void previous(Sprite s) { previous_sprite = s;}
149    public Sprite previous() { return previous_sprite;}
150 }
```

A **Sprite** has two **Image** objects, shown in lines 17 and 18:

◆ The sprite's image on a black background (line 17).

◆ A black silhouette of the sprite's image on a white background (line 18). This is known as the mask.

As you can see in the **animate()** method of the **SpriteAnimation** class, both the image and the mask are needed to allow the sprite's outline to be drawn without affecting the background. In fact, the **SpriteAnimation** class needs the actual pixels from the image and mask of a sprite. These are stored in integer arrays **ipix** and **mpix** (lines 20 and 21). In addition to the image and the mask, a sprite has an x position, a y position, and several other variables to keep track of its motion on the background.

A sprite also has a *display priority* associated with it. The display priority is an integer, stored in the variable **disp_priority** (line 22), that determines the order in which overlapping sprites are drawn—a sprite with a higher priority is drawn over one with a lower priority.

To make it easy for the **SpriteAnimation** class to store many **Sprite** objects, each **Sprite** also has **next_sprite** and **previous_sprite** variables (lines 29 and 30) that can be used to create doubly linked lists of **Sprite** objects.

Lines 54 through 86 create a sprite with a given image, mask, width, height, and display priority. A key step in the **Sprite** initialization is to get the pixels of the image and the mask into the **ipix** and **mpix** arrays. For example, lines 69 through 76 load the pixels of the image into the **ipix** array:

```
69      ipix = new int[w*h];
70      PixelGrabber pg = new PixelGrabber(image, 0, 0,
71                              w, h, ipix, 0, w);
72      try
73      {
74          pg.grabPixels();
75      }
76      catch(InterruptedException e){ipix = null;}
```

Similarly, lines 78 through 85 load the pixels of the mask into the **mpix** array.

The **Sprite** class includes a number of methods to perform various operations on a **Sprite**. For example, there are a number of **boolean** variables, such as **sprite_update** and **sprite_overlap**, to indicate whether a sprite needs updating or is overlapping another **Sprite**. The **Sprite** class includes methods such as **update()**, **overlap()**, **needs_update()**, and **is_overlapping()** to set or retrieve these **boolean** variables.

Sprite also includes methods such as **move()** and **newpos()** to move the sprite and other methods such as **xpos()** and **ypos()** to retrieve the position of the sprite.

THE SPRITEANIMATION CLASS   The **SpriteAnimation** class, defined in the file **SpriteAnimation.java**, manages a number of sprites and a background and also provides the capability to animate the sprites. The following listing shows the **SpriteAnimation.java** file. After the listing, you will find an explanation of how sprites are animated and how the key methods in the **SpriteAnimation** class perform their tasks. In the following discussion, line numbers refer to the line numbers in the listing of **SpriteAnimation.java**.

```
1  //-----------------------------------------------------------------
2  // File: SpriteAnimation.java
3  // A class that can display sprites (small images) over
4  // a background image. Each sprite is drawn by AND-ing the
5  // pixels of the mask, followed by an OR operation with the
6  // pixels of the sprite's image.
7  //-----------------------------------------------------------------
8  import java.applet.*;
9  import java.awt.*;
10 import java.awt.image.*;
11 /** Animates sprites on a background image displayed on a Canvas
12  *
13  *  @author Naba Barkakati
14  *  @version 1.0 April 1998
15  */
16 public class SpriteAnimation extends Canvas
17 {
18     Sprite          first_sprite;
19     Sprite          last_sprite;
20     int             numsprites;
21     boolean         refresh;
22     Image           background; // The background image
23     Image           scratch;    // Images prepared here before
24                                 // copying to window
25     int             top, left;  // Top left corner and
26     int             width;      // dimensions of background
27     int             height;     // being displayed
28     int             ws, hs;     // Dimensions of scratch image
29     int[]           pix_scratch;
30     int[]           pix_bg;
31     /** Constructs a SpriteAnimation with a specified background
32      *  @param w Width of canvas
33      *  @param h Height of canvas
34      */
35     SpriteAnimation(int w, int h, Image bg)
36     {
37         super();
38         // Set up coordinates of rectangle to be displayed
39         top = left = 0;
40         width = w;
41         height = h;
42         ws = w;
```

```
43          hs = h;
44          refresh = true;
45          // Initialize all other variables
46          numsprites = 0;
47          background = bg;
48          if(background == null)
49          {
50              background = createImage(width, height);
51              Graphics gc_bg = background.getGraphics();
52              gc_bg.setColor(Color.white);
53              gc_bg.fillRect(0, 0, width, height);
54          }
55          // Get the pixels from the background image
56          pix_bg = new int[width*height];
57          PixelGrabber pg = new PixelGrabber(background, 0, 0,
58                              width, height, pix_bg, 0, width);
59          try
60          {
61              pg.grabPixels();
62          }
63          catch(InterruptedException e){pix_bg = null;}
64          scratch = null;
65          pix_scratch = new int[width*height];
66      }
67      /** Marks the SpriteAnimation for refresh
68       */
69      public void set_refresh(boolean flag) { refresh = flag;}
70      /** Adds a sprite to the animation (keeps sprites sorted
71       *  in ascending order of priority)
72       */
73      public void add(Sprite s)
74      {
75          numsprites++;
76          if(first_sprite == null)
77          {
78              first_sprite = s;
79              last_sprite = s;
80          }
81          else
82          {
83              Sprite t;
84              for(t = first_sprite; t != null; t = t.next())
```

```
85              if(s.priority() >= t.priority()) break;
86          if(t == null)
87          {
88              s.next(first_sprite);
89              first_sprite.previous(s);
90              first_sprite = s;
91          }
92          else
93          {
94              if(t.next() == null) // last sprite
95              {
96                  last_sprite.next(s);
97                  s.previous(last_sprite);
98                  last_sprite = s;
99              }
100             else
101             {
102                 t.next().previous(s);
103                 s.next(t.next());
104                 t.next(s);
105                 s.previous(t);
106             }
107         }
108      }
109  }
110  public Sprite first() { return first_sprite;}
111  public Sprite last() { return last_sprite;}
112  // Utility functions
113  public boolean rects_overlap(int x1, int y1, int w1, int h1,
114                               int x2, int y2, int w2, int h2)
115  {
116      if((x2 - x1) > w1) return false;
117      if((x1 - x2) > w2) return false;
118      if((y2 - y1) > h1) return false;
119      if((y1 - y2) > h2) return false;
120      return true;
121  }
122  // Returns sprite of highest priority that encloses point (x,y)
123  public Sprite sprite_at(int x, int y)
124  {
125      Sprite rs = null, spr;
126      for(spr = last_sprite; spr != null; spr = spr.previous())
```

```
127              {
128                  if(!spr.is_active()) continue;
129                  int xs = spr.xpos();
130                  int ys = spr.ypos();
131                  if(x < xs) continue;
132                  if(y < ys) continue;
133                  int ws = spr.width();
134                  int hs = spr.height();
135                  if(x > (xs + ws - 1)) continue;
136                  if(y > (ys + hs - 1)) continue;
137                  rs = spr;
138                  break;
139              }
140          return rs;
141      }
142      public int sprite_count() { return numsprites;}
143      public Image bgimage() { return background;}
144      public int[] bg_pixels() { return pix_bg;}
145      /** Displays the entire background and draws all sprites
146       */
147      public void redisplay_all(Graphics gc, int x, int y)
148      {
149          // Copy the background image pixels into scratch image
150          System.arraycopy(pix_bg, 0, pix_scratch, 0, width*height);
151          // Draw the active sprites on the scratch image
152          for(Sprite spr = first_sprite; spr != null;
153              spr = spr.next())
154          {
155              int xs = spr.xpos() - left;
156              int ys = spr.ypos() - top;
157              int w = spr.width();
158              int h = spr.height();
159              int w2 = w;
160              int h2 = h;
161              if(xs+w > width) w2 = width-xs;
162              if(ys+h > height) h2 = height-ys;
163              if(spr.is_active())
164              {
165                  // AND the mask
166                  int[] mask = spr.mask_pixels();
167                  if(mask != null)
168                  {
```

```
169                 for(int i=0; i < h2; i++)
170                     for(int j=0; j < w2; j++)
171                         pix_scratch[(i+ys)*width+j+xs] &=
172                                         mask[i*w+j];
173             }
174             // OR the image
175             int[] image = spr.image_pixels();
176             if(image != null)
177                 for(int i=0; i < h2; i++)
178                     for(int j=0; j < w2; j++)
179                         pix_scratch[(i+ys)*width+j+xs] |=
180                                         image[i*w+j];
181         }
182         spr.update_done();
183         spr.no_overlap();
184     }
185     // Create the scratch image and display it
186     scratch = createImage(new MemoryImageSource(
187                 width, height, pix_scratch, 0, width));
188     // Display the scratch image
189     gc.drawImage(scratch, x, y, ws, hs, this);
190     scratch.flush(); // Release all resources used by scratch
191     refresh = false;
192 }
193 /** Animates the sprites on the background image
194  */
195 public void animate(Graphics gc, int x, int y)
196 {
197     if(refresh) redisplay_all(gc, x, y);
198     for(Sprite spr = first_sprite; spr != null;
199         spr = spr.next())
200     {
201         if(spr.needs_update())
202         {
203             int xdel = spr.xmove();
204             int ydel = spr.ymove();
205             int w = spr.width() + Math.abs(xdel);
206             int h = spr.height() + Math.abs(ydel);
207             int xold = spr.xpos();
208             int xnew = xold + xdel;
209             int yold = spr.ypos();
210             int ynew = yold + ydel;
```

```
211             int xfrom = Math.min(xold, xnew);
212             int yfrom = Math.min(yold, ynew);
213             // Mark this sprite as the overlapping sprite
214             spr.overlaps();
215          // Find other sprites that intersect this sprite
216          for(Sprite spr2 = first_sprite; spr2 != null;
217              spr2 = spr2.next())
218          {
219              if(!spr2.is_overlapping() &&
220                 spr2.needs_update())
221              {
222                  int xdel2 = spr2.xmove();
223                  int ydel2 = spr2.ymove();
224                  int w2 = spr2.width() + Math.abs(xdel2);
225                  int h2 = spr2.height() + Math.abs(ydel2);
226                  int xold2 = spr2.xpos();
227                  int xnew2 = xold2 + xdel2;
228                  int yold2 = spr2.ypos();
229                  int ynew2 = yold2 + ydel2;
230                  int xfrom2 = Math.min(xold2, xnew2);
231                  int yfrom2 = Math.min(yold2, ynew2);
232
233                  if(rects_overlap(xfrom, yfrom, w, h,
234                              xfrom2, yfrom2, w2, h2))
235                  {
236                      spr2.overlaps();
237                  // Adjust dimensions to be copied
238                      int oldw = w;
239                      w = Math.max(xfrom2+w2,xfrom+w) -
240                          Math.min(xfrom,xfrom2);
241                      if(w != oldw) spr2 = first_sprite;
242                      int oldh = h;
243                      h = Math.max(yfrom2+h2,yfrom+h) -
244                          Math.min(yfrom,yfrom2);
245                      if(h != oldh) spr2 = first_sprite;
246                      if(xfrom2 < xfrom) xfrom = xfrom2;
247                      if(yfrom2 < yfrom) yfrom = yfrom2;
248                  }
249              }
250          }
251          // Adjust xfrom, yfrom, w, and h by comparing
252          // with the region of background (top, left,
```

```
253        // width, height) that is currently being
254        // displayed
255        if(rects_overlap(xfrom, yfrom, w, h,
256                           left, top, width, height))
257        {
258            w = Math.min(xfrom+w,left+width) -
259                Math.max(xfrom,left);
260            h = Math.min(yfrom+h,top+height) -
261                Math.max(yfrom,top);
262            xfrom = Math.max(xfrom,left);
263            yfrom = Math.max(yfrom,top);
264        }
265        else
266            continue;
267        // Check for intersection of the rectangle
268        // xfrom, yfrom, w, h with stationary sprites.
269        for(Sprite spr2 = first_sprite; spr2 != null;
270            spr2=spr2.next())
271        {
272            if((!spr2.needs_update() ||
273                !spr2.is_overlapping()) &&
274                spr2.is_active())
275            {
276                int w2 = spr2.width();
277                int h2 = spr2.height();
278                int xfrom2 = spr2.xpos();
279                int yfrom2 = spr2.ypos();
280
281                if(rects_overlap(xfrom, yfrom, w, h,
282                                   xfrom2, yfrom2, w2, h2))
283                    spr2.overlaps();
284            }
285        }
286        // Get a piece of the background
287        // into the scratch bitmap
288        for(int m=0; m < h; m++)
289            for(int n=0; n < w; n++)
290                pix_scratch[m*w+n] =
291                        pix_bg[(m+yfrom)*width+n+xfrom];
292        // Loop through all sprites and
293        // draw the ones that overlap
294
```

```
295              for(Sprite spr2 = first_sprite; spr2!= null;
296                  spr2 = spr2.next())
297              {
298                  if(!spr2.is_overlapping()) continue;
299                  int xdel2 = spr2.xmove();
300                  int ydel2 = spr2.ymove();
301                  int w2 = spr2.width() + Math.abs(xdel2);
302                  int h2 = spr2.height() + Math.abs(ydel2);
303                  int xold2 = spr2.xpos();
304                  int xnew2 = xold2 + xdel2;
305                  int yold2 = spr2.ypos();
306                  int ynew2 = yold2 + ydel2;
307                  int xto2 = xnew2 - xfrom;
308                  int yto2 = ynew2 - yfrom;
309                  if(xto2 < 0)
310                  {
311                      xto2 = 0;
312                      xnew2 = xfrom;
313                  }
314                  if(yto2 < 0)
315                  {
316                      yto2 = 0;
317                      ynew2 = yfrom;
318                  }
319                  // AND sprite's mask onto the scratch bitmap
320                  // AND the mask
321                  int[] mask = spr2.mask_pixels();
322                  int wspr = spr2.width();
323                  int hspr = spr2.height();
324                  w2 = wspr;
325                  h2 = hspr;
326                  if(xto2+wspr > w) w2 = w-xto2;
327                  if(yto2+hspr > h) h2 = h-yto2;
328                  if(mask != null)
329                  {
330                      for(int m=0; m < h2; m++)
331                          for(int n=0; n < w2; n++)
332                              pix_scratch[(m+yto2)*w+n+xto2]
333                                  &= mask[m*wspr+n];
334                  }
335                  // Now OR the sprite's image
336                  int[] image = spr2.image_pixels();
```

```
337                        if(image != null)
338                        {
339                            for(int m=0; m < h2; m++)
340                                for(int n=0; n < w2; n++)
341                                    pix_scratch[(m+yto2)*w+(n+xto2)]
342                                        |= image[m*wspr+n];
343                        }
344                        // Update the sprite's position
345                        // and change its status bits
346                        spr2.newpos(xnew2, ynew2);
347                        spr2.update_done();
348                        spr2.no_overlap();
349                    }
350                    // Create an image from the scratch pixels
351                    scratch = createImage(new MemoryImageSource(
352                                    w, h, pix_scratch, 0, w));
353                    // Display the scratch image
354                    gc.drawImage(scratch, x+xfrom-left, y+yfrom-top,
355                                    w, h, this);
356                    scratch.flush(); // Release resources
357                }
358            }
359        }
360 }
```

As you can see from line 16 of the listing, the **SpriteAnimation** class is a subclass of **Canvas**, a Java AWT component class. As such, **SpriteAnimation** provides a drawing area on which a background image is displayed and sprites are animated. **SpriteAnimation** has the following key variables for displaying the images:

◆ **Sprite first_sprite** (line 18) refers to the first **Sprite** in a doubly linked list that holds the sprites being animated.

◆ **Sprite last_sprite** refers to the last **Sprite** in the linked list.

◆ **int numsprites** keeps count of the total number of sprites.

◆ **boolean refresh** redraws the entire image with all of the sprites when **true**.

◆ **Image background** is the background image over which the sprites are animated.

◆ **Image scratch** serves as the scratch area where images are prepared before copying to the applet's onscreen display area (to be described later).

- int[] **pix_scratch** holds the pixels of the scratch image.

- int[] **pix_bg** holds the pixels of the background image (all image operations are done on this array).

To create an instance of **SpriteAnimation**, you have to use the constructor method—**SpriteAnimation()**—shown in lines 35 through 66. The **SpriteAnimation()** method expects to receive the width and height of the scratch bitmap and an image that will be used as the background of the animation:

```
35    SpriteAnimation(int w, int h, Image bg)
```

Because **SpriteAnimation** is a subclass of **Canvas**, the **SpriteAnimation()** method first calls the **super** class constructor, as shown in line 37:

```
37        super();
```

This initializes the **Canvas** class. The rest of the **SpriteAnimation()** method performs initializations specific to the **SpriteAnimation** class. As you can see in lines 39 through 65, the constructor loads the background image, loads the pixels of the background image into the **pix_bg** array, and creates the **pix_scratch** array to hold scratch pixels.

After creating a **SpriteAnimation**, you can add **Sprite** objects to the animation by calling the **add()** method, shown in lines 73 through 109. The **add()** method adds the new **Sprite** to the linked list in an appropriate position so that all **Sprite**s are in ascending order of display priority.

To move the sprites, you call the **move()** method of each **Sprite** (as shown in the **AnimateSprites** applet's code). To animate the sprites, call the **animate()** method.

The **animate()** method, shown in lines 195 through 359, is at the heart of the process of animating sprites on a background image. Before looking into the problem of animating the sprites in an efficient way, consider the problem of redrawing the entire background image with the sprites. If you look at the beginning of the **animate()** method in the **SpriteAnimation.java** listing, you'll see this line:

```
197        if(refresh) redisplay_all(gc, x, y);
```

When the **refresh** variable is **true**, the **animate()** method calls **redisplay_all()** to update the entire image.

In the **SpriteAnimation.java** listing, lines 147 through 192 show the source code for the **redisplay_all()** method that draws the background and the sprites. In a Java-like pseudocode notation, the **refresh_all()** method uses the following steps to draw the sprites on the background:

```
Copy the background image pixels into scratch pixel array
using System.arraycopy().

for(all Sprite objects in the animation)
```

```
{
    Perform a bitwise-AND operation between the Sprite's mask
        pixels and the scratch pixel array
    Perform a bitwise-OR operation between the Sprite's image
        pixels and the scratch pixel array
}

Create a scratch image from the scratch pixels by calling
    createImage() and MemoryImageSource()
Draw the scratch image by calling drawImage()
```

As you can see, the basic idea is to copy the background pixels into a scratch array and draw all of the sprites on the background. Because the **SpriteAnimation** class stores the **Sprite**s in order by display priority, this step draws the sprites in the correct order. Figure 4-2 illustrates the process of drawing a sprite on a background.

As the figure shows, the steps for drawing a sprite are as follows:

1. Combine the pixels of the sprite's mask with the background image pixels, using a bitwise-AND operation. Remember that the mask is a silhouette of the sprite's image—it is black (all bits 0) on a white (all bits 1) background. This step will essentially punch a hole the shape of the sprite in the background image.

2. Combine the pixels of the sprite's image with the modified background image pixels, using a bitwise-OR operation. Because the image is on a white (all bits 1) background, this step will fill the hole created in the previous step.

When the entire background does not need to be updated, the **animate()** method (lines 195 through 359) draws the sprites by using an algorithm that updates the display area in an efficient manner. It uses the following algorithm for efficient sprite animation:

1. For a sprite *S* that needs updating, find all other sprites that touch sprite *S* and are also in need of update. Determine the largest rectangle that encloses all sprites that satisfy these conditions.

2. Find all stationary sprites that also touch the rectangle, and mark them as overlapping.

3. Copy from the background to the scratch pixel array an area corresponding to the rectangle determined in step 1.

4. Draw all overlapping sprites in the scratch pixel array (using the steps illustrated in Figure 4-2). Set the status of the sprites to indicate that they have been updated so that they are not included again.

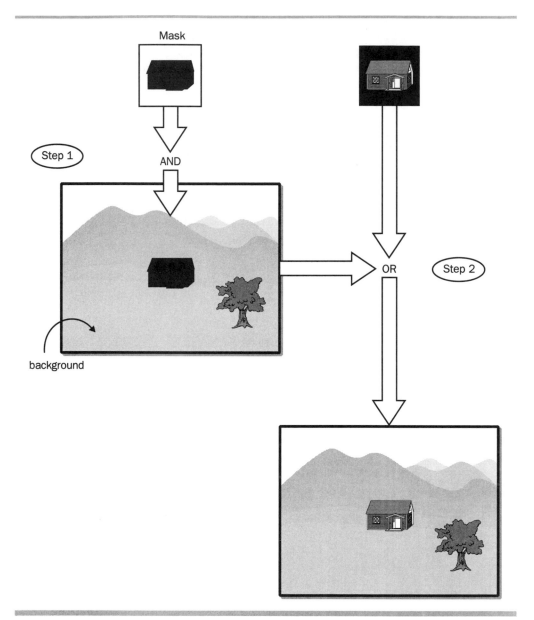

FIGURE 4-2.   Drawing a sprite on a background.

5. Create an image from the scratch pixels, and draw that image in the display area.

6. Repeat steps 1 through 5 for all sprites.

Figure 4-3 depicts these steps for sprite animation.

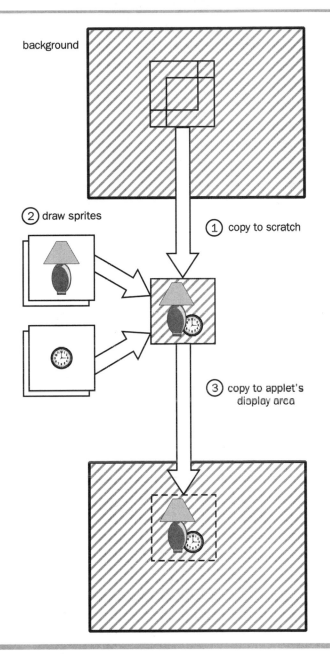

FIGURE 4-3. Animating sprites.

Displaying a Three-Dimensional Object

So far you have seen how to play sound and animate sprites. This section presents the **Viewer3D** applet, which can display a three-dimensional object whose coordinates are stored in a specific format known as an OFF file.

Viewer3D was written by Daeron Meyer and is copyrighted by The Geometry Center, University of Minnesota and distributed under the terms of the GNU Library General Public License. You'll find the terms of the license in the files named **COPYING** and **COPYING.LIB** in the **ch04\Viewer3D** directory of this book's companion CD-ROM.

After explaining how you can try out **Viewer3D**, I will briefly describe how the applet and its supporting classes work. Note that the OFF file format is a part of a larger family of 3-D file formats known as OOGL, which stands for Object Oriented Graphics Library. OOGL is the basis of a well-known 3-D visualization software package known as **Geomview** that was developed by the staff at the Geometry Center, University of Minnesota. To learn more about **Geomview**, visit the **Geomview** home page at **http://www.geom.umn.edu/software/geomview/**.

Using Viewer3D

The files for **Viewer3D** are in the **ch04\Viewer3D** directory of the companion CD-ROM. A subdirectory named **models** contains several objects in OFF files that you can display with **Viewer3D**.

To try out **Viewer3D**, open the **index.html** file (from the **ch04\Viewer3D** directory) in a Java-capable Web browser. Figure 4-4 shows the list of 3-D objects you can view with **Viewer3D**. To view all of the objects, click on the last item, labeled **All of the above**. Four 3-D objects will appear on a single Web page. You can grab any of the objects with the mouse (move the pointer on top of an object and hold down the left mouse button) and then reorient the object by moving the mouse. Figure 4-5 shows the objects after each has been moved around some.

The output shown in Figure 4-5 is produced by four **<applet>** tags in the **all.html** file in the **ch04\Viewer3D** directory of the CD-ROM. Here are the four **<applet>** tags from that file:

```
<applet code=Viewer3D.class width=300 height=300>
<param name=model value=models/chemi.off>
</applet>
<applet code=Viewer3D.class width=300 height=300>
<param name=model value=models/mushroom.off>
</applet>
<BR>
<applet code=Viewer3D.class width=300 height=300>
```

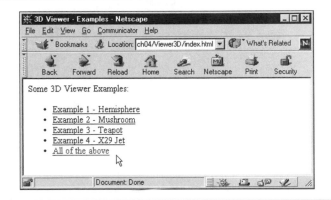

FIGURE 4-4. Sample 3-D objects you can view with **Viewer3D**.

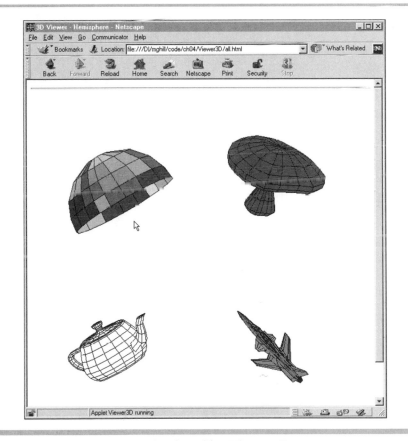

FIGURE 4-5. Four 3-D objects displayed by **Viewer3D**.

```
<param name=model value=models/teapot.off>
</applet>
<applet code=Viewer3D.class width=300 height=300>
<param name=model value=models/x29.off>
</applet>
```

As you can see, each **<applet>** tag runs an instance of the **Viewer3D** applet in a display area 300 pixels wide by 300 pixels tall. **Viewer3D** accepts the name of an OFF file in a parameter named **model**. In this case, the **<param>** tags refer to different OFF files in the **models** subdirectory.

Viewer3D

Understanding Viewer3D

The following listing shows the file **Viewer3D.java** that implements the **Viewer3D** applet. Subsequent sections briefly explain the applet's code as well as the code of other classes used by **Viewer3D**.

```
1  /**
2   *
3   * Author: Daeron Meyer
4   * Copyright (c) 1995 by The Geometry Center, University of Minnesota
5   * Distributed under the terms of the GNU Library General Public
6   * License 12-14-95
7   *
8   */
9
10 import java.applet.Applet;
11 import java.awt.Image;
12 import java.awt.Graphics;
13 import java.awt.Color;
14 import java.awt.Event;
15 import java.lang.*;
16 import java.io.InputStream;
17 import java.net.URL;
18
19 /**
20  * Viewer3D: An applet that displays and rotates a 3D OFF object
21  *           interactively, in response to user mouse events.
22  */
23
24 public class Viewer3D extends Applet {
25
26   OOGL_OFF    obj;
27   boolean     painted = true;
```

```
28   String      objname = null,
29       message = null;
30   float        xfac, scaleval = 0.1f;
31   Matrix3D     amat = new Matrix3D(),
32       tmat = new Matrix3D();
33
34   Image        bbuffer;
35   Graphics    bgc;
36   int         prevx, prevy;
37
38   public void init() {
39
40     objname = null;
41     objname = getParameter("model"); // get the object name
42     if (objname == null) objname = "models/chemi.off";
43
44     try {
45       scaleval = Float.valueOf(
                        getParameter("scale")).floatValue() * 0.1f;
46     } catch (Exception e) { };
47
48     amat.yrot(20);                    // set initial rotation
49     amat.xrot(20);
50
51     resize(size().width <=20 ? 400 : size().width,
52         size().height <= 20 ? 400 : size().height);
53
54   }
55
56   public void start() {
57
58     try {
59
60       OOGL_OFF x = new OOGL_OFF (new URL(getDocumentBase(),
                                      objname));
61                           // read object from URL
62       obj = x;
63       obj.findBB();                       // find bounding box
64       float xw = obj.xmax - obj.xmin; // so we can scale
65       float yw = obj.ymax - obj.ymin; // the object to fit
66       float zw = obj.zmax - obj.zmin; // in our window
67       if (yw > xw) xw = yw;
68       if (zw > xw) xw = zw;
```

```
69      float f1 = 250 / xw;
70      float f2 = 250 / xw;
71      xfac = 0.7f * (f1 < f2 ? f1 : f2) * scaleval;
72
73      bbuffer = createImage(size().width, size().height);
74      bgc = bbuffer.getGraphics(); // create image to do
75                                   //    double buffering
76
77    } catch(Exception e) {
78      obj = null;
79      message = e.toString();
80    }
81
82    repaint();
83
84  }
85
86
87 /* handle mouse events */
88
89  public boolean mouseDown(Event e, int x, int y) {
90
91    prevx = x;
92    prevy = y;
93    return true;
94
95  }
96
97  public boolean mouseDrag(Event e, int x, int y) {
98
99    tmat.unit();
100   float xtheta = (prevy - y) * 360.0f / size().width;
101   float ytheta = (prevx - x) * 360.0f / size().height;
102   tmat.xrot(xtheta);
103   tmat.yrot(ytheta);
104   amat.mult(tmat);
105
106   if (painted) {
107
108     painted = false;
109     repaint();
```

```
110
111      }
112
113      prevx = x; prevy = y;
114      return true;
115
116    }
117
118    public void update(Graphics g) {
119
120      if (bbuffer == null)
121        g.clearRect(0, 0, size().width, size().height);
122
123      paint(g);
124
125    }
126
127 /* transform and paint the object to the graphics context */
128
129    public void paint(Graphics g) {
130
131      if (obj != null) {
132
133        obj.mat.unit();
134        obj.mat.translate(-(obj.xmin + obj.xmax) / 2,
135              -(obj.ymin + obj.ymax) / 2,
136              -(obj.zmin + obj.zmax) / 2);
137        obj.mat.mult(amat);
138
139        int scale = (int)( xfac * size().width / 25 );
140
141        obj.mat.scale(scale, scale, 16 * xfac / size().width);
142        obj.mat.translate(size().width / 2, size().height / 2, 8);
143        obj.transformed = false;
144
145        if (bbuffer != null) {
146
147          bgc.setColor(getBackground());
148          bgc.fillRect(0,0,size().width,size().height);
149          obj.paint(bgc);
150          g.drawImage(bbuffer, 0, 0, this);
151
```

```
152        } else
153            obj.paint(g);
154
155        setPainted();
156
157    } else if (message != null)
158        g.drawString("Error reading OFF file", 3, 20);
159
160  }
161
162  private synchronized void setPainted() {
163
164    painted = true;
165    notifyAll();
166
167  }
168
169 }
```

ANNOTATIONS

Viewer3D uses two other classes—**Matrix3D** and **OOGL_OFF**—to do its job. The **Matrix3D** class performs matrix transformations, and the **OOGL_OFF** class reads and parses the contents of an OFF file that contains the description of a 3-D object. These classes are described in later sections.

Lines 26 through 36 declare a number of variables used in the **Viewer3D** class. Line 26 declares an **OOGL_OFF** object named **obj** that will hold the digital representation of the 3-D object. Lines 31 and 32 declare two **Matrix3D** objects named **amat** and **tmat** that are used for coordinate transformations (to rotate the 3-D object around various axes). Line 34 declares the **Image bbuffer** used for double buffering. (This means that the 3-D object is first rendered on **bbuffer** and then **bbuffer** is drawn on the applet's display area.)

During initialization, the **init()** method (see lines 38 through 54) gets the name of the OFF file from the parameter named **model**. Line 41 stores the OFF filename in the **String** named **objname**. Lines 48 and 49 initialize the **amat Matrix3D** object with initial angles of rotation.

When the applet starts to run, the **start()** method (lines 56 through 84) creates an **OOGL_OFF** object with the OFF file whose name is in the **String objname**. Line 60 performs this step:

```
60        OOGL_OFF x = new OOGL_OFF (new URL(getDocumentBase(),
                                            objname));
```

As you can see, you have to pass a URL as argument to the **OOGL_OFF()** constructor method. In this case, that URL is constructed by appending the object's OFF filename to the URL that the applet's code has been loaded from.

Lines 63 through 71 determine the bounding box (the length, width, and height) of the object and compute some factors used to scale the object's coordinates so that everything will fit in the applet's display area. Lines 73 and 74 initialize the off-screen image, **bbuffer**, and set up a graphics context, **bgc**, for that image.

The applet's **paint()** method, shown in lines 129 through 160, translates and rotates the object (using the current contents of the transformation matrix **amat**) and then draws it by calling the **OOGL_OFF** object's **paint()** method.

When the user holds down the mouse on the object and moves it around, the **mouseDrag()** method, shown in lines 97 through 116, is called. Based on the mouse movement, the **mouseDrag()** method computes two angles and sets up a transformation matrix corresponding to rotations around the x and y axes by those angles. It then calls **repaint()** to redraw the rotated object.

THE MATRIX3D CLASS   The **Matrix3D** class represents a 3x3 matrix that can transform a 3-D point (represented by x, y, and z coordinates) by rotating it around the x, y, and z axes by different amounts. You will find the source code for **Matrix3D** in the **Matrix3D.java** file in the **ch04\Viewer3D** directory of the CD-ROM. I don't show the entire file here, because you can use the class without having to understand all of the details.

Create a **Matrix3D** object by calling its constructor method:

```
Matrix3D amat = new Matrix3D();
```

To rotate about the x, y, and z axes, you have to apply each rotation by calling the **xrot()**, **yrot()**, and **zrot()** methods, like this:

```
// Assume tmat is a Matrix3D object used for temporary calculations
tmat.xrot(xtheta);
tmat.yrot(ytheta);
tmat.zrot(ztheta);
```

where the arguments *xtheta*, *ytheta*, and *ztheta* are angles in degrees. After the rotations, you would typically accumulate the transformations by calling the **mult()** method:

```
// Assume amat is the Matrix3D object with current transformations
amat.mult(tmat);
```

THE OOGL_OFF CLASS   The OOGL_OFF class is used to read and parse an OFF file that contains information about the 3-D object. You will find the source code in the **OOGL_OFF.java** file in the **ch04\Viewer3D** directory of the CD-ROM. I do not show the complete listing because you can use the **OOGL_OFF** class without knowing the internal details of that class. All you have to do is follow the example shown in the **Viewer3D** applet's source code.

    The **OOGL_OFF** class reads OFF files that store the description of a 3-D object. You might be curious about the format of those files. In fact, the OFF files are in text format, so you can open them in a word processor and take a look. For example, here are some lines from the **teapot.off** file from the **model** subdirectory (I don't show the entire file, because it contains close to a thousand lines of data):

```
OFF
480    448    926

0    0    0.488037
0.00390625    0.0421881    0.476326
0.00390625    -0.0421881    0.476326
0.0107422    0    0.575333
(476 more lines with vertices)

4        324 306 304 317
4        306 283 281 304
4        283 248 246 281
4        248 172 171 246
(444 more lines with faces)
```

The file starts with a line containing the text *OFF*. This means that the file contains a list of polygons (defined by vertices and faces that are made up of sequences of vertices). The second line says that there are 480 vertices, 448 faces, and 926 edges in the teapot object. The number of edges is not used, so you could set it to zero.

    After a blank line, the file contains the vertices, one per line. The coordinates of each vertex are three floating-point numbers representing the x, y, and z coordinates of the vertex. There should be 480 lines with coordinates of vertices in the **teapot.off** file.

    After the list of vertices comes another blank line followed by 448 lines of information about the faces. Each face is specified as follows: the first number is the number of vertices in that face, and the rest of the numbers on the line are indices into the list of vertices. For example, consider the following face:

```
4        324 306 304 317
```

This face has four vertices (it's a quadrilateral). The next four numbers refer to the vertices at indices 324, 306, 304, and 317 (where index 0 refers to the first vertex, index 1 to the second vertex, and so on).

Note that an OFF file can also include color information for each face. The color is specified in terms of red, green, and blue components, with the values ranging from 0.0 to 1.0. For example, here is a four-sided face with a blue color:

```
4     324 306 304 317   0.0 0.0 1.0
```

Playing an MPEG-1 Video

In addition to sound and image animation, video is another key ingredient of multimedia presentations. There are several video formats. Some of the common ones are:

◆ MPEG—a set of standards for compressing video and audio data, developed by the Motion Picture Experts Group.

◆ Apple QuickTime—a popular format for audio and video, developed by Apple Computer.

◆ AVI (Audio Video Interleaved)—a format for storing video interleaved with audio, developed by Microsoft.

MPEG is a popular format for movies. The MPEG-1 standard can produce images that are 352 pixels wide by 240 pixels tall at 30 frames per second, with CD-quality audio. This section presents the **MPEG_Play** applet, which can play the video portion of an MPEG-1 file (it ignores the audio).

MPEG_Play was developed by J. Anders, *Professur Rechnernetz u. verteilte Systeme*, TU-Chemnitz, and is distributed under the GNU General Public License (**http://www.fsf.org/copyleft/gpl.html**). The original home page of the MPEG_Play applet is **http://rnvs.informatik.tu-chemnitz.de/~ja/MPEG/MPEG_Play.html**.

Using MPEG_Play

The files for the **MPEG_Play** applet are in the **ch04\MPEGPlay** directory of the companion CD-ROM. To try out the applet, open the **PlayMPEG.html** file from a Java-capable Web browser. The **MPEG_Play** applet loads and plays a sample MPEG file named **dreh.mpg**. Figure 4-6 shows a typical frame of the resulting output. You can control the playback by clicking on the buttons along the bottom part of the view. Clicking on the Stop button stops the playback. The buttons with the double arrows allow you to play the file in the forward or backward direction. If you click on the buttons with single arrows, the display moves forward or backward by a single frame.

Here is the **PlayMPEG.html** file used to generate the display shown in Figure 4-6:

```
<HTML>
<TITLE>MPEG_Play applet</TITLE>
<BODY>
<H1>MPEG-1 player in Java</H1>

This is an MPEG-1 player written by J. Anders,
Professur <em>Rechnernetz u. verteilte Systeme</em>,
TU-Chemnitz and distributed under the GNU General
Public License (GPL). The original Web page for
the MPEG_Play applet is at:
<a href="http://rnvs.informatik.tu-chemnitz.de/~ja/MPEG/MPEG_Play.html">
http://rnvs.informatik.tu-chemnitz.de/~ja/MPEG/MPEG_Play.html</a>
<br>
<APPLET ARCHIVE="classfils.zip" CODE="MPEG_Play.class" WIDTH=260 HEIGHT=240>
<PARAM NAME=FILENAME VALUE="dreh.mpg">
<PARAM NAME=DELAY VALUE="user">
If you had a Java-capable browser, you would have seen the
MPEG_Play applet here!
</APPLET>
</BODY>
</HTML>
```

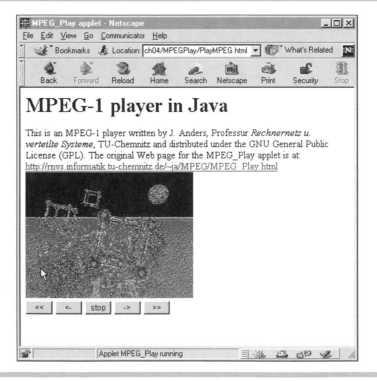

FIGURE 4-6. **MPEG_Play** displaying a frame of a sample MPEG file.

As you can see, the **<APPLET>** tag uses an **ARCHIVE** attribute to specify a Zip file (**classfils.zip**) containing the classes used by the **MPEG_Play** applet. You have to specify the name of the MPEG file through a **<PARAM>** tag named **FILENAME**. The other parameter, **DELAY**, determines the delay between frames. If that parameter is a numeric value, **MPEG_Play** uses it as the delay in milliseconds between two successive frames of the file. If you set **DELAY** to **"user"**, **MPEG_Play** displays the control panel with buttons, as shown in Figure 4-6. The user can then control the MPEG playback.

The easiest way to use **MPEG_Play** on your Web page is to copy the **classfils.zip** file to your Web site and then use an **<APPLET>** tag with the **ARCHIVE="classfils.zip"** attribute, as shown in the **PlayMPEG.html** file. You will probably want to specify your own MPEG file through the **FILENAME** parameter.

Understanding MPEG_Play

MPEG_Play

MPEG_Play is a fairly complex applet, and it uses quite a few classes that are in their own source files. You will find the complete source distribution of **MPEG_Play** in the **ch04\MPEGPlay\mpeg_java-3.3** directory of the companion CD-ROM.

PROGRAMMER'S NOTE   *To build **MPEG_Play** from scratch, you'll need a UNIX system that has the tools yacc and sed as well as a C preprocessor and C compiler installed. Copy the **mpeg_java-3_3.tgz** file (from the ch04\MPEGPlay directory) to a UNIX system, unpack using the **tar zxvf mpeg_java-3_3.tgz** command, and then type **make** in the source directory. This builds the **IDCT.java** file—one of the classes that **MPEG_Play** needs. After that you can use the Java compiler to compile the Java source files.*

Due to limited space, I do not show all of the Java source files used by MPEG_Play here. Instead, I focus on the MPEG_Play class, whose source file, **MPEG_Play.java**, appears in the following listing. When describing this code, I'll briefly mention the other classes that the **MPEG_Play** applet uses. You can see a complete list of the other classes and their source filenames in the "Annotations" section that follows.

```
1  /**********************************************************************************/
2  /*                                                                              */
3  /*              "MPEG_Play.java"                                                 */
4  /*                                                                              */
5  /* This file contains the main applet class and the class "Element" which stores */
6  /* pixel information of a single frame. Furthermore a class "dispatch" is implemented */
7  /* The object of this class controls the threads:                               */
8  /*         - ScanThread : Scanning of the MPEG Stream                           */
9  /*         - AnimatorThread: which shows in scan phase how many                 */
10 /*                 frames are already scanned.                                  */
11 /*                                                                              */
12 /* In case of an application a method "main()" is implemented.                  */
13 /*------------------------------------------------------------------------------*/
14 /*                                                                              */
15 /*       Joerg Anders, TU Chemnitz, Fakultaet fuer Informatik, GERMANY          */
16 /*       ja@informatik.tu-chemnitz.de                                           */
17 /*                                                                              */
```

```
18  /*                                                                          */
19  /*--------------------------------------------------------------------------*/
20  /*                                                                          */
21  /* This program is free software; you can redistribute it and/or modify it under the   */
22  /* terms of the GNU General Public License as published by the Free Software    */
23  /* Foundation; either version 2 of the License, or (at your option) any later version.  */
24  /*                                                                          */
25  /* This program is distributed in the hope that it will be useful, but WITHOUT ANY    */
26  /* WARRANTY; without even the implied warranty of MERCHANTABILITY or FITNESS FOR A  */
27  /* PARTICULAR PURPOSE. See the GNU General Public License for more details.     */
28  /*                                                                          */
29  /* You should have received a copy of the GNU General Public License along with this  */
30  /* program; (See "LICENSE.GPL"). If not, write to the Free Software Foundation, Inc.,  */
31  /* 59 Temple Place - Suite 330, Boston, MA  02111-1307, USA.                */
32  /*                                                                          */
33  /*--------------------------------------------------------------------------*/
34  /*                                                                          */
35  /* If the program runs as Java applet it isn't "interactive" in the sense of the GNU  */
36  /* General Public License. So paragraph 2c doesn't apply.                   */
37  /*                                                                          */
38  /****************************************************************************/
39
40  import java.awt.*;                   // Image, Frame, BorderLayout
41  import java.io.*;                    // DataInputStream, IOException
42  import java.net.*;                   // URL, MalformedURLException
43  import java.applet.Applet;
44  import java.awt.image.*;             // ColorModel, DirectColorModel, MemoryImageSource
45
46  /* The class "Element" can store the information of a single frame. By means of the   */
47  /* property "next" it can build a list whose anchor is "Frame_List" in class    */
48  /* "MPEG_Play".                                                             */
49  /* The pixels are given as YUV values and they are then translated into the Java-AWT  */
50  /* RGB model.                                                               */
51
52  class Element {
53      public Element next = null, before = null;   // To make the list
54      private boolean b_type_seen = false;          // Was there already a B-Frame ???
55      public Image Picture;              // The Image
56      public int Frame_idx;              // notice the frame number (display order)
57      public int Frame_type;                // I, B or P
58      public int Pix_Map[];              // The pixels in Java RGB model
59      private final int CR_FAC = 0x166EA; /* 1.402*2^16 */
60      private final int CB_FAC = 0x1C5A2; /* 1.772*2^16 */
61      private final int CR_DIFF_FAC = 0xB6D2; /* 0.71414 * 2^16 */
62      private final int CB_DIFF_FAC = 0x581A; /* 0.34414 * 2^16 */
63
64      /* The constructor is called every time the scanner has decoded a frame. It     */
65      /* expects the frame information as YUV values and translates them into the Java */
66      /* RGB color system. The Applet (app) object is necessary to call the      */
67      /* "createImage" routine. The dispatcher "s" is informed of the existence of a   */
68      /* new frame.                                                           */
69
70      Element (Applet app, int Pixels[][], ColorModel cm, int f_idx, int f_type, int w, int h, int o_w, int o_h) {
71          int red, green, blue, luminance, cr, cb, cr_g, cb_g, i, j;
72          Frame_idx = f_idx; Frame_type = f_type; // notice
73          Element ptr;
74
75          /* because one crominance information is applied to 4 luminace values
76           * 2 "pointers" are established, which point to the 2 lines containing
77           * the appropriate luminace values:
78           */
79
80          int lum_idx1 = 0, lum_idx2 = w;
81          int size = w * h;
```

```
 82        Pix_Map = new int[size]; // memory for the translated RGB values
 83
 84        /*
 85         *  expand the list
 86         */
 87
 88        size >>>= 2;            // the size of the crominance values
 89
 90        for (i = 0; i < size; i++) { // for all crominance values ...
 91            cb = Pixels[2][i] - 128; // extract the
 92            cr = Pixels[1][i] - 128;// chrominace information
 93
 94            cr_g = cr * CR_DIFF_FAC;
 95            cb_g = cb * CB_DIFF_FAC;
 96
 97            cb *= CB_FAC;
 98            cr *= CR_FAC;
 99
100            for (j = 0; j < 2; j++) { // apply to 2 neighbouring points
101                luminance = Pixels[0][lum_idx1] << 16; // extract lum.
102                red = (luminance + cr);
103                blue = (luminance + cb) >> 16;
104                green = (luminance - cr_g - cb_g) >> 8;
105
106                red = (red > 0xff0000) ? 0xff0000 : (red < 0) ? 0 : red & 0xff0000;    // CLAMP
107                green = (green > 0xff00)  ? 0xff00 : (green < 0) ? 0 : green & 0xff00;//CLAMP
108                blue = (blue > 255)  ? 255 : (blue < 0) ? 0 : blue;    //CLAMP
109
110                Pix_Map[lum_idx1] = ( red | green  | blue);
111
112                lum_idx1++; // next point in first line
113
114                luminance = Pixels[0][lum_idx2] << 16; // extract lum.
115                red = (luminance + cr);
116                blue = (luminance + cb) >> 16;
117                green = (luminance - cr_g - cb_g) >> 8;
118
119                red = (red > 0xff0000) ? 0xff0000 : (red < 0) ? 0 : red & 0xff0000;    // CLAMP
120                green = (green > 0xff00)  ? 0xff00 : (green < 0) ? 0 : green & 0xff00;//CLAMP
121                blue = (blue > 255)  ? 255 : (blue < 0) ? 0 : blue;    //CLAMP
122
123                Pix_Map[lum_idx2] = ( red | green | blue);
124                lum_idx2++; // next point in second line
125                if (lum_idx2 % w == 0) { // end of line ?
126                    lum_idx2 += w;
127                    lum_idx1 += w;
128                }
129            }
130        }
131 /*+++ JAVA offers 2 possibilities to create an image:                    +++*/
132 /*+++                                                                     +++*/
133 /*+++               1. createImage(int width, int height);               +++*/
134 /*+++               2. createImage(ImageProducer producer);              +++*/
135 /*+++                                                                     +++*/
136 /*+++ The first method isn't suitable here because it requires to draw the  +++*/
137 /*+++ pixel values by means of a sequence of "draw...()" methods into the image.+++*/
138 /*+++ Since all the pixel values and the color model are known, the images  +++*/
139 /*+++ are produced according to the second method by means of objects of the  +++*/
140 /*+++ class "MemoryImageSource", which implements the interface "ImageProducer".+++*/
141 /*+++ An image producer is an object which supplies the pixel values on demand  +++*/
142 /*+++ of an image consumer. The pixel values are delivered in respect of a  +++*/
143 /*+++ certain color model. The "MemoryImageSource" objects uses a Direct Color  +++*/
144 /*+++ model.                                                              +++*/
145
```

```
146            Picture = app.createImage(new MemoryImageSource(o_w, o_h, cm, Pix_Map, 0, w));
147      }
148 }
149
150 /* An object of class "dispatch" is used to control the "ScanThread" and the      */
151 /* "AnimatorThread" during scan phase. The "AnimatorThread" displays information   */
152 /* on the state of the scanning process. It waits as long as no new frame          */
153 /* is available. The "ScanThread" never waits. The (pardonable) effect is:         */
154 /* The user isn't necessarily informed of all scanned frames.                      */
155
156 class dispatch {
157      private Element newframe = null;
158      private boolean available = false;
159
160      public synchronized Element get() {
161          if (available == false) {
162              try {
163                  wait();
164              } catch (InterruptedException e) {
165                  Err.Msg = "Exception : " + e.toString();
166              }
167          }
168          available = false;
169          notifyAll();
170          return newframe;
171      }
172
173      public synchronized void put(Element akEle) {
174          newframe = akEle;
175          available = true;
176          notifyAll();
177      }
178 }
179
180
181 /* The class "MPEG_Play" is the main applet. Its work is divides into 2 phases:    */
182 /*    - scanning: A "ScanThread" and an "AnimatorThread" work concurrently         */
183 /*               The "ScanThread" produces a list of frames (images) and           */
184 /*               informs the "AnimatorThread" if a frame is decoded.               */
185 /*    - display:  By means of the method "Element.close_chain()" the list          */
186 /*               of frames is closed to a ring of frames. After that               */
187 /*               the frames are displayed. The "ScanThread" dies and the           */
188 /*               "AnimatorThread" begins to display the frames.                    */
189
190 public class MPEG_Play extends Applet implements Runnable {
191      private int h, w;                    // width and height
192      private int o_h, o_w;                       // width and height of the original pictures
193      private Element ak_pic = null;              // No. of the actual frame
194      public boolean inApplet = true;             // Is it an applet or an application ?
195      private Frame the_frame;             // THE frame (in application)
196      private InputStream in_stream = null;       // THE MPEG resource
197      private dispatch Dispatcher = new dispatch();    // THE dispatcher
198      private Element akElement = null;           // the actual element
199      private final int R = 55;              // a border
200
201        private Thread AnimatorThread = null;  // the animation runs as thread
202        private Thread ScanThread = null;       // the scanner runs as thread
203      private boolean Scanning = true;         // in scan phase ???
204      private boolean first = true;               // for the first time in display phase ?
205
206      boolean painted = false;          // "true", if the frame "ak_pic_nr" is painted
207      private static int delay = 50;         // default delay between 2 frames (in ms)
208      private boolean userdelay = false;
209
```

```
210     private Element Frame_List = null;        // The anchor
211     private Element last_Element = null;      // last element in list
212     private Element last_P_or_I = null;       // last P or I frame;
213     private boolean b_type_seen = false;
214     private DirectColorModel cm = new DirectColorModel(24, 0xff0000, 0xff00, 0xff);
215
216     private final int MINDELAY = 50, MAXDELAY = 400, DELTA = 20;
217     private final int LEFT = 1, RIGHT = 2;
218     private final int BU_W = 40, BU_H = 20, SPA = 5, BU_SPACE = 5;
219     private int playdir;                      // direction of animation
220     private Button stop = new Button("stop");
221     private Button leftleft = new Button("<<");
222     private Button left = new Button("<-");
223     private Button right= new Button("->");
224     private Button rightright= new Button(">>");
225     private Button qb    = new Button("Quit");
226     private URL old_url = null;       // to what URL belongs the decoded list
227     private URL source_url = null;        // to build the URL to MPEG resource
228
229     /* This constructor is only called in application */
230
231     MPEG_Play(InputStream s, myFrame f, boolean ud) {
232         in_stream = s;           // notice
233         the_frame = f;           // notice
234         inApplet = false;        // notice
235         userdelay = ud;          // notice
236     }
237
238
239     public MPEG_Play() {}         // This constructor is only called in applet
240
241     /* The method "init()" opens up the MPEG resource and produces and */
242     /* starts the "ScanThread"                          */
243
244     public void start () {7
245         MPEG_scan M_Scan;       // The scanner object
246         String s_delay;          // to read the delay parameter
247         boolean io = true;       // everything OK ????
248         String f_name = null;     // to read the filename parameter
249
250         if (inApplet) {// otherwise the file is already opened
251             try {                 // obtain parameters
252                 f_name = getParameter("FILENAME");
253                 s_delay = getParameter("DELAY");
254                 if (s_delay != null) {
255                     if (s_delay.compareTo("user") == 0) {
256                         userdelay = true;
257                     }
258                     else {
259                             try {
260                                 delay = Integer.parseInt(s_delay);
261                             } catch (NumberFormatException e) {
262                         io = false;
263                         Err.Msg = s_delay + " is not a number";
264                     }
265                     }
266                 }
267                 source_url = new URL(getCodeBase(), f_name);
268                 in_stream = source_url.openStream();
269             }
270         catch (NullPointerException e) {
271             Err.Msg = "no parameter \"FILENAME\"";
272             io = false;
273                 }
```

```
274              catch (MalformedURLException e) {
275                  Err.Msg = "MalformedURLException";
276                  io = false;
277              }
278              catch (IOException e) {
279                  Err.Msg = "Cannot open: " + getCodeBase() + "/" + f_name;
280                  io = false;
281              }
282              if (f_name == null) {
283                  Err.Msg = "no parameter \"FILENAME\"";
284                   io = false;
285              }
286              if (Frame_List != null && inApplet) {
287                  if (!source_url.sameFile(old_url)) { // already scanned ?
288                      Frame_List = last_Element = last_P_or_I = null; // clear up for scanning process
289                      Scanning = true;
290                  }
291              }
292          }
293          if (io && Frame_List == null) { // create the scanner object and start the scanner thread:
294              M_Scan = new MPEG_scan(this, in_stream);
295              ScanThread = new Thread(M_Scan);
296              ScanThread.start();
297          }
298
299          playdir = RIGHT;
300          if (AnimatorThread == null) {
301                  AnimatorThread = new Thread(this); // create the "AnimatorThread"
302                  AnimatorThread.start();              // pass the thread to the scheduler;
303                      // At first the "AnimatorThread" works
304                          // concurrently with the
305          }                   // "ScanThread"
306      }
307
308      public void stop() {
309          AnimatorThread = null; // stop animation loop
310          if (ScanThread != null) ScanThread.stop();      // stop Scanning
311          if (Scanning) {          // reset all in scanning process
312              Frame_List = last_Element = last_P_or_I = null; // clear up for scanning process
313              try {
314                  if (in_stream != null) in_stream.close(); // the stream must be opened again
315              }
316              catch (IOException e) {}
317          }
318      }
319
320      /* The method "close_chain()" is called after the scanner is ready.     */
321      /* It closes the list of Elements and establishes a ring of Images      */
322      /* this way.                                      */
323
324      public void close_chain() {
325          last_Element.next = last_P_or_I;
326          last_P_or_I.before = last_Element;
327          last_Element = last_P_or_I;
328          last_Element.next = Frame_List;
329          Frame_List.before = last_Element;
330          ak_pic = Frame_List;
331          Scanning = false;          // inform the "AnimatorThread"
332          Dispatcher.put(Frame_List);    // unlock the "AnimatorThread"
333          try {
334              in_stream.close();
335          }
336          catch (Exception e) {};
337          if (inApplet) {
```

```
338           try {
339               old_url = new URL(source_url.toString()); // notice;
340           }
341           catch (Exception e) {
342               Err.Msg = e.toString();
343           }
344       }
345   }
346
347
348   /* The method "run()" implements the "AnimatorThread". During scan phase */
349   /* it waits in "Dispatcher.get()". Then it calls "repaint()" to activate */
350   /* "update()". In scan phase "update()" only prints a decoder status      */
351   /* information to the user.                                               */
352   /* After scan phase the frames are displayed.                            */
353
354   public void run() {
355       while (AnimatorThread != null && Scanning) { // not dead; in scan phase
356           akElement = Dispatcher.get();  // wait till a new frame arrives
357           repaint();                     // activate (probably) "update"
358           try {
359               Thread.yield();            // give "ScanThread" a chance
360           }
361           catch (Exception e) { // don't know what to do in applet
362               Err.Msg = "Exception: " + e.toString();
363           }
364       }
365
366       if (userdelay && AnimatorThread != null) { // avoid the buttons in case
367                               // of stopping the scanner
368           removeAll(); // make sure the buttons do not exist
369           try {
370               Thread.yield();            // give the browser a chance to
371           }                  // remove the buttons
372           catch (Exception e) { // don't know what to do in applet
373               Err.Msg = "Exception: " + e.toString();
374           }
375           leftleft.reshape(0, o_h + BU_SPACE, BU_W, BU_H);
376           add(leftleft);
377           left.reshape(BU_W + SPA, o_h + BU_SPACE, BU_W, BU_H);
378           add(left);
379           stop.reshape(2 * (BU_W + SPA), o_h + BU_SPACE, BU_W, BU_H);
380           add(stop);
381           right.reshape(3 * (BU_W + SPA), o_h + BU_SPACE, BU_W, BU_H);
382           add(right);
383           rightright.reshape(4 * (BU_W + SPA), o_h + BU_SPACE, BU_W, BU_H);
384           add(rightright);
385           if (!inApplet) {
386               qb.reshape(4 * (BU_W + SPA) / 2, o_h + BU_SPACE + BU_H, BU_W, BU_H);
387               add(qb);
388           }
389       }
390       long starttime = System.currentTimeMillis();  // notice the start time
391
392       while (AnimatorThread != null) { // Is it me ?
393           repaint(); // sets the flag for "update()" -> "paint()"
394           painted = false;
395           try { // "sleep()" throws the "InterruptedException"
396               starttime += delay; // compute the destination time
397               // if destination time isn't reached -> sleep
398               Thread.sleep(Math.max(0,starttime - System.currentTimeMillis()));
399           }
400           catch (InterruptedException e) { // must be; otherwise it leads to an error
401               break;    // because "sleep()" throws the "InterruptedException"
```

```
402                    }
403
404                    /* "ak_pic" is only incremented if the Web browser    */
405                    /* had the opportunity to paint the current image.      */
406                    /* ("repaint()" sets only a flag: "Please repaint       */
407                    /* occasionally!")                                      */
408
409                    if (painted) {
410                        if (playdir == RIGHT) {
411                            ak_pic = ak_pic.next;
412                        }
413                        else {
414                            ak_pic = ak_pic.before;
415                        }
416                    }
417            }
418        }
419
420        /* This method is necessary because the scanner must be able        */
421        /* to resize the applet and (possibly) the frame once it has recognized */
422        /* the dimensions of the MPEG frames.                              */
423        /* This method is called by the "ScanThread".                      */
424
425        public void set_dim (int width, int height, int o_width, int o_height) {
426            w = width; h = height; // The width in MPEG stream
427            o_w = o_width; o_h = o_height; // The original width
428            resize(width < 250 ? 250 : o_width, o_height + R);
429            if (!inApplet) {
430                the_frame.resize(width < 250 ? 250 : o_width, o_height + R + 20);
431                the_frame.setLayout( new BorderLayout());
432                the_frame.add("Center", this);
433                the_frame.setTitle("JAVA-MPEG-Player");
434                the_frame.show();
435            }
436        }
437
438
439        /* The method "set_Pixels" expects the pixel data, the type and number */
440        /* of the next frame in display order to produce a new frame-"Element". */
441        /* Then it places the new Element at the appropriate position in List. */
442        /* It is called in "ScanThread".                                   */
443
444        public void set_Pixels(int Pixels[][], int f_idx, int f_type) {
445
446            Element newElement = new Element(this, Pixels, cm, f_idx, f_type, w, h, o_w, o_h);
447
448            /* put the frame into the list in display order: */
449
450            if (Frame_List == null) { // first Element
451                b_type_seen = false;
452                Frame_List = last_Element = newElement;
453                Dispatcher.put(newElement); // inform the dispatcher of the arrival of a new frame
454            }
455            else if (f_type == MPEG_video.B_TYPE) { // B - Frames are already in display order
456                b_type_seen = true;
457                last_Element.next = newElement;
458                newElement.before = last_Element;
459                last_Element = newElement;
460                Dispatcher.put(newElement); // inform the dispatcher of the arrival of a new frame
461            }
462            else { // a P or I frame; they are not necessarily in display order
463                if (last_P_or_I != null) { // last I or P frame
464                    last_Element.next = last_P_or_I; // place behind B-Frames
465                    last_P_or_I.before = last_Element;
```

```
466              last_Element = last_P_or_I;
467              Dispatcher.put(last_P_or_I); // inform the dispatcher of the arrival of a new frame
468          }
469          last_P_or_I = newElement;              // notice for later insertion;
470       }
471
472       try {                    // give the "AnimatorThread"
473           Thread.sleep(50);    // 50 msec to inform the user
474       }                        // of the arrival of the new frame
475       catch (Exception e) {    // don't know what to do in applet
476           Err.Msg = "Exception : " + e.toString();
477       }
478    }
479
480    /* The method "action" is the event handler and is called whenever the    */
481    /* user pushes a button. It determines the button and changes the         */
482    /* behaviour of the animation.                                            */
483
484    public boolean action(Event  evt, Object  what) {
485        if (evt.target == leftleft) {
486            moreleft();
487            return super.action(evt, what);
488        }
489        else if(evt.target == left) {
490            stopanim();
491            ak_pic = ak_pic.before;
492            repaint();
493            return super.action(evt, what);
494        }
495        else if (evt.target == stop) {
496            stopanim();
497            return super.action(evt, what);
498        }
499        else if(evt.target == right) {
500            stopanim();
501             ak_pic = ak_pic.next;
502            repaint();
503            return super.action(evt, what);
504        }
505        else if (evt.target == rightright) {
506            moreright();
507            return super.action(evt, what);
508        }
509        else if (evt.target == qb) {
510            System.exit(10);
511        }
512        return super.action(evt, what);
513    }
514
515    /* The method "moreleft()" increases the speed of backward    */
516    /* playing or decreases the speed of forward playing          */
517
518    private void moreleft() {
519        if (AnimatorThread == null) {
520            delay = 50;
521            playdir = LEFT;
522            AnimatorThread = new Thread(this);
523            AnimatorThread.start();
524            return;
525        }
526        if (playdir == LEFT) {
527            if ((delay -= DELTA) < MINDELAY) delay = MINDELAY;
528            return;
529        }
```

```
530        if ((delay += DELTA) > MAXDELAY) stopanim();
531    }
532
533    /* The method "moreleft()" increases the speed of forward   */
534    /* playing or decreases the speed of backward playing       */
535
536
537    private void moreright() {
538        if (AnimatorThread == null) {
539            delay = 50;
540            playdir = RIGHT;
541            AnimatorThread = new Thread(this);
542            AnimatorThread.start();
543            return;
544        }
545        if (playdir == RIGHT) {
546            if ((delay -= DELTA) < MINDELAY) delay = MINDELAY;
547            return;
548        }
549        if ((delay += DELTA) > MAXDELAY) stopanim();
550    }
551
552    private void stopanim() {
553        AnimatorThread = null;
554    }
555
556    /* The method "update" must decide whether the program is in   */
557    /* scan phase or not. If so, it displays the actual scan state */
558    /* to the user. Otherwise it displays the next frame.          */
559    /* If an error occurred it calls "paint()" to show the error   */
560    /* message.                                                    */
561
562    public void update(Graphics g) {  // overrides the "update()" - method of Applet
563        if (Err.Msg != null) { // error ?
564            paint(g);
565            return;
566        }
567        if (Scanning) {
568            if (akElement != null) {
569                String Type_s = null;
570                switch(akElement.Frame_type) {
571                    case MPEG_video.I_TYPE: Type_s = " (I_FRAME) decoded"; break;
572                    case MPEG_video.B_TYPE: Type_s = " (B_FRAME) decoded"; break;
573                    case MPEG_video.P_TYPE: Type_s = " (P_FRAME) decoded"; break;
574                    default: Type_s = "unknown"; break;
575                }
576                g.setColor(getBackground()); // clear background
577                g.fillRect(0, o_h, 250, R + 20);
578                g.setColor(Color.red);
579                g.drawString("Decoding WAIT!!!" , 10, o_h + 15);
580                g.setColor(Color.black);
581                g.drawString("Frame Nr. " + akElement.Frame_idx + Type_s, 10, o_h + 30);
582                g.drawImage(akElement.Picture, 0, 0, this);
583
584                return;
585            }
586        }
587        if (ak_pic == null) return;
588        g.drawImage(ak_pic.Picture, 0, 0, this);
589        painted = true; // "is painted" -> see "run()"
590        if (first) { // change the status string to "Playing"
591            first = false;
592            g.setColor(getBackground());
593                g.fillRect(0, o_h, 250, R + 20);
```

```
594                        g.setColor(Color.black);
595              if (!userdelay) {
596                        g.drawString("Playing", 10, o_h + 15);
597              }
598          }
599      }
600
601      /* The method "paint()" is only called in error case. It displays the    */
602      /* error message.                                                         */
603
604      public void paint(Graphics g) {
605          if (Err.Msg != null) {
606              if (!inApplet) {
607                  the_frame.resize(200, 60);
608              }
609              resize(200, 60);
610              g.setColor(getBackground());
611              g.fillRect(0, 0, o_w, o_h);
612              g.setColor(Color.black);
613              g.drawString(Err.Msg, 1, 15);
614              if (!inApplet) {
615                  System.out.println(Err.Msg);
616                  System.exit(10);
617              }
618          }
619      }
620
621      /* If the program runs as application, the method "main()" is called at first.  */
622      /* It creates a frame to get a display surface.                                 */
623
624      public static void main( String args[] ) {
625          InputStream fis = null;
626          boolean userdelay = false;
627
628          if (args.length < 1) {
629              System.err.println("wrong argument count");
630              System.exit(10);
631          }
632          try {
633              fis = new DataInputStream(new FileInputStream(args[0]));
634          }
635          catch (IOException e) {
636              System.out.println("can't open " + args[0]);
637              System.exit(10);
638          }
639          if (args.length == 2) {
640              if (args[1].compareTo("user") == 0) {
641                  userdelay = true;
642              }
643              else {
644                  try {
645                      delay = Integer.parseInt(args[1]);
646                  }
647                  catch (Exception e) {
648                      System.out.println(args[1] + " is not a number");
649                      System.out.println("Usage: Mpeg_Play <file>.mpg [<delay> | user]");
650                      System.exit(10);
651                  }
652              }
653          }
654          new myFrame(fis, userdelay);
655      }
656 }
```

ANNOTATIONS

The **MPEG_Play** applet uses a dozen or so classes, defined in ten different source files. To help you locate the files and understand the following discussions, Table 4-1 summarizes each class and lists the file where that class is defined. Note that all Java source files are in the **ch04\MPEGPlay\mpeg_java-3.3** directory of the companion CD-ROM.

As you can see from Table 4-1, the **MPEG_Play.java** file defines the following three classes:

◆ The **Element** class (lines 52 through 148) represents the pixels for a single frame from the MPEG file. Each **Element** object has a variable named **next**

Class Name	File	Description
dispatch	MPEG_Play.java	Provides the capability to control the scanning and animation threads.
Element	MPEG_Play.java	Represents the pixels in a single frame of animation.
Err	Err.java	Holds any error messages.
Huffmann	Huffmann.java	Decodes variable-length Huffmann code.
IDCT	IDCT.java	Performs the inverse discrete cosine transform (IDCT), used in decoding MPEG video. (Note that this source file is generated by a C program. For more information, consult the files **README** and **Makefile** in the **ch04\MPEGPlay\mpeg_java-3.3** directory.)
MPEG_Play	MPEG_Play.java	Represents the applet that displays the MPEG video frames.
MPEG_scan	MPEG_scan.java	Scans MPEG files and passes data to an **MPEG_video** object to decode.
MPEG_video	MPEG_video.java	Decodes an MPEG video data stream.
io_tool	io_tool.java	Implements an I/O stream to read the bit-oriented data from the MPEG file.
motion_data	motion_data.java	Stores and computes motion information embedded in the MPEG file.
myFrame	myFrame.java	Provides a frame that should be used when **MPEG_Play** is used in an application (rather than as an applet).
semaphor	semaphor.java	Toggles between two threads, each decoding a different layer of the MPEG file.

TABLE 4-1.   Summary of Classes Used in the **MPEG_Play** Applet.

that refers to another **Element**. The **next** variable is used to store **Element** objects in a linked list.

◆ The **dispatch** class (lines 156 through 178) is used to control the threads that scan and display the frames.

◆ The **MPEG_Play** class (lines 190 through 656) represents the applet that processes the MPEG file and displays the MPEG frames.

Unlike other applets, **MPEG_Play** does not include an **init()** method. When **MPEG_Play** runs, everything starts in its **start()** method, shown in lines 244 through 306. Lines 252 and 253 call **getParameter()** to get the **FILENAME** and **DELAY** parameters from the HTML file. The **FILENAME** parameter specifies the name of the MPEG file. Lines 267 and 268 construct a URL and an input data stream, using the specified MPEG filename:

```
267               source_url = new URL(getCodeBase(), f_name);
268               in_stream = source_url.openStream();
```

If the MPEG file has not yet been scanned, lines 294 through 296 start the scanner thread:

```
294          M_Scan = new MPEG_scan(this, in_stream);
295          ScanThread = new Thread(M_Scan);
296           ScanThread.start();
```

Line 294 creates an **MPEG_scan** object, **M_scan**, to scan the MPEG file. Line 295 creates the thread that uses the **M_scan** object to perform the scanning. Notice that the **Thread()** constructor uses the **MPEG_scan** object as its argument. This means that the thread executes the **run()** method of the **MPEG_scan** class.

After the scanner thread has started, lines 300 through 305 of the **start()** method create an animation thread (called **AnimatorThread**) and get it running. The **AnimatorThread** executes **MPEG_Play**'s **run()** method (defined in lines 354 through 418). This method essentially changes from one frame to another and displays the frame by calling the **repaint()** method.

The **update()** method, in lines 562 through 599, displays the current frame's image in the applet's display area. If there is any error, lines 563 through 566 call the **paint()** method to display an error message and return. In fact, **MPEG_Play**'s **paint()** method, shown in lines 604 through 619, is meant only to display error messages. The image display is handled by **update()**.

While the MPEG file is still being scanned, lines 567 through 586 of the **update()** method display a message stating that the applet is waiting for decoding to complete. After that, line 588 displays the image for the current frame:

```
588          g.drawImage(ak_pic.Picture, 0, 0, this);
```

The **ak_pic** variable, defined on line 193, is an **Element**. The **Picture** variable of the **Element** class is an **Image** containing the pixels for a frame extracted from the MPEG file.

Java 2

Java 2 includes an extension package called Java Media Framework, or JMF for short. JMF provides a simple Application Programming Interface (API) that you can use to play audio and video (in various formats) in your Java application or applet. For example, JMF lets you create a **Player** object that can play any of the multimedia file formats supported by JMF. Among other formats, JMF supports several types of video (such as MPEG-1, AVI, and QuickTime) and a wide variety of audio (such as AIFF, AU, MIDI, RMF, and WAV). You can learn more about JMF and download beta versions from the Web site at **http://www.javasoft.com/products/java-media/jmf/**. You can download and use JMF with older versions of Java (JDK 1.1 or later) as well.

Games

Y ou will find computer games in practically every programming environment, and Java is no exception. Soon after the Web became popular in 1993, there were many Web pages with simple HTML-based interactive games like tic-tac-toe. These games were rather cumbersome to play because they worked by downloading a new HTML page every time you made a move. When Java applets came along, it became possible to provide true interaction using an applet. You could put the game's logic into an applet, which would respond promptly to the user's input (through the mouse or the keyboard) because it ran locally in the Web browser.

Java applets are quite suitable for interactive games like tic-tac-toe, simple arcade games, and puzzles. This chapter presents the following representative game applets:

- **TicTacToe**—the classic two-player game of tic-tac-toe

- **Minesweeper**—the well-known Minesweeper game, where you try to find the mines in a minefield (a similar game comes with Windows 95/98)

- **Tetris**—the popular game involving stacking falling blocks of different shapes

- **Missile Commando II**—a game of missile defense where your goal is to shoot down bombs and missiles before they blow up your cities

Tic-Tac-Toe

Tic-tac-toe is a classic two-player game that you probably know well. To play the game, you draw a pair of horizontal lines that intersect a pair of vertical lines. This forms nine squares. One player uses an X mark, and the other uses an O mark. Players take turn marking squares. Whoever manages to draw three marks in a line (horizontally, vertically, or diagonally) wins. The game is a draw if no one can place three marks in a line.

Sun's Java Development Kit (JDK) comes with a **TicTacToe** applet (written by Arthur van Hoff) that implements the classic tic-tac-toe game. Because Sun allows anyone to use and distribute the code, I present Sun's **TicTacToe** applet here. The next few sections show you how to use the applet and how it's implemented.

Playing TicTacToe

You will find all of the files for the **TicTacToe** applet in the **ch05\TicTacToe** directory of the companion CD-ROM. There are two subdirectories—**images** and **audio**—that contain the image and audio files used by **TicTacToe**. To try out **TicTacToe**, open the **playtt.html** file in a Java-capable Web browser. The applet draws pairs of horizontal and vertical lines, forming the classic nine-square display of tic-tac-toe. You play X and the applet plays O. To start the game, click on the square where you want to mark an X. The applet draws an X, and then it draws an

O at another square. Then it's your turn again, and so it goes. Figure 5-1 shows a typical **TicTacToe** game. In this case, the game is a draw because neither player managed to place three marks in a line.

PROGRAMMER'S NOTE *The **TicTacToe** applet uses Java 1.1–style event handling. To run the applet, you need a Web browser that supports Java 1.1.*

Using the **TicTacToe** applet on an HTML page is simple because the applet does not accept any parameters. Here is the complete listing of the **playttt.html** file that produces the display shown in Figure 5-1.

```html
<html>
<head>
<title>TicTacToe (from JDK 1.2, also known as Java 2)</title>
</head>
<body>
<hr>
<applet code=TicTacToe.class width=120 height=120>
</applet>
<hr>
<a href="TicTacToe.txt">The source.</a>
<br>
</body>
</html>
```

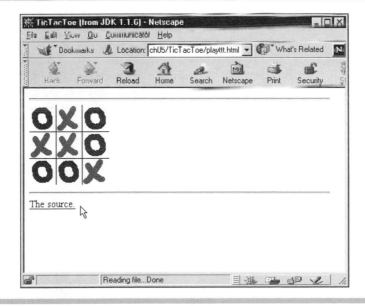

FIGURE 5-1. A typical session with the **TicTacToe** applet.

As you can see, the applet is inserted in the HTML file with an **<applet>** tag that specifies a display area 120 pixels wide by 120 pixels tall. Two **<hr>** tags are used to draw the horizontal rulers above and below the applet. This HTML file also includes a link to the applet's source code. Note that the link is to the **TicTacToe.txt** file (which is simply a copy of **TicTacToe.java**) so that the Web browser displays the source code as a plain text file.

TicTacToe

Understanding TicTacToe

Now that you have tried out the **TicTacToe** applet, you can turn your attention to how the game is implemented. The following listing shows the **TicTacToe.java** file that implements the applet. You will find this file in the **ch05\TicTacToe** directory of the companion CD-ROM. The sections following the listing describe key features of the **TicTacToe** applet.

```
1  /*
2   * @(#)TicTacToe.java        1.4 98/06/29
3   *
4   * Copyright (c) 1997, 1998 Sun Microsystems, Inc. All Rights Reserved.
5   *
6   * Sun grants you ("Licensee") a non-exclusive, royalty free, license to use,
7   * modify and redistribute this software in source and binary code form,
8   * provided that i) this copyright notice and license appear on all copies of
9   * the software; and ii) Licensee does not utilize the software in a manner
10  * which is disparaging to Sun.
11  *
12  * This software is provided "AS IS," without a warranty of any kind. ALL
13  * EXPRESS OR IMPLIED CONDITIONS, REPRESENTATIONS AND WARRANTIES, INCLUDING ANY
14  * IMPLIED WARRANTY OF MERCHANTABILITY, FITNESS FOR A PARTICULAR PURPOSE OR
15  * NON-INFRINGEMENT, ARE HEREBY EXCLUDED. SUN AND ITS LICENSORS SHALL NOT BE
16  * LIABLE FOR ANY DAMAGES SUFFERED BY LICENSEE AS A RESULT OF USING, MODIFYING
17  * OR DISTRIBUTING THE SOFTWARE OR ITS DERIVATIVES. IN NO EVENT WILL SUN OR ITS
18  * LICENSORS BE LIABLE FOR ANY LOST REVENUE, PROFIT OR DATA, OR FOR DIRECT,
19  * INDIRECT, SPECIAL, CONSEQUENTIAL, INCIDENTAL OR PUNITIVE DAMAGES, HOWEVER
20  * CAUSED AND REGARDLESS OF THE THEORY OF LIABILITY, ARISING OUT OF THE USE OF
21  * OR INABILITY TO USE SOFTWARE, EVEN IF SUN HAS BEEN ADVISED OF THE
22  * POSSIBILITY OF SUCH DAMAGES.
23  *
24  * This software is not designed or intended for use in on-line control of
25  * aircraft, air traffic, aircraft navigation or aircraft communications; or in
26  * the design, construction, operation or maintenance of any nuclear
27  * facility. Licensee represents and warrants that it will not use or
28  * redistribute the Software for such purposes.
29  */
```

```
30
31   import java.awt.*;
32   import java.awt.event.*;
33   import java.awt.image.*;
34   import java.net.*;
35   import java.applet.*;
36
37   /**
38    * A TicTacToe applet. A very simple, and mostly brain-dead
39    * implementation of your favorite game! <p>
40    *
41    * In this game a position is represented by a white and black
42    * bitmask. A bit is set if a position is ocupied. There are
43    * 9 squares so there are 1<<9 possible positions for each
44    * side. An array of 1<<9 booleans is created, it marks
45    * all the winning positions.
46    *
47    * @version       1.2, 13 Oct 1995
48    * @author Arthur van Hoff
49    * @modified 04/23/96 Jim Hagen : winning sounds
50    * @modified 02/10/98 Mike McCloskey : added destroy()
51    */
52   public
53   class TicTacToe extends Applet implements MouseListener {
54       /**
55        * White's current position. The computer is white.
56        */
57       int white;
58
59       /**
60        * Black's current position. The user is black.
61        */
62       int black;
63
64       /**
65        * The squares in order of importance...
66        */
67       final static int moves[] = {4, 0, 2, 6, 8, 1, 3, 5, 7};
68
69       /**
70        * The winning positions.
71        */
```

```
72      static boolean won[] = new boolean[1 << 9];
73      static final int DONE = (1 << 9) - 1;
74      static final int OK = 0;
75      static final int WIN = 1;
76      static final int LOSE = 2;
77      static final int STALEMATE = 3;
78
79      /**
80       * Mark all positions with these bits set as winning.
81       */
82      static void isWon(int pos) {
83          for (int i = 0 ; i < DONE ; i++) {
84              if ((i & pos) == pos) {
85                  won[i] = true;
86              }
87          }
88      }
89
90      /**
91       * Initialize all winning positions.
92       */
93      static {
94          isWon((1 << 0) | (1 << 1) | (1 << 2));
95          isWon((1 << 3) | (1 << 4) | (1 << 5));
96          isWon((1 << 6) | (1 << 7) | (1 << 8));
97          isWon((1 << 0) | (1 << 3) | (1 << 6));
98          isWon((1 << 1) | (1 << 4) | (1 << 7));
99          isWon((1 << 2) | (1 << 5) | (1 << 8));
100         isWon((1 << 0) | (1 << 4) | (1 << 8));
101         isWon((1 << 2) | (1 << 4) | (1 << 6));
102     }
103
104     /**
105      * Compute the best move for white.
106      * @return the square to take
107      */
108     int bestMove(int white, int black) {
109         int bestmove = -1;
110
111       loop:
112         for (int i = 0 ; i < 9 ; i++) {
113             int mw = moves[i];
114             if (((white & (1 << mw)) == 0) && ((black & (1 << mw)) == 0)) {
```

```
115                      int pw = white | (1 << mw);
116                  if (won[pw]) {
117                      // white wins, take it!
118                      return mw;
119                  }
120                  for (int mb = 0 ; mb < 9 ; mb++) {
121                      if (((pw & (1 << mb)) == 0) && ((black & (1 << mb)) == 0)) {
122                          int pb = black | (1 << mb);
123                          if (won[pb]) {
124                              // black wins, take another
125                              continue loop;
126                          }
127                      }
128                  }
129                  // Neither white nor black can win in one move, this will do.
130                  if (bestmove == -1) {
131                      bestmove = mw;
132                  }
133              }
134          }
135      if (bestmove != -1) {
136          return bestmove;
137      }
138
139      // No move is totally satisfactory, try the first one that is open
140      for (int i = 0 ; i < 9 ; i++) {
141          int mw = moves[i];
142          if (((white & (1 << mw)) == 0) && ((black & (1 << mw)) == 0)) {
143              return mw;
144          }
145      }
146
147      // No more moves
148      return -1;
149  }
150
151  /**
152   * User move.
153   * @return true if legal
154   */
155  boolean yourMove(int m) {
156      if ((m < 0) || (m > 8)) {
157          return false;
```

```
158          }
159          if (((black | white) & (1 << m)) != 0) {
160              return false;
161          }
162          black |= 1 << m;
163          return true;
164      }
165
166      /**
167       * Computer move.
168       * @return true if legal
169       */
170      boolean myMove() {
171          if ((black | white) == DONE) {
172              return false;
173          }
174          int best = bestMove(white, black);
175          white |= 1 << best;
176          return true;
177      }
178
179      /**
180       * Figure what the status of the game is.
181       */
182      int status() {
183          if (won[white]) {
184              return WIN;
185          }
186          if (won[black]) {
187              return LOSE;
188          }
189          if ((black | white) == DONE) {
190              return STALEMATE;
191          }
192          return OK;
193      }
194
195      /**
196       * Who goes first in the next game?
197       */
198      boolean first = true;
199
200      /**
```

```
201          * The image for white.
202          */
203         Image notImage;
204
205         /**
206          * The image for black.
207          */
208         Image crossImage;
209
210         /**
211          * Initialize the applet. Resize and load images.
212          */
213         public void init() {
214             notImage = getImage(getCodeBase(), "images/not.gif");
215             crossImage = getImage(getCodeBase(), "images/cross.gif");
216
217             addMouseListener(this);
218         }
219
220         public void destroy() {
221             removeMouseListener(this);
222         }
233
224         /**
225          * Paint it.
226          */
227         public void paint(Graphics g) {
228             Dimension d = getSize();
229             g.setColor(Color.black);
230             int xoff = d.width / 3;
231             int yoff = d.height / 3;
232             g.drawLine(xoff, 0, xoff, d.height);
233             g.drawLine(2*xoff, 0, 2*xoff, d.height);
234             g.drawLine(0, yoff, d.width, yoff);
235             g.drawLine(0, 2*yoff, d.width, 2*yoff);
236
237             int i = 0;
238             for (int r = 0 ; r < 3 ; r++) {
239                 for (int c = 0 ; c < 3 ; c++, i++) {
240                     if ((white & (1 << i)) != 0) {
241                         g.drawImage(notImage, c*xoff + 1, r*yoff + 1, this);
242                     } else if ((black & (1 << i)) != 0) {
243                         g.drawImage(crossImage, c*xoff + 1, r*yoff + 1, this);
```

```
244                    }
245                }
246            }
247    }
248
249    /**
250     * The user has clicked in the applet. Figure out where
251     * and see if a legal move is possible. If it is a legal
252     * move, respond with a legal move (if possible).
253     */
254    public void mouseReleased(MouseEvent e) {
255        int x = e.getX();
256        int y = e.getY();
257
258        switch (status()) {
259          case WIN:
260          case LOSE:
261          case STALEMATE:
262            play(getCodeBase(), "audio/return.au");
263            white = black = 0;
264            if (first) {
265                white |= 1 << (int)(Math.random() * 9);
266            }
267            first = !first;
268            repaint();
269            return;
270        }
271
272        // Figure out the row/column
273        Dimension d = getSize();
274        int c = (x * 3) / d.width;
275        int r = (y * 3) / d.height;
276        if (yourMove(c + r * 3)) {
277            repaint();
278
279            switch (status()) {
280              case WIN:
281                play(getCodeBase(), "audio/yahoo1.au");
282                break;
283              case LOSE:
284                play(getCodeBase(), "audio/yahoo2.au");
285                break;
286              case STALEMATE:
```

```
287                    break;
288                default:
289                  if (myMove()) {
290                      repaint();
291                      switch (status()) {
292                        case WIN:
293                          play(getCodeBase(), "audio/yahoo1.au");
294                          break;
295                        case LOSE:
296                          play(getCodeBase(), "audio/yahoo2.au");
297                          break;
298                        case STALEMATE:
299                          break;
300                        default:
301                          play(getCodeBase(), "audio/ding.au");
302                      }
303                  } else {
304                      play(getCodeBase(), "audio/beep.au");
305                  }
306              }
307          } else {
308              play(getCodeBase(), "audio/beep.au");
309          }
310      }
311
312      public void mousePressed(MouseEvent e) {
313      }
314
315      public void mouseClicked(MouseEvent e) {
316      }
317
318      public void mouseEntered(MouseEvent e) {
319      }
320
321      public void mouseExited(MouseEvent e) {
322      }
323
324      public String getAppletInfo() {
325          return "TicTacToe by Arthur van Hoff";
326      }
327  }
```

ANNOTATIONS

The unique aspects of **TicTacToe** are the various tricks used to represent the tic-tac-toe game in a computer program. The applet assigns a number to each of the nine squares in the game. Figure 5-2 shows the numbering scheme used in **TicTacToe**. As the figure shows, the squares are numbered sequentially from 0 through 8.

The applet's design uses the concept of a *position*, which represents a specific sequence of marks made by one player. Because there are 9 squares and each square can be either marked or unmarked, there are 2^9 or 512 possible positions for each side (X or O). To better understand the meaning of a position, imagine a 9-bit number in which each bit (with 0 representing the least significant bit and 8 the most significant) corresponds to a numbered square in Figure 5-2. For example, the least significant bit—bit 0—corresponds to square 0, and bit 4 corresponds to the middle square. If a square is marked, you should set that square's bit to 1. Thus, if square 4 is marked, you should set bit 4 to 1. With this scheme, a sequence of moves by one player will mark some bits in the 9-bit number, and that number will be the current position for that player.

When no squares are marked, all bits are 0. Thus, position 0 means no squares are marked. Suppose that after two moves you have marked squares 0 and 4 and that bits 0 and 4 are set to 1. To find the position for this case, you simply need to left-shift 1 by the appropriate square numbers and bitwise-OR the result. This means that the position corresponding to marks in squares 0 and 4 is (1<<0) | (1<<4),

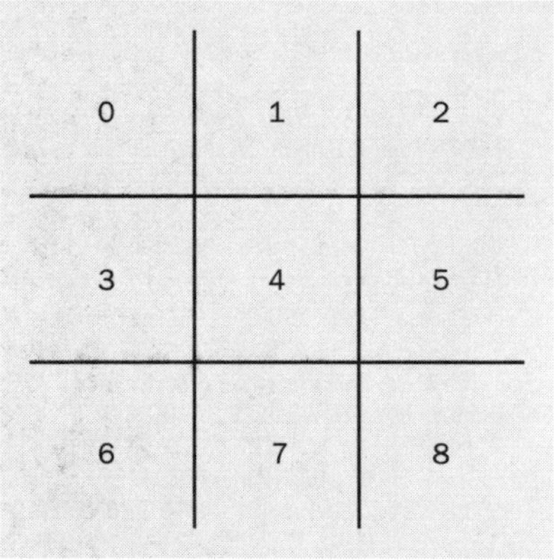

FIGURE 5-2. The nine squares are numbered 0 through 8.

or 17. As you can see, the position captures information about all of the squares a player has marked so far.

The applet uses an array of 512 **boolean** variables, one for each possible position that the applet could play. The **boolean** variables corresponding to the winning positions are set to **true**. For example, when squares 0, 1, and 2 are marked, the position is denoted by (1 << 0) | (1 << 1) | (1 << 2), or 7. Because this is a winning position (squares 0, 1, and 2 form a line), the **boolean** variable at index 7 is set to **true**.

TICTACTOE DESIGN The **TicTacToe** applet needs to keep track of each player's moves and decide which moves are winning moves. For starters, the applet uses two integer variables named **white** and **black** to keep track of each player's position (the sequence of moves, as explained in the previous section). The **white** variable represents the computer's (the **TicTacToe** applet's) position, whereas **black** holds the user's position. These two variables are at the heart of the **TicTacToe** applet because they store each player's moves. The applet updates these variables as the user and the applet make their moves. The **paint()** method uses these variables when painting the game board and the X and O marks on the board.

To figure out its moves, the applet uses an array called **moves[]** to store the square numbers in decreasing order of importance. Line 67 defines this array, using the square numbers shown in Figure 5-2:

```
67      final static int moves[] = {4, 0, 2, 6, 8, 1, 3, 5, 7};
```

As you probably know from experience, the middle square is the most important square in tic-tac-toe, meaning that you should mark it first if it's available. Then come the diagonal corners (0, 2, 6, and 8). Finally, the squares on the sides (1, 3, 5, and 7) are the last priority. When selecting a move, the **TicTacToe** applet tries to pick the first available square from this array.

The final design element is to figure out a way to tell when the game is over. This happens when either player marks three squares in a line. **TicTacToe** uses a 512-element boolean array named **won[]** that holds information about all winning positions. Line 72 defines the **won[]** array:

```
72      static boolean won[] = new boolean[1 << 9];
```

Note that this statement uses 1<<9 (that's 1 left-shifted by 9 bit positions) as the array size. That's because with 9 squares, there can be at most 1<<9 or 512 positions, and the applet needs a **boolean** variable for each position.

To make the **won[]** array useful, each winning position needs to be set to **true**. This is done by calling the **isWon()** method, defined in lines 82 through 88. This method is designed to set an element of the **won[]** array at a specified index to **true**. In other words, if you call **isWon()** with 7 as argument, **isWon()** sets **won[7]** to **true**.

It's interesting the way the applet's code calls the **isWon()** method to initialize all winning positions in the **won[]** array to true. This initialization step does not happen in the **init()** method. Instead, the **isWon()** method is called inside a **static** block (also called a static initializer), as shown in lines 93 through 102:

```
93    static {
94        isWon((1 << 0) | (1 << 1) | (1 << 2));
95        isWon((1 << 3) | (1 << 4) | (1 << 5));
96        isWon((1 << 6) | (1 << 7) | (1 << 8));
97        isWon((1 << 0) | (1 << 3) | (1 << 6));
98        isWon((1 << 1) | (1 << 4) | (1 << 7));
99        isWon((1 << 2) | (1 << 5) | (1 << 8));
100       isWon((1 << 0) | (1 << 4) | (1 << 8));
101       isWon((1 << 2) | (1 << 4) | (1 << 6));
102   }
```

The **static** block calls **isWon()** for eight winning positions (representing winning moves). This initializes the **won[]** array for those positions to **true**.

PROGRAMMER'S NOTE   *You can use a **static** block to initialize **static** variables. Note that the methods and variables appearing in a **static** block must be declared as **static**.*

In case you are wondering, the **static** block in lines 93 through 102 initializes the **won[]** array entries for the following eight winning positions:

- ◆   A horizontal line through squares 0, 1, and 2
- ◆   A horizontal line through squares 3, 4, and 5
- ◆   A horizontal line through squares 6, 7, and 8
- ◆   A vertical line through squares 0, 3, and 6
- ◆   A vertical line through squares 1, 4, and 7
- ◆   A vertical line through squares 2, 5, and 8
- ◆   A diagonal line through squares 0, 4, and 8
- ◆   A diagonal line through squares 2, 4, and 6

In addition to these variables used for keeping track of players' positions and figuring out winning positions, **TicTacToe** also implements a simple algorithm to select the next move. The **bestMove()** method, shown in lines 108 through 149, computes the best move for white (the computer) given the current white and black positions (these are the squares marked so far). Essentially, this method tries to find the best square for the computer to mark. It loops over the nine squares (as listed in the **moves[]** array) and tries to find a position such that the entry in the **won[]** array for that position is **true** (meaning that the position is a winning one). If no such position exists, it selects the first available square from the **moves[]** array.

TICTACTOE GAME START   When the **TicTacToe** applet starts, its **init()** method, shown in lines 213 through 218, loads two images—**images/not.gif** representing an O and **images/cross.gif** representing an X. Both images are expected to be in the **images** subdirectory. The **init()** method then calls the **addMouseListener()** method to ensure that mouse clicks are handled by the applet. This is important because the user plays the **TicTacToe** game by clicking on the squares.

The **paint()** method, shown in lines 227 through 247, paints the game board with the current set of X and O marks. These are based on the current positions stored in the **white** and **black** variables. Initially, these variables are zero, so the **paint()** method simply draws the game board with the vertical and horizontal lines delineating the nine squares.

At this point, the game can begin as soon as the user clicks on a square.

TICTACTOE GAME PLAY   When the user clicks on a square, the **mouseReleased()** method, shown in lines 254 through 310, is called. This method essentially plays the game. Lines 255 and 256 of this method get the x and y coordinates of the mouse click:

```
255         int x = e.getX();
256         int y = e.getY();
```

Here, **e** is the **MouseEvent** argument for the **mouseReleased()** method.

Lines 273 through 275 compute the row and column numbers of the square where the user has clicked:

```
273         Dimension d = getSize();
274         int c = (x * 3) / d.width;
275         int r = (y * 3) / d.height;
```

Line 273 gets the dimensions of the applet's display area. The game squares (which are actually rectangles) are created by dividing the applet's display area into three parts along the width and three parts along the height. The formulas in lines 274 and 275 find the column and row numbers of the square. These numbers range from 0 to 2. The column and row numbers are such that you can get the square number (as shown in Figure 5-2) with the formula (c + r * 3).

After the row and column location of the mouse click has been computed, line 276 calls the **yourMove()** method to check whether it's a legal move. If it is, line 162 of the **yourMove()** method updates the **black** variable that represents the user's positions thus far:

```
162         black |= 1 << m;
```

The **yourMove()** method returns **true** if the move is legal. Line 277 then calls **repaint()**, which schedules a call to **paint()** to redraw the X and O marks on the game board:

```
277             repaint();
```

Line 279 calls **status()** to determine the game's status. If the game is a win, a loss, or a stalemate, it plays an appropriate audio clip.

If no one has won yet, line 289 calls **myMove()** to compute the applet's move in response to the user's mouse click. The **myMove()** method, shown in lines 170 through 177, finds a move for the computer by calling **bestMove()** and then updates the **white** position.

Minesweeper

Minesweeper is another popular game that you may have played on your PC (because it comes with Microsoft Windows). In the Minesweeper game, your goal is to locate all of the hidden mines in a minefield, represented by squares arranged in a grid. You are supposed to uncover all of the squares that do not contain mines and mark the squares that contain mines.

This section presents the **Minesweeper** applet that implements the well-known Minesweeper game. The **Minesweeper** applet is copyrighted by Andrew D. Birrell. The applet and its source code are available free under the terms of the GNU General Public License. The original **Minesweeper** home page is at **http://www.research.digital.com/SRC/personal/Andrew_Birrell/minesweeper/**.

In the next few sections, you'll learn how to play **Minesweeper** and how the applet is implemented.

Playing Minesweeper

The **Minesweeper** applet's class file and other associated files are in the **ch05\Mineswpr** directory of the companion CD-ROM. To try out **Minesweeper**, open the **mines.html** file in a Java-capable Web browser. You will see a square grid—that's the minefield. Along the top edge are three items:

◆ On the left is the number of mines that you have not yet found.

◆ In the middle is a button with a yellow face.

◆ On the right is a counter that counts the elapsed time.

That elapsed time counter does not start running until you click on a square. The counter essentially serves as the game's score; the lower the score the better. The yellow face looks bored while the game is in progress, changes to a happy face if you win, and turns sad if you uncover a square that has a mine in it (in which case you lose the game).

Your goal is to uncover all squares that do not contain any mines and to mark all of the squares that contain mines—and to do this as quickly as possible. To uncover a square, click the left mouse button on the square. When you uncover a square that does not have any adjacent mines, **Minesweeper** clears out all other neighboring squares that also do not touch any squares containing mines.

To mark a square that you suspect has a mine, click the right mouse button on that square. When you mark a square by right-clicking, a red flag appears on that square. Every time you mark a mine, the count of mines in the upper-left corner decreases by 1. This happens even if you mark a mine incorrectly, thinking that a square has a mine when it actually does not.

If you are unsure about a square, click it twice with the right mouse button. A question mark appears on the square, and the mine count remains unchanged. Later on, you can uncover that square with a left click or get rid of the question mark by right-clicking.

If you uncover all of the squares without mines, you win. If you uncover a square with a mine instead of marking it, you lose. When you accidentally uncover a mine, **Minesweeper** displays all of the mine locations, shows X marks where you incorrectly marked mines, and turns the button into a sad face. To restart the game, click on the sad face.

Figure 5-3 shows a typical game in progress, with many uncovered squares without mines, some squares marked with flags, and a few squares with question marks.

The trick to playing **Minesweeper** is determining which squares to mark as mines. **Minesweeper** gives you hints to help you locate the mines. In Figure 5-3, notice that some of the uncovered squares have a number (for example, many have a 1 or a 2, and some have a 3). The number on a square represents the total number

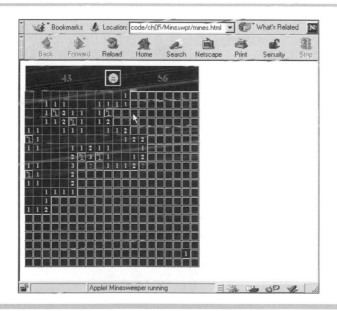

FIGURE 5-3. A typical **Minesweeper** game in progress.

of mines in the surrounding eight squares. You should use this number to decide which squares to mark as mines. For example, if there is only one covered square touching one or more squares labeled 1, then that covered square must be a mine.

To see how to use the **Minesweeper** applet on a Web page, here is the complete listing of the **mines.html** file that results in the output shown in Figure 5-3:

```html
<html>
<head>
<title>Minesweeper</title>
</head>
<body>
<applet code=Minesweeper.class width=300 height=350>
    <param name=COLUMNS value=20>
    <param name=ROWS value=20>
    <param name=PIXELS value=15>
    <param name=MINES value=50>
</applet>
</body>
</html>
```

The **<applet>** tag lists **Minesweeper.class** as the applet's class file and specifies a display area 300 pixels wide by 350 pixels tall. The height of the display area should be somewhat bigger than the width because the applet has to display the mine count and the score along the top edge. As this listing shows, **Minesweeper** accepts four parameters:

◆ **COLUMNS** is the number of columns in the minefield grid (this is the width of the minefield).

◆ **ROWS** represents the number of rows in the minefield (this is the height of the minefield).

◆ **PIXELS** denotes the size of each square in the grid by specifying the length, in pixels, of one side of a square.

◆ **MINES** indicates the number of mines hidden in the minefield (these are randomly scattered across the minefield).

As you might expect, the greater the number of mines (specified through the **MINES** parameter), the harder the game becomes because there are fewer safe squares.

Understanding Minesweeper

The following listing shows the file **Minesweeper.java** that implements the **Minesweeper** applet. I discuss the code in the sections that follow the listing.

```
1    /* Andrew's version of Minesweeper .... just for fun */
2    /* Minesweeper.java */
3    /* Copyright 1997, Andrew D. Birrell */
4    /* This program and source code are available free, under the terms of the GNU
5      general public license.  Use at your own risk!  The GNU general public
6      license is available at http://www.gnu.org/copyleft/gpl.html */
7
8    import java.applet.*;
9    import java.awt.*;
10   import java.util.*;
11
12   public class Minesweeper extends Applet implements Runnable {
13
14   /* */
15   /* State information, generally protected by our mutex */
16   /* */
17
18   int edge = 16;              /* pixels on the edge of a square */
19   int width = 16;             /* width in squares */
20   int height = 16;            /* height in squares */
21   int mines = 40;             /* number of mines */
22   int scoreHeight = 48;       /* pixels at top used for scores */
23   int faceSize = 32;          /* pixels size of smiley face */
24
25   /* "adjacent" and "exposed" are indexed by square number = y*width+x */
26
27   /* "adjacent" contains the board layout and derived state.  adjacent[i] is
28      the count of mines adjacent to square i, or "mine" if square i contains
29      a mine.  */
30   int[] adjacent = null;      /* count of adjacent mines */
31   static final int mine = 9;  /* adjacency count for mine */
32
33   /* "exposed" contains the exposure state of the board.  Values > "unexposed"
34      represent exposed squares; these either have the distinguished values
35      "exploded" or "incorrect", or some greater value (left over from the
36      pending exposure queue) for plain old exposed squares.  Values <=
37      "unexposed" include plain old unexposed squares, or one of the markers.
38      ----
```

```
39        During the "expose" method, the queue of pending exposures is a linked
40        list through this array, using array indexes.  The method holds the head
41        and tail.  "listEnd" is the tail marker.
42        ----
43        "initOffscreen" assumes that the distinguished values in "exposed" are
44        distinct integers from the adjacency counts, for simplicity in calling
45        initOneOffscreen. */
46     int[] exposed = null;              /* exposure state / pending exposures */
47     static final int listEnd = -1;    /* end marker in "exposed" */
48     static final int incorrect = -2; /* incorrect flag, at end of game */
49     static final int exploded = -3;  /* exploded mine (at end of game!) */
50     static final int unexposed = -4; /* default state at start of game */
51     static final int flagged = -5;    /* marker flag by user */
52     static final int queried = -6;    /* query flag by user */
53
54     int flags = 0;               /* count of flags currently set */
55     int remaining = 0;           /* count of unexposed squares */
56     int sadness = 0;             /* whether smiley is sad */
57     static final int sad = -1; /* smiley value after loss */
58     static final int bored = 0;/* smiley value during game */
59     static final int happy = 1;/* smiley value after win */
60
61     /* Various states used in painting.  There are offscreen images for each state
62        of the squares */
63     Color[] colors = null;       /* color for exposed counts */
64     Color baseColor;             /* color for unexposed squares */
65     Color baseShadow;            /* slightly darker than baseColor */
66     Color mineColor;             /* color for mine itself */
67     Color numberColor;           /* color for score digits */
68     Color dangerousColor;        /* color for flag, explode, incorrect */
69     Image[] exposedRect = null;
70     Image incorrectRect = null;
71     Image explodedRect = null;
72     Image unexposedRect = null;
73     Image flaggedRect = null;
74     Image queriedRect = null;
75     Image boredSmiley = null;
76     Image happySmiley = null;
77     Image sadSmiley = null;
78     Font theMainFont;
79     Font theScoreFont;
80     int numberSize;              /* Pixels for number display */
81     final static int numberMargin = 2;
```

```
82
83
84   long startTime = 0;          /* time of first click; 0 if stopped */
85   int elapsed = 0;             /* elapsed time; -1 if not started */
86
87
88   /* */
89   /* Game play */
90   /* */
91
92   private void add1(int x, int y) {
93     /* Increase adjacency count, if it's in range */
94     if (x<0 || x>=width || y<0 || y>=height) return;
95     int t = y*width+x;
96     if (adjacent[t] != mine) adjacent[t]++;
97   }
98
99   private synchronized void erase() {
100    /* Start of new game. Includes implicit initialization. */
101    if (adjacent == null) adjacent = new int[width*height];
102    if (exposed == null) exposed = new int[width*height];
103    for (int i = 0; i < width*height; i++) {
104      adjacent[i] = 0;
105      exposed[i] = unexposed;
106    };
107    int laid = 0;
108    while (laid < mines) {
109      int target = (short)Math.floor(Math.random()*height*width);
110      if (target>=0 && target < height*width && adjacent[target] != mine) {
111        adjacent[target] = mine;
112        int tx = target%width;
113        int ty = target/width;
114        add1(tx-1, ty-1);
115        add1(tx-1, ty);
116        add1(tx-1, ty+1);
117        add1(tx, ty-1);
118        add1(tx, ty+1);
119        add1(tx+1, ty-1);
120        add1(tx+1, ty);
121        add1(tx+1, ty+1);
122        laid++;
123      };
124    }
```

```
125    flags = 0;
126    remaining = width*height;
127    startTime = 0;
128    elapsed = -1;
129    sadness = bored;
130    repaint();
131  }
132
133  int tail = listEnd;                    /* tail of pending exposures */
134
135  private void expose1(Graphics g, int x, int y) {
136    /* expose single square at (x,y) and add to list. */
137    if (x<0 || x>=width || y<0 || y>=height) return;
138    int e = y*width+x;
139    if (exposed[e] <= unexposed && exposed[e] != flagged) {
140      remaining--;
141      exposed[e] = listEnd;
142      exposed[tail] = e;
143      tail = e;
144      paintSquare(g, x, y);
145    }
146  }
147
148  private void expose(int x, int y) {
149    /* Expose given square, if not already exposed.  If square has 0 adjacency,
150       expose surrounding squares, iteratively. */
151    int thisSquare = y*width+x;
152    if (thisSquare<0 || thisSquare >= width*height) return;
153    if (exposed[thisSquare] > unexposed) return;
154    Graphics g = getGraphics();
155    if (adjacent[thisSquare] == mine) {
156      /* End of game: explode it and expose other mines */
157      remaining--;
158      exposed[thisSquare] = exploded;
159      paintSquare(g, x, y);
160      for (int y2 = 0; y2<height; y2++) {
161        for (int x2 = 0; x2<width; x2++) {
162          int i = y2*width+x2;
163          if (i==thisSquare) {
164          } else if (adjacent[i] == mine && exposed[i] != flagged) {
165            remaining--;
166            exposed[i] = listEnd;
167            paintSquare(g, x2, y2);
```

```
168        } else if (adjacent[i] != mine && exposed[i] == flagged) {
169          remaining--;
170          exposed[i] = incorrect;
171          paintSquare(g, x2, y2);
172        }
173      }
174    }
175    startTime = 0; /* turn off timer */
176    sadness = sad;
177    paintFace(g);
178  } else {
179    /* Initialize pending exposure list to this square */
180    remaining--;
181    exposed[thisSquare] = listEnd;
182    tail = thisSquare;
183    paintSquare(g, x, y);
184    int pending = thisSquare;
185    /* Until pending reaches the end of the exposure list, expose neighbors */
186    while (pending != listEnd) {
187      if (adjacent[pending]==0) {
188        int px = pending%width;
189        int py = pending/width;
190        expose1(g, px-1, py-1);
191        expose1(g, px-1, py);
192        expose1(g, px-1, py+1);
193        expose1(g, px, py-1);
194        expose1(g, px, py+1);
195        expose1(g, px+1, py-1);
196        expose1(g, px+1, py);
197        expose1(g, px+1, py+1);
198      }
199      pending = exposed[pending];
200    }
201    if (remaining==mines) {
202      /* End of game: flag all remaining unflagged mines */
203      for (int y2 = 0; y2<height; y2++) {
204        for (int x2 = 0; x2<width; x2++) {
205          int i = y2*width+x2;
206          if (adjacent[i] == mine && exposed[i] <= unexposed &&
207                                exposed[i] != flagged ) {
208            exposed[i] = flagged;
209            flags++;
210            paintSquare(g, x2, y2);
```

```
211                }
212              }
213            }
214          paintFlags(g);
215          startTime=0;
216          sadness=happy;
217          paintFace(getGraphics());
218        }
219      }
220    }
221
222
223
224    /* */
225    /* Applet public methods, including the daemon thread */
226    /* */
227
228    public void init() {
229      try {
230        String wStr = getParameter("COLUMNS");
231        String hStr = getParameter("ROWS");
232        String pStr = getParameter("PIXELS");
233        String mStr = getParameter("MINES");
234        if (wStr != null) width = Integer.parseInt(wStr);
235        if (hStr != null) height = Integer.parseInt(hStr);
236        if (pStr != null) edge = Integer.parseInt(pStr);
237        if (mStr != null) mines = Integer.parseInt(mStr);
238      } catch (NumberFormatException e) {
239      }
240      scoreHeight = edge*3;
241      faceSize = edge*2;
242      erase();
243    }
244
245    Thread daemon = null;
246
247    public synchronized void start() {
248      daemon = new Thread(this);
249      daemon.start();
250    }
251
252    public synchronized void stop() {
253      daemon = null;
```

```
254    }
255
256    public void destroy() {
257    }
258
259    public void run() {
260      while (true) {
261        synchronized(this) {
262          if (daemon != Thread.currentThread()) return;
263          if (startTime != 0) {
264            long now = System.currentTimeMillis();
265            int oldElapsed = elapsed;
266            elapsed = Math.round((0.0f+(now-startTime))/1000);
267            if (elapsed != oldElapsed) paintTime(getGraphics());
268          }
269        }
270        try { Thread.sleep(100); } catch (InterruptedException e) { };
271      }
272    }
273
274
275    /* */
276    /* Painting */
277    /* */
278
279    private Image initOneOffscreen(int i) {
280      /* Create offscreen image for a square.  "i" is either an adjacency count,
281         or a distinguished value of "exposed". */
282      Image off = createImage(edge, edge);
283      Graphics g = off.getGraphics();
284      g.setColor(i==exploded ? dangerousColor : baseColor);
285      if (i > unexposed) {
286        g.fillRect(0, 0, edge, edge);
287        g.setColor(baseShadow);
288      } else {
289        g.fill3DRect(0, 0, edge-1, edge-1, true);
290        g.setColor(Color.black);
291      };
292      g.drawLine(edge-1, 0, edge-1, edge-1);
293      g.drawLine(0, edge-1, edge-1, edge-1);
294      int halfWidth = edge/2;
295      int quarterPos = (edge-1)/4;
296      if (i==unexposed || i==0 ) {
```

```
297      } else if (i==mine || i==exploded) {
298        /* A circle with four lines through it, and a highlight */
299        g.setColor(mineColor);
300        g.drawLine(2, 2, edge-4, edge-4);
301        g.drawLine(edge-4, 2, 2, edge-4);
302        g.drawLine(halfWidth-1, 1, halfWidth-1, edge-3);
303        g.drawLine(1, halfWidth-1, edge-3, halfWidth-1);
304        g.fillOval(quarterPos, quarterPos, halfWidth+1, halfWidth+1);
305        g.setColor(Color.white);
306        g.fillOval(halfWidth-3, halfWidth-3, edge/8, edge/8);
307      } else if (i==incorrect) {
308        /* A diagonal cross, 3 pixels wide */
309        g.setColor(dangerousColor);
310        g.drawLine(2, 2, edge-4, edge-4);
311        g.drawLine(2, 3, edge-5, edge-4);
312        g.drawLine(3, 2, edge-4, edge-5);
313        g.drawLine(edge-4, 2, 2, edge-4);
314        g.drawLine(edge-4, 3, 3, edge-4);
315        g.drawLine(edge-5, 2, 2, edge-5);
316      } else if (i==flagged) {
317        /* A flag on a pole with a base */
318        g.setColor(dangerousColor);
319        g.fillRect(halfWidth-4, halfWidth-5, halfWidth-4, halfWidth-4);
320        g.setColor(mineColor);
321        g.drawLine(halfWidth, 3, halfWidth, edge-4);
322        g.drawLine(5, edge-4, edge-5, edge-4);
323      } else {
324        /* A question mark or the adjacency count */
325        FontMetrics fm = this.getFontMetrics(theMainFont);
326        int fontAscent = fm.getAscent();
327        String s = i==queried ? "?" : ""+i;
328        g.setColor(i==queried ? new Color(0,0,255) : colors[i]);
329        g.setFont(theMainFont);
330        g.drawString(s, (edge-fm.stringWidth(s))/2, fontAscent);
331      };
332      return off;
333    }
334
335    private Image initOneSmiley(int theSadness) {
336      Image off = createImage(faceSize, faceSize);
337      Graphics g = off.getGraphics();
338      g.setColor(Color.black);
339      g.fillRect(0, 0, faceSize, faceSize);
```

```
340    g.setColor(baseColor);
341    g.fill3DRect(1, 1, faceSize-2, faceSize-2, true);
342    g.fill3DRect(2, 2, faceSize-4, faceSize-4, true);
343    g.setColor(Color.yellow);
344    g.fillOval(6, 6, faceSize-12, faceSize-12);
345    g.setColor(Color.black);
346    g.drawOval(6, 6, faceSize-12, faceSize-12);
347    if (theSadness==sad) {
348      g.drawArc(10, faceSize-13, faceSize-20, faceSize-20, 135, -100);
349    } else if (theSadness==happy) {
350      g.drawArc(10, 10, faceSize-20, faceSize-20, -35, -100);
351    } else {
352      g.fillRect(12, faceSize-12, faceSize-23, 1);
353    }
354    g.fillOval(13, 13, 2, 2);
355    g.fillOval(faceSize-12-2, 13, 2, 2);
356    return off;
357  }
358
359  private void initOffscreen() {
360    baseColor = new Color(204,204,204);
361    baseShadow = new Color(153,153,153);
362    mineColor = new Color(51,51,51);
363    numberColor = new Color(255,102,102);
364    dangerousColor = new Color(255,51,51);
365    colors = new Color[10];
366    colors[0] = Color.black;
367    colors[1] = new Color(51,51,204);          /* blue */
368    colors[2] = new Color(0,102,0);            /* green */
369    colors[3] = new Color(204,0,0);            /* red */
370    colors[4] = new Color(102,0,102);          /* purple */
371    colors[5] = new Color(0,102,102);          /* dark cyan */
372    colors[6] = Color.black;
373    colors[7] = Color.black;
374    colors[8] = Color.black;
375    colors[mine] = Color.black;
376    theMainFont = new Font("TimesRoman", Font.BOLD, (edge*5)/8+2);
377    theScoreFont = new Font("TimesRoman", Font.BOLD, (edge*5)/4);
378    numberSize = this.getFontMetrics(theScoreFont).stringWidth("000") +
379                numberMargin*2;
380    explodedRect = initOneOffscreen(exploded);
381    incorrectRect = initOneOffscreen(incorrect);
382    unexposedRect = initOneOffscreen(unexposed);
```

```
383        flaggedRect = initOneOffscreen(flagged);
384        queriedRect = initOneOffscreen(queried);
385        exposedRect = new Image[mine+1];
386        for (int i = 0; i<=mine; i++) exposedRect[i] = initOneOffscreen(i);
387        happySmiley = initOneSmiley(happy);
388        boredSmiley = initOneSmiley(bored);
389        sadSmiley = initOneSmiley(sad);
390      }
391
392    private void paintNumber(Graphics g, int n, int right) {
393        String s = (n>999 || n<-99 ? "---" : ""+n);
394        if (unexposedRect==null) return;
395        FontMetrics fm = this.getFontMetrics(theScoreFont);
396        int fontAscent = fm.getAscent();
397        int fontHeight = fm.getHeight();
398        int top = (scoreHeight-fontHeight)/2;
399        g.setColor(Color.black);
400        g.fillRect(right-numberSize, top-numberMargin, numberSize, fontHeight+numberMargin*2);
401        g.setColor(numberColor);
402        g.setFont(theScoreFont);
403        g.drawString(s, right-fm.stringWidth(s)-numberMargin, top+fontAscent);
404      }
405
406    private void paintFlags(Graphics g) {
407        paintNumber(g, mines-flags, numberSize+(width*edge-faceSize-numberSize*2)/4);
408      }
409
410    private void paintTime(Graphics g) {
411        paintNumber(g, elapsed<0?0:elapsed,
412                    width*edge-(width*edge-faceSize-numberSize*2)/4);
413      }
414
415    private void paintSquare(Graphics g, int x, int y) {
416        /* Paint given square. */
417        if (unexposedRect==null) return;
418        int n = y*width+x;
419        int exposure = exposed[n];
420        Image im = exposure==exploded ? explodedRect :
421                    exposure==incorrect ? incorrectRect :
422                    exposure==unexposed ? unexposedRect :
423                    exposure==flagged ? flaggedRect :
424                    exposure==queried ? queriedRect :
425                    exposedRect[adjacent[n]];
```

```
426      g.drawImage(im, x*edge, y*edge+scoreHeight, this);
427    }
428
429    private void paintFace(Graphics g) {
430      g.drawImage(sadness==sad?sadSmiley:sadness==happy?happySmiley:boredSmiley,
431                 (width*edge-faceSize)/2, (scoreHeight-faceSize)/2, this);
432    }
433
434    public synchronized void paint(Graphics g) {
435      if (unexposedRect==null) initOffscreen();
436      g.setColor(baseColor);
437      g.fill3DRect(0, 0, width*edge, scoreHeight, true);
438      paintFlags(g);
439      paintFace(g);
440      paintTime(g);
441      for (int y = 0; y<height; y++) {
442        for (int x = 0; x<width; x++) {
443          paintSquare(g, x, y);
444        }
445      }
446    }
447
448    public void update(Graphics g) {
449      paint(g);
450    }
451
452
453    /* */
454    /* User input */
455    /* */
456
457    public synchronized boolean mouseDown(Event evt, int xCoord, int yCoord) {
458      if (yCoord<scoreHeight) {
459        int smileyX = (width*edge-faceSize)/2;
460        int smileyY = (scoreHeight-faceSize)/2;
461        if (xCoord >= smileyX && xCoord < smileyX+faceSize &&
462            yCoord >= smileyY && yCoord < smileyY+faceSize) {
463          erase(); /* start new game */
464        }
465      } else if (sadness != bored) {
466        /* Game over */
467      } else if (xCoord>=0 && xCoord<width*edge) {
468        if (elapsed<0) {
```

```
469        startTime = System.currentTimeMillis();
470       elapsed = 0;
471    };
472    int x = xCoord/edge;
473    int y = (yCoord-scoreHeight)/edge;
474    int n = y*width+x;
475    if (evt.shiftDown() || evt.metaDown() ) {
476      if (exposed[n] == unexposed) {
477        exposed[n] = flagged; flags++; paintFlags(getGraphics());
478      } else if (exposed[n] == flagged) {
479        exposed[n] = queried; flags--; paintFlags(getGraphics());
480      } else if (exposed[n] == queried) {
481        exposed[n] = unexposed;
482      }
483      paintSquare(getGraphics(), x, y);
484    } else if (exposed[n] != flagged) {
485      expose(x, y);
486    };
487    };
488    return true;
489  }
490
491  }
```

ANNOTATIONS

The **Minesweeper** applet uses two integer arrays—**adjacent[]** and **exposed[]**—to store state information. These are one-dimensional arrays that you can think of as being the rows of the minefield laid one row after another. Thus, the information about a square at location (x,y) is stored at the array index **y*width+x**, where **width** is the number of pixels across the minefield (**width** is the same as the value of the **COLUMN** parameter). Figure 5-4 illustrates how the location of a square in the minefield maps to an array index.

The **adjacent[]** array, defined on line 30, is used to store the count of mines adjacent to each square in the minefield. This count can be a value from 0 to 8 because a square can have at most 8 adjacent mines. If a square actually contains a mine, a 9 is stored in the array index corresponding to that square. Therefore, a 9 is stored in those locations in the **adjacent[]** array that correspond to squares that contain mines.

The **exposed[]** array, defined in line 46, is used to store the state of each square in the minefield. The state represents whether the square is covered, uncovered, or

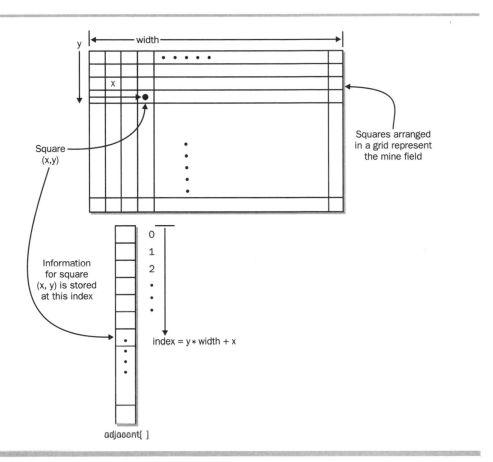

FIGURE 5-4. Information about squares is stored in arrays.

marked as a mine, or whether it has an exploded mine. Each square can have one of the integer constants shown in lines 47 through 52:

```
46    int[] exposed = null;           /* exposure state / pending exposures */
47    static final int listEnd = -1;   /* end marker in "exposed" */
48    static final int incorrect = -2; /* incorrect flag, at end of game */
49    static final int exploded = -3;  /* exploded mine (at end of game!) */
50    static final int unexposed = -4; /* default state at start of game */
51    static final int flagged = -5;   /* marker flag by user */
52    static final int queried = -6;   /* query flag by user */
```

Initially all squares are unexposed, so each element of the **exposed[]** array is set to the constant **unexposed**. After a mouse click on a square, when the applet has to figure out which squares to expose, the **exposed[]** array is used as a linked list to keep track of the squares to be exposed. When used this way, the entry for a square contains the index corresponding to the next exposed square. A special value—**listEnd**—marks the entry corresponding to the last exposed square in the list.

As you'll see later, the **adjacent[]** and **exposed[]** arrays are used extensively by various methods that implement the game's algorithms.

MINESWEEPER GAME START   During initialization, the **Minesweeper** applet's **init()** method, shown in lines 228 through 243, gets the **COLUMNS, ROWS, PIXELS,** and **MINES** parameters from the HTML file. Then line 242 calls the **erase()** method to initialize the game:

```
242     erase();
```

The **erase()** method, shown in lines 99 through 131, sets up the minefield. First, lines 101 through 106 create and initialize the **adjacent[]** and **exposed[]** arrays:

```
101     if (adjacent == null) adjacent = new int[width*height];
102     if (exposed == null) exposed = new int[width*height];
103     for (int i = 0; i < width*height; i++) {
104       adjacent[i] = 0;
105       exposed[i] = unexposed;
106     };
```

The **while** loop in lines 108 through 124 then places the mines at random locations in the minefield. Line 109 computes a random location, and if that location does not already have a mine, line 111 sets the entry corresponding to that square to the constant **mine** (which is defined to be 9):

```
111         adjacent[target] = mine;
```

After that, lines 112 through 121 increment the entries for all neighboring squares in the **adjacent[]** array. Line 122 increments the number of mines laid so far. The **while** loop continues until the number of mines specified by the **MINES** parameter have been laid.

The remainder of the **erase()** method, from line 125 through line 129, resets various variables that keep track of the mine count and the time elapsed. Lastly, line 130 calls **repaint()**, which causes the browser to call the **update()** method. The **update()** method, in turn, calls **paint()**. The **paint()** method, shown in lines 434 through 446, draws the game board.

MINESWEEPER TIMER THREAD   **Minesweeper** uses a thread to run the game's timer. The thread is named **daemon** (*daemon* is a term used in UNIX to describe processes that typically run in the background for as long as the operating system is up and running). The applet's **start()** method, shown in lines 247 through 250, starts the **daemon** thread. Lines 248 and 249 perform this task:

```
248     daemon = new Thread(this);
249     daemon.start();
```

The **daemon** thread executes the **run()** method shown in lines 259 through 272. The **run()** method uses a **while** loop (lines 260 through 271) to repeatedly update the elapsed time and then sleep for 100 milliseconds before checking the elapsed time again.

Lines 263 through 268 of the **run()** method compute the elapsed time and display the new time once every second:

```
263         if (startTime != 0) {
264             long now = System.currentTimeMillis();
265             int oldElapsed = elapsed;
266             elapsed = Math.round((0.0f+(now-startTime))/1000);
267             if (elapsed != oldElapsed) paintTime(getGraphics());
268         }
```

All of this happens only if **startTime** is not zero. Initially, **startTime** is set to zero. As soon as the user clicks on a square, the **mouseDown()** method sets **startTime** to the time (of the mouse click) in milliseconds. From that instant, the code in lines 264 through 267 will be executed.

Notice how the elapsed time is computed. First, line 264 gets the current time in a **long** integer variable named **now**. Line 265 saves the old elapsed time (this is in seconds). Then line 266 computes the new elapsed time in seconds. (That's why the difference between **now** and **startTime** is divided by 1000.) Line 267 calls the **paintTime()** method if the new elapsed time is different from the old value (this will happen when a second has elapsed). The **paintTime()** method displays the elapsed time.

After that, line 270 calls **Thread.sleep()** to stop the processing for 100 milliseconds:

```
270         try { Thread.sleep(100); } catch (InterruptedException e) { };
```

After the 100-millisecond wait, the thread checks the elapsed time again.

MINESWEEPER GAME PLAY   The game starts when the user clicks on a square to expose it. At that point, the **mouseDown()** method, shown in lines 457 through 489, is called.

Because the user may click on the yellow smiley face to restart a game, the **mouseDown()** method first checks the y coordinate of the mouse click. Lines 459 through 464 handle the case when the user has clicked on the smiley face. In this case, line 463 calls **erase()** to reset the game and display a new minefield.

If the user has clicked somewhere on the squares, lines 472 through 486 handle that mouse click. First, lines 472 and 473 compute the x and y coordinates of the square:

```
472     int x = xCoord/edge;
473     int y = (yCoord-scoreHeight)/edge;
```

Note that **edge** is the length of one side of a square in the minefield. The **scoreHeight** variable is the height of the area along the top of the applet where the smiley face and elapsed time appear.

Line 474 computes the index **n** of the element in the **adjacent[]** and **exposed[]** arrays corresponding to the square on which the user has clicked:

```
474     int n = y*width+x;
```

This index is used to access the **adjacent[]** and **exposed[]** array elements in subsequent lines of code.

Line 475 calls the **shiftDown()** method of the **Event** class to check whether the user clicked the right mouse button or held down the SHIFT key while left-clicking (this is the equivalent of right-clicking). In case of a right-click (or a SHIFT-left click), line 477 marks that square with a flag, indicating that it is one that the user suspects is a mine:

```
477        exposed[n] = flagged; flags++; paintFlags(getGraphics());
```

Notice that the marking is done by storing the constant **flagged** in the **exposed[]** array element that corresponds to the square on which the user has clicked. Line 477 also increments the **flags** variable, which keeps track of how many squares the user has marked as mines. The last part of line 477 calls the **paintFlags()** method, which simply displays an updated number of mines in the status area along the top edge of the applet's display area.

If the user clicks with the left mouse button, and if that square is not already marked as a suspected mine, line 485 calls the **expose()** method to uncover one or more squares:

```
485        expose(x, y);
```

The **expose()** method, shown in lines 148 through 220, starts by exposing the square at location (x,y) and adding it to the **exposed[]** array. Then, if that square has no adjacent mines, this method exposes all surrounding squares until it runs into squares that have adjacent mines. Each of the lines 190 through 197 calls the **expose1()** method to expose the surrounding squares one by one. This method also checks whether the game has ended (this happens when the remaining uncovered squares are the ones with mines).

As the **expose()** method exposes squares, it also calls **paintSquare()** to draw an appropriate image at the exposed square. The image will be a blank square if there is no mine in that square. If a square with a mine is exposed, **paintSquare()** draws a mine.

MINESWEEPER GAME DISPLAY The **paint()** method is responsible for drawing the minefield. Some methods call **paintSquare()** and **paintFlags()** directly to update the game display as the user clicks on squares.

The **paint()** method, shown in lines 434 through 446, draws a new game board in the beginning and whenever the user starts a new game. When it's called for the first time, line 435 of the **paint()** method calls **initOffscreen()** to initialize a number of off-screen images:

```
435    if (unexposedRect==null) initOffscreen();
```

The **unexposedRect** object is an **Image** that holds one of the off-screen images. If **unexposedRect** is **null**, that means **initOffscreen()** has not been called yet. After a call to **initOffscreen()**, the **unexposedRect Image** will be initialized (and not **null**), and **initOffscreen()** won't be called again.

The **initOffscreen()** method, shown in lines 359 through 390, calls two other methods—**initOneOffscreen()** and **initOneSmiley()**—several times to create the off-screen images of various types of squares and faces. Later on, the **paintSquare()** method uses these off-screen images to draw the squares on the applet's display area.

Lines 436 and 437 draw the rectangle where the smiley face, timer, and mine count appear:

```
436    g.setColor(baseColor);
437    g.fill3DRect(0, 0, width*edge, scoreHeight, true);
```

Lines 438 through 440 then call **paintFlags()**, **paintFace()**, and **paintTime()** to display the mine count, the sad or smiley face, and the elapsed time:

```
438    paintFlags(g);
439    paintFace(g);
440    paintTime(g);
```

Each of these methods uses the off-screen images prepared by **initOffscreen()** to draw their part of the applet's display area.

Finally, lines 441 through 445 use two **for** loops to draw all of the squares in the minefield by calling **paintSquare()**:

```
441    for (int y = 0; y<height; y++) {
442      for (int x = 0; x<width; x++) {
443        paintSquare(g, x, y);
444      }
445    }
```

The **paintSquare()** method, shown in lines 415 through 427, draws an appropriate image for the square at location (x, y), depending on the contents of the **exposed[]** array at the index corresponding to this square.

Tetris

Tetris is a remarkably simple yet difficult game. As you probably know from first-hand experience, when you play Tetris you have to arrange blocks of various shapes that gradually fall from the top of the game board to the bottom. As each block falls, you can rotate it or move it to the left and right. The block stops when it reaches the bottom or touches other pieces resting at the bottom. Your goal is to stack the blocks as tightly as possible. The more blocks you can fit into the game board, the higher your score.

Tetris was created in 1985 by Alexey Pajitnov of Moscow (in what was then the USSR). It was quickly ported to the IBM PC and eventually found its way to the Nintendo Game Boy machine.

PROGRAMMER'S NOTE   *It's a long story — how Tetris went from the hands of its original developer in Moscow to Nintendo and others. To learn more about the history of Tetris, visit one or more of the following Web sites:*
http://atarihq.com/tsr/special/tetrishist.html,
http://www.geocities.com/Athens/3672/intro.html, or
http://vadim.www.media.mit.edu/Tetris.htm.

Tetris continues to be very popular; it is available for virtually every kind of computer or game machine. Even though Java has been around for only a few years, there are already many variants of Tetris implemented in the form of Java applets. This section presents a **Tetris** applet written and copyrighted by Andrew D. Birrell. The applet's program and source code are available free, under the terms of the GNU General Public License. You can visit the applet's original home page at **http://www.research.digital.com/SRC/personal/Andrew_Birrell/tetris/**.

The next few sections show how to play **Tetris**, present the source code, and explain the important features of that source code.

Playing Tetris

The files for the **Tetris** applet are in the **ch05\Tetris** directory of the companion CD-ROM. To play **Tetris**, open the **play.html** file in a Java-capable Web browser. You will see a rectangular game board with a square grid drawn on it. There are two lines of text along the top edge. These lines display your best score so far, your current score, and the current level. The level denotes the current level of difficulty; the initial level is 5.

As the game starts, blocks of different shapes gradually drift down from the top of the game board toward the bottom. Each block is made up of four squares. You can rotate and move the falling block and control the game using the following keys:

♦ **p** pauses the game (press **p** again to continue).

♦ **s** starts a new game at the current level.

♦ **LEFT ARROW** or **j** moves the block to the left by one square.

♦ **RIGHT ARROW** or **l** (the letter L key) moves the block to the right by one square.

♦ **UP ARROW** or **k** rotates the block counterclockwise by a quarter turn (90 degrees).

♦ **DOWN ARROW** or **SPACEBAR** drops the block down until it hits bottom or another block (you can still slide it left or right).

♦ **a** toggles between smooth animation and abrupt animation (the block moves one square at a time when animation is abrupt).

♦ **u** goes one level up in difficulty (the current level is shown in the upper-right corner of the applet).

♦ **d** goes down to the next lower level of difficulty.

Press the arrow keys (or the **j**, **k**, and **l** keys) to rotate and move each block so that you can pack in as many of them as you can. If you manage to completely fill up one or more rows with blocks, those rows disappear and the rows above them move down. That gives you more room to pack blocks and get a higher score.

You get points for every block you place. You get more points for placing a block quickly. You can do so by pressing the DOWN ARROW or SPACEBAR as soon as you are sure it's in the right place and has the right orientation.

After you play well enough at the current level of difficulty, **Tetris** automatically moves to the next higher level. At higher levels of difficulty the blocks move faster and you score more for placing the blocks.

Figure 5-5 shows the **Tetris** applet in a Web browser during a pause in a game.

To see how the **Tetris** applet is embedded in an HTML file, here is the full listing of the **play.html** file that was used when running the applet as shown in Figure 5-5:

```
<html>
<body>
<applet code=Tetris.class width=160 height=360>
<param name=COLUMNS value=10>
<param name=ROWS value=20>
```

```
<param name=PIXELS value=16>
You need a Java-capable browser to run applets.
</applet>
</body>
</html>
```

Tetris accepts three parameters through **<param>** tags:

- ◆ **COLUMNS** specifies the number of columns in the **Tetris** game board (this is the width of the board).

- ◆ **ROWS** is the number of rows in the game board (this is the height of the board).

- ◆ **PIXELS** is the length, in pixels, of one side of a square on the game board.

When you specify the dimensions of the applet, make sure there is enough room for the specified number of rows and columns. For example, if **PIXELS** is 16 and **COLUMNS** is 10, you need at least a 160-pixel-wide display area for the applet. For the applet height, you should also factor in additional space for the two lines of text that appear along the top edge of the applet.

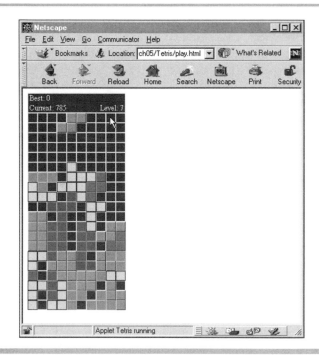

FIGURE 5-5. Playing a game of **Tetris**.

Tetris

Understanding Tetris

The following listing shows the **Tetris.java** file—the complete source code for the **Tetris** applet. I describe the salient features of the source code in the "Annotations" section that follows the listing.

```
1   /* Andrew's version of Tetris .... just for fun */
2   /* Tetris.java */
3   /* Copyright 1997, Andrew D. Birrell */
4   /* This program and source code are available free, under the terms of the GNU
5    general public license. Use at your own risk! The GNU general public
6    license is available at http://www.gnu.org/copyleft/gpl.html */
7
8   import java.applet.*;
9   import java.awt.*;
10  import java.util.*;
11
12  public class Tetris extends Applet implements Runnable {
13
14  /* */
15  /* State information, generally protected by our mutex */
16  /* Some of these value get overridden during the .init or .erase methods */
17  /* */
18
19  int edge = 16;        /* pixels on the edge of a block */
20  int width = 10;        /* width in blocks */
21  int height = 20;        /* height in blocks */
22  int textSquares = 2;    /* extra square heights used for scores */
23
24  int shapes = 8;         /* number of shapes, including blank */
25  int empty = 0;         /* shape number for blank square */
26  Color[] colors = null;  /* color of each shape */
27
28  int[][] occupant = null; /* shape number in each square */
29  boolean[][] piece = null; /* shape of current piece */
30  int kind = 0;          /* shape number of current piece */
31  int pieceSize = 4;      /* width and height of current piece, for rotation */
32  Point place = null;     /* coordinate of current piece top left */
33  int value = 0;         /* current score value of current piece */
34  boolean moved;         /* did piece move recently? */
35
36  int score = 0;         /* score for current game */
37  int maxLevel = 10;      /* highest possible level */
```

```
38  int[] high = null;    /* highest score in this run */
39  int level = 5;      /* current level */
40  int fallCount = 0;     /* blocks since last level change */
41  int fallEnough = 200;    /* threshold for increasing level based on fallCount */
42
43  /* All timing is in milliseconds */
44  boolean paused = false;  /* nothing changes */
45  boolean animate = true;  /* smooth animation of downward moves */
46  int sleepTime = 33;     /* interval between daemon activations */
47  int moveTime;        /* interval between moves */
48  long movieEnd;        /* real time of end of "drop" movie */
49
50  Thread daemon = null;    /* block-moving thread */
51  Image offscreen = null;   /* offscreen board, to prevent flicker */
52  Image images[] = null;    /* offscreen images of squares, for speed */
53  boolean boardInvalid = true; /* offscreen image doesn't match data */
54  Font theFont;          /* font for scores */
55
56
57  /* */
58  /* Game play */
59  /* */
60
61  private synchronized void erase(int levelDelta) {
62   /* Start of new game. Includes implicit initialization. */
63   if (colors==null) {
64    colors = new Color[shapes];
65    colors[empty] = new Color(102,102,102); /* darkish gray */
66    colors[1]   = new Color(153,51,51);  /* red */
67    colors[2]   = new Color(204,204,0);  /* yellow */
68    colors[3]   = new Color(51,153,51);  /* green */
69    colors[4]   = new Color(0,204,204);  /* cyan */
70    colors[5]   = new Color(51,102,204);  /* blue */
71    colors[6]   = new Color(153,0,153);  /* magenta */
72    colors[7]   = new Color(204,102,51);  /* orange */
73   }
74   if (high==null) {
75    high = new int[maxLevel+1];
76    for (int i=0; i<=maxLevel; i++) high[i] = 0;
77   }
78   if (occupant==null) occupant = new int[width][height];
79
```

```
80    /* deal with result of previous game */
81    high[level] = Math.max(high[level], score);
82    level = Math.max(0, Math.min(maxLevel, level+levelDelta));
83
84    /* Now erase the board and force repaint of blank board */
85    for (int x = 0; x<width; x++) {
86      for (int y = 0; y<height; y++) { occupant[x][y] = empty; }
87    }
88    piece = null;
89    moved = false;
90    score = 0;
91    fallCount = 0;
92    moveTime = 50; /* must be non-zero; will be set correctly in newPiece */
93    boardInvalid = true;
94    repaint();
95  }
96
97  private boolean clearRow() {
98    /* Clear a full row, if there is one */
99    int found = -1;
100   for (int y=0; y<height; y++) {
101     found = y;
102     for (int x=0; x<width; x++) {
103       if (occupant[x][y] == empty) { found=-1; break; }
104     }
105     if (found >= 0) break;
106   }
107   if (found<0) return false;
108   /* We found a full row: move higher rows down */
109   for (int y=found; y>0; y--) {
110     for (int x=0; x<width; x++) occupant[x][y] = occupant[x][y-1];
111   }
112   for (int x=0; x<width; x++) occupant[x][0] = empty;
113     moved = true;
114     boardInvalid = true;
115     repaint();
116     return true;
117   }
118
119   private boolean[][] initPiece() {
120     /* Part of rotation and piece creation: creates piece with no squares */
121     boolean[][] newPiece = new boolean[4][4];
122     for (int x=0; x<4; x++) for (int y=0; y<4; y++) newPiece[x][y] = false;
```

```
123      return newPiece;
124   }
125
126   private boolean putPiece(boolean[][] newPiece, Point newPlace) {
127      /* If new place and piece are feasible, set piece and place and do
128         appropriate state updates. Return true iff feasible. */
129      for (int x=0; x<pieceSize; x++) {
130        for (int y=0; y<pieceSize; y++) {
131          int newX = x+newPlace.x;
132          int newY = y+newPlace.y;
133          /* Allow squares off top of board, but not edges or bottom */
134          if ( newPiece[x][y] && newY>=0 && (
135                  newX<0 || newX>=width || newY>=height ||
136                  occupant[newX][newY] != empty ) ) {
137            return false;
138          }
139        }
140      }
141      piece = newPiece;
142      place = newPlace;
143      moved = true;
144      repaintPiece();
145      return true;
146   }
147
148   private synchronized boolean newPiece() {
149      /* Convert any existing piece to occupant, and create new piece.
150         Returns true iff new piece is feasible. */
151      if (piece != null) {
152        for (int x=0; x<pieceSize; x++) {
153          for (int y=0; y<pieceSize; y++) {
154            if (piece[x][y] && place.y+y >= 0) occupant[place.x+x][place.y+y] = kind;
155          }
156        }
157        score += value;
158      }
159
160      while (clearRow()) { }
161
162      if (fallCount >= fallEnough) {
163        high[level] = Math.max(high[level], score); /* we're moving: record high score */
164        level = Math.min(maxLevel, level+1);
```

```
165    fallCount -= fallEnough;
166    }
167    moveTime = Math.max(100, 600-level*50);
168
169    paintScore();
170    repaint();
171    boolean[][] newPiece = initPiece();
172    kind = (short)(Math.floor(Math.random()*(shapes-1)+1));
173    value = 24 + 2*level;
174    int initX = 0;
175    switch (kind) {
176    case 1:
177      newPiece[0][1] = true;    /* . . . . */
178      newPiece[1][1] = true;    /* X X X X */
179      newPiece[2][1] = true;    /* . . . . */
180      newPiece[3][1] = true;    /* . . . . */
181      initX = -1;
182      pieceSize = 4;
183      break;
184    case 2:
185      newPiece[0][1] = true;    /* . . . . */
186      newPiece[1][1] = true;    /* X X X . */
187      newPiece[1][2] = true;    /* . X . . */
188      newPiece[2][1] = true;    /* . . . . */
189      initX = -1;
190      pieceSize = 3;
191      break;
192    case 3:
193      newPiece[0][2] = true;    /* . . . . */
194      newPiece[1][1] = true;    /* . X X . */
195      newPiece[1][2] = true;    /* X X . . */
196      newPiece[2][1] = true;    /* . . . . */
197      initX = -2;
198      pieceSize = 3;
199      break;
200    case 4:
201      newPiece[0][1] = true;    /* . . . . */
202      newPiece[1][1] = true;    /* X X . . */
203      newPiece[1][2] = true;    /* . X X . */
204      newPiece[2][2] = true;    /* . . . . */
205      initX = -2;
```

```
206        pieceSize = 3;
207        break;
208      case 5:
209        newPiece[0][1] = true;     /* . . . . */
210        newPiece[0][2] = true;     /* X X X . */
211        newPiece[1][1] = true;     /* X . . . */
212        newPiece[2][1] = true;     /* . . . . */
213        initX = -1;
214        pieceSize = 3;
215        break;
216      case 6:
217        newPiece[0][1] = true;     /* . . . . */
218        newPiece[1][1] = true;     /* X X X . */
219        newPiece[2][1] = true;     /* . . X . */
220        newPiece[2][2] = true;     /* . . . . */
221        initX = -1;
222        pieceSize = 3;
223        break;
224      case 7:
225        newPiece[0][0] = true;     /* X X . . */
226        newPiece[0][1] = true;     /* X X . . */
227        newPiece[1][0] = true;     /* . . . . */
228        newPiece[1][1] = true;     /* . . . . */
229        initX = -1;
230        pieceSize = 2;
231        break;
232      default:
233        System.err.println("unexpected shape kind "+kind);
234        return false;
235      }
236      return putPiece(newPiece, new Point((width-pieceSize)/2, initX));
237    }
238
239    private boolean movePiece(int dx, int dy) {
240      /* Move piece one square in some direction, if feasible */
241      if (piece==null) return false;
242      return putPiece(piece, new Point(place.x+dx, place.y+dy));
243    }
244
245    private boolean rotatePiece() {
246      /* Rotate piece anti-clockwise, if feasible */
```

```
247    if (piece==null) return false;
248    boolean[][] newPiece = initPiece();
249    for (int x=0; x<pieceSize; x++) {
250      for (int y=0; y<pieceSize; y++) {
251        newPiece[x][y] = piece[pieceSize-1-y][x];
252      }
253    }
254    return putPiece(newPiece, place);
255  }
256
257
258  /* */
259  /* Applet public methods, including the daemon thread */
260  /* */
261
262  public void init() {
263    try {
264      String wStr = getParameter("COLUMNS");
265      String hStr = getParameter("ROWS");
266      String pStr = getParameter("PIXELS");
267      if (wStr != null) width = Integer.parseInt(wStr);
268      if (hStr != null) height = Integer.parseInt(hStr);
269      if (pStr != null) edge = Integer.parseInt(pStr);
270    } catch (NumberFormatException e) {
271    }
272    erase(0);
273  }
274
275  public synchronized void start() {
276    daemon = new Thread(this);
277    daemon.start();
278    requestFocus();
279  }
280
281  public synchronized void stop() {
282    daemon = null;
283  }
284
285  public void destroy() {
286  }
287
```

```
288   public void run() {
289     /* On each wakeup, if it's time for another move, make it (if possible);
290        if there's a "drop movie" in progress, advance it one step. */
291     long nextMove = System.currentTimeMillis();
292     while (true) {
293       synchronized(this) {
294         long now = System.currentTimeMillis();
295         if (daemon != Thread.currentThread()) return;
296         /* All paths paint the current piece in its final or new place */
297         if (now >= nextMove && !paused) {
298           nextMove = Math.max(now, nextMove+moveTime);
299           long newMovieEnd = animate ? nextMove : now;
300           if (moved) {
301             /* We're still making progress, either automatically or by the
302                user moving the piece around.  Try another move downwards. */
303             moved = false;
304             movieEnd = newMovieEnd;
305             if (movePiece(0,1)) {
306               value = Math.max(0, value-1);
307               fallCount+=1;
308             } else {
309               /* We're still showing the old piece: kill the movie and
310                  paint the piece in its final place. */
311               movieEnd = now;
312               repaintPiece();
313             };
314           } else {
315             /* Last automatic move did nothing, and user hasn't intervened.
316                Try generating another piece, and if that fails end the game. */
317             movieEnd = now;
318             repaintPiece();
319             movieEnd = newMovieEnd;
320             if (!newPiece()) erase(0);
321           }
322         } else {
323           repaintPiece();
324         }
325       }
326       try { Thread.sleep(sleepTime);
327       } catch (InterruptedException e) { };
328     };
329   }
330
```

```
331
332    /* */
333    /* Painting */
334    /* */
335
336    /* The general strategy is to paint into "offscreen" to avoid flicker,
337       then paint appropriate subsets of that onto the screen.  Most painting
338       is synchronous through calls of "repaintPiece", since that way we know
339       how few squares to copy to the screen.  An alternative would be to call
340       "repaint" in "repaintPiece", but that is slower, and its timing depends
341       on when the runtime system feels like calling "update".
342
343       Additionally, there are offscreen images called "images" to hold the
344       pixels for each color of square.  This might be marginally faster than
345       constructing squares on demand, and it also is structured in a way that
346       would work if we used, e.g., a GIF for the squares' images.
347       */
348
349    private void paintSquare(Graphics g, int x, int y, int delta, int shape) {
350      /* Paint a single square from "images", in fact into offscreen image */
351      g.drawImage(images[shape], x*edge, (y+textSquares)*edge+delta, this);
352    }
353
354    private void paintScore() {
355      /* Update offscreen image because score or pause state has changed */
356      if (offscreen == null) return;
357      Graphics g = offscreen.getGraphics();
358      int margin = 1+edge/8;
359      g.setColor(colors[empty]);
360      g.fill3DRect(0, 0, width*edge, textSquares*edge, true);
361      g.setFont(theFont);
362      FontMetrics fm = this.getFontMetrics(theFont);
363      int fontHeight = fm.getHeight();
364      int fontAscent = fm.getAscent();
365      int leading = (textSquares*edge-2*fontHeight)/3;
366      String left = "Best: "+high[level];
367      String right = paused ? "Paused" : "";
368      String left2 = "Current: "+score;
369      String right2 = "Level: "+level;
370      int baseline = leading + fontAscent;
371      g.setColor(Color.white);
372      g.drawString(left, margin, baseline);
```

```
373      g.setColor(Color.red);

374      g.drawString(right, width*edge-margin-fm.stringWidth(right), baseline);

375      g.setColor(Color.white);

376      baseline += fontHeight+leading;

377      g.drawString(left2, margin, baseline);

378      g.drawString(right2, width*edge-margin-fm.stringWidth(right2), baseline);

379    }

380

381  private void paintPiece(boolean doRepaint) {

382      /* Update offscreen image because piece has changed or moved.

383         Paints piece, and enough surround to deal with recent 1-square move

384         and previous in-progress movie.  Iff "doRepaint", synchronously paints

385         affected squares onto the screen. */

386      long now = System.currentTimeMillis();

387      int moviePos = -(int)((Math.max(movieEnd-now,0)*edge+moveTime/2)/moveTime);

388      if (piece == null || offscreen == null ) return;

389      int minX = Math.max(place.x-1, 0);

390      int limX = Math.min(place.x+pieceSize+1, width);

391      int minY = Math.max(place.y-2, 0);

392      int limY = Math.min(place.y+pieceSize, height); /* piece didn't move up! */

393      {

394        Graphics g = offscreen.getGraphics();

395        g.clipRect(0, textSquares*edge, width*edge, height*edge);

396        for (int x = minX; x<limX; x++) {

397          for (int y = minY; y<limY; y++) {

398            paintSquare(g, x, y, 0, occupant[x][y]);

399          };

400        };

401        for (int x = minX; x<limX; x++) {

402          for (int y = minY; y<limY; y++) {

403            if ( x >= place.x && x < place.x+pieceSize &&

404                 y >= place.y && y < place.y+pieceSize &&

405                 piece[x-place.x][y-place.y] ) {

406              paintSquare(g, x, y, moviePos, kind);

407            }

408          }

409        }

410      }

411      if (doRepaint) {

412        Graphics g = getGraphics();

413        g.clipRect(minX*edge, (minY+textSquares)*edge,
```

```
414                (limX-minX)*edge, (limY-minY)*edge);
415      g.drawImage(offscreen, 0, 0, this);
416    }
417  }
418
419  private void repaintPiece() {
420    /* Update offscreen image with piece in its current state and ensure the
421       pixels make their way to the screen. */
422    paintPiece(!boardInvalid);
423  }
424
425  private void paintBoard() {
426    /* Construct offscreen image from scratch */
427    Graphics g = offscreen.getGraphics();
428    g.clipRect(0, textSquares*edge, width*edge, height*edge);
429    for (int x = 0; x<width; x++) {
430      for (int y = 0; y<height; y++) {
431        paintSquare(g, x, y, 0, occupant[x][y]);
432      };
433    }
434    paintPiece(false);
435    paintScore();
436  }
437
438  private void initOffscreen() {
439    /* Allocate the offscreen images, and initialize the "images" one. */
440    offscreen = createImage(width*edge, (textSquares+height)*edge);
441    theFont = new Font("TimesRoman", Font.PLAIN, (edge*3)/4);
442    images = new Image[shapes];
443    for (int i = 0; i<shapes; i++) {
444      images[i] = createImage(edge, edge);
445      Graphics imageG = images[i].getGraphics();
446      imageG.setColor(colors[i]);
447      imageG.fill3DRect(0, 0, edge, edge, true);
448    }
449    boardInvalid = true;
450  }
451
452  public synchronized void paint(Graphics g) {
453    /* Generally, we have the complete image offscreen */
454    if (offscreen == null) initOffscreen();
```

```
455    if (boardInvalid) {
456      boardInvalid = false;
457      paintBoard();
458    }
459    g.drawImage(offscreen, 0, 0, this);
460  }
461
462  public void update(Graphics g) {
463    paint(g);
464  }
465
466
467  /* */
468  /* User input */
469  /* */
470
471  public synchronized boolean keyDown(Event evt, int key) {
472    switch (key) {
473    case 'a':
474      animate = !animate;
475      return true;
476    case 'd':
477      if (level > 0) erase(-1);
478      return true;
479    case 'j':
480    case Event.LEFT:
481      movePiece(-1,0);
482      return true;
483    case 'k':
484    case Event.UP:
485      rotatePiece();
486      return true;
487    case 'l':
488    case Event.RIGHT:
489      movePiece(1,0);
490      return true;
491    case 'p':
492      paused = !paused;
493      paintScore();
494      repaint();
495      return true;
496    case 's':
497      erase(0);
```

```
498      return true;
499    case 'u':
500      if (level < maxLevel) erase(+1);
501      return true;
502    case ' ':
503    case Event.DOWN:
504      movieEnd = System.currentTimeMillis();
505      while (movePiece(0,1)) {}
506      return true;
507    }
508    return false;
509  }
510
511 }
```

ANNOTATIONS

The **Tetris** applet uses a separate thread to animate the current piece so that it gradually moves down the game board. That's why line 12 declares that the **Tetris** class implements the **Runnable** interface:

```
12 public class Tetris extends Applet implements Runnable {
```

The **run()** method, shown in lines 288 through 329, moves the current piece in a **while** loop. After each move, the thread sleeps for 33 milliseconds before moving the piece again.

Tetris uses a two-dimensional integer array named **occupant[][]** to keep track of the pieces that occupy each specific cell in the game's grid. There is an entry in the **occupant[][]** array for each cell in the grid. When a cell is occupied by a game piece, the shape type of that piece is stored in the corresponding integer in **occupant[][]**. As described in the next section, each game piece can have any one of seven distinct shapes. These are represented by the numbers 1 through 7. Shape type 0 is used to mean an unoccupied cell. Thus, entries in the **occupant[][]** array are the numbers between 0 and 7.

THE GAME PIECES IN TETRIS In **Tetris,** each game piece is made out of four squares. A shape is created by attaching the squares to one another along sides. For example, a piece might have all four squares laid in a horizontal line.

In the applet's code, each game piece is represented by a two-dimensional **boolean** array with four rows and four columns. The **initPiece()** method, shown in lines 119 through 124, creates an empty piece:

```
119    private boolean[][] initPiece() {
120      /* Part of rotation and piece creation: creates piece with no squares */
```

```
121      boolean[][] newPiece = new boolean[4][4];
122      for (int x=0; x<4; x++) for (int y=0; y<4; y++) newPiece[x][y] = false;
123      return newPiece;
124  }
```

Line 121 creates a 4 by 4 **boolean** array, and line 122 sets all entries in that array to **false**. This represents an empty piece.

Basically, you can think of each shape as being built by placing squares in a 4 by 4 grid of cells. The 4 by 4 **boolean** array represents the presence or absence of a square in each cell. If an element in the **boolean** array is **true**, there is a square at that cell location; otherwise that cell is empty. That's why an empty shape is represented by setting all elements of the **boolean** array to **false**.

To see how a specific shape is represented by the 4 by 4 **boolean** array, take a look at the **newPiece()** method that creates a new game piece. First, line 171 creates the **boolean** array **newPiece[][]** that represents an empty piece:

```
171      boolean[][] newPiece = initPiece();
```

Next, line 172 selects a random number between 1 and 7:

```
172      kind = (short)(Math.floor(Math.random()*(shapes-1)+1));
```

Note that the **shapes** variable is set to 8. The **Math.random()** method returns a random number between 0.0 and 1.0. That value is multiplied by 7, 1 is added to the result, and finally, **Math.floor()** is called to get the largest integer. The resulting number should be between 1 and 7.

A **switch** statement in lines 175 through 235 then initializes the **newPiece[][]** array for the random shape type represented by **kind**. For example, when **kind** is 2, lines 184 through 191 create a specific shape:

```
184      case 2:
185        newPiece[0][1] = true;  /* . . . . */
186        newPiece[1][1] = true;  /* X X X . */
187        newPiece[1][2] = true;  /* . X . . */
188        newPiece[2][1] = true;  /* . . . . */
189        initX = -1;
190        pieceSize = 3;
191        break;
```

The four Xs in the comment lines show the positions of the four squares that make up the piece. From these comment lines, you can see what the shape looks like. Notice that the **newPiece[][]** array elements corresponding to the locations with an X are set to **true**. The **pieceSize** variable is the horizontal extent of the piece (in this case, it's three squares wide). The **initX** variable is actually the initial y coordinate of the piece (even though the variable name has an X in it). These values are used when the piece is placed on the game board by the **putPiece()** method.

TETRIS GAME START   During initialization, the **Tetris** applet's **init()** method, shown in lines 262 through 273, gets the **COLUMNS, ROWS,** and **PIXELS** parameter values from the HTML file. The **COLUMNS** and **ROWS** parameters specify the **width** and **height** of the game board (expressed as a number of squares). The **PIXELS** parameter specifies the number of pixels on each edge of a square. Line 272 of the **init()** method calls the **erase()** method to initialize the game:

```
272     erase(0);
```

The argument to the **erase()** method indicates the amount by which the current level of difficulty should be changed. When called from **init()**, the argument is set to zero. However, **erase()** is also called during the game to restart the game at a different level. In those cases, **erase()** is called with a nonzero argument.

The **erase()** method, shown in lines 61 through 95, initializes all necessary variables to start a new game. Lines 63 through 73 initialize an array of **Color** objects called **colors[]**:

```
63   if (colors==null) {
64      colors = new Color[shapes];
65      colors[empty] = new Color(102,102,102);  /* darkish gray */
66      colors[1]    = new Color(153,51,51);     /* red */
67      colors[2]    = new Color(204,204,0);     /* yellow */
68      colors[3]    = new Color(51,153,51);     /* green */
69      colors[4]    = new Color(0,204,204);     /* cyan */
70      colors[5]    = new Color(51,102,204);     /* blue */
71      colors[6]    = new Color(153,0,153);     /* magenta */
72      colors[7]    = new Color(204,102,51);     /* orange */
73   }
```

Note that line 63 proceeds with the initialization only if the **colors[]** array is **null**. This happens when the game is initialized for the first time. The **shapes** variable is set to 8 (line 24), and **empty** is set to zero (line 25). Thus, the **colors[]** array has eight entries: it sets up a dark gray color for the empty spaces and seven other colors for use when displaying the blocks.

Lines 74 through 77 of the **erase()** method initialize the high scores for each level; the applet tracks the highest scores at each level of difficulty. Line 78 then initializes the **occupant[][]** array that holds information about the shape number that currently occupies each square in the Tetris game board:

```
78   if (occupant==null) occupant = new int[width][height];
```

Initially, lines 85 through 87 set all elements in the **occupant[][]** array to **empty** (which is an integer initialized to zero):

```
85   for (int x = 0; x<width; x++) {
86     for (int y = 0; y<height; y++) { occupant[x][y] = empty; }
87   }
```

This means that the squares are blank and there are no pieces in the game board. Finally, line 94 of the **erase()** method calls **repaint()** to draw the new game board:

```
94  repaint();
```

After initialization is complete, the **Tetris** applet's **start()** method, shown in lines 275 through 279, creates a thread (called **daemon**) and starts that thread. Line 278 calls the **requestFocus()** method to request that the applet receive all keyboard events:

```
278     requestFocus();
```

This is known as receiving *input focus*—that means the applet will receive all keypresses in the form of events. This step is necessary because users use the keyboard to play **Tetris**.

GAME PIECE MOVEMENT   After the applet starts, the **daemon** thread starts executing the **run()** method, shown in lines 288 through 329. To ensure that none of the applet's variables are altered while the thread is doing its job, the code is enclosed in a **synchronized()** block that encloses lines 293 through 325:

```
293     synchronized(this) {
// Code that manipulates variables in Tetris applet
325        }
```

PROGRAMMER'S NOTE   *When you program with threads, the use of a **synchronized()** block is a good way to ensure that another thread does not change the variables while this thread is working with them.*

The **run()** method performs a set of tasks repeatedly in a **while** loop. It calls **movePiece()** to advance the current piece (or block) by a specified amount in the horizontal (x) and vertical (y) directions. The **movePiece()** method, in turn, calls **putPiece()** to change the position of the piece, if possible, and then paint the piece at the new position. If there is nothing to move, line 320 calls **newPiece()** to generate a new piece.

The **newPiece()** method, shown in lines 148 through 237, does much more than just create a new piece. If there is a current piece, lines 151 through 158 of the **newPiece()** method place that piece in the game grid by marking the appropriate entries in the **occupant[][]** array; they then update the **score** variable that tracks the current score:

```
151     if (piece != null) {
152       for (int x=0; x<pieceSize; x++) {
153         for (int y=0; y<pieceSize; y++) {
154           if (piece[x][y] && place.y+y >= 0) occupant[place.x+x][place.y+y] = kind;
155         }
156       }
157       score += value;
158     }
```

Line 154 essentially marks the appropriate element of the **occupant[][]** array with the shape type (indicated by the variable named **kind**). Note in line 157 that **score** is incremented by **value**, which is set to **24 + 2*level**, where **level** is the current level of difficulty (a number between 0 and 10).

Line 160 then calls **clearRow()** to clear any rows that are completely filled up. Lines 169 and 170 display the new score and repaint the game board:

```
169    paintScore();
170    repaint();
```

After that, the **newPiece()** method generates a new piece, as described in the section "The Game Pieces in Tetris."

After the move has been performed (or a new piece generated to move), lines 326 and 327 of the **run()** method call **Thread.sleep()** to wait a while:

```
326       try { Thread.sleep(sleepTime);
327       } catch (InterruptedException e) { };
```

Specifically, the thread sleeps for the number of milliseconds specified by the **sleepTime** variable (initialized to 33 on line 46) before repeating the **while** loop in lines 292 through 328.

TETRIS GAME PLAY   The user plays the game by pressing keys on the keyboard. All keyboard input from the user is handled by the **keyDown()** method, shown in lines 471 through 509. The **keyDown()** method has the following form:

```
471  public synchronized boolean keyDown(Event evt, int key) {
472     switch (key) {
// case statement for the a and d keys
479     case 'j':
480     case Event.LEFT:
481       movePiece(-1,0);
482       return true;
// case statement for the k, l, p, s, u, and the spacebar keys ...
507     }
508     return false;
509  }
```

The **switch** statement in lines 472 through 507 handles each individual keypress. For example, line 479 shows the **case** statement for the **j** key, and line 480 shows the **case** statement for the LEFT ARROW key (denoted by **Event.LEFT**). Because both of these keypresses result in moving the piece to the left, they are handled together. Line 481 calls **movePiece()** with appropriate x and y displacements to perform the shift. Notice that in this case, the x displacement is -1, which means move to the left by 1 square.

TETRIS GAME DISPLAY   The **paint()** method, shown in lines 452 through 460, draws the game board as the pieces move. The game board is prepared in an off-screen image named **offscreen**. Lines 455 through 459 of the **paint()** method draw the **offscreen** image on the applet:

```
455    if (boardInvalid) {
456      boardInvalid = false;
457      paintBoard();
458    }
459    g.drawImage(offscreen, 0, 0, this);
```

Line 455 checks the **boolean** variable **boardInvalid**, which is **true** whenever the **offscreen** image does not match the current state of the pieces. If **boardInvalid** is **true**, line 456 resets this **boolean** variable to **false**, and line 457 calls **paintBoard()** to update the **offscreen** image. Then line 459 draws the **offscreen** image on the applet's display area.

The **paintBoard()** method, shown in lines 425 through 436, draws the entire **offscreen** image from scratch. Lines 427 through 435 do this job:

```
427    Graphics g = offscreen.getGraphics();
428    g.clipRect(0, textSquares*edge, width*edge, height*edge);
429    for (int x = 0; x<width; x++) {
430      for (int y = 0; y<height; y++) {
431        paintSquare(g, x, y, 0, occupant[x][y]);
432      };
433    }
434    paintPiece(false);
435    paintScore();
```

Line 427 gets the **Graphics** object for the **offscreen** image. Line 428 sets the clip rectangle to the area containing the game board (excluding the area at the top where text is displayed). Lines 429 through 433 paint all of the squares by calling the **paintSquare()** method for each square. Line 434 calls **paintPiece()** to draw the pieces on the **offscreen** image. Line 435 calls **paintScore()** to draw the text messages in the text area of the image.

In addition to updating the entire **offscreen** image and then letting the **paint()** method draw that image on the applet, many methods call **repaintPiece()**, which in turn calls **paintPiece()** with an argument that updates **offscreen** and also draws the affected parts of the image directly on the applet. You can see this code in lines 411 through 416 of the **paintPiece()** method:

```
411    if (doRepaint) {
412      Graphics g = getGraphics();
413      g.clipRect(minX*edge, (minY+textSquares)*edge,
414                 (limX-minX)*edge, (limY-minY)*edge);
415      g.drawImage(offscreen, 0, 0, this);
416    }
```

Here, line 413 sets the clip rectangle to an area affected by the current piece. Line 415 then calls **drawImage()** to draw only that clip rectangle on the applet's display area.

PROGRAMMER'S NOTE *Using a clip rectangle is an efficient way to update small parts of an image. Call the* ***clipRect()*** *method of the* ***Graphics*** *object to set up the clip rectangle.*

Missile Commando II

A popular class of games is the arcade-style missile defense game. In this type of game, missiles and bombs rain down toward some cities. Your goal is to protect the cities by shooting down the incoming missiles and bombs. In PC versions of a missile defense game, you simply click where you want to shoot.

Missile Commando II is a classic missile defense game implemented as a Java applet. It's modeled after the well-known arcade game called Missile Command that was Atari's first major arcade hit. Missile Commando II is copyrighted by Mark Boyns and distributed under the terms of the GNU General Public License. The official home page for Missile Commando II is at **http://www.sdsu.edu/~boyns/java/mcii/**.

The next few sections shows you how to play Missile Commando II and explain the source code of the applet.

Playing Missile Commando II

The companion CD-ROM's **ch05\mcii** directory contains the entire distribution of Missile Commando II version 1.2. The applet is named **MissileCommando**. To try **MissileCommando**, open the **mcii.html** file in a Java-capable Web browser.

The applet displays a panel with a line of text above and three buttons—labeled **Start**, **Suspend**, and **Sound Off**—along the bottom edge. The words **Game Over** appear in the middle of the panel. If you do nothing, **MissileCommando** starts running in a demo mode (just as arcade games typically do). You'll see streams of missiles and bombs coming down on some cities. The applet simulates some defending shots that knock out some incoming missiles. This goes on until you start the game.

To begin playing, click on the **Start** button. **MissileCommando** will begin at level 1. After a short pause, you'll see red streaks of incoming missiles. Occasionally, bombs and bomb debris will drift down. Simply point and click to destroy incoming missiles, bombs, and bomb debris. **MissileCommando** displays a graphic and plays an appropriate audio clip for each explosion and gives you points for shooting down missiles. As you click, you'll use up your shots. The line of text along the applet's top edge shows the remaining shots, number of incoming missiles (that are yet to come), and your current score. When there are no more incoming missiles, the level ends. At the end of a level, **MissileCommando** awards bonus points for any remaining cities and shots. It displays a message about the bonus points and then starts a new game at the next level.

Figure 5-6 shows a screen shot of the Missile Commando II game in progress.

As you move to higher levels, the incoming missile count increases. The shot counts decrease at certain levels, making it difficult to shoot down all of the incoming missiles. However, if you are like me, you probably won't notice any of these details as you get caught up in the frenzy of clicking and shooting down all of the incoming missiles and bombs that the game throws at you. That frenzied reaction essentially sums up the attraction of Missile Commando II.

Using **MissileCommando** in a Web page is quite simple. For example, here is the **<applet>** tag from the **mcii.html** file that results in the display shown in Figure 5-6:

```
<html>
<head>
<title>Missile Commando II</title>
</head>
<body bgcolor="#FFFFFF">
<center>
<applet code=MissileCommando.class width=500 height=375>
</applet>
<br>
Graphics by <b>Keith Parks</b><br>
Programming by <a href="http://www.sdsu.edu/~boyns/">Mark Boyns</a><br>
<p>
<h2>HINTS</h2>
<ul>
<li>The object is to defend the bases from incoming missiles
<li>Extra bases awarded every 10,000 points
<li>Incoming missile count increases every level
<li>Shot count decreases at level 7, 15, 30, ...
<li>Bonus points awarded for remaining bases and shots
</ul>
<p>
<a href="index.html">[Go Back]</a>
<br>
<a href="mailto:boyns@sdsu.edu">[Send Feedback]</a>
<br>
<a href="mcii.zip">[Download (Java source included)]</a>
<br>
Accesses: <img align=absmiddle src="/cgi-bin/nph-
counter?type=alt&size=medium&width=0&url=http://www.sdsu.edu/~boyns/
java/mcii/mcii.html">
</center>
</body>
</html>
```

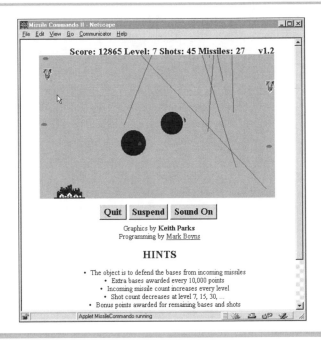

FIGURE 5-6. The Missile Commando II game in progress.

MissileCommando does not accept any **<param>** tags. All you need is the **<applet>** tag with the **MissileCommando.class** file in the **code** attribute and a reasonable **width** and **height**.

Understanding Missile Commando II

MissileCommando

MissileCommando uses a number of classes, each implemented in its own source file. Because of limited space, this book does not show the complete listings of all source files (you'll find all of the files in the **ch05\mcii** directory of the companion CD-ROM). Instead, the following listing shows the **MissileCommando.java** file that implements the **MissileCommando** applet class. I describe the applet's code in the sections that follow the listing.

```
1  /* MissileCommando.java - based on the arcade game Missile Command. */
2
3  /*
4   * Copyright (C) 1996 Mark Boyns <boyns@sdsu.edu>
5   *
6   * Missile Commando II
7   * <URL:http://www.sdsu.edu/~boyns/java/mcii/>
8   *
```

```
9   * This program is free software; you can redistribute it and/or modify
10  * it under the terms of the GNU General Public License as published by
11  * the Free Software Foundation; either version 2 of the License, or
12  * (at your option) any later version.
13  *
14  * This program is distributed in the hope that it will be useful,
15  * but WITHOUT ANY WARRANTY; without even the implied warranty of
16  * MERCHANTABILITY or FITNESS FOR A PARTICULAR PURPOSE.  See the
17  * GNU General Public License for more details.
18  *
19  * You should have received a copy of the GNU General Public License
20  * along with this program; if not, write to the Free Software
21  * Foundation, Inc., 675 Mass Ave, Cambridge, MA 02139, USA.
22  */
23
24  import java.applet.Applet;
25  import java.applet.AudioClip;
26  import java.util.*;
27  import java.awt.*;
28
29  public
30  class MissileCommando extends java.applet.Applet implements Runnable
31  {
32      final String version = "v1.2";
33      final int worldWidth = 500;
34      final int worldHeight = 300;
35      final int scoreHeight = 25;
36      final int controlsHeight = 50;
37      final int screenWidth = worldWidth;
38      final int screenHeight = worldHeight + scoreHeight + controlsHeight;
39
40      final int baseWidth = 64;
41      final int baseHeight = 32;
42      final int baseGap = 30;
43      final int maxBases = 5;
44
45      final int missilePoints = 75;
46      final int mrvPoints = 150;
47      final int bombPoints = 0;
48      final int extraShotPoints = 10;
49      final int extraBasePoints = 50;
50      final int rebuildBasePoints = 10000;
51
```

```
52      AudioClip missileSound = null;
53      AudioClip missileExplosionSound = null;
54      AudioClip mrvExplosionSound = null;
55      AudioClip baseExplosionSound = null;
56      AudioClip bombSound = null;
57
58      boolean playing = false;
59      boolean readyToPlay = false;
60      boolean clearScreen = false;
61      boolean paused = false;
62      boolean soundEnabled = true;
63
64      Thread thread = null;
65      GameObjectMover mover = null;
66
67      Controls controls;
68
69      Vector bases;
70      Vector missiles;
71      Vector shots;
72      Vector mrvs;
73      Vector explosions;
74      Vector bombs;
75      Vector bombDebris;
76
77      int score = 0;
78      int extraBaseScore = 0;
79      int level = 0;
80
81      int shotCount = 0;
82      int missileCount = 0;
83      int missileSpeed = 0;
84      int missileDelay = 0;
85      int mrvSpeed = 0;
86      int bombSpeed = 0;
87
88      Color skyColor = new Color (148, 198, 231);
89      Graphics world = null;
90
91      MediaTracker tracker;
92      Image baseImage;
93      Image mrvImage;
94      Image bombImage;
```

```
95
96      Font font;
97      FontMetrics fontMetrics;
98
99      String screenMessage;
100
101     public
102     void init ()
103     {
104         int i, x;
105
106         font = new Font ("TimesRoman", Font.BOLD, 20);
107         fontMetrics = getFontMetrics (font);
108         setFont (font);
109
110         tracker = new MediaTracker (this);
111         baseImage = getImage (getDocumentBase (), "images/base.gif");
112         tracker.addImage (baseImage, 1);
113         mrvImage = getImage (getDocumentBase (), "images/mrv.gif");
114         tracker.addImage (mrvImage, 1);
115         bombImage = getImage (getDocumentBase (), "images/bomb.gif");
116         tracker.addImage (bombImage, 1);
117
118         /* Load all the sounds. */
119         missileSound = getAudioClip (getDocumentBase (), "sounds/Rocket.au");
120         missileExplosionSound = getAudioClip (getDocumentBase (), "sounds/Oomph.au");
121         mrvExplosionSound = getAudioClip (getDocumentBase (), "sounds/Oomph.au");
122         baseExplosionSound = getAudioClip (getDocumentBase (), "sounds/Explosion-2.au");
123         bombSound = getAudioClip (getDocumentBase (), "sounds/ship_alarm.au");
124
125         setBackground (Color.white);
126
127         setLayout (new BorderLayout ());
128         controls = new Controls (this);
129         add ("South", controls);
130
131         resize (screenWidth, screenHeight);
132
133         /* Start the game! */
134         thread = new Thread (this);
135         thread.start ();
136     }
137
```

```
138     public
139     void start ()
140     {
141         if (thread == null)
142         {
143             thread = new Thread (this);
144             thread.start ();
145         }
146     }
147
148     public
149     void stop ()
150     {
151         if (thread != null && thread.isAlive ())
152         {
153             thread.stop ();
154             thread = null;
155         }
156         if (mover != null && mover.isAlive ())
157         {
158             mover.stop ();
159             mover = null;
160         }
161     }
162
163     public
164     boolean mouseDown (Event e, int x, int y)
165     {
166         if (playing)
167         {
168             createShot (x, y - scoreHeight);
169         }
170         return true;
171     }
172
173     void startGame ()
174     {
175         readyToPlay = true;
176     }
177
178     void quitGame ()
179     {
```

```
180          playing = false;
181      }
182
183      void resetScore ()
184      {
185          clearScreen = true;
186
187          score = 0;
188          extraBaseScore = 0;
189          level = 0;
190
191          message (null);
192      }
193
194      void resetGame ()
195      {
196          clearScreen = true;
197
198          missiles = new Vector (100);
199          shots = new Vector (100);
200          mrvs = new Vector (100);
201          explosions = new Vector (100);
202          bombs = new Vector (100);
203          bombDebris = new Vector (100);
204
205          // controls.playButton.setLabel ("Start");
206          // controls.suspendButton.setLabel ("Suspend");
207          // controls.soundButton.setLabel ("Sound Off");
208
209          createBases ();
210          message (null);
211      }
212
213      void suspendGame ()
214      {
215          if (thread != null && playing)
216          {
217              thread.suspend ();
218              if (mover != null && mover.isAlive ())
219              {
220                  mover.suspend ();
221              }
```

```
222            paused = true;
223            clearScreen = true;
224            repaint ();
225        }
226    }
227
228    void resumeGame ()
229    {
230        if (thread != null && playing)
231        {
232            thread.resume ();
233            if (mover != null && mover.isAlive ())
234            {
235                mover.resume ();
236            }
237            paused = false;
238            clearScreen = true;
239        }
240    }
241
242    void enableSound ()
243    {
244        soundEnabled = true;
245    }
246
247    void disableSound ()
248    {
249        soundEnabled = false;
250    }
251
252    public
253    void run ()
254    {
255        showStatus ("Loading images...");
256        tracker.checkAll (true);
257        try
258        {
259            tracker.waitForAll ();
260        }
261        catch (Exception e)
262        {
263            return;
264        }
```

```
265        showStatus ("");
266
267        resetGame ();
268        resetScore ();
269
270        for (;;)
271        {
272            if (!playing && readyToPlay)
273            {
274                resetGame ();
275                resetScore ();
276                playing = true;
277                readyToPlay = false;
278            }
279
280            if (playing)
281            {
282                level++;
283            }
284            else if (level == 0)
285            {
286                level = 1;
287            }
288
289            /* Set the delay between missiles. */
290            if (playing)
291            {
292                missileDelay = 2000 - ((level-1)*200);
293                if (missileDelay < 500)
294                {
295                    missileDelay = 500;
296                }
297            }
298            else
299            {
300                missileDelay = 500;
301            }
302
303            /* Set the missile speed. */
304            missileSpeed = 5;
305
306            /* Set the MRV speed. */
307            mrvSpeed = 6;
```

```
308
309              /* Set the bomb speed. */
310              bombSpeed = 4;
311
312              /* Set the number of missiles to be fired. */
313              missileCount = 5 + ((level-1) * 5);
314
315              /* Set the maximum number of shots. */
316              if (level < 7)
317              {
318                  shotCount = missileCount * 2;
319              }
320              else if (level < 15)
321              {
322                  shotCount = missileCount + (2 * level);
323              }
324              else if (level < 30)
325              {
326                  shotCount = missileCount;
327              }
328              else
329              {
330                  shotCount = missileCount - level;
331              }
332
333              /* Display the new level message. */
334              message ("Level " + level);
335              try
336              {
337                  Thread.sleep (3000);
338              }
339              catch (Exception e)
340              {
341              }
342              message (null);
343
344              /* Start the object mover thread to move all the
345                 game objects. */
346              mover = new GameObjectMover (100, this);
347              mover.start ();
348
349              while (missileCount > 0)
350              {
```

```
351         /* Fire a missile. */
352         int speed = missileSpeed;
353         if (level > 1 && Math.random () > 0.75)
354         {
355             speed += (int) (Math.random () * missileSpeed);
356         }
357         createMissile (speed);
358         missileCount--;
359
360         /* Maybe create a mrv. */
361         if (mrvs.size () < level)
362         {
363             double chance = Math.random ();
364             if (chance > 0.70)
365             {
366                 createMRV (mrvSpeed);
367             }
368         }
369
370         /* Maybe drop a bomb. */
371         if (level > 1 && bombs.size () < 2)
372         {
373             double chance = Math.random ();
374             if (chance > 0.85)
375             {
376                 createBomb (bombSpeed);
377             }
378         }
379
380         if (!playing)
381         {
382             starWars ();
383         }
384
385         if (!playing && readyToPlay)
386         {
387             break;
388         }
389
390         try
391         {
392             Thread.sleep (missileDelay);
393         }
```

```
394             catch (Exception e)
395             {
396             }
397         }
398
399         if (!playing && readyToPlay)
400         {
401             mover.stop ();
402             continue;
403         }
404
405         /* Wait for everything to disappear. */
406         while (missiles.size () > 0
407             || mrvs.size () > 0
408             || explosions.size () > 0
409             || bombs.size () > 0
410             || bombDebris.size () > 0
411             || shots.size () > 0)
412         {
413             if (!playing && readyToPlay)
414             {
415                 break;
416             }
417             if (!playing && (missiles.size () > 0 || mrvs.size () > 0 || bombs.size () > 0))
418             {
419                 starWars ();
420             }
421             try
422             {
423                 Thread.sleep (500);
424             }
425             catch (Exception e)
426             {
427             }
428         }
429
430         /* Stop the object mover thread. */
431         mover.stop ();
432
433         /* Calculate bonus points. */
434         int bonus = 0;
435         bonus += shotCount * extraShotPoints;
```

```
436         bonus += countAliveBases () * extraBasePoints;
437         incrementScore (bonus);
438
439         if (playing)
440         {
441             /* Display the bonus points message. */
442             message ("Bonus: " + bonus);
443             try
444             {
445                 Thread.sleep (2000);
446             }
447             catch (Exception e)
448             {
449             }
450             message (null);
451         }
452
453         /* Possibly rebuild any destroyed bases. */
454         rebuildBases ();
455
456         /* The game is over when no bases are left. */
457         if (countAliveBases () == 0)
458         {
459             playing = false;
460
461             /* Destroy the world. */
462             mover = new GameObjectMover (400, this);
463             mover.start ();
464             destroyWorld ();
465             while (explosions.size () > 0)
466             {
467                 try
468                 {
469                     Thread.sleep (500);
470                 }
471                 catch (Exception e)
472                 {
473                 }
474             }
475             mover.stop ();
476
477             resetGame ();
478
```

```
479              controls.playButton.setLabel ("Start");
480              controls.suspendButton.setLabel ("Suspend");
481          }
482       }
483    }
484
485    void starWarsFireAt (Vector v)
486    {
487       int x, y;
488       Enumeration objs = v.elements ();
489       while (objs.hasMoreElements ())
490       {
491          GameObject o = (GameObject) objs.nextElement ();
492          if (o instanceof Missile)
493          {
494              Missile m = (Missile) o;
495              x = (int) m.x;
496              y = (int) m.y;
497          }
498          else if (o instanceof MRV)
499          {
500              MRV m = (MRV) o;
501              x = m.x;
502              y = m.y;
503          }
504          else if (o instanceof Bomb)
505          {
506              Bomb b = (Bomb) o;
507              x = b.x;
508              y = b.y;
509          }
510          else
511          {
512              x = worldWidth/2;
513              y = worldHeight/2;
514          }
515
516          if (y > worldHeight/5)
517          {
518              int d;
519              if (Math.random () > 0.5)
520              {
521                  d = 1;
```

```
522                    }
523                    else
524                    {
525                        d = -1;
526                    }
527                    shots.addElement (new Shot (x+d*(int)(Math.random ()*40),
528                                                y+d*(int)(Math.random ()*40),
529                                                60));
530            }
531        }
532
533    }
534
535    void starWars ()
536    {
537        starWarsFireAt (missiles);
538        starWarsFireAt (mrvs);
539        starWarsFireAt (bombs);
540    }
541
542    void createShot (int x, int y)
543    {
544        if (shotCount > 0)
545        {
546            shots.addElement (new Shot (x, y, 60));
547            shotCount--;
548        }
549    }
550
551    void createMissile (int x1, int y1, int speed)
552    {
553        int x2 = baseGap + (int) (Math.random () * (worldWidth - baseGap));
554        int y2 = worldHeight - 1;
555
556        if (soundEnabled && missileSound != null && playing)
557        {
558            missileSound.play ();
559        }
560
561        missiles.addElement (new Missile (x1, y1, x2, y2, speed));
562    }
563
```

```
564    void createMissile (int speed)
565    {
566        int x1 = (int) (Math.random () * worldWidth);
567        int y1 = 1;
568        createMissile (x1, y1, speed);
569    }
570
571    void destroyMissile (Missile m)
572    {
573        if (soundEnabled && missileExplosionSound != null && playing)
574        {
575            missileExplosionSound.play ();
576        }
577        m.explode ();
578        createExplosion ((int)m.x, (int)m.y, 20);
579        incrementScore (missilePoints);
580    }
581
582    void createMRV (int speed)
583    {
584        int x1 = (int) (Math.random () * worldWidth);
585        int y1 = 1;
586        int y2 = worldHeight - 1;
587
588        mrvs.addElement (new MRV (x1, y1, y2, speed, mrvImage, this));
589    }
590
591    void destroyMRV (MRV m)
592    {
593        if (soundEnabled && mrvExplosionSound != null && playing)
594        {
595            mrvExplosionSound.play ();
596        }
597        m.explode ();
598        createExplosion (m.x, m.y, 10);
599        incrementScore (mrvPoints);
600    }
601
602    void createBomb (int speed)
603    {
604        if (soundEnabled && bombSound != null && playing)
605        {
```

```
606              bombSound.play ();
607          }
608
609          int x1 = (int) (Math.random () * worldWidth);
610          int y1 = 1;
611          int y2 = worldHeight - 1;
612
613          bombs.addElement (new Bomb (x1, y1, x1, y2, speed, bombImage, this));
614      }
615
616      void destroyBomb (Bomb b)
617      {
618          b.explode ();
619          createBombDebris (b.x, b.y);
620      }
621
622      void createBombDebris (int x, int y)
623      {
624          bombDebris.addElement (new BombDebris (x, y, 200));
625      }
626
627      void createBases ()
628      {
629          bases = new Vector (maxBases);
630          for (int i = 0, x = baseGap; i < maxBases; i++)
631          {
632              bases.addElement (new Base (x, worldHeight - baseHeight,
633                                          baseWidth, baseHeight, baseImage, this));
634              x += baseWidth + baseGap;
635          }
636      }
637
638      int countAliveBases ()
639      {
640          int count = 0;
641          for (int i = 0; i < maxBases; i++)
642          {
643              Base b = (Base) bases.elementAt (i);
644              if (b.alive ())
645              {
646                  count++;
647              }
648          }
```

```
649        return count;
650    }
651
652    void destroyBase (Base b, Missile m)
653    {
654        if (soundEnabled && baseExplosionSound != null && playing)
655        {
656            baseExplosionSound.play ();
657        }
658        m.explode ();
659        b.explode ();
660        createExplosion ((int)m.x, (int)m.y, 100);
661    }
662
663    void destroyBase (Base b, MRV m)
664    {
665        if (soundEnabled && baseExplosionSound != null && playing)
666        {
667            baseExplosionSound.play ();
668        }
669        m.explode ();
670        b.explode ();
671        createExplosion (m.x, m.y, 100);
672    }
673
674    void destroyBase (Base b, BombDebris debris)
675    {
676        if (soundEnabled && baseExplosionSound != null && playing)
677        {
678            baseExplosionSound.play ();
679        }
680        b.explode ();
681        createExplosion (b.x + b.w/2,
682                         b.y + b.h/2, 100);
683    }
684
685    void rebuildBases ()
686    {
687        int order[] = new int[maxBases];
688        int i;
689
690        for (i = 0; i < order.length; i++)
691        {
```

```
692                    order[i] = -1;
693                }
694
695            for (i = 0; i < maxBases; i++)
696            {
697                int n = (int) (Math.random () * maxBases);
698                while (order[n] != -1)
699                {
700                    n++;
701                    if (n == maxBases)
702                    {
703                        n = 0;
704                    }
705                }
706                order[n] = i;
707            }
708
709            for (i = 0; i < maxBases; i++)
710            {
711                Base b = (Base) bases.elementAt (order[i]);
712                if (! b.alive ())
713                {
714                    if (extraBaseScore >= rebuildBasePoints)
715                    {
716                        extraBaseScore -= rebuildBasePoints;
717                        b.rebuild ();
718                    }
719                }
720            }
721        }
722
723        void createExplosion (int x, int y, int size)
724        {
725            explosions.addElement (new Explosion (x, y, size));
726        }
727
728        void incrementScore (int points)
729        {
730            if (playing)
731            {
732                score += points;
733                extraBaseScore += points;
734            }
735        }
```

```
736
737    void destroyWorld ()
738    {
739        for (int i = 0; i < 10; i++)
740        {
741            int x = (int)(Math.random () * worldWidth);
742            int y = (int)(Math.random () * worldHeight);
743            createExplosion (x, y, 100);
744        }
745    }
746
747    public
748    void update (Graphics g)
749    {
750        paint (g);
751    }
752
753    void paintGameObjects (Vector objs, Graphics g)
754    {
755        if (objs == null)
756        {
757            return;
758        }
759
760        Enumeration e = objs.elements ();
761        while (e.hasMoreElements ())
762        {
763            GameObject o = (GameObject) e.nextElement ();
764            o.paint (g);
765        }
766    }
767
768    void message (String message)
769    {
770        if (message != null)
771        {
772            screenMessage = message;
773        }
774        else
775        {
776            screenMessage = null;
777            clearScreen = true;
778        }
```

```
779        repaint ();
780    }
781
782    void paintMessage (String message, Graphics g)
783    {
784        int h = fontMetrics.getHeight ();
785        int w = fontMetrics.stringWidth (message);
786        g.setColor (Color.black);
787        g.drawString (message, worldWidth/2 - w/2, worldHeight/2);
788    }
789
790    void paintStatus (Graphics g)
791    {
792        StringBuffer s = new StringBuffer ();
793        s.append ("Score: ");
794        s.append (score);
795        s.append (" Level: ");
796        s.append (level);
797        s.append (" Shots: ");
798        s.append (shotCount);
799        s.append (" Missiles: ");
800        s.append (missileCount);
801
802        int h = fontMetrics.getHeight ();
803        int w = fontMetrics.stringWidth (s.toString ());
804        int n = screenWidth/2 - w/2;
805
806        g.setColor (Color.white);
807        g.fillRect (0, 0, screenWidth, scoreHeight);
808
809        g.setColor (Color.black);
810        g.drawString (s.toString (), n, h);
811
812        w = fontMetrics.stringWidth (version);
813        g.drawString (version, screenWidth - w, h);
814    }
815
816    public
817    void paint (Graphics g)
818    {
```

```
819        if (world == null)
820        {
821            world = g.create (0, scoreHeight, worldWidth, worldHeight);
822        }
823
824        if (clearScreen)
825        {
826            g.setColor (Color.white);
827            g.fillRect (0, 0, worldWidth, worldHeight);
828
829            world.setColor (skyColor);
830            world.fillRect (0, 0, worldWidth, worldHeight);
831            clearScreen = false;
832        }
833
834        if (paused)
835        {
836            paintMessage ("PAUSED", world);
837            return;
838        }
839
840        paintStatus (g);
841        paintGameObjects (mrvs, world);
842        paintGameObjects (missiles, world);
843        paintGameObjects (bombs, world);
844        paintGameObjects (bases, world);
845        paintGameObjects (shots, world);
846        paintGameObjects (explosions, world);
847        paintGameObjects (bombDebris, world);
848
849        if (!playing)
850        {
851            paintMessage ("GAME OVER", world);
852        }
853        else if (screenMessage != null)
854        {
855            paintMessage (screenMessage, world);
856        }
857    }
858 }
```

ANNOTATIONS

MissileCommando uses 11 different classes that are implemented in as many different source files. These classes represent various objects such as bombs, missiles, and bases that appear in the game. Table 5-1 lists all of the classes that make up **MissileCommando**, shows the name of the file where you can find the source code for that class, and briefly describes the class. As I explain the applet's code in the next few sections, you will see how these classes are used in **MissileCommando**.

While the classes represent various objects in the **MissileCommando** game, the game itself is executed by two separate threads. The first thread executes the **run()** method in **MissileCommando.java** and runs the game by creating objects as needed and showing the game's effects, such as explosions. The other thread is the **GameObjectMover** class, a subclass of **Thread**, which moves the game objects.

Class	Source file	Description
MissileCommando	MissileCommando.java	Represents the applet.
GameObjectMover	GameObjectMover.java	A subclass of **Thread**; moves the various objects (bases, missiles, etc.) in the game.
GameObject	GameObject.java	An abstract game object that serves as superclass of all other game objects.
Bomb	Bomb.java	A subclass of **GameObject**; represents a bomb.
Explosion	Explosion.java	A subclass of **GameObject**; represents a generic explosion.
BombDebris	BombDebris.java	A subclass of **Explosion**; represents debris from a bomb.
Shot	Shot.java	A subclass of **Explosion**; represents a defensive shot.
MRV	MRV.java	A subclass of **GameObject**; represents a maneuvering reentry vehicle (MRV).
Missile	Missile.java	A subclass of **GameObject**; represents an incoming missile.
Base	Base.java	A subclass of **GameObject**; represents a base (or a city).
Controls	Controls.java	A subclass of **Panel**; displays the panel with the control buttons.

TABLE 5-1. List of Classes Used by the **MissileCommando** Applet.

Because **MissileCommando** uses a thread, it implements the **Runnable** interface, as shown in the class declaration in lines 29 and 30:

```
29 public
30 class MissileCommando extends java.applet.Applet implements Runnable
```

To implement the **Runnable** interface, **MissileCommando** defines a **run()** method where all of the game's actions take place.

Following the class declaration, lines 32 through 99 define all of the variables used by the **MissileCommando** applet. These variables include the game's version number (1.2), the dimensions (width and height) of the game's world, and the height of the panel where the controls will be drawn. Other variables relate to the bases (or cities) that appear along the bottom edge of the game and to the points assigned to various situations, such as shooting down a missile or an MRV (maneuvering reentry vehicle).

MissileCommando uses several **AudioClip** objects—one for each type of situation such as incoming missile, missile explosion, and bomb explosion. A number of **boolean** variables are used to control various aspects of the game such as whether the sound is on and whether the user is playing the game.

The key game objects are stored in **Vector** objects that are defined in lines 69 through 75:

```
69     Vector bases;
70     Vector missiles;
71     Vector shots;
72     Vector mrvs;
73     Vector explosions;
74     Vector bombs;
75     Vector bombDebris;
```

These seven **Vector** objects store the seven types of objects that appear in the game. The **bases** refer to the cities that the player defends. The **missiles, bombs, bombDebris,** and **mrvs** represent different types of incoming projectiles. The **shots** are what the player uses to defend the bases. As game objects are created, they are added to the appropriate **Vector**.

MissileCommando also uses a **MediaTracker** object to load the images used in the game. Lines 92 through 94 define the **Image** objects for bases, MRVs, and bombs. The missiles, shots, bomb debris, and explosions do not have explicit images; they are drawn using lines and filled circles.

MISSILECOMMANDO GAME START   When the applet is initialized, the **init()** method, shown in lines 101 through 136, starts by using a **MediaTracker** to load the images needed in the game. Note that the images are assumed to be in a subdirectory named **images**. Three image files are loaded: **base.gif, mrv.gif,** and **bomb.GIF**. As the names imply, these images represent the cities (bases) being defended, the MRVs, and bombs.

Next, lines 119 through 123 of the **init()** method call **getAudioClip()** to load seven audio clips from the **sounds** subdirectory: **Oomph.au, beep_multi.au, bzzzt.au, missile.au, Rocket.au, ship_alarm.au**, and **Explosion-2.au**. These are played as specific events occur in the game.

The **init()** method then creates an instance of the **Controls** class and adds that to the bottom edge of the applet. This **Controls** object represents the panel with three buttons along the bottom edge of the applet. This class handles mouse clicks on the **Start, Suspend**, and **Sound Off** buttons.

Finally, the **init()** method starts a thread to begin the game. If the applet has to stop (for example, when the user opens a different Web page), the **stop()** method, shown in lines 148 through 161, halts both threads—the one executing **MissileCommando**'s **run()** method as well as the **GameObjectMover** thread. Then, when the applet has to start again, the **start()** method, shown in lines 138 through 146, re-creates the thread that executes **MissileCommando**'s **run()** method. The **run()** method contains code that, in turn, creates a new **GameObjectMover** thread to start moving the game objects.

MISSILECOMMANDO GAME PLAY   The **run()** method, shown in lines 252 through 483, is at the heart of the **MissileCommando** applet. This method essentially runs the game. First, lines 256 through 264 call the **checkAll()** and **waitForAll()** methods of the **MediaTracker** to check and wait for all of the images to finish loading. Then lines 267 and 268 initialize the game and the score:

```
267         resetGame ();
268         resetScore ();
```

Lines 270 through 482 are a huge **for** loop that runs the game as long as the thread is active. This **for** loop performs a number of tasks. If the user has pressed the **Start** button, the **readyToPlay** variable will have been set to **true**. Lines 272 through 278 then reset the game and the score:

```
272         if (!playing && readyToPlay)
273         {
274             resetGame ();
275             resetScore ();
276             playing = true;
277             readyToPlay = false;
278         }
```

These lines also set **readyToPlay** back to **false** and the **boolean** named **playing** to **true**. This indicates that the user is playing the game now.

Next, the level is set to 1 for the first game or to the next higher level for continuing games. The delay between successive incoming missiles is set based on the selected level. The speeds of objects and the counts of missiles and shots are also set according to the level.

The **run()** method then displays a message with the current level number (for example "Level 1"), and the thread sleeps for 3 seconds (3000 milliseconds). After that, the message about the level is erased.

Lines 346 and 347 create a new **GameObjectMover** thread and start that thread:

```
346        mover = new GameObjectMover (100, this);
347        mover.start ();
```

This thread executes the **run()** method of the **GameObjectMover** class. Recall from Table 5-1 that the **GameObjectMover** class is defined in the **GameObjectMover.java** file. The **run()** method in that class moves the objects according to the speeds set in the **MissileCommando** class.

Lines 349 through 397 contain a **while** loop that runs as long as there are incoming missiles left. Lines 352 through 358 create a new incoming missile with a random speed and reduce the missile count by 1:

```
352        int speed = missileSpeed;
353        if (level > 1 && Math.random () > 0.75)
354        {
355            speed += (int) (Math.random () * missileSpeed);
356        }
357        createMissile (speed);
358        missileCount--;
```

Line 352 picks an initial speed for the missile. If the level is greater than 1, lines 353 through 355 increase the speed based on a random number. Then line 357 calls the **createMissile()** method to create a missile with a specific speed. The **createMissile()** method, shown in lines 564 through 569, first picks a random x coordinate for the missile (the y coordinate is 1). Then line 568 calls an overloaded form of **createMissile()** to create the missile:

```
568        createMissile (x1, y1, speed);
```

An overloaded method is a method with the same name but different arguments or return values. The overloaded version of **createMissile()**, shown in lines 551 through 562, accepts three arguments: the x and y coordinates of the missile's initial position and its speed. The overloaded **createMissile()** method picks a random x coordinate for the missile's end point and starts playing an audio clip for the missile. Line 561 then creates a new **Missile** object and adds that missile to the **Vector** of missiles:

```
561        missiles.addElement (new Missile (x1, y1, x2, y2, speed));
```

Notice that the argument to **addElement()** is a newly created **Missile** object. The **Missile** is represented by the starting point (**x1, y1**), the end point (**x2, y2**), and the **speed**. In the game, the missile is represented by a straight line that's drawn slowly from point (**x1, y1**) to point (**x2, y2**), giving the impression of a moving point (representing the missile). The missile is moved by the **GameMover** thread, which goes through all of the **Vector**s and moves each item according to its set speed.

Getting back to the **run()** method in **MissileCommando**, lines 361 through 368 create a new MRV, but based on a random number:

```
361            if (mrvs.size () < level)
362            {
363                double chance = Math.random ();
364                if (chance > 0.70)
365                {
366                    createMRV (mrvSpeed);
367                }
368            }
```

Line 363 gets a random number. If the random number is greater than 0.70, lines 364 through 367 create a new **MRV** object by calling the **createMRV()** method. That method works in the same way as **createMissile()**, explained earlier in this section.

Lines 371 through 378 use similar logic to create a bomb, but in this case the bomb is created only if the random number exceeds 0.85:

```
371            if (level > 1 && bombs.size () < 2)
372            {
373                double chance = Math.random ();
374                if (chance > 0.85)
375                {
376                    createBomb (bombSpeed);
377                }
378            }
```

If the user is not playing (meaning that the **playing** variable is **false**), lines 380 through 383 call the **starWars()** method to run the game in demo mode:

```
380            if (!playing)
381            {
382                starWars ();
383            }
```

The **starWars()** method, shown in lines 535 through 540, essentially fires shots at the incoming missiles and bombs (just as a user would, but more accurately).

Next, lines 390 through 396 call **Thread.sleep()** to wait for some time before sending in the next missile:

```
390            try
391            {
392                Thread.sleep (missileDelay);
393            }
```

```
394            catch (Exception e)
395            {
396            }
```

After all of the incoming missiles have been created, another **while** loop in lines 406 through 428 waits until all of the game objects—missiles, MRVs, explosions, bombs, bomb debris, and shots—disappear from the game. Each object disappears as it reaches the end point or when the user clicks to fire a shot and destroy the object. Once the objects are gone, line 431 stops the **GameObjectMover** thread:

```
431            mover.stop ();
```

Lines 434 through 437 then calculate the bonus points, and lines 439 through 451 display the bonus points on the screen and sleep for 2 seconds. This ends the game at the current level.

If the user had extra points to build bases, line 454 calls **rebuildBases()** to build destroyed bases. If there are no more bases left, lines 457 through 482 end the game. Line 459 sets the **playing** variable to **false**. This stops normal operation of the game. Line 477 resets the game.

Once the game ends, the user can start the game again by clicking on the **Start** button on the control panel. The user uses mouse clicks for these user actions as well as for the most important action of clicking to shoot down incoming missiles. The **mouseDown()** method, shown in lines 163 through 171, handles all mouse clicks during the game. If the user is playing the game, lines 166 through 169 call the **createShot()** method to create a shot at the location of the click:

```
166       if (playing)
167       {
168            createShot (x, y    scoreHeight);
169       }
```

The **createShot()** method, shown in lines 542 through 549, works the same way as the **createMissile()** method described earlier in this section:

```
542       void createShot (int x, int y)
543       {
544            if (shotCount > 0)
545            {
546                 shots.addElement (new Shot (x, y, 60));
547                 shotCount--;
548            }
549       }
```

If the user still has shots left, line 546 creates a new **Shot** object and adds it to the **Vector** named **shots**. Line 547 decrements the shot count so that the user has one less shot to fire. Once the shot is added to the **Vector**, the **GameObjectMover** thread takes care of moving the shot and exploding it.

MISSILECOMMANDO GAME DISPLAY   The **MissileCommando** applet's **paint()** method, shown in lines 816 through 857, handles the drawing of the game area by calling the **paintMessage()**, **paintStatus()**, and **paintGameObjects()** methods. The **paintMessage()** method draws a string of text in the middle of the game area. This method is used to display messages such as "GAME OVER" and "PAUSED." The **paintStatus()** method displays the score, level, shots, and missile count along the top of the game. The **paintGameObjects()** method draws all of the game objects—the missiles, bombs, MRVs, and shots—by calling the **paint()** method of each object. These game objects are represented by the **GameObject** class. All other game object classes are subclasses of **GameObject**.

Because **MissileCommando** uses **Vector**s to store all **GameObject**s, the applet's code often uses the **Enumeration** interface to go through the elements in a **Vector**. For example, here is how all **GameObject**s in a **Vector objs** are drawn:

```
760        Enumeration e = objs.elements ();
761        while (e.hasMoreElements ())
762        {
763            GameObject o = (GameObject) e.nextElement ();
764            o.paint (g);
765        }
```

Line 760 initializes the **Enumeration e** by calling the **elements()** method of the **Vector**. Then the **while** loop, in lines 761 through 765, goes through the elements one by one. The **e.hasMoreElements()** method returns **true** as long as there are elements left in the **Vector**. The **e.nextElement()** method returns the next object from the **Vector**. As line 763 shows, you have to cast this as a **GameObject** before invoking its **paint()** method in line 764.

PROGRAMMER'S NOTE   *You can use the **Enumeration** interface to sequentially access elements of a **Vector**. With an **Enumeration** you do not have to know how many elements are in the **Vector**. However, you do have to cast the returned objects to appropriate types before using them.*

Tools and Utilities

I n Chapters 1 through 5 you saw a wide variety of Java applets, from business and finance applets to games. This chapter turns to another broad category of applets—tools and utilities. This catchall category covers all types of useful applets such as clocks, an HTML color selector, and Web page search tools. If you browse through the list of applets at a Web site such as EarthWeb's **http://www.developer.com/directories/pages/dir.java.html**, you'll see the variety and number of applets in the tools and utilities category. Because of limited space, I have selected a few representative tools and utilities for this chapter. Each applet illustrates some aspect of Java programming that you have not yet seen.

You will find the following applets in this chapter:

♦ **Clock2**—displays the local time as a text string and as an analog clock

♦ **VisitCount**—displays the visitor count for a Web page (requires a CGI program on the Web server)

♦ **HTMLColor**—lets user interactively select colors for an HTML page and generates the **<BODY>** tag with appropriate attributes

♦ **HomePageSearch**—provides the ability to search a Web page (including all links) without using any CGI program on the Web server

A Clock

Many Web pages include a clock that displays the date and time. You can use a Java applet to get the date and time from the user's computer—the one on which the Web browser is running—and display them on the Web page. The Java applet can also keep the clock running and update the time display continuously.

The demo applets in Sun's Java Development Kit (JDK) include the **Clock2** applet, which demonstrates how to display a running clock. This applet, written by Rachel Gollub, is copyrighted by Sun Microsystems, Inc. Because Sun has granted permission to use and redistribute the code, I use it as an example of a clock applet and present it in this section. By studying this example, you'll learn how to use the **Date** and **GregorianCalendar** classes (introduced in Java 1.1) to get the current date and time.

Using Clock2

You will find the files for the **Clock2** applet in the **ch06\Clock2** directory of the companion CD-ROM. To try the **Clock2** applet, open the **clock.html** file in a Java-capable Web browser. Figure 6-1 shows a typical date and time display by

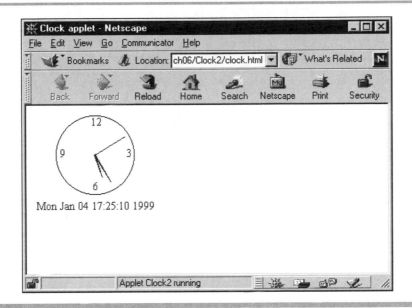

FIGURE 6-1. The **Clock2** applet displays the date and time.

Clock2. As the figure shows, **Clock2** displays an analog clock with hour, minute, and second hands. It also shows the date and time as a text string. As you watch the applet, the second hand moves and the seconds on the time display advance.

You can add the **Clock2** applet to a Web page with an <applet> tag without any parameters. For example, here is the <applet> tag from the **clock.html** file that results in the output shown in Figure 6-1:

```
<html>
<title>Clock applet</title>
<body>
<applet code="Clock2.class" width=170 height=150>
</applet>
</body>
</html>
```

By default, **Clock2** uses a white background and draws the clock and the hour and minute hands in blue. It uses a dark gray color for the text and the second hand. You can specify these colors—the background color and the colors for the clock face and text—through **<param>** tags in the HTML file. Here are the three parameters that **Clock2** accepts:

- ◆ **bgcolor** specifies the background color for the applet.
- ◆ **fgcolor1** specifies the color used to draw the clock face and the hour and minute hands.
- ◆ **fgcolor2** specifies the color used for all text and the second hand of the clock.

You specify these colors in the same way that you specify the background color in HTML files. Each color is specified in terms of the intensities of red (R), green (G), and blue (B) components of the color. For each color, specify six hexadecimal digits. The three pairs of hexadecimal digits, from left to right, represent the R, G, and B levels. The leftmost pair of hexadecimal digits is the red component, the middle pair is the green component, and the rightmost pair is the blue component. In this hexadecimal RGB notation, ff0000 denotes red and ffffff denotes white. For example, here is the HTML code you would use if you wanted a dark blue background, a gray clock face, and a yellow second hand and text:

```
<applet code="Clock2.class" width=170 height=150>
<param name=bgcolor value="000088">
<param name=fgcolor1 value="888888">
<param name=fgcolor2 value="ffff00">
</applet>
```

Clock2

Understanding Clock2

The following listing shows the file **Clock2.java** that implements the **Clock2** applet. I describe the code in the "Annotations" section.

```
 1  /*
 2   * @(#)Clock2.java        1.8 97/01/24
 3   *
 4   * Copyright (c) 1994-1996 Sun Microsystems, Inc. All Rights Reserved.
 5   *
 6   * Sun grants you ("Licensee") a non-exclusive, royalty free, license to use,
 7   * modify and redistribute this software in source and binary code form,
 8   * provided that i) this copyright notice and license appear on all copies of
 9   * the software; and ii) Licensee does not utilize the software in a manner
10   * which is disparaging to Sun.
11   *
12   * This software is provided "AS IS," without a warranty of any kind. ALL
13   * EXPRESS OR IMPLIED CONDITIONS, REPRESENTATIONS AND WARRANTIES, INCLUDING ANY
```

```
14  * IMPLIED WARRANTY OF MERCHANTABILITY, FITNESS FOR A PARTICULAR PURPOSE OR
15  * NON-INFRINGEMENT, ARE HEREBY EXCLUDED. SUN AND ITS LICENSORS SHALL NOT BE
16  * LIABLE FOR ANY DAMAGES SUFFERED BY LICENSEE AS A RESULT OF USING, MODIFYING
17  * OR DISTRIBUTING THE SOFTWARE OR ITS DERIVATIVES. IN NO EVENT WILL SUN OR ITS
18  * LICENSORS BE LIABLE FOR ANY LOST REVENUE, PROFIT OR DATA, OR FOR DIRECT,
19  * INDIRECT, SPECIAL, CONSEQUENTIAL, INCIDENTAL OR PUNITIVE DAMAGES, HOWEVER
20  * CAUSED AND REGARDLESS OF THE THEORY OF LIABILITY, ARISING OUT OF THE USE OF
21  * OR INABILITY TO USE SOFTWARE, EVEN IF SUN HAS BEEN ADVISED OF THE
22  * POSSIBILITY OF SUCH DAMAGES.
23  *
24  * This software is not designed or intended for use in on-line control of
25  * aircraft, air traffic, aircraft navigation or aircraft communications; or in
26  * the design, construction, operation or maintenance of any nuclear
27  * facility. Licensee represents and warrants that it will not use or
28  * redistribute the Software for such purposes.
29  */
30
31  // author: Rachel Gollub, 1995
32  // modified 96/04/24 Jim Hagen : use getBackground()
33  // modified 96/05/29 Rachel Gollub : add garbage collecting
34  // modified 96/10/22 Rachel Gollub : add bgcolor, fgcolor1, fgcolor2 params
35  // modified 96/12/05 Rachel Gollub : change copyright and Date methods
36  // Time!
37
38  import java.util.*;
39  import java.awt.*;
40  import java.applet.*;
41  import java.text.*;
42
43  public class Clock2 extends Applet implements Runnable {
44    Thread timer = null;
45    int lastxs=0, lastys=0, lastxm=0, lastym=0, lastxh=0, lastyh=0;
46    Date dummy = new Date();
47    GregorianCalendar cal = new GregorianCalendar();
48    SimpleDateFormat df = new SimpleDateFormat("EEE MMM dd HH:mm:ss yyyy");
49    String lastdate = df.format(dummy);
50    Font F = new Font("TimesRoman", Font.PLAIN, 14);
51    Date dat = null;
52    Color fgcol = Color.blue;
53    Color fgcol2 = Color.darkGray;
54
55  public void init() {
56    int x,y;
57
58    try {
59      setBackground(new Color(Integer.parseInt(getParameter("bgcolor"),16)));
60    } catch (Exception E) { }
61    try {
62      fgcol = new Color(Integer.parseInt(getParameter("fgcolor1"),16));
63    } catch (Exception E) { }
64    try {
```

```
65       fgcol2 = new Color(Integer.parseInt(getParameter("fgcolor2"),16));
66     } catch (Exception E) { }
67     resize(300,300);              // Set clock window size
68  }
69
70     // Plotpoints allows calculation to only cover 45 degrees of the circle,
71     // and then mirror
72
73  public void plotpoints(int x0, int y0, int x, int y, Graphics g) {
74
75     g.drawLine(x0+x,y0+y,x0+x,y0+y);
76     g.drawLine(x0+y,y0+x,x0+y,y0+x);
77     g.drawLine(x0+y,y0-x,x0+y,y0-x);
78     g.drawLine(x0+x,y0-y,x0+x,y0-y);
79     g.drawLine(x0-x,y0-y,x0-x,y0-y);
80     g.drawLine(x0-y,y0-x,x0-y,y0-x);
81     g.drawLine(x0-y,y0+x,x0-y,y0+x);
82     g.drawLine(x0-x,y0+y,x0-x,y0+y);
83  }
84
85     // Circle is just Bresenham's algorithm for a scan converted circle
86
87  public void circle(int x0, int y0, int r, Graphics g) {
88     int x,y;
89     float d;
90
91     x=0;
92     y=r;
93     d=5/4-r;
94     plotpoints(x0,y0,x,y,g);
95
96     while (y>x){
97       if (d<0) {
98         d=d+2*x+3;
99         x++;
100      }
101      else {
102        d=d+2*(x-y)+5;
103        x++;
104        y--;
105      }
106      plotpoints(x0,y0,x,y,g);
107    }
108 }
109
110
111    // Paint is the main part of the program
112
113 public void paint(Graphics g) {
114    int xh, yh, xm, ym, xs, ys, s, m, h, xcenter, ycenter;
115    String today;
```

```
116
117    dat = new Date();
118    cal.setTime(dat);
119    //  cal.computeFields(); Not needed anymore
120    s = (int)cal.get(Calendar.SECOND);
121    m = (int)cal.get(Calendar.MINUTE);
122    h = (int)cal.get(Calendar.HOUR_OF_DAY);
123    today = df.format(dat);
124    xcenter=80;
125    ycenter=55;
126
127    // a= s* pi/2 - pi/2 (to switch 0,0 from 3:00 to 12:00)
128    // x = r(cos a) + xcenter, y = r(sin a) + ycenter
129
130    xs = (int)(Math.cos(s * 3.14f/30 - 3.14f/2) * 45 + xcenter);
131    ys = (int)(Math.sin(s * 3.14f/30 - 3.14f/2) * 45 + ycenter);
132    xm = (int)(Math.cos(m * 3.14f/30 - 3.14f/2) * 40 + xcenter);
133    ym = (int)(Math.sin(m * 3.14f/30 - 3.14f/2) * 40 + ycenter);
134    xh = (int)(Math.cos((h*30 + m/2) * 3.14f/180 - 3.14f/2) * 30 + xcenter);
135    yh = (int)(Math.sin((h*30 + m/2) * 3.14f/180 - 3.14f/2) * 30 + ycenter);
136
137    // Draw the circle and numbers
138
139    g.setFont(F);
140    g.setColor(fgcol);
141    circle(xcenter,ycenter,50,g);
142    g.setColor(fgcol2);
143    g.drawString("9",xcenter-45,ycenter+3);
144    g.drawString("3",xcenter+40,ycenter+3);
145    g.drawString("12",xcenter-5,ycenter-37);
146    g.drawString("6",xcenter-3,ycenter+45);
147
148    // Erase if necessary, and redraw
149
150    g.setColor(getBackground());
151    if (xs != lastxs || ys != lastys) {
152      g.drawLine(xcenter, ycenter, lastxs, lastys);
153      g.drawString(lastdate, 5, 125);
154    }
155    if (xm != lastxm || ym != lastym) {
156      g.drawLine(xcenter, ycenter-1, lastxm, lastym);
157      g.drawLine(xcenter-1, ycenter, lastxm, lastym); }
158    if (xh != lastxh || yh != lastyh) {
159      g.drawLine(xcenter, ycenter-1, lastxh, lastyh);
160      g.drawLine(xcenter-1, ycenter, lastxh, lastyh); }
161    g.setColor(fgcol2);
162    g.drawString(today, 5, 125);
163    g.drawLine(xcenter, ycenter, xs, ys);
164    g.setColor(fgcol);
165    g.drawLine(xcenter, ycenter-1, xm, ym);
166    g.drawLine(xcenter-1, ycenter, xm, ym);
```

```
167   g.drawLine(xcenter, ycenter-1, xh, yh);
168   g.drawLine(xcenter-1, ycenter, xh, yh);
169   lastxs=xs; lastys=ys;
170   lastxm=xm; lastym=ym;
171   lastxh=xh; lastyh=yh;
172   lastdate = today;
173   dat=null;
174 }
175
176 public void start() {
177   if(timer == null)
178     {
179       timer = new Thread(this);
180       timer.start();
181     }
182 }
183
184 public void stop() {
185   timer = null;
186 }
187
188 public void run() {
189   while (timer != null) {
190     try {Thread.sleep(100);} catch (InterruptedException e){}
191     repaint();
192   }
193   timer = null;
194 }
195
196 public void update(Graphics g) {
197   paint(g);
198 }
199 }
```

ANNOTATIONS

The basic design of **Clock2** is simple. The applet essentially performs the following steps in a thread:

1. Get the date and time, using the **Date** and **GregorianCalendar** classes.

2. Format them as a text string, using the **SimpleDateFormat** class, and also figure out the positions of the hour, minute, and second hands.

3. If a second has elapsed, display the new time and redraw the hour, minute, and second hands.

4. Sleep for 100 milliseconds and repeat steps 1 through 3.

The sections that follow describe the implementation in detail.

IMPORTED CLASSES   Lines 38 through 41 show the **import** statements that incorporate packages that define classes used by the **Clock2** applet. These **import** statements include the standard **java.applet.*** and **java.awt.*** packages. **Clock2** also needs the **java.util.*** and **java.text.*** package because

♦   The **Date** and **GregorianCalendar** classes are in the **java.util** package

♦   The **SimpleDateFormat** class is in the **java.text** package

VARIABLES AND CLASS DECLARATION   Line 43 declares the **Clock2** applet class:

```
43  public class Clock2 extends Applet implements Runnable {
```

Because **Clock2** uses a thread, it implements the **Runnable** interface and, as you will see later, it includes a **run()** method.

Lines 44 through 53 define the variables used in **Clock2**. In particular, lines 46 through 49 initialize the current date and time:

```
46  Date dummy = new Date();
47  GregorianCalendar cal = new GregorianCalendar();
48  SimpleDateFormat df = new SimpleDateFormat("EEE MMM dd HH:mm:ss yyyy");
49  String lastdate = df.format(dummy);
```

Line 46 creates a **Date** object named **dummy**. **Date** represents the current date and time in binary format—as the number of milliseconds elapsed since a fixed instant (January 1, 1970, 00:00:00 GMT). Line 47 creates a **GregorianCalendar** object that will be used later to get the hours, minutes, and seconds from a binary time. Line 48 creates a **SimpleDateFormat** object named **df**. **SimpleDateFormat** parses a binary date and time (as represented by a **Date** object) and converts it to a **String**. Line 49 shows how the **SimpleDateFormat** object **df** converts the **Date** object named **dummy** to a **String** named **lastdate**.

Note that you specify the format of the date and time string in the **SimpleDateFormat()** constructor. For example, line 48 uses the format **"EEE MMM dd HH:mm:ss yyyy"**, where the fields have the following meaning:

♦   **EEE** is the 3-character abbreviation for the day of the week, such as **Sat** for Saturday.

♦   **MMM** is the 3-character abbreviation for the month, such as **Dec** for December.

♦   **dd** is the 2-digit day of the month (01 through 31, depending on the month).

♦   **HH:mm:ss** represents the current time in hour-minute-second format with the hours between 00 and 23.

♦ **yyyy** is the 4-digit year (for example, 2000 for the year 2000).

CLOCK2 INITIALIZATION   During initialization, the **init()** method gets the three color parameters—**bgcolor**, **fgcolor1**, and **fgcolor2**—from the HTML file. For example, line 59 gets the value of the **bgcolor** parameter, converts it to a hexadecimal number, creates a **Color** with that hexadecimal value, and finally sets the applet's background color—all in one line of code:

```
59      setBackground(new Color(Integer.parseInt(getParameter("bgcolor"),16)));
```

CLOCK2 TIMER THREAD   Lines 179 and 180 of the **Clock2** applet's **start()** method create a timer thread and start that thread:

```
179        timer = new Thread(this);
180        timer.start();
```

This thread executes the body of the **run()** method, shown in lines 188 through 194. The **run()** method keeps repeating two steps: it sleeps for 100 milliseconds, and then it calls **repaint()**.

DATE AND TIME DISPLAY IN CLOCK2   Whenever the **Clock2** applet's **repaint()** method is called, the Web browser calls the applet's **update()** method, shown in lines 196 through 198. In **Clock2**, the **update()** method immediately calls the **paint()** method.

The **paint()** method, shown in lines 113 through 174, draws the analog clock and displays the date and time string. Lines 117 and 118 get the current date and time information and set it in the **GregorianCalendar** object named **cal**:

```
117    dat = new Date();
118    cal.setTime(dat);
```

After that, lines 120 through 122 use the **get()** method of the **GregorianCalendar** class to get the seconds, minutes, and hours from the current date and time:

```
120    s = (int)cal.get(Calendar.SECOND);
121    m = (int)cal.get(Calendar.MINUTE);
122    h = (int)cal.get(Calendar.HOUR_OF_DAY);
```

Line 123 uses the **SimpleDateFormat** object named **df** to convert the current date and time into a **String** named **today**:

```
123    today = df.format(dat);
```

Lines 124 through 146 set up various variables (such as the center point and end points of the second, minute, and hour hands) and draw the analog clock face. In particular, line 141 calls the **circle()** method to draw a circle with a radius of 50 pixels:

```
141    circle(xcenter,ycenter,50,g);
```

The **circle()** method, shown in lines 87 through 108, uses an algorithm known as Bresenham's algorithm to calculate the points that lie on the circle and then calls the **plotpoints()** method to draw those points. Bresenham developed the circle-drawing algorithm in 1977; it essentially generates all of the points on the circle by tracing the circumference of the circle. The implementation used in **Clock2** computes the points in one octant (0 to 45 degrees) and then uses the symmetry property to find the other points on the circle.

After the circle has been drawn, lines 143 through 146 draw the numbers 9, 3, 12, and 6 on the face of the analog clock.

Then lines 150 through 154 erase the second hand and the date and time string, provided time has progressed to the next second:

```
150    g.setColor(getBackground());
151    if (xs != lastxs || ys != lastys) {
152      g.drawLine(xcenter, ycenter, lastxs, lastys);
153      g.drawString(lastdate, 5, 125);
154    }
```

Line 150 sets the color to the background color so that all drawing calls essentially result in erasing existing lines and text. The (**xs**, **ys**) and (**lastxs**, **lastys**) values are the coordinates of the second hand's endpoints, corresponding to the current second and the last second.

Lines 155 through 160 similarly erase the hour and minute hands, if necessary (if there is enough movement of the endpoints, as computed by lines 130 through 135).

Lines 161 through 168 set the colors to new values and draw the clock, its hands, and the date and time string. Lines 169 through 172 update variables that are supposed to hold old values. Line 173 sets the **Date** object **dat** to **null** to indicate to the Java Virtual Machine (JVM) that the memory used by that object may be reclaimed during garbage collection (this refers to the process used by the JVM to reclaim unused virtual memory).

An Applet That Counts Site Visitors

You have undoubtedly seen visit counters on many Web sites. The visit counter tells you how many visitors have accessed the site. Visit counters are typically implemented using CGI programs. (Because CGI programs are often implemented by Perl scripts, they are also referred to as CGI scripts.) CGI stands for Common Gateway Interface—it defines how a Web server communicates with an external program running on the same system as the Web server. In the case of a visit counter, the CGI program typically gets the number of visitors from a file, creates an image with the number, and sends that image back to the Web browser. The Web browser, in turn, displays the image with the numbers on the Web page. The CGI program also increments the visitor count stored in the file.

A Java applet coupled with a CGI program provides an interesting way to implement a visit counter. You no longer need a sophisticated CGI program; all you need is one that returns a line of text with the visitor count and then increments the count. The Java applet then displays that count as nicely formatted text on the Web page.

This section presents the **VisitCount** applet, which shows how to implement a visit counter in Java. Because you need a CGI program to use the counter, I also show a sample Perl script that you can use as the companion CGI script for **VisitCount**.

Using VisitCount

All of the files you need to use the **VisitCount** applet are in the **ch06\VCount** directory of the companion CD-ROM. To try out **VisitCount**, you need access to a Web server that allows CGI scripts. Perform the following steps to install the **VisitCount** applet on the Web server:

1. Open the file named **counter** in a text editor, and place the initial visitor count on the first line of text. For example, if you want the starting count to be 1, enter 1 on the first line.

2. Copy the **VisitCount.class** file to the Web server, and place it in the directory where the HTML files are located.

3. Copy the **count.pl** and **counter** files to the CGI directory on the Web server. If your Web service provider allows CGI programs, the Web site administrator will tell you where to place CGI programs and will let you know if there is anything else you have to do (such as changing file permissions).

To test **VisitCount**, you can use the **Counter.html** file in the **ch06\VCount** directory of the CD-ROM. Copy that file to your Web server, placing it in the same directory as the **VisitCount.class** file. You can then see **VisitCount** in action by running a Java-capable Web browser and specifying that file as the URL. For example, I tested the **VisitCount** applet on a Web server whose IP address is 192.168.1.1 (a private local area network). Figure 6-2 shows the resulting display when I visit the URL **http://192.168.1.1/Counter.html**. In this case, the Web page does not contain anything besides the visitor count. Typically, you would place the **VisitCount** applet at either the top or the bottom of a Web page that includes other useful information.

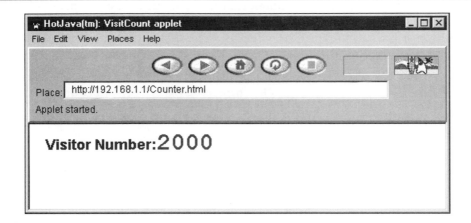

FIGURE 6-2. A sample Web page displaying a visitor count using the **VisitCount** applet.

When you want to use **VisitCount** on other Web pages, you have to insert into that Web page an **<applet>** tag with appropriate parameters. Here is the **<applet>** tag in its entirety from the **Counter.html** file:

```
<applet code=VisitCount.class width=400 height=60>
    <param name=message value="Visitor Number:">
    <param name=cgiurl value="http://192.168.1.1/cgi-bin/count.pl">
    <param name=msgfont value="Helvetica,BOLD,18">
    <param name=countfont value="Courier,BOLD,30">
    <param name=msgcolor value="0000ff">
    <param name=countcolor value="ff0000">
This is the VisitCount Java applet.
To run it you need a Java-capable browser.
</applet>
```

As this listing shows, the **<applet>** tag specifies **VisitCount.class** as the code attribute and sets aside a display area 400 pixels wide by 60 pixels tall. There are six **<param>** tags that specify parameters that **VisitCount** accepts. Just before the closing **</applet>** tag, there is some text that the user sees if the Web browser does not support Java.

The six parameters in the **Counter.html** file have the following meanings:

◆ **message** specifies text to be displayed before the visitor count (for example, **"Visitor Number:"**).

◆ **cgiurl** gives the complete URL of the CGI script that returns and increments the visitor count (for example, **"http://192.168.1.1/cgi-bin/count.pl"**).

◆ **msgfont** indicates the font to be used for the message text, specified as three comma-separated attributes: font face, style, and size (for example, **"Helvetica,BOLD,18"**).

◆ **countfont** gives the font to be used to display the count, specified in the same way as **msgfont** (for example, **"Courier,BOLD,30"**).

◆ **msgcolor** indicates the color for the message text, specified as a hexadecimal RGB value (for example, **"0000ff"** means blue).

◆ **countcolor** is the color for the count, specified in the same way as **msgcolor** (for example, **"ff0000"** means red).

Of these parameters, you must specify the **cgiurl** parameter with the complete URL of the CGI program that returns and updates the visitor count. (The other parameters use defaults if not specified.) Because of the security restrictions imposed on Java applets, **VisitCount** can access only a CGI program that runs on the same Web server as the one from which the applet's code was downloaded.

VisitCount

Understanding VisitCount

The following listing shows the **VisitCount.java** file that implements the **VisitCount** applet. As you can see from lines 12 through 26 of the listing, the applet is distributed under the GNU General Public License, which allows you to use, modify, and redistribute the code.

I describe the applet in the subsequent sections. I will also show the **count.pl** Perl script that you can use as the **VisitCount** applet's companion CGI program.

```
1  //------------------------------------------------------------------
2  // File: VisitCount.java
3  //
4  // Accesses a CGI program to update visit count and display
5  // the current count.
6  //
7  // Author: Naba Barkakati, 1998
8  //------------------------------------------------------------------
9  // VisitCount -- Java Visit Counter applet
```

```
10  // Copyright (c) 1998 Naba Barkakati (<naba@psn.net>)
11  //
12  // This program is free software; you can redistribute it
13  // and/or modify it under the terms of the GNU General Public
14  // License as published by the Free Software Foundation; either
15  // version 2 of the License, or (at your option) any later
16  // version.
17  //
18  // This program is distributed in the hope that it will be useful,
19  // but WITHOUT ANY WARRANTY; without even the implied warranty of
20  // MERCHANTABILITY or FITNESS FOR A PARTICULAR PURPOSE.  See the
21  // GNU General Public License for more details.
22  //
23  // You should have received a copy of the GNU General Public
24  // License along with this program; if not, write to the Free
25  // Software Foundation, Inc., 675 Mass Ave, Cambridge, MA 02139,
26  // USA.
27  //-------------------------------------------------------------
28  import java.awt.*;
29  import java.applet.*;
30  import java.net.*;
31  import java.io.*;
32  import java.util.*;
33  // Javadoc comments
34  /**
35   * The VisitCount class is a Java applet that accesses a CGI
36   * program at the host URL and retrieves the visitor count (the
37   * CGI program also updates the count). Then it displays the
38   * current count. Use an applet tag to embed this applet
39   * at the location where you want to display the count.
40   * You'll have to specify a CGI URL that maintains the count
41   * in a text file on the server.
42   * <p>
43   * Parameters accepted by VisitCount:
44   * <ul>
45   * <li> message - this text appears before the visit count
46   * <li> cgiurl - complete URL of CGI program that returns the
47   *               current count and updates the count
48   * <li> msgfont - font to use for message ("Helvetica,BOLD,18")
49   * <li> countfont - font to use for count, same format as msgfont
50   * <li> msgcolor - color of message text in hexadecimal RGB
51   *                 (for example, "0000ff" means blue)
```

```
52    * <li> countcolor - color of count, same format as msgcolor
53    * </ul>
54    *
55    * @author Naba Barkakati
56    * @version 1.1 August 16, 1998
57    */
58   public class VisitCount extends java.applet.Applet
59   {
60       String visitCount;   // String to store visitor count
61       String msgPrefix;    // Message to which count is appended
62       String cgiURL;       // URL of CGI script to get count
63       Font   msgFont;      // Font for message
64       Font   countFont;    // Font for the visit count
65       Color  msgColor;     // Color of message text
66       Color  countColor;   // Color for the count
67       //-----------------------------------------------------------
68       /** Gets the parameters and visit count from CGI URL */
69       public void init()
70       {
71           msgPrefix = getParameter("message");
72           String param = getParameter("msgfont");
73           if(param != null)
74               msgFont = parseFontParam(param);
75           else
76               msgFont = parseFontParam("Helvetica,BOLD,16");
77           param = getParameter("countfont");
78           if(param != null)
79               countFont = parseFontParam(param);
80           else
81               countFont = parseFontParam("Courier,BOLD,24");
82           param = getParameter("msgcolor");
83           if(param != null)
84               msgColor = parseColorParam(param);
85           else
86               msgColor = Color.black;
87           param = getParameter("countcolor");
88           if(param != null)
89               countColor = parseColorParam(param);
90           else
91               countColor = Color.red;
92           cgiURL = getParameter("cgiurl");
93           if(cgiURL == null)
```

```
94          {
95              msgPrefix = "No CGI program specified";
96              visitCount = "";
97              return;
98          }
99          try
100         {
101             // Open the URL that counts visitors to this site
102             URL url = new URL(cgiURL);
103             // Open a data stream and read a single line
104             try
105             {
106                 BufferedReader in = new BufferedReader(new
107                         InputStreamReader(url.openStream()));
108                 visitCount = in.readLine();
109             }
110             catch(IOException e)
111             {
112                 visitCount = "Error reading count!";
113             }
114         }
115         catch(MalformedURLException e)
116         {
117             visitCount = "Bad URL!";
118         }
119     }
120     //-----------------------------------------------------------
121     /** Paints the message followed by visit count */
122     public void paint(java.awt.Graphics gc)
123     {
124         // Display the visitor count that was read from the URL
125         // using whatever font style and color user has specified
126         gc.setColor(msgColor);
127         gc.setFont(msgFont);
128         FontMetrics fm = gc.getFontMetrics();
129         int xstart = 0;
130         int ystart = fm.getHeight();
131         if(msgPrefix != null)
132         {
133             gc.drawString(msgPrefix, xstart, ystart);
134             // Advance horizontally by amount needed
135             // to display message
```

```
136             xstart += fm.stringWidth(msgPrefix);
137         }
138         // Change font and display the count
139         gc.setFont(countFont);
140         gc.setColor(countColor);
141         if(visitCount != null)
142             gc.drawString(visitCount, xstart, ystart);
143     }
144     //-------------------------------------------------------------
145     /** Parses a color value passed in as a string.
146      *
147      * @param cs A 6-digit RGB color in hexadecimal ("ff0000")
148      * @return Color object based on input specifications
149      */
150     public Color parseColorParam(String cs)
151     {
152         int R = 127, G = 127, B = 127;
153         if(cs.length()==6)
154         {
155             R = Integer.valueOf(cs.substring(0,2),16).intValue();
156             G = Integer.valueOf(cs.substring(2,4),16).intValue();
157             B = Integer.valueOf(cs.substring(4,6),16).intValue();
158         }
159         return new Color(R,G,B);
160     }
161     //-------------------------------------------------------------
162     /** Creates a Font using parameters specified in a string.
163      *
164      * @param fs String with font info ("Courier,Bold,12")
165      * @return Font object created from the specifications
166      */
167     public Font parseFontParam(String fs)
168     {
169         String fontface = "Dialog";
170         int fontstyle = Font.PLAIN, fontsize = 12;
171
172         if (fs != null)
173         {
174             StringTokenizer st = new StringTokenizer(fs, ",");
175             try
176             {
177                 fontface = st.nextToken();
```

```
178          StringTokenizer stStyle = new
179                        StringTokenizer(st.nextToken());
180        fontstyle = Font.PLAIN;
181        while (stStyle.hasMoreTokens())
182        {
183          String style = stStyle.nextToken();
184          if (style.equalsIgnoreCase("plain"))
185            fontstyle |= Font.PLAIN;
186          else if (style.equalsIgnoreCase("bold"))
187            fontstyle |= Font.BOLD;
188          else if (style.equalsIgnoreCase("italic"))
189            fontstyle |= Font.ITALIC;
190        }
191        fontsize =
192          Integer.valueOf(st.nextToken()).intValue();
193      }
194    catch(Exception e)
195    {
196      fontface = "Dialog";
197      fontstyle = Font.PLAIN;
198      fontsize = 12;
199    }
200   }
201   return(new Font(fontface, fontstyle, fontsize));
202 }
203 //-------------------------------------------------- ---
204 /** Returns information about parameters accepted by applet */
205 public String[][] getParameterInfo()
206 {
207   String[][] info =
208   {
209     {"cgiurl","URL","URL that returns and updates count"},
210     {"message","String","text displayed in front of count"},
211     {"msgfont","Font","font for message (face,style,size)"},
212     {"countfont","Font","font for count (face,style,size)"},
213     {"msgcolor","RGB","color for message text (RRGGBB)"},
214     {"countcolor","RGB","color for count (RRGGBB)"}
215   };
216
217   return info;
218 }
219 //------------------------------------------------------------
220 /** Returns information about VisitCount applet */
```

```
221     public String getAppletInfo()
222     {
223         return "VisitCounter 1.1 Copyright (C) 1998 Naba Barkakati";
224     }
225 }
```

ANNOTATIONS

The basic idea behind the **VisitCount** applet is as follows:

◆ Write a CGI program that updates a count stored in a file. When run, the
CGI program updates the count and sends back a text document with the
current count.

◆ Embed a visit counter applet in your Web site's home page. Whenever a user
accesses the home page, the visit counter applet is executed. You should write
the applet so that it, in turn, executes the CGI program that updates the count
stored in a file at your Web server. The visit counter applet can also display
the current count.

I describe the applet's code next. In a later section, I present the sample Perl script,
count.pl, that sends the visitor count to the applet.

VISITCOUNT INITIALIZATION   The **VisitCount** applet does most of its work during
initialization. The **init()** method, shown in lines 69 through 119, gets the parameters
from the HTML file and accesses the CGI URL to download the visitor count as a
text document.

Lines 71 through 98 call **getParameter()** several times to retrieve the values of
parameters from the HTML file. A key parameter is **cgiurl**, which specifies the full
URL of the CGI script that updates and returns the visitor count. Note that if **cgiurl**
is not specified, lines 93 through 98 set the **String visitCount** to an empty string and
return from **init()**.

If the **cgiurl** parameter is specified, lines 99 through 118 of the **init()** method get
the visitor count from this URL. Line 102 creates a **URL** object that establishes a
connection to the specified CGI script's URL. The net effect of connecting to the URL
is to execute the CGI script that updates the visit count and returns the current
count.

Lines 106 and 107 then call the URL object's **openStream()** method and construct
a **BufferedReader** object to read from the URL:

```
106             BufferedReader in = new BufferedReader(new
107                 InputStreamReader(url.openStream()));
```

Line 108 reads a line of text from the URL:

```
108                 visitCount = in.readLine();
```

As you'll soon see in the description of the **count.pl** script, this single line should include the current visitor count for the Web site (specified in the CGI URL).

VISITOR COUNT DISPLAY   The **paint()** method, shown in lines 122 through 143, formats the visitor count and displays it on the Web page where the applet is embedded. Lines 126 through 137 set up the color and font and then display the message text that comes before the count.

Lines 139 through 142 change the color and font and display the visitor count. Because the count is returned as a **String**, all line 142 does is call the **drawString()** method to display the **String**:

```
142             gc.drawString(visitCount, xstart, ystart);
```

A PERL SCRIPT TO UPDATE THE VISITOR COUNT   The **VisitCount** applet needs a CGI script that returns the current visitor count in a text document and that also updates the visitor count. In the **ch06\Vcount** directory of the companion CD-ROM, you'll find a Perl script named **count.pl** that does this job. As you probably know, Perl is a popular scripting language, with text processing features that make it an excellent tool for writing CGI programs (which involve parsing URLs and preparing HTML text that is sent back to the Web browser).

The Perl script **count.pl** performs the following tasks:

◆ Opens a file named **counter** and reads the current count stored in that file

◆ Increments the count and stores the new count back in the **counter** file

◆ Prints the count as a single line of text preceded by a MIME header (that's how Web servers return documents requested by Web browsers)

The following listing shows my implementation of the **count.pl** script (I have removed some comments to make the listing shorter):

```perl
#!/usr/bin/perl
# Print a minimal MIME header
    print "Content-type: text/plain\n\n";
    $counterfile = "counter";
# Open the counter file and get current count
    open(COUNTER, "$counterfile");
# Lock the file to guard against another process updating the
# file as this script uses it
    $lock_exclusive = 2;
    $unlock = 8;
```

```
    flock(COUNTER, $lock_exclusive);
# Read and increment the count
    $line = <COUNTER>;
    close(COUNTER);
    chop($line);
    $count = $line;
    $count++;
# Save the new count in the file
    open(COUNTER, ">$counterfile");
    print COUNTER ("$count\n");
    close(COUNTER);
# Remember to unlock the file
    flock(COUNTER, $unlock);
# Send count to caller by printing on STDOUT
    print "$count\n";
```

Even if you don't know Perl, as a Java programmer, you can easily see what the script does. It prints a one-line MIME header with the following statement:

```
print "Content-type: text/plain\n\n";
```

The **Content-type** field specifies the MIME type of the data that the Web server sends to the Web browser. MIME stands for Multipurpose Internet Mail Extensions, an Internet standard for attaching any type of data to a mail message. (MIME is specified in RFC 1521.) Originally, MIME was developed so that the data contained in mail messages and attachments could be identified properly. Because any file can be an attachment to a mail message, MIME defines types for all kinds of data, from text and images to applications. Web servers use MIME types to identify the type of data being sent to the Web browser. In this case, the type **text/plain** means that the data is plain text.

The rest of the script opens the file named **counter** and gets a line of text from that file. That line will contain the current visitor count. The last line of the script sends back the count by printing the value:

```
print "$count\n";
```

Here **$count** is a Perl variable that holds the value of the count.

To test and use this script, place the **count.pl** file in your Web server's **cgi-bin** directory (that's the directory where your Web server looks for CGI programs). Then use a text editor to create a file named **counter**, and enter a single line with a zero. Try the script by typing the appropriate URL in a Web browser. For example, if the Web server IP address is 192.168.1.1, the URL for this CGI script would be **http://192.168.1.1/cgi-bin/count.pl**.

An HTML Color Selector

When you prepare a Web page, you use HTML's **<BODY>** tag to set various colors used on the page. For example, you can use the **BGCOLOR** attribute to specify the background color and the **TEXT** attribute to specify the color of text. Thus, **<BODY BGCOLOR="000000" TEXT="FFFFFF">** produces a Web page with white text on a black background. You are supposed to specify the colors using hexadecimal RGB values—three pairs of hexadecimal numbers denoting the intensities of red (R), green (G), and blue (B) components of the color.

It's difficult to come up with the RGB values for most colors besides the simple ones, such as blue, red, yellow, black, and white. It's relatively simple, however, to design a Java applet that lets the user select colors interactively from a palette of colors. This section presents just such an applet. **HTMLColor** allows the user to choose colors interactively for various parts of the HTML page. It also shows how the Web page will look with the selected colors and prepares a **<BODY>** tag with the selected colors.

Using HTMLColor

You'll find the files for the **HTMLColor** applet in the **ch06\HTMLColr** directory of this book's companion CD-ROM. To try out **HTMLColor**, open the **Color.html** file in a Java-capable Web browser. Figure 6-3 shows the **HTMLColor** output. The display area is divided into two halves: the left half shows a color wheel, and the right half shows a sample HTML document with the currently selected colors. There is a vertical scrollbar between these two halves. You can increase the brightness of the color by moving the scrollbar up. To select a color, just click on the color on the wheel. You'll see the color in the small patch underneath the color wheel.

Along the bottom of the applet are five checkboxes, one for each attribute of HTML's **<BODY>** tag:

- **BGCOLOR** (labeled **Background** on the checkbox) is the document's background color.
- **TEXT** is the color of text.
- **LINK** is the color of an unvisited hypertext link on the HTML document.
- **VLINK** is the color of links that have already been visited.
- **ALINK** is the color of the currently active link.

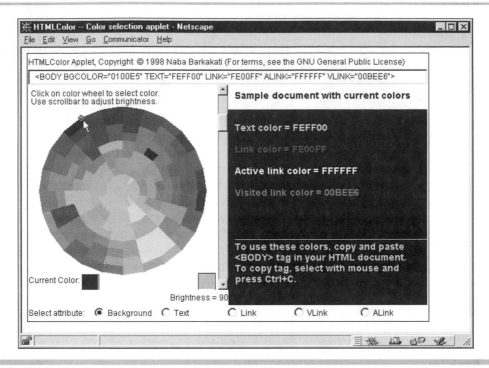

FIGURE 6-3.   HTMLColor lets you select colors for Web pages.

Initially, the **Background** checkbox is selected. This means that when you change the color, it affects the background of the HTML document. In fact, as you change the color, you'll see the background of the sample document (in the right half of the applet) change. To change the color of another attribute, click on that attribute's checkbox. The color wheel and brightness scrollbar immediately change to reflect that attribute's color. As you adjust that color, the sample document shows the change.

The complete **<BODY>** tag for the current set of colors appears along the top edge of the applet. As you change the color of any of the attributes, this tag changes as well. When you are satisfied with a set of colors, you can simply copy this tag into your HTML file. To copy, select the entire **<BODY>** tag with the mouse (hold down the mouse and drag across the line of text). Press CTRL-C to copy the text. Then open the HTML file in an editor and paste the tag into that file at the appropriate location.

The **HTMLColor** applet does not accept any parameters, making it simple to embed in an HTML file. All you need is the **<applet>** tag without any **<param>** tags. Here is the **<applet>** tag from the **Color.html** file that results in the output shown in Figure 6-3:

```
<html>
<head>
```

```
<title>HTMLColor -- Color selection applet</title>
<body>
<applet code="HTMLColor.class" width=600 height=400>
</applet>
</body>
</html>
```

In this case, the **<applet>** tag specifies a display area 600 pixels wide by 400 pixels tall. You need to provide an area that is at least that large so that there is enough room to draw everything.

If you want to use the **HTMLColor** applet on a Web site, copy all of the class files (these are the files with the **.class** extension) from the **ch06\HTMLColr** directory of the CD-ROM to your Web server. After that, you can embed the **HTMLColor** applet in a Web page, using an **<applet>** tag similar to the one in the **Color.html** file.

HTMLColor

Understanding HTMLColor

Now that you have tried out **HTMLColor**, you can study the source code to see how it is implemented. The following listing shows the **HTMLColor.java** file, the Java source file for the applet. I explain the applet's code in detail in the subsequent sections.

```
 1  //----------------------------------------------------------------
 2  // File: HTMLColor.java
 3  // Lets user select colors for the HTML <BODY> tag.
 4  // User can interactively pick the colors for background, text,
 5  // link, active link, and visited link. The applet displays the
 6  // <BODY> tag for the selected colors. To use the selected colors,
 7  // all that the user needs to do is cut and paste that <BODY> tag
 8  // into the HTML document.
 9  //
10  // Author: Naba Barkakati
11  // Date. November 26, 1998
12  //----------------------------------------------------------------
13  // HTMLColor -- Color selector for HTML <BODY> tag
14  // Copyright (C) 1998 Naba Barkakati (<naba@psn.net>)
15  //
16  // This program is free software; you can redistribute it
17  // and/or modify it under the terms of the GNU General Public
18  // License as published by the Free Software Foundation; either
19  // version 2 of the License, or (at your option) any later
20  // version.
```

```
21 //
22 // This program is distributed in the hope that it will be useful,
23 // but WITHOUT ANY WARRANTY; without even the implied warranty of
24 // MERCHANTABILITY or FITNESS FOR A PARTICULAR PURPOSE.  See the
25 // GNU General Public License for more details.
26 //
27 // You should have received a copy of the GNU General Public
28 // License along with this program; if not, write to the Free
29 // Software Foundation, Inc., 675 Mass Ave, Cambridge, MA 02139,
30 // USA.
31 //-------------------------------------------------------------------
32 import java.awt.*;
33 import java.awt.event.*;
34 import java.io.*;
35 import java.applet.*;
36 /** Displays colors using Hue-Saturation-Brightness (HSB) model */
37 class ColorSelect extends Canvas
38     implements MouseListener, MouseMotionListener
39 {
40     Image     offscreen;
41     int       w;
42     int       h;
43     int       border;
44     int       cx;
45     int       cy;
46     int       radius;
47     int       nSat;
48     int       nHue;
49     int[][]   ptx;
50     int[][]   pty;
51     float[][] ptHue;
52     float[][] ptSat;
53     float     brightness;
54     int       currentX;
55     int       currentY;
56     HTMLColor parent;
57     public ColorSelect(HTMLColor parent)
58     {
59         this.parent = parent;
60         offscreen = null;
61         border = 16;
62         nHue = 24;
```

```
63      nSat = 10;
64      brightness = (float)1.0;
65      ptx = new int[nHue][nSat];
66      pty = new int[nHue][nSat];
67      ptHue = new float[nHue][nSat];
68      ptSat = new float[nHue][nSat];
69      addMouseListener(this);
70      addMouseMotionListener(this);
71    }
72    /** Specify preferred size of Canvas (else it'll be 0x0) */
73    public Dimension getPreferredSize()
74    {
75        //  Return the parent panel's dimension
76        Component c = getParent();
77        Dimension ps = c.getSize();
78        w=ps.width;
79        h=ps.height;
80        // Compute radius of circle
81        radius = Math.min(w-2*border, h-2*border) / 2;
82        cx = w/2;
83        cy = h/2;
84        // Compute points along radials (to be used
85        // later to draw the color wheel)
86        double deltaHue = 1.0/(double)nHue;
87        float dHue2 = (float)deltaHue/(float)2.0;
88        double deltaRadians = 2.0*Math.PI*deltaHue;
89        double deltaSat = 1.0/(double)nSat;
90        float dSat2 = (float)deltaSat/(float)2.0;
91        double hue, sat;
92        float satCenter;
93        float hueCenter = dHue2;
94        for(int i = 0; i < nHue; i++)
95        {
96            hue = (double)i*deltaRadians;
97            double cosHue = radius * Math.cos(hue);
98            double sinHue = radius * Math.sin(hue);
99            satCenter = dSat2;
100           sat = 0.0;
101           for(int j = 1; j <= nSat; j++)
102           {
103               sat = j*deltaSat;
104               ptx[i][j-1] = cx + (int)(sat*cosHue);
```

```
105            pty[i][j-1] = cy + (int)(sat*sinHue);
106            ptHue[i][j-1] = hueCenter;
107            ptSat[i][j-1] = satCenter;
108            satCenter += deltaSat;
109         }
110         hueCenter += deltaHue;
111     }
112     currentX = ptx[20][nSat-2];
113     currentY = pty[20][nSat-2];
114     return ps;
115 }
116 public void update(Graphics g)
117 {
118     paint(g);
119 }
120 public void paint(Graphics g)
121 {
122     Graphics offGC;
123     // Initialize off-screen image (if not yet done)
124     if(offscreen == null)
125     {
126         offscreen = createImage(w, h);
127     }
128     offGC = offscreen.getGraphics();
129     offGC.setColor(Color.white);
130     offGC.fillRect(0, 0, w-1, h-1);
131     // Draw the polygons in appropriate color
132     int inext;
133     int cRGB;
134     for(int i = 0; i < nHue; i++)
135     {
136         for(int j = 1; j <= nSat; j++)
137         {
138             Polygon p = new Polygon();
139             inext = i+1;
140             if(i == nHue-1) inext = 0;
141             if(j == 1)
142                 p.addPoint(cx, cy);
143             else
144             {
145                 p.addPoint(ptx[inext][j-2], pty[inext][j-2]);
146                 p.addPoint(ptx[i][j-2], pty[i][j-2]);
```

```
147                     }
148                     p.addPoint(ptx[i][j-1], pty[i][j-1]);
149                     p.addPoint(ptx[inext][j-1], pty[inext][j-1]);
150                     cRGB = Color.HSBtoRGB(ptHue[i][j-1],
151                                       ptSat[i][j-1], brightness);
152                     offGC.setColor(new Color(cRGB));
153                     offGC.fillPolygon(p);
154                 }
155             }
156             // Draw the patch with current color
157             int xy[] = new int[2];
158             float hs[] = getHueSat(currentX, currentY, xy);
159             currentX = xy[0];
160             currentY = xy[1];
161             int colorSel = Color.HSBtoRGB(hs[0], hs[1], brightness);
162             offGC.setColor(new Color(colorSel));
163             offGC.fillRect(80, h-28, 24, 24);
164             offGC.setColor(Color.black);
165             offGC.drawRect(80, h-28, 25, 25);
166             // Draw current point and display label for current color
167             offGC.setColor(Color.white);
168             offGC.drawOval(currentX-3, currentY-3, 6, 6);
169             offGC.setColor(Color.black);
170             offGC.drawOval(currentX-4, currentY-4, 8, 8);
171             offGC.drawOval(currentX-2, currentY-2, 4, 4);
172             offGC.drawString("Current Color:", 0, h-15);
173             // Show brightness as a gray patch that gradually changes
174             // from black to gray to white as brightness increases
175             int blevel = (int)((float)255.0*brightness);
176             offGC.setColor(new Color(blevel,blevel,blevel));
177             offGC.fillRect(w-30, h-30, 24, 24);
178             offGC.setColor(Color.black);
179             offGC.drawRect(w-30, h-30, 25, 25);
180             // Add some instructional messages
181             offGC.drawString("Click on color wheel to select color.",
182                             4, 12);
183             offGC.drawString("Use scrollbar to adjust brightness.",4, 24);
184             // Draw offscreen image into canvas
185             g.drawImage(offscreen, 0, 0, this);
186             parent.colorChanged(hs, brightness);
187         }
188     public float[] getHueSat(int x, int y, int xy[])
```

```
189     {
190         boolean adjustXY = false;
191         double dx = (double)(x - cx);
192         double dy = (double)(y - cy);
193         float satSel = (float)(Math.sqrt(dx*dx + dy*dy) /
194                                    (double)radius);
195         double angle = Math.acos(dx/(double)radius);
196         if(dy < 0.0) angle = 2.0*Math.PI - angle;
197         float hueSel = (float)((double)angle / 2.0 / Math.PI);
198         if(satSel > (float)1.0)
199         {
200             satSel = (float)1.0;
201             adjustXY =true;
202         }
203         if(hueSel > (float)1.0)
204         {
205             hueSel = (float)1.0;
206             adjustXY =true;
207         }
208         if(adjustXY)
209         {
210             xy[0] = cx + (int)((double)radius * Math.cos(angle));
211             xy[1] = cy + (int)((double)radius * Math.sin(angle));
212         }
213         else
214         {
215             xy[0] = x;
216             xy[1] = y;
217         }
218         float[] hs = new float[2];
219         hs[0] = hueSel;
220         hs[1] = satSel;
221         return hs;
222     }
223     public void setBrightness(float b)
224     {
225         brightness = b;
226         repaint();
227     }
228     public void setCurrentHSB(float hsb[])
229     {
230         double hue = (double)hsb[0]*2.0*Math.PI;
```

```
231        double sat = (double)hsb[1]*(double)radius;
232        currentX = cx + (int)(sat*Math.cos(hue));
233        currentY = cy + (int)(sat*Math.sin(hue));
234        brightness = hsb[2];
235        repaint();
236    }
237    // Methods for MouseListener interface
238    public void mouseClicked(MouseEvent e)
239    {
240        currentX = e.getX();
241        currentY = e.getY();
242        repaint();
243    }
244    public void mousePressed(MouseEvent e){}
245    public void mouseReleased(MouseEvent e){}
246    public void mouseEntered(MouseEvent e){}
247    public void mouseExited(MouseEvent e){}
248    // Methods for MouseMotionListener interface
249    public void mouseDragged(MouseEvent e)
250    {
251        currentX = e.getX();
252        currentY = e.getY();
253        repaint();
254    }
255    public void mouseMoved(MouseEvent e){}
256
257 }
258 /** Shows how the HTML document will look with current colors */
259 class SampleDocument extends Canvas
260 {
261    int w;
262    int h;
263    float bgHSB[];
264    float textHSB[];
265    float linkHSB[];
266    float alinkHSB[];
267    float vlinkHSB[];
268    Image offscreen;
269    HTMLColor parent;
270    public SampleDocument(HTMLColor parent)
271    {
272        this.parent = parent;
```

```
273        offscreen = null;
274        setFont(new Font("Helvetica", Font.BOLD, 14));
275    }
276    /** Specify preferred size of Canvas (else it'll be 0x0) */
277    public Dimension getPreferredSize()
278    {
279        //  Return the parent panel's dimension
280        Component c = getParent();
281        Dimension ps = c.getSize();
282        w=ps.width;
283        h=ps.height;
284        offscreen = createImage(w, h);
285        return ps;
286    }
287    public void update(Graphics g)
288    {
289        paint(g);
290    }
291    public void paint(Graphics g)
292    {
293        Graphics offGC = offscreen.getGraphics();
294        int cBG = Color.HSBtoRGB(bgHSB[0], bgHSB[1], bgHSB[2]);
295        int cTxt = Color.HSBtoRGB(textHSB[0],
296                               textHSB[1], textHSB[2]);
297        int cLnk = Color.HSBtoRGB(linkHSB[0],
298                               linkHSB[1], linkHSB[2]);
299        int cAlnk = Color.HSBtoRGB(alinkHSB[0],
300                               alinkHSB[1], alinkHSB[2]);
301        int cVlnk = Color.HSBtoRGB(vlinkHSB[0],
302                               vlinkHSB[1], vlinkHSB[2]);
303        Color bgColor = new Color(cBG);
304        Color txtColor = new Color(cTxt);
305        Color linkColor = new Color(cLnk);
306        Color alinkColor = new Color(cAlnk);
307        Color vlinkColor = new Color(cVlnk);
308        int y = 16;
309        int x = 10;
310        int yStep = 16;
311        offGC.setColor(Color.black);
312        offGC.drawString("Sample document with current colors",
313                        x, y);
314        // Fill rectangle with background color
```

```
315        y += yStep;
316        offGC.setColor(bgColor);
317        offGC.fillRect(0, y, w-1, h-21);
318        // Background color (just compute the string)
319        String hexValue = Integer.toHexString(cBG).toUpperCase();
320        String bgString = hexValue.substring(2);
321        hexValue = null;
322        // Text color
323        y += 2*yStep;
324        offGC.setColor(txtColor);
325        hexValue = Integer.toHexString(cTxt).toUpperCase();
326        String txtString = hexValue.substring(2);
327        String s = "Text color = "+txtString;
328        offGC.drawString(s, x, y);
329        hexValue = null;
330        // Link color
331        y += 2*yStep;
332        offGC.setColor(linkColor);
333        hexValue = Integer.toHexString(cLnk).toUpperCase();
334        String linkString = hexValue.substring(2);
335        s = "Link color = "+linkString;
336        offGC.drawString(s, x, y);
337        hexValue = null;
338        // Active link color
339        y += 2*yStep;
340        offGC.setColor(alinkColor);
341        hexValue = Integer.toHexString(cAlnk).toUpperCase();
342        String alinkString = hexValue.substring(2);
343        s = "Active link color = "+alinkString;
344        offGC.drawString(s, x, y);
345        hexValue = null;
346        // Visited link color
347        y += 2*yStep;
348        offGC.setColor(vlinkColor);
349        hexValue = Integer.toHexString(cVlnk).toUpperCase();
350        String vlinkString = hexValue.substring(2);
351        s = "Visited link color = "+vlinkString;
352        offGC.drawString(s, x, y);
353        hexValue = null;
354        // Display a message about the <BODY> tag
355        y += 4*yStep;
356        offGC.setColor(txtColor);
```

```
357        offGC.drawLine(x, y, w-1, y);
358        y += yStep;
359        offGC.drawString("To use these colors, copy and paste",
360                          x, y);
361        y += yStep;
362        offGC.drawString("<BODY> tag in your HTML document.",
363                          x, y);
364        y += yStep;
365        offGC.drawString("To copy tag, select with mouse and",
366                          x, y);
367        y += yStep;
368        offGC.drawString("press Ctrl+C.", x, y);
369
370        // Draw offscreen image into canvas
371        g.drawImage(offscreen, 0, 0, this);
372        // Update the <BODY> tag
373        parent.setBodyTag(bgString, txtString, linkString,
374                          alinkString, vlinkString);
375    }
376    public void setbgHSB(float hsb[]) { bgHSB = hsb;}
377    public void settextHSB(float hsb[]) { textHSB = hsb;}
378    public void setlinkHSB(float hsb[]) { linkHSB = hsb;}
379    public void setalinkHSB(float hsb[]) { alinkHSB = hsb;}
380    public void setvlinkHSB(float hsb[]) { vlinkHSB = hsb;}
381 }
382 /**
383  * HTMLColor lets user select various colors for an HTML document.
384  * It constructs a <BODY> tag using selected colors and also shows
385  * how the HTML document will look with the selected colors.
386  * The applet does not accept any parameters.
387  *
388  * @author Naba Barkakati
389  * @version 1.0 November 26, 1998
390  */
391 public class HTMLColor extends Applet
392      implements AdjustmentListener, ItemListener
393 {
394    Label brightnessLabel;
395    Scrollbar brightnessSB;
396    ColorSelect cs;
397    SampleDocument sd;
398    Checkbox currentCB;
```

```
399     Checkbox bgCB;
400     Checkbox textCB;
401     Checkbox linkCB;
402     Checkbox vlinkCB;
403     Checkbox alinkCB;
404     TextField bodyTag;
405     float bgHSB[];
406     float textHSB[];
407     float linkHSB[];
408     float alinkHSB[];
409     float vlinkHSB[];
410     /** Initialized the user interface of the HTMLColor applet */
411     public void init()
412     {
413         bgHSB = new float[3];
414         textHSB = new float[3];
415         linkHSB = new float[3];
416         alinkHSB = new float[3];
417         vlinkHSB = new float[3];
418         Color.RGBtoHSB(  0,   0, 200, bgHSB);
419         Color.RGBtoHSB(255, 255,   0, textHSB);
420         Color.RGBtoHSB(255,   0, 255, linkHSB);
421         Color.RGBtoHSB(255, 255, 255, alinkHSB);
422         Color.RGBtoHSB(  0, 190, 230, vlinkHSB);
423
424         setLayout(new BorderLayout());
425         Panel pTop = new Panel();
426         pTop.setLayout(new GridLayout(2,1));
427         Label l1 = new Label(
428             "HTMLColor Applet, Copyright  (c) 1999 Naba Barkakati
                    (For terms, see the GNU General Public License)");
429         bodyTag = new TextField("<BODY>");
430         pTop.add(l1);
431         pTop.add(bodyTag);
432         add("North", pTop);
433
434         Panel pMid = new Panel();
435         pMid.setLayout(new GridLayout(1,2));
436
437         Panel pML = new Panel();
438         pML.setLayout(new BorderLayout());
439         Panel pCS = new Panel();
440         cs = new ColorSelect(this);
```

```
441        pCS.add(cs);
442        pML.add("Center", pCS);
443        brightnessSB = new Scrollbar(Scrollbar.VERTICAL,
444                                      0, 10, 0, 100);
445        brightnessSB.addAdjustmentListener(this);
446        pML.add("East", brightnessSB);
447        brightnessLabel = new Label("Brightness: 100", Label.RIGHT);
448        pML.add("South", brightnessLabel);
449        pMid.add(pML);
450
451        Panel pMR = new Panel();
452        sd = new SampleDocument(this);
453        pMR.add(sd);
454        pMid.add(pMR);
455        add("Center", pMid);
456
457        Panel pBottom = new Panel();
458        pBottom.setLayout(new BorderLayout());
459        Panel p = new Panel();
460        p.setLayout(new GridLayout(1, 5));
461        CheckboxGroup cbGroup = new CheckboxGroup();
462        bgCB    = new Checkbox("Background", cbGroup, true );
463        textCB  = new Checkbox("Text",       cbGroup, false);
464        linkCB  = new Checkbox("Link",       cbGroup, false);
465        vlinkCB = new Checkbox("VLink",      cbGroup, false);
466        alinkCB = new Checkbox("ALink",      cbGroup, false);
467        currentCB = bgCB;
468        p.add(bgCB);
469        p.add(textCB);
470        p.add(linkCB);
471        p.add(vlinkCB);
472        p.add(alinkCB);
473        pBottom.add("Center", p);
474        Label lCB = new Label("Select attribute:");
475        pBottom.add("West", lCB);
476        add("South", pBottom);
477        validate();
478        cs.setCurrentHSB(bgHSB);
479        int bLevel = (int)((float)100.0*bgHSB[2]);
480        brightnessSB.setValue(100 - bLevel);
481        brightnessLabel.setText("Brightness:"+bLevel);
482        sd.setbgHSB(bgHSB);
```

```
483        sd.settextHSB(textHSB);
484        sd.setlinkHSB(linkHSB);
485        sd.setalinkHSB(alinkHSB);
486        sd.setvlinkHSB(vlinkHSB);
487        // Add ItemListeners for each checkbox
488        bgCB.addItemListener(this);
489        textCB.addItemListener(this);
490        linkCB.addItemListener(this);
491        vlinkCB.addItemListener(this);
492        alinkCB.addItemListener(this);
493    }
494    /** Reserves room around the applet for a border */
495    public Insets getInsets()
496    {
497        return new Insets(2,2,2,2);
498    }
499    /** Draws a border around the applet */
500    public void paint(Graphics g)
501    {
502        Dimension aSize = getSize();
503        g.drawRect(0,0,aSize.width-1, aSize.height-1);
504    }
505    /** Handles mouse clicks on the scroll bar */
506    public void adjustmentValueChanged(AdjustmentEvent e)
507    {
508        int value = 100 - e.getValue();
509        float brightness = (float)value/(float)100.0;
510        cs.setBrightness(brightness);
511        brightnessLabel.setText("Brightness = "+value);
512        repaint();
513    }
514    /* Handles mouse clicks on the checkboxes */
515    public void itemStateChanged(ItemEvent e)
516    {
517        String cbName = (String)e.getItem();
518        if(cbName.equals("Background"))
519        {
520            cs.setCurrentHSB(bgHSB);
521            int bLevel = (int)((float)100.0*bgHSB[2]);
522            brightnessSB.setValue(100 - bLevel);
523            brightnessLabel.setText("Brightness:"+bLevel);
524            currentCB = bgCB;
```

```
525              }
526          else if(cbName.equals("Text"))
527          {
528              cs.setCurrentHSB(textHSB);
529              int bLevel = (int)((float)100.0*textHSB[2]);
530              brightnessSB.setValue(100 - bLevel);
531              brightnessLabel.setText("Brightness:"+bLevel);
532              currentCB = textCB;
533          }
534          else if(cbName.equals("Link"))
535          {
536              cs.setCurrentHSB(linkHSB);
537              int bLevel = (int)((float)100.0*linkHSB[2]);
538              brightnessSB.setValue(100 - bLevel);
539              brightnessLabel.setText("Brightness:"+bLevel);
540              currentCB = linkCB;
541          }
542          else if(cbName.equals("ALink"))
543          {
544              cs.setCurrentHSB(alinkHSB);
545              int bLevel = (int)((float)100.0*alinkHSB[2]);
546              brightnessSB.setValue(100 - bLevel);
547              brightnessLabel.setText("Brightness:"+bLevel);
548              currentCB = alinkCB;
549          }
550          else if(cbName.equals("VLink"))
551          {
552              cs.setCurrentHSB(vlinkHSB);
553              int bLevel = (int)((float)100.0*vlinkHSB[2]);
554              brightnessSB.setValue(100 - bLevel);
555              brightnessLabel.setText("Brightness:"+bLevel);
556              currentCB = vlinkCB;
557          }
558      }
559      /** Called by ColorSelect when color changes */
560      public void colorChanged(float hs[], float b)
561      {
562          if(currentCB == bgCB)
563          {
564              bgHSB[0] = hs[0];
565              bgHSB[1] = hs[1];
566              bgHSB[2] = b;
```

```
567              sd.setbgHSB(bgHSB);
568          }
569          else if(currentCB == textCB)
570          {
571              textHSB[0] = hs[0];
572              textHSB[1] = hs[1];
573              textHSB[2] = b;
574              sd.settextHSB(textHSB);
575          }
576          else if(currentCB == linkCB)
577          {
578              linkHSB[0] = hs[0];
579              linkHSB[1] = hs[1];
580              linkHSB[2] = b;
581              sd.setlinkHSB(linkHSB);
582          }
583          else if(currentCB == alinkCB)
584          {
585              alinkHSB[0] = hs[0];
586              alinkHSB[1] = hs[1];
587              alinkHSB[2] = b;
588              sd.setalinkHSB(alinkHSB);
589          }
590          else if(currentCB == vlinkCB)
591          {
592              vlinkHSB[0] = hs[0];
593              vlinkHSB[1] = hs[1];
594              vlinkHSB[2] = b;
595              sd.setvlinkHSB(vlinkHSB);
596          }
597      sd.repaint();
598      }
599      /** Called by SampleDocument to set the <BODY> tag */
600      public void setBodyTag(String bg, String text, String link,
601                      String alink, String vlink)
602      {
603          String tag = "<BODY BGCOLOR=\""+bg+"\" ";
604          tag = tag + "TEXT=\""+text+"\" ";
605          tag = tag + "LINK=\""+link+"\" ";
606          tag = tag + "ALINK=\""+alink+"\" ";
607          tag = tag + "VLINK=\""+vlink+"\">";
608          bodyTag.setText(tag);
```

```
609        }
610        /** Returns information about HTMLColor applet */
611        public String getAppletInfo()
612        {
613            return "HTMLColor 1.0 Copyright (C) 1998 Naba Barkakati";
614        }
615 }
```

ANNOTATIONS

The main function of the **HTMLColor** applet is to show all possible colors in a convenient manner so that users can select colors easily. One idea would be to show the colors using RGB values that show the red, green, and blue intensities of color. Unfortunately, it's difficult to show all RGB color combinations, because with three independent variables (red, green, and blue), you need a cube to show all of the colors. There is an alternate color representation using hue, saturation, and brightness (HSB for short) that's easier for interactive color selection. The **HTMLColor** applet uses the HSB color model in its design.

The HSB color model has an inverted hexagonal cone shape in which the top of the cone (the wide part) corresponds to B = 1, which represents the maximum brightness. The radial axis represents S, the saturation, and the angle is H, the hue, or color. As Figure 6-4 shows, the red, green, and blue colors occur around the top face at angles 0, 120, and 240 degrees.

The **HTMLColor** applet uses the HSB model in its user interface by representing the top face of the inverted HSB cone as a circle that shows the hue (H) along the circumference and the saturation (S) along the radius. The brightness (B) is represented by a separate scrollbar. Figure 6-5 shows the basic layout of such a color-selection user interface. As you can see, taken together, a point on the circle and a brightness value give a complete HSB color. The **HTMLColor** applet uses this layout, together with some extra features such as a patch that shows the current color and another patch that shows the brightness in terms of the gray level, where black means zero brightness and white means maximum brightness.

This idea of using the hue, saturation, and brightness for a color-selection user interface is not new. Such a color-selection dialog box was originally used in the Apple Macintosh in 1984.

Note that the Java Abstract Windowing Toolkit (AWT) supports the HSB color model. Java's HSB model represents hue, saturation, and brightness using **float**

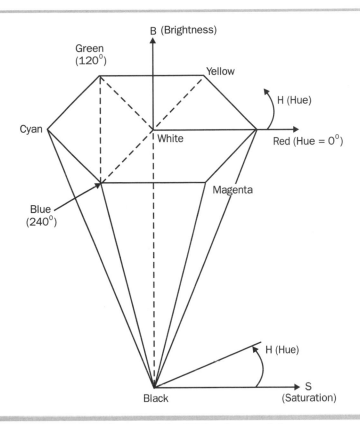

FIGURE 6-4. The hexagonal cone of the HSB color model.

variables (representing single-precision real numbers) that range in value from 0.0 to 1.0. Thus, hue values are normalized by 360 degrees (meaning that the angle in degrees is divided by 360) so that the value changes between 0.0 and 1.0.

AN OVERVIEW OF THE HTMLCOLOR CLASS   There are three classes in the **HTMLColor** applet. The first one is **HTMLColor** itself, because every applet is defined as a subclass of **Applet**. The other two classes are **ColorSelect** and **SampleDocument**. The **ColorSelect** class displays the hue-saturation circle shown in Figure 6-5. **SampleDocument** shows the appearance of an HTML document that uses the current color selections.

The three classes—**HTMLColor**, **ColorSelect**, and **SampleDocument**—need to communicate with one another. The **ColorSelect** class displays the colors in a circle,

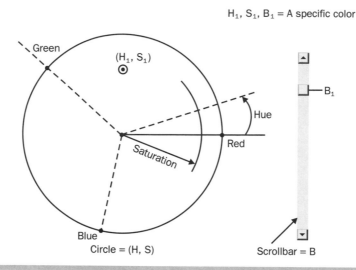

H$_1$, S$_1$, B$_1$ = A specific color

Green

(H$_1$, S$_1$)

Hue

Saturation

Red

Blue

Circle = (H, S)

B$_1$

Scrollbar = B

FIGURE 6-5.   **HTMLColor**'s color-selection user interface, based on the HSB color model.

but these colors depend on the brightness set through a scrollbar that's a component of the **HTMLColor** class. Also, when the user changes the colors through **ColorSelect**, **SampleDocument** has to display the new colors. Because instances of **ColorSelect** and **SampleDocument** are created in the **HTMLColor** class, the communication among the classes is handled through **HTMLColor**. Figure 6-6 illustrates how the color changes are coordinated among the three classes. The figure depicts the following typical sequence of color change coordination:

1. When the user moves the scrollbar to adjust the brightness, the **HTMLColor** class calls the **setBrightness()** method of the **ColorSelect** class to change the brightness.

2. The **ColorSelect** class repaints the color circle and calls the **colorChanged()** method of the **HTMLColor** class. The **colorChanged()** method is also called when the user clicks on the color circle to select a new color.

3. The **colorChanged()** method, in turn, checks which attribute's color is being changed. The attributes correspond to the **<BODY>** tag's attributes. It then calls one of the methods—**setbgHSB()**, **settextHSB()**, **setlinkHSB()**, **setalink()**, or **setvlinkHSB()**—in the **SampleDocument** class. The **SampleDocument** class repaints the sample document showing the new colors.

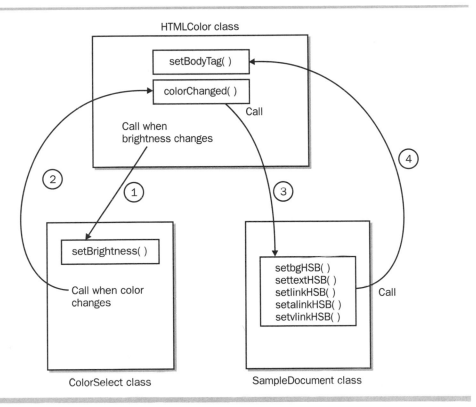

HTMLColor class

ColorSelect class

SampleDocument class

FIGURE 6-6.   Coordination of color changes among the three classes.

4.   The **SampleDocument** class calls the **setBodyTag()** method in the
     HTMLColor class to update the **<BODY>** tag that's shown in the text field
     along the top part of the applet.

Each of the classes **ColorSelect** and **SampleDocument** is a subclass of **Canvas**,
and each has a **paint()** method that takes care of drawing whatever the class is
supposed to show. **ColorSelect** displays the color wheel—the circle that shows the
hue and saturation components of color. **SampleDocument** displays how the HTML
document looks with the currently selected colors.

HTMLCOLOR INITIALIZATION   During initialization, the **HTMLColor** class lays out
the user interface you see in Figure 6-3. The **init()** method, shown in lines 411
through 493, performs these initializations.

As explained in the beginning of the "Annotations" section, **HTMLColor** uses the HSB color model. **HTMLColor** stores the colors for the five attributes of the **<BODY>** tag—background, text, link, active link, and visited link—in five arrays of **float** variables, initialized in lines 413 through 422:

```
413         bgHSB = new float[3];
414         textHSB = new float[3];
415         linkHSB = new float[3];
416         alinkHSB = new float[3];
417         vlinkHSB = new float[3];
418         Color.RGBtoHSB(  0,   0, 200, bgHSB);
419         Color.RGBtoHSB(255, 255,   0, textHSB);
420         Color.RGBtoHSB(255,   0, 255, linkHSB);
421         Color.RGBtoHSB(255, 255, 255, alinkHSB);
422         Color.RGBtoHSB(  0, 190, 230, vlinkHSB);
```

First lines 413 through 417 create five arrays, each with three **float** variables. Then lines 418 through 422 call the **RGBtoHSB()** method of the **Color** class to convert specific RGB color values into HSB format. These lines initialize the HSB color arrays **bgHSB[]**, **textHSB[]**, **linkHSB[]**, **alinkHSB[]**, and **vlinkHSB[]**, representing the initial color choices for the **<BODY>** tag's five attributes.

Lines 424 through 477 lay out various user interface components to form the user interface for the **HTMLColor** applet. The steps in laying out the user interface are similar to those in many other applets you have seen in previous chapters. The scrollbar is one user interface element that you have not seen so far. Lines 443 and 444 create a new **Scrollbar** object:

```
443         brightnessSB = new Scrollbar(Scrollbar.VERTICAL,
444                                      0, 10, 0, 100);
```

The arguments to the **Scrollbar** constructor specify the scrollbar's orientation (vertical in this case) and the minimum and maximum values represented by the scrollbar (here 0 and 100, respectively). After the scrollbar has been created, line 445 specifies the class that provides the listener objects for the scrollbar:

```
445         brightnessSB.addAdjustmentListener(this);
```

In this case, events from the scrollbar are handled by methods in the **HTMLColor** class (that's what the **this** keyword means).

The **init()** method is also where the **ColorSelect** and **SampleDocument** objects are created. Each of these classes is a subclass of **Canvas**. Each of these objects is placed in a **Panel**, and that **Panel** is then arranged inside other **Panel** objects. For example, lines 437 through 442 show how the **ColorSelect** object is created and placed in the applet:

```
437         Panel pML = new Panel();
438         pML.setLayout(new BorderLayout());
439         Panel pCS = new Panel();
440         cs = new ColorSelect(this);
441         pCS.add(cs);
442         pML.add("Center", pCS);
```

Line 437 creates a **Panel** object named **pML**. Line 438 sets the layout manager for that panel to a **BorderLayout**. Line 439 creates another **Panel** object named **pCS**. Line 440 then initializes a **ColorSelect** object. Notice that line 440 calls the **ColorSelect()** constructor with the parent class as an argument. The **ColorSelect** object needs this because it has to coordinate color changes with the **SampleDocument** object. Line 441 places the **ColorSelect** object in the **pCS** panel, and line 442 puts that panel in **pML**.

The last part of the **init()** method, lines 478 through 492, sets the color of each **<BODY>** tag attribute in the **SampleDocument** object and specifies a listener object that handles mouse clicks on the checkboxes along the bottom of the applet's display area. For example, line 482 sets the background color in the **SampleDocument** object named **sd**:

```
482         sd.setbgHSB(bgHSB);
```

Line 489 sets the listener object for the checkbox labeled **Text**:

```
489         textCB.addItemListener(this);
```

The section "The Attribute Checkboxes," later in this chapter, describes how mouse clicks on the checkboxes are handled.

THE COLORSELECT CLASS The ColorSelect class displays the color wheel that appears in the left half of the **HTMLColor** applet. Lines 37 through 257 of the listing show the **ColorSelect** class. As you can see from lines 37 and 38, **ColorSelect** is a subclass of **Canvas**, and it implements the **MouseListener** and **MouseMotionListener** interfaces:

```
37  class ColorSelect extends Canvas
38      implements MouseListener, MouseMotionListener
```

The **Canvas** class provides a drawing area where the **paint()** method of **ColorSelect** draws the color wheel. The **MouseListener** interface handles mouse clicks on the color wheel—that's how the user selects a new color. The **MouseMotionListener** interface handles mouse drags across the color wheel.

Lines 40 through 56 define the variables used in the **ColorSelect** class. Line 40 defines the **Image** object named **offscreen** that represents the off-screen image used to prepare the color wheel (and anything else that appears on the canvas) before actually displaying the output on the screen. This is done to avoid flicker as the color wheel is redrawn.

As you'll see later in this section, the **paint()** method of **ColorSelect** draws the color wheel as a series of polygons (mostly quadrilaterals). The x and y coordinates of these polygons are stored in the integer arrays **ptx[][]** and **pty[][]**, declared in lines 49 and 50:

```
49      int [] []    ptx;
50      int [] []    pty;
```

Each polygon has an associated color. The hue and saturation components of that color are stored in the following **float** arrays:

```
51      float [] []  ptHue;
52      float [] []  ptSat;
```

Lines 57 through 71 initialize a new **ColorSelect** object. Lines 65 through 68 initialize the arrays **ptx[][]**, **pty[][]**, **ptHue[][]**, and **ptSat[][]**:

```
65          ptx = new int [nHue] [nSat];
66          pty = new int [nHue] [nSat];
67          ptHue = new float [nHue] [nSat];
68          ptSat = new float [nHue] [nSat];
```

Lines 69 and 70 set up the **ColorSelect** object as the listener for mouse events (both mouse clicks and mouse motions such as dragging the mouse across the color wheel):

```
69          addMouseListener(this);
70          addMouseMotionListener(this);
```

When the **ColorSelect** object is initialized, its default size is zero (all **Canvas** objects are created with zero width and zero height). You must provide the **getPreferredSize()** method and return a **Dimension** object with the size of the canvas. Lines 73 through 115 show the **getPreferredSize()** method of the **ColorSelect** class. Line 76 gets the component that contains the **ColorSelect** object (this is the **Panel** in which the **ColorSelect** object is placed):

```
76          Component c = getParent();
```

Then line 77 gets the dimensions of that component:

```
77          Dimension ps = c.getSize();
```

Line 114 returns this dimension as the desired size of the **ColorSelect** object's display area.

Besides computing the preferred size of the **ColorSelect** object's display area, the **getPreferredSize()** method also initializes the **ptx[][]** and **pty[][]** arrays that represent the corners of the polygons that make up the color wheel. Figure 6-7 illustrates how the color wheel is divided into polygons and the coordinates that are stored in the **ptx[][]** and **pty[][]** arrays.

The calculations take place inside the two **for** loops shown in lines 94 through 111. The outer **for** loop steps over the angles that represent the hue. For each angle, the inner **for** loop steps along the radial that represents saturation. Both saturation and hue are normalized (the values are divided by their maximum) so that they range from 0.0 to 1.0, as expected by Java's HSB color model. Lines 104 and 105 compute the coordinates of one point:

```
104             ptx[i][j-1] = cx + (int)(sat*cosHue);
105             pty[i][j-1] = cy + (int)(sat*sinHue);
```

Here **cosHue** and **sinHue** represent the cosine and sine of the hue angle. Notice that the coordinates of the circle's center, (**cx, cy**), are added to the computed coordinates. This is needed because the formula for a point on the radial assumes that the center is

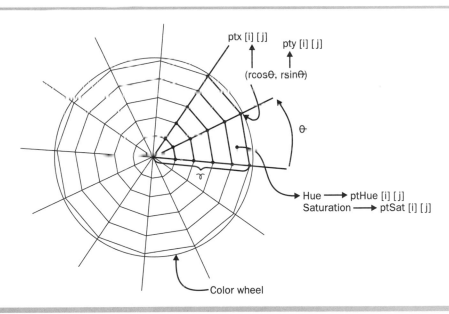

FIGURE 6-7.   The color wheel is divided into polygons.

at (0, 0), but the actual center of the circle is to be drawn at (**cx**, **cy**). For each polygon, lines 106 and 107 compute the hue and saturation:

```
106                    ptHue[i][j-1] = hueCenter;
107                    ptSat[i][j-1] = satCenter;
```

The **paint()** method, in lines 120 through 187, draws everything on the off-screen image and then draws that image on the **ColorSelect** object's display area. If the off-screen image is not initialized yet, line 126 creates the image:

```
126              offscreen = createImage(w, h);
```

Lines 132 through 155 draw the polygons, using a color for each one. Two **for** loops scan through the points in the **ptx[][]** and **pty[][]** arrays and create **Polygon** objects. First, line 138 creates a **Polygon** with no points:

```
138            Polygon p = new Polygon();
```

Then the **addPoint()** method of the **Polygon** object is called to add vertices to the polygon. The polygon's color has to be an RGB value. The **Color.HSBtoRGB()** method is used to convert an HSB color into an RGB value. Lines 150 and 151 perform this step:

```
150             cRGB = Color.HSBtoRGB(ptHue[i][j-1],
151                             ptSat[i][j-1], brightness);
```

Lines 152 and 153 then set this color and draw the filled polygon:

```
152               offGC.setColor(new Color(cRGB));
153               offGC.fillPolygon(p);
```

The entire color wheel is done once all of the polygons are drawn.

After that, lines 157 through 183 of the **paint()** method draw a bull's-eye at the point corresponding to the current color, draw a patch showing the current color, display some informational text, and draw a patch showing the brightness value in terms of a gray level. The bull's-eye is important because the user moves it around to select a new color. Lines 167 through 171 draw the bull's-eye at the location corresponding to the currently selected color:

```
167          offGC.setColor(Color.white);
168          offGC.drawOval(currentX-3, currentY-3, 6, 6);
169          offGC.setColor(Color.black);
170          offGC.drawOval(currentX-4, currentY-4, 8, 8);
171          offGC.drawOval(currentX-2, currentY-2, 4, 4);
```

As you can see, the location of the current color is the point (**currentX**, **currentY**). Lines 167 and 168 draw a white circle. Then lines 169 through 171 draw two black circles—one inside the white circle and the other outside it. The user can select a new color either by clicking at a new color on the color wheel or by dragging the bull's-eye to a new color. Whenever either of these happens, the **paint()** method is called and the bull's-eye is drawn at the new point.

Finally, line 185 of the **paint()** method draws the off-screen image on the **ColorSelect** object's display area on the screen:

```
185          g.drawImage(offscreen, 0, 0, this);
```

After all this is finished, line 186 calls the **colorChanged()** method of the **HTMLColor** class to make sure that the **SampleDocument** object shows any change in color:

```
186          parent.colorChanged(hs, brightness);
```

The **ColorSelect** class also has a few other utility methods. The **getHueSat()** method, shown in lines 188 through 222, converts an (x, y) coordinate to a hue and saturation value. This method returns the hue and saturation values in a two-element **float** array. Whenever the user clicks on the color wheel, the **getHueSat()** method is called to determine the hue and saturation value corresponding to the location where the user has clicked. The **getHueSat()** method converts the (x, y) coordinates into polar coordinates with the angle representing hue and the radius representing saturation.

The **setBrightness()** method, shown in lines 223 through 227, is called by the **HTMLColor** class whenever the user adjusts the brightness value by moving the scrollbar. This method sets the brightness variable and calls **repaint()** to redraw the color wheel for the new brightness.

The **mouseClicked()** method, shown in lines 238 through 243, is called whenever the user clicks on the color wheel:

```
238     public void mouseClicked(MouseEvent e)
239     {
240          currentX = e.getX();
241          currentY = e.getY();
242          repaint();
243     }
```

Lines 240 and 241 set the **currentX** and **currentY** variables to the x and y coordinates of the mouse click. Notice that this information is obtained by calling the **getX()** and **getY()** methods of the **MouseEvent e**. Line 242 then calls **repaint()** to redraw the color wheel along with the bull's-eye mark at the new location (**currentX**, **currentY**).

If the user drags the bull's-eye around, the **mouseDragged()** method is called. That method, shown in lines 249 through 254, is implemented in exactly the same way as **mouseClicked()**: It updates the **currentX** and **currentY** variables and then calls the **repaint()** method. This, in turn, causes a call to **paint()**, which redraws the bull's-eye mark.

The **paint()** method, in turn, calls the **colorChanged()** method of the **HTMLColor** class. The **colorChanged()** method then sets the colors in the **SampleDocument** object and calls the **repaint()** method of that object. This causes the **SampleDocument** object to display the sample document with new colors. The end result is that the user can see the effects of color selection immediately.

THE SAMPLEDOCUMENT CLASS   Just like **ColorSelect**, the **SampleDocument** class is a subclass of **Canvas**. This class is used to display a sample HTML document with the current color selections for various attributes of the **<BODY>** tag.

Lines 259 through 381 show the **SampleDocument** class. Like **ColorSelect**, **SampleDocument** also prepares all drawings in an off-screen **Image** called **offscreen** (line 268). **SampleDocument** also keeps track of the colors of the five attributes—background, text, link, active link, and visited link. These colors are stored in **float** arrays in terms of hue, saturation, and brightness.

The class constructor, shown in lines 270 through 275, requires the **HTMLColor** object as an argument. This is necessary because the **SampleDocument** needs to call the **setBodyTag()** method of the **HTMLColor** class whenever colors change. Recall that the **setBodyTag()** method displays the complete **<BODY>** tag in the text field along the top edge of the applet.

Because **SampleDocument** is a subclass of **Canvas**, it should include a **getPreferredSize()** method that returns the actual dimensions of the **SampleDocument** object's display area. If you forget the **getPreferredSize()** method, the display area will have a zero width and zero height. The end result is that nothing will show up on the screen. Lines 277 through 286 show the **getPreferredSize()** method, which returns the preferred dimensions of the **SampleDocument** object's display area and also creates the off-screen image. Like **ColorSelect**, the **getPreferredSize()** method returns the dimensions of the **Panel** object in which **SampleDocument** is placed. Lines 280 and 281 get the parent object and its dimensions:

```
280        Component c = getParent();
281        Dimension ps = c.getSize();
```

Note that line 285 returns the dimensions as the preferred size of the **SampleDocument** object.

The **SampleDocument** class's **paint()** method, shown in lines 291 through 381, draws the sample HTML document in the off-screen image. Line 293 gets a **Graphics** object for the off-screen image:

```
293        Graphics offGC = offscreen.getGraphics();
```

After this, all of the drawing operations are performed by using the **offGC** object. The result is that everything gets drawn in the off-screen image (the **Image** variable named **offscreen**).

The **Graphics** object's methods require colors in terms of RGB values. However, all of the classes in **HTMLColor**, including **SampleDocument**, store colors as HSB values. Before these colors can be used, they must be converted from RGB to HSB values by calling the **RGBtoHSB()** method of the **Color** class. Lines 294 through 302 convert the HSB colors to RGB values. For example, line 294 converts the background color in the **float** array **bgHSB[]** into a packed RGB value named **cBG**:

```
294        int cBG = Color.HSBtoRGB(bgHSB[0], bgHSB[1], bgHSB[2]);
```

The **cBG** variable is packed in the sense that the red, green, and blue components are all packed into a single integer variable.

You really don't have to understand how the RGB value is stored, because you can use it directly to create a **Color** object corresponding to the RGB value in an integer such as **cBG**. For example, line 303 creates a **Color** object named **bgColor**, using the packed RGB value in **cBG**:

```
303        Color bgColor = new Color(cBG);
```

Similarly, lines 304 through 307 create **Color** objects for the other colors.

Lines 308 through 310 initialize some variables, such as the x and y coordinates for displaying the sample document. Lines 312 and 313 display a title for the sample document:

```
312        offGC.drawString("Sample document with current colors",
313                         x, y);
```

Line 315 increments the y coordinate to move downward in the sample document's display area. Lines 316 and 317 fill a rectangle with the background color:

```
316        offGC.setColor(bgColor);
317        offGC.fillRect(0, y, w-1, h-21);
```

This rectangle, filled with the background color, becomes the sample document on which several other lines of text are shown. Each line of text is drawn using the color of a specific attribute of the **<BODY>** tag.

After the background color has been set, lines 319 and 320 convert the RGB color in **cBG** to a string representation in hexadecimal format:

```
319        String hexValue = Integer.toHexString(cBG).toUpperCase();
320        String bgString = hexValue.substring(2);
```

Line 319 converts **cBG** by calling the **Integer.toHexString()** method. The string is then converted to uppercase by calling the **toUpperCase()** method. The **hexValue** string will have eight hexadecimal digits because **cBG** is an integer with four bytes, and each byte translates to two hexadecimal digits. Line 320 extracts six hexadecimal digits, from index 2 through 7, from the **hexValue** string and copies them to **bgString**. Later, in the **paint()** method, this hexadecimal representation of background color is used as an argument when the **setBodyTag()** method of the **HTMLColor** class is called to display the updated **<BODY>** tag.

Next lines 323 through 329 display a string with the color selected for the text attribute. The steps are similar to those used for background color. However, unlike the background color, the text color is used to display a text string that shows the current text color as a hexadecimal RGB value.

Lines 331 through 353 repeat the same operations for the link, active link, and visited link attributes. These sample attributes essentially show how an HTML document will look with the currently selected colors. To help the user, lines 355 through 368 display some helpful messages suggesting how to use the current colors in an HTML document.

After the off-screen image has been prepared, line 371 draws it to the **SampleDocument** object's display area:

```
371            g.drawImage(offscreen, 0, 0, this);
```

The last line of code in the **paint()** method calls the **setBodyTag()** method of the **HTMLColor** class to update the <BODY> tag:

```
373            parent.setBodyTag(bgString, txtString, linkString,
374                              alinkString, vlinkString);
```

This method is called with the string representations of the RGB values of the colors for each attribute of the <BODY> tag. In **HTMLColor**, the **setBodyTag()** method creates a complete <BODY> tag from these strings and displays them in the text field along the top edge of the applet's display area. This ensures that the <BODY> tag always shows the colors currently being used to render the sample document in the **SampleDocument** object.

THE ATTRIBUTE CHECKBOXES   A key part of the **HTMLColor** applet's user interface is the set of checkboxes that the user can click to select colors for a specific attribute of the <BODY> tag. Lines 398 through 403 declare the **Checkbox** objects. The **currentCB** checkbox always refers to the checkbox that is currently selected. Lines 461 through 467 create these **Checkbox** objects and initialize **currentCB**:

```
461        CheckboxGroup cbGroup = new CheckboxGroup();
462        bgCB    = new Checkbox("Background", cbGroup, true );
463        textCB  = new Checkbox("Text",       cbGroup, false);
464        linkCB  = new Checkbox("Link",       cbGroup, false);
465        vlinkCB = new Checkbox("VLink",      cbGroup, false);
466        alinkCB = new Checkbox("ALink",      cbGroup, false);
467        currentCB = bgCB;
```

The first argument in each **Checkbox()** constructor is the label that appears next to the checkbox. All of the checkboxes are in a **CheckboxGroup** object named **cbGroup**. Notice that each **Checkbox()** constructor has **cbGroup** as an argument. This means that all of these checkboxes are in the same group. This grouping is necessary because the user can select only one checkbox from a group, meaning that the Java AWT has to keep track of the checkboxes that belong to a group. The **CheckboxGroup** argument provides this information to the Java AWT. The last argument in each **Checkbox()**

constructor is a **boolean** that indicates whether or not that checkbox is selected. In this case, the first checkbox, **bgCB**, is selected. Line 467 sets the **currentCB** variable to the currently selected checkbox, **bgCB**.

The **HTMLColor** class implements the listener interface for events occurring in the checkboxes. This is done by providing the **itemStateChanged()** method, which gets called whenever the user clicks on a checkbox. Lines 488 through 492 set up the listener for each **Checkbox** object by calling its **addItemListener()** method:

```
488          bgCB.addItemListener(this);
489          textCB.addItemListener(this);
490          linkCB.addItemListener(this);
491          vlinkCB.addItemListener(this);
492          alinkCB.addItemListener(this);
```

Lines 515 through 558 show the **itemStateChanged()** method. Line 517 gets the name of the checkbox (that's the label next to the checkbox):

```
517          String cbName = (String)e.getItem();
```

This line gets the label name by calling the **getItem()** method of the **ItemEvent e**.

There is a separate block of code to handle mouse clicks on each checkbox. For example, lines 518 through 525 show the code that handles mouse clicks on the checkbox labeled **Background**:

```
518          if(cbName.equals("Background"))
519          {
520              cs.setCurrentHSB(bgHSB);
521              int bLevel = (int)((float)100.0*bgHSB[2]);
522              brightnessSB.setValue(100   bLevel);
523              brightnessLabel.setText("Brightness:"+bLevel);
524              currentCB = bgCB;
525          }
```

Line 520 calls the **setCurrentHSB()** method of the **ColorSelect** object **cs**. This sets the colors on the color wheel to reflect the color associated with the background attribute. Line 521 computes the brightness level as an integer between 0 and 100. Line 522 sets the scrollbar value. In **HTMLColor**, the vertical scrollbar has the minimum value at the bottom and the maximum value at the top. This is the reverse of the normal association of minimum and maximum values for a vertical scrollbar. That's why line 522 subtracts the brightness level from 100 before setting the scrollbar's value. Line 523 displays the value of brightness as a text label. Finally, line 524 sets the **currentCB** variable to **bgCB**, the checkbox corresponding to the background attribute.

A Web Site Search Engine

Most Web sites could do with a search engine that lets users locate information easily. A typical search engine requires a CGI program at the server to perform the search and to provide the search results in the form of another Web page. Unfortunately, many Internet Service Providers (ISPs) do not allow users to run CGI programs on the server. There is, however, a way to allow users to search Web pages without using CGI programs on the server. A Java applet could download the HTML files and search through them for some text. The applet could start at the home page, download other HTML files referenced in the home page, and search all of the HTML files for the text the user wants to locate. That's exactly what the **HomePageSearch** applet does. This section shows you how to use the **HomePageSearch** applet at a Web site and describes how that applet works.

The **HomePageSearch** applet was written and copyrighted by Richard Everitt and is distributed under the terms of the GNU General Public License (GPL). You can use, modify, and redistribute it under the terms specified in the GNU GPL. For more information on the GNU GPL, read the file named **COPYING** in this book's companion CD-ROM, or visit the **HomePageSearch** applet's home page at **http://www.babbage.demon.co.uk/HomePageSearchInfo.html**.

Using HomePageSearch

The files for the **HomePageSearch** applet are in the **ch06/HPSearch** directory of the companion CD-ROM. To use the applet as the search engine for your home page, follow these steps:

1. Copy the **HomePageSearch.class** and **SearchPages.class** files to your Web server, placing them in the same directory as the other Web pages.

2. Edit the **search.html** file in a text editor. Change the **server** parameter to the name of your Web server (for example, **http://myisp.net/~myname/**). Also, change the **indexName** parameter to the name of the HTML file that represents your home page (such as **index.html** or **default.htm**). Save the edited **search.html** file (as a text file).

3. Copy the **search.html** file to your Web server, placing it in the same directory as other Web pages and the **HomePageSearch.class** file.

Now you can try out the **HomePageSearch** applet by opening the **search.html** file in a Java-capable Web browser. Figure 6-8 shows the **HomePageSearch** applet displaying the results of a search for all Web pages that contain the word *linux*. To search using **HomePageSearch**, you enter the search text in the text field labeled **Search for:** and then click the **search** button. The applet downloads HTML files one

FIGURE 6-8. **HomePageSearch** showing results of a search.

by one and searches for the text. It follows all links that refer to Web pages on the same Web server. In other words, if you have links that refer to other sites, the applet does not download any Web pages from those sites (in fact, the applet cannot do so because of security restrictions).

HomePageSearch displays the search results in the large text area. For each match, the applet shows the title of the matching Web page (taken from the **<TITLE>** tag) and the matching line of text. If you double-click on any of these lines, **HomePageSearch** loads that Web page for you.

After you try out **HomePageSearch** to perform a few searches, you'll see that it is very useful as a search engine for a small Web site. It does have to download each HTML file to perform the search, but most HTML files are not that large in size (it's the images that make Web pages slow to load). If you have numerous Web pages, you can specify the maximum number of pages that **HomePageSearch** downloads and searches.

The **HomePageSearch** applet accepts a number of parameters through <PARAM> tags. For example, here is the <APPLET> tag from the **search.html** file that results in the output shown in Figure 6-8:

```
<APPLET CODE="HomePageSearch.class" WIDTH=650 HEIGHT=400>
<PARAM NAME="server" VALUE="http://www.psn.net/~naba/">
<PARAM NAME="indexName" VALUE="index.html">
<EM>Sorry, the Search applet requires a Java aware
Web browser </EM>
</APPLET>
```

This first line specifies that the applet's display area is 650 pixels wide by 400 pixels tall. The next two <PARAM> tags specify the values of the **server** and **indexName** parameters. This is the minimum set of parameters that the **HomePageSearch** applet needs before you can use it as the search engine for a Web site.

The complete list of parameters for the **HomePageSearch** applet is as follows:

◆ **server** gives the full URL of the Web server. It must end with a slash (/) because other URLs are constructed by appending HTML filenames to this string.

◆ **hostName** indicates the host name of the Web server. The full URL is assumed to be of the form **http://www.*hostName*.demonco.uk**.

◆ **IPAddress** provides the IP address of the Web server.

◆ **indexName** gives the name of the HTML file that serves as the home page. This is where the search begins.

◆ **bgColour** specifies the background color in hexadecimal RGB format, such as **0000ff** for blue. The default is light gray.

◆ **fgColour** specifies the foreground color in hexadecimal RGB format, such as **ffffff** for white. The default is black.

◆ **maxSearch** indicates the maximum number of pages to search.

◆ **debug**, when set to any string, causes the applet to print debug information on the console. Such information can be useful in locating errors.

At minimum, you have to specify one of the parameters—**server** or **IPAddress**—that identify the Web server as well as the **indexName** parameter, which specifies the file to be downloaded first.

Understanding HomePageSearch

The source code for the **HomePageSearch** applet is in the **HomePageSearch.java** file in the **ch06\HPSearch** directory of the companion CD-ROM. The following listing shows the **HomePageSearch.java** file in its entirety.

HomePageSearch

The source file is rather lengthy because the applet needs a lot of code to parse and search through the HTML files. Despite the length of the source file, the applet's inner workings are not that complex. I explain the code in the subsequent sections.

```
 1  import java.awt.*;
 2  import java.applet.*;
 3  import java.net.*;
 4  import java.io.*;
 5  import java.util.*;
 6
 7  // v1.5 Home Page Search applet
 8  // 15th February 1998
 9
10  /*
11   * This applet provides search facilities for Web sites with no CGI access
12   *
13   * Copyright (c) 1997 Richard Everitt G4ZFE
14   *       richard@babbage.demon.co.uk
15   *
16   * This program is free software; you can redistribute it and/or modify it
17   * under the terms of the GNU General Public License as published by the
18   * Free Software Foundation; either version 2 of the License, or (at your
19   * option) any later version.
20   *
21   * This program is distributed in the hope that it will be useful, but
22   * WITHOUT ANY WARRANTY; without even the implied warranty of
23   * MERCHANTABILITY or FITNESS FOR A PARTICULAR PURPOSE.  See the GNU
24   * General Public License for more details.
25   *
26   * You should have received a copy of the GNU General Public License along
27   * with this program; if not, write to the Free Software Foundation, Inc.,
28   * 675 Mass Ave, Cambridge, MA 02139, USA.
29   *
30   *
31   */
32
33  /* Applet parameters:
34   * This applet takes two parameters
35   * a. hostname, the name of the Demon Home Page (e.g., babbage). The name is
36   *              converted to lower case and used to create the URL of the
37   *              pages to search, i.e., http://www.<hostname>.demon.co.uk.
38   *              (this parameter is required for Demon Internet users
39   *              *only*)
40   * b. IPaddress, the corresponding IP address for the Home Page. I plan to
41   *              use it as it will allow the search applet to run from
42   *              behind a firewall. Demon have stated in the HomePage AUP
43   *              that the IP address should not be directly used. I do not
44   *              recommend its use (the www.babbage.demon.co.uk IP address
45   *              has already changed once)
46   *              (this parameter is optional)
47   * c. maxSearch, the maximum number of pages to search. If your site is vast
48   *              then the search will take a long time so people will give
49   *              up. This parameter limits the number of pages to be searched
50   *              to a sensible value, reducing the search time (but also
```

```
 51  *              reducing its usefulness)
 52  *              (this parameter is optional. Defaults to 100)
 53  * d. debug,    this parameter is for my use. Set to true to display
 54  *              parameter and debug information.
 55  *              (this parameter is optional)
 56  * e. server,   this parameter allows the search applet to be used on non-
 57  *              Demon home pages. This parameter should point to the name
 58  *              of the site, e.g., "http://www.myisp.com/me/" (note use of
 59  *              trailing "/" character.
 60  *              (this parameter is required for non-Demon Internet users)
 61  * f. indexName, this parameter allows the search applet to be used on non-
 62  *              Demon home pages. This parameter should point to the name
 63  *              of the index page (e.g., home.htm). If not set, then
 64  *              "index.htm" ot "index.html" is assumed.
 65  *              (this parameter is optional)
 66  * g. bgColour,  The background colour for the applet in RGB hex format
 67  *              (rrggbb). The default is light grey.
 68  * h. fgColour,  The foreground colour for the applet in RGB hex format
 69  *              (rrggbb). The default is black.
 70  *
 71  * Example of applet use on a Demon Home Page - www.babbage.demon.co.uk
 72  * <APPLET CODE="HomePageSearch.class" WIDTH=650 HEIGHT=400>
 73  * <PARAM NAME="hostname" VALUE="babbage">
 74  * <EM>Sorry but the Search applet requires a Java aware
 75  * Web browser </EM>
 76  * </APPLET>
 77  *
 78  * Example of applet use on a non-Demon Home Page - www.myisp.co.uk/fred/
 79  * and the "index" page is called home.htm
 80  * <APPLET CODE="HomePageSearch.class" WIDTH=650 HEIGHT=400>
 81  * <PARAM NAME="server" VALUE="http://www.myisp.co.uk/fred/">
 82  * <PARAM NAME="indexName" VALUE="home.htm">
 83  * <EM>Sorry but the Search applet requires a Java aware
 84  * Web browser </EM>
 85  * </APPLET>
 86  */
 87
 88
 89  /* Modification history
 90  * xxxx  12th February - alpha version
 91  * v0.9  19th February - first beta version
 92  * v0.91 26th February - tidy up
 93  *                     - added maxSearch functionality
 94  *                     - added debugMode parameter
 95  * v0.92 03rd March    - added server and indexname parameters to
 96  *                       allow use on non-Demon home pages
 97  * v0.93 09th March    - fixed bug with lowercase filenames
 98  *                       added case insensitive/sensitive/match whole
 99  *                       word functionality
100  * v0.94 12th March    - fixed bug which resulted in "cannot connect"
101  *                       error on non-Demon sites.
102  * v0.95 15th March    - Removed some uses of debugMode. Server parameter
103  *                       can be set to http://localhost/ to simulate this.
104  *                     - Added support for working behind proxy servers/
```

```
105  *                      firewalls. This uses the IP Address rather than
106  *                      the hostname of the server for connections.
107  * v0.96 17th March    - Corrected code to parse HREFs. It was not
108  *                      understanding framed format or spaces.
109  *                    - Match whole word not working properly
110  *                    - HREF="http://server/" was not being followed
111  *                      correctly
112  * v0.97 20th March    - fixed bug where incorrect page name was being
113  *                      displayed for a match. This was due to the use
114  *                      of a global variable for the page name. As the
115  *                      stack unwound, then this variable was lost. Stack
116  *                      used to stored page name instead.
117  * v0.98 23rd March    - if match found on index page (using HTTP) then URL to
118  *                      jump to was created incorrectly.
119  * v0.99 25th March    - allow to be resized < 600 pixels
120  *                      allow handling of links such as
121  *                      "/www/page.html"
122  * v1.0 8th April      - Added bgColour, fgColour applet parameters
123  *                      Set default of 100 for maximum number pages to search
124  *                      Added option menu for number of pages to search
125  *                      Allow handling of framed links such as
126  *                      <FRAME SRC="framepage.html">
127  * v1.1 18th April     - Display Page title rather than page name in list of
128  *                      matches.
129  *                      If match found on index page (using FILE://) then
130  *                      URL to jump to was created incorrectly.
131  *                      Broke the <= 600 pixels code by adding the "Max
132  *                      Pages" option menu. Size of buttons adjusted to
133  *                      allow all widgets to be display in < 600 pixels
134  * v1.2 9th May        - Removed hard limits by using vectors rather than
135  *                      arrays.
136  *                      Search the index page and index page links first.
137  *                      Added internalisation support for titles. A subset
138  *                      of the special character entity names (e.g., &egrave;)
139  *                      are converted into Unicode characters so that they
140  *                      are displayed correctly.
141  *                      Fixed bug - "match word" did not match the last word
142  *                      on a line.
143  * v1.3 8th July       - Bug fix release
144  *                      Links with single quotes e.g.,
145  *                      <a href='page.html'>Test Page</a>
146  *                      were not being searched
147  *                      fgColour and bgColour only worked with UNIX browsers!
148  *                      Fixed to allow useage with MS Windows browsers,
149  *                      although due to limitations in Win32 AWT the colour
150  *                      of buttons and their text cannot be changed.
151  * v1.4 4th August     - Bug fix release
152  *                      Single quote HREF fix in v1.3 broke some normal
153  *                      HREF link code (no </A> on same line as HREF).
154  * v1.5 15th February  - Applet now searches .txt files
155  *                      Fixed bug for Demon internet users who use index
156  *                      pages other than index.htm and index.html
157  *                      Added further lower case localisation support
158  *
```

```
159   */
160
161   public class HomePageSearch extends Applet
162   {
163       final int MAX_NUMBER_PAGES = 100;        // default limit of number
164                           // pages to read
165       final int BACKSPACE_CHARACTER = 8;       // ASCII backspace
166       final int NUMBER_SPECIAL_CHARS = 45;     // Number of special character
167                           // entity names supported
168
169       Button search, clear, abort;     // GUI buttons
170
171       TextField inputArea;             // TextField used to enter
172                   // search text in
173       TextField statusArea;            // TextField used to display
174                   // search status
175       List  resultsArea;       .       // List to display matches in
176
177       public String hostName;          // Host name paramter read by
178                   // applet (required)
179       public String IPAddress;         // IP address parameter read by
180                   // applet (optional)
181       public int maxSearch = MAX_NUMBER_PAGES;
182                   // Maximum number of pages to
183                   // search (optional)
184
185       public boolean debugMode;        // TRUE = localhost
186                   // FALSE = on-line
187
188       Vector pageNames;                // Pages that have been visited
189
190       public String server;            // Non-Demon home page starting point
191
192       public String indexName;         // Name of index page (defaults to
193                   // index.html or index.htm)
194
195       SearchPages cp = null;           // Search thread
196
197       Checkbox caseSensitive;
198       Checkbox caseInsensitive;
199       Checkbox matchWholeWord;
200
201       public boolean matchCase = false;        // Flag to indicate if we
202                       // need to match case.
203
204
205       public boolean matchWord = false;        // Flag to indicate if we need
206                       // to match the whole word
207
208       String versionNumber = "v1.5";
209
210       boolean packComponents;                  // Set to true if size < 600
211
212       Color   bgColour;                        // Background colour of applet
```

```
213    Color    fgColour;                        // Foreground colour of applet
214
215    Choice numPagesChoice;                    // Option menu to select max
216                        // number of pages to search
217    Vector pageMatch;                         // Pages that contain the
218                        // search word
219
220    public void init ()
221    {
222        Panel p;
223
224        getParameters ();       // Read the applet parameters
225
226        setLayout (new BorderLayout ());
227
228        // If applet size is <= 600 pixels then reduce the length
229        // of text fields, labels, etc. so that the applet will
230        // display OK
231        if (size().width <= 600)
232            packComponents = true;
233        else
234            packComponents = false;
235
236        // This panel consists of a input text field where the
237        // user enters the text to search for. The buttons allow
238        // the search to be started, aborted and clear the applet's
239        // output fields.
240
241        p = new Panel();
242        p.setLayout (new FlowLayout());
243        Label lab = new Label ("Search for: ");
244        lab.setFont (new Font ("Helvetica", Font.PLAIN, 12));
245        p.add (lab);
246        if (packComponents)
247            inputArea = new TextField ("",15);
248        else
249            inputArea = new TextField ("",20);
250        p.add (inputArea);
251        if (packComponents)
252        {
253            search = new Button ("search");
254            search.setFont (new Font ("Helvetica", Font.BOLD, 12));
255        }
256        else
257        {
258            search = new Button (" search ");
259            search.setFont (new Font ("Helvetica", Font.BOLD, 14));
260        }
261        p.add (search);
262        if (packComponents)
263        {
264            clear = new Button ("clear");
265            clear.setFont (new Font ("Helvetica", Font.BOLD, 12));
266        }
```

```
267          else
268          {
269              clear = new Button (" clear ");
270              clear.setFont (new Font ("Helvetica", Font.BOLD, 14));
271          }
272          p.add (clear);
273          if (packComponents)
274          {
275              abort = new Button ("stop");
276              abort.setFont (new Font ("Helvetica", Font.BOLD, 12));
277          }
278          else
279          {
280              abort = new Button (" stop ");
281              abort.setFont (new Font ("Helvetica", Font.BOLD, 14));
282          }
283          abort.disable();
284          p.add (abort);
285          if (packComponents)
286              lab = new Label ("Pages");
287          else
288              lab = new Label (" Max. Pages:");
289          lab.setFont (new Font ("Helvetica", Font.PLAIN, 12));
290          p.add (lab);
291          numPagesChoice = new Choice();
292          p.add (numPagesChoice);
293          p.setForeground (fgColour);
294          p.setBackground (bgColour);
295          add ("North",p);
296
297          // This panel lists the results. When an item from the list
298          // box is double clicked the URL is opened up.
299          p = new Panel();
300          p.setLayout (new GridLayout(0,1));
301          resultsArea = new List (10,false);
302          p.add (resultsArea);
303          p.setForeground (fgColour);
304          p.setBackground (bgColour);
305          add ("Center",p);
306
307          p = new Panel();
308          Label labVersion = new Label (versionNumber);
309          labVersion.setFont (new Font ("Helvetica", Font.PLAIN, 12));
310          p.add (labVersion);
311          CheckboxGroup caseSense = new CheckboxGroup();
312
313          // This textfield shows the status of the search to provide
314          // some feedback to the user. The page count is displayed.
315          if (packComponents)
316              statusArea = new TextField ("",14);
317          else
318              statusArea = new TextField ("",20);
319
320          statusArea.setEditable (false);
```

```
321          p.add (statusArea);
322
323          if (packComponents)
324              caseInsensitive = new Checkbox ("in-sensitive");
325          else
326              caseInsensitive = new Checkbox ("case in-sensitive");
327
328          p.add (caseInsensitive);
329          caseInsensitive.setCheckboxGroup (caseSense);
330
331          if (packComponents)
332              caseSensitive = new Checkbox ("sensitive" );
333          else
334              caseSensitive = new Checkbox ("case sensitive" );
335
336          p.add (caseSensitive);
337          caseSensitive.setCheckboxGroup (caseSense);
338          caseSense.setCurrent (caseInsensitive);
339
340          if (packComponents)
341              matchWholeWord = new Checkbox ("whole word");
342          else
343              matchWholeWord = new Checkbox ("match whole word");
344
345          p.add (matchWholeWord);
346          p.setForeground (fgColour);
347          p.setBackground (bgColour);
348          add ("South",p);
349
350          disableButtons ();        // Disable buttons until text entered
351
352          // Create vector to hold pages that have been found
353          // and pages that contain the search text
354          pageNames = new Vector();
355          pageMatch = new Vector();
356
357          // Now that we know what the maxSearch parameter is, fill
358          // in sensible page numbers
359          for (int i=maxSearch / 5; i<= maxSearch, i += maxSearch / 5)
360          {
361              numPagesChoice.addItem (Integer.toString(i));
362          }
363
364          numPagesChoice.setFont (new Font ("Helvetica", Font.PLAIN, 12));
365
366          // Set the default number of pages to be searched
367          numPagesChoice.select (0);
368          maxSearch = maxSearch / 5;
369
370          // Set the background + foreground applet colours
371 //              setBackground(bgColour);
372 //              setForeground(fgColour);
373
374          // Always set text input field to white for readability
```

```
375              inputArea.setBackground (Color.white);
376         }
377
378         // Function enableButtons
379         // Purpose - enable use of buttons in GUI
380         public void enableButtons ()
381         {
382              search.enable();
383              clear.enable();
384         }
385
386         // Function disableButtons
387         // Purpose - disable use of buttons in GUI
388         final void disableButtons ()
389         {
390              search.disable();
391              clear.disable();
392         }
393
394         // Function getParameters
395         // Purpose - read applet parameters
396         final void getParameters ()
397         {
398              hostName = getParameter ("hostname");
399              IPAddress = getParameter ("IPAddress");
400              String num = getParameter ("maxSearch");
401              String arg = getParameter ("debug");
402              server = getParameter ("server");
403              indexName = getParameter ("indexName");
404
405              String colour = getParameter("bgColour");
406              if (colour == null)
407              {
408                   // I wish this could be locali[sz]ed so that I could
409                   // write lightGrey !!
410                   bgColour = Color.lightGray;
411              }
412              else
413              {
414                   try
415                   {
416                        bgColour = new Color(Integer.parseInt(colour, 16));
417                   }
418                   catch (NumberFormatException e)
419                   {
420                        bgColour=Color.lightGray;
421                   }
422              }
423
424              colour = getParameter("fgColour");
425              if (colour == null)
426              {
427                   fgColour = Color.black;
428              }
```

```
429          else
430          {
431              try
432              {
433                  fgColour = new Color(Integer.parseInt(colour, 16));
434              }
435              catch (NumberFormatException e)
436              {
437                  bgColour=Color.black;
438              }
439          }
440
441          // Check for missing parameters
442          if (hostName == null && server == null)
443          {
444              statusArea.setText ("Error - no host/server");
445              System.out.println (" Error: No hostname specified");
446              hostName = "none";
447          }
448
449          maxSearch = (num == null) ? MAX_NUMBER_PAGES : Integer.parseInt(num);
450          debugMode = (arg == null) ? false : true;
451
452          if (debugMode)
453          {
454              System.out.println ("hostname is " + hostName);
455              System.out.println ("IPAddress is " + IPAddress);
456              System.out.println ("maxSearch is " + maxSearch);
457              System.out.println ("debugMode is " + debugMode);
458              System.out.println ("server is " + server);
459              System.out.println ("indexName is " + indexName);
460              System.out.println ("bgColour is " + bgColour);
461              System.out.println ("fgColour is " + fgColour);
462          }
463      }
464
465      // Display parameter information
466      public String[][] getParameterInfo()
467      {
468          String[][] info =
469          {
470              {"hostname","String","hostname of site"},
471              {"IPAddress","String","IP address of site"},
472              {"maxSearch","String","maximum number of pages to search"},
473              {"debug","String","debug mode"},
474              {"server","String","Home Page URL"},
475              {"indexName","String","Name of index page"},
476              {"bgColour","Color","Background colour of applet"},
477              {"fgColour","Color","Foreground colour of applet"}
478          };
479
480          return info;
481      }
482
```

```
483      // Display applet information
484      public String getAppletInfo()
485      {
486          return "Home Page Search Applet v1.5";
487      }
488
489      // Function keyDown
490      // Purpose - enable or disable buttons. When search text is entered
491      // the search and clear buttons are enabled. When no search text has
492      // been entered the buttons are disabled.
493      public boolean keyDown (Event e, int nKey)
494      {
495          boolean boolDone = true;
496          String text;
497
498          text = inputArea.getText();        // Read the search text
499          int n = text.length();             // Count number of chars
500
501          if (nKey == BACKSPACE_CHARACTER)// catch backspace character
502          {
503              boolDone = false;
504              n--;
505          }
506          else
507          {
508              boolDone = false;
509              n++;
510          }
511
512          if (n > 0)
513          {
514              enableButtons ();
515          }
516          else
517          {
518              disableButtons ();
519          }
520
521          return (boolDone);
522      }
523
524      // Purpose - this function handles all the GUI events
525      public boolean action (Event e, Object o)
526      {
527
528          String text;                // Search text entered by user
529          String searchText;          // Lower case version of above
530          URL newURL = null;
531
532          // Check to see if the option menu has been selected
533          if (e.target instanceof Choice)
534          {
535              Choice c = (Choice) e.target;
536              try
```

```
537             {
538                 maxSearch = Integer.parseInt(c.getSelectedItem(), 10);
539             }
540         catch (NumberFormatException ex)
541             {
542                 maxSearch = MAX_NUMBER_PAGES;
543             }
544
545         if (debugMode)
546             System.out.println ("maxSearch is now " + maxSearch);
547     }
548
549     // Check to see if a checkbox has been pressed
550     if (e.target instanceof Checkbox)
551     {
552         if (caseSensitive.getState() == true)
553             matchCase = true;
554         else
555             matchCase = false;
556
557         if (matchWholeWord.getState() == true)
558             matchWord = true;
559         else
560             matchWord = false;
561     }
562
563     // A button has been pressed - determine which
564     if (e.target instanceof Button)
565     {
566         if (e.target == search)
567         {
568             // Search button pressed - read in
569             // search text entered
570             text = inputArea.getText();
571
572             // Make sure there's somthing to search for
573             if (text.length() == 0)
574                 return (false);
575
576             // New search so clear the GUI out
577             if (resultsArea.countItems() > 0)
578                 resultsArea.clear();
579
580             disableButtons ();
581             abort.enable();
582             statusArea.setText("");
583
584             // Clear out previous search data
585             pageNames.removeAllElements();
586             pageMatch.removeAllElements();
587
588             // We're off - start the search thread
589             cp = new SearchPages (this, hostName, text, maxSearch);
590             cp.start();
```

```
591                  }
592              else if (e.target == abort)
593              {
594                  // Abort button pressed - stop the thread
595                  if (cp != null)
596                      cp.stop();
597                  cp = null;
598
599                  // Enable buttons for another search
600                  enableButtons();
601                  abort.disable();
602              }
603              else
604              {
605                  // Clear button pressed - clear all the fields
606                  // and return
607                  inputArea.setText("");
608                  statusArea.setText("");
609
610                  // Clear radio buttons
611                  caseSensitive.setState(false);
612                  caseInsensitive.setState(true);
613                  matchWholeWord.setState(false);
614
615                  // Clear option menu
616                  numPagesChoice.select (0);
617                  try
618                  {
619                      maxSearch = Integer.parseInt(numPagesChoice.getSelectedItem(), 10);
620                  }
621                  catch (NumberFormatException ex)
622                  {
623                      maxSearch = MAX_NUMBER_PAGES;
624                  }
625
626                  if (debugMode)
627                      System.out.println ("maxSearch is now " + maxSearch);
628
629                  if (resultsArea.countItems() > 0)
630                      resultsArea.clear();
631
632                  cp = null;
633              }
634          }
635
636          // Selection made from the list of matches
637          if (e.target instanceof List)
638          {
639              List list = (List) e.target;
640              int index = list.getSelectedIndex();
641
642              // Extract the page name from the list
643              if (index < pageMatch.size())
644              {
```

```
645                 String URLSelected = (String)pageMatch.elementAt(index);
646
647             try
648             {
649                 // If URL stored then use it
650                 if (URLSelected.startsWith ("http:") ||
651                     URLSelected.startsWith ("file:"))
652                 newURL = new URL(URLSelected);
653                 else if (server == null)
654                     newURL = new URL("http://www." + hostName + ".demon.co.uk/" + URLSelected);
655                 else
656                     newURL = new URL (server + URLSelected);
657             }
658             catch(MalformedURLException excep)
659             {
660                 System.out.println("action(): Bad URL: " + newURL);
661             }
662
663             if (debugMode)
664                 System.out.println (" Jumping to ... " + newURL.toString());
665
666             // Display the document
667             getAppletContext().showDocument(newURL,"_self");
668         }
669     }
670
671     return true;                                      // We're done
672 }
673
674
675 // Purpose - checks to see if a page has already been
676 // visited by the search thread
677 boolean checkAlreadyFound (String page)
678 {
679     if (pageNames.size() == 0)
680         return (false);
681
682     // Check this is a new one
683     for (int i=1; i < pageNames.size() ;i++)
684     {
685         String pageName = (String) pageNames.elementAt(i);
686         if (pageName.equalsIgnoreCase (page))
687             return (true);
688     }
689
690     return (false);
691 }
692
693 // Purpose - adds a page visited by the search thread to
694 // the list of visited pages
695 // This prevents the same link from being followed if it
696 // is on multiple pages.
697 public void incrementPages (String page)
698 {
```

```
699          // Check if page already indexed
700          if (checkAlreadyFound (page))
701             return;
702
703          pageNames.addElement (page);
704
705          // Provide feedback to the user
706          statusArea.setText ("Searching page: " + pageNames.size());
707      }
708
709      // Purpose - returns the number of pages that the search
710      // thread has visited
711      public int getTotalPages ()
712      {
713          return pageNames.size() - 1;
714      }
715
716      // Purpose - convert special characters in the page title
717      // to Unicode characters so they are displayed properly
718      final protected String translateSpecialChars (String title)
719      {
720          int start;
721          int i;
722          // HTML representation of selected extended chars
723          String rawString[] = {"&aacute;","&acirc;","&aelig;",
724                          "&agrave;","&auml;","&ccedil;",
725                          "&eacute;","&ecirc;","&egrave;",
726                          "&euml;","&icirc;","&iuml;",
727                          "&ocirc;","&ouml;","&szlig;",
728                          "&uuml;","&yuml;","&copy;",
729                          "&pound;","&reg;","&lt;",
730                          "&gt;","&amp;","&quot;",
731                     "&atilde;","&aring;","&igrave;",
732                     "&iacute;","&eth;","&ntilde;",
733                     "&ograve;","&oacute;","&otilde;",
734                     "&divide;","&oslash;","&ugrave;",
735                     "&uacute;","&ucirc;","&yacute;",
736                     "&thorn;","&times;"," ",
737                     "&sect;","&cent;","&deg;"};
738          // Unicode representation of above
739          char translatedChar[] = {'\u00e1','\u00e2','\u00e6',
740                          '\u00e0','\u00e4','\u00e7',
741                          '\u00e9','\u00ea','\u00e8',
742                          '\u00eb','\u00ee','\u00ef',
743                          '\u00f4','\u00f6','\u00df',
744                          '\u00fc','\u00ff','\u00a9',
745                          '\u00a3','\u00ae','\u003c',
746                          '\u003e','\u0026','\u0022',
747                          '\u00e3','\u00e5','\u00ec',
748                          '\u00ed','\u00f0','\u00f1',
749                          '\u00f2','\u00f3','\u00f5',
750                          '\u00f7','\u00f8','\u00f9',
751                          '\u00fa','\u00fb','\u00fd',
752                          '\u00fe','\u00d7','\u00a0',
```

```
753                         '\u00a7','\u00a2','\u00b0'};
754        StringBuffer translated = new StringBuffer ("");
755        String titleString = title;
756
757        // Check the title for each of the above HTML special chars
758        for (int loop=0; loop < NUMBER_SPECIAL_CHARS; loop++)
759        {
760            if (translated.length() > 0)
761            {
762                titleString = translated.toString();
763                translated = new StringBuffer ("");
764            }
765
766            start = titleString.indexOf (rawString[loop]);
767
768            if (start != -1)
769            {
770                // HTML special character found so replace it
771                // with the Unicode equivalent for display
772                for (i=0; i < start; i++)
773                    translated.insert (i,titleString.charAt(i));
774
775                translated.append (translatedChar[loop]);
776
777                for (i=start+rawString[loop].length(); i < titleString.length(); i++)
778                    translated.append (titleString.charAt(i));
779
780            }
781        }
782
783        return (translated.length() == 0) ? titleString : translated.toString();
784    }
785
786    // Purpose - adds a page to the list of matches in the results
787    // ListBox. The page title and matching text are displayed.
788    // The page name is also stored so that the URL can be jumped
789    // to.
790    public void addToList (String Page, String line, String title)
791    {
792        String translatedTitle = title;
793        String translatedLine  = line;
794
795        if (title.indexOf("&") != -1 &&
796            title.indexOf(";") != -1)
797        {
798            // check for HTML special characters
799            // e.g., &quot; &ccedil; etc.
800            translatedTitle = translateSpecialChars (title);
801        }
802
803        if (line.indexOf("&") != -1 &&
804            line.indexOf(";") != -1)
805        {
806            // check for HTML special characters
807            // e.g., &quot; &ccedil; etc.
```

```
808                translatedLine = translateSpecialChars (line);
809            }
810
811        resultsArea.addItem ("Title:\" " + translatedTitle + "\" Text: " + translatedLine);
812
813        pageMatch.addElement(Page);
814    }
815
816 }
817
818
819 //============================================================================
820 //                          Class SearchPages
821 //============================================================================
822
823 // This thread performs the search. The search starts with the index.html or
824 // index.htm page and then follows all local links
825 // (e.g. <A HREF="fred.html">link to fred</A> or
826 // <A HREF="http://www.<hostname>.demon.co.uk/fred.html">link to fred</A>.
827 // Note external links are ignored.
828 class SearchPages extends Thread
829 {
830    // Search state transitions
831    // First find top level pages (from the index page)
832    // Search the above pages first
833    // Search all other pages
834    final byte FIND_TOP_LEVEL_PAGES = 0;
835    final byte SEARCH_TOP_LEVEL_PAGES = 1;
836    final byte SEARCH_OTHER_PAGES = 2;
837
838    String hostName;           // Host name of site e.g., babbage
839    HomePageSearch app;        // Parent applet
840    String textToFind;         // String to find
841    int maxPages;              // Maximum number of pages to visit
842    int hitsFound = 0;         // No of occurrences of search string
843    static final byte URLCOUNT = 2;
844    boolean pageOpened = false;     // Flag to indicate if index page
845                        // opened OK
846    boolean proxyDetected = false;  // Flag to indicate if a proxy server
847                    // or firewall has been detected
848    int topLevelSearch;             // Search the index page links first
849    Vector topLevelPages;           // Page names in the index page
850    Vector nextLevelPages;          // Lower level pages
851
852    // Constructor
853    SearchPages (HomePageSearch applet, String hn, String text, int maxSearch)
854    {
855        app = applet;
856        hostName = hn;
857        textToFind = text;
858        maxPages = maxSearch;
859    }
860
861    public void run()
```

```
862      {
863          // State 1: search the index page, remembering all links on
864          // the index page
865          topLevelSearch = FIND_TOP_LEVEL_PAGES;
866
867          topLevelPages = new Vector();
868          nextLevelPages = new Vector();
869
870          // Check to see if a proxy is being used. If so then we use
871          // IP address rather than hostnames
872          proxyDetected = detectProxyServer();
873
874          startSearch();
875          app.enableButtons();
876          app.abort.disable();
877
878          if (hitsFound == 0 && pageOpened == true)
879              app.statusArea.setText ("No matches found");
880          else if (hitsFound == 1)
881              app.statusArea.setText (hitsFound + " match found");
882          else
883              app.statusArea.setText (hitsFound + " matches found");
884      }
885
886      // Function: detectProxyServer
887      // Purpose: attempt to see if a proxy server or firewall is blocking
888      // a connection back to the originating server. If so then the
889      // variable proxyDetected is set to true and all future connections
890      // to the server will use the IP Address (if passed as a parameter)
891      final boolean detectProxyServer ()
892      {
893          DataInputStream dis = null;
894          String url = "";
895
896          // Allow for non-Demon Home Page
897          if (app.server == null)
898          {
899              if (app.indexName == null)
900                  url = "http://www." + hostName + ".demon.co.uk/index.html";
901              else
902                  url = "http://www." + hostName + ".demon.co.uk/" + app.indexName;
903          }
904          else
905          {
906              if (app.indexName == null)
907                  url = app.server + "index.html";
908              else
909                  url = app.server + app.indexName;
910          }
911
912          // Attempt to connect to this URL
913          try
914          {
915              URL doc = new URL (url);
```

```
916                 dis = new DataInputStream (doc.openStream());
917           }
918           catch (Exception e)
919           {
920               // Unable to connect. This may be an incorrect applet
921               // parameter. Let's assume, though, that it's a proxy server
922               // that's stopping us using the hostname.
923
924               return true;
925           }
926
927           return false;
928
929       }
930
931       final void startSearch()
932       {
933           DataInputStream dis = null;
934           String [] url = {"",""};
935           String currentPageName="";       // HTML page currently being searched
936
937           // Allow for non-Demon Home Page
938           if (app.server == null)
939           {
940               if (app.indexName == null)
941               {
942                   url[0] = "http://www." + hostName + ".demon.co.uk/index.html";
943                   url[1] = "http://www." + hostName + ".demon.co.uk/index.htm";
944               }
945               else
946               {
947                   url[0] = "http://www." + hostName + ".demon.co.uk/" + app.indexName;
948                   url[1] = "";
949               }
950           }
951           else
952           {
953               if (app.indexName == null)
954               {
955                   url[0] = app.server + "index.html";
956                   url[1] = app.server + "index.htm";
957               }
958               else
959               {
960                   // Allow for an index page other than
961                   // "index.html"
962                   url[0] = app.server + app.indexName;
963                   url[1] = "";
964               }
965           }
966
967           // If a proxy server/firewall has been detected, then use the
968           // IP address (if supplied) of the originating server rather
969           // than the hostname.
```

```
970          if (proxyDetected && app.IPAddress != null)
971          {
972              if (app.indexName == null)
973              {
974                  url[0] = "http://" + app.IPAddress + "/index.html";
975                  url[1] = "http://" + app.IPAddress + "/index.htm";
976              }
977              else
978              {
979                  url[0] = "http://"+ app.IPAddress + "/" + app.indexName;
980                  url[1] = "";
981              }
982          }
983
984          for (int i=0; i < URLCOUNT; i++)
985          {
986              try
987              {
988                  currentPageName = url[i];
989                  URL doc = new URL (url[i]);
990                  dis = new DataInputStream (doc.openStream());
991              }
992              catch (Exception e)
993              {
994                  System.out.println ("StartSearch(): Exception: " + e + " Page= " + url[i]);
995                  continue;         // Try next page
996              }
997
998              if (dis != null)          // Check page opened OK
999              {
1000                 pageOpened = true;
1001                 i = URLCOUNT;  // Exit the loop
1002             }
1003         }
1004
1005         if (pageOpened == false)
1006         {
1007             app.statusArea.setText ("Cannot connect to server");
1008             System.out.println ("StartSearch(): No pages to search");
1009             return;                     // Nothing to do
1010         }
1011         else
1012         {
1013             // Search the first page. Any links on the index page
1014             // are saved and searched next.
1015             searchPage (dis,currentPageName);
1016         }
1017
1018         // State 2: search links found on the index page
1019         topLevelSearch = SEARCH_TOP_LEVEL_PAGES;
1020
1021         for (int i=0; i < topLevelPages.size(); i++)
1022         {
1023             checkLink ((String)topLevelPages.elementAt(i));
```

```
1024
1025            // Check that the maximum number of pages to be
1026            // searched has not been reached
1027            if (app.getTotalPages () >= maxPages)
1028                return;
1029        }
1030
1031        // State 3: spider all other pages
1032        topLevelSearch = SEARCH_OTHER_PAGES;
1033
1034        for (int i=0; i < nextLevelPages.size(); i++)
1035        {
1036            checkLink ((String)nextLevelPages.elementAt(i));
1037
1038            // Check that the maximum number of pages to be
1039            // searched has not been reached
1040            if (app.getTotalPages () >= maxPages)
1041                return;
1042        }
1043    }
1044
1045    // Purpose - read all lines on a page - extracting local links
1046    // and checking for the presence of the search string
1047    final void searchPage (DataInputStream dis, String url)
1048    {
1049        try
1050        {
1051            String input;           // Raw line read in
1052            String upperCaseInput;  // Uppercase version of
1053                        // above
1054            String link;            // HTML link found
1055            String temp;
1056            String title = "";      // Page title
1057
1058            // Read a line at a time
1059            while ((input = dis.readLine()) != null)
1060            {
1061                // Convert to upper case (makes comparisons
1062                // easier)
1063                upperCaseInput = input.toUpperCase();
1064
1065                // check for document title
1066                temp = parseForTitle (input, upperCaseInput, dis);
1067                // If a title has been found, then remember it
1068                // so that it can be displayed in the list box
1069                if (temp != null && temp.length() > 0)
1070                    title = temp;
1071
1072                // check for match after title has been found
1073                // (Don't bother searching the title though)
1074                if (title.length() > 0 && temp == null)
1075                    checkMatch (input, url, title);
1076
1077                // check to see if this line contains
```

```
1078                // a link
1079                link = parseForLink (upperCaseInput, input);
1080                if (link != null)
1081                {
1082                    // Check if the maximum number
1083                    // of pages to search has been
1084                    // reached
1085                    if (app.getTotalPages () >= maxPages)
1086                        return;
1087
1088                    if (topLevelSearch == FIND_TOP_LEVEL_PAGES)
1089                        topLevelPages.addElement (link);
1090                    else if (topLevelSearch == SEARCH_TOP_LEVEL_PAGES)
1091                        nextLevelPages.addElement (link);
1092                    else
1093                        checkLink (link);
1094                }
1095
1096            }
1097        }
1098    catch (IOException e)
1099    {
1100        System.out.println ("searchPage(): Exception: " + e + " on Page: " + url);
1101    }
1102    }
1103
1104    // Purpose - scan a line of text looking for the title of the page
1105    // e.g., <TITLE> My Page </TITLE>
1106    // Titles may be multi-line so this routine reads from the document
1107    // until the </TITLE> tag has been read or 25 characters read (max
1108    // meaningful length of a title) (same as Alta Vista!)
1109    final String parseForTitle (String rawInput, String input, DataInputStream dis)
1110    {
1111        int i,j,k,l;                    // Loop counters
1112        int titleLength = 0;            // Keep track of title length
1113                        // as only first 25 characters
1114                        // are displayed
1115        int start = 0;                  // Start of title text
1116        String temp;
1117        StringBuffer title = new StringBuffer ("");
1118        boolean foundTag = false;
1119
1120        try
1121        {
1122            // Search for <TITLE> tage
1123            // Can the TITLE tag have spaces? e.g < TITLE  > (assume not!)
1124            i = input.indexOf ("<TITLE");
1125            if (i != -1)
1126            {
1127                // Allow for <HTML><HEAD><TITLE>Title</TITLE></HEAD>
1128                j = input.indexOf (">",i);
1129
1130                if (j != -1)
1131                {
```

```
1132                     while (titleLength <= 25 && foundTag == false)
1133                     {
1134                         start = j + 1;
1135                         for (k=start; k < rawInput.length(); k++)
1136                         {
1137                             if (foundTag == false && rawInput.charAt(k) != '<')
1138                             {
1139                                 titleLength++;
1140                                 title.append (rawInput.charAt(k));
1141                             }
1142                             else
1143                                 foundTag = true;
1144                         }
1145
1146                         // Continue reading from doc
1147                         // if </TITLE> not found
1148                         if (foundTag == false)
1149                         {
1150                             rawInput = dis.readLine();
1151                             j = -1;
1152                         }
1153                     }
1154
1155                     // Remove leading and trailing spaces
1156                     temp = title.toString();
1157
1158                     return (temp.trim());
1159                 }
1160             }
1161
1162         }
1163         catch (IOException e)
1164         {
1165             System.out.println ("parseForTitle(): Exception: " + e);
1166         }
1167
1168         return (null);                       // No title found
1169     }
1170
1171
1172     // Purpose - scan a line of text looking for links to other
1173     // pages. The following types of links are currently supported
1174     // 1. Normal links, e.g., <A HREF="page.html">Text</A>
1175     // 2. Frames, e.g., <FRAME scrolling=yes SRC="contents.html">
1176     final String parseForLink (String upperCaseInput, String input)
1177     {
1178         int i,j,k,l;
1179         String temp = null;
1180         String link = null;
1181
1182         // Look for links to other pages
1183         // 1. Normal links, e.g., <A HREF="page.html">Text</A>
1184         i = upperCaseInput.indexOf ("HREF");
1185         if (i != -1)
```

```
1186          {
1187              // Locate position of quote marks
1188              j = upperCaseInput.indexOf ("\"",i);
1189              k = upperCaseInput.indexOf ("\"",j+1);
1190
1191              // Locate position of </a>
1192              l = upperCaseInput.indexOf ("</A>",i);
1193
1194              // If double quotes were not found, then try using
1195              // single quote marks
1196              if (j == -1 || k == -1 || (j > l && k == -1))
1197              {
1198                  j = upperCaseInput.indexOf ("\'",i);
1199                  k = upperCaseInput.indexOf ("\'",j+1);
1200              }
1201
1202              // Remove leading and trailing spaces
1203              if (j != -1 && k != -1)
1204              {
1205                  // Extract the link name
1206                  temp = input.substring (j+1,k);
1207
1208                  // Remove leading and trailing spaces
1209                  link = temp.trim ();
1210
1211                  return (link);
1212              }
1213          }
1214
1215      // 2. Frames, e.g., <FRAME scrolling=yes SRC="contents.html">
1216      i = upperCaseInput.indexOf ("FRAME");
1217      if (i != -1)
1218      {
1219          // Locate position of SRC tag
1220          l = upperCaseInput.indexOf ("SRC",i);
1221
1222          if (l != -1)
1223          {
1224              // Locate position of quote marks
1225              j = upperCaseInput.indexOf ("\"",l);
1226              k = upperCaseInput.indexOf ("\"",j+1);
1227
1228              // If double quotes were not found, then try
1229              // single quote marks
1230              if (j == -1)
1231              {
1232                  j = upperCaseInput.indexOf ("\'",i);
1233                  k = upperCaseInput.indexOf ("\'",j+1);
1234              }
1235
1236              // Remove leading and trailing spaces
1237              if (j != -1 && k != -1)
1238              {
1239                  // Extract the link name
```

```
1240                          temp = input.substring (j+1,k);
1241
1242                          // Remove leading and trailing spaces
1243                          link = temp.trim ();
1244
1245                          return (link);
1246                      }
1247                  }
1248              }
1249
1250          return (null);
1251      }
1252
1253      // Purpose - scan a line of text to see if the search string is
1254      // present. If so then add the line to the list of matches.
1255      final void checkMatch (String input, String url, String title)
1256      {
1257          // remove HTML tags before search
1258          String searchLine = removeHTMLTags (input);
1259
1260          // If the line contains some non-HTML text
1261          // then search it
1262          if (searchLine.length() > 0)
1263          {
1264              // Check if case-sensitive search
1265              if (app.matchCase)
1266              {
1267                  // Check if attempting to match whole word
1268                  if (app.matchWord)
1269                  {
1270                      if (searchLine.indexOf (" " + textToFind + " ") != -1 ||
1271                          (searchLine.indexOf (textToFind) != -1 && searchLine.length() == textToFind.length()) ||
1272                          (searchLine.indexOf (" " + textToFind) != -1 && textToFind.charAt
1273                          (textToFind.length()-1) == searchLine.charAt(searchLine.length()-1)))
1274                      {
1275                          // Found it! Display the match
1276                          app.addToList (url, searchLine, title);
1277                          hitsFound++;
1278                      }
1279                  }
1280                  else if (searchLine.indexOf (textToFind) != -1)
1281                  {
1282                      // Found it! Display the match
1283                      app.addToList (url, searchLine, title);
1284                      hitsFound++;
1285                  }
1286              }
1287              else
1288              {
1289                  String lower1 = searchLine.toLowerCase();
1290                  String lower2 = textToFind.toLowerCase();
1291
1292                  // Check if attempting to match whole word
1293                  if (app.matchWord)
```

```
1293                    {
1294                        if (lower1.indexOf (" " + lower2 + " ") != -1 ||
1295                            (lower1.indexOf (lower2) != -1 && lower1.length() == lower2.length()) ||
1296                            (lower1.indexOf (" " + lower2) != -1 && lower2.charAt
1297                            (lower2.length()-1) == lower1.charAt(lower1.length()-1)))
1298                        {
1299                            // Found it! Display the match
1300                            app.addToList (url, searchLine, title);
1301                            hitsFound++;
1302                        }
1303                        else if (lower1.indexOf (lower2) != -1)
1304                        {
1305                            // Found it! Display the match
1306                            app.addToList (url, searchLine, title);
1307                            hitsFound++;
1308                        }
1309                    }
1310
1311                }
1312        }
1313
1314        // Purpose - remove HTML tages from a line (e.g <BR>). The
1315        // algorithm is a bit simplistic in that it cannot handle
1316        // HTML tags split over one line.
1317        final String removeHTMLTags (String inputLine)
1318        {
1319            StringBuffer outputLine = new StringBuffer ("");
1320            boolean foundTag = false;
1321
1322            for (int i=0; i < inputLine.length(); i++)
1323            {
1324                if (inputLine.charAt (i) == '<')
1325                    foundTag = true;
1326                else if (inputLine.charAt(i) == '>')
1327                    foundTag = false;
1328                else if (foundTag == false)
1329                    outputLine.append (inputLine.charAt(i));
1330            }
1331
1332            return (outputLine.toString());
1333        }
1334
1335        // Purpose - checks validity of a link. If the link is valid
1336        // it's added to the list of visited links and then followed
1337        final void checkLink (String link)
1338        {
1339            URL doc;            // URL of link
1340            DataInputStream dis = null;
1341            int i;
1342            boolean qualifiedLink = false;
1343
1344            // Skip the link if it's just an offset in this document
1345            if (link.startsWith("#"))
```

```
1346           return;
1347
1348       // Strip #offset tag off
1349       if ((i = link.indexOf ("#")) != -1)
1350       {
1351           String substr =link.substring (0,i);
1352           link = substr;
1353       }
1354
1355       // Check that this link hasn't already been followed
1356       if (app.checkAlreadyFound (link))
1357           return;
1358
1359       // Ignore non HTML links and start page
1360       if ((link.startsWith ("mailto:")) ||
1361           (link.startsWith ("wais:")) ||
1362           (link.startsWith ("gopher:")) ||
1363           (link.startsWith ("newsrc:")) ||
1364           (link.startsWith ("ftp:")) ||
1365           (link.startsWith ("nntp:")) ||
1366           (link.startsWith ("telnet:")) ||
1367           (link.startsWith ("news:")) ||
1368           (link.equalsIgnoreCase (app.indexName)) ||
1369           (link.equalsIgnoreCase ("index.html")) ||
1370           (link.equalsIgnoreCase ("index.htm")))
1371           return;
1372
1373       // Check that it is not an outside link (e.g., www.mycom.com)
1374       if (link.indexOf ("http:") != -1)
1375       {
1376           String pageName;
1377           if (app.server == null)
1378               pageName = "http://www."+ hostName + ".demon.co.uk";
1379           else
1380               pageName = app.server;
1381
1382           // Allow for local host being displayed as an
1383           // IP address rather than host name
1384           if (proxyDetected && app.IPAddress != null)
1385               pageName = "http://" + app.IPAddress;
1386
1387           // This is a "fully qualified link"
1388           // e.g., "http://www.babbage.demon.co.uk/link.html"
1389           qualifiedLink = true;
1390
1391           // If the link doesn't contain the local host name
1392           // or IP address, then it's an external link - so
1393           // ignore it
1394           if (link.indexOf (pageName) == -1)
1395               return;
1396       }
1397
1398       // Check that it's a HTML page
1399       if (link.indexOf (".htm") == -1 &&
```

```
1400            link.indexOf (".HTM") == -1 &&
1401            link.indexOf (".TXT") == -1 &&
1402            link.indexOf (".txt") == -1 &&
1403                link.indexOf (".phtml") == -1 &&
1404            link.indexOf (".PHTML") == -1)
1405            return;
1406
1407        // Valid link - add it to the array of visited links
1408        app.incrementPages (link);
1409
1410        // Follow link and read its contents
1411        try
1412        {
1413            if (app.server == null)
1414                doc = new URL ("http://www."+ hostName + ".demon.co.uk/" + link);
1415            else
1416            {
1417                if (link.startsWith ("/"))
1418                {
1419                    // Remove the "/" from the link, as the
1420                    // server name has a terminating "/"
1421                    String temp = link.substring (1, link.length());
1422                    link = temp;
1423                }
1424                doc = new URL (app.server + link);
1425            }
1426
1427            // Link may be absolute
1428            // (e.g www.babbage.demon.co.uk/fred.html")
1429            if (qualifiedLink)
1430                doc = new URL (link);
1431
1432            // If a proxy server/firewall has been detected, then use the
1433            // IP address (if supplied) of the originating server rather
1434            // than the hostname.
1435            if (proxyDetected && app.IPAddress != null)
1436                doc = new URL ("http://" + app.IPAddress + "/" + link);
1437
1438            if (app.debugMode)
1439                System.out.println ("Found link " + link);
1440
1441            dis = new DataInputStream (doc.openStream());
1442
1443            // Start searching this new link
1444            searchPage (dis, link);
1445
1446        }
1447        catch (IOException e)
1448        {
1449            System.out.println ("checkLink(): Exception: " + e + " Page: " + link);
1450        }
1451    }
1452
1453 }
```

ANNOTATIONS

The basic operation of the **HomePageSearch** applet is simple. It starts by downloading the HTML file specified by the **indexName** parameter. Typically, this is a file named **index.html** (or **index.htm**). Then **HomePageSearch** reads the lines of text from that file and locates any links, as indicated by HTML's **<A>** tag. It downloads any links that refer to Web pages located on the same server as the one from which the applet's class file was loaded and disregards any links to other Web sites. Figure 6-9 illustrates this basic idea. Subsequent sections describe key aspects of how the applet is implemented. In the case shown in the figure, **HomePageSearch** follows the links to **books.html**, **search.html**, **JavaAA.html**, and **Linux.html**, but it ignores links that refer to other Web sites, such as **http://java.sun.com**.

As you go through the **HomePageSearch** applet's source code, you will see many references to **demon.co.uk** and **www.babbage.demon.co.uk**. These refer to the domain name and Web server of the ISP used by the applet's author. If you do not explicitly specify a Web server, the applet assumes you want to search home pages on **www.babbage.demon.co.uk**.

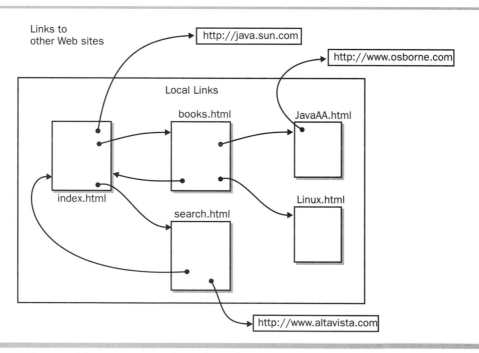

FIGURE 6-9.   The **HomePageSearch** applet downloads and searches all local links.

ORGANIZATION OF THE SOURCE FILE   You will find it easier to navigate through the **HomePageSearch.java** file if you know the organization of the file. The following listing shows a skeletal view of the **HomePageSearch.java** file (along with line numbers) to help you understand how that file is organized:

```
  1 import java.awt.*;
    // ... Import statements
  5 import java.util.*;

  7 // v1.5 Home Page Search applet
    // ... Comments and modification history
159  */

161 public class HomePageSearch extends Applet
162 {
    // ... HomePageSearch class
816 }

828 class SearchPages extends Thread
829 {
    // ... SearchPages class
1453 }
```

The file starts with the required **import** statements that makes classes from various other packages available to this source file. Following the **import** statements, more than 150 lines are devoted to comments and modification history.

The rest of the source file shows the two classes—HomePageSearch and SearchPages—that are used in the applet. The **HomePageSearch** class represents the applet. The **SearchPages** class is a subclass of **Thread** and is used by **HomePageSearch** to download Web pages and perform the search. I discuss the functionality of both of these classes in the next few sections.

HOMEPAGESEARCH INITIALIZATION   When the **HomePageSearch** applet is initialized, the **init()** method, shown in lines 220 through 376, gets the parameters from the <PARAM> tags and lays out the applet's user interface.

To get the parameter values, line 224 calls the **getParameters()** method. This method, shown in lines 396 through 463, retrieves all parameter values by calling the **getParameter()** method of the **Applet** class. If the **debug** parameter is specified, the **getParameters()** method also prints the values of all parameters as debugging information.

Lines 231 through 375 of the initialization code are devoted to laying out the user interface components in the applet's display area. The code is lengthy because it is designed to use one layout when the display area is wider than 600 pixels and another layout when the width is less than 600 pixels. Notice that lines 231 through 234 set the **boolean** variable named **packComponents** according to the width of the applet's display area:

```
231        if (size().width <= 600)
232            packComponents = true;
233        else
234            packComponents = false;
```

Here, **size().width** is the width of the applet's display area. If this width is less than or equal to 600 pixels, line 232 sets **packComponents** to **true**. Otherwise, line 234 sets **packComponents** to **false**.

The rest of the initialization code uses **packComponents** to make sure that the user interface is well laid out even when the display area is less than 600 pixels wide. When **packComponents** is **true**, the initialization code packs the components closer together. This is done by shortening text input areas and using smaller fonts. For example, lines 246 through 250 define a text input area (where the user enters the search text) and add it to a **Panel** object named **p**:

```
246        if (packComponents)
247            inputArea = new TextField ("",15);
248        else
249            inputArea = new TextField ("",20);
250        p.add (inputArea);
```

Notice that when **packComponents** is **true**, line 247 specifies a text field that is 15 characters wide; otherwise, line 249 creates a 20-character-wide text field.

Along the top of the user interface, there is a label followed by a text field and then three buttons—**search**, **clear**, and **stop**—that allow the user to initiate a search, clear the search text, or stop the search. The applet uses the methods **enableButtons()**, shown in lines 380 through 384, and **disableButtons()**, shown in lines 388 through 392, to enable or disable the **search** and **clear** buttons. For example, the **search** and **clear** buttons are initially disabled; they are enabled as soon as the user enters the search text.

To the right of the buttons, there is a **Label** component with the **Max Pages:** label followed by a **Choice** component that lets the user set the maximum number of pages to search.

To display the search results, the applet uses a **List** component that can display a scrolling list of text items. Line 301 creates the **List** component:

```
301        resultsArea = new List (10,false);
```

The first argument to the **List()** constructor indicates that there are 10 visible lines; the second argument specifies that the user cannot select multiple lines from the **List**.

PROGRAMMER'S NOTE *If you try to compile **HomePageSearch.java** in Java 2, you'll get errors because Java 2 includes an interface named **List** (in the **java.util** package). This makes the name **List** ambiguous to the Java 2 compiler. To avoid this problem, change all occurrences of **List** to **java.awt.List**—this makes it clear that the code is referring to the **List** component class and not the **List** interface.*

Underneath this **List** is another line of components that show the version number, the status of the search (how many pages have been searched or the number of matches found), and three checkboxes that control how the search is performed. Lines 307 through 348 prepare this part of the user interface.

The rest of the **init()** method sets the colors and initializes the **Vector** objects **pageNames** and **pageMatch** that will be used to hold the pages that have been found and pages that contain the search text.

SEARCH INITIATION IN HOMEPAGESEARCH   The user prepares for a search by typing the search text into the text field at the top of the applet's display area. The **HomePageSearch** applet handles events by using the older Java 1.0 approach, in which all keyboard events are handled by a method named **keyDown()**.

The **keyDown()** method, shown in lines 493 through 522, is called whenever the user types something in the text field. Lines 496 through 499 get the current contents of the text field:

```
496        String text;
497
498        text = inputArea.getText();      // Read the search text
499        int n = text.length();           // Count number of chars
```

Lines 501 through 510 then reduce the number of characters by 1 if the current key is a BACKSPACE. Once there is more than one character in the text field, the **keyDown()** method also enables the **search** and **clear** buttons by calling **enableButtons()**.

To initiate the search, the user clicks on the **search** button. In **HomePageSearch**, mouse clicks on all user interface components are handled by the **action()** method, shown in lines 525 through 672 (this is Java 1.0–style event handling for mouse clicks on the user interface). The **action()** method checks where the mouse click occurred and then takes appropriate action.

Lines 566 through 591 contain the code that handles mouse clicks on the **search** button. This is where the search gets started. First, line 570 gets the search text from the **TextField** component named **inputArea**:

```
570            text = inputArea.getText();
```

Lines 577 and 578 clear out the **List** component named **resultsArea** that will hold the results of the search:

```
577            if (resultsArea.countItems() > 0)
578                resultsArea.clear();
```

Then line 580 disables the **search** and **clear** buttons by calling **disableButtons()**, and line 581 enables the **abort** button:

```
580                    disableButtons ();
581                    abort.enable();
```

This is done because once the search starts, the user does not have to click the **search** and **clear** buttons anymore. On the other hand, the **abort** button is enabled because the user may want to cancel the search.

Next lines 585 and 586 remove all previous pages from the **Vector** objects that store the pages being searched and the pages that contain the search text:

```
585                    pageNames.removeAllElements();
586                    pageMatch.removeAllElements();
```

Finally, lines 589 and 590 create a **SearchPages** thread and start running that thread:

```
589                    cp = new SearchPages (this, hostName, text, maxSearch);
590                    cp.start();
```

Note that the first argument to the **SearchPages()** constructor is the **HomePageSearch** applet itself. This is needed because the **SearchPages** class uses the variables and methods in **HomePageSearch** to perform a search and store the search results.

The code that does the actual work of downloading and searching the Web pages is in the **SearchPages** class, which is described in the next section.

THE RUN() METHOD OF THE SEARCHPAGES CLASS   The **SearchPages** class, shown in lines 819 through 1453, is a subclass of **Thread**. When the thread's **start()** method is called from the **HomeSearchPage** class in line 590, the code in the **run()** method of the **SearchPages** class starts executing.

The **run()** method, shown in lines 861 through 884, performs the search by calling the **startSearch()** method. However, before starting the search, the **run()** method performs a few additional tasks to prepare for the search.

Line 865 sets the **topLevelSearch** variable to the constant **FIND_TOP_LEVEL_PAGES**:

```
865            topLevelSearch = FIND_TOP_LEVEL_PAGES;
```

The **topLevelSearch** variable controls what goes on during the search. Setting it to **FIND_TOP_LEVEL_PAGES** means that the **startSearch()** method should search for all of the links on the home page (the home page is the HTML file specified by the **indexName** parameter) and save these links in an array.

The **SearchPages** class uses two **Vector** objects—**topLevelPages** and **nextLevelPages**—to store the URLs of Web pages found on the home page and the lower-level pages. Lines 867 and 868 define these two **Vector** objects:

```
867            topLevelPages = new Vector();
868            nextLevelPages = new Vector();
```

In the final step before the search, line 872 calls the **detectProxyServer()** method to detect whether the applet is accessing the Web server through a proxy server:

```
872        proxyDetected = detectProxyServer();
```

A proxy server (also referred to as application gateway) acts as an intermediary between a protected network and the Internet. In the case of the World Wide Web, the Web browser essentially communicates with any Web server through the proxy server. Depending on a company's security policy, the proxy server can screen those requests and disallow some of them. Because the **HomePageSearch** applet runs in the Web browser, it will also have to go through the proxy server when it tries to download Web pages to perform the search. The **detectProxyServer()** method, shown in lines 891 through 929, attempts to detect the presence of a proxy server by trying to open a connection to the Web server. You'll see a lot of different URL strings being used in the **detectProxyServer()** method, but the one of interest to us is the URL string constructed in line 909:

```
909            url = app.server + app.indexName;
```

This is the URL string corresponding to the **server** and **indexName** parameters. The **app** object refers to the **HomePageSearch** applet where these strings are defined. Lines 913 through 917 attempt to open the Web page specified by the **url** string:

```
913        try
914        {
915            URL doc = new URL (url);
916            dis = new DataInputStream (doc.openStream());
917        }
```

Line 915 creates a **URL** object, and line 916 opens a **DataInputStream** using that **URL** object. If this fails, the **catch** block in lines 918 through 925 returns **true** to indicate that the applet is trying to access the Web server through a proxy server:

```
918        catch (Exception e)
919        {
920            // Unable to connect. This may be an incorrect applet
921            // parameter. Let's assume, though, that it's a proxy server
922            // that's stopping us using the hostname.
923
924            return true;
925        }
```

As the comments on lines 920 through 922 show, the connection could fail due to bad **server** and **indexName** parameters. However, if those parameters are correct, the failure could be because of a proxy server.

Getting back to the **run()** method again, after these preliminary preparations, line 874 calls **startSearch()** to perform the search:

```
874        startSearch();
```

AN OVERVIEW OF WEB PAGE SEARCHES   The **startSearch()** method, shown in lines 931 through 1043, orchestrates the Web page searches. The search is performed in three steps:

1. Call **searchPage()** to search the home page (the **index.html** file or the file specified by the **indexName** parameter) for any lines that contain the search text. Add the matching lines of text to the results list in the applet. Look for links and save any local links in the **Vector** named **topLevelPages** to be searched during later steps. Note that local links are URLs (appearing in <A> tags) that refer to the same Web site as the one where the home page is located. During this step, the **topLevelSearch** variable has **FIND_TOP_LEVEL_PAGES** as its value. After this step, the **topLevelSearch** variable is set to **SEARCH_TOP_LEVEL_PAGES**.

2. Go through all URL strings stored in the **topLevelPages** array, download each one, and search for any lines that contain the search text. If any page contains the text, add it to the list of matches in the applet's display area. Look for any links, and save the local links in the **nextLevelPages** array. After this step, set the **topLevelSearch** variable to **SEARCH_OTHER_PAGES**.

3. Go through all of the URL strings in the **nextLevelPages** array, download each one, and look for lines containing the search text. Add any matching lines to the results list in the applet's display area. For any local links, this step calls **searchPage()**, thus repeating steps 1 through 3 for each link. This step recursively searches the links on each page until there are no more links to search.

Of course, in all of these steps, the **startSearch()** method counts the number of pages that have been searched. As soon as that count exceeds the value stored in **maxPages**, the method returns.

The end result of the three-step search process is that all of the local links, starting with the ones on the home page, are searched for the text specified by the user. Figure 6-10 illustrates the search sequence for a hypothetical home page with a number of links. The rectangles represent Web pages, and the lines are hypertext links. The numbered circles show the sequence in which these pages are searched. The horizontal lines divide the search sequence into the three steps corresponding to the three values of the **toplevelSearch** variable—**FIND_TOP_LEVEL_PAGES**, **SEARCH_TOP_LEVEL_PAGES**, and **SEARCH_OTHER_PAGES**.

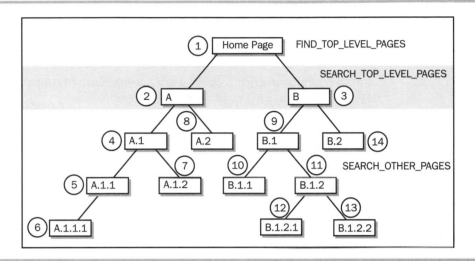

FIGURE 6-10. A Web page search sequence in the **SearchPages** class.

WEB PAGE SEARCHING IN THE SEARCHPAGES CLASS   Before calling other methods to perform the text search, the **startSearch()** method opens a connection to the Web server and gets ready to read the home page. The first part of the **startSearch()** method constructs the URL string for the Web page for a variety of special cases. The case of interest to us is the one in which the **server** and **indexName** parameters are specified in the **<APPLET>** tag, because this is the most general case when the applet is being used at a typical Web site. The other cases are for various types of use within the **demon.co.uk** domain (the applet author's Internet domain). Line 962 constructs the URL string for the case of interest:

962   `url[0] = app.server + app.indexName;`

For some cases, the method constructs two URL strings—**url[0]** and **url[1]**. Lines 984 through 1003 show a **for** loop that tries to open a connection using each of these URL strings. The method uses whichever connection is successful.

If the home page is opened successfully, line 1015 calls the **searchPage()** method to search that page and save all of the links to be searched next:

1015   `searchPage (dis,currentPageName);`

Here **dis** refers to the **DataInputStream** for the connection, and **currentPageName** is the URL string for the home page.

The **seachPage()** method, shown in lines 1047 through 1102, uses a **while** loop to read and process one line at a time from the specified Web page. The following listing shows the skeleton of the **while** loop with comments that summarize the processing steps performed for each line of text:

```
1059        while ((input = dis.readLine()) != null)
1060        {
            // Convert input to upper case, look for <TITLE>
            // tag, check if input contains search text,
            // check if input contains a link (<A>), and handle
            // the link depending on the current value of
            // the topLevelSearch variable.
1096        }
```

Line 1063 converts the input to uppercase and saves it in a separate **String** variable. The uppercase input is used to search for the HTML tags such as **<TITLE>** and **<A>**, which can be in mixed case:

```
1063        upperCaseInput = input.toUpperCase();
```

Line 1066 calls **parseForTitle()** to extract the title from the uppercase input, if the line happens to contain the **<TITLE>** tag:

```
1066        temp = parseForTitle (input, upperCaseInput, dis);
```

After a title has been found, line 1075 calls the **checkMatch()** method to see if the original input line contains the search text:

```
1075        checkMatch (input, url, title);
```

If **checkMatch()** finds any line with the matching text, it calls the **HomePageSearch** applet's **addToList()** method to insert the Web page title and the matching line into the list that displays the results of the search.

Line 1079 calls **parseForLink()** to find any links in the uppercase version of the input line:

```
1079        link = parseForLink (upperCaseInput, input);
```

Links are embedded in **<A>** tags and are of the following form:

```
<A HREF="http://java.sun.com">Java</a>
```

The **parseForLink()** method extracts the URL within quotes following the **HREF** attribute and returns it as a **String**.

If a link is found, the next step depends on the value of the **topLevelSearch** variable:

◆ If **topLevelSearch** is **FIND_TOP_LEVEL_PAGES**, line 1089 saves the link in the **topLevelPages** array. These are processed in the second step, when **startSearch()** goes through these links and calls **checkLink()** for each one.

◆ If **topLevelSearch** is **SEARCH_TOP_LEVEL_PAGES**, line 1091 saves the link in the **nextLevelPages** array. These are processed in the third step, when **startSearch()** goes through these links and calls **checkLink()** for each one.

◆ Otherwise, **topLevelSearch** is **SEARCH_OTHER_PAGES**, and line 1093 calls the **checkLink()** method to process the link.

The **checkLink()** method, shown in lines 1337 through 1451, ignores links whose URL begins with text such as **ftp:**, **news:**, **mailto:**, and so on that are not HTTP links used to download HTML pages. It also ignores any external links. It then ensures that the link refers to an HTML file or to a text file (valid filenames end with **.html**, **.htm**, **.txt**, and **.phtml**).

If it's a valid link, **checkLink()** adds the link to the array of visited links by calling the **incrementPages()** method of the **HomePageSearch** applet. Then it opens a connection to that link. Finally, line 1444 of the **checkLink()** method calls **searchPage()** to search through that link:

```
1444            searchPage (dis, link);
```

Because **checkLink()** was initially called from **searchPage()**, this is an example of recursion, where a method calls itself. This causes all of the processing steps in the **searchPage()** method to be performed for this link. If the HTML file corresponding to this link has other links, **searchPage()** will be called for each of those links as well. The end result is that the **seachPage()** method downloads and searches all of the links for the search text.

## PART 2

JavaBeans

Visible Java Beans

Invisible Java Beans

Visible Java Beans

Chapters 1 through 6 cover a wide variety of Java applets. Applets are an important class of Java programs because they allow Java-capable Web browsers to be used as universal clients. Developers can implement custom processing in one or more applets, and these applets can execute in any Java-capable Web browser. This chapter introduces Java *beans*—Java software components that can be visually manipulated, customized, and assembled into applications in Java application builder tools such as Symantec's Visual Cafe, IBM's Visual Age for Java, Inprise Corporation's JBuilder, SunSoft's Java Workshop, and many others.

Many Java beans are simple GUI (graphical user interface) elements, such as buttons and gauges. Others are more complex objects, such as a spreadsheet or a text editor. Many beans—for example, the GUI elements—have a visual representation, but there are beans (called *invisible beans*) that do not have any visual representation at all. For example, a Java bean might implement an algorithm that simply transforms some input data into some other output data according to the algorithm. This chapter shows examples of visible Java beans; the next chapter presents some invisible beans.

Regardless of whether a bean has a visual representation or not, all Java beans can be visually manipulated in an application builder tool. That's because all Java beans follow the JavaBeans software component model, which specifies a standard interface that lets other Java code invoke a bean's methods and access and manipulate the bean's properties (these are the bean's data).

PROGRAMMER'S NOTE *The term* JavaBeans *refers to the* Java *software component model. The term* Java bean, *or simply* bean, *refers to a software component that conforms to the JavaBeans component model.*

Because the Java software component is a relatively new and important concept, this chapter starts with a brief description of Sun's Java Bean Development Kit (BDK), followed by an overview of the JavaBeans specification and the structure of typical beans. After that, I present two simple GUI beans:

- **RainbowRuler**—A bean that displays an animated rainbow-colored horizontal ruler

- **CalendarJ**—A bean that displays a calendar that makes the user-selected date available via events

The Bean Development Kit

Before you start learning about the JavaBeans specification and various details of the JavaBeans application programming interface (API), you should experience how a developer might use a Java bean. Seeing some beans in action will help you understand why beans are useful and why they must support certain features.

Installing the BDK

To experience Java beans firsthand, you need an application builder tool and some Java beans. If you already have such a builder tool, you may have seen how to use beans. In that case you do not need to go through this section. If you don't have a builder tool, Sun provides a sample tool called the **BeanBox** with the BDK, which you can download from Sun's Web site at **http://java.sun.com/beans/software/ bdk_download.html**. Follow the instructions on that Web page to download the BDK. The Windows version of BDK is distributed as an executable (.**exe**) file that's nearly 4MB in size.

Note that to use the BDK, you need to have the Java Development Kit (JDK) version 1.1 or later installed on your system. (The JDK is available from **http://java.sun.com/products/**.) To install the BDK on a Windows system, simply run the .**exe** file that you have downloaded.

The BDK includes the JavaBeans API, the **BeanBox** application to test beans and create applets, and some sample beans complete with source code. To see beans in action, you have to run the **BeanBox**.

Using the BeanBox

The **BeanBox** is a Java application that acts as a container for beans. In Microsoft Windows, you can run the **BeanBox** from an MS-DOS window. First, change to the **BeanBox** subdirectory of the location in which you installed the BDK, and then type **run**. For example, if you installed the BDK in the default directory of **c:\bdk**, you would type the following commands in the MS-DOS window:

```
c:
cd \bdk\beanbox
run
```

The **run** command executes the **Run.bat** file, which sets the **CLASSPATH** environment variable with the following command:

```
set CLASSPATH=classes;\JavaScope.zip;infobus.jar
```

It then starts the **BeanBox** with the command

```
java sun.beanbox.BeanBoxFrame
```

When the **BeanBox** starts, you will see three windows, as shown in Figure 7-1. On the left is a ToolBox window that lists a number of Java beans. Some of the beans have icons that appear to the left of the bean's name. The larger window in the middle is the **BeanBox** work area. It's a simple container for beans. This is where

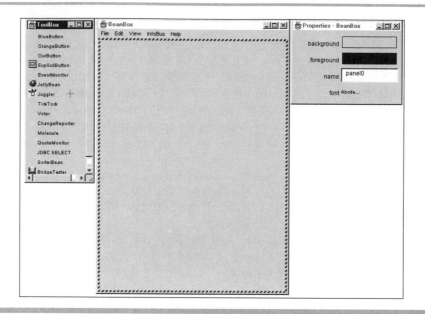

FIGURE 7-1. Initial windows displayed by the **BeanBox.**

The Duke logo is a trademark or registered trademark of Sun Microsystems, Inc. in the United States and other countries.

you will place beans and connect them to create applets. The Properties window on the right shows the attributes of the currently selected Java bean. In this case, the Properties window shows the attributes of the empty panel in the BeanBox window.

To try out some Java beans, perform these steps:

1. Click on the **Juggler** bean in the ToolBox window. The mouse pointer changes to a crosshair.

2. Position the crosshair in the BeanBox window and click once. The **Juggler** bean appears and starts juggling three beans. The Properties window shows the **Juggler** bean's properties.

3. Click on the **OrangeButton** bean and place it in the BeanBox window, underneath the **Juggler** bean. An orange button labeled Press appears.

4. The Properties window shows the **OrangeButton** bean's attributes. One of the attributes is the button's label. Click on the text field next to the label and change the string from Press to Stop.

5. Click the Edit->Events->Button Push-> actionPerformed menu item. A red line appears from the **OrangeButton** bean. The line moves as you move the mouse.

6. Move the mouse onto the **Juggler** bean and click. The red line disappears, and a dialog box with a list of methods appears. Click on the **stopJuggling** method, and then click OK. A message appears that says "Generating and compiling adaptor class," and after a while the dialog box goes away. This step generates the code needed to associate the button press with the **stopJuggling** method of the **Juggler** bean. This means that when you click the button labeled Stop, the **Juggler** bean will stop juggling.

7. Select the **BlueButton** bean from the ToolBox window, place it next to the **OrangeButton**, and change its label to Start. Also, click on the Foreground attribute in the Properties window and change the foreground color to white.

8. Using steps similar to steps 5 and 6, associate the **actionPerformed** event of the Start button with the **startJuggling** method of the **Juggler** bean.

After you complete steps 1 through 8, the three beans appear in the BeanBox window, as shown in Figure 7-2. Try out the Start and Stop buttons. When you click on the Start button, the **Juggler** starts juggling. It stops juggling when you click on the Stop button.

The next step is to create an applet from these three beans that you have connected together in the **BeanBox**. To create an applet, select MakeApplet from the File menu in the BeanBox window. A dialog box appears showing you the default name of the applet and the location of the Jar file (this is a Java archive file that will store the applet's code). You can simply accept the default names and click the OK button. You will see a message stating that the applet's code is being generated and

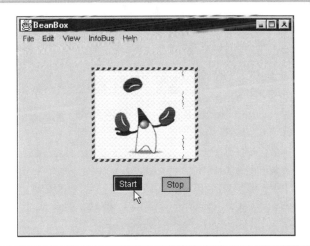

FIGURE 7-2. The **Juggler** bean with Start and Stop buttons.

The Duke logo is a trademark or registered trademark of Sun Microsystems, Inc. in the United States and other countries.

compiled. After completing this step, you can quit the **BeanBox** by selecting Exit from the File menu.

By default, all of the files needed for the new applet will be in the **c:\bdk\beanbox\tmp\myApplet** directory (assuming that you installed the BDK in the **c:\bdk** directory). That directory will have all of the Jar files as well as an HTML file, **myApplet.html**, that you can use to try out the applet. You can use the **appletviewer** tool (included with Sun's JDK) to test the newly generated applet. Change the directory to **c:\bdk\beanbox\tmp\myApplet**, and type **appletviewer myApplet.html** to run the applet. Figure 7-3 shows the resulting **appletviewer** window. You should be able to stop and start the juggling by clicking on the Stop and Start buttons.

As you can see from this session with the **BeanBox**, you can use Java beans to create an applet without writing a single line of code.

PROGRAMMER'S NOTE   *If, after running the **BeanBox**, you have trouble compiling Java programs with the JDK's **java** command, you should unset the **CLASSPATH** environment variable. In the MS-DOS Prompt window, type **set CLASSPATH=** to unset the **CLASSPATH** variable.*

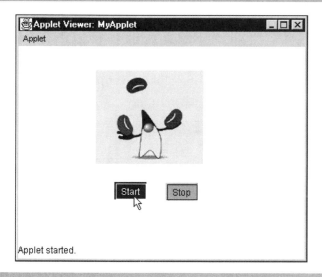

FIGURE 7-3.   Running the newly generated applet in **appletviewer**.

The Duke logo is a trademark or registered trademark of Sun Microsystems, Inc. in the United States and other countries.

The JavaBeans Component Model

JavaBeans is a specification for software components (called beans) written in Java. Like everything else in Java, these software components are objects that are implemented by Java classes. However, software components differ from other objects in that an application builder tool can manipulate and assemble the components into an application without having to recompile the component's code. This is similar to the way one would build a hardware component such as a PC. You can build a PC by buying the various components, from the motherboard to disk drives and a power supply, and then connecting everything together. Building an application with software components is supposed to work the same way.

Hardware components work because each component has well-defined interfaces. The same is true for software components; they need standard interfaces so that different software components can be connected to one another in applications. This is where the JavaBeans specification comes in. JavaBeans specifies how developers can write the software components and distribute them in the form of compiled Java bytecode (that's the object code of the Java Virtual Machine). The idea is to create a market for Java software components that can be easily plugged into applications.

The concept of such software components is not new. Microsoft Visual Basic, Inprise (formerly Borland) Delphi, Sybase PowerBuilder, TI Composer, and Forté are some well-known systems that support software components. Visual Basic programmers have been using VBX (Visual Basic Extensions) components for years. Although originally designed for custom controls (user interface components such as dialog boxes), enterprising software developers discovered that they could use the VBX architecture to package a variety of software as reusable components. Soon there were many different types of VBXs that offered a variety of add-on capabilities, such as text editing, image processing, database access, facsimile (FAX) send/receive, and various types of graphing and charting. Because the VBX architecture is closely tied to 16-bit Windows, Microsoft came up with OLE (Object Linking and Embedding) Custom Controls (OCX) as the successor to VBX in the 32-bit Windows world. You probably know of OCX by its new name — ActiveX. Developers writing ActiveX components follow Microsoft's Component Object Model (COM).

Java beans are software components just like ActiveX components. The advantage of Java beans is that they are written in Java and, therefore, can be used wherever a Java Virtual Machine is available.

Understanding Java Bean Characteristics

The JavaBeans specification essentially lays out the API for the Java software components, called beans. All Java beans support the following features:

◆ **Introspection** allows application builder tools or any Java class to find out the methods, properties, and events of a bean. To support introspection, beans must use standard naming conventions for methods used to get or set properties. Builder tools use the Java Core Reflection APIs to analyze the methods of a bean to figure out a bean's properties and events. You can also provide a bean information class along with the other bean classes.

◆ **Customization** allows a developer to visually alter the behavior or appearance of a bean in an application builder tool. Application builder tools display property sheets with a bean's properties and allow the developer to edit those properties. Developers can also include a **Customizer** class that can provide a GUI-based interface to edit the bean's properties.

◆ **Events** are used by a bean to communicate with other beans. Beans use the Java 1.1 event model, in which an event source generates events and one or more listeners provide methods that handle the event. An event source, such as a Java bean, has to provide a way of registering and unregistering event listeners. In an application builder, you can connect a bean's event to another bean's methods. The events provide a way to connect beans and send information from one bean to another.

◆ **Properties** are the attributes of a bean that control a bean's behavior or appearance. For example, the properties of a button bean would include its color, label, and font. Properties are a bean's data elements that can be accessed through public methods of the bean class. Developers can change the properties through customization.

◆ **Persistence** refers to the ability to modify a bean's properties and then save its state for future use. Because a bean is customizable, it must be able to save and restore its customized properties. For example, a developer might alter a button bean's label and color in an application builder tool and then save that bean for future use. When that button is loaded the next time, it should appear with the changed label and color. Persistence makes this possible. Beans support persistence by implementing the **Serializable** interface.

Most of these features, such as introspection and customization, are designed to allow an application builder tool to access and manipulate beans. However, Java beans can be used directly by human programmers. After all, a bean is simply a Java class that follows some rules.

PROGRAMMER'S NOTE *This is not a tutorial about the JavaBeans specification. The complete JavaBeans specification is available at **http://java.sun.com/beans/spec.html**. You can download the document in either PostScript or Adobe's Portable Document Format (PDF). On the same Web page, you will also find a link to download a 30-page tutorial about the BDK.*

Understanding Java Bean Structure

A Java bean is simply a class that follows some specific rules. This section gives you an overview of the typical form of a Java bean. As you will see, you can easily convert an existing Java class or an applet into a Java bean.

For a typical visible Java bean, you have to declare the bean as a subclass of **java.awt.Component** so that it can be placed inside other components such as **Panel**. The bean can be declared as a subclass of **Component** or any subclass of **Component**. For example, the **Applet** class is a subclass of **Component** (to be precise, the exact subclass sequence is **java.awt.Component->java.awt.Container->java.awt.Panel->java.applet.Applet**). This means that you can convert a Java applet into a Java bean.

You should use the **package** statement to assign a package name to the bean. Many application builder tools require a package name for a bean before you can use that bean in that tool. Note that the **package** statement must be the first noncomment statement in a Java file. Also, the package name implies a directory structure for the location of the Java class. For example, if you give a bean the package name **beans.demo.calendar**, that bean's source file and class file should be in the **beans\demo\calendar** subdirectory (in a Windows system).

To support persistence, the Java bean should implement the **java.io.Serializable** interface. Because the **java.awt.Component** class already implements the **Serializable** interface, your Java bean class does not have to provide the **writeObject()** and **readObject()** methods that the interface requires. You do have to provide a constructor that takes no arguments. For example, if you are defining the **MyBean** class, you have to provide a **MyBean()** constructor.

You also have to attend to another detail related to persistence. You should use the **transient** keyword to qualify information that does not have to be saved along with the bean. For example, if your bean creates an **Image** object and uses a **Thread** for animation, those objects should be declared as **transient**:

```
private transient Image image;
private transient Thread animationThread;
```

You should declare all variables as **private** and provide public methods to get and set the values of those variables that have to be manipulated to make the bean work. For example, if the bean has a background color variable named **bgColor** and you want the application developer to manipulate that variable using the property name **backGround**, you would define the get and set methods as follows:

```
private Color bgColor;
public void setBackGroundColor(Color c)
{
    bgColor = c;
    // Other code to actually change the bean's background color
}
public Color getBackGroundColor() { return bgColor; }
```

The naming convention is very important. Note that the first letter of the property name is capitalized and that name is then appended to the words *get* and *set* to arrive at the method names. Also note that the internal variable name need not match the property name that you choose to expose to the application developers who use the bean.

Beans communicate using events. In a builder tool, an application developer may tie events of one bean to any public methods in your bean. Conversely, your bean can send information to other beans by generating events. You would use an event object, which is a subclass of **java.util.EventObject**, to package the information. You then have to use public methods to add and remove listeners. Typically, you would store the registered listeners in a **Vector**. When the event occurs, your bean should call each of the registered listeners. For example, if you are writing a calendar bean (that allows users to select a date from a calendar), you might define an event called **DateEvent**. You would also define a **DateListener** interface that specifies the functions that the **DateEvent** listeners must implement. Finally, you would define public methods named **addDateListener()** and **removeDateListener()** that can be called to register and unregister objects that want to receive events from your bean.

When you write a bean, you should always assume that the bean will be running in a multithreaded environment. This means that several threads may be simultaneously calling methods in the bean and setting properties. You must ensure that the bean behaves properly in such an environment. You should use the **synchronized** keyword to protect sections of code that should not be accessed by multiple threads at the same time. In particular, you must be careful when handling events. For example, suppose you use a **Vector dateListeners** to store the **DateListener** objects in the calendar bean example. You would use the **synchronized** qualifier for the **addDateListener()** and **removeDateListener()** methods as follows:

```
public synchronized void addDateListener(DateListener l)
{
    dateListeners.addElement(l);
}
public synchronized void removeDateListener(DateListener l)
{
    dateListeners.removeElement(l);
}
```

Another important programming point is to make a copy of the **Vector** of registered listeners before sending the events to those listeners. For the calendar bean example, here is how you might do this in a **sendDateEvent()** method that sends a date change notification to all **DateListener** objects stored in a vector:

```
public void fireAction()
{
    Vector l;
    synchronized(this)    // protected section of code
    {  // Make a copy of the listener vector
        l = (Vector)dateListeners.clone();
    }
    // Create a DateEvent object with the new date
    DateEvent dateEvt = new DateEvent(this);
    // Call the dateChanged() method of each registered listener
    for(int i = 0; i < l.size(); i++)
    {
        DateListener target = (ActionListener)l.elementAt(i);
        target.dateChanged(dateEvt);
    }
}
```

Note that the code that copies the **Vector dateListeners** is protected from multiple thread access by using the **synchronized** keyword.

The final step in getting a bean ready for use is to compile its source files and package the compiled class files into a Jar file. (A Jar file is a Zip-format archive file.) As with a Zip archive, you can use a Jar file to store any type of file. When you package Java beans in a Jar file, you must include a manifest file, which is a text file that identifies the classes for each bean. For example, if you are creating a Java bean named **MyBean** with a package named **sample.mybean**, you should first compile the source file **MyBean.java** and place that file in the **sample\mybean** directory. Next, you would create a manifest file, **mybean.mf**, containing the following lines:

```
Name: sample/mybean/MyBean.class
Java-Bean: True
```

Note that you must use a forward slash (/) as the directory name separator, even if you are on a Windows system where the backslash character (\) is normally used to separate directory names. Assuming that you have Sun's JDK (which includes the **jar** utility program to create Jar files) installed, you can then prepare the **mybean.jar** file with the following command:

```
jar cfm mybean.jar mybean.mf sample\mybean\MyBean.class
```

The **mybean.jar** file is what you would provide to anyone who wants to use the Java bean named **MyBean**. You will see an example of a manifest file in the next section.

A Bean That Displays a Rainbow-Colored Ruler

This section shows you how to convert an applet into a Java bean. Specifically, I take a simple applet—the **RainbowRuler** applet from Chapter 1, which displays an animated rainbow-colored horizontal ruler—and convert that applet into a Java bean. I will explain the code later. First you should try out the bean in an application builder tool and learn how to compile and package the bean in a Jar file.

Using the RainbowRuler Bean

The files for the **RainbowRuler** bean are in the **ch07\hruler** directory of the companion CD-ROM. To try out the bean, you need an application builder tool. In this section, I explain how to use the bean in Sun's **BeanBox** application, which Sun provides with the BDK (see the section "The Bean Development Kit" earlier in this chapter). If you are using some other Java application builder tool, you should install the bean following that tool's instructions.

The **RainbowRuler** bean is packaged in the **hruler.jar** file (the **.jar** extension is used for Java archive files created using the **jar** utility program). As you can see, the Jar file containing a bean can have an arbitrary name (it does not have to match the name of the Java bean). In fact, a Jar file can contain more than one Java bean; it can also contain any image files that the beans might need.

To use the **RainbowRuler** bean in the **BeanBox**, copy the **hruler.jar** file from the CD-ROM's **ch07\hruler** directory to the **jars** subdirectory of the location in which you have installed the BDK. For example, if you installed the BDK in the default location (**c:\bdk**), you can copy the Jar file with the command **copy X:\ch07\hruler\hruler.jar c:\bdk\jars**, where *X* is the drive letter for your CD-ROM drive.

After you copy the **hruler.jar** file to the BDK's **jars** subdirectory, open an MS-DOS window and start the **BeanBox** by changing the directory to **c:\bdk\beanbox** and then typing the **run** command. You will see the ToolBox, BeanBox, and Properties windows, as shown previously in Figure 7-1. Note, however, that the list of beans in the ToolBox window now includes **RainbowRuler**. Click on the **RainbowRuler** item in the ToolBox, and then click somewhere in the BeanBox window. The **RainbowRuler** bean appears in the BeanBox window, as shown in Figure 7-4. The bean displays a rainbow-colored horizontal ruler with the colors gradually shifting to the right. You can use the Properties window to change various properties of the **RainbowRuler** bean. For example, if you change the **moveRight** property to **false**, the colors will begin moving to the left. You can add several instances of **RainbowRuler** beans to the **BeanBox**. Following the steps outlined in the section "Using the BeanBox," you can also create applets that include the **RainbowRuler** bean.

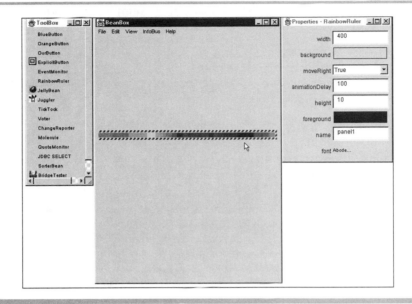

FIGURE 7-4. Adding the **RainbowRuler** bean to the **BeanBox**.

The Duke logo is a trademark or registered trademark of Sun Microsystems, Inc. in the United States and other countries.

Because Java beans are relatively new, you may want to learn the steps involved in compiling and packaging a bean. For the **RainbowRuler** bean, the source file **RainbowRuler.java** and the manifest file **hruler.mf** are in the **ch07\hruler** directory of the companion CD-ROM. You can follow these steps to compile and package the **RainbowRuler** bean in the **hruler.jar** file:

1. Copy **RainbowRuler.java** and **hruler.mf** files to some directory on your hard drive. (As you might have guessed, this step is necessary because you cannot create any new files on the CD-ROM, as it's a read-only medium.)

2. Assuming that you have Sun's JDK installed, compile the file with the **javac RainbowRuler.java** command.

3. Because **RainbowRuler** uses **ch07.hruler** as the package name, create the **ch07\hruler** subdirectory (in the hard drive directory where you have placed **RainbowRuler.java**).

4. Copy the **RainbowRuler.class** file to the **ch07\hruler** subdirectory.

5. Create the Jar file with the command **jar cfm hruler.jar hruler.mf ch07\hruler\RainbowRuler.class**.

When I am creating a new bean, I usually place all of the commands in a batch file so that I can compile the bean, create the Jar file, and copy the file to the BDK's

jars directory. For instance, the batch file for this example, **makejar.bat**, contains the following commands:

```
javac RainbowRuler.java
copy RainbowRuler.class ch07\hruler
jar cfm hruler.jar hruler.mf ch07\hruler\RainbowRuler.class
copy hruler.jar c:\bdk\jars
```

For a larger project, you would want to use a makefile to compile only those files that have changed, but for small projects this approach works fine. Note that you need the **make** (or Microsoft **nmake**) utility if you decide to use a makefile.

PROGRAMMER'S NOTE   *If you are familiar with makefiles and want to use them to compile and package beans, you can download Microsoft's* **nmake** *utility from* **ftp://ftp.microsoft.com/Softlib/ MSLFILES/nmake15.exe** *(it's a 50K file). The* **nmake15.exe** *file is a self-extracting archive; just run it to extract the* **nmake.exe** *file—the executable file for the* **nmake** *utility. If you want to see samples of makefiles, look in the demo subdirectory of the BDK (if you installed it in* **C:\BDK**, *look at the* **c:\bdk\demo** *directory). In that directory you will find the makefiles for the sample beans that Sun distributes with the BDK.*

The manifest file, **hruler.mf**, contains the following lines of text:

```
Name: ch07/hruler/RainbowRuler.class
Java-Bean: True
```

The first line specifies the name of the Java bean class file, with the package name added as the directory path. The second line indicates that this is a Java bean. When you create a Jar file with Java beans, the manifest file is the first file in the list of files being added to the archive.

RainbowRuler

Understanding the RainbowRuler Bean

Now that you have seen the **RainbowRuler** bean in action, you will want to study its source code. The following listing shows the **RainbowRuler.java** file that implements the bean. I explain the source code in subsequent sections.

```
1  //-------------------------------------------------------------------
2  // RainbowRuler.java
3  //
4  // A Java bean that displays an animated rainbow-colored
5  // horizontal ruler.
6  //
7  // Author: Naba Barkakati, January 1999
8  //-------------------------------------------------------------------
```

```
 9 package ch07.hruler;
10 import java.awt.*;
11 import java.applet.Applet;
12 public class RainbowRuler extends Applet implements Runnable
13 {
14     private int appletWidth=400, appletHeight=10;
15     private int delay = 100;
16     private int shift = 4;
17     private boolean stopped = false;
18     private boolean moveRight = true;
19     private transient int offset;
20     private transient Thread colorShiftThread = null;
21     private transient Image oIm = null;
22     private transient Graphics oGC = null;
23     //-----------------------------------------------------------
24     /** Starts the applet by starting the animation thread */
25     public void start()
26     {
27         if(colorShiftThread == null)
28         {
29             colorShiftThread = new Thread(this);
30             colorShiftThread.start();
31         }
32         stopped = false;
33     }
34     //-----------------------------------------------------------
35     /** Stops the applet by stopping the animation thread */
36     public void stop()
37     {
38         stopped = true;
39     }
40     //-----------------------------------------------------------
41     /** Update the display by calling paint() */
42     public void update(Graphics g) { paint(g);}
43     //-----------------------------------------------------------
44     /** Copies appropriate parts of off-screen image to applet */
45     public synchronized void paint(Graphics g)
46     {
47         if (oIm != null)
48         {
49             g.drawImage(oIm, -offset, 0, this);
50             g.drawImage(oIm, appletWidth-offset, 0, this);
51         }
```

```
52          else
53              makeNewImage();  // create the off-screen image
54      }
55      //------------------------------------------------------------
56      /** Animate the ruler by repainting at regular intervals */
57      public void run()
58      {
59          while(!stopped)
60          {
61              repaint();
62              if(moveRight)
63              {
64                  offset -= shift;
65                  if(offset < 0) offset = appletWidth;
66              }
67              else
68              {
69                  offset += shift;
70                  if (offset >= appletWidth) offset = 0;
71              }
72              try
73              {
74                  // Sleep until it's time for next repainting
75                  Thread.sleep(delay);
76              }
77              catch(InterruptedException e){}
78          }
79      }
80      //------------------------------------------------------------
81      /** Creates a new off-screen rainbow-colored image */
82      private void makeNewImage()
83      {
84          if(oGC != null) oGC.dispose();
85          if(oIm != null) oIm = null;
86          oIm = createImage(appletWidth, appletHeight);
87          oGC = oIm.getGraphics();
88          int xpos;
89          for(xpos = 0; xpos < appletWidth; xpos++)
90          {
91              oGC.setColor(computeColor(xpos));
92              oGC.drawLine(xpos, 0, xpos, appletHeight);
93          }
94      }
```

```
95      //-----------------------------------------------------------
96      /** Returns a rainbow color for a specified x position */
97      private Color computeColor(int x)
98      {
99          if (x >= appletWidth) x %= appletWidth;
100         double f = (double)x * 6. / (double)(appletWidth);
101         double r, g, b;
102
103         if(f < 1)      { r = 1;      g = 0;      b = 1.0-f;}
104         else if(f < 2) { r = 2.0-f; g = 0;      b = 1;}
105         else if(f < 3) { r = 0;     g = f-2.0;  b = 1;}
106         else if(f < 4) { r = 0;     g = 1;      b = 4.0-f;}
107         else if(f < 5) { r = f-4.0; g = 1;      b = 0;}
108         else           { r = 1;     g = 6.0-f;  b = 0;}
109
110         return new Color((float)r, (float)g, (float)b);
111     }
112     //-----------------------------------------------------------
113     /** Returns the desired size of the component */
114     public Dimension getPreferredSize()
115     {
116         return new Dimension(appletWidth, appletHeight);
117     }
118     //-----------------------------------------------------------
119     // Set and get methods for the exposed properties
130     public void setAnimationDelay(int x) { delay = x;}
121     public int getAnimationDelay() { return delay;}
122     public void setWidth(int x)
123     {
124         appletWidth = x;
125         updateSize();
126     }
127     public int getWidth() { return appletWidth;}
128     public void setHeight(int x)
129     {
130         appletHeight = x;
131         updateSize();
132     }
133     void updateSize()
134     {
135         makeNewImage();
136         setSize(appletWidth, appletHeight);
```

```
137        Container c = getParent();
138        if(c != null)
139        {
140            c.invalidate();
141            c.doLayout();
142        }
143    }
144    public int getHeight() { return appletHeight;}
145    public void setMoveRight(boolean x) { moveRight = x;}
146    public boolean isMoveRight() { return moveRight;}
147 }
```

ANNOTATIONS

The **RainbowRuler** bean's design is the same as that of the **RainbowRuler** applet discussed in Chapter 1. You should browse through that applet's description to learn how the rainbow colors are prepared and animated. In this section, I primarily describe the changes I made to convert the applet to a Java bean. You can use the ideas presented here to convert other applets to Java beans (and make them more readily usable in building other applications and applets with builder tools).

The first step is to add a package name to the class. Line 9 specifies **ch07.hruler** as the package name for this sample bean:

```
9 package ch07.hruler;
```

Some application builder tools require beans to have a package name before you can use the beans in the tool.

Line 12 declares the **RainbowRuler** class:

```
12 public class RainbowRuler extends Applet implements Runnable
```

Note that the class is still declared exactly as it was for the applet. That's because a Java bean is simply a class that follows certain rules. A visible bean such as **RainbowRuler** must be a subclass of **java.awt.Component**. Because **Applet** is a subclass of **Component**, you can declare a visible bean such as **RainbowRuler** as a subclass of **Applet**.

The **RainbowRuler** class no longer has an **init()** method. The **init()** method initializes applets, and most applets read parameters from HTML files in the **init()** method. As a bean, **RainbowRuler** does not accept any parameters through HTML **<applet>** tags.

RainbowRuler includes the **start()** and **stop()** methods that are part of typical applets. The **start()** method, shown in lines 25 through 33, creates the **colorShiftThread** that animates the colors in the ruler.

Because **RainbowRuler** uses a thread to animate the rainbow colors, it includes a **run()** method that the thread executes. The **run()** method, shown in lines 57 through 79, is nearly the same as the one used in the **RainbowRuler** applet in Chapter 1. I simplified the code by using only one **boolean** variable, **moveRight**, to control the direction of color shift. If **moveRight** is **true**, the colors shift to the right; otherwise the **run()** method shifts the colors to the left.

The rainbow-colored image is prepared and stored in an off-screen **Image** object named **oIm**. The initial off-screen image is prepared by calling the **makeNewImage()** method from line 53 of the **paint()** method. From then on, lines 47 through 51 draw the rainbow-colored ruler by copying appropriate parts of the image from **oIm** to the bean's display area:

```
47          if (oIm != null)
48          {
49              g.drawImage(oIm, -offset, 0, this);
50              g.drawImage(oIm, appletWidth-offset, 0, this);
51          }
```

Lines 114 through 117 show the **getPreferredSize()** method that is called by the bean's container to determine the extent of the bean's display area:

```
114     public Dimension getPreferredSize()
115     {
116         return new Dimension(appletWidth, appletHeight);
117     }
```

You must add this method when converting an applet to a Java bean. In the case of an applet, you do not need this method, because the width and height of the applet are specified through the <applet> tag in the HTML file in which you embed the applet.

The final set of additions to the applet are the get and set methods for the parameters that you want to expose to the application builder tool. For example, I decided to expose **animationDelay** as a property that can be used to get or set the internal variable named **delay** (which controls the pause between successive color shifts). Lines 120 and 121 show these methods:

```
120     public void setAnimationDelay(int x) { delay = x;}
121     public int getAnimationDelay() { return delay;}
```

Note that the method names follow the naming convention of capitalizing the first letter of the property name and appending it to the word *set* or *get*.

Two other properties, **width** and **height**, can be used to get or set the internal variables **appletWidth** and **appletHeight**. Lines 122 through 127 show the **setWidth()** and **getWidth()** methods:

```
122    public void setWidth(int x)
123    {
124        appletWidth = x;
125        updateSize();
126    }
127    public int getWidth() { return appletWidth;}
```

The **getWidth()** method simply returns **appletWidth**, but **setWidth()** is a bit more involved. It sets **appletWidth**, but it also calls **updateSize()** to actually change the bean's size.

Lines 133 through 143 show the **updateSize()** method, which resizes the bean's display area to match the new values of **appletWidth** and **appletHeight**:

```
133    void updateSize()
134    {
135        makeNewImage();
136        setSize(appletWidth, appletHeight);
137        Container c = getParent();
138        if(c != null)
139        {
140            c.invalidate();
141            c.doLayout();
142        }
143    }
```

Line 135 calls **makeNewImage()** to construct a new off-screen image (this is necessary whenever the dimensions of the bean change). Then line 136 calls **setSize()** to set the bean's size. Line 137 gets the bean's parent component. Finally, if the container is not null, lines 140 and 141 call the **invalidate()** method followed by **doLayout()** to force a new layout of all components inside the parent. You should use such a technique whenever you change a bean's size.

Note that programmers typically follow a slightly different naming convention for methods that get the value of a **boolean** property. Instead of using *get* as the prefix, it's common practice to use an *is* prefix (although you can use the standard *get* prefix if you choose). The **RainbowRuler** bean exposes **moveRight** as a **boolean** property. Lines 145 and 146 show the set and get methods for the **moveRight** property:

```
145    public void setMoveRight(boolean x) { moveRight = x;}
146    public boolean isMoveRight() { return moveRight;}
```

As you can see from line 146, the method for getting the value of **moveRight** is named **isMoveRight()**.

A Calendar Bean

A calendar Java bean can be very useful in applications and applets that require the user to enter one or more dates. For example, a hotel reservation application typically requires the user to enter the arrival and departure dates. As the application developer, you can force the user to type in the date in a text field, but then the user probably has to consult a real calendar to figure out the correct date. A better way is to display a calendar and let the user click on the dates. That's where you can use the calendar bean.

This section converts the **Calendar** applet, presented in Chapter 2, into the **CalendarJ** bean. The bean displays a calendar and, when the user selects a date, the selected date is provided to other beans via a **DateListener** interface and a **DateEvent** object. First I will show you how to use the **CalendarJ** bean in Sun's **BeanBox**. Then I will explain the bean's source code as well as the source of the **DateEvent** and **DateListener** classes.

To test the **CalendarJ** bean, I also created a simple bean named **tdisp** that implements the **DateListener** interface and displays the date from the **DateEvent** sent by the **CalendarJ** bean. In the following sections, you will learn about the **tdisp** bean as well.

Using the CalendarJ Bean

All files for the **CalendarJ** bean are in the **ch07\calendar** directory of this book's companion CD-ROM. In addition to the Java source code for all necessary classes, you will find the **calendar.jar** file with the packaged **CalendarJ** and **tdisp** beans. To try the beans, copy **calendar.jar** to the **jars** subdirectory of the location in which you have installed Sun's Bean Development Kit. For example, if you installed the BDK in **c:\bdk**, you would copy the **calendar.jar** file to the **c:\bdk\jars** directory. Then change the directory to **c:\bdk\beanbox** and type **run** to start the **BeanBox**.

In the ToolBox window, you will see the **CalendarJ** and **tdisp** beans listed. Click on **CalendarJ** in the ToolBox window, and then click inside the BeanBox window to create an instance of the calendar. Create an instance of **tdisp** as well. Connect the **dateChanged** event of the **CalendarJ** bean to the **dateChanged** method in **tdisp**. (To learn how to connect events to methods, see the description in the section "Using the BeanBox," earlier in this chapter.)

Now try out the **CalendarJ** bean. Select a month from the drop-down list of months. To see the calendar for a specific year, type the year in the text field. To pick a specific date, click on the buttons that show the dates. When you select a date, that date appears in the **tdisp** bean, as shown in Figure 7-5.

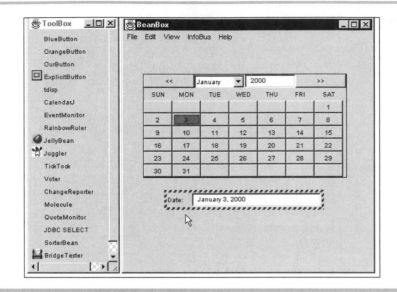

FIGURE 7-5. Selecting dates from the **CalendarJ** bean in the **BeanBox**.

The Duke logo is a trademark or registered trademark of Sun Microsystems, Inc. in the United States and other countries.

If you want to build and package the **CalendarJ** and **tdisp** beans from scratch, perform the following steps:

1. Copy all Java files (files with a **.java** extension) and the **calendar.mf** file from the **ch07\calendar** directory of the CD-ROM to a directory of your choice on your system's hard drive.

2. Assuming that you have the JDK installed, use the **javac** command to compile the **DateEvent.java** file.

3. Create a **ch07\calendar** subdirectory in the same directory where you have placed the Java source files.

4. Copy **DateEvent.class** to the **ch07\calendar** directory.

5. Compile **DateListener.java** with the **javac DateListener.java** command.

6. Copy **DateListener.class** to the **ch07\calendar** directory.

7. Compile **CalendarJ.java** with the **javac CalendarJ.java** command.

8. Copy **CalendarJ.class** to the **ch07\calendar** directory.

9. Compile **tdisp.java**, and copy **tdisp.class** to the **ch07\calendar** directory.

10. Use the command **jar cfm calendar.jar calendar.mf ch07\calendar*.class** to package the classes into the **calendar.jar** file.

11. Copy **calendar.jar** to the **jars** subdirectory of the location in which you have installed the BDK. For example, if the BDK is in **c:\bdk**, use the command **copy calendar.jar c:\bdk\jars**.

After these steps, the **CalendarJ** and **tdisp** beans will be ready for use in the **BeanBox**. To make it easy to rebuild the beans, I place these commands in a batch file, **makejar.bat**, and then type **makejar** whenever I want to perform these steps. The **makejar.bat** file in the **ch07\calendar** directory of the CD-ROM includes the following commands:

```
javac DateEvent.java
copy DateEvent.class ch07\calendar
javac DateListener.java
copy DateListener.class ch07\calendar
javac CalendarJ.java
javac tdisp.java
copy CalendarJ.class ch07\calendar
copy tdisp.class ch07\calendar
jar cfm calendar.jar calendar.mf ch07\calendar\*.class
copy calendar.jar c:\bdk\jars
```

Note that the manifest file, **calendar.mf**, defines the beans that are packaged in the **calendar.jar** file with the **jar** command. The following listing shows the contents of the **calendar.mf** file used to specify the **CalendarJ** and **tdisp** beans:

```
Name: ch07/calendar/CalendarJ.class
Java-Bean: True


Name: ch07/calendar/tdisp.class
Java-Bean: True
```

CalendarJ

Understanding the CalendarJ Bean

The following listing shows the **CalendarJ.java** file, the source code for the **CalendarJ** bean. I explain this code in the next section and present the source code for other supporting classes.

```
1  //-------------------------------------------------------------
2  // Calendar.java
3  // A Java bean that displays a calendar for any month and
4  // any year (up to 9999) and lets the user select a date. It
5  // sends a DateEvent to any registered DateListeners.
6  //
```

```
7  // Uses DateEvent and DateListener classes (defined in separate
8  // files).
9  //------------------------------------------------------------------
10 package ch07.calendar;
11 import java.applet.*;
12 import java.awt.*;
13 import java.awt.event.*;
14 import java.util.*;
15 /** CalendarJ class represents the Calendar bean */
16 public class CalendarJ extends Applet implements
17 ActionListener, ItemListener, TextListener
18 {
19     private transient Choice    monthChoice;
20     private transient TextField year;
21     private transient Button    previousButton;
22     private transient Button    nextButton;
23     private transient int       currentMonth;
24     private transient int       currentYear;
25     private transient String    currentDayString = "1";
26     private transient String    currentDateString;
27     private transient int       appletWidth;
28     private transient int       appletHeight;
29     private transient Font helvP10 =
30                 new Font("Helvetica", Font.PLAIN, 10);
31     private transient Font helvB10 =
32                 new Font("Helvetica", Font.BOLD, 10);
33     private String days[] = {"SUN", "MON", "TUE", "WED", "THU",
34                         "FRI", "SAT"};
35     private String months[] = {
36                     "January", "February", "March", "April",
37                     "May", "June", "July", "August", "September",
38                     "October", "November", "December"};
39     private int daysInMonth[] = {31, 28, 31, 30, 31, 30, 31, 31,
40                                 30, 31, 30, 31};
41     private transient Button[][] monthButtons = new Button[6][7];
42     private transient Button highlightedBtn = null;
43     private transient Vector dateListeners = new Vector();
44     /** Adds a DateListener */
45     public synchronized void addDateListener(DateListener dl)
46     {
47         dateListeners.addElement(dl);
48     }
```

```
49      /** Removes a DateListener */
50      public synchronized void removeDateListener(DateListener dl)
51      {
52          dateListeners.removeElement(dl);
53      }
54      /** Sends DateEvents to all registered DateListeners */
55      public void notifyDateChanged()
56      {
57          Vector l;
58          currentDateString = months[currentMonth]+" "+
59                              currentDayString+", "+currentYear;
60          DateEvent de = new DateEvent(this, currentDateString);
61          synchronized(this) { l = (Vector)dateListeners.clone();}
62          for(int i = 0; i < l.size(); i++)
63          {
64              ((DateListener)l.elementAt(i)).dateChanged(de);
65          }
66      }
67      /** Initializes CalendarJ's user interface */
68      public void init()
69      {
70          appletWidth = 100;
71          appletHeight = 100;
72          Calendar today = Calendar.getInstance();
73          currentMonth = today.get(Calendar.MONTH);
74          currentYear = today.get(Calendar.YEAR);
75          setLayout(new BorderLayout());
76
77          Panel pTop = new Panel();
78          pTop.setLayout(new GridLayout(1, 4));
79          previousButton = new Button("<<");
80          previousButton.addActionListener(this);
81          pTop.add(previousButton);
82          monthChoice = new Choice();
83          monthChoice.setFont(helvP10);
84          for(int i = 0; i < months.length; i++)
85              monthChoice.addItem(months[i]);
86          monthChoice.select(currentMonth);
87          monthChoice.addItemListener(this);
88          pTop.add(monthChoice);
89          year = new TextField("" + currentYear, 4);
90          year.setFont(helvP10);
91          year.addTextListener(this);
```

```
92          pTop.add(year);
93          nextButton = new Button(">>");
94          nextButton.addActionListener(this);
95          pTop.add(nextButton);
96          add("North", pTop);
97
98          Panel pButtons = new Panel();
99          pButtons.setLayout(new GridLayout(7,7));
100         pButtons.setFont(helvB10);
101         for(int i=0; i < days.length; i++)
102             pButtons.add(new Label(days[i], Label.CENTER));
103         for(int i=0; i < 6; i++)
104             for(int j=0; j < 7; j++)
105             {
106                 monthButtons[i][j] = new Button("");
107                 monthButtons[i][j].setBackground(Color.lightGray);
108                 monthButtons[i][j].addActionListener(this);
109                 pButtons.add(monthButtons[i][j]);
110             }
111         add("Center", pButtons);
112         validate();
113         repaint(75);
114     }
115     /** Returns true if the year is a leap year. */
116     public boolean isLeapYear(int year)
117     {
118         if((year % 400) == 0) return(true);
119         if((year > 1582) && ((year % 100) == 0)) return(false);
120         if((year % 4) == 0) return(true);
121         return(false);
122     }
123     /** Displays the calendar for a specific month of a year */
124     public void displayMonth(int month, int year)
125     {
126         int day = 1; // first of the month
127         int monthNum = month - 1; // month number,1=Mar,2=Apr,...
128         if(monthNum <= 0) monthNum += 12; // Jan = 11, Feb = 12
129         int tempYear = year;
130         if(monthNum > 10) tempYear = year - 1;
131         int century = tempYear / 100;
132         int yy = tempYear - 100 * century;
```

```
133        int factor = (int)(day +
134                (int)(2.6*(double)monthNum - 0.2) -
135                2*century + yy + yy/4 + century/4.0);
136        int firstWeekday = factor % 7; // 0=Sun, 1=Mon, 2=Tue, ...
137
138        // Now draw the dates on the buttons in the calendar
139        int maxDate = daysInMonth[month];
140        if(month == 1 && isLeapYear(year)) maxDate += 1;
141        int dateNow = 1;
142        if(highlightedBtn != null)
143            highlightedBtn.setBackground(Color.lightGray);
144        String ds;
145        for(int i=0; i < 6; i++)
146        {
147            for(int j=0; j < 7; j++)
148            {
149                if(dateNow == 1 && j < firstWeekday)
150                    monthButtons[i][j].setLabel("");
151                else if(dateNow > maxDate)
152                    monthButtons[i][j].setLabel("");
153                else
154                {
155                    ds = ""+dateNow;
156                    monthButtons[i][j].setLabel(ds);
157                    if(ds.equals(currentDayString))
158                    {
159                        monthButtons[i][j].setBackground(
160                                            Color.gray);
161                        highlightedBtn = monthButtons[i][j];
162                    }
163                    dateNow++;
164                }
165            }
166        }
167    }
168    /** Processes the year entered by the user */
169    public int processYear(String yearString)
170    {
171        if((yearString.length() == 4))
172        {
173            try
174            {
```

```
175                    int year = Integer.parseInt(yearString);
176                    return year;
177                }
178            catch(NumberFormatException e)
179            {
180                    return currentYear;
181            }
182        }
183        return -1;
184    }
185    /** Updates applet by calling paint(). */
186    public void update(Graphics g) { paint(g);}
187    /** Calls displayMonth() to display the calendar */
188    public void paint(Graphics g)
189    {
190        displayMonth(currentMonth, currentYear);
191        g.setColor(Color.black);
192        Dimension d = getSize();
193        g.drawRect(0, 0, d.width-1,d.height-1);
194    }
195    /** Handles mouse clicks in the buttons and drop-down menus*/
196    public void actionPerformed(ActionEvent ev)
197    {
198        if(ev.getSource().equals(previousButton))
199        {
200            if((currentYear > 1) || (currentMonth > 0))
201            {
202                currentMonth--;
203                if(currentMonth < 0)
204                {
205                    currentMonth = 11;
206                    currentYear--;
207                }
208                monthChoice.select(currentMonth);
209                year.setText(""+currentYear);
210                currentDayString = "1";
211                notifyDateChanged();
212                repaint();
213            }
214        }
215        else if(ev.getSource() == nextButton)
216        {
```

```
217                 if((currentYear < 9999) || (currentMonth < 11))
218                 {
219                     currentMonth++;
220                     if(currentMonth > 11)
221                     {
222                         currentMonth = 0;
223                         currentYear++;
224                     }
225                     monthChoice.select(currentMonth);
226                     year.setText(""+currentYear);
227                     currentDayString = "1";
228                     notifyDateChanged();
229                     repaint();
230                 }
231             }
232         else
233         {   // check for click on a day of the month
234             String ds;
235             for(int i=0; i < 6; i++)
236             {
237                 for(int j=0; j < 7; j++)
238                 {
239                     if(ev.getSource() == monthButtons[i][j])
240                     {
241                         ds = ev.getActionCommand();
242                         if(!ds.equals(""))
243                         {
244                             highlightedBtn.
245                                 setBackground(Color.lightGray);
246                             highlightedBtn = monthButtons[i][j];
247                             monthButtons[i][j].setBackground(
248                                                 Color.gray);
249                             currentDayString = ds;
250                             notifyDateChanged();
251                         }
252                     }
253                 }
254             }
255         }
256     }
257     /** Handles selections from the month list */
258     public void itemStateChanged(ItemEvent ev)
259     {
```

```
260         if(ev.getSource() == monthChoice)
261         {
262             int m = monthChoice.getSelectedIndex();
263             year.setText(""+currentYear);
264             if(m != currentMonth)
265             {
266                 currentMonth = monthChoice.getSelectedIndex();
267                 currentDayString = "1";
268                 notifyDateChanged();
269                 repaint();
270             }
271         }
272     }
273     /** Handles changes to the year text field */
274     public void textValueChanged(TextEvent ev)
275     {
276         if(ev.getSource() == year)
277         {
278             int y = processYear(year.getText());
279             if((y > 0) && (y != currentYear))
280             {
281                 currentYear = y;
282                 currentDayString = "1";
283                 notifyDateChanged();
284                 repaint();
285             }
286         }
287     }
288     /** Makes room for a 1-pixel border. */
289     public Insets getInsets()
290     {
291         return new Insets(1,1,1,1); // 1-pixel border
292     }
293 }
```

ANNOTATIONS

The **CalendarJ** bean is based on the **Calendar** applet described in Chapter 2. You should read the description of the **Calendar** applet to understand how the calendar for a specific month is constructed. This section focuses on the changes I made to convert the **Calendar** applet into the **CalendarJ** bean. I also describe some supporting classes used in **CalendarJ** as well as the **tdisp** class used to test the bean.

I began by adding a package name for the calendar bean:

```
10  package ch07.calendar;
```

This meant that I had to place the class files in the **ch07\calendar** subdirectory because Java assumes a directory structure based on the package name.

Next I changed the event-handling methods from the old Java 1.0 model to the new listener-based Java 1.1 event-handling model (this model is used in Java 2 as well). The new event-handling model required changing the class declaration, as follows:

```
16  public class CalendarJ extends Applet implements
17  ActionListener, ItemListener, TextListener
```

As lines 16 and 17 show, **CalendarJ** implements three event listener interfaces: **ActionListener** for clicks on the buttons, **ItemListener** for the month selection list, and **TextListener** for text typed into the text field that displays the year. I also added the methods that each of these listener interfaces requires. The **ActionListener** interface requires the **actionPerformed()** method, **ItemListener** needs the **itemStateChanged()** method, and the **TextListener** interface requires the **textValueChanged()** method. For the body of these methods I used appropriate parts of the event-handling code from the **Calendar** applet. The final step in using the new event-handling model is to call the appropriate methods to add the **CalendarJ** class as the listener for the appropriate user interface components. For example, line 87 calls **addItemListener()** to add **CalendarJ** as a listener for month selections from the **monthChoice** drop-down list:

```
87          monthChoice.addItemListener(this);
```

Java 2

Although I retain the same calendar algorithms as in the **Calendar** applet, I had to change the way **CalendarJ** gets the current month and year. The **getMonth()** and **getYear()** methods of the **Date** class are deprecated in Java 2. Instead, the recommended way to get the current date and then retrieve the month and year are as shown in lines 72 through 74:

```
72          Calendar today = Calendar.getInstance();
73          currentMonth = today.get(Calendar.MONTH);
74          currentYear = today.get(Calendar.YEAR);
```

Line 72 gets the current calendar by calling the **getInstance()** method of Java 2's new **Calendar** class (I changed this bean's name to **CalendarJ** to differentiate it from the Java 2 **Calendar** class). Line 73 gets the current month; line 74 gets the current year.

I also added new code to make **CalendarJ** an event source so that it can send the currently selected date to other beans. The date is sent through a **DateEvent**, which is defined in the **DateEvent.java** file as follows:

```
package ch07.calendar;
import java.util.*;
import java.awt.*;

public class DateEvent extends EventObject
{
    String date;
    DateEvent(Component source, String d)
    {
        super(source);
        date = d;
    }
    public String getDate() { return date;}
}
```

Note that **DateEvent** is a subclass of **EventObject**. The **DateEvent** class stores the date as a string. You have to provide the date string as an argument when creating an instance of **DateEvent**. Besides the constructor, **DateEvent** includes the **getDate()** method, which returns the date.

In the new event model, each type of event has an associated listener interface that specifies the methods to be defined in any class that wants to receive the event. For example, **ActionEvent** is associated with the **ActionListener** interface. Similarly, I define a **DateListener** interface for classes that need to process **DateEvent** objects:

```
package ch07.calendar;
import java.awt.event.*;
import java.util.*;

public interface DateListener extends EventListener
{
    public void dateChanged(DateEvent de);
}
```

This interface specifies that a class that implements **DateListener** must define the **dateChanged()** method, which accepts a **DateEvent** object as argument.

Lines 43 through 66 of **CalendarJ**'s listing show the code used to dispatch **DateEvent** to registered **DateListener** objects. Line 43 defines the **dateListeners** vector used to keep track of all registered **DateListener** objects:

```
43      private transient Vector dateListeners = new Vector();
```

Lines 44 through 53 define the **addDateListener()** and **removeDateListener()** methods for adding and removing **DateListener** objects:

```
44      /** Adds a DateListener */
45      public synchronized void addDateListener(DateListener dl)
46      {
47          dateListeners.addElement(dl);
48      }
49      /** Removes a DateListener */
50      public synchronized void removeDateListener(DateListener dl)
51      {
52          dateListeners.removeElement(dl);
53      }
```

These two methods are implemented in a straightforward manner using the **addElement()** and **removeElement()** methods of the **Vector** class. Note that the names of the methods—**addDateListener()** and **removeDateListener()**—use the naming conventions mandated by the JavaBeans specification.

Whenever the user selects a new date in the **CalendarJ** bean, I call the **notifyDateChanged()** method to send that date to all registered **DateListener** objects. Lines 55 through 66 define the **notifyDateChanged()** method:

```
55      public void notifyDateChanged()
56      {
57          Vector l;
58          currentDateString = months[currentMonth]+" "+
59                              currentDayString+", "+currentYear;
60          DateEvent de = new DateEvent(this, currentDateString);
61          synchronized(this) { l = (Vector)dateListeners.clone();}
62          for(int i = 0; i < l.size(); i++)
63          {
64              ((DateListener)l.elementAt(i)).dateChanged(de);
65          }
66      }
```

Lines 58 and 59 create a string representation of the selected date. Line 60 creates a new **DateEvent** object with that date string. Line 61 makes a copy of the vector of **DateListener** objects. This step uses the **synchronized** keyword to protect it from simultaneous access by several threads. Lines 62 through 65 show the **for** loop that calls the **dateChanged()** method of all **DateListener** objects. That's how the **CalendarJ** bean sends events to other classes. In fact, this is the same mechanism you would use to send any type of event from a bean.

I created another bean named **tdisp** to test the **CalendarJ** bean in Sun's **BeanBox**. The **tdisp** bean implements the **DateListener** interface and displays the date from a

DateEvent in a text field. The following listing shows the **tdisp.java** file, which implements the **tdisp** bean:

```
//------------------------------------------------------------
// File: tdisp.java
// A sample text display bean that implements the DateListener
// interface. You can use this bean in a builder to receive and
// display date change events from the CalendarJ bean.
//
// Uses the DateListener and DateEvent classes that are defined
// in separate files.
//------------------------------------------------------------
package ch07.calendar;
import java.awt.*;
public class tdisp extends Panel implements DateListener
{
    private String labelString = "Date:";
    private String dateString = "January 1, 2000";
    private TextField tf = new TextField("", 30);
    private Label l = new Label(labelString);
    public tdisp()
    {
        super();
        this.setLayout(new BorderLayout());
        add("West", l);
        add("Center", tf);
        validate();
        tf.setText(dateString);
    }
    public void dateChanged(DateEvent de)
    {
        dateString = de.getDate();
        tf.setText(dateString);
        repaint();
    }
    public Dimension getPreferredSize()
    {
        return new Dimension(160, 20);
    }
}
```

The **tdisp** class is a subclass of **Panel**, and it implements the **DateListener** interface. This means that it defines the **dateChanged()** method. That method extracts the date string from the **DateEvent** object and displays that date in a text field that's part of the **tdisp** bean's user interface.

The code to initialize the layout of the **tdisp** bean's user interface is in the **tdisp()** constructor. I included a **getPreferredSize()** method that returns the preferred dimensions of **tdisp**'s display area.

When you hook up the date event from the **CalendarJ** bean to the **dateChanged()** method of the **tdisp** bean, the **BeanBox** adds **tdisp** as a listener by calling the **addDateListener()** method in **CalendarJ**. When the user selects a date, the **CalendarJ** bean calls the **tdisp** bean's **dateChanged()** method, which in turn gets the date string and displays it in the text field in the **tdisp** bean's user interface.

Invisible Java Beans

A Timer Bean (TimerJ) A Spell-Checker Bean (Speller)

C hapter 7, "Visible Java Beans," provides you with an overview of Java bean programming and explains how to implement some visible Java beans that can be used as GUI components in an application builder tool. This chapter presents a few more sample beans, but these are invisible beans that do not have any visual representation. Invisible beans typically implement some computational algorithm. For example, you might create a spell-check bean that performs spelling checks. Such a bean implements the spell-check algorithm, but it does not have any visual screen representation. Another example of an invisible bean might be a timer that periodically sends events to any bean that requests such events. Although invisible beans do not have any visual representation, they are useful for packaging an algorithm in the form of a reusable software component.

The key difference between a visible Java bean and an invisible Java bean is that you do not have to define an invisible Java bean as a subclass of any particular class or interface. Other than that, an invisible bean follows the same rules as a visible bean. If you are unfamiliar with Java beans, you should first browse through Chapter 7.

You will find the following Java beans in this chapter:

◆ **TimerJ**—An invisible bean that generates events at a specified rate

◆ **Speller**—An invisible bean that performs a spelling check by consulting a list of correctly spelled words

A Timer Bean

A simple invisible bean is a timer that sends out an event periodically. You could use such a bean as the timing source for an animation. Whenever an event from the timer bean arrives, you could draw the next frame of animation. This section presents a simple timer bean that sends a property change event at specified intervals.

Note that there is a similar invisible bean, named **TickTock**, in Sun's BDK. I show the code for a timer bean to illustrate how to implement invisible beans and how to generate property change events. You will also learn how to send a **PropertyChangeEvent** and implement the **Serializable** interface. In a visible bean, the **Serializable** interface is implemented by the **java.awt.Component** superclass, but in an invisible bean you have to implement that interface yourself. Otherwise, the application builder tool cannot save and restore your bean.

Java 2

Java 2 includes the **javax.swing.Timer** class, which maintains a list of **ActionListener** objects and invokes the **actionPerformed()** method of these listeners at a predefined rate. To avoid confusion with the Java 2 **Timer** class, I named this invisible bean **TimerJ**.

Using the TimerJ Bean

All of the files for the **TimerJ** bean are in the **ch08\timer** directory of the companion CD-ROM. Along with the **TimerJ** bean, I have also included a simple visual bean—**ViewTimer**—that you can use to verify whether property change events are being sent by the **TimerJ** bean. Both the **TimerJ** bean and the **ViewTimer** bean are in the **timer.jar** file.

To try the bean in Sun's **BeanBox** tool, copy **timer.jar** to the **jars** subdirectory of the directory in which you have installed the BDK. For example, if you installed the BDK in **c:\bdk**, copy the **timer.jar** file to the **c:\bdk\jars** directory. Next, run the **BeanBox** by changing the directory to **c:\bdk\beanbox** and typing **run** in an MS-DOS window. The ToolBox, BeanBox, and Properties windows appear, and you see the **TimerJ** and **ViewTimer** beans listed in the ToolBox window. Create an instance of **TimerJ** and **ViewTimer** in the BeanBox window. Then hook up the **PropertyEvent** of **TimerJ** to the **propertyChanged()** method of the **ViewTimer** bean. (Consult Chapter 7 to learn how to create instances of beans and hook up events in the BeanBox window.)

The **ViewTimer** bean displays a circle and a radial line that advances with each property change event that **ViewTimer** receives. After you hook up **TimerJ**'s property change event to **ViewTimer**, the line rotates at a rate determined by the **delay** parameter of the **TimerJ** bean. If you click on the **TimerJ** bean, you will see its properties listed in the Properties window and you will be able to enter a new value for the **delay** parameter. That parameter specifies the milliseconds of delay between successive property change events generated by the **TimerJ** bean. Figure 8-1 shows the **TimerJ** and **ViewTimer** beans as they appear in the **BeanBox**. You can use the **Make Applet** option in **BeanBox**'s File menu to create an applet from these two beans. When you run that applet, you will see the **ViewTimer** bean only; the **TimerJ** bean won't appear, because it's an invisible bean.

The **makejar.bat** file contains the commands I used to compile and package the **TimerJ** and **ViewTimer** beans. Here is a listing of this file:

```
javac ViewTimer.java
copy ViewTimer.class ch08\timer
javac TimerJ.java
copy TimerJ.class ch08\timer
jar cfm timer.jar timer.mf ch08\timer\*.class
copy timer.jar c:\bdk\jars
```

These commands assume that you have installed both the JDK and the BDK on your system and that you installed the BDK in the **c:\bdk** directory.

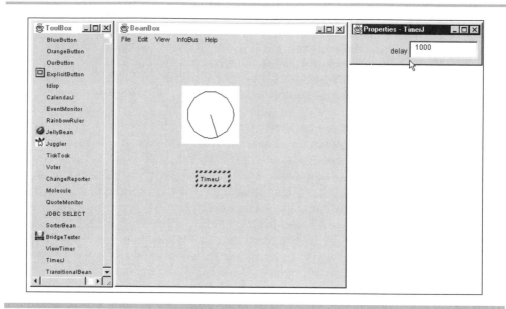

FIGURE 8-1. The **TimerJ** and **ViewTimer** beans in the **BeanBox**.
The Duke logo is a trademark or registered trademark of Sun Microsystems, Inc. in the United States and other countries.

The **timer.mf** file used with the **jar** command is called the manifest file. This text file identifies the classes that make up the **TimerJ** and **ViewTimer** beans. The following listing shows the **timer.mf** file:

```
Name: ch08/timer/ViewTimer.class
Java-Bean: True


Name: ch08/timer/TimerJ.class
Java-Bean: True
```

This manifest file lists the Java classes for two beans. Each bean has a **Name:** tag identifying the Java class and a **Java-Bean: true** line that indicates that the class is a Java bean. Notice that the Java bean name uses the directory name derived from the package name used for the bean. In this case, the Java source files used the package name **ch08.timer**, so each bean's class name has a **ch08/timer/** prefix (note the use of forward slashes as opposed to backslashes).

Understanding the TimerJ Bean

TimerJ

The following listing shows the **TimerJ.java** file that implements the **TimerJ** bean. I explain the source code in the "Annotations" section that follows the listing. In that section, I also present the **ViewTimer** bean's source code. (Even though this chapter focuses on invisible beans, it's difficult to test an invisible bean without some visual output.)

```
1  //------------------------------------------------------------------
2  // File: TimerJ.java
3  //
4  // TimerJ is an invisible bean that periodically sends a
5  // PropertyChange event to any registered PropertyListener
6  // objects. You can set the delay (in milliseconds) between
7  // successive PropertyChange events.
8  //------------------------------------------------------------------
9  package ch08.timer;
10 import java.beans.*;
11 import java.io.*;
12 public class TimerJ implements Runnable, Serializable
13 {
14     private PropertyChangeSupport pc =
15                     new PropertyChangeSupport(this);
16     private int delay = 100; // delay in milliseconds
17     private transient Thread t;
18     /** Constructs a new TimerJ object */
19     public TimerJ()
20     {
21         t = new Thread(this);
22         t.start();
23     }
24     /** Runs the timer thread */
25     public void run()
26     {
27         int oldstate = 0;
28         int newstate = 1;
29         int x;
30         while(true)
31         {
32             try
33             {
34                 Thread.sleep(delay);
35             } catch (InterruptedException ex) {}
36             // Fires a PropertyChange event
37             pc.firePropertyChange("state", new Integer(oldstate),
38                     new Integer(newstate));
38             x = oldstate;
39             oldstate = newstate;
40             newstate = x;
41         }
42     }
```

```
43    /** Registers a PropertyChangeListener */
44    public void addPropertyChangeListener(
45                              PropertyChangeListener l)
46    {
47        pc.addPropertyChangeListener(l);
48    }
49    /** Unregisters a PropertyChangeListener */
50    public void removePropertyChangeListener(
51                              PropertyChangeListener l)
52    {
53        pc.removePropertyChangeListener(l);
54    }
55    /** Writes the object to an output stream */
56    private void writeObject(java.io.ObjectOutputStream out)
57            throws java.io.IOException
58    {
59        out.defaultWriteObject();
60        out.writeInt(delay);
61    }
62    /** Reads the object from an input stream */
63    private void readObject(java.io.ObjectInputStream in)
64            throws java.lang.ClassNotFoundException,
65                java.io.IOException
66    {
67        in.defaultReadObject();
68        delay = in.readInt();
69    }
70    /** Returns the value of the "delay" property */
71    public int getDelay() { return delay;}
72    /** Sets the value of the "delay" property */
73    public void setDelay(int x)
74    {
75        synchronized(this) { delay = x;}
76        if (t != null) t.interrupt();
77    }
78 }
```

ANNOTATIONS

The very first executable statement in **TimerJ.java** is the **package** statement on line 9:

```
9 package ch08.timer;
```

This specifies the package name as **ch08.timer**. The **package** statement must be the first noncomment statement in a file. Using a package name of **ch08.timer** means that the class files must be placed in the **ch08\timer** subdirectory, and that directory name must be used when packaging the class file with the **jar** command.

The **import** statements on lines 10 and 11 include classes from the **java.beans** package and the **java.io** package. The **java.io** package defines the **Serializable** interface and includes the **ObjectOutputStream** and **ObjectInputStream** classes. These classes are used to support persistence—the ability to save and restore a bean from a permanent storage medium such as the hard drive. The **java.bean** package includes the **PropertyChangeEvent**, **PropertyListener**, and **PropertyChangeSupport** classes. These classes are used to send property change events to registered **PropertyListeners**.

The **TimerJ** class declaration specifies that it implements the **Runnable** and **Serializable** interfaces:

```
12  public class TimerJ implements Runnable, Serializable
```

The **Runnable** interface is needed because **TimerJ** uses a thread to generate property change events at a periodic rate. **TimerJ** implements the **Serializable** interface to support persistence.

Lines 14 through 17 define the internal variables of the bean:

```
14      private PropertyChangeSupport pc =
15                      new PropertyChangeSupport(this);
16      private int delay = 100; // delay in milliseconds
17      private transient Thread t;
```

Lines 14 and 15 define a **PropertyChangeSupport** object named **pc** that's used to manage **PropertyListeners** and to fire (i.e., send) property change events. Line 16 defines the **delay** variable, which refers to the number of milliseconds of delay between successive property change events. Finally, line 17 defines the **Thread t** that will run the timer.

Lines 19 through 23 define the no-argument constructor **TimerJ()**:

```
19      public TimerJ()
20      {
21          t = new Thread(this);
22          t.start();
23      }
```

The constructor creates the **Thread t** and starts it, which causes the thread **t** to execute the **run()** method.

The **run()** method, shown in lines 25 through 42, includes a **while** loop that repeatedly sends property change events. The loop starts with a call to **Thread.sleep()** to sleep for the number of milliseconds specified in the **delay** variable. Then line 37 calls the **firePropertyChange()** method in the **PropertyChangeSupport** object **pc**. This sequence keeps repeating as long as the thread runs.

The property change requires the name of the property as well as the new and old values of the property. In this case, I used **state** as the property name. The value alternates between zero and one.

TimerJ also includes the **addPropertyChangeListener()** and **removePropertyChangeListener()** methods to add and remove **PropertyListener** objects; these are the objects that want to receive the property change events. When the application builder hooks **TimerJ**'s property change event to another bean, the builder tool calls **addPropertyChangeListener()** to register the recipient. Lines 44 through 48 show the **addPropertyChangeListener()** method:

```
44    public void addPropertyChangeListener(
45                            PropertyChangeListener l)
46    {
47        pc.addPropertyChangeListener(l);
48    }
```

As you can see, line 47 calls the **addPropertyChangeListener()** method of the **PropertyChangeSupport** object to take care of the task. The **removePropertyChangeListener()** method is implemented in a similar manner.

To implement the **Serializable** interface, **TimerJ** includes the **writeObject()** and **readObject()** methods to save and restore the bean. Lines 56 through 61 define the **writeObject()** method:

```
56    private void writeObject(java.io.ObjectOutputStream out)
57                throws java.io.IOException
58    {
59        out.defaultWriteObject();
60        out.writeInt(delay);
61    }
```

Line 59 calls the **defaultWriteObject()** method of the **ObjectOutputStream** class. Then the **writeInt()** method is called to save the integer variable named **delay**. Most **writeObject()** methods have a structure similar to this one. The **readObject()** method, shown in lines 63 through 69, is similar to **writeObject()** except that it calls **defaultReadObject()** and **readInt()** to restore the object from persistent storage.

Finally, **TimerJ** exposes the **delay** property that allows application developers to alter the delay between successive property change events. To support this, **TimerJ** includes the **getDelay()** and **setDelay()** methods (see lines 71 through 78 of the listing). The **getDelay()** method simply returns the **delay** variable. The **setDelay()** method does a bit more:

```
73    public void setDelay(int x)
74    {
75        synchronized(this) { delay = x;}
76        if (t != null) t.interrupt();
77    }
```

Line 75 sets the **delay** variable. Line 76 then interrupts the thread **t** to ensure that the change in the **delay** variable takes place immediately.

Because **TimerJ** is an invisible bean, it's difficult to determine whether it is working or not without some visual output. I developed a simple visible bean, **ViewTimer**, that displays a rotating line in response to the property change events. The following listing shows the **ViewTimer.java** file that implements the **ViewTimer** bean:

```
//----------------------------------------------------------------
// File: ViewTimer.java
//
// A bean that animates a rotating line in response to
// property change events sent by the TimerJ class.
// You can hook up the propertyChanged() method of this class
// to any property change event to see how this bean works.
//----------------------------------------------------------------
package ch08.timer;
import java.awt.*;
import java.beans.*; // this defines the PropertyChangeEvent class
public class ViewTimer extends Canvas
{
    private transient Image[] images = null;
    private int x = 50, y = 50, w = 100, h = 100;
    private int radius = 40;
    private int index = 0;
    private transient Graphics oGC;
    public ViewTimer()
    {
        super();
    }
    public Dimension getPreferredSize()
    { return new Dimension(w, h);}
    public void propertyChanged(PropertyChangeEvent ev)
    {
        // property value has changed
        synchronized(this)
        {
            index++;
            if(index > 9) index = 0;
        }
        repaint();
    }
    public void update(Graphics g) { paint(g);}
    public synchronized void paint(Graphics g)
```

```
    {
        if(images == null) initialize();
        g.drawImage(images[index], 0, 0, this);
    }
    public void initialize()
    {
        setBackground(Color.white);
        images = new Image[10];
        double a = 0.0;
        double step = 36.0 * Math.PI / 180.0;
        int x1, y1;
        for(int i = 0; i < 10; i++)
        {
            images[i] = createImage(w, h);
            oGC = images[i].getGraphics();
            oGC.setColor(Color.black);
            oGC.drawOval(x-radius, y-radius, 2*radius, 2*radius);
            x1 = (int)(radius * Math.cos(a));
            y1 = (int)(radius * Math.sin(a));
            oGC.drawLine(x, y, x+x1, y+y1);
            a += step;
            oGC.dispose();
        }
    }
}
```

ViewTimer is a subclass of **Canvas**, and it uses ten off-screen images to animate the rotating line. Each image has a circle with a radial line at angles ranging from zero to 360 degrees. The **initialize()** method prepares these off-screen images. The **paint()** method simply displays the current image as indicated by the **index** variable.

ViewTimer also implements the **propertyChanged()** method, which takes a **PropertyChangeEvent** as an argument. The idea is that you would hook up the **TimerJ** bean's property change event to the **propertyChanged()** method of **ViewTimer**. That method then moves to the next image in sequence by incrementing the **index** variable.

All in all, **ViewTimer** is quite simple and rather crude, but it's nice to have something like this to visualize the timing of events generated by the **TimerJ** bean.

A Spell-Checker Bean

An interesting and useful invisible bean is a spelling checker. The idea is to create a bean that includes a dictionary (a list of correctly spelled words) and a search algorithm to compare individual words against the dictionary. Other beans can use an event to send the text to be spell-checked. After performing the spelling check, the spell-checker bean can send back the misspelled words through another event. This section presents the **Speller** bean that implements such a spell-checker bean. Although it's somewhat crude, this bean illustrates how a real spell-checker bean might be implemented.

By studying the **Speller** bean, you will learn how to receive input data through an event and send back the results through another event. You will also learn how to load data from a resource in a bean's Jar file. The **Speller** bean stores a list of correctly spelled words as a resource in its Jar file and reads these words in during initialization.

Using the Speller Bean

All of the files for the **Speller** bean are in the **ch08\speller** directory of the companion CD-ROM. Like other invisible beans, **Speller** needs a visible bean to test its output. I wrote a simple text entry and display bean called **TextMessage** that lets you enter text to be spell-checked and displays any misspelled words reported by the **Speller** bean.

Both the **Speller** and **TextMessage** classes are in the **speller.jar** file. To test the **Speller** bean with Sun's **BeanBox** tool, you should copy the **speller.jar** file to the **jars** subdirectory of the location where you installed the BDK. For example, if you installed the BDK in **c:\bdk**, copy **speller.jar** to the **c:\bdk\jars** directory. Next, start the **BeanBox** by changing to the **c:\bdk\beanbox** directory and typing **run** in an MS-DOS window.

When the **BeanBox** runs, you will see the ToolBox, BeanBox, and Properties windows. The ToolBox window will show the names of the **Speller** and **TextMessage** beans (along with any other beans in other Jar files in the **c:\bdk\jars** directory). Create instances of the **Speller** and **TextMessage** beans in the BeanBox window. (To learn how to do this, see the "Using the BeanBox" section in Chapter 7.)

Now you have to hook up events from **TextMessage** to **Speller** and vice versa. First click on **TextMessage** so that a dashed rectangular outline appears around that bean. Select Edit->Events->spellCheck->checkText from the **BeanBox** menu bar. Drag the red line to the **Speller** bean (because **Speller** is invisible, all you see is the name of the bean in the BeanBox window), and click on the bean's name. From the resulting dialog box, select **checkText**, and then click OK. That completes the hookup of spell-check events from **TextMessage** to **Speller**.

Next click on the **Speller** bean's name (a rectangular dashed outline appears around the name). Select Edit->Events->spellingReport->spellingErrors from the menu bar. Drag the resulting red line to an edge of the **TextMessage** bean, and click. Select **spellingErrors** from the resulting dialog box, and click OK. This connects the spelling report events from **Speller** to **TextMessage**.

After you complete these two event hookups, the **TextMessage** bean can send text to the **Speller** bean for spelling checks, and the **Speller** bean can report spelling errors to the **TextMessage** bean. Now you can see how the **Speller** bean works.

Type some text in the text-entry area (on the left-hand side) of the **TextMessage** bean, and click the Check button. Any spelling errors will appear in the text area on the right-hand side of the **TextMessage** bean. Figure 8-2 shows the result of a spelling check with the **Speller** bean.

You can easily convert the beans into an applet by selecting File->MakeApplet from the menu bar and then filling in the name of the applet and its directory in the resulting dialog box. After the applet is built, you can run the applet using the **appletviewer** tool that comes with Sun's JDK. Figure 8-3 shows the resulting applet. If you type any text in the text area on the left-hand side and click the Check button, the results of spelling check will appear in the text area on the right-hand side. In Figure 8-3, you do not see the **Speller** bean because it has no visual representation. However, the **Speller** bean is very much a part of the applet, and it's the component that performs the actual spelling check.

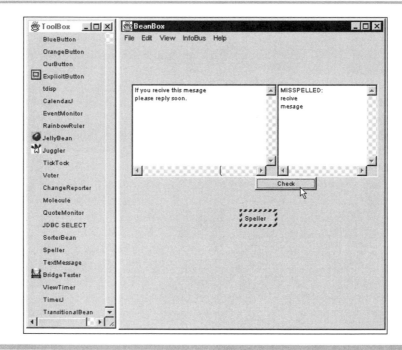

FIGURE 8-2.   The **TextMessage** bean displays the results of a spelling check by the **Speller** bean.

The Duke logo is a trademark or registered trademark of Sun Microsystems, Inc. in the United States and other countries.

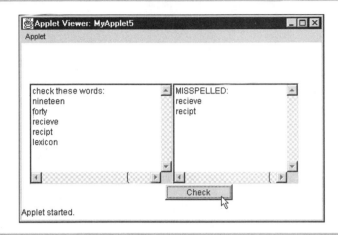

FIGURE 8-3. An applet that uses **TextMessage** and the **Speller** invisible bean.

If you want to compile the beans and package them, you should study the **makejar.bat** file that shows the commands I used when creating **speller.jar**. Here is the complete listing of this file:

```
javac SpellCheckEvent.java
copy SpellCheckEvent.class ch08\speller
javac SpellCheckListener.java
copy SpellCheckListener.class ch08\speller
javac SpellingReportEvent.java
copy SpellingReportEvent.class ch08\speller
javac SpellingReportListener.java
copy SpellingReportListener.class ch08\speller
javac Speller.java
javac TextMessage.java
copy Speller.class ch08\speller
copy TextMessage.class ch08\speller
jar cfm speller.jar speller.mf ch08\speller\*.class ch08\speller\words.txt
copy speller.jar c:\bdk\jars
```

Although there are quite a few classes, the manifest file, **speller.mf**, defines the classes that represent the **TextMessage** and **Speller** beans. Here is the **speller.mf** file I used:

```
Name: ch08/speller/Speller.class
Java-Bean: True
```

```
Name: ch08/speller/TextMessage.class
Java-Bean: True
```

The other classes—**SpellCheckEvent**, **SpellCheckListener**, **SpellingReportEvent**, and **SpellingReportListener**—are supporting classes that are needed to implement the events used for communication between **Speller** and other beans. In the following sections, you will learn about the **Speller** and **TextMessage** classes as well as the supporting classes.

Understanding the Speller Bean

Speller

The following listing shows the **Speller.java** file that implements the spell-checker bean. In subsequent sections, I describe this code and the code for the supporting classes.

```
 1  //------------------------------------------------------------
 2  // File: Speller.java
 3  //
 4  // A crude spelling checker bean that breaks up text into
 5  // words and then searches for those words in a list of
 6  // valid words. The text to be searched is provided through
 7  // a SpellCheckEvent and the results (the misspelled words)
 8  // are sent by Speller through a SpellingReportEvent.
 9  //
10  // This bean illustrates how to read from a file that has been
11  // saved in the bean's Jar file as a resource.
12  //
13  // Author: Naba Barkakati
14  // Date: January 15, 1999.
15  //------------------------------------------------------------
16  package ch08.speller;
17  import java.io.*;
18  import java.util.*;
19  public class Speller implements Serializable,
20                                  SpellCheckListener
21  {
22      private transient Vector spellingReportListeners =
23                                              new Vector();
24      private transient int nErr;
25      private transient LinkedList words = new LinkedList();
26      private transient String[] errors;
27      private String delim = " ,.;:()\"\'\t\n\r\f";
28      /** Constructs an instance of the class */
29      public Speller()
30      {
```

```
31              // Read the list of correct words from the bean's
32              // resource in the jar file
33              InputStream rawIn =
34                      getClass().getResourceAsStream("words.txt");
35              BufferedReader in
36                 = new BufferedReader(new InputStreamReader(rawIn));
37              String word;
38              try
39              {
40                  while(true)
41                  {
42                      word = in.readLine();
43                      if(word == null) break;
44                      words.add(word); // save the words in a list
45                  }
46              }
47          catch(IOException e) {}
48      }
49      /** Spell checks text by comparing with word list */
50      public void checkText(SpellCheckEvent sce)
51      {
52          String word;
53          LinkedList errorList = new LinkedList();
54          nErr = 0;
55          StringTokenizer st = new
56                  StringTokenizer(sce.getText(), delim);
57          try
58          {
59              while (st.hasMoreTokens())
60              {
61                  word = st.nextToken();
62                  int r = Collections.binarySearch(words, word,
63                              String.CASE_INSENSITIVE_ORDER);
64                  if(r < 0)
65                  {
66                      errorList.add(word);
67                      nErr++;
68                  }
69              }
70          }
71          catch(ClassCastException e){}
72          errors = new String[nErr];
73          try
74          {
```

```
75          ListIterator li = errorList.listIterator(0);
76          try
77          {
78              for(int i = 0; i < nErr; i++)
79              {
80                  errors[i] = (String)li.next();
81              }
82          }
83          catch(NoSuchElementException e){}
84      }
85      catch(IndexOutOfBoundsException e) {}
86      notifySpellingErrors();
87  }
88  /** Adds a SpellingReportListener */
89  public synchronized void addSpellingReportListener(
90                              SpellingReportListener srl)
91  {
92      spellingReportListeners.addElement(srl);
93  }
94  /** Removes a SpellingReportListener */
95  public synchronized void removeSpellingReportListener(
96                              SpellingReportListener srl)
97  {
98      spellingReportListeners.removeElement(srl);
99  }
100 /** Sends the spelling errors to all registered
101     SpellingReportListeners */
102 public void notifySpellingErrors()
103 {
104     Vector l;
105     SpellingReportEvent sre = new SpellingReportEvent(
106                                     this, nErr, errors);
107     synchronized(this)
108     {
109         l = (Vector)spellingReportListeners.clone();
110     }
111     for(int i = 0; i < l.size(); i++)
112     {
113         ((SpellingReportListener)l.elementAt(i)).
114                                 spellingErrors(sre);
115     }
116 }
```

```
117     /** Writes the object to an output stream */
118     private void writeObject(java.io.ObjectOutputStream out)
119                 throws java.io.IOException
120     {
121         out.defaultWriteObject();
122     }
123     /** Reads the object from an input stream */
124     private void readObject(java.io.ObjectInputStream in)
125                 throws java.lang.ClassNotFoundException,
126                     java.io.IOException
127     {
128         in.defaultReadObject();
129     }
130 }
```

ANNOTATIONS

You can best understand the **Speller** bean's design when you see how it exchanges information with other beans and what resources it uses to do its job. Figure 8-4 shows how the **Speller** bean is used by another bean such as the **TextMessage** bean, described later in this section. As Figure 8-4 shows, the **Speller** bean implements the **SpellCheckListener** interface (meaning that it can receive **SpellCheckEvent**s) and uses a list of correctly spelled words from a file named **words.txt** that's stored as a resource in the same Jar file as the **Speller** bean. When the other bean (such as **TextMessage**) has to check the spelling of words in some text, that bean sends the text to the **Speller** bean in a **SpellCheckEvent**. The **Speller** bean checks each word against the list of correctly spelled words in **words.txt**. It then reports back the results of the spelling check in a **SpellingReportEvent**. This means that the other bean has to implement the **SpellingReportListener** interface so that it can receive the results of the spell check.

Note that whenever a bean sends out a specific type of event, that bean must implement the add and remove methods for listeners of that event type. This means that the **Speller** bean has to include the **addSpellingReportListener()** and **removeSpellingReportListener()** methods so that it can keep track of all beans that want to receive **SpellingReportEvent**s. Similarly, the **TextMessage** bean has to implement the **addSpellCheckListener()** and **removeSpellCheckListener()** methods to add or remove listeners for **SpellCheckEvent**s.

As you can see, before you start reading the source code for the **Speller** or **TextMessage** bean, you need to learn about the supporting classes— **SpellCheckEvent**, **SpellCheckListener**, **SpellingReportEvent**, and **SpellingReportListener**—because they feature prominently in the operation of the **Speller** and **TextMessage** beans. Luckily, these classes are fairly simple and easy to understand. I will go over these supporting classes next.

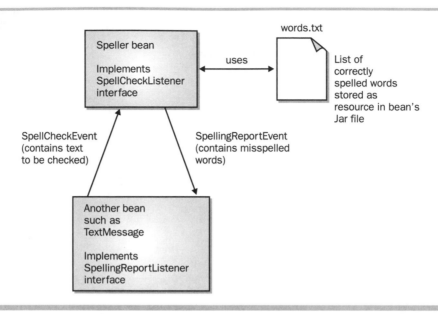

FIGURE 8-4. The basic operation of the **Speller** bean.

The following listing shows the **SpellCheckEvent** class, which is used to send some text (to be spell-checked) to the **Speller** bean:

```
//-----------------------------------------------------------------
// File: SpellCheckEvent.java
//
// Beans provide text for spell check through SpellCheckEvent.
// The Speller bean implements a SpellCheckListener to receive
// these events.
//-----------------------------------------------------------------
package ch08.speller;
import java.util.*;
public class SpellCheckEvent extends EventObject
{
    String text;
    SpellCheckEvent(Object source, String text)
    {
        super(source);
        this.text = text;
    }
    public String getText() { return text;}
}
```

SpellCheckEvent is a subclass of **EventObject** and has a **String** object that stores the text to be spell-checked. Any class that receives a **SpellCheckEvent** can call the **getText()** method to retrieve the text. The receiving class must implement any methods specified by the **SpellCheckListener** interface, which is shown next.

The following listing shows the **SpellCheckListener** interface, which specifies the method that the **Speller** class implements in order to receive and process **SpellCheckEvent**:

```
//------------------------------------------------------------
// File: SpellCheckListener.java
//
// Specifies method to be implemented by classes that want
// to receive text for spell check.
//------------------------------------------------------------
package ch08.speller;
import java.util.*;
public interface SpellCheckListener extends EventListener
{
    public void checkText(SpellCheckEvent sce);
}
```

SpellCheckListener is a subclass of **EventListener**, and it specifies a single method, **checkText()**, that must be implemented to handle a **SpellCheckEvent**.

The result of the spelling check is reported through **SpellingReportEvent**, shown in the following listing:

```
//------------------------------------------------------------
// File: SpellingReportEvent.java
//
// The Speller bean reports results of spell check through
// SpellingRepotEvents. Beans that want to receive reports
// should implement the SpellingReportInterface interface.
//------------------------------------------------------------
package ch08.speller;
import java.util.*;
public class SpellingReportEvent extends EventObject
{
    int numErrors;
    String[] words;
    SpellingReportEvent(Object source, int numErrors,
                        String[] words)
    {
        super(source);
        this.numErrors = numErrors;
        this.words = words;
```

```
    }
    public int getErrorCount() { return numErrors;}
    public String[] getWrongWords() { return words;}
}
```

SpellingReportEvent includes two data items: an integer with the count of misspelled words and an array of **String**s with the misspelled words themselves. Two public methods, **getErrorCount()** and **getWrongWords()**, allow the event recipients to extract the information about misspelled words.

SpellingReportListener is the listener interface for the **SpellingReportEvent**. As the following listing shows, the **SpellingReportListener** interface specifies the method that a recipient of **SpellingReportEvent** must implement:

```
//-------------------------------------------------------------
// File: SpellingReportListener.java
//
// Specifies method to be implemented by classes that want
// to report of spell check.
//-------------------------------------------------------------
package ch08.speller;
import java.util.*;
public interface SpellingReportListener extends EventListener
{
    public void spellingErrors(SpellingReportEvent sre);
}
```

This interface requires **SpellingReportEvent** recipients to implement the **spellingErrors()** method.

You will see sample usage of these events and listeners in the source code of the **Speller** and **TextMessage** beans.

Returning to the **Speller** bean's source code, lines 29 through 48 show the public constructor for this bean:

```
29      public Speller()
30      {
31          // Read the list of correct words from the bean's
32          // resource in the jar file
33          InputStream rawIn =
34                  getClass().getResourceAsStream("words.txt");
35          BufferedReader in
36             = new BufferedReader(new InputStreamReader(rawIn));
37          String word;
38          try
39          {
```

```
40            while(true)
41            {
42                word = in.readLine();
43                if(word == null) break;
44                words.add(word); // save the words in a list
45            }
46        }
47        catch(IOException e) {}
48    }
```

Java 2

This constructor loads the list of correctly spelled words from the **words.txt** resource into a linked list structure maintained in the bean. Note that line 25 declares a **LinkedList** object named **words**. The **LinkedList** class is new in Java 2; it implements a linked list data structure in which you can store any type of object. Here, lines 33 and 34 call the **getResourceAsStream()** method to create an **InputStream** to load the resource named **words.txt**. Following Java conventions, this looks for a file named **ch08/speller/words.txt** (as line 16 shows, the package name is **ch08.speller**) in the **Speller** bean's Jar file. Lines 35 and 36 create a **BufferedReader** object from this **InputStream**.

The **words.txt** file stores the words, one word per line. The **while** loop in lines 40 through 45 reads the words and saves them in the **LinkedList** object named **words**. Line 42 reads a word by calling the **readLine()** method of the **BufferedReader** object. Then line 44 calls **words.add()** to save the word in the **LinkedList** named **words**.

Lines 49 through 87 show the **checkText()** method, which handles a **SpellCheckEvent** containing text to be spell-checked. This is where the **Speller** bean does its job.

Lines 55 and 56 create a **StringTokenizer** to split the text into words:

```
55        StringTokenizer st = new
56                StringTokenizer(sce.getText(), delim);
```

The **delim** string defines the delimiting characters that mark the end of words. Line 27 defines **delim** as follows:

```
27    private String delim = " ,.;:()\"\'\t\n\r\f";
```

Note that **delim** includes punctuation characters such as the comma and period so that words can be extracted from typical sentences.

Lines 59 through 69 perform the actual dictionary lookup: the **while** loop gets a token from the input text (a token should be a word) and then searches for that word in the internal **LinkedList** named **words**:

```
59        while (st.hasMoreTokens())
60        {
61            word = st.nextToken();
62            int r = Collections.binarySearch(words, word,
63                        String.CASE_INSENSITIVE_ORDER);
```

```
64              if(r < 0)
65              {
66                  errorList.add(word);
67                  nErr++;
68              }
69          }
```

Java 2

Lines 62 and 63 perform the actual search by using the **binarySearch()** method of the **Collections** class, which is another new class in Java 2. That method takes three arguments: the name of the linked list, the object you want to locate, and a **Comparator** that specifies how objects are to be compared. In this case, the objects are **String**s. Therefore, I use the **static Comparator** named **String.CASE_INSENSITIVE_ORDER** to perform a case-insensitive search. If the search is not successful, the **binarySearch()** method returns a negative value. This means that the word is misspelled (or, more accurately, that the word is not in the **words.txt** file). Line 66 adds any misspelled word to a **LinkedList** object named **errorList** (defined on line 53). Line 67 increments the **nErr** variable that keeps a count of spelling errors.

After all of the words have been spell-checked, lines 72 through 85 copy the list of misspelled words into a **String** array because the **SpellingReportEvent** requires the words to be in a **String[]**:

```
72      errors = new String[nErr];
73      try
74      {
75          ListIterator li = errorList.listIterator(0);
76          try
77          {
78              for(int i = 0; i < nErr; i++)
79              {
80                  errors[i] = (String)li.next();
81              }
82          }
83          catch(NoSuchElementException e){}
84      }
85      catch(IndexOutOfBoundsException e) {}
```

Line 72 creates a **String** array large enough to hold all of the misspelled words. Line 75 gets a **ListIterator** for the **LinkedList** named **errorList**. Then the **for** loop in lines 78 through 81 copies the misspelled words from the linked list to the **errors** array. Notice that line 80 calls the **next()** method of the **ListIterator** to get the next word in the linked list. Also, the code uses **try-catch** blocks to handle exceptions generated by the **listIterator()** and **next()** methods of the **ListIterator** class.

Line 86 implements the last step in the **checkText()** method:

```
86      notifySpellingErrors();
```

It calls the **notifySpellingErrors()** method to send out the results of the spelling check to all registered **SpellingReportListener** objects.

Lines 102 through 116 show the **notifySpellingErrors()** method, which calls the **spellingErrors()** method of all registered **SpellingReportListener** objects:

```
102    public void notifySpellingErrors()
103    {
104        Vector l;
105        SpellingReportEvent sre = new SpellingReportEvent(
106                                        this, nErr, errors);
107        synchronized(this)
108        {
109            l = (Vector)spellingReportListeners.clone();
110        }
111        for(int i = 0; i < l.size(); i++)
112        {
113            ((SpellingReportListener)l.elementAt(i)).
114                                        spellingErrors(sre);
115        }
116    }
```

Lines 105 and 106 create a new **SpellingReportEvent** with the current spelling error information. Line 109 makes a copy of the **Vector spellingReportListeners** by calling the **clone()** method of the **Vector** class. Line 109 is enclosed in a **synchronized** block to protect it against simultaneous access by multiple threads. The **for** loop in lines 111 through 115 gets each **SpellingReportListener** object and calls its **spellingErrors()** method. The **SpellingReportEvent** is passed as the argument to the **spellingErrors()** method. That's how the **Speller** bean sends back the results of the spelling check to other beans.

To test the **Speller** bean, I wrote a simple visible bean, **TextMessage**, that provides a user interface for typing in text that has to be spell-checked. **TextMessage** is designed to communicate using **SpellCheckEvent** and **SpellingReportEvent**. **TextMessage** also displays the results of spelling check. The following listing shows the **TextMessage.java** file, which implements the **TextMessage** bean:

```
//----------------------------------------------------------------
// File: TextMessage.java
//
// Allows user to type some text and press a button to
// initiate spell check and then displays the results.
// Sends the text to the Speller bean through SpellCheckEvent
// and receives results from Speller through SpellingReportEvent.
//----------------------------------------------------------------
package ch08.speller;
```

```java
import java.awt.*;
import java.awt.event.*;
import java.util.*;
public class TextMessage extends Panel implements
                        ActionListener, SpellingReportListener
{
    private transient Vector spellCheckListeners = new Vector();
    private transient TextArea taIn, taOut;
    private String text;
    /** Lays out the user interface for this bean */
    public TextMessage()
    {
        this.setLayout(new BorderLayout());
        taIn = new TextArea(10, 36);
        add("Center", taIn);
        taOut = new TextArea(10, 24);
        add("East", taOut);
        Panel p = new Panel();
        p.setLayout(new GridLayout(1, 4));
        Label l1 = new Label("      ");
        p.add(l1);
        Label l2 = new Label("      ");
        p.add(l2);
        Button b = new Button("Check");
        b.addActionListener(this);
        p.add(b);
        Label l3 = new Label("     ");
        p.add(l3);
        add("South", p);
        validate();
    }
    /** Sends text for spelling check */
    public void actionPerformed(ActionEvent ae)
    {
        text = taIn.getText();
        checkSpelling();
    }
    /** Displays results of spell check */
    public void spellingErrors(SpellingReportEvent sre)
    {
        String msg;
        taOut.setText("");
        if(sre.getErrorCount() == 0)
        {
```

```java
            msg = "NO ERRORS.";
        }
        else
        {
            msg = "MISSPELLED:";
        }
        taOut.append(msg);
        String[] words = sre.getWrongWords();
        for(int i = 0; i < sre.getErrorCount(); i++)
        {
            msg = "\n"+words[i];
            taOut.append(msg);
        }
    }
    /** Adds a SpellCheckListener */
    public synchronized void addSpellCheckListener(
                            SpellCheckListener scl)
    {
        spellCheckListeners.addElement(scl);
    }
    /** Removes a SpellCheckListener */
    public synchronized void removeSpellCheckListener(
                            SpellCheckListener scl)
    {
        spellCheckListeners.removeElement(scl);
    }
    /** Sends SpellCheckEvents to all registered
        SpellCheckListeners */
    public void checkSpelling()
    {
        Vector l;
        SpellCheckEvent sce = new SpellCheckEvent(this, text);
        synchronized(this)
        {
            l = (Vector)spellCheckListeners.clone();
        }
        for(int i = 0; i < l.size(); i++)
        {
            ((SpellCheckListener)l.elementAt(i)).checkText(sce);
        }
    }
}
```

The **TextMessage** bean lets you type some text in a text-entry area and click on a button to send that text to the **Speller** bean in a **SpellCheckEvent**. For that matter, **TextMessage** can send the **SpellCheckEvent** to any bean that implements the **SpellCheckListener** interface. It includes the **addSpellCheckListener()** and **removeSpellCheckListener()** methods, which allow application builder tools to hook it up to beans such as **Speller**.

TextMessage has two **TextArea** objects—**taIn** and **taOut**—one for entering the text to be checked and the other for displaying the results of the spelling check. A Button labeled Check is provided to initiate a spelling check. When the user clicks on that button, the **actionPerformed()** method is called. The **actionPerformed()** method is implemented as follows:

```
public void actionPerformed(ActionEvent ae)
{
    text = taIn.getText();
    checkSpelling();
}
```

This method gets the text from the **taIn** text-entry area and calls **checkSpelling()**. The **checkSpelling()** method places the text in a **SpellCheckEvent** and calls the **checkText()** method of all registered **SpellCheckListener** objects (such as the **Speller** bean).

The **TextMessage** bean also implements the **SpellingReportListener** interface by providing a **spellingErrors()** method. This means that it can display the spell-check reports sent by the **Speller** bean. The following code in the **spellingErrors()** method extracts the misspelled words from the **SpellingReportEvent** and displays them in the **taOut** text area:

```
String[] words = sre.getWrongWords();
for(int i = 0; i < sre.getErrorCount(); i++)
{
    msg = "\n"+words[i];
    taOut.append(msg);
}
```

The first line gets all misspelled words into a **String[]** array named **words** by calling the **getWrongWords()** method of the **SpellingReportEvent** object. Then the **for** loop displays each misspelled word in the **taOut** text area by calling the **append()** method of the **TextArea** class.

## PART 3

Java Applications

GUI Applications

Command-Line Applications

Client/Server Applications

Database Applications (TextView)

GUI Applications

A Calendar Application (ViewCal)   A Text Viewer (TextView)

In the previous chapters you saw many examples of Java applets and Java beans. This chapter turns to stand-alone Java applications that do not have the limitations of applets. I call them stand-alone applications because, unlike applets, you do not need a Web browser to run them. Also, these applications are not burdened by the strict security restrictions that are imposed on applets. Like other applications on your system, these Java applications can perform all operations. For example, stand-alone Java applications can read and write files and establish a TCP/IP connection with any Internet host.

There are two broad categories of Java applications: those that implement graphical user interfaces (GUIs) just as applets do and those that you run from the command line. This chapter covers the GUI applications; Chapter 10 presents several command-line applications written in Java.

Java 2

This chapter's GUI applications differ from the applets of previous chapters in another respect. These GUI applications use the new Swing GUI components that are part of Java 2. The previous chapters' applets and beans use GUI components from the older Abstract Windowing Toolkit (AWT). The AWT includes a limited selection of components that may have been adequate for applets, but stand-alone GUI applications require many more user interface components, such as menu bars and tables, that the older AWT lacks. Swing extends AWT by adding an extensive collection of GUI components that are on a par with other popular windowing systems. Additionally, the Swing architecture supports what is known as *pluggable look-and-feel* that allows users to change the appearance of the user interface without having to restart the application.

PROGRAMMER'S NOTE   *You will see the word **plaf** in the package name of Swing classes. That word is an acronym for "pluggable look-and-feel."*

Because the Swing classes are new, this chapter starts with a brief introduction to the Swing GUI components, including a description of the modified Model-View-Controller (MVC) architecture of the Swing classes. Then it presents a few sample GUI applications that illustrate how to use many GUI components. The first application shows how you can convert an applet into a stand-alone application.

You will find the following Java applications in this chapter:

◆   **ViewCal**—A GUI application that displays a calendar

◆   **TextView**—A GUI application that lets the user open and view text files

An Overview of Swing

To understand the Swing class library, you need to know a bit about how Java's GUI classes came about. Java 1.0 came with the Abstract Windowing Toolkit, or AWT for short. AWT is a set of classes that allows you to build GUIs for applets and applications. AWT classes include the basic components such as buttons, labels, checkboxes, frames, text-input areas, scrollbars, and panels. AWT also provides graphics classes to handle drawing and image rendering. You can see examples of AWT classes in the applets presented in the earlier chapters of this book.

Each of the GUI components in AWT has two parts: a Java class representing the component and a peer object that renders the component using the capabilities of the native windowing system on which the Java Virtual Machine is running. For example, in Microsoft Windows, AWT's **Button** component is drawn using a button from a Microsoft Windows library. This means that the button should look the same as other buttons in Microsoft Windows. On the other hand, the **Button** on a Macintosh will look like other buttons in the Macintosh user interface. The AWT components are known as *heavyweight* components because each component has a platform-specific implementation that is directly supported by a user interface component of the underlying windowing system. Typically, each component is rendered in a window from the windowing system.

The Swing components are a high-level collection of GUI components, implemented entirely in Java. (Swing was the name of the project that developed these components.) Swing renders components such as buttons and labels in a container such as a frame or a dialog box. The container is a heavyweight component that does rely on the underlying windowing system, but the components themselves do not make use of any user interface components from the underlying windowing system. The container provides the drawing area where various Swing components render themselves. Swing components are called *lightweight* because they do not have any representation in the underlying windowing system. For example, on a Microsoft Windows system, a Swing button does not use a Windows button. Instead, the button is drawn using graphics primitives such as lines and rectangles. This means that a Swing component should look the same on any system. In fact, as you will see later in this section, Swing allows you to change the look and feel of the user interface (UI) on the fly.

The following sections summarize Swing's UI components, describe the modified Model-View-Controller architecture used in Swing, and provide some Swing programming tips.

The SwingSet Demo

Before you read the rest of this chapter, you need to experience the user interface components and the functionality that Swing offers. You can explore the Swing components if you have installed Sun's Java Development Kit (JDK) 1.2 (which implements Java 2) on your system. If you have not yet done so, visit Sun's JDK 1.2 Web site at **http://java.sun.com/products/jdk/1.2/**, download the software, and install it on your system.

Assuming that you have installed JDK1.2 on your Windows system, you will find a demo program named **SwingSet** in the **c:\jdk1.2\demo\jfc\SwingSet** directory.

From an MS-DOS window, change to that directory and then type **java SwingSet** to start the program.

SwingSet immediately displays a dialog box with a progress bar that shows the items it is loading. When it finishes loading, the dialog box disappears and **SwingSet** displays the window shown in Figure 9-1.

The **SwingSet** window has a menu bar and a large tabbed pane with numerous tabs. As the figure shows, **SwingSet** initially displays the **Swing!** tab with an opening screen. Each of the other tabs contains samples of various Swing components. The tab headings tell you what types of components appear on a tab. For example, to see the Swing component that provides a tree view of hierarchical data, click on the TreeView tab. You will see what amounts to a directory structure in an outline view. Click on a folder to open it and see its contents. By drilling down through folders, you can see the contents of a specific folder. Figure 9-2 shows a typical tree view. Figure 9-2 also shows another key feature of the

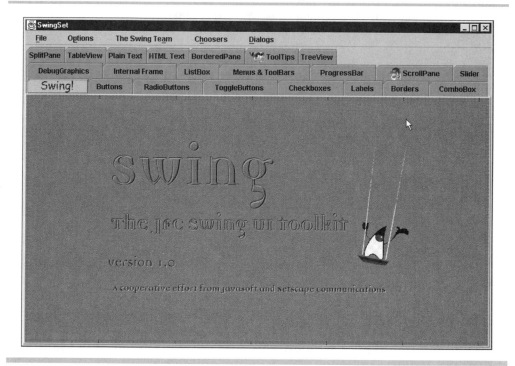

FIGURE 9-1.   Exploring the Swing components in the **SwingSet** program.

The Duke logo is a trademark or registered trademark of Sun Microsystems, Inc. in the United States and other countries.

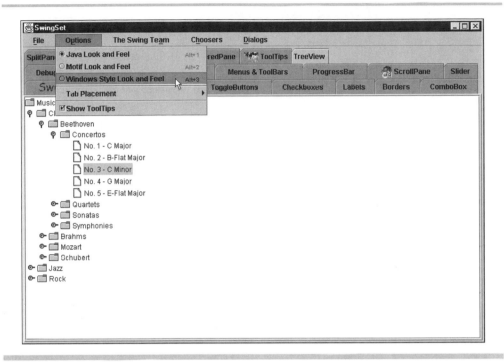

FIGURE 9-2. A typical tree view in the TreeView tab of the **SwingSet** program.

SwingSet demo program. **SwingSet** allows you to try out pluggable look-and-feel, which lets you change the appearance and behavior of a Swing user interface without having to restart the application. As you can see in Figure 9-2, the Options menu lets you choose between the Java, Motif, and Windows styles of look-and-feel. The figure shows the default Java look-and-feel. If you select Windows Style Look and Feel from the Options menu, the user interface immediately changes to a Windows-style appearance, as shown in Figure 9-3. Notice that the tree view of Figure 9-3 resembles the views you see in Windows Explorer, and the appearance of the folders matches the ones you see in the Microsoft Windows user interface.

The ability to switch from one type of look-and-feel to another is a significant advantage of the Swing GUI components. It means that, as an application developer, if you develop a GUI application with Swing components, your users can choose whatever look-and-feel they want.

To fully explore the other Swing components, you should experiment with each of the tabs in **SwingSet**. You should also try the items listed in the Choosers and

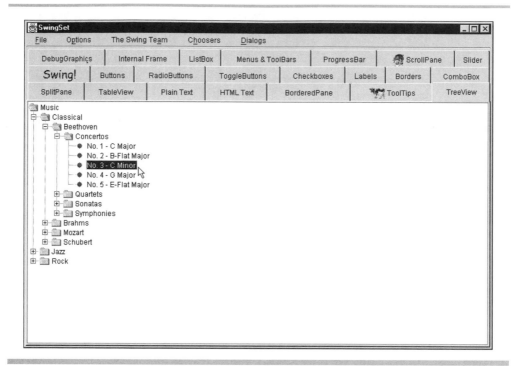

FIGURE 9-3. The tree view after switching to Windows-style look-and-feel.

Dialogs menus on the menu bar. In particular, the Choosers menu allows you to try out a File Chooser (to browse directories and select a file) and a Color Chooser (to select a color from a palette).

Java Foundation Classes and Swing

You may have heard about Java Foundation Classes (JFC), which is a collection of classes that provide everything you need to develop GUI applications. Swing happens to be a part of JFC, and JFC itself is now incorporated into Java 2.

JFC does not replace AWT. Rather, it extends the AWT by adding the Swing classes and several other class libraries that support all aspects of GUI programming. In particular, JFC includes the following major components:

♦ **Swing GUI components** are lightweight GUI components for Java applications and applets. You have already explored the components in the **SwingSet** demo program, and you will see more examples of them later in this chapter. For the latest information on Swing classes and some programming tips, see *The Swing Connection,* an online newsletter at **http://java.sun.com/products/jfc/tsc/**.

◆ **Accessibility APIs** allow developers to create GUI applications that can support people with disabilities such as limited sight or the inability to operate a mouse. For more information on the accessibility features, visit Sun's Web site at **http://java.sun.com/products/jfc/jaccess-1.2/doc/** and browse the online accessibility documentation.

◆ **Java 2D API** is a set of classes for two-dimensional (2D) graphics and imaging. In particular, Java 2D API provides more control over the image rendering process. For more information on Java 2D API, visit the Java 2D API home page at **http://java.sun.com/products/java-media/2D/**. If you have JDK 1.2 installed, you can see what Java2D offers by running the **Java2Demo** program, which should be in the **demo\jfc\Java2D** subdirectory of the location where you installed JDK 1.2. (Use the command **java Java2Demo** to start the demo program.)

◆ **Drag and Drop** refers to the ability to cut and paste text and images between Java applications (as well as other applications running on your system). You can download the latest Drag and Drop specification from **http://java.sun.com/ beans/glasgow/#draganddrop**. In Java 2, the **java.awt.dnd** package includes the interfaces and classes for supporting drag-and-drop operations.

Swing happens to be the largest part of JFC. Originally, Swing was released as a separate class library that could be used with Java 1.1 class libraries. You had to download the Swing class library and install it separately. However, when Java 2 was officially released in December 1998, the Swing classes were included in it. If you downloaded JDK 1.2 (that's the version that supports Java 2), you will find the Swing classes in various packages with names that begin with **javax.swing**.

JFC is essentially layered on the AWT, which, in turn, relies on the native windowing system (such as Microsoft Windows or Motif) to render the user interface on the display. Figure 9-4 illustrates the layered model of JFC. As the figure shows, the Swing components rely on parts of the AWT but not all of it. AWT components use the native windowing system to display output and receive user input from the mouse and keyboard. AWT components such as buttons, labels, panels, and frames are still available for use. The Accessibility APIs are closely tied to Swing components, but Java2D API and Drag and Drop also rely on the native windowing system. Finally, Java GUI applications rely on the Swing components (although they can also use the AWT components, if necessary).

Swing Classes

Because this book focuses on explaining Java programming through sample programs, you may not encounter all of the Swing classes here. Only the most commonly used Swing components show up in the various examples. However, it's

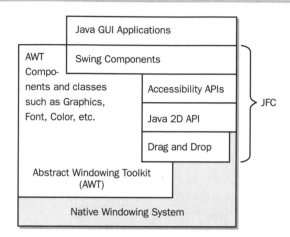

FIGURE 9-4.   The layered model of Java Foundation Classes (JFC).

useful to know the names of the various components, so you know what's available in Swing. Accordingly, Table 9-1 summarizes the Swing classes.

Class	Description
JApplet	Implements a Java applet capable of using Swing components. Any applet that uses Swing classes must be a subclass of **JApplet**.
JButton	Displays a button with some text and, optionally, an icon.
JCheckBox	Displays a checkbox.
JCheckBoxMenuItem	Displays a menu item that can be selected or deselected.
JColorChooser	Displays a complex dialog box from which the user can select a color.
JComboBox	Displays a combo box that includes a text field and a button to view a drop-down list of items.
JComponent	Represents the superclass of most Swing classes.
JDesktopPane	Implements a **DesktopManager** object that can be plugged into a **JInternalFrame** object.
JDialog	Provides a container in which Swing components can be laid out to create custom dialog boxes.

TABLE 9-1.   Summary of Swing Component Classes.

Class	Description
JEditorPane	Provides a text component to edit various types of content such as plain text, HTML, and Rich Text Format (RTF).
JFileChooser	Displays a complex dialog box in which the user can browse through folders and select a file.
JFrame	Provides a container in which other Swing components can be laid out. Most stand-alone GUI applications use a **JFrame** as the top-level container for laying out other Swing components.
JInternalFrame	Implements a lightweight frame object that can be placed inside a **JDesktopPane** object.
JLabel	Displays a label showing text or an image or both.
JLayeredPane	Allows the display of multiple layered panes in a frame so that components can be overlaid.
JList	Displays a list of objects (text or icons) from which the user can select one or more items.
JMenu	Implements a drop-down menu that can be attached to a menu bar (the menu can show text or images or both).
JMenuBar	Implements a menu bar.
JMenuItem	Implements a menu item that appears in a **JMenu**.
JOptionPane	Displays a dialog box that prompts the user for input and then provides that input to the program.
JPanel	Provides a lightweight container for arranging other components such as **JButton**, **JLabel**, and **JComboBox**.
JPasswordField	Displays a text field in which the user can type a password (the characters typed by the user are not displayed).
JPopupMenu	Implements a pop-up menu.
JProgressBar	Displays a progress bar that can be used to indicate the progress of an operation.
JRadioButton	Implements a radio button that can display text or an image or both.
JRadioButtonMenuItem	Implements a menu item that is part of a group of menu items, only one of which can be selected at any time.
JRootPane	Creates an object with a glass pane, a layered pane, an optional menu bar, and a content pane.
JScrollBar	Displays a scrollbar.
JScrollPane	Implements a scrolled pane that can scroll objects placed inside the pane.

TABLE 9-1. Summary of Swing Component Classes *(continued).*

Class	Description
JSeparator	Implements a separator that can be placed in a **JMenu** to separate one group of menu items from another.
JSlider	Displays a slider bar from which the user can select a value.
JSplitPane	Implements a pane that can be split horizontally or vertically.
JTabbedPane	Implements tabbed pane components that allow the user to view different pages by clicking on tabs (much like the tabs on file folders).
JTable	Implements a table that can display tabular data (ideal for displaying the results of database searches).
JTableHeader	Implements the column header part of a **JTable** (shares the same **TableColumnModel** with the **JTable**).
JTextArea	Implements a multiline text area that can be used to display read-only or editable text.
JTextField	Provides a single-line text entry and editing area.
JTextPane	Provides a text component that can be marked up with attributes that are represented graphically.
JToggleButton	Implements a button that can display text or an image and that can be in one of two states (on or off).
JToolBar	Implements a toolbar that can either be attached to a frame or stand alone.
JToolTip	Displays a short help message (attached to a component to provide help when the user moves the mouse onto that component).
JTree	Displays a set of hierarchical data in the form of a tree (similar to the directory structure in Windows Explorer).
JViewport	Displays a clipped view of a component (used by **JScrollPane**).
JWindow	Implements a container that can be displayed anywhere on the user's desktop (**JWindow** does not have the title bar and window-management buttons associated with a **JFrame**).

TABLE 9-1.　Summary of Swing Component Classes *(continued)*.

The Model-View-Controller Architecture and Swing

Swing components use a modified form of the Model-View-Controller (MVC) architecture. The classic MVC architecture of Smalltalk-80 breaks an application up into three separate layers:

◆ **Model**—The *application layer* or the *model* implements the application's functionality. All application-specific code is in this layer.

◆ **View**—The *presentation layer* or the *view* implements the mechanisms for presenting various aspects of the application layer to the user. In a graphical user interface, the view provides the windows.

◆ **Controller**—The *virtual terminal layer* or the *controller* handles the user's interactions with the application. This is a graphics library that presents a device-independent interface to the presentation layer.

Figure 9-5 illustrates this classic MVC architecture of Smalltalk-80.

The MVC architecture does an excellent job of separating the responsibilities of the objects in the system. The application-specific details are insulated from the user interface. Also, the user interface itself is broken down into two parts, with the presentation handled by the view and the user interaction (mouse and keyboard input) handled by the controller.

Each Smalltalk-80 application consists of a model and an associated view-controller pair. Figure 9-6 shows the usual interactions in Smalltalk-80's MVC architecture. The controller accepts the user's inputs and invokes the appropriate methods from the model to perform the task requested by the user. When the work is done, the method in the model sends messages to the view and controller. The view updates the display in response to this message, accessing the model for further information, if necessary Thus, the model has a view and a controller, but it never directly accesses either of them. The view and controller, on the other hand, access the model's functions and data when necessary.

As Figure 9-6 illustrates, in actual implementations, the view and controller are tightly coupled and typically treated as a single view-controller pair. This is the way Swing uses the MVC model. Each Swing component collapses the view and controller into a single user interface (UI) object, but retains the model as a separate entity. The model maintains state information such as the maximum, minimum, and current values of a scrollbar. The UI object handles the view and controller responsibilities by rendering the component and processing user input in the form of mouse and keyboard events. Additionally, Swing introduces a UI manager that handles the look-and-feel characteristics of each component. Figure 9-7 depicts the *Model-UI object-UI manager* architecture of Swing components. The UI manager

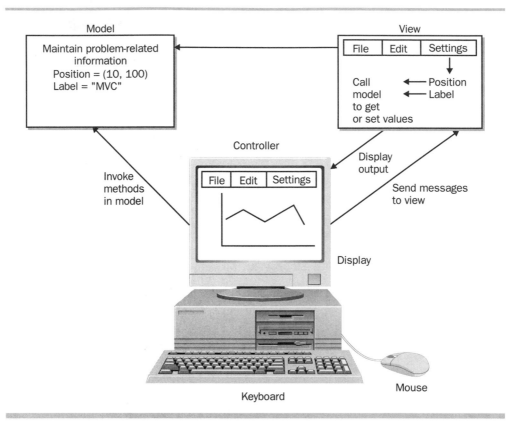

FIGURE 9-5. The Model-View-Controller (MVC) architecture of Smalltalk-80.

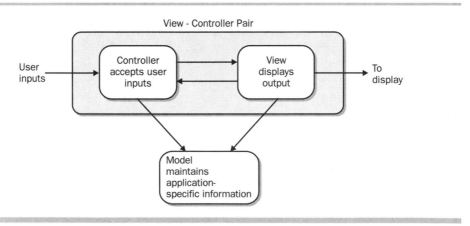

FIGURE 9-6. Interactions among model, view, and controller in Smalltalk-80.

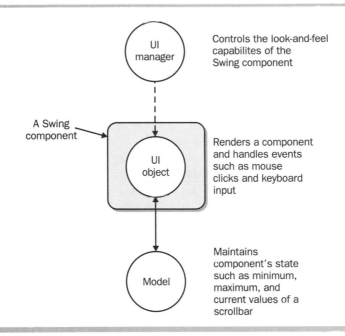

UI manager — Controls the look-and-feel capabilites of the Swing component

A Swing component

UI object — Renders a component and handles events such as mouse clicks and keyboard input

Model — Maintains component's state such as minimum, maximum, and current values of a scrollbar

FIGURE 9-7. The modified MVC architecture used by Swing components.

controls the look-and-feel capabilities of a Swing component by communicating with the component's UI object, as shown in Figure 9-7.

If you think about look-and-feel, *look* refers to how the component appears on the display, and *feel* refers to how the component reacts to user inputs. In other words, look and feel are the responsibilities of the view and controller components of the MVC architecture. In each Swing component, the UI object handles the look-and-feel of the component. Because the class representing the component delegates the look-and-feel responsibilities to the UI object, that object is also referred to as the *UI delegate*.

You should remember that all Swing components use a separate model. Many simple components provide a default model that maintains the information you provide when you create the Swing component. For more-complex Swing components, such as **JTable**, you have to provide a model that represents the tabular data and implements the interface expected by **JTable**.

Swing Programming Tips

When you use AWT components to create a user interface, you place AWT components such as buttons, labels, and checkboxes inside various AWT containers such as frames and panels. Typically, you end up with a hierarchical containment structure, grouping several components in a panel and then placing several panels inside another panel. You do not have to worry much about how the components paint themselves, because the AWT components are heavyweight components that rely on the underlying windowing system for rendering themselves.

The situation changes when you create a user interface with the lightweight Swing components. Swing components rely on Java code (as opposed to the underlying windowing system) to support the windowing features such as showing, hiding, moving, and resizing the components. The upshot is that you have to follow certain rules when constructing user interfaces with Swing components, and you have to follow a few key rules to ensure that the user interface is painted properly.

The first rule is to avoid mixing heavyweight and lightweight components when they may overlap. In other words, do not place an AWT component inside a Swing component and vice versa. When these two types of components overlap, they are not painted correctly. (If you must use both AWT and Swing components, the article at **http://java.sun.com/products/jfc/tsc/archive/tech_topics_arch/mixing/ mixing.html** explains the rules for doing so.)

To use Swing components properly, you must start with one of the container classes in Swing. The most commonly used container classes are

♦ **JApplet** for any applet that uses Swing components

♦ **JFrame** for GUI applications that use Swing components

♦ **JDialog** for dialog boxes that contain Swing components

These Swing containers use an appropriate heavyweight AWT component to create the display area where the lightweight Swing components can be arranged. Each of these containers has a content pane in which the rest of the components are placed. You must add other Swing components to the content pane. Call the **getContentPane()** method of the Swing container to get the content pane and then add the components to that pane. For example, here is how you would create a **JFrame** and add a **JDesktopPane** to that frame:

```
JFrame frame = new JFrame("Main Application Frame");
JDesktopPane jdp = new JDesktopPane();
frame.getContentPane().add(jdp);
```

To add lightweight components to other lightweight components, such as **JPanel**, you simply need to call the **add()** method of the **JPanel** object.

Whenever you want to redraw any Swing component, call that component's **repaint()** method. As with AWT components, do not call **paint()** directly. For example, here's how the **repaint()** method of a **JButton** is called in a mouse listener to repaint the button as the user presses and releases the button:

```
MouseListener l = new MouseAdapter()
{
    public void mousePressed(MouseEvent ev)
    {
        JButton b = (JButton)ev.getSource();
        b.setSelected(true);
        b.repaint();
    }
    public void mouseReleased(MouseEvent ev)
    {
        JButton b = (JButton)ev.getSource();
        b.setSelected(false);
        b.repaint();
    }
};
```

When you define any class as a subclass of the Swing container classes (**JApplet**, **JFrame**, or **JDialog**) and override the **paint()** method, you must insert a call to **super.paint()**, as shown in the following example:

```
public class MyApplet extends JApplet
{
    public void paint(Graphics g)
    {
        // Paint my applet's contents first. Then make sure
        // lightweight Swing components are painted.
            super.paint(g);
    }
}
```

If you do not call **super.paint()**, the lightweight Swing components inside the container won't show up. This is a common problem with beginners to Swing programming.

Additionally, each Swing component breaks down the **paint()** processing into three distinct parts by calling three methods in the following sequence:

1. **paintComponent()** to draw this component

2. **paintBorder()** to draw this component's border

3. **paintChildren()** to draw this component's children

When you define any class as a subclass of a lightweight Swing component such as **JPanel,** you should override the **paintComponent()** method to perform any additional painting you want done. You should first call **super.paintComponent()** to properly draw the component, as shown in the following example:

```
public class MyPanel extends JPanel
{
    protected void paintComponent(Graphics g)
    {
        // First call the superclass' paintComponent() to
        // ensure correct painting of the component
        super.paintComponent(g);
        // Now paint anything MyPanel needs ...
    }
}
```

Because Swing components draw themselves in a pane—a drawing area—provided by a container, Swing uses double buffering to avoid flickering when components are drawn. This means that the user interface is drawn in an off-screen buffer and then the off-screen image is copied to the screen. The **doubleBuffered** property of the **JComponent** class controls whether double buffering is enabled. By default, the **doubleBuffered** property is set to **true**. Although you can change this property by calling the **setDoubleBuffered()** method, you should leave double buffering enabled for all Swing components.

A Calendar Application

This section presents **ViewCal**, a GUI application derived from the **Calendar** applet that I described in Chapter 2. To create this application, I replaced all of the AWT user interface components in **Calendar** with similar Swing components. Then I converted that applet to run as an application by providing a static **main()** method that creates the frame necessary to display the calendar. By studying this application, you will learn how to use a number of different Swing components. You will also learn how to convert an applet to an application.

Using ViewCal

The files for the **ViewCal** application are in the **ch09\ViewCal** directory of the companion CD-ROM. Assuming that you have Sun's JDK 1.2 installed on your system, you can run the application by typing **java ViewCal** from an MS-DOS window after changing to the **ch09\ViewCal** directory of the CD-ROM. **ViewCal** displays a calendar for the current year and current month and highlights the current date. You can change the year by typing a new year into the text field and pressing ENTER. You can also click on the buttons next to the text field to move forward and backward by a month. Another way to select a new month is by clicking on the down arrow next to the month and then selecting a month from the list that appears. Figure 9-8 shows a typical monthly calendar displayed by the **ViewCal** application. When you move the mouse over the text field and buttons, a small pop-up help message (called a *tool tip*) appears that tells you what that GUI component does. Figure 9-8 shows the tool tip associated with the text field in which you enter a new year. As you will learn later, these tool tips are a feature of Swing components.

Because **ViewCal** is an applet, you can run it as an applet. However, you have to run it in a Web browser that supports the Swing classes. If you have JDK 1.2 installed on your system, use the command **appletviewer cal.html** to run **ViewCal** as an applet. (The file **cal.html** is in the **ch09\ViewCal** directory of the CD-ROM.)

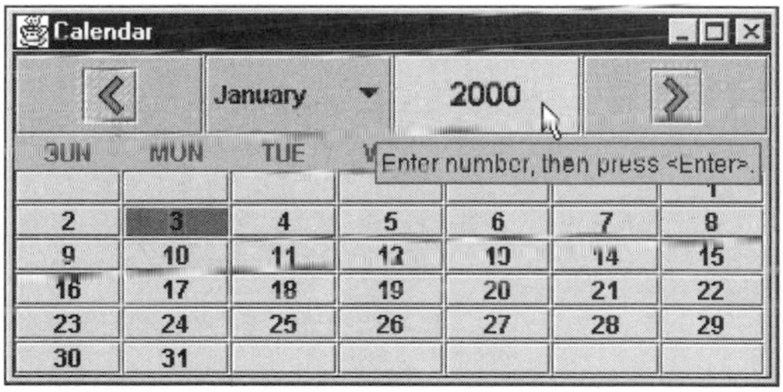

FIGURE 9-8.   **ViewCal** displays a calendar for a selected month and year.

Understanding ViewCal

The following listing shows the **ViewCal.java** file that implements the **ViewCal**
application. I describe the code in the section that follows the listing.

```java
1  //------------------------------------------------------------------
2  // ViewCal.java
3  //
4  // A calendar applet that you can run as a stand-alone
5  // application. Uses a GUI built with the Swing classes in
6  // Java 2. Shows how you can convert an applet into a
7  // stand-alone GUI application.
8  //------------------------------------------------------------------
9  import java.applet.*;
10 import java.awt.*;
11 import java.util.*;
12 import java.awt.event.*;
13 import javax.swing.*;
14 /** ViewCal is an applet that includes a main() method so it
15  *  can run as a stand-alone application. Use the command
16  *  "java ViewCal" to run the application. Note that ViewCal
17  *  is a subclass of JApplet because it uses Swing components.
18  */
19 public class ViewCal extends JApplet implements ActionListener,
20                                                 ItemListener
21 {
22     private JComboBox   monthChoice;
23     private JTextField  year;
24     private JButton     previousButton;
25     private JButton     nextButton;
26     private int         currentMonth;
27     private int         currentYear;
28     private String      currentDayString;
29     private String      currentDateString;
30     private Font helvB16 =
31                 new Font("Helvetica", Font.BOLD, 16);
32     private String days[] = {"SUN", "MON", "TUE", "WED", "THU",
33                             "FRI", "SAT"};
34     private String months[] = {
35                     "January", "February", "March", "April",
36                     "May", "June", "July", "August", "September",
37                     "October", "November", "December"};
```

```
38    private int daysInMonth[] = {31, 28, 31, 30, 31, 30, 31, 31,
39                                 30, 31, 30, 31};
40    private JButton[][] monthButtons = new JButton[6][7];
41    private JButton highlightedBtn = null;
42    private JLabel[] dayLabels = new JLabel[7];
43    /** Initializes the calendar's user interface */
44    public void init()
45    {
46        Calendar today = Calendar.getInstance();
47        currentMonth = today.get(Calendar.MONTH);
48        currentYear = today.get(Calendar.YEAR);
49        currentDayString = ""+today.get(Calendar.DAY_OF_MONTH);
50        // In JApplet everything is inside a ContentPane
51        Container cp = this.getContentPane();
52        cp.setLayout(new BorderLayout());
53
54        JPanel pTop = new JPanel();
55        pTop.setLayout(new GridLayout(1, 4));
56        Icon prevIcon = new ImageIcon("prev.gif");
57        previousButton = new JButton(prevIcon);
58        previousButton.addActionListener(this);
59        previousButton.setToolTipText("Previous month");
60        pTop.add(previousButton);
61        monthChoice = new JComboBox();
62        for(int i = 0; i < months.length; i++)
63            monthChoice.addItem(months[i]);
64        monthChoice.setSelectedIndex(currentMonth);
65        monthChoice.setMaximumRowCount(6);
66        monthChoice.addItemListener(this);
67        pTop.add(monthChoice);
68        year = new JTextField("" + currentYear, 4);
69        year.setFont(helvB16);
70        year.setBackground(Color.lightGray);
71        year.setHorizontalAlignment(JTextField.CENTER);
72        year.addActionListener(this);
73        year.setToolTipText("Enter number, then press <Enter>.");
74        pTop.add(year);
75        Icon nextIcon = new ImageIcon("next.gif");
76        nextButton = new JButton(nextIcon);
77        nextButton.addActionListener(this);
78        nextButton.setToolTipText("Next month");
79        pTop.add(nextButton);
```

```
80        cp.add("North", pTop);
81
82      JPanel pButtons = new JPanel();
83      pButtons.setLayout(new GridLayout(7,7));
84      for(int i=0; i < days.length; i++)
85      {
86          dayLabels[i] = new JLabel(days[i], JLabel.CENTER);
87          pButtons.add(dayLabels[i]);
88      }
89      for(int i=0; i < 6; i++)
90          for(int j=0; j < 7; j++)
91          {
92              monthButtons[i][j] = new JButton("");
93              monthButtons[i][j].setBackground(Color.lightGray);
94              monthButtons[i][j].addActionListener(this);
95              pButtons.add(monthButtons[i][j]);
96          }
97      cp.add("Center", pButtons);
98      validate();
99      repaint();
100   }
101   /** Returns true if the year is a leap year. */
102   public boolean isLeapYear(int year)
103   {
104       if((year % 400) == 0) return(true);
105       if((year > 1582) && ((year % 100) == 0)) return(false);
106       if((year % 4) == 0) return(true);
107       return(false);
108   }
109   /** Displays the calendar for a specific month of a year */
110   public void displayMonth(int month, int year)
111   {
112       int day = 1; // first of the month
113       int monthNum = month - 1; // month number,1=Mar,2=Apr,...
114       if(monthNum <= 0) monthNum += 12; // Jan = 11, Feb = 12
115       int tempYear = year;
116       if(monthNum > 10) tempYear = year - 1;
117       int century = tempYear / 100;
118       int yy = tempYear - 100 * century;
119       int factor = (int)(day +
120               (int)(2.6*(double)monthNum - 0.2) -
121               2*century + yy + yy/4 + century/4.0);
```

```
122        int firstWeekday = factor % 7; // 0=Sun, 1=Mon, 2=Tue, ...
123
124        // Now draw the dates on the buttons in the calendar
125        int maxDate = daysInMonth[month];
126        if(month == 1 && isLeapYear(year)) maxDate += 1;
127        int dateNow = 1;
128        if(highlightedBtn != null)
129            highlightedBtn.setBackground(Color.lightGray);
130        String ds;
131        for(int i=0; i < 6; i++)
132        {
133            for(int j=0; j < 7; j++)
134            {
135                if(dateNow == 1 && j < firstWeekday)
136                    monthButtons[i][j].setText("");
137                else if(dateNow > maxDate)
138                    monthButtons[i][j].setText("");
139                else
140                {
141                    ds = ""+dateNow;
142                    monthButtons[i][j].setText(ds);
143                    if(ds.equals(currentDayString))
144                    {
145                        monthButtons[i][j].setBackground(
146                                        Color.gray);
147                        highlightedBtn = monthButtons[i][j];
148                    }
149                    dateNow++;
150                }
151            }
152        }
153    }
154    /** Processes the year entered by the user */
155    public int processYear(String yearString)
156    {
157        if((yearString.length() == 4))
158        {
159            try
160            {
161                int year = Integer.parseInt(yearString);
162                return year;
163            }
```

```
164            catch(NumberFormatException e)
165            {
166                return currentYear;
167            }
168        }
169        return -1;
170    }
171    /** Calls displayMonth() to display the calendar */
172    public void paint(Graphics g)
173    {
174        g.setColor(Color.black);
175        Dimension d = getSize();
176        g.drawRect(0, 0, d.width-1,d.height-1);
177        displayMonth(currentMonth, currentYear);
178        super.paint(g);    // Important step for Swing components
179    }
180    /** Handles mouse clicks in the buttons and drop-down menus*/
181    public void actionPerformed(ActionEvent ev)
182    {
183        if(ev.getSource().equals(previousButton))
184        {
185            if((currentYear > 1) || (currentMonth > 0))
186            {
187                currentMonth--;
188                if(currentMonth < 0)
189                {
190                    currentMonth = 11;
191                    currentYear--;
192                }
193                monthChoice.setSelectedIndex(currentMonth);
194                year.setText(""+currentYear);
195                currentDayString = "1";
196                repaint();
197            }
198        }
199        else if(ev.getSource() == nextButton)
200        {
201            if((currentYear < 9999) || (currentMonth < 11))
202            {
203                currentMonth++;
204                if(currentMonth > 11)
205                {
```

```
206                     currentMonth = 0;
207                     currentYear++;
208                 }
209             monthChoice.setSelectedIndex(currentMonth);
210             year.setText(""+currentYear);
211             currentDayString = "1";
212             repaint();
213         }
214     }
215     else if(ev.getSource() == year)
216     {
217 // called when user presses Enter in text field
218         int y = processYear(year.getText());
219         if((y > 0) && (y != currentYear))
220         {
221             currentYear = y;
222             currentDayString = "1";
223             repaint();
224         }
225     }
226     else
227     {   // check for click on a day of the month
228         String ds;
229         for(int i=0; i < 6; i++)
230         {
231             for(int j=0; j < 7; j++)
232             {
233                 if(ev.getSource() == monthButtons[i][j])
234                 {
235                     ds = ev.getActionCommand();
236                     if(!ds.equals(""))
237                     {
238                         highlightedBtn.
239                             setBackground(Color.lightGray);
240                         highlightedBtn = monthButtons[i][j];
241                         monthButtons[i][j].setBackground(
242                                             Color.gray);
243                         currentDayString = ds;
244                     }
245                 }
246             }
247         }
```

```
248          }
249      }
250      /** Handles selections from the month list */
251      public void itemStateChanged(ItemEvent ev)
252      {
253          if(ev.getSource() == monthChoice)
254          {
255              int m = monthChoice.getSelectedIndex();
256              year.setText(""+currentYear);
257              if(m != currentMonth)
258              {
259                  currentMonth = monthChoice.getSelectedIndex();
260                  currentDayString = "1";
261                  repaint();
262              }
263          }
264      }
265      /** Makes room for a 1-pixel border. */
266      public Insets getInsets()
267      {
268          return new Insets(1,1,1,1); // 1-pixel border
269      }
270      /** Provides a frame so ViewCal can run stand-alone */
271      public static void main(String s[])
272      {
273          WindowListener l = new WindowAdapter()
274          {
275              public void windowClosing(WindowEvent e)
276              {System.exit(0);}
277          };
278
279          JFrame frame = new JFrame("Calendar");
280          frame.addWindowListener(l);
281          ViewCal c = new ViewCal();
282          c.init();
283          frame.getContentPane().add("Center", c);
284          frame.pack();
285          frame.setVisible(true);
286      }
287 }
```

ANNOTATIONS

I created the **ViewCal** application from the **Calendar** applet discussed in Chapter 2. Both **ViewCal** and **Calendar** use the same underlying algorithm to compute the day of the week for a given date. Consult Chapter 2 for information about that algorithm. Here I will focus on the changes that I made to the applet.

I changed all of the AWT components to Swing components and converted the event-handling approach to the listener-based model used in Java 2. I then added a static **main()** method so that the class can run as a stand-alone application. The remainder of this section describes these changes in detail.

To support the new event-handling model and to use the Swing classes, I added the **import** statements on lines 12 and 13:

```
12 import java.awt.event.*;
13 import javax.swing.*;
```

The **java.awt.event** package contains the classes needed for listener-based event handling, and the **javax.swing** package defines the basic Swing classes.

I define **ViewCal** as a subclass of **JApplet** (instead of **Applet**) because applets that use Swing components must be defined in this way:

```
19 public class ViewCal extends JApplet implements ActionListener,
20                                                  ItemListener
```

ViewCal also implements the **ActionListener** and **ItemListener** interfaces to handle mouse clicks on various GUI components. The **ViewCal** class implements these interfaces by providing the required **actionPerformed()** and **itemStateChanged()** methods. The implementations of these methods are the same as in the **Calendar** Java bean (see Chapter 7), which is also derived from the **Calendar** applet of Chapter 2.

In the body of the **ViewCal** class, I changed all AWT classes, such as **Label**, **Button**, **TextField**, and **Choice**, to equivalent Swing classes. For the most part, you can simply add a **J** prefix to the AWT class name to get the equivalent Swing class. Thus, I use **JLabel**, **JButton**, and **JTextField** in place of **Label**, **Button**, and **TextField**. You have to be careful, however; not all AWT classes have similarly named equivalent Swing classes. For example, the Swing class that provides the functionality of AWT's **Choice** component is named **JComboBox**. (Windows provides a similar GUI component.)

As is typical in an applet, the **init()** method, shown in lines 44 through 100, lays out the user interface. Most of the **init()** method is similar to that in the **Calendar** applet except for the use of Swing components. There is, however, a key difference. Because **ViewCal** is a subclass of **JApplet**, you must add all GUI components to its content pane. Line 51 gets the content pane (which is a **Container** object), and line 52 sets the layout manager for the content pane:

```
51        Container cp = this.getContentPane();
52        cp.setLayout(new BorderLayout());
```

Later on, other high-level containers are added to the content pane named **cp**. For example, lines 54 through 79 prepare a set of GUI components in a **JPanel** named **pTop**. Then line 80 adds **pTop** to the north position of the content pane (in the **BorderLayout** manager, the north position is the top edge of the container):

```
80        cp.add("North", pTop);
```

The Swing components have capabilities above and beyond what AWT components support. For example, the **JButton** component allows you to create buttons with a label or an icon or both. Additionally, you can associate tool tips with many Swing components (as was mentioned previously, a tool tip is a help message that appears in a pop-up window when the user moves the mouse over the component). For example, lines 56 through 59 illustrate how a button with an icon is set up:

```
56        Icon prevIcon = new ImageIcon("prev.gif");
57        previousButton = new JButton(prevIcon);
58        previousButton.addActionListener(this);
59        previousButton.setToolTipText("Previous month");
```

Line 56 creates an icon from an image file named **prev.gif**. Line 57 creates a **JButton** object named **previousButton** with that icon (meaning that the button will display the icon). Line 58 assigns an action event listener to the newly created button. In this case, the listener is the **ViewCal** class (represented by the **this** keyword), which means that the **actionPerformed()** method of **ViewCal** is called whenever the user clicks on **previousButton**. Line 59 calls the **setToolTipText()** method to associate a short help message with that button. To see the result of calling **setToolTipText()**, run **ViewCal** and move the mouse over the button that shows an icon of a left-pointing arrow.

I made another important addition in the **paint()** method, shown in lines 172 through 179:

```
172   public void paint(Graphics g)
173   {
174        g.setColor(Color.black);
175        Dimension d = getSize();
176        g.drawRect(0, 0, d.width-1,d.height-1);
177        displayMonth(currentMonth, currentYear);
178        super.paint(g);   // Important step for Swing components
179   }
```

Lines 174 through 176 draw a border around the calendar. Then line 177 calls **displayMonth()** to draw the current month's calendar. After these steps, I inserted line 178, which calls **super.paint()** to ensure that all Swing components are painted properly.

The final addition to the applet's code is a static **main()** method that prepares a frame and provides the context where the applet can run. Lines 271 through 286 show the **main()** method:

```
271     public static void main(String s[])
272     {
273         WindowListener l = new WindowAdapter()
274         {
275             public void windowClosing(WindowEvent e)
276             {System.exit(0);}
277         };
278
279         JFrame frame = new JFrame("Calendar");
280         frame.addWindowListener(l);
281         ViewCal c = new ViewCal();
282         c.init();
283         frame.getContentPane().add("Center", c);
284         frame.pack();
285         frame.setVisible(true);
286     }
```

As line 271 shows, the **main()** method accepts an array of **String** objects as argument—these are the arguments that the user specifies on the command line. For example, if the user were to start the application with a command such as **java ViewCal arg1 arg2**, the **String** array would contain **arg1** and **arg2**. (Although **ViewCal** does not make any use of command-line arguments, the **main()** method must be declared with a **String** array for the arguments.)

Lines 273 through 277 define a **WindowListener**, using a **WindowAdapter** class that provides the **windowClosing()** method that handles a window closing event by exiting the application. Line 279 creates a **JFrame** object that provides the window where **ViewCal**'s user interface is displayed. Line 280 associates the **WindowListener** object with the **JFrame** (meaning that the application exits when the user closes the **JFrame**).

Lines 281 and 282 create an instance of **ViewCal** and initialize it by calling the **init()** method. Line 283 adds the applet to the center of the **JFrame** (notice that you have to add the applet to the content pane). Line 284 calls **pack()** to resize the **JFrame** to accommodate the preferred size and layouts of its subcomponents. Finally, line 285 makes the **JFrame** visible (this causes the **ViewCal** user interface to appear on the display screen).

A Text Viewer

The rest of this chapter presents the **TextView** application, which demonstrates a typical GUI created with Swing components. **TextView** is similar to Windows Notepad except that it does not support the editing and printing of files. You can use **TextView** to open and browse through a text file. You can also change the text color. By studying **TextView**'s source code, you will learn how to lay out a full-fledged user interface using Swing components. You will see how to create a menu bar and the drop-down menus, display a dialog box, and use more-complicated Swing components, such as **JFileChooser** for selecting files and **JColorChooser** for picking a color.

Using TextView

The files for the **TextView** application are in the **ch09\TextView** directory of this book's companion CD-ROM. To run **TextView**, you will need a version of Java Virtual Machine that supports Java 2. If you have JDK 1.2 installed on your system, switch to the CD-ROM's **ch09\TextView** directory and run **TextView** with the **java TextView** command. (Type this command in an MS-DOS window.) The initial window of the **TextView** application appears. To open a text file, select File | Open from the menu bar. The Open dialog box appears, as shown in Figure 9-9. The dialog box shows all text files (as indicated by a **.txt** extension in the filename) in the current directory. Click on a file and then click the Open button. **TextView** loads the text file. You can use the scrollbar to move back and forth in the text.

Click on the Options menu to try out the other features of **TextView**. As Figure 9-10 shows, the Options menu in **TextView** allows you to change the color of the text and select a different look-and-feel. To try out a different look-and-feel, click on the Windows Look and Feel item in the Options menu. You will see some changes in the **TextView** window's appearance. For example, the text font changes, and all dialog boxes appear similar to other Windows dialog boxes. If you choose File | Open again, you'll see that the Open dialog box looks like a Windows-style dialog box. Each of the look-and-feel menu items also has an accelerator key associated with it. For example, ALT-1 is the accelerator key for the first look-and-feel menu item (Java Look and Feel). This means that you can switch to the Java look-and-feel

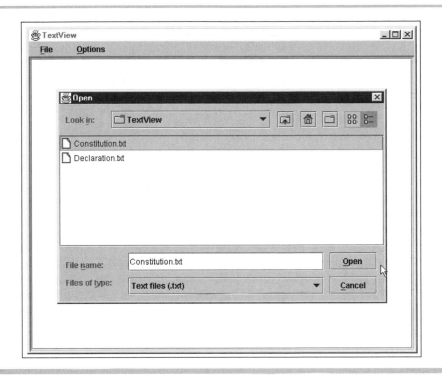

FIGURE 9-9. The Open dialog box in **TextView**.

by pressing ALT-1. Pressing ALT-2 changes to the Motif look-and-feel, and ALT-3 changes to the Windows look-and-feel.

To change the text color, select Options | Text Color. **TextView** displays a Select Text Color dialog box, as shown in Figure 9-11. The dialog box shows a large grid of color swatches from which you can choose a color. To select a color, click on a color swatch. The preview area of the dialog box shows how that color looks. As you click on color swatches, the most recent selections appear in a smaller grid of swatches marked Recent. After you are satisfied with a color, click the OK button to select the color. **TextView** then displays the text in the selected color. If you do not want to change the text color, click the Cancel button.

TextView implements another feature commonly found in GUI applications—an About dialog box, or About box for short, that displays information about the application. Select File | About to see **TextView's** About box. Figure 9-12 shows the resulting display. Click the OK button to dismiss the About box. When I discuss the code, you'll see how the About box is implemented.

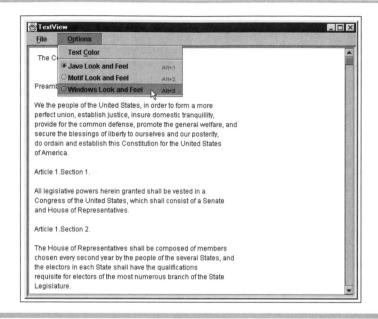

FIGURE 9-10. The Options menu in **TextView**.

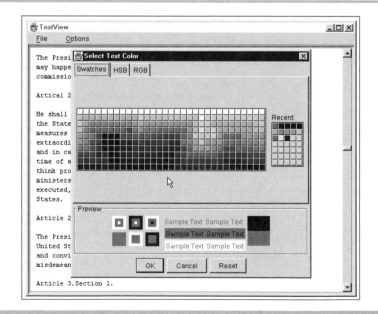

FIGURE 9-11. The Select Text Color dialog box in **TextView**.

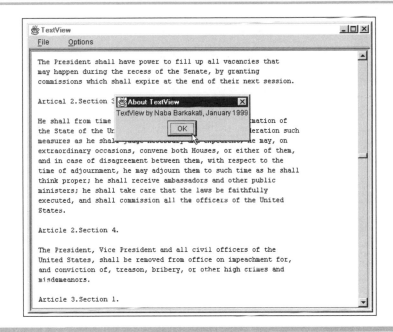

FIGURE 9-12. The About box in **TextView**.

Understanding TextView

TextView

The following listing shows the **TextView.java** file that implements the **TextView** application. I describe the code in the sections that follow this listing.

```
1  //-------------------------------------------------------------
2  // File: TextView.java
3  //
4  // A simple Swing application that lets the user view text files.
5  //-------------------------------------------------------------
6  import javax.swing.*;
7  import javax.swing.event.*;
8  import javax.swing.text.*;
9  import javax.swing.border.*;
10 import javax.swing.filechooser.*;
11 import java.awt.*;
12 import java.awt.event.*;
13 import java.util.*;
```

```
14  import java.io.*;
15      /** The TextView application class */
16  public class TextView extends JPanel
17  {
18      // The width and height of the main frame
19      private static int WIDTH = 600;
20      private static int HEIGHT = 500;
21      public static Dimension screenSize;
22      private static JFrame frame;
23      private JDialog aboutBox;
24      private JScrollPane textScroller;
25      private JPanel textPanel;
26      private JTextArea textArea = null;
27      public final static Border loweredBorder =
28                  new SoftBevelBorder(BevelBorder.LOWERED);
29      private String text; // String to store file content
30      // Rabio button menu items for different look-and-feel
31      private JRadioButtonMenuItem metalMenuItem;
32      private JRadioButtonMenuItem motifMenuItem;
33      private JRadioButtonMenuItem windowsMenuItem;
34      /** Creates an instance of the application */
35      public TextView()
36      {
37          super(true); // enable double buffer
38          setLayout(new BorderLayout());
39          // Add the menu bar
40          add(createMenuBar(), BorderLayout.NORTH);
41          // Add the scrolling text display area
42          textPanel = new JPanel(new BorderLayout());
43          textPanel.setBorder(loweredBorder);
44          textArea = new JTextArea();
45          textArea.setMargin(new Insets(10, 10, 10, 10));
46          textArea.setEditable(false);
47          textScroller = new JScrollPane();
48          textScroller.getViewport().add(textArea);
49          textPanel.setFont(new Font("Dialog", Font.PLAIN, 12));
50          textPanel.add(textScroller, BorderLayout.CENTER);
51          // Add the text panel to the main panel
52          add(textPanel);
53      }
54      /** Creates the application's menu bar */
55      JMenuBar createMenuBar()
56      {
```

```
57    JMenuBar menuBar = new JMenuBar();
58    JMenuItem mi;
59    //---------------
60    // File Menu
61    JMenu file = (JMenu) menuBar.add(new JMenu("File"));
62    file.setMnemonic('F');
63    // Menu item - "About"
64    mi = (JMenuItem) file.add(new JMenuItem("About"));
65    mi.setMnemonic('b');
66    mi.addActionListener(new ActionListener()
67    {
68        public void actionPerformed(ActionEvent e)
69        {
70            if(aboutBox == null)
71            {
72                aboutBox = new JDialog(frame,
73                                    "About TextView", false);
74                JPanel aboutPanel = new JPanel(
75                                    new BorderLayout());
76                JLabel aboutLabel = new JLabel(
77                 "TextView by Naba Barkakati, January 1999");
78                aboutPanel.add(aboutLabel);
79                aboutBox.getContentPane().add(aboutPanel,
80                                    BorderLayout.CENTER);
81                JPanel buttonPanel = new JPanel(true);
82                aboutPanel.add(buttonPanel,
83                                    BorderLayout.SOUTH);
84                JButton okBtn = new JButton("OK");
85                buttonPanel.add(okBtn);
86                okBtn.addActionListener(new ActionListener()
87                {
88                    public void actionPerformed(ActionEvent e)
89                    {
90                        aboutBox.setVisible(false);
91                    }
92                }); // end of okBtn.addActionListener()
93            }
94            Point fp = frame.getLocationOnScreen();
95            Dimension fs = frame.getSize();
96            aboutBox.setLocation(fp.x + fs.width/4,
97                                fp.y+ fs.height/4);
98            aboutBox.pack();
99            aboutBox.show();
```

```
100              }
101          }); // end of mi.addActionListener()
102          // Insert a separator between menu items
103          file.addSeparator();
104          // Menu item - "Open"
105          mi = (JMenuItem) file.add(new JMenuItem("Open"));
106          mi.setMnemonic('O');
107          mi.setEnabled(true);
108          ActionListener fileOpen = new ActionListener()
109          {
110              public void actionPerformed(ActionEvent e)
111              {
112                  JFileChooser chooser = new JFileChooser();
113                  SimpleFileFilter filter = new SimpleFileFilter(
114                          new String[] {"txt"}, "Text files");
115                  chooser.addChoosableFileFilter(filter);
116                  chooser.setFileFilter(filter);
117                  File currentFile = new File(".");
118                  chooser.setCurrentDirectory(currentFile);
119                  int rv = chooser.showOpenDialog(TextView.this);
120                  if(rv == JFileChooser.APPROVE_OPTION)
121                  {
122                      File theFile = chooser.getSelectedFile();
123                      if(theFile != null)
124                      {
125                          text = readTextFile(
126                      chooser.getSelectedFile().getAbsolutePath());
127                          textArea.setText(text);
128                      }
129                  }
130              }
131          };
132          mi.addActionListener(fileOpen);
133          // Several other sample menu items (all disabled)
134          mi = (JMenuItem) file.add(new JMenuItem("Save"));
135          mi.setMnemonic('S');
136          mi.setEnabled(false);    // disable this item
137          mi = (JMenuItem) file.add(new JMenuItem("Save As..."));
138          mi.setMnemonic('A');
139          mi.setEnabled(false);   // disable this item
140          file.addSeparator();
141          mi = (JMenuItem) file.add(new JMenuItem("Exit"));
```

```
142        mi.setMnemonic('x');
143        mi.addActionListener(new ActionListener()
144        {
145            public void actionPerformed(ActionEvent e)
146            {
147                System.exit(0);
148            }
149        });
150        //-------------
151        // Options Menu
152        JMenu options = (JMenu) menuBar.add(new JMenu("Options"));
153        options.setMnemonic('O');
154        // Menu item - "Text Color"
155        mi = (JMenuItem) options.add(new JMenuItem("Text Color"));
156        mi.setMnemonic('C');
157        ActionListener selectColor = new ActionListener()
158        {
159            public void actionPerformed(ActionEvent e)
160            {
161                Color color = JColorChooser.showDialog(
162                                TextView.this,
163                                "Select Text Color",
164                                textArea.getForeground());
165                textArea.setForeground(color);
166                textArea.repaint();
167            }
168        };
169        mi.addActionListener(selectColor);
170        options.addSeparator();
171        // Menu items that let user change the look-and-feel
172        ButtonGroup uiGroup = new ButtonGroup();
173        UIChangeListener uiListener = new UIChangeListener();
174        // Menu item - "Java Look and Feel"
175        metalMenuItem = (JRadioButtonMenuItem) options.add(
176                new JRadioButtonMenuItem("Java Look and Feel"));
177        metalMenuItem.setSelected(
178            UIManager.getLookAndFeel().getName().equals("Metal"));
179        uiGroup.add(metalMenuItem);
180        metalMenuItem.addItemListener(uiListener);
181        metalMenuItem.setAccelerator(
182            KeyStroke.getKeyStroke(KeyEvent.VK_1,
183                ActionEvent.ALT_MASK));
```

```
184         // Menu item - "Motif Look and Feel"
185         motifMenuItem = (JRadioButtonMenuItem) options.add(
186             new JRadioButtonMenuItem("Motif Look and Feel"));
187         motifMenuItem.setSelected(
188             UIManager.getLookAndFeel().getName().equals("CDE/Motif"));
189         uiGroup.add(motifMenuItem);
190         motifMenuItem.addItemListener(uiListener);
191         motifMenuItem.setAccelerator(
192             KeyStroke.getKeyStroke(KeyEvent.VK_2,
193                 ActionEvent.ALT_MASK));
194         // Menu item - "Windows Look and Feel"
195         windowsMenuItem = (JRadioButtonMenuItem) options.add(
196             new JRadioButtonMenuItem("Windows Look and Feel"));
197         windowsMenuItem.setSelected(
198             UIManager.getLookAndFeel().getName().equals("Windows"));
199         uiGroup.add(windowsMenuItem);
200         windowsMenuItem.addItemListener(uiListener);
201         windowsMenuItem.setAccelerator(
202             KeyStroke.getKeyStroke(KeyEvent.VK_3,
203                 ActionEvent.ALT_MASK));
204         return menuBar;
205     }
206     /** Changes the user interface look-and-feel */
207     class UIChangeListener implements ItemListener
208     {
209         public void itemStateChanged(ItemEvent e)
210         {
211             frame.setCursor(Cursor.getPredefinedCursor(
212                                     Cursor.WAIT_CURSOR));
213             JRadioButtonMenuItem rb =
214                     (JRadioButtonMenuItem) e.getSource();
215             try
216             {
217                 if(rb.isSelected() && rb == windowsMenuItem)
218                 {
219                     UIManager.setLookAndFeel(
220         "com.sun.java.swing.plaf.windows.WindowsLookAndFeel");
221                     SwingUtilities.updateComponentTreeUI(frame);
222                 } else if(rb.isSelected() && rb == motifMenuItem)
223                 {
224                     UIManager.setLookAndFeel(
225             "com.sun.java.swing.plaf.motif.MotifLookAndFeel");
```

```
226              SwingUtilities.updateComponentTreeUI(frame);
227          } else if(rb.isSelected() && rb == metalMenuItem)
228          {
229              UIManager.setLookAndFeel(
230               "javax.swing.plaf.metal.MetalLookAndFeel");
231              SwingUtilities.updateComponentTreeUI(frame);
232          }
233      }
234      catch (UnsupportedLookAndFeelException ex)
235      {// Unsupported look and feel
236          rb.setEnabled(false);
237          System.err.println("Unsupported LookAndFeel: " +
238                              rb.getText());
239          // Reset look and feel to Java look-and-feel
240          try
241          {
242              metalMenuItem.setSelected(true);
243              UIManager.setLookAndFeel(
244          UIManager.getCrossPlatformLookAndFeelClassName());
245              SwingUtilities.updateComponentTreeUI(frame);
246          }
247          catch (Exception e1)
248          {
249              e1.printStackTrace();
250              System.err.println(
251                  "Could not load LookAndFeel: " + e1);
252              e1.printStackTrace();
253          }
254      }
255      catch (Exception e2)
256      {
257          rb.setEnabled(false);
258          e2.printStackTrace();
259          System.err.println("Could not load LookAndFeel: "
260                              + rb.getText());
261          e2.printStackTrace();
262      }
263      frame.setCursor(
264          Cursor.getPredefinedCursor(Cursor.DEFAULT_CURSOR));
265  }
266
267  }
```

```
268    /** Sets up the user interface and starts the application */
269    public static void main(String[] args)
270    {
271        String version = System.getProperty("java.version");
272        if (version.compareTo("1.1.2") < 0)
273        {
274            System.out.println("WARNING: Swing components require"
275                                    + "Java version 1.1.2 or higher");
276        }
277        WindowListener l = new WindowAdapter()
278        {
279            public void windowClosing(WindowEvent e)
280            {System.exit(0);}
281        };
282        TextView tv = new TextView();
283        frame = new JFrame("TextView");
284        frame.addWindowListener(l);
285        frame.getContentPane().setLayout(new BorderLayout());
286        frame.getContentPane().add(tv, BorderLayout.CENTER);
287        screenSize = Toolkit.getDefaultToolkit().getScreenSize();
288        frame.setLocation(screenSize.width/2 - WIDTH/2,
289                            screenSize.height/2 - HEIGHT/2);
290        frame.setSize(WIDTH, HEIGHT);
291        frame.setCursor(Cursor.getPredefinedCursor(
292                                        Cursor.DEFAULT_CURSOR));
293        frame.validate();
294        frame.show();
295        tv.requestDefaultFocus();
296    }
297    /** Returns contents of a file in a String object */
298    public static String readTextFile(String filename)
299    {
300        String s = new String();
301        File infile;
302        char[] buffer = new char[50000];
303        InputStream is;
304        InputStreamReader isr;
305        // Open and read the file's content
306        try
307        {
308            infile = new File(filename);
309            isr = new FileReader(infile);
```

```
310             int n;
311             while((n = isr.read(buffer, 0, buffer.length)) != -1)
312             { // Append buffer to String
313                 s = s + new String(buffer, 0, n);
314             }
315         }
316         catch (java.io.IOException e)
317         {
318             s = "Error loading file: " + filename;
319         }
320         return s;
321     }
322 }
323 //------------------------------------------------------------------
324 // A simple file filter used by JFileChooser to display files
325 // with a specified extension (such as .txt).
326 //------------------------------------------------------------------
327 class SimpleFileFilter extends javax.swing.filechooser.FileFilter
328 {
329     private Hashtable extensions = null;
330     private String description = null;
331     private String fullDescription = null;
332     /** Creates a file filter from a string array of file
333      *  extensions and a description. For example, to create a
334      *  text fiile filter, create an instance as follows:
335      *      new SimpleFileFilter(String {"txt"}, "Text files");
336      *  Note that you don't need the " " before the file
337      *  extension.
338      */
339     public SimpleFileFilter(String[] extensions,
340                             String description)
341     {
342         this.extensions = new Hashtable(extensions.length);
343         for (int i = 0; i < extensions.length; i++)
344         {
345             // Add the extensions one by one
346             addExtension(extensions[i]);
347         }
348         this.description = description;
349         fullDescription = null;
350     }
351     /** Returns true is file is a directory or the file
```

```
352        *   extension matches one of the allowed extensions.
353        */
354      public boolean accept(File f)
355      {
356          if(f != null)
357          {
358              if(f.isDirectory()) return true;
359              String extension = getExtension(f);
360              if(extension != null &&
361                  extensions.get(getExtension(f)) != null)
362                      return true;
363          }
364          return false;
365      }
366      /** Returns the extension portion of a file's name */
367      public String getExtension(File f)
368      {
369          if(f != null)
370          {
371              String filename = f.getName();
372              int i = filename.lastIndexOf('.');
373              if(i > 0 && i < filename.length()-1)
374                  return filename.substring(i+1).toLowerCase();
375          }
376          return null;
377      }
378      /** Returns a description of acceptable file extensions */
379      public String getDescription()
380      {
381          if(fullDescription == null)
382          {
383              if(description != null)fullDescription = description;
384              // Add a comma-separated list fo extensions
385              // within parentheses
386              fullDescription += " (";  // opening parenthesis
387              Enumeration extlist = extensions.keys();
388              if(extlist != null)
389              {
390                  fullDescription += "." +
391                                  (String)extlist.nextElement();
392                  while(extlist.hasMoreElements())
```

```
393                     {
394                         fullDescription += ", " +
395                                     (String)extlist.nextElement();
396                     }
397                 }
398             fullDescription += ")";  // closing parenthesis
399         }
400         return fullDescription;
401     }
402     /** Adds a file extension to the table of extensions. */
403     public void addExtension(String extension)
404     {
405         if(extensions == null) extensions = new Hashtable(8);
406         extensions.put(extension.toLowerCase(), this);
407         fullDescription = null;
408     }
409 }
```

ANNOTATIONS

Designing a GUI application involves laying out the GUI components that make up the user interface. You can understand the code better if you see the containment hierarchy—which components contain what—of the Swing components that make up **TextView**'s user interface. Figure 9-13 shows how the various Swing components are organized in **TextView**.

Many components in Figure 9-13 appear with the same names as those used in the program listing. As you read the description of the code, you can refer back to this figure to see where a particular component fits into the user interface.

Figure 9-13 does not show three significant user interface components—the **JFileChooser** component, which allows the user to select a file; the **JColorChooser** component, which lets the user select a color; and the About box, which is created using other Swing components. However, these components are also described in the sections that follow.

DEFINING THE TEXTVIEW CLASS   Like any application in Java, the **TextView** GUI application is implemented by a class that includes a static **main()** method. This method creates the **JFrame** component, which holds the rest of the user interface components. In fact, a good place to start reading the code is the **main()** method, shown in lines 269 through 296.

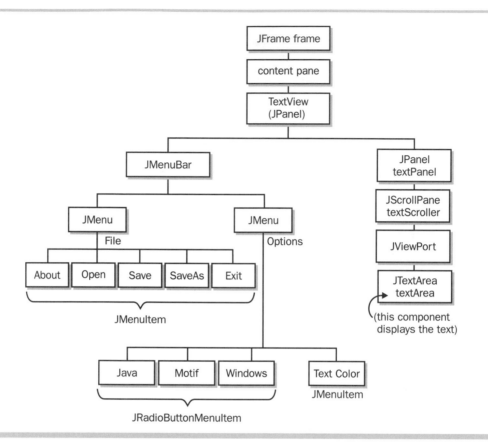

FIGURE 9-13. The containment hierarchy of Swing components in **TextView**.

Lines 271 through 276 of the **main()** method check the current version of Java and print a warning message if the version is lower than 1.1.2:

```
271    String version = System.getProperty("java.version");
272    if (version.compareTo("1.1.2") < 0)
273    {
274        System.out.println("WARNING: Swing components require"
275                         + "Java version 1.1.2 or higher");
276    }
```

Line 271 shows how you can get the Java version number by calling the **System.getProperty()** method with the property name **java.version**.

Lines 277 through 281 create a **WindowListener** object by using the **WindowAdapter** class, which can receive window events. Lines 279 and 280 define the **windowClosing()** method, which handles the **WindowEvent** that occurs when the user closes a window. Line 283 creates a **JFrame** component that acts as the main window for the application, and line 284 associates the **WindowListener** object of line 277 with the frame:

```
283            frame = new JFrame("TextView");
284            frame.addWindowListener(1);
```

This means that when the user closes the frame, the **windowClosing()** method of the **WindowListener** is invoked, and that method exits the application.

Line 282 of the **main()** method creates an instance of the **TextView** class:

```
282            TextView tv = new TextView();
```

As you will learn later in this section, the **TextView()** constructor sets up the rest of the user interface in a **JPanel** component. Line 285 sets the layout manager for the frame, and line 286 adds the **TextView** component to the frame:

```
285            frame.getContentPane().setLayout(new BorderLayout());
286            frame.getContentPane().add(tv, BorderLayout.CENTER);
```

Lines 287 through 290 set the size and location of the frame:

```
287            screenSize = Toolkit.getDefaultToolkit().getScreenSize();
288            frame.setLocation(screenSize.width/2 - WIDTH/2,
289                              screenSize.height/2 - HEIGHT/2);
290            frame.setSize(WIDTH, HEIGHT);
```

First line 287 calls a **Toolkit** method to determine the screen size (in terms of the number of pixels horizontally and vertically). Lines 288 and 289 place the frame so that it appears in the middle of the screen. Finally, line 290 sets the frame's size, as specified by static integer variables **WIDTH** and **HEIGHT**.

Lines 291 and 292 set the cursor for the frame, and line 294 makes the frame visible by calling its **show()** method:

```
294            frame.show();
```

This step is essential; if you forget this step, nothing will appear on the screen.

Now that you know what the **main()** method does, you can focus your attention on other parts of the **TextView** class. Because **TextView** uses a number of Swing components, it imports a number of classes from several packages. Lines 6 through 10 contain the **import** statements that refer to various Swing packages (note that the package names begin with **javax.swing**):

```
 6 import javax.swing.*;
 7 import javax.swing.event.*;
 8 import javax.swing.text.*;
 9 import javax.swing.border.*;
10 import javax.swing.filechooser.*;
```

Line 16 defines the **TextView** class:

```
16 public class TextView extends JPanel
```

As line 16 shows, **TextView** extends the **JPanel** class, which is a lightweight Swing container where other Swing components can be laid out. In fact, as explained in the next section, the **TextView()** constructor lays out the application's user interface in this **JPanel** container.

LAYING OUT THE SWING COMPONENTS   The **TextView()** constructor, shown in lines 35 through 53, lays out the user interface. Line 37 starts initializing the **TextView** component by calling the constructor of **JPanel**, **TextView**'s superclass:

```
37        super(true); // enable double buffer
```

This constructor initializes the **JPanel** with double buffering turned on (meaning that the panel uses an off-screen image to prepare the user interface before displaying everything on the screen).

By default, **JPanel** uses a flow layout manager that places components one next to the other and wraps around when a component extends beyond the horizontal extent of the panel. **TextView** uses a border layout manager instead; line 38 sets the new layout manager:

```
38        setLayout(new BorderLayout());
```

Line 40 calls the **createMenuBar()** method to prepare a menu bar and add it to the top edge of the **TextView** component (**BorderLayout.NORTH** refers to the north position or top edge of a component):

```
40        add(createMenuBar(), BorderLayout.NORTH);
```

You will learn more about the **createMenuBar()** method in the next section.

Lines 42 through 50 prepare the text display area, place it inside a scroll pane, and place that scroll pane inside another panel:

```
42        textPanel = new JPanel(new BorderLayout());
43        textPanel.setBorder(loweredBorder);
44        textArea = new JTextArea();
45        textArea.setMargin(new Insets(10, 10, 10, 10));
46        textArea.setEditable(false);
47        textScroller = new JScrollPane();
48        textScroller.getViewport().add(textArea);
49        textPanel.setFont(new Font("Dialog", Font.PLAIN, 12));
50        textPanel.add(textScroller, BorderLayout.CENTER);
```

Line 42 creates a **JPanel** named **textPanel** with a border layout manager. Line 43 sets that panel's border to a previously defined border of the **SoftBevelBorder** class (see lines 27 and 28). Lines 44 through 46 initialize a **JTextArea** object—this is the component that will display the contents of a text file. Line 47 creates a **JScrollPane** that manages a viewport and optional scrollbars. To support scrolling, all you need to do is place a Swing component inside the viewport, which is what line 48 does. Notice that line 48 calls the **getViewport()** method to access the viewport managed by the **JScrollPane**. Line 49 sets the text panel's font, and line 50 places the **JScrollPane** component in the center position of the **TextView** component (that's what **BorderLayout.CENTER** means).

Finally, line 52 adds the **textPanel** to **TextView**:

```
52    add(textPanel);
```

After this step, the entire user interface is laid out in the **TextView** component. The only remaining user interface elements are the dialog boxes, but, as you will learn in the following sections, these dialog boxes are created as they are needed.

CREATING THE MENU BAR   The **createMenuBar()** method, shown in lines 55 through 205, sets up the menu bar and returns a **JMenuBar** object. As you can see, it takes quite a few lines of Java code to set up the menu bar with the simple menus used in the **TextView** application. Even though it takes a lot more code to create more complicated menus, you can learn the basic steps for creating menus by studying the **createMenuBar()** method. For more-complicated menus, you simply need to repeat some of the steps.

The basic steps in creating a menu bar with pull-down menus are as follows:

1. Create a **JMenuBar** object. This is the menu bar that you see along the top edge of the user interface of a typical GUI application. Initially, the **JMenuBar** object is empty—it does not have any menus associated with it.

2. Create a **JMenu** object representing a pull-down menu, and add it to the **JMenuBar**.

3. Create instances of **JMenuItem** objects, one for each menu item in the current pull-down menu (the menu items can also be represented by **JRadioButtonMenuItem** objects). Then add each **JMenuItem** to the **JMenu** representing the current pull-down menu.

4. For each **JMenuItem**, define an appropriate listener and add the listener to the menu item. For example, for a **JMenuItem**, you would add an **ActionListener** with the **actionPerformed()** method that will be called when the user selects that **JMenuItem** object.

5. Repeat steps 2 and 4 for each pull-down menu.

Because the steps are repetitive for each pull-down menu and each menu item, I will describe only a few of the steps from the **createMenuBar()** method in detail.

Line 57 of **createMenuBar()** creates an instance of a **JMenuBar** object named **menuBar**:

```
57        JMenuBar menuBar = new JMenuBar();
```

This is the menu bar to which two pull-down menus (representing the File and Options menus) will be added. After the menu bar is set up, line 204 of **createMenuBar()** returns **menuBar**.

Line 61 creates the first pull-down menu and adds it to the menu bar:

```
61        JMenu file = (JMenu) menuBar.add(new JMenu("File"));
```

This line creates a new **JMenu** object with the File label and then calls the **add()** method of the **JMenuBar** class to add the **JMenu** object to the menu bar. The **add()** method returns its argument, which in this case is the newly created **JMenu** object. The return value is assigned to a **JMenu** variable named **file** for later use.

Line 62 sets the mnemonic for the File menu as the letter *F*:

```
62        file.setMnemonic('F');
```

This means that when the user presses ALT-F on the keyboard, the File menu will appear.

Lines 64 through 149 set up the menu items that appear on the File menu. For example, line 64 adds a **JMenuItem** for the About menu item:

```
64        mi = (JMenuItem) file.add(new JMenuItem("About"));
```

Line 65 sets the mnemonic of this item to the letter *b* (meaning that when this menu is visible, the user can select About by pressing the B key):

```
65        mi.setMnemonic('b');
```

Lines 66 through 100 define and add an **ActionListener** to this menu item. The **ActionListener** creates and displays the About box. You can learn more about this code in the section "Displaying the About Box," later in this chapter.

After the About menu item is added, line 103 inserts a separator between the About menu item and the other menu items:

```
103       file.addSeparator();
```

Lines 105 through 132 add the Open menu item, whose **ActionListener** uses a **JFileChooser** component to let the user select a file. You will learn more about this code in the section "Displaying a File-Selection Dialog Box," later in this chapter.

After the File pull-down menu is done, lines 152 through 203 create the Options menu in a similar manner. Line 152 creates and adds the menu to the menu bar. Then lines 155 through 169 create the Text Color menu item. The **ActionListener** for this menu item uses a **JColorChooser** component to allow the user to select a color.

The section "Displaying a Color-Selection Dialog Box," later in this chapter, explains this code.

A new feature in the Options menu is the use of **JRadioButtonMenuItem** objects for the three look-and-feel menu items. This involves defining the three **JRadioButtonMenuItem** objects and adding them to a **ButtonGroup**. Each **JRadioButtonMenuItem** is associated with an object that implements the **ItemListener** interface. The **itemStateChanged()** method of that object handles the event that occurs when the user clicks on one of the look-and-feel menu items. You can learn more about the look-and-feel menu items in the section "Changing the Look-and-Feel," later in this chapter.

Although the details of the **createMenuBar()** method can be overwhelming, the basic steps for setting up a menu bar are straightforward. In a nutshell, you have to create one **JMenuBar** for the menu bar, one **JMenu** for each pull-down menu, and as many **JMenuItem** (or **JRadioButtonMenuItem**) objects as there are menu items in the pull-down menus. The code becomes lengthy because you have to define a separate listener class for each menu item.

DISPLAYING A FILE-SELECTION DIALOG BOX   In **TextView**, the file-selection dialog box appears when the user selects File | Open from the menu bar. The Open menu item is created and the **ActionListener** is associated with that item using the following code (some lines have been deleted to emphasize code structure):

```
105        mi = (JMenuItem) file.add(new JMenuItem("Open"));
106        mi.setMnemonic('O');
107        mi.setEnabled(true);
108        ActionListener fileOpen = new ActionListener()
109        {
110             public void actionPerformed(ActionEvent e)
111             {
... code to display file-selection dialog box ...
130             }
131        };
132        mi.addActionListener(fileOpen);
```

Line 105 creates the Open menu item. Line 106 sets the mnemonic to the letter *O*, and line 107 enables the menu item (this is superfluous because menu items are enabled by default, but it does not do any harm). The code that handles mouse clicks on the Open menu item is the **actionPerformed()** method in the **ActionListener** class defined in lines 108 through 131. Line 132 associates this **ActionListener** with the Open menu item.

Note that lines 108 through 131 define a local class (without an explicit name) that implements the **ActionListener** interface by providing the **actionPerformed()** method. This approach of defining local classes for event handling is a typical programming technique used in Java programs.

The **actionPerformed()** method, shown in lines 110 through 130, uses the **JFileChooser** component to display a file-selection dialog box from which the user can select a file. Lines 112 through 119 demonstrate how **JFileChooser** is used:

```
112            JFileChooser chooser = new JFileChooser();
113            SimpleFileFilter filter = new SimpleFileFilter(
114                        new String[] {"txt"}, "Text files");
115            chooser.addChoosableFileFilter(filter);
116            chooser.setFileFilter(filter);
117            File currentFile = new File(".");
118            chooser.setCurrentDirectory(currentFile);
119            int rv = chooser.showOpenDialog(TextView.this);
```

Line 112 creates a **JFileChooser** object named **chooser**. Lines 113 and 114 create an instance of the **SimpleFileFilter** class (a subclass of **javax.swing.filechooser.FileFilter**) to act as the filter for filenames. Essentially, **JFileChooser** calls methods in the file filter class to determine what filenames to list in the dialog box. Lines 115 and 116 set the **SimpleFileFilter** object as the file filter for **chooser**. Lines 117 and 118 set the current directory of the file-selection dialog box. Line 119 calls the **showOpenDialog()** method to display the file-selection dialog box (see Figure 9-9). The argument for **showOpenDialog()** is the parent component of the dialog box, which in this case is the **TextView** component.

Lines 120 through 129 open the selected file if the user clicks the Open button in the dialog box:

```
120            if(rv == JFileChooser.APPROVE_OPTION)
121            {
122                File theFile = chooser.getSelectedFile();
123                if(theFile != null)
124                {
125                    text = readTextFile(
126                  chooser.getSelectedFile().getAbsolutePath());
127                    textArea.setText(text);
128                }
129            }
```

If the user clicks the Open button, the **showOpenDialog()** method (see line 119) returns the static integer value **JFileChooser.APPROVE_OPTION**. Line 120 checks for this return value. Line 122 creates a **File** object with the file selected in the dialog box. If the user has selected a file, lines 125 and 126 call the **readTextFile()** method to read the text from that file into a **String** variable named **text**. Finally, line 127 assigns the text to the **JTextArea** component named **textArea**. At this point, the file's contents appear in the **TextView** application.

The **SimpleFileFilter** class is defined in lines 327 through 409. **SimpleFileFilter** is a subclass of the abstract class **javax.swing.filechooser.FileFilter**. In addition to a constructor, this class must provide two methods—**accept()** and **getDescription()**. **JFileChooser** calls the **accept()** method with a **File** object. If the return value is **true**, **JFileChooser** displays the filename in the dialog box; otherwise it skips the file. **JFileChooser** calls the **getDescription()** method to get a **String** that contains a description of the file filter.

SimpleFileFilter provides a constructor that accepts an array of filename extensions (such as **.txt**, **.jpg**, **.gif**, and so on) and a description of the filter (such as "Text files"). The class maintains the file extensions in a **Hashtable**. The **accept()** method, shown in lines 354 through 365, returns **true** whenever the file is a directory or the file's extension matches one of the extensions stored in the internal **Hashtable**.

The other key method in selecting and loading a file is the **readTextFile()** method, shown in lines 298 through 322. Lines 308 through 314 show the Java code that loads the file's contents into the **String s**:

```
308        infile = new File(filename);
309        isr = new FileReader(infile);
310        int n;
311        while((n = isr.read(buffer, 0, buffer.length)) != -1)
312        { // Append buffer to String
313            s = s + new String(buffer, 0, n);
314        }
```

Line 308 creates a **File** object for the file specified by **filename**. Line 309 creates a **FileReader** to read from the file. The **while** loop in lines 311 through 314 reads blocks of characters from the file into a buffer and then appends that buffer to the **String s**. These lines of code are enclosed in a **try** block because some of this code can throw an **IOException**, which is handled by the **catch** block in lines 316 through 319.

Line 320 returns the **String** s that contains the contents of the file:

```
320     return s;
```

DISPLAYING A COLOR-SELECTION DIALOG BOX   The Text Color menu item on the Options menu displays a color-selection dialog box. Lines 155 through 169 show how the Text Color menu item is set up and how that menu selection is handled:

```
155        mi = (JMenuItem) options.add(new JMenuItem("Text Color"));
156        mi.setMnemonic('C');
157        ActionListener selectColor = new ActionListener()
158        {
159            public void actionPerformed(ActionEvent e)
160            {
161                Color color = JColorChooser.showDialog(
162                            TextView.this,
163                            "Select Text Color",
```

```
164                                              textArea.getForeground());
165                    textArea.setForeground(color);
166                    textArea.repaint();
167                }
168            };
169            mi.addActionListener(selectColor);
```

Line 155 creates the Text Color menu item. Line 156 sets up its mnemonic as the letter C. Lines 157 through 168 define the **ActionListener** that handles mouse clicks on the Text Color menu item. Line 169 associates this **ActionListener** with the Text Color menu item; this means that the **actionPerformed()** method of the **ActionListener** is called when the user selects the Text Color menu item.

The **actionPerformed()** method, shown in lines 159 through 167, uses the **JColorChooser** component to display the Select Text Color dialog box. Compared to the **JFileChooser** component for selecting files, the **JColorChooser** dialog box is much simpler to use. Essentially, you can create the component and show the dialog box with a single statement, as shown in lines 161 through 164. In this case, the **showDialog()** method is called with three arguments: **TextView** as the parent component, Select Text Color as the dialog box title, and the text area's foreground color as the initial color selection. The **showDialog()** method displays the Select Text Color dialog box (see Figure 9-11) and returns a **Color** object with the color selected by the user. Line 165 uses that color to set the color of the text. Finally, line 166 calls the text area's **repaint()** method to show the text using the new color.

DISPLAYING THE ABOUT BOX   **TextView** displays the About box when the user selects File | About (see Figure 9-12). Lines 64 through 101 of the **createMenuBar()** method set up the About menu item. The following listing provides an overview of this code (excluding some of the details):

```
64            mi = (JMenuItem) file.add(new JMenuItem("About"));
65            mi.setMnemonic('b');
66            mi.addActionListener(new ActionListener()
67            {
68                public void actionPerformed(ActionEvent e)
69                {
70                    if(aboutBox == null)
71                    {
... code to create the About box ...
93                    }
... code to position and show the About box
100                }
101            });    // end of mi.addActionListener()
```

Line 64 creates the About menu item. Line 65 sets the mnemonic to the letter *b*. Lines 66 through 101 add an **ActionListener** that handles the user's selection of this menu item. In this case, the **ActionListener** class is defined directly as an argument of the **addActionListener()** method. In other words, the class definition is embedded in the parentheses that would have enclosed the argument in the **addActionListener()** call.

Lines 72 through 92 create the About dialog box the first time the user selects File | About. Lines 72 and 73 create a **JDialog** as the container that will hold the other Swing components that make up the About box:

```
72              aboutBox = new JDialog(frame,
73                              "About TextView", false);
```

Lines 74 through 78 create another panel and place in it a label with some information about the **TextView** application:

```
74              JPanel aboutPanel = new JPanel(
75                              new BorderLayout());
76              JLabel aboutLabel = new JLabel(
77               "TextView by Naba Barkakati, January 1999");
78              aboutPanel.add(aboutLabel);
```

Lines 74 and 75 create the **JPanel** named **aboutPanel** with a border layout manager. Lines 76 and 77 create a **JLabel** with the informative text. Line 78 places the label in the **JPanel**.

Lines 79 and 80 add the **aboutPanel** to the content pane of the **JDialog** named **aboutBox**:

```
79              aboutBox.getContentPane().add(aboutPanel,
80                              BorderLayout.CENTER);
```

As with other top-level containers such as **JFrame**, you must call the **getContentPane()** method of the **JDialog** container to get the content pane and then add the **aboutPanel** to that content pane. In this case, the **JDialog** named **aboutBox** uses the border layout manager. Lines 79 and 80 add the **aboutPanel** in the center position of the component (that's what the argument **BorderLayout.CENTER** signifies).

Next, lines 81 through 85 set up the OK button that appears in the About box:

```
81              JPanel buttonPanel = new JPanel(true);
82              aboutPanel.add(buttonPanel,
83                              BorderLayout.SOUTH);
84              JButton okBtn = new JButton("OK");
85              buttonPanel.add(okBtn);
```

Line 81 creates the **JPanel** named **buttonPanel** to hold the button. Lines 82 and 83 add **buttonPanel** to **aboutPanel**, which holds the informative label about **TextView**. Line 84 creates the OK button, and line 85 adds the button to **buttonPanel**.

Lines 86 through 92 add an **ActionListener** to the OK button:

```
86                          okBtn.addActionListener(new ActionListener()
87                          {
88                              public void actionPerformed(ActionEvent e)
89                              {
90                                  aboutBox.setVisible(false);
91                              }
92                          }); // end of okBtn.addActionListener()
```

The **actionPerformed()** method, shown in lines 88 through 91, simply hides the About box when the user clicks the OK button.

After the About box is ready, lines 94 through 99 position it on the screen and make it visible:

```
94                          Point fp = frame.getLocationOnScreen();
95                          Dimension fs = frame.getSize();
96                          aboutBox.setLocation(fp.x + fs.width/4,
97                                               fp.y+ fs.height/4);
98                          aboutBox.pack();
99                          aboutBox.show();
```

Line 94 gets the location of the main frame of the **TextView** application by calling the **getLocationOnScreen()** method of the frame. This returns a **Point** with the coordinates of the upper-left corner of the frame. Line 95 gets the dimensions of the frame itself. Lines 96 and 97 then position the About box inside the frame. Line 98 resizes the About box to accommodate the preferred sizes of the components inside the box. Line 99 calls the **show()** method to make the About box visible.

Once the About box is created, it is reused whenever the user selects File | About.

CHANGING THE LOOK-AND-FEEL   The user can change the look-and-feel of the **TextView** user interface by clicking the radio button menu items on the Options menu (see Figure 9-10). Lines 172 through 203 of the **createMenuBar()** method create the three menu items—**JRadioButtonMenuItem** objects named **metalMenuItem**, **motifMenuItem**, and **windowsMenuItem**. These radio button menu items are placed in a button group so that only one of them can be selected at any time.

Line 172 creates a **ButtonGroup** for the look-and-feel menu items:

```
172       ButtonGroup uiGroup = new ButtonGroup();
```

Line 173 creates an instance of the **UIChangeListener** class, which handles mouse clicks on the look-and-feel menu items:

```
173       UIChangeListener uiListener = new UIChangeListener();
```

The code that changes the look-and-feel is in the **itemStateChanged()** method of the **UIChangeListener** class, described later in this section.

Lines 175 through 183 create the **metalMenuItem**, which refers to the default Java look-and-feel:

```
175        metalMenuItem = (JRadioButtonMenuItem) options.add(
176                new JRadioButtonMenuItem("Java Look and Feel"));
177        metalMenuItem.setSelected(
178            UIManager.getLookAndFeel().getName().equals("Metal"));
179        uiGroup.add(metalMenuItem);
180        metalMenuItem.addItemListener(uiListener);
181        metalMenuItem.setAccelerator(
182            KeyStroke.getKeyStroke(KeyEvent.VK_1,
183                ActionEvent.ALT_MASK));
```

Lines 175 and 176 create and add a radio button menu item labeled Java Look and Feel. Lines 177 and 178 call **UIManager.getLookAndFeel().getName()** to get the name of the current look-and-feel style. If the name is **Metal** (which is what the default Java look-and-feel is called), these lines set **metalMenuItem** as the selected item. Line 180 sets up the listener for this menu item. Finally, lines 181 through 183 set ALT-1 as the accelerator key for this menu item (meaning that the user can select this menu item by pressing the ALT-1 key combination).

Lines 185 through 193 set up the **motifMenuItem** in a similar manner. The **motifMenuItem** is for selecting the user interface style of the Motif Common Desktop Environment (CDE) that's popular on UNIX workstations. Lines 195 through 203 create the **windowsMenuItem** that allows the user to select the Microsoft Windows look-and-feel.

The code that changes the look-and-feel is defined in the **UIChangeListener** class that serves as the listener for these radio button menu items. Lines 207 through 267 define the **UIChangeListener** class. This class implements the **ItemListener** interface by defining the **itemStateChanged()** method, shown in lines 209 through 265.

Lines 211 and 212 start by setting the cursor to a wait cursor (in case it takes some time to change the look-and-feel):

```
211        frame.setCursor(Cursor.getPredefinedCursor(
212                        Cursor.WAIT_CURSOR));
```

Lines 213 and 214 get the menu item that was selected by the user:

```
213        JRadioButtonMenuItem rb =
214                (JRadioButtonMenuItem) e.getSource();
```

A **try** block spanning lines 215 through 233 sets the look-and-feel, depending on which menu item the user selected. For example, when the user selects the

windowsMenuItem, the **if** statement in lines 217 through 222 switches the
look-and-feel:

```
217                    if(rb.isSelected() && rb == windowsMenuItem)
218                    {
219                        UIManager.setLookAndFeel(
220              "com.sun.java.swing.plaf.windows.WindowsLookAndFeel");
221                        SwingUtilities.updateComponentTreeUI(frame);
222                    } else if(rb.isSelected() && rb == motifMenuItem)
```

Line 217 checks that the selected radio button is indeed the
windowsMenuItem. Then lines 219 and 220 call **UIManager.setLookAndFeel()**
to set the look-and-feel. The Windows look-and-feel is referred to by a long name:
com.sun.java.swing.plaf.windows.WindowsLookAndFeel. After that, line 221 calls
the **SwingUtilities.updateComponentTreeUI()** method to set the look-and-feel
style of all of the components contained in the **TextView** application's frame.

The steps for changing the look-and-feel are similar when the user selects
motifMenuItem or **metalMenuItem**. Only the name of the look-and-feel differs.

## CHAPTER 1

Command-Line Applications

hapter 9 showed you how to create applications with graphical user interfaces (GUIs). For many useful tasks, however, you do not need a GUI. For example, to compile a Java source file with Sun's Java Development Kit (JDK), you would type the command **javac filename.java** at the operating system's command prompt (for instance, in an MS-DOS window). The compiler would then translate the source file into Java bytecode and save the bytecode in another file named **filename.class**. The Java compiler is a command-line or console application. Other common command-line applications are the operating system commands such as **xcopy** in MS-DOS and **ls** in UNIX. This chapter shows you examples of command-line applications written in Java.

Command-line applications typically read user input from the keyboard and display output on the console. You can also provide input through arguments that you supply on the command line. Many command-line applications also read and write files. In general, command-line applications are simpler than GUI applications because GUI code tends to be lengthy and complicated. They also tend to be simple utility programs, designed for a single task.

You will find the following command-line applications in this chapter:

◆ **lnum**—A command-line application that numbers lines in a text file (used to number the listings that appear in this book)

◆ **jprop**—A command-line application that lists the current set of Java system properties

◆ **rdate**—A command-line application that gets the date and time from a remote host

◆ **rseq**—A command-line application that generates a random sequence of all of the numbers between 1 and a specified upper limit

Numbering Lines in a Text File

A good example of a command-line application is the one I used to add line numbers to the program listings you see in this book. I wrote a Java program, **lnum**, that opens a specified text file and prints out each line after adding a line number at the beginning of each line. The following sections describe the **lnum** program and explain how **lnum** is implemented.

Using lnum

The files for the **lnum** application are in the **ch10\lnum** directory of the companion CD-ROM. Assuming that you have Sun's JDK installed, you can try out **lnum** by changing to the **ch10\lnum** directory of the CD-ROM and typing the command **java**

lnum lnum.java in an MS-DOS window. The **lnum** program then opens the **lnum.java** file (the source file for the application) and prints out the lines with line numbers. If the lines stream by too fast, type **java lnum lnum.java | more** to view the output one screenful at a time.

The **lnum** application accepts a filename as a command-line argument (the argument is anything that follows **java lnum**). It then opens that file, reads a line at a time, and prints out each line along with a line number. The lines are printed to the standard output. By default, the standard output is the same window of terminal where you typed in the command to start the program. However, you can use the redirection operator of operating systems such as UNIX or MS-DOS to associate the standard output with a file. For example, if you want to save the numbered lines in a file named **c:\out.java**, you would use the command **java lnum lnum.java > c:\out.java** (if you are on a UNIX system, use a filename with appropriate syntax). The greater-than sign (**>**) is the output redirection operator. The output of the command preceding the greater-than sign is sent to the filename that follows the greater-than sign.

If you want to compile the program, copy the **lnum.java** file from the **ch10\lnum** directory of the CD-ROM to a directory on your system's hard disk. Then type **javac lnum.java** to compile the program using the Java compiler in Sun's JDK.

Inum

Understanding lnum

The following listing shows the **lnum.java** file that implements the **lnum** application. As you can see, it's much simpler than a typical applet or GUI application. I will describe the salient features of this application in the section that follows the listing.

```
1  //------------------------------------------------------------------
2  // File: lnum.java
3  //
4  // Reads lines from a text file, adds a line number to each line,
5  // and prints each line to the console (standard output). You
6  // have to use the operating system's output redirection feature
7  // to save the output in a file, with a command like this:
8  //
9  //     java lnum filein.java > fileout.java
10 //------------------------------------------------------------------
11 import java.io.*;
12 class lnum
13 {
14     public static void main(String arg[])
15     {
16         BufferedReader infile;
```

```
17          if(arg.length < 1)
18          {
19              System.err.println(
20                  "Syntax: java lnum infile > outfile");
21              System.exit(0);
22          }
23          try
24          {
25              infile = new BufferedReader(new FileReader(arg[0]));
26              int num = 1;
27              while(true)
28              {
29                  String line = infile.readLine();
30                  if(line == null) break;
31                  if(num < 10)
32                      System.out.println("  "+num+" "+line);
33                  else if(num > 9 && num < 100)
34                      System.out.println(" "+num+" "+line);
35                  else if(num > 99 && num < 1000)
36                      System.out.println(num+" "+line);
37                  else if(num > 999 && num < 10000)
38                      System.out.println(num+" "+line);
39                  num++;
40              }
41              // If more than 999 lines, display an error message
42              if(num > 999) System.err.println(
43                              "WARNING: More than 999 lines!!!");
44              infile.close();
45          }
46          catch(IOException e)
47          {
48              System.err.println("Error reading from: "+arg[0]);
49              System.err.println(e.toString());
50          }
51      }
52  }
```

ANNOTATIONS

Like any other Java applet or application, the **lnum** application is implemented by a Java class of the same name. Because **lnum** opens and reads from a file, it needs classes from the **java.io** package. Line 11 imports classes from the **java.io** package:

```
11 import java.io.*;
```

As a stand-alone application, **lnum** is required to have a static **main()** method. In fact, **lnum** has only this method, shown in lines 14 through 51. Line 14 declares the **main()** method as follows:

```
14    public static void main(String arg[])
```

As you can see, **main()** takes a **String** array named **arg[]** as its argument. This **String** array contains the command-line arguments that you type when you run the program. For example, if you were to run the **lnum** program by typing the command **java lnum one two three**, the **String** array would have **one** as the first element, **two** as the second element, and **three** as the third element. In other words, **arg[0]** would be **one**, **arg[1]** would be **two**, and **arg[2]** would be **three**. You can use the command-line arguments to pass information to a Java application. In the case of **lnum**, the first command-line argument is the filename (this is the text file whose lines will be numbered by **lnum**). You can provide more arguments on the command line, but **lnum** will ignore everything beyond the first argument.

Because **lnum** requires a filename as argument, lines 17 through 22 in **main()** check whether the user has provided an argument and, if not, display an error message and quit the program:

```
17            if(arg.length < 1)
18            {
19                System.err.println(
20                    "Syntax: java lnum infile > outfile");
21                System.exit(0);
22            }
```

The **if** statement on line 17 checks the value of **arg.length**, the number of command-line arguments. If the number is less than 1, lines 19 and 20 print an error message. **System.err** is a **PrintStream** object that represents the standard error output stream. The concept of standard input, standard output, and standard error streams are common in many operating systems, including UNIX and MS-DOS. Essentially, applications read input from standard input, print output to standard output, and print error messages to the standard error streams. By default, the standard input is the keyboard; the standard output and standard error streams go to the display screen (or, more precisely, to the window from which the user runs the application). However, the user can use operating system capabilities to redirect the input and output streams to files.

The **try** block in lines 23 through 45 encloses the code that does the line numbering, provided **lnum** was started with a filename argument. The code is enclosed in a **try** block because when opening a file or reading from a file, an **IOException** may be thrown. The **catch** block in lines 46 through 50 catches any **IOException** and prints an error message.

Line 25 starts the processing by opening the file and creating a **BufferedReader** object named **infile**:

```
25              infile = new BufferedReader(new FileReader(arg[0]));
```

A lot is happening in line 25. The name of the text file to be processed by **lnum** is in **arg[0]**, the first element of the array of command-line arguments. First, a new **FileReader** object is created for reading characters from that file. That **FileReader** object is then used as an argument to the **BufferedReader()** constructor to create the **BufferedReader** object named **infile**. The **BufferedReader** class provides the **readLine()** method as an efficient way to read lines of text from a text file. The **BufferedReader** reads blocks of characters from the file into an internal buffer, refilling the buffer when necessary. Then, when you call **readLine()**, the **BufferedReader** class returns a line of text from its internal buffer. This is efficient because reading characters from a file on the hard drive takes much longer than accessing characters that are in an in-memory buffer.

Line 26 initializes the integer variable **num**, which keeps track of the line numbers:

```
26              int num = 1;
```

The **while** loop in lines 27 through 40 reads a line at a time and prints it out with a line number:

```
27              while(true)
28              {
29                  String line = infile.readLine();
30                  if(line == null) break;
31                  if(num < 10)
32                      System.out.println("  "+num+" "+line);
33                  else if(num > 9 && num < 100)
34                      System.out.println(" "+num+" "+line);
35                  else if(num > 99 && num < 1000)
36                      System.out.println(num+" "+line);
37                  else if(num > 999)
38                      System.out.println(num+" "+line);
39                  num++;
40              }
```

Line 29 calls the **readLine()** method of the **BufferedReader infile** to read a line of text into the **String line**. When the file ends, the **String line** will be **null**. The **if** statement in line 30 checks for this condition and breaks the **while** loop when the file ends. Lines 31 through 38 print a line number followed by the line itself. The **lnum** application assumes that there are at most 999 lines in the file, and it allows three spaces for the number, then a blank space, and then the line. The **if-else** statements are needed to handle the cases as the digits in the line number increase from one to three. Lines 31 and 32 print a single-digit number with two preceding spaces. Lines 33 and 34 handle double-digit line numbers. Lines 35 and 36 are for three-digit numbers from 100 to 999. If the line number exceeds 999, lines 37 and 38 simply print them out with the line number followed by a space. Line 39 increments the line number before reading the next line.

When the line number exceeds 999, the output formatting is ruined because the line number does not fit within three character spaces. Although **lnum** prints out the lines beyond line number 999, it also prints a warning message, as shown in lines 42 and 43:

```
42          if(num > 999) System.err.println(
43                          "WARNING: More than 999 lines!!!");
```

Finally, line 44 closes the input stream by calling the **close()** method:

```
44          infile.close();
```

Displaying the Java System Properties

Java includes a number of system properties that contain useful information, such as the version number of the Java run-time environment and the name of the operating system. The properties are like the environment variables in various operating systems such as UNIX and MS-DOS. Like an environment variable, a property has a name (called a *key*) and a value. Both the key and the value are text strings. The **jprop** application, described in this section, displays the current set of Java properties.

Using jprop

The files for the **jprop** application are in the **ch10\jprop** directory of the companion CD-ROM. Assuming that you have Sun's JDK installed, you can run the program by changing to that directory of the CD-ROM and typing **java jprop** in an MS-DOS window. You will see a listing of the Java properties. For example, when I type **java jprop** on the Windows 95 system where I have JDK 1.2 installed, I get the following output:

```
Current Java properties:
-----------------------
Java Runtime Environment version = 1.2
Java Runtime Environment vendor = Sun Microsystems Inc.
Java Vendor's URL = http://java.sun.com/
Java installation directory = C:\JDK1.2\JRE
Java Virtual Machine specification version = 1.0
Java Virtual Machine specification vendor = Sun Microsystems Inc.
Java Virtual Machine specification name = Java Virtual Machine Specification
Java Virtual Machine implementation version = 1.2
```

```
Java Virtual Machine implementation vendor = Sun Microsystems Inc.
Java Virtual Machine implementation name = Classic VM
Java Runtime Environment specification version = 1.2
Java Runtime Environment specification vendor = Sun Microsystems Inc.
Java Runtime Environment specification name = Java Platform API Specification
Java class format version number = 46.0
Java class path = .
Operating system name = Windows 95
Operating system architecture = x86
Operating system version = 4.0
File separator = \
Path separator = ;
Line separator = \r\n
User's account name = naba
User's home directory = C:\WINDOWS
User's current working directory = D:\javaaa\code\ch10\jprop
```

As you can see, **jprop** prints each property with a descriptive string followed by an equals sign (=) and the property's value. Note that the file separator is the character used to separate directory names in a path name. The path separator is a character that separates names of directories in a PATH environment variable. The line separator refers to one or more characters that mark the end of line in a text file. On a Windows system, the file separator is a backslash (\), the path separator is a semicolon (;), and the line separator is a carriage return followed by a linefeed (represented by \r\n). Because you cannot see a carriage return or linefeed when it is printed on the console, **jprop** shows them in a notation that programmers understand. Carriage return is shown as \r and linefeed (also called newline) appears as \n.

When you run **jprop** on your system, the property values will differ depending on the version of the Java run-time environment and your operating system. For example, if you are using an older JDK (such as JDK 1.1.6 or JDK 1.1.7A), you will see a different run-time version number, and none of the specification and implementation properties (such as Java Virtual Machine specification version) will be defined.

If you run **jprop** on a UNIX system, the file separator, path separator, and line separator properties will be different from those you see on a Windows system. For example, on my Linux system I run the JDK 1.1.7A from Blackdown (**http://www.blackdown.org/java-linux.html**). Here is a relevant portion of the **jprop** output from that system :

```
Operating system name = Linux
Operating system architecture = x86
Operating system version = 2.0.34
File separator = /
```

```
Path separator = :
Line separator = \n
```

As you can see, **jprop** shows the operating system name and version. The system architecture is shown as x86, meaning that the system uses an Intel 80x86 or Pentium (or similar) processor. The file separator is a forward slash (/) as opposed to the backslash in Windows. The path separator is a colon (:), and the line separator is a single newline character (represented by **\n**), not the two characters (**\r\n**) used in Windows.

If **jprop**'s output scrolls by too fast, type **java jprop | more** to see the output a screenful at a time. You can also save the output in a file by using the operating system's redirection operator. For example, in UNIX or MS-DOS, type **java jprop >** *filename* to save the property listing in the specified file. (If you are trying this command from the CD-ROM's directory, remember to specify a filename on the hard drive because you cannot create files on the CD-ROM.)

jprop

Understanding jprop

The following listing shows the **jprop.java** file that implements the **jprop** application. I explain the code in the section that follows the listing.

```
1  //-----------------------------------------------------------------
2  // File: jprop.java
3  // Prints the Java properties.
4  //-----------------------------------------------------------------
5  public class jprop
6  {
7      private static String[][] properties =
8      {
9          {"java.version", "Java Runtime Environment version"},
10         {"java.vendor", "Java Runtime Environment vendor"},
11         {"java.vendor.url", "Java Vendor's URL"},
12         {"java.home", "Java installation directory"},
13         {"java.vm.specification.version",
14            "Java Virtual Machine specification version"},
15         {"java.vm.specification.vendor",
16            "Java Virtual Machine specification vendor"},
17         {"java.vm.specification.name",
18            "Java Virtual Machine specification name"},
19         {"java.vm.version",
20            "Java Virtual Machine implementation version"},
21         {"java.vm.vendor",
22            "Java Virtual Machine implementation vendor"},
23         {"java.vm.name",
24            "Java Virtual Machine implementation name"},
```

```
25        {"java.specification.version",
26            "Java Runtime Environment specification version"},
27        {"java.specification.vendor",
28            "Java Runtime Environment specification vendor"},
29        {"java.specification.name",
30            "Java Runtime Environment specification name"},
31        {"java.class.version",
32            "Java class format version number"},
33        {"java.class.path", "Java class path"},
34        {"os.name", "Operating system name"},
35        {"os.arch", "Operating system architecture"},
36        {"os.version", "Operating system version"},
37        {"file.separator", "File separator"},
38        {"path.separator", "Path separator"},
39        {"line.separator", "Line separator"},
40        {"user.name", "User's account name"},
41        {"user.home", "User's home directory"},
42        {"user.dir", "User's current working directory"}
43    };
44    public static void main(String[] arg)
45    {
46        String propValue;
47        System.out.println("Current Java properties:");
48        System.out.println("------------------------");
49        for(int i = 0; i < properties.length; i++)
50        {
51            try
52            {
53                propValue = System.getProperty(properties[i][0]);
54                // Need to show linefeed and carriage return
55                // as \n and \r (otherwise it'll look like a
56                // blank line)
57                System.out.print(properties[i][1]+" = ");
58                if(properties[i][0].equals("line.separator"))
59                {
60                    for(int j = 0; j < propValue.length(); j++)
61                    {
62                        if(propValue.charAt(j) == '\n')
63                            System.out.print("\\n");
64                        if(propValue.charAt(j) == '\r')
65                            System.out.print("\\r");
66                    }
67                    System.out.println("");
```

```
68                    }
69                else
70                {
71                    if(propValue != null)
72                        System.out.println(propValue);
73                    else
74                        System.out.println("--NOT DEFINED--");
75                }
76            }
77            catch(SecurityException se)
78            {
79                System.err.println(
80                    "Could not get value of: "+properties[i][0]);
81                System.err.println(se.toString());
82            }
83        }
84    }
85 }
```

ANNOTATIONS

The **jprop** application is implemented by the **jprop** class, which includes a single static **main()** method. Lines 7 through 43 define a two-dimensional array of **Strings** named **properties** (see Table 10-1). Each row of this array holds a property key and a description of the property. For example, **properties[0][0]** is the property key **java.version**, and **properties[0][1]** is set to **Java Runtime Environment version**,

Property Key	Description
java.version	The version number of the Java Runtime Environment
java.vendor	The name of the vendor who provided the Java Runtime Environment
java.vendor.url	The Uniform Resource Locator (URL) of the Java vendor's Web site
java.home	The path name of the directory where the Java Runtime Environment is installed
java.vm.specification.version	The version number of the Java Virtual Machine specification (defined in Java 2 and later)

TABLE 10-1. Java System Properties Collected by **jprop**.

Property Key	Description
java.vm.specification.vendor	The name of the vendor who provided the Java Virtual Machine specification (defined in Java 2 and later)
java.vm.specification.name	The Java Virtual Machine specification name (defined in Java 2 and later)
java.vm.version	The version number of the Java Virtual Machine implementation (defined in Java 2 and later)
java.vm.vendor	The name of the vendor who implemented the Java Virtual Machine (defined in Java 2 and later)
java.vm.name	The name of this Java Virtual Machine (defined in Java 2 and later)
java.specification.version	The version number of the Java Runtime Environment specification (defined in Java 2 and later)
java.specification.vendor	The vendor who provided the Java Runtime Environment specification (defined in Java 2 and later)
java.specification.name	The name of the Java Runtime Environment specification (defined in Java 2 and later)
java.class.version	The version number of the Java class format (46.0 in Java 2)
java.class.path	The list of directories where the Java Runtime Environment looks for Java classes (set through the **CLASSPATH** environment variable)
os.name	The name of the operating system (for example, Windows 95 or Linux)
os.arch	The name of the operating system architecture (for example, x86 for Intel 80x86 and Pentium systems)
os.version	The version number of the operating system (for example, 4.0 for Windows 95)
file.separator	The character used to separate directory names (\ in Windows and / in UNIX)
path.separator	The character used to separate path names in the PATH environment variable (**;** in Windows and **:** in UNIX)
line.separator	One or more characters that mark the end of a line in a text file (**\r\n** in Windows and \n in UNIX)
user.name	The user's name (the login name in UNIX)
user.home	The user's home directory
user.dir	The user's current working directory

TABLE 10-1. Java System Properties Collected by **jprop** *(continued).*

which describes **java.version**. The **jprop** application uses the property key to get the property value. When printing the property value, however, **jprop** prints the descriptive text instead of the cryptic property key. Table 10-1 shows the property keys that are defined in the **properties** array in lines 7 through 43. These are the properties whose values **jprop** displays. Note that some of the properties are defined in Java 2 (JDK 1.2) only.

The **main()** method, shown in lines 44 through 84, is quite simple. It uses a **for** loop, shown in lines 49 through 83, to get the value of each property listed in the **properties** array and then print the value next to a description of the property. Before starting the **for** loop, lines 47 and 48 print the first two lines of output:

```
47        System.out.println("Current Java properties:");
48        System.out.println("-------------------------");
```

Line 49 defines the **for** loop that goes through all of the entries in the **properties** array:

```
49        for(int i = 0; i < properties.length; i++)
```

Lines 53 through 75 show the code that gets the property value and prints it. This code is enclosed in a **try** block because the code can raise a **SecurityException**. Specifically, the **System.getProperty()** method may throw a **SecurityException** if the Java security manager does not allow access to a property. Lines 77 through 82 contain the **catch** block, which handles the **SecurityException** by printing an error message.

Line 53 gets the value of a property by calling **System.getProperty()** and stores the value in the **String propValue**:

```
53            propValue = System.getProperty(properties[i][0]);
```

System.getProperty() requires a property key as its argument. In this case, line 53 uses **properties[i][0]** to get the property key corresponding to the ith entry in the **properties** array.

At this point, it would be a simple matter to print the description of the property from **properties[i][1]** and the property value in **propValue**. However, for the **line.separator** property, the value is a combination of carriage return and linefeed characters—users may not be able to see these characters if they are printed as is. Lines 58 through 68 handle this special case. First line 57 prints the description of the property by calling the **print()** method, which does not advance to the next line:

```
57            System.out.print(properties[i][1]+" = ");
```

If the current property key is **line.separator**, the **for** loop in lines 60 through 66 goes through the **String propValue** and prints any carriage return character as **\r** and any linefeed (or newline) character as **\n**. The **else** clause in lines 69 through 75 prints the property value in **propValue** for all other cases. If **propValue** is **null**, the property value is shown as not defined.

Getting a Remote Date and Time

The **rdate** application, described in this section, is another example of a simple command-line utility program. With **rdate** you can get the date and time from a remote system (provided that the system supports the time service on port 37). UNIX already includes a similar **rdate** command; this Java version of **rdate** performs the same function as the UNIX counterpart.

Using rdate

The files for the **rdate** application are in the **ch10\rdate** directory of this book's companion CD-ROM. To try out the program, you will need access to a system that supports TCP/IP services and has the time service running at port 37. (You do not need login privileges on the remote system; all you need is a system that allows the time service.) You will also need the JDK installed so that you can run the **rdate** program from the command line. Assuming that you know of a host that has the time service enabled, switch to the CD-ROM's **ch10\rdate** directory and then type **java rdate** *hostname*, where *hostname* is the name of the host from which you want **rdate** to get the current date and time. Specify either the fully qualified domain name of the host (a name of the form **your.isp.com**) or an IP address. For example, if you have a host with the IP address **192.168.1.1** running TCP/IP services (and with the time service enabled at port 37), you can run **rdate** with the command **java rdate 192.168.1.1**. Here is the typical output of a successful **rdate** run:

```
Time at 192.168.1.1 is: Sat Feb 06 17:26:19 EST 1999
```

If the host runs the time service at a different port, you can specify the port number as an additional command-line argument to **rdate**. For example, if the time service is set to respond at port 1037, run **rdate** with the command **java rdate** *hostname* **1037**.

rdate

Understanding rdate

The following listing shows the **rdate.java** file that implements the **rdate** application. I explain the code in the section that follows the listing.

```
1  //------------------------------------------------------------
2  // File: rdate.java
3  // Gets and prints the date and time at a remote system.
4  // To use:  java rdate hostname-or-IPaddress
5  //------------------------------------------------------------
6  import java.net.*;
```

```
7  import java.io.*;
8  import java.util.*;
9  public class rdate
10 {
11     static int timePort = 37;
12     // Seconds from 1/1/1900 to Jan 1, 1970 00:00 GMT
13     // That's 70 years plus 17 extra days for leap years
14     // 70*365*24*3600 + 17*24*3600 = 2208988800
15     static final long offset = 2208988800L;
16     public static void main(String[] arg)
17     {
18         if(arg.length < 1)
19         {
20             System.out.println(
21                 "Syntax: java rdate hostname [port]");
22             System.exit(0);
23         }
24         try
25         {
26             int port = timePort;
27             if(arg.length > 1)
28                 port = Integer.valueOf(arg[1]).intValue();
29             Socket sock = new Socket(arg[0], port);
30             DataInputStream in = new DataInputStream(
31                                     sock.getInputStream());
32             int time = in.readInt();
33             sock.close();
34             Date d = new Date();
35             // Time returned from host is an unsigned int
36             // Convert to milliseconds since 1/1/1970 00:00 GMT
37             d.setTime(((((1L << 32) + time) - offset) * 1000);
38             System.out.println("Time at "+arg[0]+" is: "+d);
39         }
40         catch(IOException e)
41         {
42             System.err.println(
43                 "Error reading time from: "+arg[0]);
44             System.err.println(e.toString());
45         }
46     }
47 }
```

ANNOTATIONS

The **rdate** class, shown in lines 9 through 47, implements the **rdate** application. The class includes a static **main()** method, which a stand-alone Java application must have.

Lines 18 through 22 of **main()** print an error message if the **rdate** application is run without a host name in the argument.

Lines 26 through 38 show the code that gets the date and time at the remote host. This code opens a socket connection to the remote host and reads the time information. The code is enclosed in a **try** block because it can throw an **IOException**. The **catch** block, shown in lines 40 through 45, handles any such exceptions by printing an error message.

Lines 26 through 28 set the port number to 37 or to a number specified by the user on the command line:

```
26          int port = timePort;
27          if(arg.length > 1)
28              port = Integer.valueOf(arg[1]).intValue();
```

Line 26 sets the **port** variable to **timePort**, a static variable whose value is set to 37 earlier in the program (see line 11). If the user has specified both a host name and a port number on the command line, line 28 sets **port** to the integer in **arg[1]**, the second command-line argument (the first one, **arg[0]**, is the host name).

Line 29 opens a socket connection to the specified port number at the host whose name (or IP address) is in **arg[0]**:

```
29          Socket sock = new Socket(arg[0], port);
```

Lines 30 and 31 open a data stream using that socket's **InputStream**:

```
30          DataInputStream in = new DataInputStream(
31                              sock.getInputStream());
```

DataInputStream allows programs to read primitive Java data types (such as integer or float) from an input stream.

Line 32 calls the **readInt()** method of the **DataInputStream** to read an integer value from the remote host and then stores it in an integer named **time**:

```
32          int time = in.readInt();
```

The returned value is a 4-byte unsigned value that represents the number of seconds elapsed since January 1, 1900, 00:00 GMT. Now you have to interpret this returned value.

One way to interpret the value is to create a **Date** object and then set its time by calling the **setTime()** method. The **setTime()** method expects the time information in the form of a long integer that expresses the current time in terms of the number of milliseconds that have elapsed since January 1, 1970, 00:00 GMT. This means that we have to first subtract the number of seconds between January 1, 1900, and January 1,

1970. That's 70 years plus 17 additional days due to the 17 leap years between 1900 and 1970. You can then compute the number of seconds between 1900 and 1970 by evaluating (70 * 365 * 24 * 3600) + (17 * 24 * 3600), or 2,207,520,000 + 1,468,800 = 2,208,988,800 seconds. You will notice that line 15 initializes a long integer named **offset** with this value:

```
15      static final long offset = 2208988800L;
```

Recall that the **time** variable that holds the value returned by the remote host's time service has to be interpreted as a 4-byte unsigned integer. However, Java treats the **int** data type as a signed integer. One way to convert the returned value to a unsigned value is to perform the following operation in a long integer: **((1L << 32) + time)**. The **offset** can then be subtracted from this value to get the number of seconds elapsed since January 1, 1970, 00:00 GMT. Finally, that value has to be multiplied by 1000 to get the number of milliseconds. Line 37 shows this entire operation. Line 34 creates a **Date** object, and line 37 calls that object's **setTime()** method with the number of milliseconds:

```
37          d.setTime((((1L << 32) + time) - offset) * 1000);
```

After line 37 sets the time in the **Date** object named **d**, line 38 displays the date and time simply by calling **System.out.println()** as follows:

```
38          System.out.println("Time at "+arg[0]+" is: "+d);
```

System.out.println() calls the **toString()** method of the **Date** object **d** to get a textual representation of the time and displays that on the standard output. The result is an output line that takes the following form:

```
Time at 192.168.1.1 is: Sat Feb 06 17:43:40 DOT 1999
```

Everything following the blank space after the colon (:) is a string returned by the **Date** object's **toString()** method.

Generating a Random Sequence

Suppose that your office has 20 employees and that you assign each a number from 1 through 20. As a community service, each employee is going to volunteer a weekend at a local nursing home, and you want a fair way to decide who gets to volunteer when. A good way would be to generate a random sequence of numbers between 1 and 20. The sequence must contain only the numbers 1 through 20 in random order, with no number appearing more than once. The **rseq** program does just that. It's a command-line application that uses Java's **Math.random()** method, along with some logic, to generate a random sequence of numbers.

Using rseq

You'll find the files for the **rseq** application in the **ch10\rseq** directory of the companion CD-ROM. Assuming that you have Sun's JDK installed, you can try out **rseq** by typing **java rseq** in an MS-DOS window. The program will display a sequence of 20 random numbers consisting of the numbers 1 through 20 in random order. Here is a typical output from **rseq**:

```
Random sequence (1 - 20) =
17 12 14 6 10 7 20 13 4 1 9 16 2 5 3 18 8 19 15 11
```

If you want to generate a shorter or longer random sequence, simply specify the number as an argument when you run **rseq**. For example, to generate a random sequence with numbers from 1 through 10, type **java rseq 10**. The program then prints a sequence like this:

```
Random sequence (1 - 10) =
2 10 1 4 6 5 7 3 9 8
```

You can use such a random sequence to assign tasks among workers in a group.

rseq

Understanding rseq

The following listing shows **rseq.java**, the source code for the **rseq** application. I explain the code in the section that follows the listing.

```
1  //------------------------------------------------------------
2  // File: rseq.java
3  // Generates a random sequence containing the numbers 1 through
4  // a specified maximum number. By default, rseq generates a
5  // random sequence from 1 through 20. Run it with the command:
6  //       java rseq N    (where N is the maximum number)
7  //------------------------------------------------------------
8  public class rseq
9  {
10     private static final int MAXNUM = 20;
11     private static int max = MAXNUM;
12     public static void main(String[] arg)
13     {
14         if(arg.length >= 1)
15         {
16             max = Integer.valueOf(arg[0]).intValue();
17         }
18         int seq[] = new int[max];
```

```
19          int count = 0;
20          int randnum;
21          while(count < max)
22          {
23              randnum = (int)((double)max*Math.random()) + 1;
24              int i;
25              for(i = 0; i < count; i++)
26              {
27                  if(randnum == seq[i]) break;
28              }
29              if(i >= count) // not in seq[]
30              {
31                  seq[count] = randnum;
32                  count++;
33              }
34          }
35          // Print the random sequence
36          System.out.println("Random sequence (1 - "+max+") =");
37          for(int i = 0; i < count; i++)
38              System.out.print(seq[i]+" ");
39          System.out.println("");
40      }
41  }
```

ANNOTATIONS

The **rseq** class, shown in lines 8 through 41, represents the **rseq** application. The static **main()** method, in lines 12 through 40, implements the logic that generates the random sequence.

Lines 14 through 17 set up the range of numbers for the random sequence. The default maximum number is 20 (as specified by the static integer variable **MAXNUM**). If the user specifies a number on the command line, line 16 sets the variable **max** to that new number:

```
16          max = Integer.valueOf(arg[0]).intValue();
```

Notice that line 16 calls the **Integer.valueOf()** method to convert the command-line argument **arg[0]** into an **Integer** object. Then the **intValue()** method returns the value of that **Integer** as an **int** variable.

Line 18 defines an array, **seq[]**, to hold the random sequence:

```
18          int seq[] = new int[max];
```

Lines 21 through 34 contain the **while** loop that generates the random sequence containing the numbers 1 through **max**:

```
21      while(count < max)
22      {
23          randnum = (int)((double)max*Math.random()) + 1;
24          int i;
25          for(i = 0; i < count; i++)
26          {
27              if(randnum == seq[i]) break;
28          }
29          if(i >= count) // not in seq[]
30          {
31              seq[count] = randnum;
32              count++;
33          }
34      }
```

Line 23 shows how the random number between 1 and **max** is generated:

```
23          randnum = (int)((double)max*Math.random()) + 1;
```

The **Math.random()** method returns a random number greater than or equal to 0.0 and less than 1.0. Line 23 multiplies that random number by **max** and adds 1 to get a floating-point number that ranges from 1 through **max**. This floating-point number is then cast as an **int** variable. That's how line 23 gets a random integer that ranges from 1 through **max**.

The **for** loop, shown in lines 25 through 28, checks whether the number is already in the **seq[]** array. If not, lines 31 and 32 add the number to the **seq[]** array; otherwise, a new random number is generated.

After the random sequence is generated, lines 36 through 39 print the results:

```
36      System.out.println("Random sequence (1 - "+max+") =");
37      for(int i = 0; i < count; i++)
38          System.out.print(seq[i]+" ");
39      System.out.println("");
```

Line 36 prints a line showing the range of numbers in the random sequence. The **for** loop in lines 37 and 38 prints each number in the **seq[]** array. Line 39 calls **System.out.println()** with an empty string to print a newline character.

Client/Server Applications

revious chapters have shown Java applets that act as clients to other servers, such as HTTP or FTP servers. This chapter turns to Java client/server applications—where both the client and the server are written in Java. It starts with a brief tutorial on client/server programming in Java and how to use Java RMI (Remote Method Invocation) and Common Object Request Broker Architecture (CORBA). Database applications, in which a Java client application (or applet) uses the services of a database server, are not discussed here. Chapter 12 covers such applications.

This chapter presents several example programs to illustrate how to write client and server applications in Java. The brief tutorials on RMI and CORBA also include simple examples of RMI and CORBA programming, using tools that come with Sun's JDK 1.2 (Java 2).

You will find the following programs in this chapter:

♦ **jPOP3**—A client that can get mail from a POP3 (Post Office Protocol) server

♦ **jChat**—A Java chat application that demonstrates client/server programming

An Overview of Client/Server Programming

Client/server programming partitions an application into two distinct parts—a server and a client—so that the processing can be distributed to multiple computers. Typically, the server application provides a well-defined set of services. For example, a server might accept a file from a client and then print that file. Networked PCs in a local area network (LAN) use such a print server to share a printer among many users. In this case, the client application runs on each user's PC, and the print server runs on a different PC that has a printer attached to it. The print server is designed to accept files from all clients on the network and print the files one by one. The server might also provide other services, such as responding to queries from a client about all files that are currently queued for printing.

This example highlights a common use of client/server applications. The server usually provides access to a shared resource such as a printer, a disk, or a database. Clients and the server communicate by sending data over the network. The exact meaning of the data is left up to the server and the clients that are designed to work with that server. Typically, the server and client follow a well-defined protocol that specifies what sort of data the client must send to request services and what data the server sends back in response to a request.

Client/server applications form the foundation of the Internet. You already know and use many of these applications. Electronic mail, File Transfer Protocol (FTP), and the World Wide Web are all examples of client/server applications. Chapter 3 describes various Internet services as well as how the client/server applications communicate using the TCP/IP suite of protocols. It also shows applets that act as clients to various Internet servers, such as FTP and SMTP. As you will see from the

jPOP3 example presented later in this chapter, you can easily write a Java application that can act as a client to an Internet server. All you need to know is the protocol that the client must follow when requesting service from the server. In the case of **jPOP3**, the client and server follow the Post Office Protocol (POP3), which specifies how to read mail from a remote host.

You can also design and implement client/server applications with your own protocol. In some cases the protocol may be very simple. For example, in a chat application the server simply echoes all incoming text back to the clients. The **jChat** example, shown later in this chapter, illustrates how chat applications work.

Whether you implement a client that interacts with an Internet server or write a client/server pair with your own protocol, you have to use sockets for the data exchange between the client and the server. The following section outlines the steps involved in socket-based client/server programming in Java.

Java 2 also supports Java Remote Method Invocation (RMI) and Common Object Request Broker Architecture (CORBA)—two more approaches to constructing distributed client/server applications. RMI and CORBA are covered in separate sections following the discussion of socket-based programming.

| Java 2

Socket-Based Client/Server Communications

Client/server applications such as Web servers and browsers use TCP/IP to communicate. These Internet applications perform TCP/IP communications using the Berkeley Sockets interface (so named because the sockets interface was introduced in Berkeley UNIX around 1982). In the C and C++ programming languages, the sockets interface consists of a library of routines that an application developer can use to create applications that can communicate with other applications on the Internet. There is even a Windows Sockets API (application programming interface—a fancy name for a library of functions) that's modeled after the Berkeley Sockets interface. The Winsock interface, as it's known, provides a standard API that Windows programmers can use to write network applications.

Client/server applications use sockets to communicate over a TCP/IP network. A *socket* is an abstraction that represents a bidirectional endpoint of a connection. Because a socket is bidirectional, data can be sent as well as received through a socket. A socket has three attributes:

◆ The network address (the IP address) of the system

◆ The port number, identifying the process (a process is a computer program running on a computer) that exchanges data through the socket

◆ The type of socket (such as stream or datagram), identifying the protocol for data exchange

Figure 11-1 illustrates client/server communications using sockets.

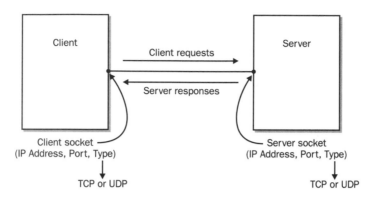

FIGURE 11-1. Client/server communications using sockets.

Essentially, the IP address identifies a network node, the port number identifies a process on the node, and the socket type determines the manner in which data is exchanged—through a connection-oriented or a connectionless protocol.

The sockets model has two types of sockets, stream and datagram. Stream sockets are connection oriented, whereas datagram sockets are connectionless.

A connection-oriented protocol works like a normal phone conversation. When you want to talk to your friend, you first have to dial your friend's phone number and establish a connection. In the same way, connection-oriented data exchange requires both the sending and the receiving processes to establish a connection before data exchange can begin. In the TCP/IP protocol suite, TCP (Transmission Control Protocol) supports a connection-oriented data transfer between two processes running on two computers on the Internet. TCP provides a reliable two-way data exchange between processes. As the name TCP/IP suggests, TCP relies on IP (Internet Protocol) for delivery of packets. IP does not guarantee delivery of packets, nor does it deliver packets in any particular sequence. It simply delivers a packet from one network to another in an efficient manner. It is TCP's responsibility to arrange the packets in the proper sequence, detect whether errors occurred, and request retransmission of packets in case of any error. TCP is useful for applications that plan to exchange large amounts of data at a time, as well as for applications that need reliable data exchange. For example, the Simple Mail Transfer Protocol (SMTP) uses TCP to transfer mail messages.

A connectionless data exchange protocol does not require the sender and receiver to explicitly establish a connection. In the TCP/IP protocol suite, the User Datagram Protocol (UDP) provides connectionless service for sending and receiving packets known as datagrams. Unlike TCP, UDP does not guarantee that datagrams ever reach their intended destination. Nor does UDP ensure that datagrams are delivered in the order in which they were sent. UDP is used by applications that exchange small amounts of data at a time, or by applications that do not need the reliability and sequencing of data delivery. For example, SNMP (Simple Network Management Protocol) uses UDP to transfer data.

It takes two sockets to complete a communication path between a client process and a server process. The server application listens on a specific port on the system. The client initiates a connection from any available port and tries to connect to the server (identified by the server's IP address and port number). Once the connection is established, the client and the server can exchange data according to their own protocol.

Java includes a number of classes to support data communications using stream and datagram sockets. The **DatagramPacket** and **DatagramSocket** classes are meant for client/server data exchanges using datagram sockets. For the connection-oriented stream sockets, Java provides the **ServerSocket** class to represent server-side sockets and the **Socket** class for client-side sockets.

The basic programming steps in sockets-based data exchanges depend on whether the transfer is connection oriented (stream) or connectionless (datagram).

For connectionless datagram servers, the basic steps are as follows:

1. Create a new **DatagramSocket** to listen on a specified port number.

2. Create a **DatagramPacket** and call the datagram socket's **receive()** method with that **DatagramPacket** as an argument.

3. Process the received packet according to the agreed-upon protocol.

4. Create another **DatagramPacket** and call the datagram socket's **send()** method to send information back to the client.

5. Repeat steps 2 through 4 as often as necessary. When it's time to end the connection (this depends on the protocol), go to step 6.

6. Call the datagram socket's **close()** method to close the connection.

The datagram client follows similar steps:

1. Create a new **DatagramSocket** on any available port.

2. Create an **InetAddress** object with the host address of the server.

3. Create a **DatagramPacket** with the server's address and port number and the data to be sent to the server. Then call the datagram socket's **send()** method to send the **DatagramPacket** to the server.

4. Create another **DatagramPacket** and call the datagram socket's **receive()** method to receive data in that **DatagramPacket**.

5. Repeat steps 3 and 4 as required by the agreed-upon protocol. When it's time to end the connection, go to step 6.

6. Call the datagram socket's **close()** method to close the connection.

Connection-oriented stream sockets are more commonly used for Internet services than connectionless datagram sockets. For a connection-oriented server, the basic programming steps are as follows:

1. Create a **ServerSocket** with a specified port number.

2. Call the socket's **accept()** method to wait for a new client connection. When a client successfully connects to the server, the server's **accept()** method returns a **Socket** object representing the client's end of the connection.

3. Create a new thread to exchange data with the client. (A new thread is necessary so that the server can serve multiple clients.) In the thread, create input and output streams for the client socket returned by the **accept()** method. Then send and receive data on these streams according to the agreed-upon protocol. Close the streams and the socket when done.

The programming steps in a connection-oriented client application are as follows:

1. Create a **Socket** with the server's host name and the port number at which the server accepts connection.

2. Create input and output streams for the socket.

3. Send and receive data using the streams, as required by the protocol. If necessary, create two separate threads, one to receive data from the server and the other to send data to the server.

4. When the data exchanges are done, close the streams and close the socket.

Servers typically listen on a well-known port number so that clients can connect to that port to access the server. Chapter 3 lists the port numbers for some common Internet services such as FTP, SMTP, and HTTP (Web server). If you design your own client/server application, you can select an unused port number for the server. On UNIX systems, the **/etc/services** text file contains a list of all known services and their associated port numbers. On Microsoft Windows systems, you'll find similar information in the **Services** text file in the Windows directory (usually **C:\Windows**). You might want to browse through this file to learn more about various well-known (and many not so well-known) port numbers.

In the client/server model, the server has to be up and running before the client can run. After creating a socket associated with a port, the server application calls the socket's **accept()** method to wait for a connection from a client.

Establishing the connection from the client side is somewhat simpler. The client simply creates a socket with the host name (or IP address) and the port number on which the server accepts connections.

After a client establishes a connection to a server using a connection-oriented stream socket, the client and server can exchange data by opening input and output streams and then reading from and writing to these streams. Like a conversation between two persons, the server and client alternately send and receive data. The meaning of the data depends on the message protocol used by the server and the clients. Usually, a server is designed for a specific task, and inherent in that design is a message protocol that the server and clients use to exchange the necessary data. For example, the Web server and the Web browser (client) communicate using the Hypertext Transfer Protocol (HTTP).

Java Remote Method Invocation

As was explained in the previous section, traditional socket-based client/server applications have to use a protocol that specifies the sequence and meaning of data that the client and server exchange. In contrast to socket-based applications, Java Remote Method Invocation, or RMI for short, provides an API that lets you write distributed client/server applications that are similar to other stand-alone applications. For example, in a typical Java application, you create various objects and call their methods to perform some programming task. Similarly, Java RMI lets an object in one Java Virtual Machine (JVM) call (or invoke) a method in another JVM that may be running on a different computer on the network. That remote method can also return results in the form of Java objects.

PROGRAMMER'S NOTE *To learn more about RMI, visit Sun's Java RMI home page at* ***http://java.sun.com/products/jdk/rmi/***. *This page includes links to a variety of information, including the RMI specification and some real-world applications.*

In RMI terminology, *local objects* are objects in a specific JVM. All objects in other JVMs are *remote objects*. Typically, the remote objects are in a JVM running on a different computer on the network. A local object that invokes a remote object's method is referred to as a *client*, and the remote object is called a *server* (because it provides services by allowing the client to invoke its methods).

A remote object exports itself by registering with a remote registry. The remote registry maintains a list of names and the objects associated with those names. JDK 1.2 comes with a remote registry application called **rmiregistry**. You will be using that program when you run any program that uses RMI.

In RMI, the client object does not directly access the server object. Instead, the client calls methods in a local stub object. The stub serves as a local proxy for the remote object. The stub then communicates with a skeleton on the remote JVM through lower-layer networking protocols. The skeleton interprets the network requests, invokes the appropriate method of the server object, and passes any return value back to the stub, which passes it back to the client. Figure 11-2 illustrates how Java RMI uses stubs and skeletons to support client/server communications. The stub and skeleton code can be complicated, but fortunately for us programmers, it is generated automatically by the **rmic** tool that comes with JDK.

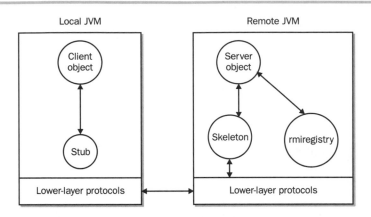

FIGURE 11-2. Stubs and skeletons support client/server communications in Java RMI.

Unlike socket-based client/server applications, RMI works only when both client and server are written in Java. Also, you need to follow these steps when writing client/server applications that use RMI:

1. Define an interface that extends the **java.rmi.Remote** interface. In the interface, define the methods implemented by the remote object. (These are the methods that the client can invoke remotely.) Each method must throw a **java.rmi.RemoteException**.

2. Write the server object as a subclass of **java.rmi.server.UnicastRemoteObject**. The server must implement the interface defined in step 1. Define a **public static main()** method in the server class so that you can run it as an application. In the **main()** method, call **Naming.rebind()** to assign a name to the server object and export it so that client objects can access the server by name. Compile the server application using **javac**.

3. Use the **rmic** tool to generate a stub and a skeleton for the server. Run **rmic** with the name of the server class as an argument. The **rmic** tool then generates two new classes whose names are constructed by appending **_Stub** and **_Skel** to the server class name. These are the stub and skeleton classes for this server.

4. Write the client program. Call **Naming.lookup()** to access the remote server object. Specifically, you will get the interface implemented by the server. You can then call any of the methods defined in the server's interface. Compile the client application with **javac**.

5. Start the remote registry. On 32-bit Windows systems, type **start rmiregistry** to run the registry. On UNIX systems, type **rmiregistry &** to start the registry and run it as a background process.

6. Run the server application.

7. Run the client application.

To see these steps in action, let's look at a simple RMI example where the server object provides a method that returns the date and time at the remote host. You will find the files for this example in the **ch11\rmi** directory of the companion CD-ROM. The remainder of this section takes you through the steps that you would follow when writing this client/server application.

The first step is to define the interface for the server. The following listing shows the **RemoteTime.java** file, which defines an interface with three methods:

```
//-----------------------------------------------------------------
// File: RemoteTime.java
// Defines the RemoteTime interface for an RMI time server.
//-----------------------------------------------------------------
import java.rmi.*;
public interface RemoteTime extends Remote
{
    public long getBinaryTime() throws RemoteException;
    public String getTimestampString() throws RemoteException;
    public String getDateTimeString() throws RemoteException;
}
```

As you can see, each method must throw **RemoteException**. The first method returns the time in terms of the milliseconds elapsed since 00:00 January 1, 1970. The second and third methods return two different string representations of the date and time at the server.

Next, you would implement the server that provides the methods specified in the **RemoteTime** interface. The following listing shows the **TimeServer.java** file, which implements a server application with the **RemoteTime** interface:

```
1  //-----------------------------------------------------------------
2  // File: TimeServer.java
3  // Server that implements the RemoteTime interface.
4  //-----------------------------------------------------------------
5  import java.util.*;
6  import java.text.*;
7  import java.rmi.*;
8  import java.rmi.server.*;
9
10 public class TimeServer extends UnicastRemoteObject
11     implements RemoteTime
12 {
13     static SimpleDateFormat tstamp =
```

```
14              new SimpleDateFormat("yyyyMMMdd-HHmmss");
15      static SimpleDateFormat datetime =
16              new SimpleDateFormat("EEE MMM dd HH:mm:ss z yyyy");
17      public TimeServer() throws RemoteException
18      {
19          super();
20      }
21      public long getBinaryTime() throws RemoteException
22      {
23          Date d = new Date();
24          return d.getTime();
25      }
26      public String getTimestampString() throws RemoteException
27      {
28          Date d = new Date();
29          String tstampString = tstamp.format(d);
30          return tstampString;
31      }
32      public String getDateTimeString() throws RemoteException
33      {
34          Date d = new Date();
35          String dtString = datetime.format(d);
36          return dtString;
37      }
38      public static void main(String args[])
39      {
40          try
41          {
42              TimeServer ts = new TimeServer();
43              Naming.rebind("rmiTime", ts);
44              System.out.println("rmiTime service started");
45          }
46          catch(Exception e)
47          {
48              System.err.println(e);
49              System.exit(1);
50          }
51      }
52  }
```

As line 8 shows, you have to import classes from the **java.rmi.server** package. Lines 10 and 11 show the class declaration. The **TimeServer** class is a subclass of **UnicastRemoteObject**, and it implements the **RemoteTime** interface.

Lines 13 through 37 implement the methods specified in the **RemoteTime** interface and provide a constructor for the **TimeServer** class. Each method, including the constructor, throws **RemoteException**, as required by the Java RMI specification. The methods get the current time by creating a **Date** object. The time is formatted into a string by using the **SimpleDateFormat** class. For example, the time is formatted as a timestamp by creating a **SimpleDateFormat** object as follows:

```
13    static SimpleDateFormat tstamp =
14            new SimpleDateFormat("yyyyMMMdd-HHmmss");
```

The **getTimestampString()** method then gets the current time and converts that time into a timestamp with the following code:

```
28        Date d = new Date();
29        String tstampString = tstamp.format(d);
```

Notice that line 29 calls the **format()** method of the **SimpleDateFormat** object named **tstamp** to create the formatted string. In this case, the returned string has the form **1999Feb27-202611** (when the time is 20:26:11 on February 27, 1999). Note that such a compact time string can be used as a timestamp for a log file or as part of an automatically generated filename.

Lines 38 through 51 show the **public static main()** method of the server application. Lines 42 and 43 perform the crucial steps:

```
42            TimeServer ts = new TimeServer();
43            Naming.rebind("rmiTime", ts);
```

Line 42 creates an instance of the TimeServer object, and line 43 associates the name **rmiTime** with this server object. As you will see later in this section, the client accesses the TimeServer object by using the **rmiTime** name.

After preparing the **TimeServer.java** file, compile it by typing the **javac TimeServer.java** command in an MS-DOS window. Then type **rmic TimeServer** to run the Java RMI compiler. This command creates the files **TimeServer_Stub.class** and **TimeServer_Skel.class** — the stub and skeleton classes for **TimeServer**. The skeleton class must be on the same computer on which the server will run. The stub class runs on the client side and acts as a proxy for the remote server object. The stub takes care of forwarding method invocations to the server object, which may be on a different computer on the network.

The last step is to write a client application to test the server. A simple client would call the remote methods and print out the results. The following listing shows the **CheckTime.java** file, which implements such a client application:

```
1 //-----------------------------------------------------------------
2 // File: CheckTime.java
3 // Client application that uses RMI to get date/time information
4 // from a remote server.
```

```
 5  //------------------------------------------------------------
 6  import java.rmi.*;
 7  public class CheckTime
 8  {
 9      public static void main(String args[])
10      {
11          try
12          {
13              RemoteTime rts = (RemoteTime)Naming.lookup(args[0]);
14              // Get date/time from remote server in various forms
15              String datetime = rts.getDateTimeString();
16              String timestamp = rts.getTimestampString();
17              long bintime = rts.getBinaryTime();
18              // Print the results
19              System.out.println("At the server ["+args[0]+"]");
20              System.out.println("---------------------------");
21              System.out.println("Date/time   = "+datetime);
22              System.out.println("Time stamp  = "+timestamp);
23              System.out.println("Binary time = "+bintime);
24              System.out.println("                    "+
25                      "(milliseconds since Jan 1, 1970)");
26          }
27          catch(RemoteException e)
28          {
29              System.err.println(e);
30          }
31          catch(Exception e)
32          {
33              System.err.println(e);
34              System.err.println(
35                  "Usage: java CheckTime server-URL"
36                  +" where URL= rmi://host/rmiTime");
37          }
38      }
39  }
```

Line 6 imports the classes from the **java.rmi** package. These are needed in the RMI client application. This application assumes that the first command-line argument specifies the URL of the RMI server. The URL is of the form **rmi://*hostname*/*servicename*,** where *hostname* is the name of the host where the server object is running and *servicename* is the name associated with the server object. Line 13 calls **Naming.lookup()** with the first command-line argument to get the remote server's interface:

```
13                RemoteTime rts = (RemoteTime)Naming.lookup(args[0]);
```

Naming.lookup() locates the server object by contacting the **rmiregistry** on the host identified in the URL specified in **args[0]**. The **Naming.lookup()** method returns an object that you should cast as the interface implemented by the server. In this case, line 13 casts the returned object as a **RemoteTime** interface named **rts**.

After getting a reference to the **RemoteTime** interface, lines 15 through 17 simply call the server's methods, using that reference:

```
15                String datetime = rts.getDateTimeString();
16                String timestamp = rts.getTimestampString();
17                long bintime = rts.getBinaryTime();
```

Lines 19 through 25 then print out the result on the console.

Now that you have both the server and the client ready, you can try out the applications. You can run everything—the **rmiregistry**, the server, and the client—on the same system, or you may want to run them on two systems on a TCP/IP network to confirm that the client and server really can be distributed.

If you decide to run the applications on two networked computers, you will need the JDK installed on both systems. You will need the **TimeServer.class** and **TimeServerSkel.class** files on the server host. On the client host, you'll need the **CheckTime.class** and **TimeServerStub.class** files.

Start the **rmiregistry** on the server host. On Windows 95/98/NT systems, type **start rmiregistry** in an MS-DOS window. On UNIX systems, type **rmiregistry &** at the shell prompt. Then run **TimeServer** on the server, with the command **java TimeServer**. After **TimeServer** is ready, it displays the following message:

```
rmiTime service started
```

On the client host, run **CheckTime** with the command **java CheckTime rmi://*hostname*/rmiTime**, where *hostname* is the name of the server host (or its IP address). For example, if the server host's IP address is 192.168.1.200, you would use the command **java CheckTime rmi://192.168.1.200/rmiTime**. When **CheckTime** runs, it displays its result on the console. For example, here is a typical output from **CheckTime**:

```
At the server [rmi://192.168.1.200/rmiTime]
---------------------------
Date/time   = Sat Feb 27 21:52:17 EST 1999
Time stamp  = 1999Feb27-215217
Binary time = 920170337890
              (milliseconds since Jan 1, 1970)
```

If you are running everything—**rmiregistry**, **TimeServer**, and **CheckTime**—on the same system, you can use the command **java CheckTime rmi://localhost/rmiTime** to start **CheckTime**. The host name **localhost** refers to the local host where the programs are running.

Java and CORBA

Common Object Request Broker Architecture (CORBA) is an approach to distributed client/server programming that works with many different types of computers, operating systems, and programming languages. Essentially, CORBA allows client/server applications to find and communicate with each other no matter who developed them or where they are running on a network. In 1991, a nonprofit consortium of companies called the Object Management Group (OMG) introduced CORBA 1.1, which defined the following:

◆ The Interface Definition Language (IDL) used to define an object's interface (the methods that client objects can call)

◆ An API that allows client and server objects to interact with an Object Request Broker (ORB), the software through which clients and servers communicate

In 1994, OMG adopted CORBA 2.0, which specifies how ORBs from different vendors can interoperate. In a TCP/IP network such as the Internet or any intranet, ORBs running on different hosts can communicate using the Internet Inter-ORB Protocol (IIOP). IIOP is based on standard TCP/IP protocols, and it defines how CORBA-compliant ORBs pass information back and forth.

The key to CORBA is the ORB—the middleware through which clients and servers communicate. Using an ORB, a client object can invoke a method in a server object's interface. The server object may be on the same machine or on another system on the network.

CORBA uses stubs and skeletons just as Java RMI does. The stub serves as a proxy for a server object; it presents the same public interface as the server but runs on the computer where the client is running. The skeleton represents the remote interface to the server, and it runs on the same computer where the server is running. Additionally, CORBA uses an object adapter that also runs on the same system as the server. The server object accesses the services of the ORB through the object adapter.

When a client object wants to invoke a method in the remote server object, the client calls that method in the local stub. The stub then communicates with the ORB and provides the name of the server object, the method being invoked, and the arguments for the method. The ORB finds the server object by using a name service and forwards the method invocation to the server-side ORB using IIOP. On the server, the ORB communicates with the server object through the object adapter. The object adapter invokes the server's method via the skeleton. When the method returns, the skeleton sends any return values or errors back to the client via the ORBs. Figure 11-3 illustrates client/server communications in CORBA.

As the figure shows, the ORBs are the glue that binds everything together in CORBA. The client-side ORB takes care of finding the server object, invoking the

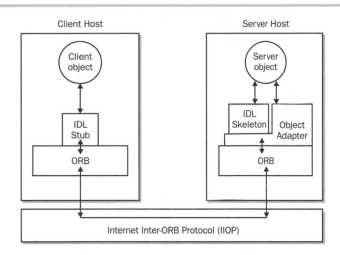

FIGURE 11-3. Client/server communications in CORBA.

server's method by communicating with the server-side ORBs, and getting the result back to the client. The client does not have to know the server object's location, its programming language, or the operating system for which it is designed. Essentially, the ORB provides a language-neutral, system-independent interface between the client and server objects. As you will learn next, that interface is defined using IDL.

PROGRAMMER'S NOTE *To learn more about CORBA, visit the Object Management Group's Web site at http://www.omg.org, and click on the CORBA links. If you are new to CORBA, you may want to go to the CORBA for Beginners Page at http://www.omg.org/corba/beginners.html.*

JDK 1.2 comes with *Java IDL*, a term that refers to a collection of classes and tools that you can use to write Java client/server applications using CORBA. Java IDL includes an IIOP-compliant ORB in the form of an ORB class library and a tool called **tnameserv** that implements the CORBA Common Object Services (COS) naming service.

In addition to what's already in JDK 1.2, you'll also need the **idltojava** compiler, which processes a CORBA IDL file and generates stub and skeleton code. You can download the **idltojava** compiler from **http://developer.javasoft.com/developer/ earlyAccess/jdk12/idltojava.html**. You will also find a link to HTML documentation for Java IDL at this site.

PROGRAMMER'S NOTE *To read more about Java IDL, visit http://java.sun.com/products/jdk/idl/index.html on the Web. This page also includes links to download JDK 1.2 and the **idltojava** compiler—the two items you need to develop CORBA applications using Java IDL.*

If you have not already done so, you should download and install JDK 1.2 and the **idltojava** compiler on your system. Then you can try out a simple example of a client/server application based on Java IDL. First I present an overview of the Java IDL development process.

To design, develop, and run a distributed object application using Java IDL, you will follow these basic steps:

1. Define the remote interface using CORBA IDL. The interface definition is similar to a Java interface, except that you must follow CORBA IDL syntax. In the interface, you also define any data structures used by the methods listed in the interface.

2. Compile the CORBA IDL file, using the **idltojava** compiler. For example, if the IDL file is named **sample.idl**, you would compile it with the command **idltojava -fno-cpp sample.idl**. The **idltojava** compiler generates a Java version of the interface as well as a number of Java source files, including the stub and skeleton classes.

3. Implement the servant class. In the Java IDL approach, the servant class refers to the object that implements the remote interface. If your interface name is **xyz**, you would define an **xyzServant** class as a subclass of **_xyzImplBase** class. In the **xyzServant** class, you would implement each method shown in the interface. These are the methods that a client application may invoke. After writing the servant class, compile it with **javac**.

4. Create the server class. In the Java IDL programming model, the server class represents the server application that initializes the ORB, registers the servant object, and handles client requests. For an interface named **xyz**, you would implement the **xyzServer** class that creates an instance of **xyzServant** and registers the servant with the naming service. Compile the server with **javac**.

5. Write the client application. The client initializes the ORB, gets a reference to the remote object, and invokes the remote object's methods. Compile the client with the **javac** compiler.

6. Start the Java IDL naming service. In Windows, type **start tnameserv** in an MS-DOS window. The **tnameserv** program comes with JDK 1.2.

7. Start the server application. For example, to start the **xyzServer** application in Windows, type **java xyzServer** in an MS-DOS window.

8. Start the client application in another MS-DOS window or on another host.

To help you better understand the specific steps, let's walk through a simple example that implements a server that returns the date and time information in several different formats. The client gets the time information and prints it out. I use the same example as was used to illustrate Java RMI programming in the "Java

Remote Method Invocation" section to enable you to easily compare CORBA and RMI programming.

You will find the files for this example in the **ch11\corba** directory of the companion CD-ROM.

The first step in writing a client/server application is to define the interface for the server objects. This specifies the methods that the server implements and that the clients can invoke. The following listing shows the **RemoteTime.idl** file, which defines the **RemoteTime** interface using CORBA IDL syntax:

```
//------------------------------------------------------------
// File: RemoteTime.idl
//
// Specifies the remote time service interface in CORBA-compliant
// Interface Definition Language (IDL).
//
// Compile using idltojava compiler with following command line:
//       idltojava -fno-cpp RemoteTime.idl
//------------------------------------------------------------
interface RemoteTime
{
    long long getBinaryTime();
    string getTimestampString();
    string getDateTimeString();
};
```

The syntax is similar to a Java interface declaration except for various subtle deviations from Java syntax. For example, notice the semicolon (;) after the closing curly brace. That's a required punctuation mark in CORBA IDL.

Also note that the return value for the **getBinaryTime()** method is shown as **long long**. That's not a typographical error; **long long** is the CORBA IDL type equivalent to Java's **long** type. Similarly, in an IDL file you have to use **string** (all lowercase) for Java's **String** class. Table 11-1 shows the mapping of various CORBA IDL constructs to Java language constructs.

CORBA IDL Construct	Java Construct
Module	package
Interface	**interface**, holder, and helper classes
Constant	**public static final**
Boolean	**boolean**

TABLE 11-1. Mapping of CORBA IDL Constructs to Java Constructs.

CORBA IDL Construct	Java Construct
char, wchar	char
Octet	byte
string, wstring	java.lang.String
short, unsigned short	short
long, unsigned long	int
long long, unsigned long long	long
Float	float
Double	double
enum, struct, union	class
sequence, array	array
Exception	class
readonly attribute	method for accessing value of attribute
readwrite attribute	methods for accessing and setting value of attribute
Operation	method

TABLE 11-1.   Mapping of CORBA IDL Constructs to Java Constructs *(continued)*.

After you prepare the **RemoteTime.idl** file, you have to compile that file with the **idltojava** compiler. To perform this task on a Windows system, type **idltojava -fno-cpp RemoteTime.idl** in an MS-DOS window. The **-fno-cpp** option is required if you do not have a C or C++ preprocessor installed on your system. You have a C/C++ preprocessor only if you have a C/C++ compiler on your system. In that case, you can skip the **-fno-cpp** option.

The **idltojava** compiler will generate several files, including **RemoteTime.java**—the Java interface file—as follows:

```
/*
 * File: ./REMOTETIME.JAVA
 * From: REMOTETIME.IDL
 * Date: Sat Feb 27 15:31:36 1999
 *   By: C:\JDK1.2\BIN\IDLTOJ~2.EXE Java IDL 1.2 Aug 18 1998 16:25:34
 */

public interface RemoteTime
    extends org.omg.CORBA.Object, org.omg.CORBA.portable.IDLEntity {
    long getBinaryTime()
;
```

```
    String getTimestampString()
;
    String getDateTimeString()
;
}
```

As you can see, the **idltojava** tool adds a comment showing the date and time when the IDL file was compiled. You can tell that the file was generated automatically because a human programmer would not have placed each semicolon on its own line.

In addition to the **RemoteTime.java** file with the Java interface specification, **idltojava** generates the following files:

◆ **_RemoteTimeStub.java** defines the stub that acts as a proxy for the server.

◆ **RemoteTimeHolder.java** is the holder class for the interface. A holder class supports parameter passing between Java and CORBA.

◆ **RemoteTimeHelper.java** is the helper class for the **RemoteTime** interface. It contains static methods for reading, writing, and locating objects. It is used by the client and the holder class.

◆ **_RemoteTimeImplBase.java** is the skeleton class. This class serves as the superclass for the servant class that implements the server object.

The next step is to write the **RemoteTimeServant** class and implement the methods that were specified in the **RemoteTime** interface. You have to define this class as a subclass of the **_RemoteTimeImplBase** class. The following listing shows the **RemoteTimeServant.java** file, which implements the **RemoteTimeServant** class:

```
//-------------------------------------------------------------
// File: RemoteTimeServant.java
// The servant object that implements the RemoteTime interface.
// Used by RemoteTimeServer (see RemoteTimeServer.java file).
//-------------------------------------------------------------
import java.util.*;
import java.text.*;
public class RemoteTimeServant extends _RemoteTimeImplBase
{
    static SimpleDateFormat tstamp =
            new SimpleDateFormat("yyyyMMMdd-HHmmss");
    static SimpleDateFormat datetime =
            new SimpleDateFormat("EEE MMM dd HH:mm:ss z yyyy");
    public RemoteTimeServant()
    {
        super();
    }
```

```
public long getBinaryTime()
{
    Date d = new Date();
    return d.getTime();
}
public String getTimestampString()
{
    Date d = new Date();
    String tstampString = tstamp.format(d);
    return tstampString;
}
public String getDateTimeString()
{
    Date d = new Date();
    String dtString = datetime.format(d);
    return dtString;
}
}
```

The methods that implement the **RemoteTime** interface are similar to the ones used when implementing the Java RMI version of the time server (described in the section "Java Remote Method Invocation," earlier in this chapter). Each method gets the current time by using a **Date** object. The **getDateTimeString()** and **getTimestampString()** methods format the time by using a **SimpleDateFormat** object with a specific format. The **getBinaryTime()** method calls the **getTime()** method of the **Date** class to get the number of milliseconds elapsed since January 1, 1970.

After writing the **RemoteTimeServant** class, you can compile with the **javac RemoteTimeServant.java** command. You may get a warning saying that **_RemoteTimeImplBase.java** uses or overrides a deprecated API. That's because **idltojava** generates code that contains deprecated methods. Future versions of **idltojava** may correct the code that generates the warnings. For now, the deprecated methods are still supported, so you should be able to run the compiled programs.

Next you should implement the server class, **RemoteTimeServer**. This class represents the server application. It includes a **public static main()** method that initializes the ORB, creates an instance of the **RemoteTimeServant**, registers that servant object, and handles client requests. When you write, you need to call various API methods in a specific order. The following listing shows the **RemoteTimeServer** class:

```
1  //-------------------------------------------------------------
2  // File: RemoteTimeServer.java
3  // Implements a CORBA-based remote time service that provides
4  // the server's time in different formats.
5  //-------------------------------------------------------------
6  import org.omg.CORBA.*;
```

```
 7 import org.omg.CosNaming.*;
 8 import org.omg.CosNaming.NamingContextPackage.*;
 9 import java.util.*;
10 import java.text.*;
11
12 public class RemoteTimeServer
13 {
14     public static void main(String args[])
15     {
16         try
17         {
18             ORB orb = ORB.init(args, null);
19             RemoteTimeServant servant = new RemoteTimeServant();
20             orb.connect(servant);
21             org.omg.CORBA.Object obj =
22                 orb.resolve_initial_references("NameService");
23             NamingContext nc = NamingContextHelper.narrow(obj);
24             NameComponent c = new NameComponent("corbaTime", "");
25             NameComponent path[] = {c};
26             // Bind this path name with the servant
27             nc.rebind(path, servant);
28             // Wait for client connections
29             java.lang.Object sync = new java.lang.Object();
30             synchronized(sync)
31             {
32                 System.out.println("RemoteTimeServer (CORBA): "
33                                     +"waiting for connection...");
34                 sync.wait();
35             }
36         }
37         catch(Exception e)
38         {
39             System.err.println("Error: "+e);
40             System.exit(1);
41         }
42     }
43 }
```

Lines 6 through 8 show the new packages you must import when writing CORBA applications in Java. Lines 14 through 42 define the **main()** method for the server application. The **try** block in lines 16 through 36 contains the important steps you must perform in a server. The **catch** block in lines 37 through 41 handles any exceptions that might occur in the steps being performed in the **try** block. As you will see later in this section, these steps are implemented similarly in the client.

Line 18 creates a new ORB. Line 19 creates an instance of the servant class—
RemoteTimeServant. Line 20 calls the ORB's **connect()** method to connect the
servant object to the ORB. Lines 21 through 25 deal with setting a name for the
servant object in the name server. These lines set up a path name for the servant,
and line 27 associates that name with the servant object. In this case, line 27
associates the name **corbaTime** with the servant object. After the servant object is
connected to the ORB and named in the name server, lines 29 through 35 wait for a
connection from a client.

After writing the server, you can compile it by typing the **javac
RemoteTimeServer.java** command in an MS-DOS window.

The final step in developing the client/server time service is to write a client
application so that you can try out the server. The following listing shows the
CheckTime.java file, which implements a client that calls the methods in the
RemoteTimeServer:

```
1  //------------------------------------------------------------
2  // File: CheckTime.java
3  // Client application that gets date/time from RemoteTimeServer
4  //------------------------------------------------------------
5  import org.omg.CORBA.*;
6  import org.omg.CosNaming.*;
7
8  public class CheckTime
9  {
10     public static void main(String args[])
11     {
12         try
13         {
14             ORB orb = ORB.init(args, null);
15             org.omg.CORBA.Object obj =
16                 orb.resolve_initial_references("NameService");
17             NamingContext nc = NamingContextHelper.narrow(obj);
18             NameComponent c = new NameComponent("corbaTime", "");
19             NameComponent path[] = {c};
20             RemoteTime rts = RemoteTimeHelper.narrow(
21                                      nc.resolve(path));
22             // Get date/time from remote server in various forms
23             String datetime = rts.getDateTimeString();
24             String timestamp = rts.getTimestampString();
25             long bintime = rts.getBinaryTime();
26             // Print the results
27             System.out.println("From corbaTime server:");
28             System.out.println("----------------------");
29             System.out.println("Date/time   = "+datetime);
```

```
30          System.out.println("Time stamp  = "+timestamp);
31          System.out.println("Binary time = "+bintime);
32          System.out.println("                    "+
33                  "(milliseconds since Jan 1, 1970)");
34      }
35      catch(Exception e)
36      {
37          System.err.println("Error: "+e);
38          System.err.println(
39          "Usage: java CheckTime [-ORBInitialHost hostname]");
40      }
41  }
42 }
```

Notice that the client's **main()** method also has a **try** block (lines 12 through 34) that encloses the code that interacts with the ORB and the remote object. If you compare lines 14 through 19 with the corresponding lines in **RemoteTimeServer.java**, you will notice that they are very similar. The only difference is that the client does not do anything with the servant class. Instead, lines 20 and 21 of the client get a **RemoteTime** object through which the client can call the methods of the server. After that **RemoteTime** object is obtained, the client code is identical to that in the Java RMI client shown in the "Java Remote Method Invocation" section.

After implementing the client, compile it with the **javac CheckTime.java** command. Now you are ready to try out the programs. You can run everything—the server, the client, and the name server—on the same system. You may, however, need an active Internet connection for everything to work. When I tested these applications on a Windows 95 PC, they worked only when the PC had an Internet connection. Otherwise, the server and client could not seem to find the name server.

On a Windows system, first run the **tnameserv** program. Type **start tnameserv** in an MS-DOS window. The program opens another MS-DOS window and displays a message about the initial naming context with a long string of hexadecimal numbers followed by the line

TransientNameServer: setting port for initial object references to: 900

TransientNameServer happens to be the name of the Java IDL name server, and the message says that it listens on port number 900. On UNIX and Windows NT systems, you need administrator privileges to start any service that listens on port numbers less than 1024. If you want the name server to listen on another port, simply start with a command of the form **start tnameserv -ORBInitialPort 2087**. This will cause the name server to listen on port 2087.

Next start the server by typing the command **java RemoteTimeServer** in an MS-DOS window. If you used a port number other than 900 for **tnameserv**, specify the same port number when starting **RemoteTimeServer** with a command of the form **java RemoteTimeServer -ORBInitialPort 2087**. After the server starts, it displays the following line:

```
RemoteTimeServer (CORBA): waiting for connection...
```

Now start the client application from another MS-DOS window. If you used the default port for **tnameserv**, type **java CheckTime** to start the program. Otherwise, specify the port explicitly with a command of the form **java CheckTime -ORBInitialPort 2087**. In fact, you can even run the client from a different system on the network. In that case, add the host name in the command, with the syntax **java CheckTime -ORBInitialHost** *hostname*.

After the client runs and successfully gets the results back from the remote object, it displays the result. Here is the typical format of the output:

```
From corbaTime server:
---------------------
Date/time   = Sat Feb 27 18:26:11 EST 1999
Time stamp  = 1999Feb27-182611
Binary time = 920157971630
            (milliseconds since Jan 1, 1970)
```

The date and time are shown in three different forms: the first one is a typical date string, the second one does not have any embedded spaces (and thus can be used as a timestamp or in a filename), and the third form is an integer representing the number of milliseconds since 00:00 January 1, 1970.

A POP3 Client

POP3 refers to Post Office Protocol version 3, an Internet protocol for downloading e-mail messages from a POP3 server. The protocol specifies a simple set of messages that a client can send to log on to a POP3 account and then retrieve messages from the server. The **jPOP3** application is a POP3 client with a graphical user interface to let users download and read POP3 mail. It communicates with the POP3 server using sockets, as explained in the section "Socket-Based Client/Server Communications," earlier in this chapter. You will first try out the application and then learn how it is implemented.

Using jPOP3

The files for the **jPOP3** application are in the **ch11\jPOP3** directory of the companion CD-ROM. You will need JDK 1.2 installed on your system because **jPOP3** uses the Swing GUI classes. You will also need access to a POP3 account. Typically, your regular e-mail account will be a POP3 account because most mail readers (such as the ones in Netscape Communicator and Internet Explorer) download e-mail using POP3. You can safely test **jPOP3** with your regular ISP-provided mail account. Note, however, that **jPOP3** sends your POP3 password in the clear. If you are uncomfortable with this, you should not test **jPOP3** with your regular mail account.

PROGRAMMER'S NOTE *Normally, POP3 mail readers download the messages and then send a command to the POP3 server to delete the downloaded messages. Because jPOP3 is not a full-fledged mail reader, it downloads the mail messages but does not delete them. This means that you can access the same messages again using your favorite mail reader.*

Assuming that you have JDK 1.2 installed, type **java jPOP3** in an MS-DOS window to run the application. The **jPOP3** application displays a window with a menu bar, a toolbar, a tabbed pane, and a text area underneath the tabbed pane. The toolbar has two buttons: the leftmost one is for downloading mail, and the one with a question mark provides a brief help dialog box. Click on the button with a question mark icon. Figure 11-4 shows the dialog box that pops up. After reading the information, click on the OK button to close the dialog box. As the dialog box states, you first have to provide some POP3 server information in the Settings tab, and then you click on the get mail button on the toolbar and browse the messages on the Inbox tab. Finally, you can click on a message in the Inbox to view its contents in the text area underneath the Inbox.

Click on the Settings tab. This tab contains text fields where you enter information about the POP3 server and the POP3 user account. Specifically, you have to provide the host name or IP address of the POP3 server, the POP3 port number (the default is 110), the POP3 user name, and the POP3 password. Figure 11-5 shows the **jPOP3** window after information has been entered on the Settings tab. As you might expect, the password field shows the password as a series of asterisks.

After you enter the settings in the text fields, click on the Inbox tab, because that's where the list of messages will appear. Now click on the leftmost button on the toolbar. This causes **jPOP3** to contact the POP3 server and download any messages

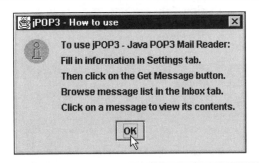

FIGURE 11-4. The dialog box with information on how to use **jPOP3**.

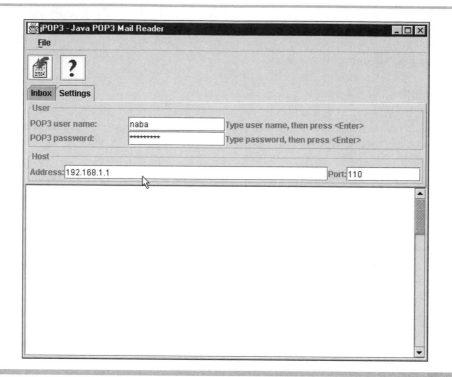

FIGURE 11-5. Entering POP3 settings in the **jPOP3** application.

on the server. If there are any errors, an error dialog box appears. Figure 11-6 shows a typical error dialog box when **jPOP3** is unable to reach a POP3 host.

If all goes well and **jPOP3** is able to download messages from the server, it displays a list of messages in the Inbox tab. To view any of the messages in the Inbox, click on the message in the list. The **jPOP3** application then displays the contents in the text area underneath the list, as shown in Figure 11-7.

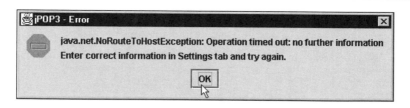

FIGURE 11-6. An error dialog box from **jPOP3**.

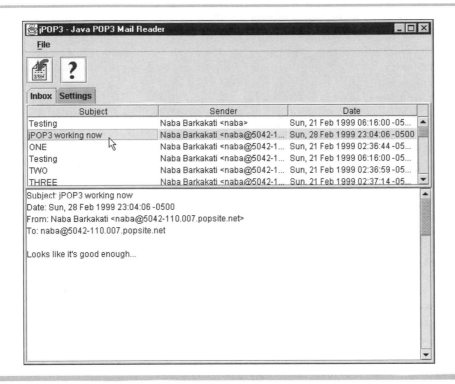

FIGURE 11-7. Viewing a mail message in **jPOP3**.

When you are done experimenting with **jPOP3**, select File | Exit to quit the application.

jPOP3

Understanding jPOP3

The following listing shows the **jPOP3.java** file that implements the **jPOP3** application. I explain the code in the section that follows the listing.

```
1 //-----------------------------------------------------------------
2 // File: jPOP3.java
3 // A client for downloading and reading mail messages from
4 // a Post Office Protocol (POP3 server). Uses Swing classes
5 // for user interface. Requires Java 2 compiler and JVM.
6 //-----------------------------------------------------------------
7 import java.awt.*;
8 import java.awt.event.*;
9 import javax.swing.*;
```

```java
10  import javax.swing.border.*;
11  import javax.swing.table.*;
12  import java.net.*;
13  import java.io.*;
14  import java.util.*;
15  /** The jPOP3 application class */
16  class jPOP3 extends JFrame
17  {
18      static jPOP3 jPOP3App;
19      static final int MAXMSG = 200;
20      JTextField pop3ID;
21      JPasswordField pop3Pwd;
22      JTextField pop3Add;
23      JTextField pop3PortText;
24      JTable table;
25      String[][] msgInfo = new String[MAXMSG][3];
26      JMenuBar menuBar;
27      JToolBar toolbar;
28      JTextArea msgArea;
29      static int WIDTH = 600;
30      static int HEIGHT = 500;
31      int tableRow = 0;
32      POP3 pop3 = null;          // Connection to the POP3 server
33      int pop3Port = 110;                    // POP3 port
34      String pop3Address = "192.168.1.1"; // POP3 host
35      String pop3UserName;     // POP3 user name
36      String pop3Password;     // POP3 password
37      Hashtable mailMessages; // Hash table for storing messages
38      /** Creates the user interface */
39      public jPOP3()
40      {
41          super("jPOP3 - Java POP3 Mail Reader");
42          this.addWindowListener(new WindowAdapter()
43          {
44              public void windowClosing(WindowEvent e)
45              {
46                  dispose();
47                  System.exit(0);
48              }
49          });
50          mailMessages = new Hashtable();
51          // Construct the application's user interface
52          createMenuBar();
```

```
53          setJMenuBar(menuBar);
54          JPanel p = new JPanel();
55          p.setLayout(new BorderLayout());
56          p.add("North", createToolbar());
57          JTabbedPane tp = new JTabbedPane(JTabbedPane.TOP)
58          {
59              public Dimension getPreferredSize()
60              {
61                  Dimension d = new Dimension();
62                  d.width = 200;
63                  d.height = 150;
64                  return d;
65              }
66          };
67          setupMsgTable();
68          JScrollPane scrollpane = new JScrollPane(table);
69          tp.addTab("Inbox", scrollpane);
70          JPanel settingsPanel = createPOP3SettingsPanel();
71          tp.addTab("Settings",settingsPanel);
72          p.add("Center", tp);
73          getContentPane().add("North",p);
74          msgArea = new JTextArea(60, 30);
75          JScrollPane scrollPane = new JScrollPane(msgArea);
76          getContentPane().add("Center", scrollPane);
77          setSize(WIDTH, HEIGHT);
78          show();
79      }
80      /** Initialize the POP3 object */
81      private void initPOP3()
82      {
83          try
84          {
85              pop3 = new POP3(pop3Address, pop3Port,
86                              pop3UserName, pop3Password);
87          }
88          catch (Exception e) {}
89      }
90      /** Set up the table for displaying message info */
91      private  void setupMsgTable()
92      {
93          final String columnNames[] = {"Subject", "Sender","Date"};
94          TableModel msgInfoModel = new AbstractTableModel()
95          {
```

```
96          public int getColumnCount()
97              { return columnNames.length;}
98          public int getRowCount() { return msgInfo.length;}
99          public Object getValueAt(int row, int col)
100             { return msgInfo[row][col];}
101         public String getColumnName(int column)
102             {return columnNames[column];}
103     };
104     // Create a table with this model
105     table = new JTable(msgInfoModel);
106     table.getSelectionModel().setSelectionMode(
107             ListSelectionModel.SINGLE_SELECTION);
108     table.setShowGrid(false);
109     table.addMouseListener(new MouseAdapter()
110     {
111         public void mousePressed(MouseEvent e)
112         {
113             int selRow = table.getSelectedRow();
114             if(msgInfo[selRow][0]!=null)
115             {
116                 // Display selected message content
117                 MailMsg m = (MailMsg)jPOP3App.getMailMsg(
118                                     msgInfo[selRow][0]+
119                                     msgInfo[selRow][1]+
120                                     msgInfo[selRow][2]);
121                 msgArea.setText(m.toString());
122             }
123         }
124     });
125 }
126 /** Fill the table with mail message info */
127 private void fillMsgTable()
128 {
129     Enumeration e = getMailMessages().elements();
130     while(e.hasMoreElements())
131     {
132         MailMsg m = (MailMsg)e.nextElement();
133         msgInfo[tableRow%MAXMSG][0] = m.subject();
134         msgInfo[tableRow%MAXMSG][1] = m.sender();
135         msgInfo[tableRow%MAXMSG][2] = m.date();
136         tableRow++;
137     }
138 }
```

```
139    /** Creates a panel for POP3 settings */
140    private JPanel createPOP3SettingsPanel()
141    {
142        JPanel p = new JPanel(new BorderLayout());
143        p.add("North", createPop3UserPanel());
144        p.add("South", createPop3HostPanel());
145        return p;
146    }
147    /** Creates the panel for user name and password */
148    private JPanel createPop3UserPanel()
149    {
150        JPanel pop3User = new JPanel(new GridLayout(2,1));
151        pop3User.setBorder(new TitledBorder("User"));
152        JLabel pop3Acct = new JLabel("POP3 user name:");
153        pop3ID = new JTextField();
154        pop3ID.setText(pop3UserName);
155        pop3ID.addActionListener(new ActionListener()
156        {
157            public void actionPerformed(ActionEvent e)
158            {
159                pop3UserName = pop3ID.getText();
160                initPOP3();
161                pop3Pwd.requestFocus();
162            }
163        });
164        JPanel pTop1 = new JPanel(new GridLayout(1,2));
165        pTop1.add(pop3Acct);
166        pTop1.add(pop3ID);
167        JLabel pad1 = new JLabel(
168                "Type user name, then press <Enter>");
169        JPanel p1 = new JPanel(new GridLayout(1,2));
170        p1.add(pTop1);
171        p1.add(pad1);
172        JLabel pad2 = new JLabel(
173                "Type password, then press <Enter>");
174
175        JLabel pop3Pass = new JLabel("POP3 password:");
176        pop3Pwd = new JPasswordField();
177        pop3Pwd.setText(pop3Password);
178        pop3Pwd.addActionListener(new ActionListener()
179        {
180            public void actionPerformed(ActionEvent e)
181            {
```

```
182                         pop3Password =
183                             new String(pop3Pwd.getPassword());
184                     initPOP3();
185                     pop3Add.requestFocus();
186                 }
187         });
188         JPanel pTop2 = new JPanel(new GridLayout(1,2));
189         pTop2.add(pop3Pass);
190         pTop2.add(pop3Pwd);
191         JPanel p2 = new JPanel(new GridLayout(1,2));
192         p2.add(pTop2);
193         p2.add(pad2);
194         pop3User.add(p1);
195         pop3User.add(p2);
196         return pop3User;
197     }
198     /** Creates the panel for POP3 host and port number */
199     private JPanel createPop3HostPanel()
200     {
201         JPanel POP3panel = new JPanel(new BorderLayout());
202         POP3panel.setBorder(new TitledBorder("Host"));
203         JLabel addressL = new JLabel("Address:");
204         JLabel portL = new JLabel("Port:");
205         pop3Add = new JTextField(pop3Address);
206         pop3Add.addActionListener(new ActionListener()
207         {
208             public void actionPerformed(ActionEvent e)
209             {
210                 pop3Address = pop3Add.getText();
211                 initPOP3();
212                 pop3PortText.requestFocus();
213             }
214         });
215         pop3PortText = new JTextField(""+pop3Port, 10);
216         pop3PortText.addActionListener(new ActionListener()
217         {
218             public void actionPerformed(ActionEvent e)
219             {
220                 pop3Port = Integer.parseInt(pop3PortText.
221                                     getText().trim());
222                 initPOP3();
223                 pop3ID.requestFocus();
224             }
```

```
225            });
226            JPanel p1 = new JPanel(new BorderLayout());
227            p1.add("West", addressL);
228            p1.add("Center", pop3Add);
229            JPanel p2 = new JPanel(new BorderLayout());
230            p2.add("West", portL);
231            p2.add("East", pop3PortText);
232            POP3panel.add("Center", p1);
233            POP3panel.add("East", p2);
234            return POP3panel;
235        }
236    /**
237     * Create the toolbar with two buttons: Get Messages, Help
238     */
239     /** Creates the toolbar with two buttons */
240     private JToolBar createToolbar()
241     {
242            toolbar = new JToolBar();
243            toolbar.setFloatable(false);
244            JButton gmBtn = new JButton(new ImageIcon("getmail.gif"));
245            gmBtn.setToolTipText("Get messages");
246            gmBtn.addActionListener(new ActionListener()
247            {
248                public void actionPerformed(ActionEvent e)
249                {
250                    Vector newMailMessages=null;
251                    if(pop3 == null) initPOP3();
252                    try
253                    {
254                        newMailMessages = pop3.getMailMessages();
255                        for(int i=0; i < newMailMessages.size(); i++)
256                        {
257                            addMailMsg((MailMsg)newMailMessages.
258                                               elementAt(i));
259                        }
260                        msgInfo = new String[MAXMSG][3];
261                        tableRow = 0;
262                        fillMsgTable();
263                        repaint();
264                        if(newMailMessages.size() == 0)
265                            JOptionPane.showMessageDialog(toolbar,
266                                    "No new message on server",
```

```
267                                      "jPOP3 - Error",
268                             JOptionPane.INFORMATION_MESSAGE);
269                 }
270             catch(Exception ex)
271             {
272                 JOptionPane.showMessageDialog(toolbar,
273                                     ex.toString()+"\n"+
274             "Enter correct information in "+
275             "Settings tab and try again.",
276             "jPOP3 - Error", JOptionPane.ERROR_MESSAGE);
277             }
278         }
279     });
280     JButton helpBtn = new JButton(new ImageIcon("help.gif"));
281     helpBtn.setToolTipText("Help for jPOP3...");
282     helpBtn.addActionListener(new ActionListener()
283     {
284         public void actionPerformed(ActionEvent e)
285         {
286             JOptionPane.showMessageDialog(toolbar,
287                 "To use jPOP3 - Java POP3 Mail Reader:\n"+
288                 "Fill in information in Settings tab.\n"+
289                 "Then click on the Get Message button.\n"+
290                 "Browse message list in the Inbox tab.\n"+
291                 "Click on a message to view its contents.",
292                 "jPOP3 - How to use",
293                 JOptionPane.INFORMATION_MESSAGE);
294         }
295     });
296     toolbar.add(gmBtn);
297     toolbar.addSeparator();
298     toolbar.add(helpBtn);
299     return toolbar;
300 }
301 /** Creates the menu bar */
302 private void createMenuBar()
303 {
304     menuBar = new JMenuBar();
305     JMenu file = new JMenu("File");
306     file.setMnemonic('F');
307     JMenuItem mi;
308     mi = new JMenuItem("About jPOP3...", 'A');
309     mi.addActionListener(new ActionListener()
310     {
```

```
311         public void actionPerformed(ActionEvent e)
312         {
313             JOptionPane.showMessageDialog(menuBar,
314               "jPOP3 - Java POP3 Mail Reader\n"+
315               "Copyright (c) 1999 - Naba Barkakati\n",
316               "About jPOP3",JOptionPane.INFORMATION_MESSAGE);
317         }
318     });
319     file.add(mi);
320     file.addSeparator();
321     mi = new JMenuItem("Exit", 'x');
322   mi.addActionListener(new ActionListener()
323     {
324         public void actionPerformed(ActionEvent e)
325         {
326             System.exit(0);
327         }
328     });
329     file.add(mi);
330     menuBar.add(file);
331 }
332 /** Adds a mail message to the hash table */
333 public void addMailMsg(MailMsg m)
334 {
335     mailMessages.put(m.subject() + m.sender() + m.date(), m);
336 }
337 /** Returns a message from the hash table */
338 public MailMsg getMailMsg(String s)
339 {
340     return (MailMsg)mailMessages.get(s);
341 }
342 /** Returns the hash table containing mail messages */
343 public Hashtable getMailMessages()
344 {
345     return mailMessages;
346 }
347 /** The main() method of the jPOP3 application */
348 public static void main(String[] args)
349 {
350     jPOP3App = new jPOP3();
351 }
352 } // End of jPOP3 class
```

```
353   /** A class that represents a mail message */
354   class MailMsg
355   {
356       String subject = "";
357       String sender = "";
358       String message = "";
359       String date = "";
360       String header = "";
361       /** Creates a mail message using specified parts */
362       public MailMsg(String subject, String date, String from,
363                       String to, String cc, String content,
364                       String header)
365       {
366           this.header = header;
367           this.subject = subject;
368           sender = from;
369           if(date.equals(""))
370               this.date = new Date().toString();
371           else
372               this.date = date;
373           // Construct the message to be displayed
374           // The order of header fields is up to you
375           message = "Subject: "+subject+"\n"+
376                       "Date: "+ date +"\n" +
377                       "From: "+sender+"\n" +
378                       "To: "+to+"\n";
379           if(!cc.equals(""))
380               message = message + "Cc: "+cc+"\n";
381           message = message + content;
382       }
383       public String sender() { return sender;}
384       public String date() { return date;}
385       public String subject() { return subject;}
386       public String toString() { return message;}
387   }
388   /** POP3 class implements a client that gets mail messages
389    *  from a POP3 server using the POP3 protocol (defined
390    *  in RFC 1939). The default port number for POP3
391    *  service is 110.
392    */
393   class POP3
394   {
```

```
395    InetAddress pop3Server;
396    int port = 110;
397    String user;   // User name
398    String passwd; // Password
399    Socket socket;
400    BufferedReader in = null;
401    PrintWriter out = null;
402    // POP3 protocol messages
403    String quit = "QUIT";
404    String reset ="RSET";
405    String usr ="USER ";
406    String pass = "PASS ";
407    String stat = "STAT";
408    String list = "LIST";
409    String retr = "RETR ";
410    String dele = "DELE ";
411    boolean startOfMessage = false;
412    /** Constructs a POP3 client
413     *   @param pop3Srv = pop3 server address
414     *   @param p = port number
415     *   @param uid = user name
416     *   @param pwd = user password (warning: sent in cleartext)
417     */
418    public POP3(String pop3Srv, int p, String uid, String pwd)
419    {
420        try
421        {
422            pop3Server = InetAddress.getByName(pop3Srv);
423            port = p;
424            user = uid;
425            passwd = pwd;
426        }
427        catch(UnknownHostException e)
428        {
429            System.err.println("Unknown host: "+pop3Srv);
430        }
431    }
432    /** Returns a Vector containing of MailMsg objects */
433    public Vector getMailMessages() throws Exception
434    {
435        String line = "";
436        Vector msgVec = new Vector();
```

```
437        // Open a socket connection to the POP3 server
438        try
439        {
440            socket = new Socket(pop3Server,port);
441            // Set up the input and output streams
442            in = new BufferedReader(new
443                    InputStreamReader(socket.getInputStream()));
444            out = new PrintWriter(new
445                    BufferedWriter(new
446                OutputStreamWriter(socket.getOutputStream())));
447            // Read first response from server (should be "+OK")
448            while((line  = in.readLine()) == null);
449            if(!line.substring(0,3).equalsIgnoreCase("+OK"))
450                throw new Exception(
451                    "POP3 service not available on the server\n");
452            // Send user name and read server's response
453            out.println(usr+user);
454            out.flush();
455            while((line  = in.readLine()) == null);
456            if(!line.substring(0,3).equalsIgnoreCase("+OK"))
457                throw new Exception(line);
458            // Send password and read server's response
459            // WARNING: password is sent in cleartext
460            out.println(pass+passwd);
461            out.flush();
462            while((line  = in.readLine()) == null);
463            if(!line.substring(0,3).equalsIgnoreCase("+OK"))
464                throw new Exception(line);
465            // Get messages
466            out.println(stat);
467            out.flush();
468            while((line  = in.readLine()) == null);
469            if(!line.substring(0,3).equalsIgnoreCase("+OK"))
470                throw new Exception(line);
471            // Get message list
472            Vector ids = new Vector();
473            out.println(list);
474            out.flush();
475            if(!(line=in.readLine()).
476                    substring(0,3).equalsIgnoreCase("+OK"))
477                        throw new Exception(line);
478            while(!(line  = in.readLine()).equals("."))
```

```
479             {
480                 ids.addElement(line.
481                     substring(0,line.indexOf(" ")));
482             }
483         if(!line.substring(0,1).equalsIgnoreCase("."))
484             throw new Exception(line);
485         // Get the messages one by one
486         for(int i = 0; i < ids.size(); i++)
487         {
488             String header ="";
489             String content ="";
490             String subject ="";
491             String date ="";
492             String from="";
493             String to ="";
494             String cc="";
495             String retrieve = retr + ids.elementAt(i);
496             out.println(retrieve);
497             out.flush();
498             // Read the +OK response
499             if(!(line=in.readLine()).
500                 substring(0,3).equalsIgnoreCase("+OK"))
501                     throw new Exception(line);
502             // Next read the message
503             while(!(line  = in.readLine()).equals("."))
504             {
505                 if(line.startsWith("Subject:"))
506                     subject = line.substring(line.
507                     indexOf(":")+1,line.length()).trim();
508                 if(line.startsWith("From:"))
509                     from = line.substring(line.
510                     indexOf(":")+1,line.length()).trim();
511                 if(line.startsWith("Date:"))
512                     date = line.substring(line.
513                     indexOf(":")+1,line.length()).trim();
514                 if(line.startsWith("To:"))
515                     to = line.substring(line.
516                     indexOf(":")+1,line.length()).trim();
517                 if(line.startsWith("Cc:"))
518                     cc = line.substring(line.
519                     indexOf(":")+1,line.length()).trim();
520                 if(line.equals("")) startOfMessage = true;
```

```
521                    if(startOfMessage)
522                        content = content + line +"\n";
523                    else
524                        header = header + line + "\n";
525                }
526                try
527                {
528                    msgVec.addElement(new MailMsg(subject, date,
529                                  from, to, cc, content, header));
530                } catch (Exception e){}
531                startOfMessage = false;
532                // Expect a period that indicates end of message
533                if(!line.substring(0,1).equalsIgnoreCase("."))
534                    throw new Exception("No end of message");
535            }
536        // Typically, at this point you would delete the
537        // messages with the following code, but I won't
538        // delete because this is not a full-blown POP3
539        // client:
540        // for(int i = 0; i < ids.size(); i++)
541        // {
542        // out.println(dele+ids.elementAt(i));
543        // out.flush();
544        // while((line  = in.readLine()) == null);
545        // if(!line.substring(0,3).
546        //     equalsIgnoreCase("+OK"))
547        //         throw new Exception(line);
548        // }
549        // Send QUIT command to POP3 server
550        out.println(quit);
551        out.flush();
552        while((line  = in.readLine()) == null);
553        if(!line.substring(0,3).equalsIgnoreCase("+OK"))
554            throw new Exception(line);
555    }
556    catch(Exception ex)
557    {
558        try
559        {
560            System.err.println(ex.toString());
561            out.println(reset);
562            out.flush();
563            in.readLine();
```

```
564              out.println(quit);
565              out.flush();
566              socket.close();
567          }
568          catch(Exception f) {}
569          throw(ex);  // Throw the exception again
570      }
571      // Close the connection
572      try
573      {
574          socket.close();
575      } catch (IOException e){ throw e;}
576      return msgVec;
577      }
578  }
```

ANNOTATIONS

When you write a GUI client for an Internet service such as POP3, you have to write three broad categories of code:

◆ The GUI code that presents information to the user and accepts user input

◆ The sockets-based communication code that exchanges data with the Internet service, using the standard protocol

◆ Supporting code that stores and manages the application's data, including the information (such as mail messages) received from the Internet server

The **jPOP3** application is no exception; it has these three types of code embodied in three distinct classes:

◆ The **jPOP3** class, shown in lines 16 through 352, primarily represents the GUI code. This class also includes some supporting code for managing the mail messages received from the POP3 server.

◆ The **POP3** class, shown in lines 393 through 578, handles the sockets-based communication with a POP3 server. In particular, the **getMailMessages()** method, in lines 433 through 577, takes care of all of the protocol exchanges involved in downloading mail messages from the POP3 server.

◆ The **MailMsg** class, shown in lines 354 through 387, represents a mail message. Various methods in the **jPOP3** class maintain **MailMsg** objects in a **Hashtable** (which is a Java container capable of storing objects by a key).

The next few sections give you an overview of each category of code in **jPOP3**.

HANDLING USER INTERACTIONS   The **jPOP3** class is defined as a subclass of **JFrame**, the Swing class that must be the container for a Swing-based GUI. The entire user interface is laid out in the **jPOP3()** constructor, shown in lines 39 through 79. First, line 41 calls the **JFrame** constructor and sets the title that appears in the application window's title bar:

```
41        super("jPOP3 - Java POP3 Mail Reader");
```

Lines 42 through 49 set up a **WindowListener** for the **WindowEvent** that occurs when the user closes the window. The listener calls **dispose()** to get rid of the frame and then calls **System.exit()** to exit the application.

Line 50 sets up the **Hashtable** used to store mail messages. This is described further in the section "Managing the Application's Data," later in this chapter.

Line 52 calls **createMenuBar()** to create the menu bar, and line 53 attaches the menu bar to this frame:

```
52        createMenuBar();
53        setJMenuBar(menuBar);
```

The **createMenuBar()** method, shown in lines 302 through 331, creates the File menu with two menu items: **About jPOP3** and **Exit**. Each menu item has its **ActionListener** to handle the event that occurs when the user clicks on the menu item. The programming for these items is similar to the way Swing menus are typically set up (as described in Chapter 9, "GUI Applications").

Line 54 creates a new **JPanel** to hold the toolbar and the tabbed pane that appears in the upper part of the application's window:

```
54        JPanel p = new JPanel();
```

Line 55 sets this panel's layout manager to **BorderLayout** and adds a toolbar to the **"North"** position of the layout:

```
55        p.setLayout(new BorderLayout());
56        p.add("North", createToolbar());
```

The toolbar is created by calling the **createToolbar()** method, shown in lines 240 through 300. The toolbar is made up of a **JToolBar** Swing component that contains two buttons. One button has an icon that uses an image file named **getmail.gif**, and the other has an icon from an image named **help.gif**. As the image filenames imply, the button with the **getmail.gif** icon is meant for getting mail, and the other button displays a help dialog box. Each button has an **ActionListener** that takes care of the tasks that the button must perform. In particular, line 254 in the **ActionListener** for the button with the **getmail.gif** icon calls the **getMailMessages()** method of the **POP3** class to download messages from the POP3 server:

254   **newMailMessages = pop3.getMailMessages();**

This line is the link between the user interface and the **POP3** class that handles the sockets-based communications with the POP3 server.

Lines 57 through 66 create the tabbed pane using the **JTabbedPane** Swing component and override the **getPreferredSize()** method to limit the size (especially the vertical extent) of the tabbed pane.

Line 67 calls **setupMsgTable()** to create the table that will display the list of messages:

67   **setupMsgTable();**

The **setupMsgTable()** method, shown in lines 91 through 125, creates a **JTable** component with a simple model of the table's data represented by a local class named **TableModel** (shown in lines 94 through 103). As described in Chapter 9, "GUI Applications," Swing GUI classes use the Model-View-Controller architecture, in which a component's state information is maintained in the model while the screen representation and user interaction are handled by a separate class. In this case, the table model is required to provide a specific set of methods, which the **TableModel** class does in lines 96 through 102.

After the table has been created, line 68 places the table inside a **JScrollPane** (so that users can scroll up and down a long list), and line 69 adds that scroll pane in a tab labeled Inbox:

68   **JScrollPane scrollpane = new JScrollPane(table);**
69   **tp.addTab("Inbox", scrollpane);**

Next, line 70 creates another panel for the POP3 settings and line 71 adds that to the tabbed pane with the label Settings:

70   **JPanel settingsPanel = createPOP3SettingsPanel();**
71   **tp.addTab("Settings",settingsPanel);**

The settings panel is created by the **createPOP3SettingsPanel()** method, shown in lines 140 through 146. That method creates a **JPanel** with a **BorderLayout** layout manager. Line 143 calls **createPop3UserPanel()** to create the panel with text fields for the user name and password and add it to the **"North"** position. Line 144 calls **createPop3HostPanel()** to create another panel where the user enters the POP3 host name (or IP address) and port number. That panel is added to the **"South"** position. Finally, the **createPOP3SettingsPanel()** method returns the **JPanel** containing the two panels.

Once the tabbed pane **tp** is ready, it is placed in the **"Center"** position of the **JPanel** containing the toolbar:

72   **p.add("Center", tp);**

Line 73 then adds that panel to the **"North"** position of the frame's content pane:

```
73          getContentPane().add("North",p);
```

As explained in Chapter 9, "GUI Applications," you must add Swing components to a **JFrame** object's content pane. That's why line 73 calls **getContentPane()** to get the content pane and add that panel. Note that the **JFrame** content pane uses a **BorderLayout** by default.

The remainder of the user interface involves adding a text area where the currently selected mail message can be displayed. Lines 74 through 76 take care of this part of the user interface:

```
74          msgArea = new JTextArea(60, 30);
75          JScrollPane scrollPane = new JScrollPane(msgArea);
76          getContentPane().add("Center", scrollPane);
```

Line 74 creates the **JTextArea**, and line 75 places it inside a **JScrollPane** so that users can scroll through long messages. Line 76 adds the scrolled pane to the **JFrame** content pane.

The final step in finishing up the user interface is to set the size of the frame and make it visible. These steps are performed by lines 77 and 78:

```
77          setSize(WIDTH, HEIGHT);
78          show();
```

These two steps are very important. Line 77 sets the size of the frame to the width and height specified by the **WIDTH** and **HEIGHT** variables. Line 78 then calls **show()** to make the frame visible.

PROGRAMMER'S NOTE   *It can be very confusing if you forget to call **show()** to make the **JFrame** visible in a GUI application, because nothing appears when you run the program, not even an error message.*

INTERACTING WITH THE POP3 SERVER   To implement a POP3 client, you have to understand the POP3 protocol. The POP3 protocol is documented in RFC 1939, "Post Office Protocol—Version 3," S. J. Myers and M. Rose, 1996, and is available on the Web at **http://www.cis.ohio-state.edu/htbin/rfc/rfc1939.html**.

The basic interactions with the POP3 server are simple. The server listens on a specific port on the host (the standard POP3 port number is 110). When a client establishes a TCP connection to that port, the server sends a greeting message that begins with the string **+OK**. The client then sends the user name and password. After that the client sends text commands (typically followed by one or more arguments) to get information from the server. The server always begins its responses with one of two status indicators: **+OK** if all goes well and **-ERR** if there are any problems. For example, the following listing is an annotated transcript of message exchanges between a client and a POP3 server. (Note that comments appear in italics; each server response is shown with an **S:** prefix and **C:** marks the client commands, but the **S:** and **C:** are not part of the protocol.)

```
S: +OK POP3 somehost v4.45 server ready
C: USER someuser
S: +OK User name accepted, password please
C: PASS pwd(cleartext)
S: +OK Mailbox open, 7 messages
C: STAT
S: +OK 7 4457   (this means that there are 7 messages with 4457 bytes)
C: LIST
S: +OK Mailbox scan listing follows
(Server sends a list of messages with length of each message)
S: .    (a period marks the end of lists and message text)
C: RETR 1     (this says to retrieve message number 1)
S: +OK 433 octets
(Server sends all lines of message 1 and ends with a period)
S: .
C: RETR 2     (this says to retrieve message number 2)
S: +OK 433 octets
(Server sends all lines of message 2 and ends with a period)
S: .
(Typically client downloads all messages and then quits)
C: QUIT
S: +OK Sayonara
```

The **POP3** class, shown in lines 393 through 578, handles the interactions with the POP3 server. This class is at the heart of the POP3 client application. The **POP3()** constructor, shown in lines 418 through 431, simply stores the settings information: the host name, port number, POP3 user name, and POP3 password.

The actual interactions with the POP3 server are handled by the **getMailMessages()** method, shown in lines 433 through 577. The sequence of POP3 protocol exchanges mimics the sample transcript shown in the listing earlier in this section. Line 440 creates a socket connection to the POP3 server at the specified port number:

```
440         socket = new Socket(pop3Server,port);
```

Lines 442 through 446 set up a **BufferedReader** named **in** and a **PrintWriter** named **out** to conduct the protocol conversation with the POP3 server:

```
442         in = new BufferedReader(new
443             InputStreamReader(socket.getInputStream()));
444         out = new PrintWriter(new
445             BufferedWriter(new
446             OutputStreamWriter(socket.getOutputStream())));
```

Specifically, the client can call **in.readLine()** to read a line of text from the server, and it can call **out.println()** to send a line of text to the server.

Right after the socket connection has been opened, line 448 listens for the server's response:

```
448          while((line  = in.readLine()) == null);
```

Line 449 checks whether the response begins with **+OK**; if not, lines 450 and 451 throw an exception:

```
449          if(!line.substring(0,3).equalsIgnoreCase("+OK"))
450              throw new Exception(
451                  "POP3 service not available on the server\n");
```

You will see this pattern of code repeated throughout the **getMailMessages()** method.

Lines 453 and 454 send the POP3 command **USER** followed by the user name:

```
453          out.println(usr+user);
454          out.flush();
```

After that, lines 455 through 457 wait for a response that begins with **+OK**. If a good response is received, lines 460 and 461 send the **PASS** command followed by the password:

```
460          out.println(pass+passwd);
461          out.flush();
```

It's important to note that the POP3 password is sent in the clear. If you feel uncomfortable about this, you should not use **jPOP3** with your ISP-provided POP3 mail account.

The rest of the protocol exchanges in **getMailMessages()** follow the pattern illustrated in the listing shown earlier in this section. Each downloaded message is stored in a **MailMsg** object (see the next section, "Managing the Application's Data"), and these **MailMsg** objects, in turn, are placed in a **Vector** named **msgVec**. After all messages have been downloaded, lines 550 and 551 send a **QUIT** command:

```
550          out.println(quit);
551          out.flush();
```

Finally, line 576 returns the **msgVec** vector with all of the **MailMsg** objects containing the downloaded mail messages:

```
576      return msgVec;
```

If there are any errors during the interactions with the POP3 server, the **getMailMessages()** method throws an exception. The exception is caught by a **catch** block embedded in the **ActionListener** of the toolbar button that initiates the downloading of messages from the POP3 server. Lines 270 through 277 show this **catch** block:

```
270                     catch(Exception ex)
271                     {
272                         JOptionPane.showMessageDialog(toolbar,
273                                              ex.toString()+"\n"+
274                         "Enter correct information in "+
275                         "Settings tab and try again.",
276                         "jPOP3 - Error", JOptionPane.ERROR_MESSAGE);
277                     }
```

As you can see, this **catch** block creates a **JOptionPane** and displays a dialog box with an error message.

MANAGING THE APPLICATION'S DATA   The **jPOP3** application has several important data elements to manage. First, it has to keep track of the POP3 data: the server name, the port number, the user name, and the password. Lines 32 through 36 show the variables used to store this information:

```
32    POP3 pop3 = null;        // Connection to the POP3 server
33    int pop3Port = 110;                  // POP3 port
34    String pop3Address = "192.168.1.1"; // POP3 host
35    String pop3UserName;     // POP3 user name
36    String pop3Password;     // POP3 password
```

The **POP3** object is initialized later on by the **initPOP3()** method, shown in lines 81 through 89. Whenever the user changes any POP3 parameter, **initPOP3()** is called to reset the **POP3** object.

The other important data elements are the mail messages. Line 37 declares a **Hashtable** for the mail messages:

```
37    Hashtable mailMessages; // Hash table for storing messages
```

Mail messages are read from the server by code embedded in the **ActionListener** for the toolbar button with the **getmail.gif** icon (the leftmost button on the toolbar). Lines 254 through 259 show the code that gets the mail messages and then adds them to the **Hashtable** named **mailMessages**:

```
254                     newMailMessages = pop3.getMailMessages();
255                     for(int i=0; i < newMailMessages.size(); i++)
256                     {
257                         addMailMsg((MailMsg)newMailMessages.
258                                                elementAt(i));
259                     }
```

Line 254 gets the mail messages in a **Vector** named **newMailMessages**. The **for** loop in lines 255 through 259 calls **addMailMsg()** to insert each mail message into the hash table.

Lines 333 through 336 show the **addMailMsg()** method:

```
333    public void addMailMsg(MailMsg m)
334    {
335        mailMessages.put(m.subject() + m.sender() + m.date(), m);
336    }
```

Line 335 calls the **put()** method of the **Hashtable mailMessages** to add the mail message with a key that consists of the subject, sender, and date of the message. Later on, messages are extracted using the same key.

Another important data structure is the two-dimensional array **msgInfo** that holds the subject, sender, and date of all received messages. Line 25 creates the **msgInfo** array:

```
25    String[][] msgInfo = new String[MAXMSG][3];
```

MAXMSG is set to 200. This means that the application can display information about at most 200 mail messages. The **msgInfo** array is used in the data model for the table that appears in the tabbed pane labeled Inbox. The **fillMsgTable()** method, shown in lines 127 through 138, fills the **msgInfo** array from the messages currently in the **mailMessages** hash table.

A Java Client/Server Chat Application

A simple client/server application is a chat program that allows people to have communal conversations. The protocol for the chat client/server communication is very simple. All that a chat server does is echo back each line of text from a client to all other clients. The client application, on the other hand, reads lines of text from the server and sends to the server anything that the user types. The following sections present the **jChatServer** and **jChatClient** applications, which constitute a Java client/server chat system. You will first try out the chat application and then learn how to implement the server and the client.

Using jChatServer and jChatClient

You will find the files for the **jChat** applications in the **ch11\jChat** directory of this book's companion CD-ROM. You will need JDK 1.2 to try the client application, **jChatClient**, because it uses the Swing classes. However, you can compile and run the server, **jChatServer**, using older versions of the JDK.

PROGRAMMER'S NOTE *When you compile jChatServer.java using a pre–Java 2 compiler, you may get a warning indicating that jChatServer.java uses a deprecated API. If you recompile with the javac -deprecation jChatServer.java command, the message tells you that the PrintStream(java.io.OutputStream) constructor is deprecated. Surprisingly, the Java 2 compiler in JDK 1.2 does not show this warning. I assume that this is something that changed between Java 1.1.x and Java 2.*

You can run both the client application and the server application on the same system. If you have multiple networked systems, you should run them on separate hosts. If you want to run the applications on another system (that has JDK installed), first copy the class files to that system.

Start by running the server with the command **java jChatServer**. By default, the server listens on port number 8299. When the server starts, it will print an opening message in the following form:

```
jChatServer 1.0 Copyright 1999 Naba Barkakati
java jChatServer -port 8299 -timeout 300 -logfile jchat.1999Mar01-044649.log
```

The first line is a copyright notice. The second line displays the command line that started the server. As you can see, you can add a number of command-line options. If you don't specify any options, the command line shows the default values used to start the server. Here is how you can interpret the command-line options:

- **-port 8299** specifies the port number as 8299.

- **-timeout 300** means that any client idle for more than 300 seconds (5 minutes) will be disconnected.

- **-logfile jchat.1999Mar01-044649.log** specifies the name of the log file where the server records information about the chat session (by default, the log filename is created by inserting a timestamp between the words **jchat** and **log**).

If you want the server to listen on a different port, simply start with a command line such as **java jChatServer -port 2087** (where 2087 is the port on which the server should listen).

After the server is running, run the client with the command **java jChatClient -host** *hostname* **-port** *portnum*, where *hostname* is the name (or IP address) of the host on which the **jChatServer** is running and *portnum* is the port number being used by the server. If you run everything on the same system, you can skip the **-host** option. You do not have to specify the port number if you want to use the default port (8299). In any case, even if you start **jChatClient** with the default parameters, you will be able to enter all of the information after the application displays its window.

The chat client displays a main window with text fields along the top where you can enter the host name, the port number, and the name you want to use for the chat.

Type the necessary information, and then click on the Connect button next to the Port field. This will cause the client to connect to the chat server. The status field under the Connect button will show the status of the connection. If the connection is successful, you'll see some messages in the large text area that occupies most of the window. To chat with others, start typing in the text field along the bottom edge of the window, pressing ENTER to send each line to the server. Anything you type will go to all chat clients, including yourself. When anyone else joins the chat, you'll see messages in the text area about the new user. Figure 11-8 shows a typical chat session.

You can also chat using the Telnet application. Simply connect to the host running **jChatServer** at the port where the server listens. Thus everyone participating in the chat does not have to use the **jChatClient** application. They can chat as long as everyone connects to the same **jChatServer**.

The server prints out various information in a log file. You can study the log file to see the history of how participants joined and left the chat. The log also includes any error conditions encountered by the server. Here are some lines from a typical log file:

```
jChatServer 1.0 Copyright 1999 Naba Barkakati
java jChatServer -port 8299 -timeout 300 -logfile jchat.1999Mar01-044649.log
[1999Mar01-044649] jChatServer started.
[1999Mar01-044937]
  Currently Connected:
  lnbp200/192.168.1.200:1056 (from lnbp200/192.168.1.200:1056)
[1999Mar01-044942]
  Currently Connected:
  naba (from lnbp200/192.168.1.200:1056)
[1999Mar01-045005]
  Currently Connected:
  lnbp75/192.168.1.1:4680 (from lnbp75/192.168.1.1:4680)
  naba (from lnbp200/192.168.1.200:1056)
[1999Mar01-045014]
  Currently Connected:
  naba-telnet (from lnbp75/192.168.1.1:4680)
  naba (from lnbp200/192.168.1.200:1056)
[1999Mar01-045416] naba-telnet left the chat.
```

As the listing shows, each entry in the log is prefixed with a timestamp made up of the year, month, day, and current time (the hours, minutes, and seconds are concatenated).

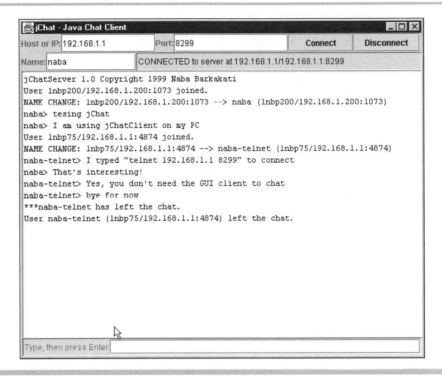

FIGURE 11-8. A typical chat session using **jChatClient** and **jChatServer**.

jChatServer

Understanding jChatServer

There are two parts to the client/server chat application: **jChatServer** and **jChatClient**. I will describe **jChatServer** first. A later section presents **jChatClient**.

The following listing shows the **jChatServer.java** file, which implements the **jChatServer** application. The code is described in the sections that follow the listing.

```
1 //-----------------------------------------------------------------
2 // File: jChatServer.java
3 // A Java Chat Server.
4 //-----------------------------------------------------------------
5 import java.io.*;
6 import java.net.*;
7 import java.util.*;
8 import java.text.*;
```

```java
 9  /** The main server thread */
10  public class jChatServer extends Thread
11  {
12      public static jChatServer server;
13      public static final String jChatAnnounce =
14          "jChatServer 1.0 Copyright 1999 Naba Barkakati";
15      public final static int JCHAT_PORT = 8299;
16      public String commandLine;
17      // Number of seconds of inactivity allowed before
18      // server ends a "conversation" with a client
19      public final static int INACTIVITY_TIMEOUT = 300;
20      // How often to check for inactivity (every 10 seconds)
21      public final static int TIMEOUT_CHECK_INTERVAL = 10000;
22      private int inactivityTimeout = INACTIVITY_TIMEOUT;
23      private int warningTimeout = INACTIVITY_TIMEOUT*4/5;
24      private int disconnectTimeout = INACTIVITY_TIMEOUT/5;
25      private int port = JCHAT_PORT;
26      private String logFileName = "jchat." +
27                                  TimeStamp.timeNow() + ".log";
28      private ServerSocket socket;
29      private Thread timeout;
30      protected PrintStream log;
31      protected Hashtable conversations;
32      /** The main() method of the server application */
33      public static void main(String[] args)
34      {
35          System.out.println(jChatAnnounce);
36          server = new jChatServer(args);
37      }
38      /** Parses the command-line arguments of the form
39       *  -port portnum -logfile filename etc.
40       */
41      public void parseOptions(String[] args)
42      {
43          int i = 0;
44          while(i < args.length)
45          {
46              if(args[i].equals("-port"))
47              {
48                  i++;
49                  try
50                  {
```

```
51                          port = Integer.parseInt(args[i++]);
52                      }
53                      catch(NumberFormatException e) { showUsage();}
54              }
55              else if(args[i].equals("-logfile"))
56              {
57                  i++;
58                  logFileName = args[i++];
59              }
60              else if(args[i].equals("-timeout"))
61              {
62                  try
63                  {
64                      inactivityTimeout = Integer.parseInt(args[i++]);
65                      warningTimeout = inactivityTimeout*4/5;
66                      disconnectTimeout = inactivityTimeout/5;
67                  }
68                  catch(NumberFormatException e) { showUsage();}
69              }
70              else
71                  showUsage();
72          }
73      }
74      /** Prints command-line syntax for server */
75      public static void showUsage()
76      {
77          System.out.println("jChatServer command line syntax.\n"
78              + "java jChatServer  port portNum -timeout tSec "
79              + "-logfile filename\n"
80              + "  portNum = port number where server "
81              + "listens for connections\n"
82              + "  tSec = seconds after which to end "
83              + "inactive connections\n"
84              + "  fileName = name of log file\n");
85          System.exit(1);
86      }
87      /** Creates a jChatServer */
88      public jChatServer(String[] args)
89      {
90          parseOptions(args);
```

```
91          // Print out the command line options
92          commandLine = "java jChatServer -port "+port +
93                       " -timeout "+inactivityTimeout +
94                       " -logfile "+logFileName;
95      System.out.println(commandLine);
96          // Convert the timeout values into milliseconds
97      inactivityTimeout *= 1000;
98      warningTimeout *= 1000;
99      disconnectTimeout *= 1000;
100         // Open the log file
101     try
102     {
103         log = new PrintStream(new FileOutputStream(logFileName));
104
105     }
106     catch(IOException e)
107     {
108         System.err.println(e+"\nError opening log file: "+
109                         logFileName);
110         System.exit(1);
111     }
112     log.println(jChatAnnounce);
113     log.println(commandLine);
114     Date d = new Date();
115     log.print("["+  TimeStamp.timeNow() + "] " +
116                     "jChatServer started.\n");
117     log.flush();
118     try
119     {
120         socket = new ServerSocket(port);
121     }
122     catch(IOException e)
123     {
124         System.err.println(e +
125             "\nError creating server socket");
126     }
127     conversations = new Hashtable();
128         // A thread that monitors any inactive conversations
129     timeout = new Thread()
130     {
131         public void run()
132         {
```

```
133                     while(true)
134                     {
135                         server.checkTimeouts();
136                         try
137                         {
138                             sleep(TIMEOUT_CHECK_INTERVAL);
139                         }
140                         catch(InterruptedException e)
141                         {
142                             System.err.println(
143                                 "Timeout thread interrupted: " + e);
144                         }
145                     }
146                 }
147         };
148         timeout.start();
149         this.start();
150     }
151     /** Listen to client connections and launch new threads */
152     public void run()
153     {
154         try
155         {
156             while(true)
157             {
158                 Socket client_socket = socket.accept();
159                 Conversation c = new Conversation(client_socket,
160                                                     this);
161             }
162         }
163         catch(IOException e)
164         {
165             System.err.println(
166                 e+"\nError while waiting for connections");
167             System.exit(1);
168         }
169     }
170     /** Check for any conversations that have timed out */
171     public void checkTimeouts()
172     {
173         Vector idleList = new Vector();
174         Date d = new Date();
175         long now = d.getTime();\
176         Enumeration keys = conversations.keys();
```

```
177            while(keys.hasMoreElements())
178            {
179                String key = (String)keys.nextElement();
180                Conversation thisClient = (Conversation)
181                                 conversations.get(key);
182                long inactivity = now - thisClient.timeOfLastActivity;
183                if(inactivity > inactivityTimeout)
184                {
185                    idleList.addElement(thisClient);
186                }
187                else if(inactivity > warningTimeout)
188                {
189                    thisClient.out.println("WARNING: you have been "+
190                    "inactive for "+inactivity/1000+" seconds "+
191                    "(you'll be disconnected after "+
192                    inactivityTimeout/1000+" seconds)");
193                    thisClient.out.flush();
194                }
195            }
196            // Close all conversations that have timed out
197            for(int i= 0; i < idleList.size(); i++)
198            {
199                Conversation thisClient =
200                    (Conversation)idleList.elementAt(i);
201                try
202                {
203                    thisClient.client.close();
204                }
205                catch(IOException e)
206                {
207                    System.err.println(e +
208                        "\nError closing conversation");
209                }
210            }
211        }
212 }
213 /** A thread to conduct a conversation with a chat client */
214 class Conversation extends Thread
215 {
216     private String clientName;
217     private InetAddress clientAddress;
218     private int clientPort;
219     protected Socket client;
```

```
220    private BufferedReader in;
221    protected PrintStream out;
222    private PrintStream log;
223    protected long timeOfLastActivity;
224    protected boolean cannotStart = false;
225    private Hashtable conversations;
226    /** Initializes the streams and starts the thread */
227    public Conversation(Socket client_socket,
228                        jChatServer server)
229    {
230        client = client_socket;
231        timeOfLastActivity = (new Date()).getTime();
232        conversations = server.conversations;
233        log = server.log;
234        try
235        {
236            in = new BufferedReader(new InputStreamReader(
237                                    new DataInputStream(
238                               client.getInputStream())));
239            out = new PrintStream(client.getOutputStream());
240        }
241        catch(IOException e)
242        {
243            try
244            {
245                client.close();
246            }
247            catch(IOException e2){}
248            logPrint(
249              e+" Exception while getting socket streams\n");
250            cannotStart = true;
251        }
252        if(cannotStart) return;
253        clientAddress = client.getInetAddress();
254        clientPort = client.getPort();
255        clientName = clientAddress + ":" + clientPort;
256        conversations.put(clientName, this);
257        out.println(server.jChatAnnounce);
258        sendtoAll("User " + clientName + " joined.");
259        logPrint(listUsers());
260        this.start();
261    }
262    /** Returns a string with all current users */
263    public String listUsers()
```

```
264         {
265             String users ="\n  Currently Connected:\n";
266             Enumeration keys = conversations.keys();
267             while(keys.hasMoreElements())
268             {
269                 String key = (String)keys.nextElement();
270                 Conversation thisClient = (Conversation)
271                                 conversations.get(key);
272                 users += "  " + thisClient.clientName
273                         + " (from " + key + ")\n";
274             }
275             return users;
276         }
277     /** Reads client input and send it to everyone */
278     public void run()
279     {
280         String line;
281         int len;
282         try
283         {
284             while(true)
285             {
286                 // Read in a line
287                 line = in.readLine();
288                 timeOfLastActivity = (new Date()).getTime();
289                 if(line == null) break;
290                 // The "@@name name" command changes user's name
291                 if(line.startsWith("@@name "))
292                 {
293                     String msg;
294                     msg = "NAME CHANGE: " + clientName + " --> "
295                         + line.substring(7) + " ("
296                         + clientAddress + ":" + clientPort + ")";
297                     clientName = line.substring(7);
298                     sendtoAll(msg);
299                     logPrint(listUsers());
300                     continue;
301                 }
302                 // The @@list command lists all users
303                 if(line.startsWith("@@list"))
304                 {
```

```
305                    out.println(listUsers());
306                    out.flush();
307                    continue;
308                }
309                // The @@quit command ends this conversation
310                if(line.startsWith("@@quit"))
311                {
312                    logPrint(clientName+" left the chat.\n");
313                    sendtoAll(
314                        "***"+clientName+" has left the chat.");
315                    in.close();
316                    out.close();
317                    client.close();
318                    break;
319                }
320                // No command, just text. Send to everyone.
321                sendtoAll(clientName + "> " + line);
322            }
323        }
324        catch(IOException e)
325        {
326            logPrint(e+" Error during conversation with "
327                + clientName + "(" + clientAddress
328                + ":" + clientPort + ")\n");
329        }
330        finally
331        {
332            try
333            {
334                client.close();
335            }
336            catch(IOException e2)
337            {
338                logPrint(e2+" Error closing socket for "
339                    + clientAddress + ":" + clientPort+"\n");
340            }
341            finally
342            {
343                client = null;
344                conversations.remove(clientAddress + ":" +
345                                        clientPort);
```

```
346                    sendtoAll("User " + clientName + " ("
347                        + clientAddress + ":" + clientPort
348                        + ") left the chat.");
349                    logPrint(listUsers());
350                }
351            }
352        }
353        /** Prints a message to the log file */
354        public void logPrint(String message)
355        {
356            log.print("["+  TimeStamp.timeNow() + "] " + message);
357            log.flush();
358        }
359        /** Sends a line of text to all chat participants */
360        public void sendtoAll(String s)
361        {
362            Enumeration keys = conversations.keys();
363            while(keys.hasMoreElements())
364            {
365                String key = (String)keys.nextElement();
366                Conversation thisClient =
367                    (Conversation) conversations.get(key);
368                thisClient.out.println(s);
369                thisClient.out.flush();
370            }
371        }
372 }
373 /** Provides a time stamp */
374 class TimeStamp
375 {
376     static SimpleDateFormat df =
377                 new SimpleDateFormat("yyyyMMMdd-HHmmss");
378     public static String time(Date d)
379     {
380         String dateString = df.format(d);
381         return dateString;
382     }
383     public static String timeNow()
384     {
385         return TimeStamp.time(new Date());
386     }
387 }
```

ANNOTATIONS

As line 10 shows, the **jChatServer** class is a subclass of **Thread**:

```
10 public class jChatServer extends Thread
```

You'll see later in this section that this thread listens for incoming connections. Whenever a client connects, this thread launches a **Conversation** thread that takes over the communications with that client. **Conversation** is another class that is defined to be a subclass of **Thread**. The **Conversation** thread receives lines of text from the client and simply echoes them back to all currently connected clients. Thus, there is a separate thread for each chat client connected to the server. The **jChatServer** thread also creates another thread that periodically checks each client connection and times out those that are inactive for longer than a specified timeout interval. That, in a nutshell, is the design of the **jChatServer** application. The code, of course, looks more complicated because, as always, there are many details that must be handled. I will highlight the important ones in the next few sections.

PARSING COMMAND-LINE OPTIONS When you run the **jChatServer** application, the **main()** method runs first. Lines 33 through 37 show the **main()** method:

```
33    public static void main(String[] args)
34    {
35        System.out.println(jChatAnnounce);
36        server = new jChatServer(args);
37    }
```

Line 35 of the **main()** method prints an announcement, and line 36 then creates a new **jChatServer** object, passing the command-line arguments to the **jChatServer()** constructor.

The **jChatServer()** constructor, shown in lines 88 through 150, calls **parseOptions()** to parse the command-line arguments and set the internal variables based on command-line arguments. If there is any error during parsing, the **parseOptions()** method calls **showUsage()** to print the command-line syntax and then quits.

STARTING CONVERSATIONS The **jChatServer** thread uses sockets-based communication to converse with the client. The first step for a server is to create a **ServerSocket**. Line 120 in the **jChatServer()** constructor creates a **ServerSocket** to listen on the specified port:

```
120        socket = new ServerSocket(port);
```

After this step, the **jChatServer()** constructor performs several other steps, including starting a thread to monitor inactive conversations, and then it starts its own thread:

```
149        this.start();
```

This causes the **jChatServer** thread to start executing the code in the **run()** method, shown in lines 152 through 169. Lines 156 through 161 are at the heart of the server thread:

```
156          while(true)
157          {
158              Socket client_socket = socket.accept();
159              Conversation c = new Conversation(client_socket,
160                                          this);
161          }
```

Line 158 calls the **accept()** method of the **ServerSocket** to wait for a connection from a client. When a client establishes a TCP connection to the server socket, the **accept()** method returns the client socket. Then line 159 starts a new **Conversation** thread to handle all conversations with that client. It passes the client socket and a reference to the **jChatServer** as arguments to the **Conversations()** constructor. After that, the **while** loop continues and the server thread again calls **socket.accept()** to wait for another client connection.

MANAGING CONVERSATIONS   Because the server creates a new **Conversation** thread for each client, it needs a way to track these threads. The **jChatServer** class uses a **Hashtable** to store the **Conversation** threads. Line 127 creates a **Hashtable** named **conversations**:

```
127          conversations = new Hashtable();
```

When it creates a new **Conversation** thread, the server passes a reference to itself as an argument to the **Conversation()** constructor. The **Conversation()** constructor, shown in lines 227 through 261, stores a reference to the server's **conversations** hash table in a local variable with the same name:

```
232          conversations = server.conversations;
```

Lines 253 through 256 in the **Conversations()** constructor then create a name for the client (using the client's host name and port number) and insert this particular **Conversation** thread into the **conversations** hash table:

```
253          clientAddress = client.getInetAddress();
254          clientPort = client.getPort();
255          clientName = clientAddress + ":" + clientPort;
256          conversations.put(clientName, this);
```

In this way, each **Conversation** thread is stored in the hash table.

Another aspect of managing the conversations is to get rid of clients that have been inactive for longer than a specified timeout period. Lines 129 through 147 of the **jChatServer()** constructor create a thread named **timeout** that checks for inactive threads periodically. Lines 131 through 146 show the **run()** method of the **timeout** thread:

```
131        public void run()
132        {
133            while(true)
134            {
135                server.checkTimeouts();
136                try
137                {
138                    sleep(TIMEOUT_CHECK_INTERVAL);
139                }
140                catch(InterruptedException e)
141                {
142                    System.err.println(
143                        "Timeout thread interrupted: " + e);
144                }
145            }
146        }
```

As this method shows, the **timeout** thread calls the **checkTimeouts()** method of the server after every 10000 milliseconds or 10 seconds (that's the value of **TIMEOUT_CHECK_INTERVAL**).

The **checkTimeouts()** method, shown in lines 171 through 211, checks for clients that should be timed out. Each **Conversation** thread has a long integer named **timeOfLastActivity** that contains the time when the client last sent a line of text. (That time is expressed as milliseconds since 00:00 January 1, 1970.)

In the **checkTimeouts()** method, lines 174 and 175 get the current time, also in terms of the number of milliseconds since 00:00 January 1, 1970:

```
174        Date d = new Date();
175        long now = d.getTime();
```

Line 176 then gets an **Enumeration** of the keys from the hash table that holds all **Conversation** threads:

```
176        Enumeration keys = conversations.keys();
```

After that, the **while** loop shown in lines 177 through 195 goes through all **Conversation** threads in the hash table and finds those that have been inactive for too long. Specifically, line 182 calculates the inactive period:

```
182            long inactivity = now - thisClient.timeOfLastActivity;
```

If the inactivity exceeds the timeout period, that **Conversation** thread is added to a **Vector** named **idleList**:

```
183             if(inactivity > inactivityTimeout)
184             {
185                 idleList.addElement(thisClient);
186             }
```

A warning message is sent to the client if the inactivity exceeds a warning period but is not yet greater than the timeout period.

Finally, the **for** loop shown in lines 197 through 210 closes all of the connections to all of the clients that are in the **idleList** vector.

CONDUCTING CONVERSATIONS   The **Conversation** thread's **run()** method, shown in lines 278 through 352, conducts the conversation with the client. A **while** loop reads a line of text from the client and updates the **timeOfLastActivity**.

The **while** loop also checks whether the line is a command to the server. The server accepts three special commands:

◆ **@@name** *newname* sets the name of the client to *newname*.

◆ **@@list** sends a string with the list of current chat participants.

◆ **@@quit** closes the connection to the client.

PROGRAMMER'S NOTE   *If you want, you can enhance the chat server by adding more commands to perform other tasks, such as sending the current time at the server or allowing a private conversation with a selected chat participant.*

If the line is not a command to the chat server, line 321 sends it to all chat participants by calling **sendtoAll()**:

```
321             sendtoAll(clientName + "> " + line);
```

Lines 360 through 371 show the **sendtoAll()** method:

```
360     public void sendtoAll(String s)
361     {
362         Enumeration keys = conversations.keys();
363         while(keys.hasMoreElements())
364         {
365             String key = (String)keys.nextElement();
366             Conversation thisClient =
367                 (Conversation) conversations.get(key);
368             thisClient.out.println(s);
369             thisClient.out.flush();
370         }
371     }
```

Line 362 gets an **Enumeration** of all of the keys from the hash table **conversations**. Then the **while** loop in lines 363 through 370 goes through each key and retrieves the **Conversation** thread corresponding to the key. Lines 368 and 369 write out the string to that thread's output stream. This is how each client's input goes back to all of the clients currently connected to the server.

KEEPING A LOG FILE   The **jChatServer** application keeps a log of important activities in a log file. You can specify a log filename through the **-log filename** option. By default, lines 26 and 27 of the program initialize the log filename as follows:

```
26      private String logFileName = "jchat." +
27                                  TimeStamp.timeNow() + ".log";
```

This creates a name of the form **jchat.***timestamp***.log**, where *timestamp* is the current date and time in the form of a timestamp.

Line 103 opens a **PrintStream** named **log** that is used later to write text to the log file:

```
103          log = new PrintStream(new FileOutputStream(logFileName));
```

The **TimeStamp** class provides the timestamp for the default name of the log file as well as the timestamp used in recording information in the log file. Lines 376 through 382 show the basic code for this class:

```
376     static SimpleDateFormat df =
377                 new SimpleDateFormat("yyyyMMMdd-HHmmss");
378     public static String time(Date d)
379     {
380         String dateString = df.format(d);
381         return dateString;
382     }
```

Lines 376 and 377 initialize a **SimpleDateFormat** object that is used to format the date and time string in the form of a timestamp. In the **time()** method of the class, line 380 uses the **SimpleDateFormat** object to format a **Date** into a timestamp string. Line 381 returns that timestamp string to the caller.

Another method named **timeNow()** simply calls **TimeStamp.time()** with the current time and thereby returns a timestamp for the current time:

```
383     public static String timeNow()
384     {
385         return TimeStamp.time(new Date());
386     }
```

Whenever the server has to log anything in the log file, it calls the **logPrint()** method with the string to print. Lines 354 through 358 show the **logPrint()** method, which simply prints to the stream connected to the log file:

```
354    public void logPrint(String message)
355    {
356        log.print("["+  TimeStamp.timeNow() + "] " + message);
357        log.flush();
358    }
```

You can see in line 356 the format of entries in the log file. Each line begins with the timestamp enclosed in square brackets followed by a message string. Here is a typical entry from a log file created by **jChatServer**:

```
[1999Mar01-044649] jChatServer started.
```

jChatClient

Understanding jChatClient

The previous sections describe the **jChatServer** code. The next few sections focus on **jChatClient**—the GUI client that interacts with the **jChatServer**. The following listing shows the **jChatClient.java** file, which implements the **jChatClient** application. I describe the code in the sections that follow the listing.

```
1  //------------------------------------------------------------------
2  // File: jChatClient.java
3  // A chat client that works with jChatServer.
4  //------------------------------------------------------------------
5  import java.io.*;
6  import java.net.*;
7  import java.awt.*;
8  import java.awt.event.*;
9  import java.util.*;
10 import javax.swing.*;
11 import javax.swing.border.*;
12 /** Lays out the user interface for the chat client */
13 public class jChatClient extends JFrame
14 {
15     private static final String jChatAnnounce =
16         "jChatClient 1.0 Copyright 1999 Naba Barkakati";
17     private static final String JCHAT_HOST = "localhost";
18     private static final int JCHAT_PORT = 8299;
19     private static final int WIDTH = 600, HEIGHT = 500;
20     private Receiver receiver = null;
```

```
21      private Sender sender = null;
22      private String host = JCHAT_HOST;
23      private int port = JCHAT_PORT;
24      private String username = "naba";
25      private Socket s = null;
26      private String connectInfo;
27      private static jChatClient client;
28      private static String commandLine;
29      private static String notConnectedMsg =
30          "NOT CONNECTED. Enter host, port and click on Connect";
31      private JTextField inputTF;
32      private JTextArea msgArea;
33      private JTextField hostTF;
34      private JTextField portTF;
35      private JTextField nameTF;
36      private JTextField statusTF;
37      private SoftBevelBorder sbb = new SoftBevelBorder(
38                                      BevelBorder.LOWERED);
39      /** The main() method of the chat client application */
40      public static void main(String[] args)
41      {
42          System.out.println(jChatAnnounce);
43          client = new jChatClient(args);
44          client.addWindowListener(new WindowAdapter()
45          {
46              public void windowClosing(WindowEvent e)
47              {
48                  System.exit(0);
49              }
50          });
51      }
52      /** Parses command-line options of the form
53       *   -host hostname_or_IP -port portnum
54       */
55      public void parseOptions(String[] args)
56      {
57          int i = 0;
58          while(i < args.length)
59          {
60              if(args[i].equals("-port"))
61              {
```

```
62              i++;
63              try
64              {
65                  port = Integer.parseInt(args[i++]);
66              }
67              catch (NumberFormatException e) { showUsage();}
68          }
69          else if(args[i].equals("-host"))
70          {
71              i++;
72              host = args[i++];
73          }
74          else
75              showUsage();
76      }
77  }
78  /** Displays the command-line syntax */
79  public static void showUsage()
80  {
81      System.out.println ("jChatClient command-line syntax:\n"
82          + "java jChatClient -host hostname_or_IP "
83          + "-port portNum\n"
84          + "  hostname_or_IP = hostname or IP address of "
85          + "jChat server\n"
86          + "  portNum = port number where server "
87          + "listens for connections\n");
88      System.exit(1);
89  }
90  /** Lays out the user interface for the application */
91  public jChatClient(String[] args)
92  {
93      super("jChat - Java Chat Client");
94      parseOptions(args);
95      // Print out the command line options
96      commandLine = "java jChatClient -host "+host+
97                  " -port "+port;
98      System.out.println (commandLine);
99      setSize(WIDTH, HEIGHT);
100     getContentPane().setLayout(new BorderLayout());
101     JPanel pTop = new JPanel(new GridLayout(2,1));
102     JPanel pTop1 = new JPanel(new GridLayout(1,2));
103     JPanel pTopL = new JPanel(new BorderLayout());
104     JLabel hostL = new JLabel("Host or IP:");
```

```
105        hostTF = new JTextField(host);
106        pTopL.add("West", hostL);
107        pTopL.add("Center", hostTF);
108        JPanel pTopR = new JPanel(new GridLayout(1,2));
109        JPanel pTopM = new JPanel(new BorderLayout());
110        JLabel portL = new JLabel("Port:");
111        portTF = new JTextField(""+port, 6);
112        pTopM.add("West", portL);
113        pTopM.add("Center", portTF);
114        JButton connectBtn = new JButton("Connect");
115        connectBtn.setToolTipText("Connect to server");
116        JButton quitBtn = new JButton("Disconnect");
117        quitBtn.setToolTipText("Disconnect from server");
118        pTopR.add(connectBtn);
119        pTopR.add(quitBtn);
120        pTop1.add(pTopL);
121        pTop1.add(pTopM);
122        pTop1.add(pTopR);
123        JPanel pTop2 = new JPanel(new BorderLayout());
124        JPanel pTop2L = new JPanel(new BorderLayout());
125        JLabel nameL = new JLabel("Name:");
126        nameTF = new JTextField("naba", 12);
127        pTop2L.add("West", nameL);
128        pTop2L.add("Center", nameTF);
129        statusTF = new JTextField(jChatAnnounce, 120);
130        statusTF.setEditable(false);
131        statusTF.setBorder(sbb);
132        pTop2.add("West", pTop2L);
133        pTop2.add("Center", statusTF);
134        pTop.add(pTop1);
135        pTop.add(pTop2);
136        getContentPane().add("North", pTop);
137        msgArea = new JTextArea(19,60);
138        msgArea.setFont(new Font("Courier",Font.PLAIN,12));
139        msgArea.setEditable(false);
140        msgArea.setBorder(sbb);
141        getContentPane().add("Center", msgArea);
142        JPanel pBottom = new JPanel(new BorderLayout());
143        inputTF = new JTextField(80);
144        inputTF.setFont(new Font("Courier",Font.PLAIN,12));
145        pBottom.add("Center", inputTF);
146        JLabel prompt = new JLabel("Type, then press Enter:",
147                                 JLabel.RIGHT);
```

```
148        prompt.setFont(new Font("Helvetica",Font.PLAIN,12));
149        pBottom.add("West", prompt);
150        pBottom.setBorder(sbb);
151        getContentPane().add("South", pBottom);
152        show();
153        // Set up listeners for event handling
154        inputTF.addActionListener(new ActionListener()
155        {
156            public void actionPerformed(ActionEvent e)
157            {
158                if(sender != null)
159                    sender.sendLine();
160            }
161        });
162        nameTF.addActionListener(new ActionListener()
163        {
164            public void actionPerformed(ActionEvent e)
165            {
166                username = nameTF.getText();
167                if(sender != null)
168                {
169                    inputTF.setText("@@name "+username);
170                    sender.sendLine();
171                }
172            }
173        });
174        connectBtn.addActionListener(new ActionListener()
175        {
176            public void actionPerformed(ActionEvent e)
177            {
178                host = hostTF.getText();
179                try
180                {
181                    port = Integer.parseInt(portTF.getText());
182                }
183                catch (NumberFormatException e2)
184                {
185                    port = 8299;
186                    portTF.setText(""+port);
187                    setStatus("Resetting port to: "+port);
188                }
189                connect();
190            }
```

```
191          });
192          quitBtn.addActionListener(new ActionListener()
193          {
194              public void actionPerformed(ActionEvent e)
195              {
196                  disconnect();
197              }
198          });
199          setStatus(notConnectedMsg);
200      }
201      /** Connects to the chat server */
202      public void connect()
203      {
204          // First, disconnect if already connected
205          disconnect();
206          // Open the socket
207          try
208          {
209              setStatus("Connecting to: "+host+":"+port);
210              s = new Socket(host, port);
211              connectInfo = s.getInetAddress() + ":"+ s.getPort();
212          }
213          catch (IOException e)
214          {
215              setStatus("ERROR creating socket: "+  e);
216              return;
217          }
218          receiver = new Receiver(s, msgArea, this);
219          sender = new Sender(s, inputTF, this);
220          if(sender != null) // send user name to server
221          {
222              inputTF.setText("@@name "+username);
223              sender.sendLine();
224          }
225          try
226          {
227              Thread.sleep(1000);
228          }catch(InterruptedException e){}
229          setStatus("CONNECTED to server at "+connectInfo);
230      }
231      /** Disconnects from the chat */
232      public void disconnect()
233      {
```

```
234          if(sender == null && receiver == null) return;
235          if(sender != null)
236          {
237              inputTF.setText("@@quit");
238              sender.sendLine();
239              sender.close();
240              sender = null;
241          }
242          if(receiver != null)
243          {
244              receiver.close();
245              receiver = null;
246          }
247          s = null;
248          setStatus(notConnectedMsg);
249      }
250      /** Displays a message in the status text field */
251      public void setStatus(String msg)
252      {
253          statusTF.setText(msg);
254      }
255  }
256  /** Thread that sends text to the chat server */
257  class Sender extends Thread
258  {
259      private PrintStream out;
260      private JTextField tf;
261      private boolean isRunning = false;
262      private jChatClient client;
263      public Sender(Socket s, JTextField tf, jChatClient client)
264      {
265          client.setStatus("Creating Sender thread...");
266          this.tf = tf;
267          this.client = client;
268          try
269          {
270              out = new PrintStream(s.getOutputStream());
271              client.setStatus("Opened output stream to server");
272          }
273          catch (IOException e)
274          {
275              client.setStatus("ERROR: opening output stream: "+e);
276              isRunning = false;
```

```
277              client.disconnect();
278              return;
279          }
280          this.start();
281      }
282      /** Sets a flag indicating the thread is running */
283      public void run()
284      {
285          client.setStatus("Sender thread running...");
286          isRunning = true;
287      }
288      /** Closes output stream */
289      public void close()
290      {
291          out.close();
292          out = null;
293          isRunning = false;
294          client.setStatus("Sender thread closed output stream.");
295      }
296      /** Sends a line to the chat server over the socket */
297      public void sendLine()
298      {
299          String line = tf.getText();
300          tf.setText("");
301          if (line != null)
302          {
303              line = line.trim() + "\n";
304              out.print(line);
305              out.flush();
306          }
307      }
308 }
309 /** Thread that receives text from the chat server */
310 class Receiver extends Thread
311 {
312      private BufferedReader in;
313      private JTextArea tf;
314      private boolean isRunning = false;
315      private jChatClient client;
316      /** Creates a new Receiver thread */
317      public Receiver(Socket s, JTextArea tf, jChatClient client)
318      {
```

```
319        client.setStatus("Creating Receiver thread...");
320        this.tf = tf;
321        this.client = client;
322        try
323        {
324            in = new BufferedReader(new InputStreamReader(
325                                            s.getInputStream())));
326            client.setStatus("Opened input stream...");
327        }
328        catch (IOException e)
329        {
330            client.setStatus("ERROR opening input stream: "+e);
331            isRunning = false;
332            client.disconnect();
333            return;
334        }
335        this.start();
336    }
337    /** Reads lines and displays them in text area */
338    public void run()
339    {
340        client.setStatus("Receiver thread running...");
341        isRunning = true;
342        String line;
343        while (isRunning)
344        {
345            try
346            {
347                line = in.readLine();
348                // If line is null, probably disconnected
349                if (line == null)
350                {
351                    client.setStatus(
352                    "ERROR: Probably disconnected from server.");
353                    isRunning = false;
354                    client.disconnect();
355                }
356                tf.append(line+"\n");
357            }
358            catch (IOException e)
359            {
360                client.setStatus(
361                    "ERROR reading from socket: "+e);
```

```
362                     isRunning = false;
363                     client.disconnect();
364                 }
365
366             }
367     }
368     /** Closes the input stream */
369     public void close()
370     {
371         try
372         {
373             in.close();
374         }
375         catch(IOException e){}
376         in = null;
377         isRunning = false;
378     }
379 }
```

ANNOTATIONS

The **jChatClient** application uses two threads to hold the conversation with the chat server. The **Sender** thread sends any text typed by the user to the server. The **Receiver** thread reads lines of text from the server and displays them in a text area in the application's user interface.

The application's user interface is created and managed by the **jChatClient** class. This class is defined to be a subclass of **JFrame**, the Swing class that is supposed to be the container for other Swing components:

```
13 public class jChatClient extends JFrame
```

I explain the user interface and the two threads—**Sender** and **Receiver**—in the sections that follow.

HANDLING THE USER INTERACTIONS   The **jChatClient()** constructor, shown in lines 91 through 200, lays out the user interface and sets up everything needed to manage user interactions. Line 93 starts by calling the superclass (**JFrame**) constructor and setting the text that appears in the window's title bar:

```
93          super("jChat - Java Chat Client");
```

Line 99 sets the size of the frame:

```
99          setSize(WIDTH, HEIGHT);
```

Lines 100 through 151 then create a hierarchy of Swing components and add everything to the frame's content pane. I won't go into the details of the GUI layout because Chapter 9, "GUI Applications," covers these topics.

Line 152 performs the crucial step of calling the **show()** method to make the frame visible:

```
152         show();
```

The important aspect of the user interface is the connection between the GUI components and the chat client functions of the application. This connection happens through the various event listeners.

Lines 154 through 161 show the **ActionListener** for the text field where the user types text to be sent to the chat server:

```
154         inputTF.addActionListener(new ActionListener()
155         {
156             public void actionPerformed(ActionEvent e)
157             {
158                 if(sender != null)
159                     sender.sendLine();
160             }
161         });
```

Notice that line 159 of the **actionPerformed()** method calls the **sendLine()** method of the sender thread to send the line of text to the server. The sender thread is described later in the section "Sending User Input to the Server."

Lines 174 through 191 show the **ActionListener** for the Connect button. This listener gets the current host name and port number from the appropriate text fields and calls the **connect()** method to establish a socket connection to the chat server.

CONNECTING TO THE CHAT SERVER   The **connect()** method, shown in lines 202 through 230, sets up the socket connection to the chat server. This method also creates the sender and receiver threads that take care of exchanging text with the server.

Line 205 starts by calling the **disconnect()** method to end the current connection. This is necessary because the user might want to change the host and port parameters and try to connect to a different chat server. In that case, the program should first disconnect from the currently active connection. The **disconnect()** method does not do anything if the sender and receiver threads are not present. If these threads are active, **disconnect()** closes the threads.

Lines 210 and 211, inside a **try** block, create a new socket and initialize a string with information about the connection:

```
210         s = new Socket(host, port);
211         connectInfo = s.getInetAddress() + ":"+ s.getPort();
```

Lines 218 and 219 create the receiver and sender threads that take over the communications with the server:

```
218        receiver = new Receiver(s, msgArea, this);
219        sender = new Sender(s, inputTF, this);
```

After these steps, the client is connected to the server.

SENDING USER INPUT TO THE SERVER   The **Sender** thread, shown in lines 257 through 308, provides the facilities to send lines of text to the chat server. The **Sender()** constructor, shown in lines 263 through 281, receives as its arguments the socket, the text field where the user types text, and a reference to the **jChatClient** object:

```
263    public Sender(Socket s, JTextField tf, jChatClient client)
```

The constructor creates a **PrintStream** named **out** for sending text to the server:

```
270        out = new PrintStream(s.getOutputStream());
```

The **Sender** thread's **run()** method does not do anything, because the text is ready to be sent only when the user types something in the input field. Instead, the thread provides a **sendLine()** method that the **ActionListener** of the input text field can call whenever there is something to send to the server.
Lines 297 through 307 show the **sendLine()** method:

```
297    public void sendLine()
298    {
299        String line = tf.getText();
300        tf.setText("");
301        if (line != null)
302        {
303            line = line.trim() + "\n";
304            out.print(line);
305            out.flush();
306        }
307    }
```

Line 299 gets the user input from the text field (**tf** refers to the input text field where the user types text). Line 300 clears the text field so that the user can type the next line. If the string is not null, line 303 calls **trim()** to remove white space from both ends of the string. Then line 304 writes the line to the output stream and line 305 makes sure that the text is actually written to the stream instead of being accumulated in a buffer.

RECEIVING TEXT FROM THE SERVER   The **Receiver** thread, shown in lines 310 through 379, reads lines of text from the socket connection to the chat server and appends these lines to the text area in the user interface.

The **Receiver()** constructor, shown in lines 317 through 336, is provided with the socket, the text area where chat output appears, and a reference to the **jChatClient** object:

```
317        public Receiver(Socket s, JTextArea tf, jChatClient client)
```

The constructor then creates a **BufferedReader** named **in** for reading lines of text from the server:

```
324            in = new BufferedReader(new InputStreamReader(
325                                        s.getInputStream()));
```

Line 335 of the constructor starts the **Receiver** thread:

```
335            this.start();
```

This causes the thread to begin executing the **run()** method, shown in lines 338 through 367. A **while** loop in the **run()** method repeatedly reads lines of text and appends them to the text area in the user interface. Specifically, line 347 reads a line from the stream connected to the server:

```
347            line = in.readLine();
```

Line 356 then calls the **append()** method of the text area to add this line to the display:

```
356            tf.append(line+"\n");
```

Database
Applications

C hapter 11 presented some client/server applications written in Java. A unique type of client/server application is one in which the server is a database server. A database server is software that manages the data in a database, typically using a model such as the relational model. Client applications access the data by sending commands to the database server. These commands are usually in Structured Query Language (SQL), the standard language of database servers.

This chapter focuses on how to write database applications in Java. Specifically, it covers how to write client applications that use the Java Database Connectivity (JDBC) API to access databases that may be on a remote system on the network. The chapter starts with an overview of database programming that introduces the concepts of relational databases and SQL and explains JDBC programming with a sample program. Following this overview, the chapter presents some Java database applications.

You will find the following JDBC applications in this chapter:

◆ **dbtst**—A sample program that accesses a Microsoft Access database

◆ **comcal**—An application for using and maintaining a community calendar of events

An Overview of Database Programming

Most business applications access and use databases because business information is stored in databases. Employee records, sales records, and financial records are all examples of data stored in databases. In the not too distant past, database programming and database management were in the realm of mainframe computers. Data was typically stored in files with custom-designed record structures and custom APIs (often called access methods) for accessing the data in those files. More recently, however, databases have evolved into database servers that store data using a relational model. Database applications that access the database are clients to the database server. These database applications use Structured Query Language (SQL, often pronounced "sequel") to send commands to the database server and receive requested data.

The next few sections briefly explain the relational model, SQL, and how Java provides access to SQL database servers through JDBC.

The Relational Model

SQL views a database as being organized into a collection of tables. This table-based model of data is known as a *relational model*. A database that follows the relational model is referred to as a *relational database*.

The columns in a relational model's table represent attributes (such as name, identification number, and salary in an employee database) that apply to the rows. Each row in the table is a database record (for instance, the record of a specific employee in an employee database). Figure 12-1 shows how employee information might be organized in a number of tables—note that the employee ID ties the two tables together.

When you work with a relational database, you work with tables. The database structure—the collection of tables and the attributes in each table—is known as the schema.

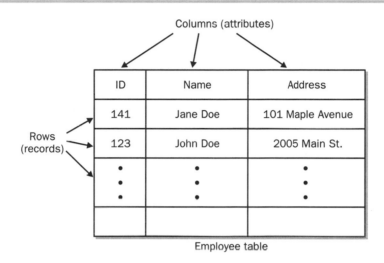

FIGURE 12-1. Data is organized in tables in the relational model.

The relational model was developed by E. F. Codd, a mathematician at IBM, in 1969. (A classic reference on the relational model is *The Relational Model for Database Management: Version 2*, by E. F. Codd, Addison-Wesley, 1990.)

Informally, you can think of each relation as a table of values. However, more formally, the relational model lets you view data at several different levels:

◆ The *external* level constitutes the user's view of the data.

◆ The *conceptual* level models the data as a collection of entities and relationships between entities (through entity-relationship diagrams).

◆ The *logical* level is the database schema—a collection of relational tables and the attributes of each table.

◆ The *physical* level refers to the actual storage of data (for example, UNIX files, raw disk partitions, or B-trees).

SQL lets you access the data at the logical level. Thus, SQL-based applications do not need to be changed when the physical implementation of the database is changed.

A Taste of SQL

SQL originated from the relational data model, which is based on organizing data into tables. It was developed by IBM in the 1970s. SQL was adopted as an industry standard in 1989 and was subsequently revised in 1992. The 1992 SQL standard is known as SQL-92 or SQL2. Another revision, called SQL3, is now in progress. SQL3 will support objects (a higher-level abstraction of data than relational tables). By now, SQL is a widely accepted industry standard for defining, manipulating, and managing tables. Even databases that do not use the relational data model support SQL.

SQL is not a programming language. It lacks flow control (such as the "if-else" statements in Java). Essentially, SQL provides operators for manipulating tables. For example, the SQL SELECT statement queries tables with the following general syntax:

```
SELECT attributes
FROM table1, table2, ...
WHERE condition
```

Here *attributes* refer to the columns you want to retrieve from the tables. The FROM clause identifies the tables with the specified columns (*table1, table2,* and so on), and the WHERE clause specifies the rows you want to see. The SELECT query returns the rows for which the *condition* is true. A typical query from a database (with two tables named **employees** and **benefits**) might be as follows:

```
SELECT employees.name, benefits.base_salary
FROM employees, benefits
```

```
WHERE employees.id = benefits.id
and benefits.base_salary > 65000
```

This returns the employee name and salary for all employees whose salary exceeds 65,000. The SELECT statement can have many other clauses, such as GROUP BY and ORDER BY.

In addition to SELECT, there are many more SQL statements that perform a wide variety of database operations, from creating a new table to inserting rows of information into tables. You will find it useful to learn some SQL because you have to use SQL when writing Java database applications using JDBC. Table 12-1 summarizes the syntax of some commonly used SQL statements.

SQL Statement	Description
CREATE TABLE *tableName (* *columnName1 columnType1 modifiers,* *... ,* *columnName2 columnType2 modifiers)*	Creates a table with the specified columns. For example, to create a table named **books**, use **CREATE TABLE books (isbn CHAR(10) NOT NULL, title CHAR(50), pubyear INT, pagecount INT)**.
DELETE FROM *tableName* **WHERE** *columnName1 = value1* [**AND** *columnName2 = value2 ...*]	Deletes one or more rows that meet the condition specified in the WHERE clause. For example, to delete all books published before 1990, use **DELETE FROM books WHERE pubyear < 1990**.
**SELECT ALL	DISTINCT |** *columnName1, columnName2, ...* **FROM** *tableName1, tableName2,* **WHERE** *columnName1 = value1* [**AND** *columnName2 = value2 ...*] **GROUP BY** *columnNameN* **HAVING** *columnName1 = value1* [**AND** *columnName2 = value2 ...*] **ORDER BY** *columnNameN*	Selects rows from a table based on criteria specified in the WHERE clause. For example, to pick any book with "Linux" in the title, use the query **SELECT isbn, title, pubyear from books WHERE title like '%Linux%' ORDER BY isbn**.
INSERT INTO *tableName (columnName1, ..., columnNameN)* **VALUES** *(value1, ..., valueN)*	Inserts a row with the specified values into a table. For example, to add a book into the books table, you might write **INSERT INTO books (pubyear, title, pagecount, isbn) VALUES (1999, 'Java Annotated Archives', 800, '007882902-0')**.
UPDATE *tableName* **SET** *columnName1 = value1, ..., columnNameN = valueN* **WHERE** *columnName1 = value1* [**AND** *columnName2 = value2 ...*]	Modifies data previously entered into the database. For example, to change the page count of a book, you would write **UPDATE books SET pagecount=809 WHERE title='Java Annotated Archives'**.

TABLE 12-1. Commonly Used SQL Statements.

When you create a table using the JDBC API, you need to specify the data type for the columns. JDBC supports a set of generic SQL data types and specifies the mapping between JDBC and Java data types. Table 12-2 shows the Java types corresponding to common JDBC data types. From this table, you can get an idea about the types of data that a SQL database can store and how you can represent these data types in your Java applications.

JDBC Data Type	Java Type	Description
CHAR	**String**	Small, fixed-length character string (usually databases support at least 254 characters in a **CHAR**)
VARCHAR	**String**	Small, variable-length character string (could be up to 32K)
LONGVARCHAR	**String**	Large, variable-length character string (could be megabytes or even gigabytes)
NUMERIC	**java.math.BigDecimal**	Fixed-precision decimal value (typically used for currency)
DECIMAL	**java.math.BigDecimal**	Similar to **NUMERIC**
BIT	**boolean**	Single-bit value that can be zero or one
TINYINT	**byte**	8-bit unsigned integer value between 0 and 255
SMALLINT	**short**	16-bit signed integer value between −32768 and 32767
INTEGER	**int**	32-bit signed integer value between −2147483648 and 2147483647
BIGINT	**long**	64-bit signed integer value between −9223372036854775808 and 9223372036854775807
REAL	**float**	Single-precision floating-point number that supports 7 digits of mantissa
FLOAT	**double**	Same as **DOUBLE**
DOUBLE	**double**	Double-precision floating-point number that supports 15 digits of mantissa
BINARY	**byte[]**	Small, fixed-length binary value (typically up to 254 bytes)

TABLE 12-2.   JDBC Data Types and Their Corresponding Java Types.

JDBC Data Type	Java Type	Description
VARBINARY	byte[]	Small, variable-length binary value (also limited to 254 bytes)
LONGVARBINARY	byte[]	Large, variable-length binary value (up to a gigabyte of binary data)
DATE	java.sql.Date	Date, consisting of day, month, and year (usually in YYYY-MM-DD format; for example, 1999-12-31)
TIME	java.sql.Time	Time, consisting of hours, minutes, and seconds (usually in the form HH:MM:SS; for example, 11:54:30)
TIMESTAMP	java.sql.Timestamp	DATE plus TIME plus a nanosecond field

TABLE 12-2. JDBC Data Types and Their Corresponding Java Types *(continued)*.

Table names are usually limited to 31 characters, and table names and column names cannot include a period. Also, table and column names are case-sensitive, but SQL keywords are not.

When you specify any text values, they must be enclosed in single quotes—for example, **'New York'**. If the string happens to contain a single quote, you have to replace that single quote with a pair of single quotes, as in **'New Year''s Eve'**.

Note that SQL has many keywords, such as CATALOG and TIME, that might conceivably be used as table or column names. If table or column names conflict with SQL keywords, you must enclose those names between two backquotes or grave accent marks (`). For example, you would write `` `Time` `` instead of just **Time**. If a column name needs to be enclosed in backquotes and the name is qualified by a table name with the syntax **TableName.ColumnName**, you must individually enclose the table and column names in backquotes, like this: `` `TableName`.`ColumnName` ``.

What Is JDBC?

PCs running Windows are a common choice for the client systems on which database applications run. On these systems, you will generally find Windows applications that let the user access data through a graphical front end. Many Windows database applications use Microsoft's Open Database Connectivity (ODBC) drivers to access data stored in many different types of databases. As the name Open Database Connectivity implies, ODBC provides a common framework for applications accessing many disparate databases using a standard API.

Traditionally, database applications have been written to access a specific database, often using an API specific to the database. In recent years, embedded SQL (where SQL statements are placed in a program) has been used to standardize the application's code. Although embedded SQL makes the application code portable, the source code must be compiled for each database because the usual method for compiling embedded SQL is to use a preprocessor that converts the embedded SQL statements into database-specific code. ODBC uses a layered architecture that isolates applications from database-specific code by providing a standard SQL-based API and placing the database-specific code in ODBC drivers. The only problem with ODBC is that it's Windows-specific and not portable to other platforms.

This is where Java Database Connectivity (JDBC) comes in. JDBC has the same design goals as ODBC and uses a similar architecture. Additionally, JDBC is a Java API and therefore is portable to all systems that can run Java. Like ODBC, JDBC provides a way for applications to access data stored in many different databases, using its SQL-based API. Java 2 includes database classes (in the **java.sql** package) that simplify database programming and hide some of the details of SQL.

Figure 12-2 illustrates the JDBC architecture, which allows you to write a database application capable of accessing any database for which a JDBC driver is available. JDBC makes the application independent of the specific details of the database by providing an API that presents a standard table-oriented view of the underlying data, regardless of how the data is actually stored in the database.

The JDBC architecture consists of the following major components:

♦ *JDBC applications* store and retrieve data by calling the JDBC API functions. Usually, applications process and display the data in various formats that make the data more useful to the user.

♦ The *JDBC API* provides a standard Java API that applications can use to access data. The access method is similar to that provided by SQL.

♦ The *JDBC driver manager* loads drivers on behalf of the application.

♦ The *JDBC driver* is a collection of Java classes that connect to the database, send SQL statements to a specific database server, and return results to the application. If the database does not support SQL, the driver translates the SQL statements into requests that conform to the syntax supported by the database.

♦ The *database server* represents the server that manages the files or database tables accessed by the JDBC driver.

Because of the similarity between ODBC and JDBC, it is possible to write a JDBC driver that maps JDBC calls to ODBC calls. In fact, such a JDBC–ODBC bridge was

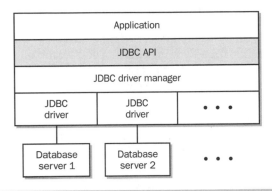

FIGURE 12-2. The JDBC architecture.

one of the early JDBC drivers made available by Sun. JDK 1.2 includes this JDBC–ODBC driver; you can use it to access any database that supports ODBC. By now there are JDBC drivers available for many more databases. You can get the latest list of JDBC drivers from Sun's Web site at **http://java.sun.com/products/ jdbc/jdbc.drivers.html**.

When you look at the list of JDBC drivers at Sun's Web site, you will see that there are several different types of drivers. Based on the way drivers are implemented, Sun has broken down the various JDBC drivers into four types:

◆ A type 1 driver is a JDBC–ODBC bridge that accesses a database through Microsoft's ODBC driver. You can use type 1 drivers on Windows systems to access any database for which an ODBC driver is available. JDK 1.2 comes with a type 1 JDBC–ODBC bridge.

◆ A type 2 driver communicates with the database using APIs specific to the database. Typically, type 2 drivers contain Java code that calls C or C++ APIs for a specific database such as Oracle, Sybase, Informix, DB2, or other database management system (DBMS).

◆ A type 3 driver is a pure Java client that uses a generic network API to communicate with a server that accesses the database and returns the requested information. This type of driver is very flexible because a single driver can provide access to many different databases (at the expense of having a server that can access that many different databases).

◆ A type 4 driver is a pure Java client that translates the JDBC calls into network protocols built into a database server. This type of driver requires knowledge of database-specific network protocols. Because such protocols are often proprietary, type 4 drivers are usually provided by the database vendors themselves.

JDBC Programming

JDBC programming refers to the task of writing database applications using the JDBC API. To write a JDBC program, you'll need a database, a JDBC driver for the database, and JDK 1.2 (the JDBC API is part of JDK 1.2).

If you have JDK 1.2 and Microsoft Access installed on your Windows system, you are all set to try out JDBC programming. Microsoft provides an ODBC driver for Access (and other databases), and Sun includes a JDBC–ODBC bridge that allows you to write JDBC programs that access databases through an ODBC driver.

If you have Microsoft Access, you don't even have to build a database; you can simply use the sample database file **Northwind.mdb** that Microsoft ships with its Access database product. Before you get started with the JDBC program, you have to set up **Northwind.mdb** as an ODBC data source. Perform the following steps to accomplish this task:

1. Open the Windows Control Panel (Start -> Settings -> Control Panel), and double-click on the 32-bit ODBC icon. This brings up the ODBC Data Source Administrator dialog box with a number of tabbed panes.

2. Click on the User DSN tab, and then click on the Add button on that tab. This brings up the Create New Data Source dialog box.

3. Select the Microsoft Access Driver (*.mdb) from the list in the Create New Data Source dialog box, and then click on the Finish button. The ODBC Microsoft Access 97 Setup dialog box appears.

4. In the field labeled Data Source Name, type **northwind** (this is the data source name the example program will use). Then click on the Select button to select the database to be associated with the source name. The Select Database dialog box appears.

5. From the Select Database dialog box, change the directory to **c:\Program Files\Microsoft Office\Office\Samples**, and then select the **Northwind.mdb** file. Click OK to close this dialog box.

6. Click OK two more times to close the other dialog box.

Now you are ready to access that database from a Java program using the JDBC API. You will find a sample program, **dbtst**, in the **ch12\dbtst** directory of the companion CD-ROM. To try out the program, first set up the ODBC data source name (using the steps outlined earlier in this section), and then type **java dbtst 60** in an MS-DOS window. Here is the expected output from the program:

Category	Product	Price
Meat/Poultry	Mishi Kobe Niku	$97.0
Seafood	Carnarvon Tigers	$62.5
Confections	Sir Rodney's Marmalade	$81.0
Meat/Poultry	Thüringer Rostbratwurst	$123.79
Beverages	Côte de Blaye	$263.5

5 products cost over $60.0

As you might guess from the output, the **dbtst** program is designed to display the list of products that cost more than the amount you specify on the command line. In this case, the output shows five products that cost over $60. If you run the program without any command-line arguments, it prints the products that cost more than $40.

PROGRAMMER'S NOTE   *For those readers who may not have Microsoft Access, I have included an Access database named **Products.mdb** that you can use to test the **dbtst** program. If you do not have Microsoft Access, follow the steps outlined earlier and, in step 5, select the **Products.mdb** file (located in the **ch12\dbtst** directory of the CD-ROM) as the database. The **Products.mdb** database has tables similar to those in **Northwind.mdb** but contains different data, so the output from **dbtst** will be different when you use **Products.mdb** as the database.*

Now that you have seen what the **dbtst** program does, let's look at the source code to see how the program uses JDBC API to get data from the Microsoft Access database. The following listing shows the **dbtst.java** file—the source code for the **dbtst** program. The JDBC programming steps are outlined in the sections that follow the listing.

```
1  //-------------------------------------------------------------
2  // A sample JDBC program that accesses an ODBC data source
3  // named "northwind" associated with the Microsoft Access
4  // database file Northwind.mdb that comes with the Access
5  // database product. It displays products that cost more
6  // than a specified price (provide the price on the command
7  // line).
8  //
9  // To use, you must first set up ODBC in Windows Control Panel.
10 //-------------------------------------------------------------
11 import java.sql.*;
12 public class dbtst
13 {
```

```
14    static Connection theConnection;
15    static float highPrice = (float)40.0;
16    public static void main(String args[])
17    {
18        if(args.length >= 1)
19        {
20            try
21            {
22                float f = Float.parseFloat(args[0]);
23                highPrice = f;
24            }
25            catch(NumberFormatException e){}
26        }
27        try
28        {
29            Class.forName("sun.jdbc.odbc.JdbcOdbcDriver");
30            theConnection = DriverManager.getConnection(
31                            "jdbc:odbc:northwind","","");
32            Statement select = theConnection.createStatement();
33            // Make the SQL query (you need to study the
34            // Northwind.mdb database to formulate the query)
35            ResultSet result = select.executeQuery(
36                "SELECT Products.ProductName, "+
37                "Categories.CategoryName, Products.UnitPrice "+
38                "FROM Products, Categories WHERE "+
39                "Products.CategoryID = Categories.CategoryID "+
40                "AND Products.UnitPrice > "+highPrice);
41            // Now display the result in a nice format :-)
42            System.out.println(
43                "Category\t\tProduct\t\t\t\tPrice");
44            for(int i = 0; i < 5; i++)
45                System.out.print("-------------");
46            System.out.println();
47            int count = 0;
48            while(result.next())
49            {
50                String name = result.getString(1);
51                String category = result.getString(2);
52                float price = result.getFloat(3);
53                System.out.print(category);
54                int len = category.length();
55                if(len < 15)
56                    for(int i=0; i < 15-len; i++)
```

```
57                        System.out.print(" ");
58                len = name.length();
59                System.out.print(" "+name);
60                if(len < 40)
61                    for(int i=0; i < 40-len; i++)
62                        System.out.print(" ");
63                System.out.println(" $"+price);
64                count++;
65            }
66            for(int i = 0; i < 5; i++)
67                System.out.print("-------------");
68            System.out.println();
69            System.out.println(
70                count+" products cost over $"+highPrice);
71            select.close();
72            theConnection.close();
73        }
74        catch(ClassNotFoundException e1) { e1.printStackTrace(); }
75        catch(SQLException e2) { e2.printStackTrace(); }
76    }
77 }
```

ANNOTATIONS

The **dbtst** program uses the following steps to get data from a database using JDBC:

1. Load the JDBC driver by calling the **Class.forName()** method. You have to specify the name of the driver class as an argument to this method.

2. Create a **Connection** object (that represents the connection to the database) by calling the **DriverManager.getConnection()** method. This method requires the database name (in the form of a special URL) as well as a user name and password as arguments.

3. Call the **createStatement()** method of the **Connection** object to create a **Statement** object that represents a SQL statement.

4. Call the **executeQuery()** method of the **Statement** object with a SQL statement as argument. This method returns the results in a **ResultSet** object.

5. Call various methods such as **next()**, **getString()**, and **getInt()** of the **ResultSet** object to retrieve each row returned by the SQL query performed in step 4.

6. When done, close the **Statement** and then close the **Connection**.

This is the basic sequence of steps you must follow in all JDBC-based Java database applications. Next, I will go through the code in the **dbtst.java** file and highlight the key JDBC programming steps.

When you use the JDBC API, you have to import the classes in the **java.sql** package. Line 11 shows the required **import** statement:

```
11  import java.sql.*;
```

Because **dbtst** is a simple command-line application, it has only a static **main()** method. The program accepts an optional argument through which the user can specify a price threshold (the program then shows all products that cost more than the threshold amount). Lines 18 through 26 process the command-line argument, if any.

The **try** block, shown in lines 27 through 73, contains all JDBC API calls. The **catch** blocks in lines 74 and 75 process any exceptions caused by the code inside the **try** block.

Line 29 loads the JDBC–ODBC driver by calling the **Class.forName()** method:

```
29          Class.forName("sun.jdbc.odbc.JdbcOdbcDriver");
```

In fact, you can load any class with the **Class.forName()** method. That method requires the name of the class as an argument. For Sun's JDBC–ODBC driver, use the name **"sun.jdbc.odbc.JdbcOdbcDriver"**. If the named class is not found, the **Class.forName()** method throws a **ClassNotFoundException**. The **catch** block in line 74 handles this exception. This should not happen for the JDBC–ODBC driver, however, because JDK 1.2 includes that driver class.

Lines 30 and 31 call the **getConnection()** method of the **DriverManager** to create a **Connection** object that establishes a connection to a database:

```
30          theConnection = DriverManager.getConnection(
31                          "jdbc:odbc:northwind","","");
```

The **getConnection()** method accepts three arguments: the database name, the user name, and the password. For a Microsoft Access database, you do not have to specify the user name and password, but most databases will require a valid user name and password. The database name is a URL of the form **jdbc:*subprotocol*:*subname*,** where *subprotocol* is the name of the driver and *subname* is a way to identify the database. (The *subname* depends on the database driver you are using.)

For the JDBC–ODBC driver, the database URL is of the form **jdbc:odbc:*dsn*,** where *dsn* refers to the data source name you assign to a database through the ODBC control panel.

For a remote database server, *subname* typically has the form *//hostname:port/remoteDBname,* where *hostname* identifies the host where the database server runs and *port* is the port number where the server accepts socket connections from clients. (Chapter 11 describes socket-based client/server communications.) The *remoteDBname* part of the *subname* is the name by which the remote database server identifies the database you want to access.

After a connection is established, line 32 creates a **Statement** object named **select** by calling the **createStatement()** method of the **Connection** object:

```
32          Statement select = theConnection.createStatement();
```

The **Statement** is what you would use to make a SQL query.

Lines 35 through 40 show how the **Statement** object's **executeQuery()** method is used to run a SQL query against the database:

```
35          ResultSet result = select.executeQuery(
36              "SELECT Products.ProductName, "+
37              "Categories.CategoryName, Products.UnitPrice "+
38              "FROM Products, Categories WHERE "+
39              "Products.CategoryID = Categories.CategoryID "+
40              "AND Products.UnitPrice > "+highPrice);
```

At this point, you need detailed knowledge of the database tables to construct the SQL query. I ran Microsoft Access, opened the **Northwind.mdb** database, and checked the design of the **Products** and **Categories** tables before writing the query. The **Categories** table essentially holds a category name for each category identifier (ID). Among the fields that the **Products** table contains are category ID, product name, and unit price of each product. I wanted to display the category name, the product name, and the unit price when that price exceeds the value stored in the variable named **highPrice**. That's what is accomplished by the SQL statement constructed in lines 35 through 40.

The **executeQuery()** method returns the results in a **ResultSet** object, which is a new table with zero or more rows that satisfy the conditions in the SQL statement. The **ResultSet** class contains methods you can use to access the rows of the result table and extract individual fields from each row.

PROGRAMMER'S NOTE   *For SQL statements such as INSERT, UPDATE, or DELETE that do not return multiple rows of results as SELECT does, you have to call the **executeUpdate()** method instead of **executeQuery()**. The **executeUpdate()** method returns an integer value denoting the number of rows affected by the SQL statement.*

After the **ResultSet** has been received, lines 42 through 70 format and display the result in tabular form. Just as in **dbtst**, a large part of a database application is typically devoted to formatting and displaying the output in a nice format.

The key task of extracting the rows from the **ResultSet** is done by the **while** loop shown in lines 48 through 65. Here are the key lines of code from that **while** loop:

```
48              while(result.next())
49              {
50                  String name = result.getString(1);
51                  String category = result.getString(2);
52                  float price = result.getFloat(3);
... code that prints out these fields has been omitted
65              }
```

On line 48, the **while** loop advances through successive rows of the **ResultSet** named **result** by calling the **next()** method. Lines 50 through 52 call various **getXXX()** methods (where **XXX** denotes a Java data type) of the **ResultSet** to get individual fields from the current row. You refer to each field by its position in the SELECT statement. For example, in this program, the SELECT statement requests the product name, the category, and the unit price, in that order. That's why line 50 calls **getString()** with argument 1 to get the product name, line 51 calls **getString()** with argument 2 to get the category, and line 52 calls **getFloat()** with argument 3 to get the unit price. For each field, you must call an appropriate method—**getString()** to get a **String**, **getInt()** to get an integer, and **getFloat()** to get a **float** value. Otherwise, these methods throw a **SQLException**, which you have to handle with a **catch** block.

The **ResultSet** class is key to extracting and using the results you get from the SQL query. In particular, you need to know which **getXXX()** method to call to retrieve a JDBC data type (which is same as the generic SQL data type). Table 12-3 lists the recommended **ResultSet** method to call to retrieve a specific type of JDBC data.

To Retrieve JDBC Data of Type	The Best ResultSet Method to Call Is
BIGINT	getLong()
BINARY or VARBINARY	getBytes()
BIT	getBoolean()
CHAR or VARCHAR	getString()
DATE	getDate()
DECIMAL or NUMERIC	getBigDecimal()
FLOAT or DOUBLE	getDouble()
INTEGER	getInt()
LONGVARBINARY	getBinaryStream()

TABLE 12-3.   The Recommended **ResultSet** Method to Call for Various JDBC Data Types.

To Retrieve JDBC Data of Type	The Best ResultSet Method to Call Is
LONGVARCHAR	getAsciiStream()
LONGVARCHAR	getUnicodeStream()
REAL	getFloat()
SMALLINT	getShort()
TIME	getTime()
TIMESTAMP	getTimestamp()
TINYINT	getByte()

TABLE 12-3. The Recommended **ResultSet** Method to Call for Various JDBC Data Types *(continued)*.

After extracting, formatting, and displaying all of the rows from the **ResultSet**, lines 71 and 72 close the **Statement** and the **Connection** to end the database access:

```
71      select.close();
72      theConnection.close();
```

An Alternate Database and JDBC Driver for UNIX

As I explained in the previous section, if you are using a PC running Microsoft Windows 95/98/NT, you can get started with JDBC programming provided you have the following:

◆ **JDK 1.2**: This latest version of the Java 2 software development kit (Java 2 SDK) comes with the JDBC classes and the JDBC–ODBC driver that you can use to develop and test your database applications.

◆ **Microsoft 32-bit ODBC drivers**: You can also download version 3.5 of the ODBC Desktop Database Drivers from the Microsoft Software Library at **ftp://ftp.microsoft.com/Softlib/MSLFILES/WX1350.EXE**. (This file is a 4,367K self-extracting archive.)

To create new databases, you also need any database that has an ODBC driver. However, you can test this chapter's examples by using the Microsoft Access database files I have provided on the CD-ROM. Your JDBC applications can access these Access databases even if you do not have Microsoft Access on your PC.

You can use the JDBC–ODBC driver to develop and test JDBC applications that can access any other databases for which you have an ODBC driver installed on your system. You probably already have the ODBC drivers for Microsoft Fox Pro, dBase, and Excel files (in addition to Microsoft Access). ODBC drivers are available from various vendors for a wide variety of databases, including IBM DB2, IBM AS/400, VSAM, ISAM, IMS, IDMS, Rdb, Oracle, Microsoft SQL Server, Informix, Sybase, C-ISAM, OpenIngres, R:BASE, Paradox, Progress, Model 204, ADABAS, and FOCUS, to name some. You should be able to get more information about the availability of ODBC drivers for a specific database by contacting that database vendor. Otherwise, visit a Web search engine such as **http://www.altavista.com** and search for the phrase "list of ODBC drivers," and you should get some links to sources of up-to-date ODBC drivers.

If you are running a UNIX system such as Linux or Solaris, you may consider using one of the low-cost databases that you can download and try out. A good choice is mSQL—the Mini SQL database engine that supports a subset of ANSI standard SQL as its query interface. You can download a 14-day evaluation copy by visiting **http://www.hughes.com.au/**. If you decide to use it, you can purchase a license for a nominal fee.

When you download mSQL, you'll get a compressed UNIX tar file (nearly 1MB in size) that contains the mSQL source code and documentation. You have to unpack the files and then build mSQL from the source files. The basic steps are as follows:

1. Use the command **tar zxvf** *filename* to uncompress and extract the contents of the archive. The files will be extracted into a subdirectory with a name like **msql-2.0.6.** (The directory name depends on the version of mSQL you download; this is the name for mSQL version 2.0.6.)

2. Go to the directory where the mSQL files reside and type **make target** at the UNIX prompt. This will create a directory named **targets**, which will contain a subdirectory whose name matches the name of your operating system. For example, on a PC that runs Linux 2.0.32 kernel, the directory will be **Linux-2.0.32-i586**.

3. Go to the directory whose name matches your operating system, and type **setup** to prepare a makefile for use in building mSQL.

4. Type **make all** to compile and link mSQL.

5. Type **make install** to place the mSQL program files in appropriate locations. By default, all files are installed in the **/usr/local/Hughes** directory.

After you build and install mSQL, you can create databases and populate the database with tables. First, log in as **root** (the super user) and start the database server with the command **/usr/local/Hughes/bin/msqld &**. The database server is a daemon (a background process that runs continuously) that accepts database queries from the **msql** program (or from Java programs that use a JDBC driver to access the mSQL database).

You should also add the mSQL binary directory to your PATH environment variable. If you installed mSQL in the default location, you need to add the **/usr/local/Hughes/bin** directory to the PATH. The exact command for this depends on the UNIX shell you use. In Korn shell or Bash, use the command **export PATH=$PATH:/usr/local/Hughes/bin** to modify the PATH. That way you will be able to run the mSQL programs without having to specify the full path name.

If you want to try out a database, type the command **msqladmin create booklist** to create an empty database named **booklist**. I have included a file named **makedb.sql** that contains the appropriate SQL commands (using the syntax required by mSQL) to create a table named **books** and add some book entries to that table. To set up the table, copy the **makedb.sql** file to the UNIX system and then type **msql booklist < makedb.sql**. After this step, you can check out the table with the **msql** program, which allows you to type SQL commands at a prompt. Here is a typical session with the **msql** program (the text shown in italic is what you have to type):

```
msql booklist
Welcome to the miniSQL monitor.  Type \h for help.

mSQL > select title from books where pubyear > 1995\g

Query OK.  5 row(s) modified or retrieved.

+-------------------------------------------------------+
| title                                                 |
+-------------------------------------------------------+
| Red Hat Linux SECRETS, 2e                             |
| Discover Perl 5                                       |
| UNIX Webmaster Bible                                  |
| Linux SECRETS                                         |
| Success with Windows 95                               |
+-------------------------------------------------------+

mSQL > \q

Bye!
```

To access an mSQL database from a JDBC application, you need a JDBC driver for mSQL. An mSQL–JDBC driver is available from **www.imaginary.com/Java/**. Note that you'll need to place the mSQL–JDBC driver on the same system as the one on which you plan to run the JDBC application. In other words, if you are running the JDBC application on a PC running Windows while the mSQL database is on a Linux system on the network, you have to place the mSQL–JDBC driver files on the PC.

After you download and unpack the mSQL–JDBC driver, you'll find a Jar file with a name that starts with **msql-jdbc** and ends with a **.jar** extension. To use this driver in your JDBC program, place this Jar file in the **jre\lib\ext** subdirectory of the directory where you have installed JDK 1.2. For example, if you installed JDK 1.2 in **c:\jdk1.2**, you should place the mSQL–JDBC Jar file in the **c:\jdk1.2\jre\lib\ext** directory. You need to perform this step so that the Java run-time environment can find the JDBC driver classes.

To allow you to try out the mSQL–JDBC driver, I have included the **dbmsql** program in the **ch12\dbtst** directory of this book's companion CD-ROM. That program accesses the **booklist** database you created earlier in this section. Type **java dbmsql** to run the program. Here is the output from that program:

```
Year    Title
-------------------------------
1998 Red Hat Linux SECRETS, 2e
1997 Discover Perl 5
1996 UNIX Webmaster Bible
1996 Linux SECRETS
1996 Success with Windows 95
-------------------------------
5 books since  1995
```

The source code of the **dbmsql** program—**dbmsql.java**—is similar to **dbtst.java** (the program that uses the JDBC–ODBC driver). The primary differences are in the name of the JDBC driver, the database URL, and the SQL statement used to extract data. Here is how the **dbmsql** program loads the driver:

```
Class.forName("com.imaginary.sql.msql.MsqlDriver");
```

The JDBC driver name depends on the package name used for the classes that make up the driver. The convention is to construct a package name by reversing the parts of the developer's domain name. In this case, the developer's domain name is **imaginary.com**. That's why the package name starts with **com.imaginary**. The developer is free to choose the remaining parts of the package.

After loading the mSQL–JDBC driver, you can connect to an mSQL database as follows:

```
theConnection = DriverManager.getConnection(
    "jdbc:msql://192.168.1.1:1114/booklist","naba","");
```

The mSQL JDBC driver expects a database URL of the form **jdbc:msql://** *your.host.com:***1114/***dbname*, where *your.host.name* is the host name, 1114 is the port number (by default, the mSQL database server listens on port 1114), and *dbname* is the name of the mSQL database. If you want, you can replace the host name with an IP address so that the URL is of the form **jdbc:msql://192.168.1.1:1114/***dbname*, as I have done in this example.

The SQL query used in the **dbmsql** program is executed by the following lines of code:

```
ResultSet result = select.executeQuery(
                "SELECT pubyear, title FROM books "+
                "WHERE pubyear > 1995");
```

As you might expect, the SQL query depends on the columns in the table from which you are extracting data. In this case, the query retrieves data from a table named **books**.

After getting the results, the following **while** loop gets each row of the result, extracts the fields, and displays the publication year and title of each book:

```
while(result.next())
{
    String title = result.getString("title");
    int pubyear = result.getInt("pubyear");
    System.out.println(pubyear+" "+title);
    count++;
}
```

Note that in this case the **getString()** and **getInt()** methods are called with the names of the columns as they were used in the SQL query. This is another way to access the fields in the rows. (In the previous example, these methods were called with integers that denoted positions of the column names in the SQL query statement.)

Maintaining a Community Calendar

A community calendar is a useful database application. You can set up a simple database that keeps track of events and provide a JDBC application that allows users to add events or view events for a specific date. The next few sections present **comcal**—a JDBC-based community calendar application.

Using comcal

The files for the **comcal** application are in the **ch12\comcal** directory of this book's companion CD-ROM. If you are using a Microsoft Windows 95, 98, or NT system and you have JDK 1.2 installed, you can try out **comcal** with the **Events.mdb** Microsoft Access database file. First copy the **Events.mdb** file from the CD-ROM's **ch12\comcal** directory to your system's hard disk. Then use the ODBC control panel to set up the **Events.mdb** file on the hard disk as a data source named **events**. For step-by-step instructions on setting up an ODBC data source, see the section "JDBC Programming," earlier in this chapter.

After you have set up **Events.mdb** as an ODBC data source, you can run the application by typing **java comcal** in an MS-DOS window. The application's user interface consists of a calendar with two tabbed panes under the window. Initially, the application displays the events for the current date in the default tab of the tabbed pane. You can also click on any date to view the events for that day. Figure 12-3 shows the **comcal** application window with the events for a selected date. In this case, the database contains only one event for this date. Notice that the tab's label tells you which day's events are currently being displayed. Of course, you can also tell this from the selected date (marked with a darker shade of gray) in the calendar.

To enter an event, use the calendar to go to the date you want, and then click on the Add Event tab in the tabbed pane. Figure 12-4 shows the tab on which you type information about the new event.

After you fill in the requested information about an event, click on the Add It! button in the upper-right corner of the tab (see Figure 12-4). The **comcal** application then inserts the event in the database and clears up the event-entry fields. If there is an error, the application displays an error message in a dialog box.

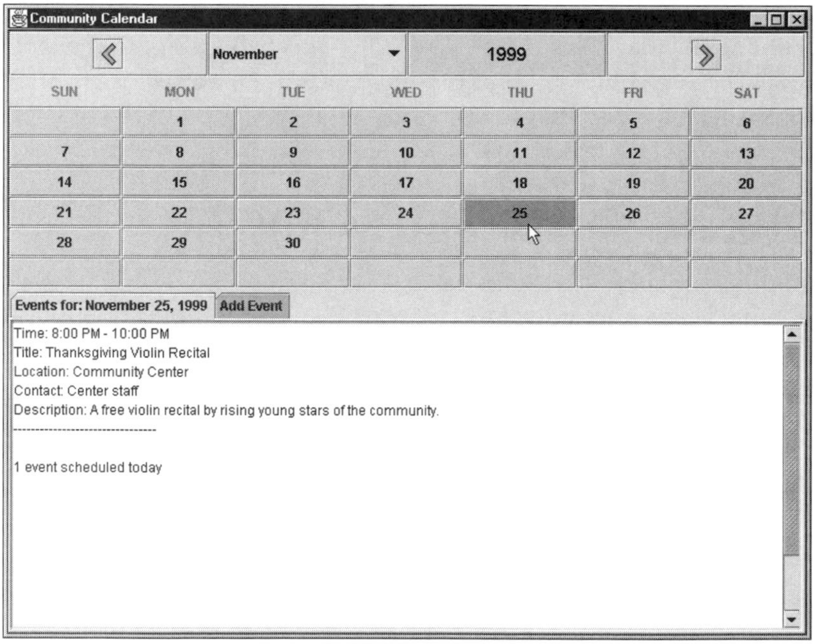

FIGURE 12-3.   The **comcal** application displays the events for the selected date.

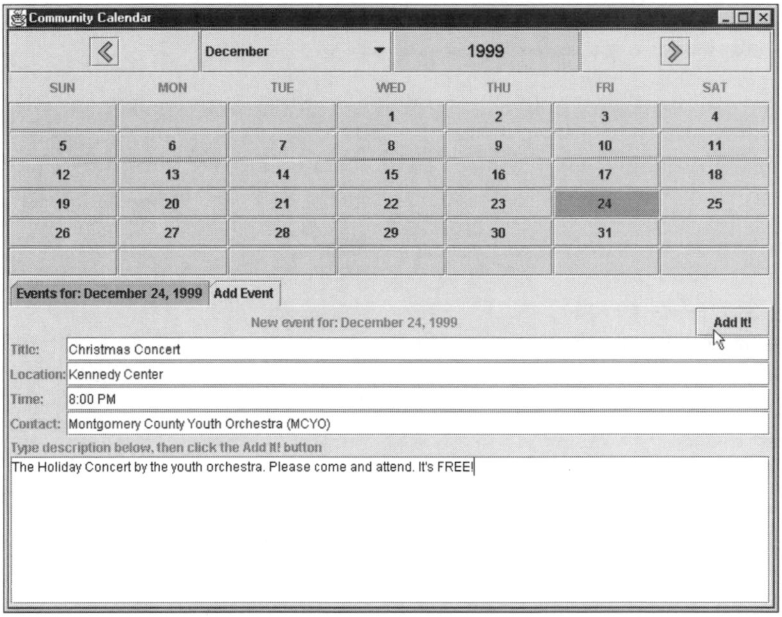

FIGURE 12-4. Entering information about a new event in **comcal**.

The **comcal** application expects the name of the JDBC driver and the database URL (that identifies the database to the JDBC driver) to be in a text file named **comcal.ini**. In that file, you can provide the driver name and database URL, as well as an optional user name and password (many databases require a user name and password to establish a connection). For example, here is how the **comcal.ini** file looks when you use the JDBC–ODBC driver with the ODBC data source named **events**:

```
// Initialization file for comcal application
// All lines except those that begin with "driver",
// "database", "username", and "password" are ignored.

driver = sun.jdbc.odbc.JdbcOdbcDriver
database = jdbc:odbc:events

// Add lines for "username" and "password" if your
// database requires user name and password.
```

```
// The syntax is:
//    username = username-for-database
//    password = password-for-database
```

If you want to try out a different database, simply create another text configuration file with the appropriate JDBC driver name and database URL. Make sure that the database has a table called **EventList** created with the following SQL statement:

```
CREATE TABLE EventList (
    Title CHAR(70),
    Location CHAR(70),
    EventTime CHAR(70),
    Contact CHAR(70),
    Description CHAR(255),
    Month INT,
    Day INT,
    Year INT,
    EnteredBy CHAR(70)
)
```

I tested **comcal** with a database in mSQL (running on a Linux system on the network) using the Imaginary mSQL–JDBC driver (available from **www.imaginary.com/Java/**). I created a configuration file named **msql.ini** with the following lines in it:

```
// Initialization file for comcal application
// For use with mSQL-JDBC driver
// You'll need an mSQL database named Events
// with an EventList table

  driver = com.imaginary.sql.msql.MsqlDriver
  database = jdbc:msql://192.168.1.1:1114/Events
  username = naba
// If you need it, add a password = somepwd line
```

Note that the database URL is specific to my local network.

I then ran the application with the command **java comcal msql.ini**. This command causes **comcal** to read the initialization parameters from the filename specified on the command line. The user interface looks the same as before; the only difference is that **comcal** now accesses a different database.

comcal

Understanding comcal

Now that you have seen how the **comcal** application works, you can go through the source code. The following listing shows the file **comcal.java**, which implements the application. I explain the code in the sections that follow the listing.

```
1  //-----------------------------------------------------------------
2  // comcal.java   (Community Calendar)
3  //
4  // A community calendar GUI application that lets users
5  // add events to a calendar. The events are stored in
6  // a database. The program uses JDBC to access the database.
7  // The JDBC driver name and the database name are read from
8  // a file named comcal.ini. In that file, place two lines
9  // with the following syntax:
10 //     driver = sun.jdbc.odbc.JdbcOdbcDriver
11 //     database = jdbc:odbc:events
12 //     username = database username [optional]
13 //     password = password to log in [optional]
14 // These are the default driver and database names (in case
15 // you don't provide a comcal.ini file). If you use a different
16 // database driver or database, change these values. You can run
17 // this program with the Events.mdb (Microsoft Access database)
18 // included in the ch12\comcal directory. If you decide to use
19 // a different database, you have to make sure that the database
20 // includes a table named "EventList" that has the following
21 // columns:
22 //     Title       CHAR(70)  -- Stores event title
23 //     Location    CHAR(70)  -- Location of event
24 //     EventTime   CHAR(70)  -- Time of event
25 //     Contact     CHAR(70)  -- Name of contact
26 //     Description CHAR(255) -- Description of event
27 //     Month       INT       -- Month number (0 = Jan, 1=Feb,...)
28 //     Day         INT       -- Day (1, 2, through 31)
29 //     Year        INT       -- Year (1999, 2000, etc.)
30 //     EnteredBy   CHAR(70)  -- Who entered the event
31 //-----------------------------------------------------------------
32 import java.applet.*;
33 import java.awt.*;
34 import java.util.*;
35 import java.awt.event.*;
36 import javax.swing.*;
37 import javax.swing.border.*;
```

```java
38  import java.sql.*;
39  import java.text.*;
40  import java.io.*;
41  /** A community calendar application built from an old applet */
42  public class comcal extends JApplet implements ActionListener,
43                                                    ItemListener
44  {
45      private static String appName = "Community Calendar";
46      private static comcal thisApp;
47      private static JFrame mainFrame;
48      private static final int WIDTH = 350;
49      private static final int HEIGHT = 400;
50      private JComboBox  monthChoice;
51      private JTextField year;
52      private JButton    previousButton;
53      private JButton    nextButton;
54      private int        currentMonth;
55      private int        currentYear;
56      private int        currentDay;
57      private String     currentDayString;
58      private String     currentDateString;
59      private Font helvB16 =
60                  new Font("Helvetica", Font.BOLD, 16);
61      private Font helvP12 =
62                  new Font("Helvetica", Font.PLAIN, 12);
63      private String days[] = {"SUN", "MON", "TUE", "WED", "THU",
64                          "FRI", "SAT"};
65      private String months[] = {
66                      "January", "February", "March", "April",
67                      "May", "June", "July", "August", "September",
68                      "October", "November", "December"};
69      private int daysInMonth[] = {31, 28, 31, 30, 31, 30, 31, 31,
70                          30, 31, 30, 31};
71      private JButton[][] monthButtons = new JButton[6][7];
72      private JButton highlightedBtn = null;
73      private JLabel[] dayLabels = new JLabel[7];
74      private JTextArea eventsArea;
75      private JTabbedPane tPane;
76      private JButton evtAddBtn;
77      private JLabel evtLabel;
78      private JTextField evtTitleTF;
79      private JTextField evtLocTF;
```

```
80      private JTextField evtTimeTF;
81      private JTextField evtContactTF;
82      private JTextArea evtDescArea;
83      private SoftBevelBorder sbb = new SoftBevelBorder(
84                                  BevelBorder.LOWERED);
85      private static SimpleDateFormat df =
86                  new SimpleDateFormat("MMM dd, yyyy HH:mm:ss");
87      private static String iniFileName = "comcal.ini";
88      private static String driverName =
89                  "sun.jdbc.odbc.JdbcOdbcDriver";
90      private static String databaseURL = "jdbc:odbc:events";
91      private static String username = "";
92      private static String password = "";
93      private static Connection theConnection = null;
94      private static Statement sqlStmt = null;
95      /** Initializes the community calendar's user interface */
96      public void init()
97      {
98          Calendar today = Calendar.getInstance();
99          currentMonth = today.get(Calendar.MONTH);
100         currentYear = today.get(Calendar.YEAR);
101         currentDay = today.get(Calendar.DAY_OF_MONTH);
102         currentDayString = ""+currentDay;
103         currentDateString = months[currentMonth]+" "+
104                             currentDayString+", "+currentYear;
105         Container cp = this.getContentPane();
106         cp.setLayout(new BorderLayout());
107         JPanel pAll = new JPanel();
108         pAll.setLayout(new BorderLayout());
109         JPanel pUpper = new JPanel();
110         pUpper.setLayout(new BorderLayout());
111         JPanel pTop = new JPanel();
112         pTop.setLayout(new GridLayout(1, 4));
113         Icon prevIcon = new ImageIcon("prev.gif");
114         previousButton = new JButton(prevIcon);
115         previousButton.addActionListener(this);
116         previousButton.setToolTipText("Previous month");
117         pTop.add(previousButton);
118         monthChoice = new JComboBox();
119         for(int i = 0; i < months.length; i++)
120             monthChoice.addItem(months[i]);
121         monthChoice.setSelectedIndex(currentMonth);
122         monthChoice.setMaximumRowCount(6);
```

```
123        monthChoice.addItemListener(this);
124        pTop.add(monthChoice);
125        year = new JTextField("" + currentYear, 4);
126        year.setFont(helvB16);
127        year.setBackground(Color.lightGray);
128        year.setHorizontalAlignment(JTextField.CENTER);
129        year.addActionListener(this);
130        year.setToolTipText("Enter number, then press <Enter>.");
131        pTop.add(year);
132        Icon nextIcon = new ImageIcon("next.gif");
133        nextButton = new JButton(nextIcon);
134        nextButton.addActionListener(this);
135        nextButton.setToolTipText("Next month");
136        pTop.add(nextButton);
137        pUpper.add("North", pTop);
138        JPanel pButtons = new JPanel();
139        pButtons.setLayout(new GridLayout(7,7));
140        for(int i=0; i < days.length; i++)
141        {
142            dayLabels[i] = new JLabel(days[i], JLabel.CENTER);
143            pButtons.add(dayLabels[i]);
144        }
145        for(int i=0; i < 6; i++)
146            for(int j=0; j < 7; j++)
147            {
148                monthButtons[i][j] = new JButton("");
149                monthButtons[i][j].setBackground(Color.lightGray);
150                monthButtons[i][j].addActionListener(this);
151                pButtons.add(monthButtons[i][j]);
152            }
153        pUpper.add("Center", pButtons);
154        pAll.add("North", pUpper);
155        JPanel pLower = new JPanel();
156        pLower.setLayout(new BorderLayout());
157        eventsArea = new JTextArea(20, 50);
158        eventsArea.setFont(helvP12);
159        tPane = new JTabbedPane(JTabbedPane.TOP);
160        JScrollPane scrollPane = new JScrollPane(eventsArea);
161        scrollPane.setBorder(sbb);
162        tPane.addTab(currentDateString, scrollPane);
163        tPane.addTab("Add Event", createAddEvtPanel());
164        pLower.add("Center", tPane);
```

```
165         pAll.add("Center", pLower);
166         cp.add("Center", pAll);
167         validate();
168         repaint();
169         try
170         {
171             BufferedReader infile = new BufferedReader(
172                             new FileReader(iniFileName));
173             while(true)
174             {
175                 String line = infile.readLine();
176                 if(line == null) break;
177                 line = line.trim();
178                 if(line.startsWith("driver"))
179                 {
180                     int i = line.indexOf("=");
181                     String drname = line.substring(i+1).trim();
182                     driverName = drname;
183                 }
184                 else if(line.startsWith("database"))
185                 {
186                     int i = line.indexOf("=");
187                     String dbname = line.substring(i+1).trim();
188                     databaseURL = dbname;
189                 }
190                 else if(line.startsWith("username"))
191                 {
192                     int i = line.indexOf("=");
193                     String uname = line.substring(i+1).trim();
194                     username = uname;
195                 }
196                 else if(line.startsWith("password"))
197                 {
198                     int i = line.indexOf("=");
199                     String pwd = line.substring(i+1).trim();
200                     password = pwd;
201                 }
202             }
203         }
204         catch(IOException e){}
205         try
```

```
206        {    // Load the database driver and connect to database
207            Class.forName(driverName);
208            theConnection = DriverManager.getConnection(
209                               databaseURL, username, password);
210            sqlStmt = theConnection.createStatement();
211        }
212        catch(ClassNotFoundException e1) { e1.printStackTrace();}
213        catch(SQLException e2) { e2.printStackTrace(); }
214        displayEvents();
215    }
216    /** Returns true if the year is a leap year. */
217    public boolean isLeapYear(int year)
218    {
219        if((year % 400) == 0) return(true);
220        if((year > 1582) && ((year % 100) == 0)) return(false);
221        if((year % 4) == 0) return(true);
222        return(false);
223    }
224    /** Displays the calendar for a specific month of a year */
225    public void displayMonth(int month, int year)
226    {
227        int day = 1; // first of the month
228        int monthNum = month - 1; // month number,1=Mar,2=Apr,...
229        if(monthNum <= 0) monthNum += 12; // Jan = 11, Feb = 12
230        int tempYear = year;
231        if(monthNum > 10) tempYear = year - 1;
232        int century = tempYear / 100;
233        int yy = tempYear - 100 * century;
234        int factor = (int)(day +
235                (int)(2.6*(double)monthNum - 0.2) -
236              2*century + yy + yy/4 + century/4.0);
237        int firstWeekday = factor % 7; // 0=Sun, 1=Mon, 2=Tue, ...
238
239        // Now draw the dates on the buttons in the calendar
240        int maxDate = daysInMonth[month];
241        if(month == 1 && isLeapYear(year)) maxDate += 1;
242        int dateNow = 1;
243        if(highlightedBtn != null)
244            highlightedBtn.setBackground(Color.lightGray);
245        String ds;
246        for(int i=0; i < 6; i++)
247            {
```

```
248              for(int j=0; j < 7; j++)
249              {
250                   if(dateNow == 1 && j < firstWeekday)
251                        monthButtons[i][j].setText("");
252                   else if(dateNow > maxDate)
253                        monthButtons[i][j].setText("");
254                   else
255                   {
256                        ds = ""+dateNow;
257                        monthButtons[i][j].setText(ds);
258                        if(ds.equals(currentDayString))
259                        {
260                             monthButtons[i][j].setBackground(
261                                                 Color.gray);
262                             highlightedBtn = monthButtons[i][j];
263                        }
264                        dateNow++;
265                   }
266              }
267         }
268    }
269    /** Processes the year entered by the user */
270    public int processYear(String yearString)
271    {
272         if((yearString.length() == 4))
273         {
274              try
275              {
276                   int year = Integer.parseInt(yearString);
277                   return year;
278              }
279              catch(NumberFormatException e)
280              {
281                   return currentYear;
282              }
283         }
284         return -1;
285    }
286    /** Calls displayMonth() to display the calendar */
287    public void paint(Graphics g)
288    {
```

```
289        g.setColor(Color.black);
290        Dimension d = getSize();
291        g.drawRect(0, 0, d.width-1,d.height-1);
292        displayMonth(currentMonth, currentYear);
293        super.paint(g);    // Important step for Swing components
294    }
295  /** Handles mouse clicks in the buttons and drop-down menus*/
296    public void actionPerformed(ActionEvent ev)
297    {
298        if(ev.getSource().equals(previousButton))
299        {
300            if((currentYear > 1) || (currentMonth > 0))
301            {
302                currentMonth--;
303                if(currentMonth < 0)
304                {
305                    currentMonth = 11;
306                    currentYear--;
307                }
308                monthChoice.setSelectedIndex(currentMonth);
309                year.setText(""+currentYear);
310                currentDay = 1;
311                currentDayString = "1";
312                // Display events for new date
313                displayEvents();
314                repaint();
315            }
316        }
317        else if(ev.getSource() == nextButton)
318        {
319            if((currentYear < 9999) || (currentMonth < 11))
320            {
321                currentMonth++;
322                if(currentMonth > 11)
323                {
324                    currentMonth = 0;
325                    currentYear++;
326                }
327                monthChoice.setSelectedIndex(currentMonth);
328                year.setText(""+currentYear);
329                currentDay = 1;
330                currentDayString = "1";
```

```
331                        // Display events for new date
332                        displayEvents();
333                        repaint();
334                    }
335                }
336            else if(ev.getSource() == year)
337            {
338            // called when user presses Enter in text field
339                int y = processYear(year.getText());
340                if((y > 0) && (y != currentYear))
341                {
342                    currentYear = y;
343                    currentDay = 1;
344                    currentDayString = "1";
345                    // Display events for new date
346                    displayEvents();
347                    repaint();
348                }
349            }
350            else
351            {   // check for click on a day of the month
352                String ds;
353                for(int i=0; i < 6; i++)
354                {
355                    for(int j=0; j < 7; j++)
356                    {
357                        if(ev.getSource() == monthButtons[i][j])
358                        {
359                            ds = ev.getActionCommand();
360                            if(!ds.equals(""))
361                            {
362                                highlightedBtn.
363                                    setBackground(Color.lightGray);
364                                highlightedBtn = monthButtons[i][j];
365                                monthButtons[i][j].setBackground(
366                                                    Color.gray);
367                                currentDayString = ds;
368                                try
369                                {
370                                    int day = Integer.parseInt(ds);
371                                    currentDay = day;
372                                    // Display events for new date
373                                    displayEvents();
374                                }
```

```
375                              catch(NumberFormatException ex){}
376                        }
377                    }
378                }
379            }
380        }
381    }
382    /** Handles selections from the month list */
383    public void itemStateChanged(ItemEvent ev)
384    {
385        if(ev.getSource() == monthChoice)
386        {
387            int m = monthChoice.getSelectedIndex();
388            year.setText(""+currentYear);
389            if(m != currentMonth)
390            {
391                currentMonth = monthChoice.getSelectedIndex();
392                currentDayString = "1";
393                currentDay = 1;
394                // Display events for new date
395                displayEvents();
396                repaint();
397            }
398        }
399    }
400    /** Makes room for a 1-pixel border. */
401    public Insets getInsets()
402    {
403        return new Insets(1,1,1,1); // 1-pixel border
404    }
405    /** Provides a frame so the program can run stand-alone */
406    public static void main(String args[])
407    {
408        if(args.length > 0) iniFileName = args[0];
409        WindowListener l = new WindowAdapter()
410        {
411            public void windowClosing(WindowEvent e)
412            {
413                try
414                {
415                    sqlStmt.close();
```

```
416                    theConnection.close();
417                }
418                catch(SQLException ex){ex.printStackTrace();}
419                System.exit(0);
420            }
421        };
422        mainFrame = new JFrame("Community Calendar");
423        mainFrame.addWindowListener(1);
424        thisApp = new comcal();
425        thisApp.init();
426        mainFrame.setSize(WIDTH, HEIGHT);
427        mainFrame.getContentPane().add("Center", thisApp);
428        mainFrame.pack();
429        mainFrame.setVisible(true);
430    }
431    /** Gets today's events from database and displays them */
432    private void displayEvents()
433    {
434        currentDateString = months[currentMonth]+" "+
435                            currentDayString+", "+currentYear;
436        tPane.setTitleAt(0, "Events for: "+currentDateString);
437        evtLabel.setText("New event for: "+currentDateString);
438        eventsArea.setText("");
439        try
440        {   // Make the SQL query to get today's events
441            String selectStmt =
442                "SELECT Title, Location, EventTime, Contact, "+
443                "Description FROM EventList WHERE "+
444                "Month = "+currentMonth+" AND "+
445                "Day = "+currentDay+" AND "+
446                "Year = "+currentYear+" "+
447                "ORDER BY EventTime";
448            ResultSet result = sqlStmt.executeQuery(selectStmt);
449            int count = 0;
450            while(result.next())
451            {
452                String title = result.getString(1);
453                String location = result.getString(2);
454                String time = result.getString(3);
455                String contact = result.getString(4);
456                String descr = result.getString(5);
457                String es = "Time: ";
```

```
458                    if(time != null) es += time;
459                    es += "\nTitle: ";
460                    if(title != null) es += title;
461                    es += "\nLocation: ";
462                    if(location != null) es += location;
463                    es += "\nContact: ";
464                    if(contact != null) es += contact;
465                    es += "\nDescription: ";
466                    if(descr != null) es += descr+"\n";
467                    es += "--------------------------------\n\n";
468                    eventsArea.append(es);
469                    count++;
470                }
471            if(count > 0)
472            {
473                eventsArea.append(count+" ");
474                if(count > 1)
475                    eventsArea.append("events scheduled today\n");
476                else
477                    eventsArea.append("event scheduled today\n");
478            }
479            else
480                eventsArea.append(
481                    "NO events scheduled today\n"+
482                    "To add an event, click on Add Event tab, "+
483                    "fill in the requested information, and "+
484                    "click on the Add It! button");
485        }
486        catch(SQLException ex)
487        {
488            eventsArea.append(ex.toString()+"\n");
489            eventsArea.append(
490                "ERROR: Could not get events from database!\n");
491        }
492    }
493    /** Creates the user interface for adding an event */
494    private JPanel createAddEvtPanel()
495    {
496        JPanel p = new JPanel(new GridLayout(2,1));
497        JPanel pTop = new JPanel(new BorderLayout());
498        JPanel pTopT = new JPanel(new BorderLayout());
499        JPanel pTopM = new JPanel(new BorderLayout());
```

```
500        JPanel pTopML = new JPanel(new GridLayout(4,1));
501        JPanel pTopMR = new JPanel(new GridLayout(4,1));
502        evtLabel = new JLabel("New event for: "+
503                       currentDateString, JLabel.CENTER);
504        evtAddBtn = new JButton("Add It!");
505        setAddEvtListener();
506        pTopT.add("East", evtAddBtn);
507        pTopT.add("Center", evtLabel);
508        JLabel lbl2 = new JLabel("Title:");
509        JLabel lbl3 = new JLabel("Location:");
510        JLabel lbl4 = new JLabel("Time:");
511        JLabel lbl5 = new JLabel("Contact:");
512        pTopML.add(lbl2);
513        pTopML.add(lbl3);
514        pTopML.add(lbl4);
515        pTopML.add(lbl5);
516        evtTitleTF = new JTextField(60);
517        evtLocTF = new JTextField(60);
518        evtTimeTF = new JTextField(60);
519        evtContactTF = new JTextField(60);
520        pTopMR.add(evtTitleTF);
521        pTopMR.add(evtLocTF);
522        pTopMR.add(evtTimeTF);
523        pTopMR.add(evtContactTF);
524        pTopM.add("West", pTopML);
525        pTopM.add("Center", pTopMR);
526        JLabel lbl6 = new JLabel(
527          "Type description below, then click the Add It! button");
528        pTop.add("North", pTopT);
529        pTop.add("Center", pTopM);
530        pTop.add("South", lbl6);
531        p.add(pTop);
532        evtDescArea = new JTextArea(
533                "New event description goes here", 6, 40);
534        JScrollPane sp = new JScrollPane(evtDescArea);
535        p.add(sp);
536        return p;
537    }
538    /** Returns current date and time */
539    public static String getTimeString()
```

```
540         {
541             return df.format(new java.util.Date());
542         }
543     /** Defines the ActionListener for the Add It! button */
544     private void setAddEvtListener()
545         {
546             ActionListener l = new ActionListener()
547                 {
548                     public void actionPerformed(ActionEvent ev)
549                         {
550                             try
551                                 {
552                                     // Construct the SQL statement
553                                     String title = evtTitleTF.getText();
554                                     String location = evtLocTF.getText();
555                                     String time = evtTimeTF.getText();
556                                     String contact = evtContactTF.getText();
557                                     String desc = evtDescArea.getText();
558                                     String insertStmt = "INSERT INTO EventList (";
559                                     if(!title.equals("")) insertStmt += "Title, ";
560                                     if(!location.equals(""))
561                                         insertStmt += "Location, ";
562                                     if(!time.equals(""))
563                                         insertStmt += "EventTime, ";
564                                     if(!contact.equals(""))
565                                         insertStmt += "Contact, ";
566                                     if(!desc.equals(""))
567                                         insertStmt += "Description, ";
568                                     insertStmt +=
569                                         "Month, Day, Year, EnteredBy) VALUES (";
570                                     if(!title.equals(""))
571                                         insertStmt += expandSingleQuotes(title)
572                                                 + ", ";
573                                     if(!location.equals(""))
574                                         insertStmt += expandSingleQuotes(location)
575                                                 + ", ";
576                                     if(!time.equals(""))
577                                         insertStmt += expandSingleQuotes(time)
578                                                 + ", ";
579                                     if(!contact.equals(""))
580                                         insertStmt += expandSingleQuotes(contact)
581                                                 + ", ";
```

```
582                    if(!desc.equals(""))
583                        insertStmt += expandSingleQuotes(desc)
584                                     + ", ";
585                insertStmt +=
586                    currentMonth+", "+currentDay+", "+
587                    currentYear+", '"+thisApp.appName+" "+
588                    thisApp.getTimeString()+"')";
589                // Call executeUpdate() to insert row
590                int result = sqlStmt.executeUpdate(
591                                              insertStmt);
592                thisApp.displayEvents();
593                thisApp.clearAddEvtPanel();
594            }
595            catch(SQLException ex)
596            {
597                JOptionPane.showMessageDialog(
598                    thisApp.evtDescArea,
599                    ex.toString()+"\n"+
600                    "Could not update database!",
601                    "Community Calendar - Error",
602                    JOptionPane.ERROR_MESSAGE);
603            }
604        }
605    };
606    evtAddBtn.addActionListener(l);
607 }
608 /** Replaces single quotes with two single quotes */
609 private String expandSingleQuotes(String ins)
610 {
611     String outs = "";
612     if(!ins.equals(""))
613     {
614         outs += "'";
615         int to, from = 0;
616         to = ins.indexOf('\'');
617         while(to > -1)
618         {
619             outs += ins.substring(from,to)+"''";
620             from = to+1;
621             to = ins.indexOf('\'', from);
622         }
```

```
623              outs += ins.substring(from) +"'";
624          }
625          return outs;
626      }
627      /** Clears the Add Event tab */
628      private void clearAddEvtPanel()
629      {
630          evtTitleTF.setText("");
631          evtLocTF.setText("");
632          evtTimeTF.setText("");
633          evtContactTF.setText("");
634          evtDescArea.setText("New event description goes here");
635      }
636  }
```

ANNOTATIONS

I start with an overview of the **comcal** application and then provide more details in the subsequent sections.

I created the **comcal** application by expanding the **ViewCal** GUI application from Chapter 9. **ViewCal** displays a monthly calendar of any month of a selected year. A calendar happens to be an ideal user interface for a community calendar. Users can click on a date to view that day's events or enter the necessary information to add an event for the selected date. I added additional user interface elements so that the user can view the events for a date and add a new event.

Like **ViewCal**, the **comcal** class is defined as a subclass of **JApplet**, only because I did not want to change it. Because of the new code I had to add, you cannot run **comcal** as an applet. If you try to run it using **appletviewer**, you'll get a security exception when **comcal** tries to load the JDBC driver class by calling the **Class.forName()** method.

The **comcal** application retains the **ViewCal** application's calendar user interface, but it adds a tabbed pane underneath the monthly calendar. One of the two tabs on the pane is labeled with the current date and has a text area where the application displays the events for a selected date. The other tab, labeled Add Event, displays the user interface components that allow the user to add a new event. Of course, both of these operations—displaying the current date's events and adding a new event—involve using the JDBC API to get data from and send data to the database.

All of the application's initializations take place in the **init()** method because the calendar started out as an applet, and applets are initialized in the **init()** method. Specifically, the **init()** method performs the following steps:

1. Sets up the calendar display area. Adds the two tabbed panes for viewing events and adding a new event.

2. Opens a text file and reads from it the JDBC driver name, the database name, and any user name and password (needed for accessing the database).

3. Loads the JDBC driver, opens a connection with the database, and creates a **Statement** object for use when sending SQL commands to the database.

4. Displays the events for the current date.

To allow **comcal** to run as a stand-alone application, the **comcal** class includes a static **main()** method that creates a main frame (a **JFrame** component), creates an instance of the **comcal** class, calls the **init()** method, and then places the **comcal** component in the frame.

After **comcal** starts running, whenever the user selects a different date, the program sends a SQL query to get the events for the new date and displays them in the tab. To add an event, the user goes to the Add Event tab, fills in the event information, and clicks on the Add It! button. That button's event listener sends a SQL command to the database to add the new event.

In a nutshell, that's how the **comcal** application works. The next few sections describe the code for specific tasks. The focus is primarily on the JDBC API calls used to interact with the database.

READING JDBC PARAMETERS FROM THE INITIALIZATION FILE   To allow the use of different JDBC drivers and databases, the **comcal** application reads various JDBC parameters from an initialization file. Internally, the application stores the JDBC parameters in a number of static variables:

```
88      private static String driverName =
89                  "sun.jdbc.odbc.JdbcOdbcDriver";
90      private static String databaseURL = "jdbc:odbc:events";
91      private static String username = "";
92      private static String password = "";
```

Although these variables have some initial values, the idea is to read these parameters from a text file (which I am referring to as the initialization file).

Line 87 defines the name of the default initialization file as **comcal.ini**:

```
87      private static String iniFileName = "comcal.ini";
```

However, the user can also provide the initialization file's name as a command-line argument. In other words, if the user starts the application with the command **java comcal msql.ini**, the application assumes that the initialization file is **msql.ini**. Line

408 in the **main()** method checks whether the user has provided a command-line argument and if so sets the **iniFileName** variable to that argument:

```
408        if(args.length > 0) iniFileName = args[0];
```

The JDBC parameters are read in the **init()** method right after the user interface is set up. The **try** block in lines 169 through 203 encloses the code that opens the initialization file and reads the lines in that file. Lines 171 and 172 open a **BufferedReader** to read from the file:

```
171        BufferedReader infile = new BufferedReader(
172                    new FileReader(iniFileName));
```

A **while** loop reads a line at a time and parses the lines that contain the JDBC parameters. The interesting lines are the ones that start with one of the strings **driver**, **database**, **username**, and **password**. These lines specify the JDBC driver name, the database URL, and the optional user name and password that may be needed to connect to the database server. For example, lines 175 through 183 show how a line is read and processed:

```
175            String line = infile.readLine();
176            if(line == null) break;
177            line = line.trim();
178            if(line.startsWith("driver"))
179            {
180                int i = line.indexOf("=");
181                String drname = line.substring(i+1).trim();
182                driverName = drname;
183            }
```

Line 175 reads the line. Line 176 ends the **while** loop if the line is **null** (meaning that the file ended). Line 177 gets rid of any blank spaces at the beginning and end of the line. If the line starts with the string **"driver"**, line 180 finds the equals sign (=), and line 181 extracts the JDBC driver name that follows the equals sign. Finally, line 182 sets the **driverName** variable to the string extracted from the initialization file.

Values for the other JDBC parameters—**databaseURL**, **username**, and **password**—are read from the initialization file in the same manner.

SETTING UP THE INITIAL DATABASE CONNECTION   After the JDBC parameters are read from the initialization file, the **try** block in lines 205 through 211 of the **init()** method loads the JDBC driver and connects to the database:

```
205        try
206        {   // Load the database driver and connect to database
207            Class.forName(driverName);
```

```
208                    theConnection = DriverManager.getConnection(
209                                  databaseURL, username, password);
210                    sqlStmt = theConnection.createStatement();
211            }
```

Line 207 calls **Class.forName()** with the JDBC driver's name to load that driver. Lines 208 and 209 connect to the database. Line 210 creates a **Statement** object named **sqlStmt** for that connection. That **sqlStmt** object is used whenever the application has to send SQL commands to the database.

If any exceptions occur during these initial steps, an appropriate **catch** block in lines 212 and 213 prints an error message and exits the program.

GETTING EVENTS FROM THE DATABASE   After the initial connection to the database is established and a **Statement** object is available, it is straightforward to send a SQL query to retrieve the events for a specific date. The **displayEvents()** method, shown in lines 432 through 492, performs this task. This method is called whenever the user selects a different date (either by clicking on a day, selecting a new month, or typing in a new year). You'll see calls to **displayEvents()** in the **actionPerformed()** and **itemStateChanged()** methods that handle the events that occur when the user clicks on a day button, types a new year, or selects a new month.

Essentially, **displayEvents()** sends a SQL query to the database to retrieve all events whose date matches the currently selected date, as indicated by the variables **currentMonth**, **currentDay**, and **currentYear**. Each of these variables store integer values for the current month, day, and year. All of the values are as you would expect except the current month; that value is between 0 and 11, where 0 denotes January and 11 is December. The database also stores the month in the same manner.

After getting the results from the database, **displayEvents()** displays the events in the text area that appears underneath the monthly calendar.

Lines 434 through 437 of the **displayEvents()** method initialize some labels in the two tabs of the tabbed pane where events are displayed and entered. Line 438 clears the text area where the events for the current date are displayed.

The **try** block in lines 439 through 485 enclose the code that sends the SQL query to the database and processes the **ResultSet** containing the results of the query. Lines 441 through 447 construct a **String** with the SQL query to be sent to the database:

```
441            String selectStmt =
442                "SELECT Title, Location, EventTime, Contact, "+
443                "Description FROM EventList WHERE "+
444                "Month = "+currentMonth+" AND "+
445                "Day = "+currentDay+" AND "+
```

```
446                    "Year = "+currentYear+" "+
447                    "ORDER BY EventTime";
```

This is a straightforward SELECT statement that picks the relevant fields from the **EventList** table for the user-selected date. As you can see, the SELECT statement is constructed by concatenating SQL commands with the values of the variables **currentMonth**, **currentDay**, and **currentYear**. For example, if the user selects December 31, 1999, as the date, **currentMonth** will be 11 (because the application assumes that 0 = January, 1 = February, and so on), **currentDay** = 31, and **currentYear** = 1999. Therefore, the **selectStmt** string will be

```
SELECT Title, Location, EventTime, Contact, Description
FROM EventList WHERE Month = 11 AND Day = 31 AND Year = 1999
ORDER BY EventTime
```

PROGRAMMER'S NOTE *You have to watch out for any column names that are also SQL keywords. For example, I had used **Time** as a column name in the **EventList** table, but **Time** happens to be a SQL keyword. I kept getting errors until I noticed that I was using **Time** as a column name. I ended up changing that column's name to **EventTime**. The other option would have been to enclose **Time** in backquotes (also called grave accent marks) like this: `Time`. To be safe, you might want to enclose all column names in backquotes.*

After the SQL statement is ready, line 448 uses the previously prepared **Statement** object named **sqlStmt** to execute the query:

```
448            ResultSet result = sqlStmt.executeQuery(selectStmt);
```

The results of the query are returned as a new table maintained by the **ResultSet** object named **result**.

The remainder of the **try** block—lines 449 through 484—goes through the rows in the **ResultSet** and displays the event list in the text area that appears underneath the monthly calendar. The **while** loop in lines 450 through 470 calls **result.next()** to extract one row of the result at a time and then get the fields from that row. Lines 452 through 456 call **result.getString()** to retrieve the text for the five fields—**Title**, **Location**, **EventTime**, **Contact**, and **Description**:

```
452              String title = result.getString(1);
453              String location = result.getString(2);
454              String time = result.getString(3);
455              String contact = result.getString(4);
456              String descr = result.getString(5);
```

To keep the application simple, I chose to display the event list as lines of text. You could also display the events in a structured manner, perhaps summarizing the time and title in a table and then displaying the description for a selected event in a text area (similar to the way the **jPOP3** application in Chapter 11 displays mail messages).

Lines 457 through 467 construct a **String** named **es** with details for the current event. Line 468 then adds that string to the text area named **eventsArea** (that's the text area underneath the monthly calendar):

```
468         eventsArea.append(es);
```

Line 469 keeps a count of the events in a variable named **count**. After the **while** loop finishes, lines 471 through 484 add a summary statement based on the event count. If the count is greater than zero, lines 471 through 478 display the total event count. If the count is zero, lines 479 through 484 display a helpful message about how to add a new event.

If there are any errors in the SQL query, the code in the **try** block throws a **SQLException**. The **catch** block, in lines 486 through 491, displays an error message in the text area where the event details would have appeared. The program does not exit, and the user can select a new date to view other events in the database.

ADDING A NEW EVENT TO THE DATABASE   To add a new event, the user clicks on the Add Event tab. This displays the user interface through which the user can enter information about the event and add it to the database. The event being added is assumed to be for the date currently selected by the user.

To understand how a new event is added, you should start by looking through the **createAddEvtPanel()** method, which constructs the user interface through which the user enters information for a new event. That method prepares and returns a **JPanel** that contains the text fields and the button for adding an event. The **init()** method calls **createAddEvtPanel()** when the **comcal** application is being initialized. If you look at line 163 of the **init()** method, you'll see that the panel created by **createAddEvtPanel()** is added to the tabbed pane as one of the tabs.

Getting back to the **createAddEvtPanel()** method, most of that method creates a hierarchy of panels to hold the labels and text fields for various fields of the new event. I will highlight some of the GUI components that are important to adding a new event.

Lines 502 and 503 add a label that displays the date for which the user is adding an event:

```
502         evtLabel = new JLabel("New event for: "+
503                     currentDateString, JLabel.CENTER);
```

The **currentDateString** is of the form December 24, 1999, and is updated whenever the user selects a new date. Notice that line 437 of the **displayEvents()** method updates the **evtLabel** so that the label always corresponds to the currently selected date.

Lines 516 through 519 create the text fields where the user enters the event's title, location, time, and contact information:

```
516         evtTitleTF = new JTextField(60);
517         evtLocTF = new JTextField(60);
```

```
518          evtTimeTF = new JTextField(60);
519          evtContactTF = new JTextField(60);
```

Later on, when the event is added, these fields are obtained by calling the **getText()** method of these components.

Another important element of an event is the description. Lines 532 and 533 create the text area for the event description. (A text area is meant for entering multiple lines of text, whereas a text field is for a single line of text.)

```
532          evtDescArea = new JTextArea(
533              "New event description goes here", 6, 40);
```

Line 534 places this text area in a scrolling pane so that the user can scroll through the text area (in case there is no room to display the text area in its entirety):

```
534          JScrollPane sp = new JScrollPane(evtDescArea);
```

I skipped over the most important GUI component for adding an event—the Add It! button that the user clicks to add the new event. Lines 504 and 505 create the Add It! button and set up the listener with the code to insert the event into the database:

```
504          evtAddBtn = new JButton("Add It!");
505          setAddEvtListener();
```

The JDBC code for inserting the new event is embedded in the **setAddEvtListener()** method, shown in lines 544 through 607. Lines 546 through 605 of this method define a new **ActionListener** object named **l**, and line 606 adds that as the listener for the **evtAddBtn**:

```
606          evtAddBtn.addActionListener(l);
```

The **ActionListener l** includes an **actionPerformed()** method that will be called whenever the user clicks on the Add It! button. As the name implies, the **actionPerformed()** method, shown in lines 548 through 604, performs the action associated with the Add It! button—the insertion of a new event into the database.

Because the JDBC calls can throw a **SQLException**, the database code is enclosed in the **try** block shown in lines 550 through 594. Lines 553 through 557 first retrieve the event details from the appropriate text fields of the user interface:

```
553              String title = evtTitleTF.getText();
554              String location = evtLocTF.getText();
555              String time = evtTimeTF.getText();
556              String contact = evtContactTF.getText();
557              String desc = evtDescArea.getText();
```

Line 558 then starts the construction of the SQL statement in a **String** named **insertStmt**:

```
558              String insertStmt = "INSERT INTO EventList (";
```

In this case, the SQL command is INSERT INTO, and the table name is **EventList**.

The remainder of the SQL statement depends on which of the event fields were entered by the user. For example, if the **title** string is not empty, the column name **Title** is added to the **insertStmt** string:

```
559        if(!title.equals("")) insertStmt += "Title, ";
```

After all of the required column names have been added, lines 568 and 569 add the remaining columns for the selected date:

```
568        insertStmt +=
569             "Month, Day, Year, EnteredBy) VALUES (";
```

Next, lines 570 through 588 prepare the values for each of these columns. The values of all text columns are enclosed in single quotes. One consequence of enclosing the text in single quotes is that any single quote that's part of the text must be replaced with two single quotes. Thus, the string *New Year's Eve* must be included in the SQL statement as **'New Year''s Eve'**, with the apostrophe after *Year* replaced by two single quotes. I wrote the **expandSingleQuotes()** method to accept a **String** and return a new **String** after replacing all of the single quotes in the original string with pairs of single quotes. The returned string is also enclosed in a pair of single quotes, ready to use as a value in the SQL INSERT INTO statement. Lines 609 through 626 show the **expandSingleQuotes()** method, which is implemented in a straightforward manner. The code simply searches for a single quote by calling the **indexOf()** method and expands each occurrence into a pair of single quotes.

The value for each column is prepared in the same manner. For example, lines 570 through 571 show how the event title is added to the SQL statement:

```
570        if(!title.equals(""))
571             insertStmt += expandSingleQuotes(title)
572                    + ", ";
```

If the title is not an empty string, line 571 calls **expandSingleQuotes()** to expand any single quotes in the title and then appends the title to the SQL statement. Line 572 adds a comma that separates one column's value from the next.

Lines 573 through 584 append the values of the other columns. Then lines 585 through 588 append the last four values—month, day, year, and a timestamp string for the **EnteredBy** column:

```
585        insertStmt +=
586             currentMonth+", "+currentDay+", "+
587             currentYear+", '"+thisApp.appName+" "+
588             thisApp.getTimeString()+"')";
```

The **insertStmt** string can be quite long, depending on the values of each of the columns in the **EventList** table. For example, here's a sample SQL statement prepared by the code in lines 553 through 588 for a fictitious event for August 7, 1999:

```
INSERT INTO EventList (Title, Location, EventTime,
Contact, Description, Month, Day, Year, EnteredBy)
VALUES ('event title', 'where''s the event?', '9:00 AM',
'contact info', 'Here''s a description (notice single quote)',
7, 16, 1999, 'Community Calendar Mar 10, 1999 13:17:46'
```

Notice that any single quotes in the values have been replaced by a pair of single quotes. Also, the last text field shows the timestamp generated by the **getTimeString()** method that line 588 calls.

After the SQL statement is ready, lines 590 and 591 call the **executeUpdate()** method of the previously created **Statement** object named **sqlStmt** to complete the SQL INSERT operation:

```
590         int result = sqlStmt.executeUpdate(
591                                     insertStmt);
```

If you compare these lines with line 448, which performs the SQL SELECT query, you'll notice that these lines call the **executeUpdate()** method and not the **executeQuery()** method that was called in line 448. Also, the return value from **executeUpdate()** is an integer, whereas **executeQuery()** returns a **ResultSet** object. The integer value indicates the number of rows affected by the SQL statement (for example, the number of rows inserted or deleted).

You have to remember whether to call **executeQuery()** or **executeUpdate()** whenever you send SQL commands to the JDBC server. Essentially, you must call **executeUpdate()** to execute an SQL INSERT, UPDATE, or DELETE statement that returns a row count or nothing. Always call **executeQuery()** to execute a SELECT statement and receive the result in a **ResultSet**.

After the SQL INSERT statement has executed successfully, line 592 calls **displayEvents()** to retrieve and display the events for the current date:

```
592         thisApp.displayEvents();
```

This ensures that the event display reflects the latest event added by the user.

Finally, line 593 calls **clearAddEvtPanel()** to clear all of the text fields in the Add Event tab:

```
593         thisApp.clearAddEvtPanel();
```

If you browse through the **clearAddEvtPanel()** method, shown in lines 628 through 635, you'll notice that the panel is cleared by calling the **setText()** method of all text fields to set the contents of each field to an empty string.

If any error occurs in the JDBC APIs, a **SQLException** is thrown. The **catch** block in lines 595 through 603 handles any such exception:

```
595             catch(SQLException ex)
596             {
597                 JOptionPane.showMessageDialog(
598                     thisApp.evtDescArea,
599                     ex.toString()+"\n"+
600                     "Could not update database!",
601                     "Community Calendar - Error",
602                     JOptionPane.ERROR_MESSAGE);
603             }
```

This exception-handling code calls the **showMessageDialog()** method of the **JOptionPane** class to display a dialog box with the cause of the exception plus a message indicating that the database could not be updated.

Servlets

Java Servlets
Three-Tiered Web Applications

Java Servlets

The first six chapters of this book focused exclusively on applets—small Java applications that run in a Java-capable Web browser. Applets were the first Java programs to become widely used on the Web. As Java has gained popularity among programmers, it has increasingly been used for server-side applications as well. One such server-side use of Java is to develop *servlets*— applications that run in a Java-capable Web server. This chapter introduces you to servlets and explains how to develop servlets by presenting several practical examples that you can study and use as the basis for your own servlets.

To develop servlets, you need a Web server capable of supporting servlets, the JDK, and the Java Servlet Development Kit, or JSDK. The JSDK provides a set of classes that constitute the servlet API. Because servlets are relatively new, this chapter starts with a brief introduction to the tools you need to start writing servlets. Then it offers a few examples that illustrate typical uses of servlets. You can also use a servlet as a gateway to a database. Chapter 14 discusses the use of servlets for database access in Web-based applications that employ a three-tiered client/server architecture.

You will find the following servlets in this chapter:

- ◆ **OrderBooks**—A servlet that demonstrates how to read data from a form (despite the promising name, it does not actually handle any book orders)

- ◆ **VCount**—A servlet that returns and updates a site visit counter

- ◆ **wrapper**—A servlet that appends a date and visit count to an HTML file

- ◆ **Feedback**—A servlet that accepts a feedback form and saves the feedback in a file

An Overview of Java Servlets

In concept, servlets are analogous to applets. Both applets and servlets reside on a server, but an applet runs in a Java-capable Web browser after the browser downloads the applet from the Web server. Because the Web browser is a client to the Web server, applets are referred to as client-side applications. A servlet, on the other hand, runs in a Java Virtual Machine (JVM) on the Web server. Thus, servlets are server-side applications.

Another difference between applets and servlets is that an applet typically produces some visible output, whereas servlets do not display anything. Instead, servlets perform specific tasks for the Web server. They are commonly used at Web sites to support interactive and dynamic Web pages.

A static Web page is an HTML file with some preset information. In contrast, an *interactive* Web page lets the user send information to the Web server and get back a response that differs depending on user input. A Web search engine such as Alta Vista (**http://www.altavista.com/**) is a good example of an interactive Web page; the user enters one or more keywords and the Alta Vista search engine returns an HTML document containing links to other Web pages that contain the search words. The HTML document returned by the search engine is *dynamic* because the contents of that page depend on what search words the user types; it's not a predefined, static document.

Another example of an interactive and dynamic Web page might be a form where the user can enter a stock ticker symbol and receive the latest quote for that stock. Yet another example might allow the user to subscribe to a magazine or register for a conference. The interaction might be as simple as letting users fill out a feedback form and submit comments that are then recorded in a file at the Web site.

To create an interactive Web page, you have to use certain HTML codes (to display the form that solicits user input) and implement special computer programs on the Web server. These programs process the user input (sent by the Web browser) and return requested information back to the user, usually in the form of a dynamic Web page—a page that is constructed on the fly by a computer program. Such programs are known as gateways because they typically act as a conduit between the Web server and an external source of information such as a database (even if the database is simply a collection of files).

Traditionally, Web sites have used gateway programs that are started by the Web server and that exchange information with the Web server using a standard protocol known as *Common Gateway Interface* (*CGI*). These stand-alone CGI programs can be written in any language (C, C++, Perl, Tcl/Tk, and even Java). One drawback of CGI programs is that the Web server has to start a new process to run a stand-alone CGI program whenever the server receives data from an HTML form.

Servlets provide functionality similar to that of CGI programs, but servlets avoid the overhead of new process startup. Typically, the Web server runs a JVM, and that JVM, in turn, loads and runs the servlets. The JVM runs a servlet in a Java thread, which is faster and requires fewer operating system resources than a new process. Additionally, the JVM can keep a servlet loaded and running so that a single instance can handle many future requests. This makes servlets more responsive than other CGI programs, especially ones written in scripting languages such as Perl. At the same time, servlets are portable to any system that supports Java, just as Perl CGI programs can run on any system with a Perl interpreter.

Many Web sites already use servlets extensively. While browsing the Web, you may have accessed some servlets without even realizing it. A giveaway that the Web server is using a servlet is the occurrence of **/servlet/** in the URL (in the same way that **/cgi-bin/** commonly appears in URLs that refer to CGI programs). Even if you have never seen a servlet in action, you'll be familiar with them after reading this chapter.

The next few sections explain how Java servlets work and what you need to develop servlets.

The Role of Java Servlets

A servlet performs specific tasks for a Web server and typically returns the results formatted as an HTML document (if necessary, servlets can also return images and other multimedia content). Often, the servlet program acts as a bridge between the Web server and some other repository of information such as a database. Figure 13-1 highlights the interrelationships among the Web browser, Web server, servlets, applets, and HTML documents. Web servers also serve images and other multimedia content, but the figure does not show these.

As Figure 13-1 shows, the Web browser running on the user's system uses the Hypertext Transfer Protocol (HTTP) to exchange information with a Web server. The Web server (also called the HTTP server) has access to the HTML documents, applets, and servlets residing on the server. Depending on the type of request from the browser, the Web server either serves an HTML document or an applet from its

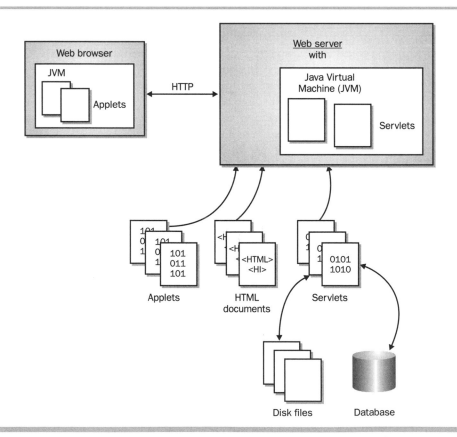

FIGURE 13-1.   The interrelationships among the Web browser, Web server, servlets, and applets.

own document directory or starts a servlet thread in its JVM. The applets run in the JVM in the Web browser, whereas servlets run in a JVM that's typically integrated with the Web server (although they may be implemented as separate but communicating processes). If necessary, the servlets may access other system resources such as disk files or databases.

When the Web browser receives a dynamic document from a Java servlet, the basic sequence of events is as follows:

1. The user clicks on some link on a Web page, and that causes the Web browser to request an HTML document that contains a form.

2. The Web server sends the HTML document with the form, which the browser displays.

3. The user fills in the fields of the form and clicks on the Submit button. The browser, in turn, sends the form's data using the GET or POST method (as specified by the **<form>** tag in the HTML form). In either method, the browser sends to the Web server the URL specified in the **<form>** tag's action attribute. That URL refers to the servlet that should process the form's data.

4. From the URL the Web server determines that it should activate the servlet listed in the URL and send the information to that servlet.

5. The servlet processes the information and returns a new MIME document to the Web browser. (MIME refers to Multipurpose Internet Mail Extension, an Internet standard described in RFC 1521 for attaching any type of data to a mail message. It is also used by Web servers when sending documents back to the Web browser.)

6. The Web browser displays the document received from the Web server. The information contained in that document depends on what the user entered in the HTML form. (Often the information may be nothing more than a confirmation from the server that the user's input has been received.)

To understand how servlets process data from an HTML form, you need to know how a Web browser sends form data to the Web server. The Web browser uses the **method** attribute of the **<form>** tag to determine how to send the form's data to the Web server. There are two submission methods:

◆ In the GET method, the Web browser submits the form's data as part of the URL.

◆ In the POST method, the Web browser sends the form's data separately from the URL.

The GET and POST methods are so called because the browser uses the HTTP GET and POST commands to submit the data. The GET command sends a URL to the Web server. This means that to send a form's contents to the server using the GET method, the browser must include all data in the URL. Because there is typically an upper limit on the length of a URL, the GET method cannot be used to transfer large amounts of form data from the browser to the server. The POST command, on the other hand, sends the form's data in a separate stream. Therefore, the POST method can send much larger amounts of data to the server.

Regardless of which method—GET or POST—is specified in the HTML form, a servlet can get the form's data by overriding specific methods in the **HttpServlet** class and calling other servlet API methods to retrieve specific parameters from the HTML form.

Because you design the form as well as the servlet that will process the form's data, you can select the method that best suits your needs. The basic guidelines for choosing a data submission method are as follows:

◆ Use GET to transfer a small amount of data, and use POST to send potentially large amounts of data. For example, GET is appropriate for a search form that solicits a few keywords from the user. On the other hand, you'd want to use POST for a feedback form with a free-form text-entry area because the user might enter considerable amounts of text.

◆ Use the GET method if you want to access the servlet without using a form. For example, if you want to access a servlet at the URL **http://www.someplace.com/ servlet/dbquery** with a parameter named **keyword** as input, you could invoke the servlet with a URL such as **http://www.someplace.com/servlet/ dbquery?keyword=Linux**. In this case, **Linux** is the value of the **keyword** parameter. If a servlet is designed to receive data with the POST method only, you cannot activate that servlet with a URL like this.

What You Need to Develop Servlets

You are probably anxious to try out some Java servlets and then learn how to write a servlet. Because servlets are used with a Web server, you'll need a Web server that supports servlets. There are two good choices:

◆ Sun's Java Web Server (**http://www.sun.com/software/jwebserver/index.html**)

◆ The Apache HTTP server (**http://www.apache.org/**) together with Apache JServ (**http://java.apache.org/**)

Additionally, if you want to develop servlets, you need the JDK and the JSDK (the Java Servlet Development Kit). The JSDK provides the servlet classes in the **javax.servlet** and **javax.servlet.http** packages. You have to use these classes when writing your own servlets.

If you want to get started quickly with servlet programming on a Windows 95/98 or NT system (or, for that matter, on a Sun Solaris/SPARC system), I recommend that you download the trial version of Sun's Java Web Server, because it's easy to install and it supports servlets right out of the box.

However, if you already run or are setting up a Web site critical to your business, you may decide to go with the Apache HTTP server. Apache happens to be the most popular Web server on the Internet (and it's free!). According to a March 1999 Netcraft Web Server Survey (**http://www.netcraft.com/survey/**), about 55 percent of the Web sites on the Internet use the Apache Web server. If you use Apache at your Web site, you can download Apache JServ and add support for Java servlets. Incidentally, the Apache Web server and Apache JServ will also work on Windows NT systems.

The next two sections briefly describe the installation and setup process for both the Java Web Server and the Apache HTTP server plus Apache JServ combination.

Sun's Java Web Server

Sun's Java Web Server is a Web server with built-in support for servlets. It's simple to set up and manage. The best part is that it comes with nearly two dozen servlets with full source code that you can try out and study. The Java Web Server is available for Solaris/SPARC and Windows 95/98/NT environments. It's a commercial product, but Sun allows you to download, install, and evaluate the Java Web Server free of charge for 30 days. To download the trial version of the Java Web Server, go to the URL **http://www.sun.com/software/jwebserver/try/index.html** and follow the appropriate links. At the time of this writing, Java Web Server is at version 1.1.3.

For a Windows system, the trial version of Java Web Server 1.1.3 comes in a self-extracting executable file named **jwsr1_1_3-win-try-gl.exe** (about 8MB in size). After downloading the file, run it either from the Start->Run menu or by typing **start jwsr1_1_3-win-try-gl.exe** in an MS-DOS prompt window. An installation program will guide you through the installation process. If you stay with the default choices, the Java Web Server will be installed in the **c:\JavaWebServer1.1.3** directory.

To start the Java Web server, switch to drive C and type **cd\JavaWebServer1.1.3\bin** in an MS-DOS prompt window. Then type **start httpd** to start the Web server. By default, the Java Web server listens on port 8080. Sun chose a port number larger than 1024 as the default so that any user can install and run the Web server. If the server had used port 80, the default specified in the HTTP specification, only system administrators would be able to install the server, at least on UNIX and Windows NT systems. (Windows 95 and 98 systems do not have the concept of a privileged user.)

To verify that the Java Web Server is working, go to the Web browser and enter **http://localhost:8080/** as the URL. (If your system is not connected to the Internet, use **http://127.0.0.1:8080/** as the URL so that the **localhost** name does not have to be translated into an IP address.) You must specify 8080 as the port number; otherwise, the browser assumes port 80 by default. Figure 13-2 shows the initial home page served by the Java Web Server.

In the left-hand column of the initial home page, you can see a link that says View Sample Servlets. Click on that link. Figure 13-3 shows the new Web page, with links for a number of sample servlets.

If you click on the link for one of the servlets, you'll see a brief description of the servlet as well as a link to try the servlet and a link to view the source code. For example, if you click on the Simple link and then the Try It link underneath the Simple Servlet header, the servlet will run and the output shown in Figure 13-4 will appear.

Next click the Back button on the browser and then click the Source link underneath the Simple Servlet header. Figure 13-5 shows the resulting display of the source code of the **SimpleServlet** servlet. (Depending on your browser, you may get a dialog box asking you to save the source file or open it; you can view the source code if you open it.)

If you study the source code for the servlet and compare it with the HTML output in Figure 13-4, you can begin to see how you prepare HTML content in a servlet.

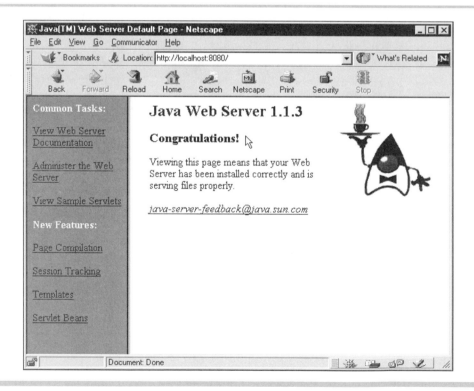

FIGURE 13-2.   Home page displayed after Java Web Server 1.1.3 has been installed.
The Duke logo is a trademark or registered trademark of Sun Microsystems, Inc. in the United States and other countries.

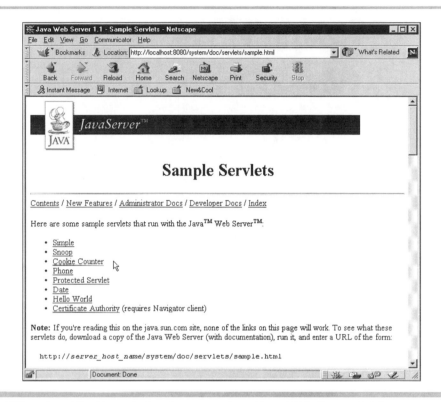

FIGURE 13-3. The Sample Servlets page from Java Web Server 1.1.3.

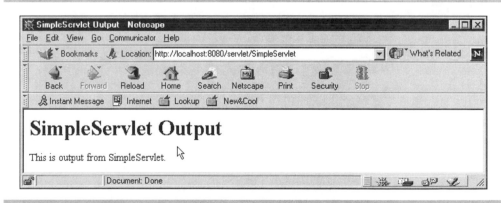

FIGURE 13-4. Output from **SimpleServlet**.

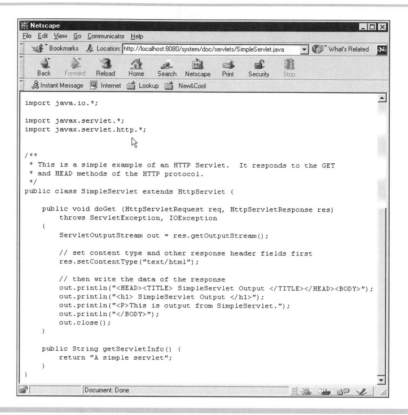

```
import java.io.*;

import javax.servlet.*;
import javax.servlet.http.*;


/**
 * This is a simple example of an HTTP Servlet.  It responds to the GET
 * and HEAD methods of the HTTP protocol.
 */
public class SimpleServlet extends HttpServlet {

    public void doGet (HttpServletRequest req, HttpServletResponse res)
        throws ServletException, IOException
    {
        ServletOutputStream out = res.getOutputStream();

        // set content type and other response header fields first
        res.setContentType("text/html");

        // then write the data of the response
        out.println("<HEAD><TITLE> SimpleServlet Output </TITLE></HEAD><BODY>");
        out.println("<h1> SimpleServlet Output </h1>");
        out.println("<P>This is output from SimpleServlet.");
        out.println("</BODY>");
        out.close();
    }

    public String getServletInfo() {
        return "A simple servlet";
    }
}
```

FIGURE 13-5. Source code for **SimpleServlet**.

PROGRAMMER'S NOTE   *If you want to develop your own servlet, download the JSDK from* **http://java.sun.com/products/servlet/index.html**. *Unpack the files and place the* **jsdk.jar** *file in the* **jre/lib/ext** *directory of the JDK install directory. (If you installed JDK1.2 in* **c:\jdk1.2**, *place the* **jsdk.jar** *file in* **c:\jdk1.2\jre\lib\ext** *directory.) To test the servlets with the Java Web Server, place them in the* **servlets** *directory in the location where the Java Web Server is installed. (The default directory is* **c:\JavaWebServer1.1.3\servlets**.)*

The Apache HTTP Server and Apache JServ

This section provides a brief overview of the installation and setup process for the Apache HTTP server and Apache JServ. I assume that you are running the server on a UNIX system (I tested these steps on a Linux system).

To add servlet support to the Apache HTTP server, download the source distribution of the latest version of Apache HTTP (1.3.4 at the time of this writing) from **http://www.apache.org/**. Assuming that you downloaded the **apache_1.3.4.tar.gz** file (approximately 1.3MB), unpack the files using the **tar zxvf apache_1.3.4.tar.gz** command in a suitable directory, such as **/usr/local**. This creates the source tree in the **/usr/local/apache_1.3.4** directory. Go to that directory and type the command **./configure —prefix=/usr/local/apache** (specifying the directory where you want to install the Apache HTTP server). After the **configure** script has finished, you can download the other components for the Apache JServ installation.

To install Apache JServ, you have to do the following:

◆ Download the latest Apache JServ source distribution from **http://java.apache.org/** (the version at the time of this writing is 1.0b3). The installation steps are explained later in this section.

◆ Download the Java Servlet Development Kit (JSDK) 2.0 from **http://java.sun.com/products/servlet/index.html**. Unpack the distribution in a directory such as **/usr/local** so that JSDK is installed in the **/usr/local/JSDK2.0** directory of the system.

◆ Download and install the latest JDK for your system.

Assuming that you downloaded the **Apache-JServ-1.0b3.tar.gz** file (approximately 351K), unpack the distribution with the command **tar zxvf Apache-JServ-1.0b3.tar.gz** in a suitable directory, such as **/usr/local**. This creates the source tree in the **/usr/local/Apache-JServ-1.0b3** directory. Go to that directory and type the following command (I placed the command in a file and then executed that file from the shell prompt):

```
./configure \
--with-apache-src=/usr/local/apache_1.3.4 \
--enable-apache-conf \
--prefix=/usr/local/jserv \
--with-jdk-home=/usr/local/jdk117_v1a \
--with-jsdk=/usr/local/JSDK2.0/lib/jsdk.jar
```

Note that this command requires the location of the Apache HTTP source, the location of the JSDK jar file, and the installation directory for the JDK. After this command finishes, type **make** to build Apache JServ. Then type **make install** to install the JServ jar file in the directory specified in the **--prefix** option.

After building Apache JServ, switch to the Apache HTTP directory (**/usr/local/apache_1.3.4**) and type the **make** command in that directory. This builds the Apache HTTP server. Finally, type **make install** to install the Apache HTTP server in the **/usr/local/apache** directory. When installed in this way, the Apache HTTP server will serve documents from the **/usr/local/apache/htdocs** directory.

Once both Apache JServ and the Apache HTTP server are built, open the Apache configuration file (**/usr/local/apache/conf/httpd.conf**) in a text editor and append the following line to it:

```
Include /usr/local/Apache-JServ-1.0b3/example/jserv.conf
```

Then save the **httpd.conf** configuration file. The newly added line incorporates the JServ configuration file into the Apache HTTP configuration.

After you have completed the configuration step, you can start the Apache HTTP server with the command **/usr/local/apache/bin/apachectl start**. To verify that Apache JServ is working, start a Web browser and enter the URL **http://*your.hostname.com*/example/Hello/** (specify your Web server's host name or IP address). You should see a Web page with a message indicating that Apache JServ is working.

You can also test the Apache server installation using a low-tech approach that does not require a browser. At the server's UNIX prompt, type **telnet localhost 80**. After the connection is made, type **GET /example/Hello/ HTTP/1.0** and press ENTER twice. (The blank line is part of the HTTP protocol; it indicates the end of an HTTP request.) The line you typed happens to be an HTTP request to retrieve a URL. In this case, the URL **/example/Hello/** refers to a servlet (included in Apache JServ). The Apache Web server responds back with some header information followed by whatever the **Hello** servlet sends back. In this case, **Hello** sends HTML text with the message that Apache JServ is working. The following listing shows a transcript of the telnet command and the response from the server (the lines you type are annotated and shown in italic):

```
telnet localhost 80              ** You type this line
Trying 127.0.0.1...
Connected to localhost.
Escape character is '^]'.
GET /example/Hello/ HTTP/1.0     ** You type this line

HTTP/1.1 200 OK
Date: Sat, 13 Mar 1999 15:09:46 GMT
Server: Apache/1.3.4 (Unix) ApacheJServ/1.0b3
Connection: close
Content-Type: text/html

<HTML><HEAD><TITLE>
Example Apache JServ Servlet
```

```
</TITLE></HEAD><BODY bgcolor="#FFFFFF">
<H1>Example Apache JServ Servlet</H1>
<H2> Congratulations, Apache JServ is working!<br>
</BODY></HTML>
Connection closed by foreign host.
```

The "Server:" line in the header identifies the Web server. In this example, the Web server is Apache 1.3.4 with Apache JServ 1.0b3. That's another clue that you have successfully installed Apache JServ.

Initially, Apache JServ is configured with only one servlet URL (**/example**). If you want to place servlets in a specific directory, say, **/usr/local/apache/servlet** and refer to them with a URL of the form **http://*your.hostname.com*/servlet/*xyz*/** (where *xyz* is the name of a servlet class), you have to log on as **root** (the super user in UNIX) and perform the following steps:

1. Open the file **/usr/local/Apache-JServ-1.0b3/example/jserv.conf** in a text editor. Insert the line **ApJServMount /servlet /servlet** in this file and save the file.

2. Open the file **/usr/local/Apache-JServ-1.0b3/example/jserv.properties** in a text editor. Locate the line that starts with **zones=**, and edit that line to read **zones=example,servlet**. Then add a new line with the text **servlet.properties=/usr/local/apache/servlet/servlet.properties**. Save the **jserv.properties** file.

3. Copy the **/usr/local/Apache-JServ-1.0b3/example/example.properties** file to **/usr/local/apache/servlet/servlet.properties**.

4. Edit the **/usr/local/apache/servlet/servlet.properties** file, changing the line that begins with **repositories=** to read **repositories=/usr/local/apache/servlet**.

5. Restart the Apache HTTP server (so that it reads the changed configuration files) by typing the command **/usr/local/apache/bin/apachectl restart**.

After performing these steps, you should be able to place servlet classes in the **/usr/local/apache/servlet** directory and refer to them with a URL of the form **http://*your.hostname.com*/servlet/*xyz*/** (where *xyz* is the name of a servlet class).

How HTML Forms Relate to Servlets

Before you jump into servlet programming, you need to learn how to prepare and use interactive Web pages—those Web pages that look like data-entry forms where you can type in the requested information and click on a Submit button to send the information back to the Web server. When writing a servlet, you would use the

JSDK classes to obtain the input that users submit through HTML forms. It can be helpful to know how to create the data-entry forms through which you solicit information from users.

There is also a relationship between servlets and HTML forms, because servlets process the data that the user enters in the form. One of the attributes of the form specifies the name of the servlet that receives the input from the form. Additionally, each element of the form has an identifying name that helps the servlet isolate the user's input for that element. This section highlights the aspects of an HTML form that matter when you are writing a servlet to handle form data.

Consider a typical book order form that lets the user sign in using an ID and password, select one or more books, select the payment option, fill out the credit card information, and submit the order. Figure 13-6 shows a simple book order form.

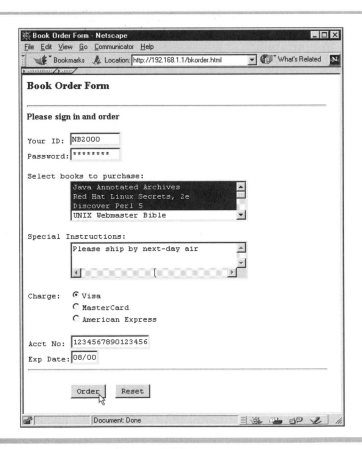

FIGURE 13-6. A book order form in HTML.

The following listing shows the HTML text used to display the book order form:

```
<html>
<head>
<title>Book Order Form</title>
</head>
<body>
<form action="/servlet/OrderBooks/" method=post>
<h3> Book Order Form</h3>
<hr>
<b>Please sign in and order</b>
<pre>
Your ID: <input type=text size=10 name=id>
Password:<input type=password size=10 name=passwd>

Select books to purchase:
        <select name=books size=4 multiple>
          <option>Java Annotated Archives
          <option>Red Hat Linux Secrets, 2e
          <option>Discover Perl 5
          <option>UNIX Webmaster Bible
          <option>Success with Windows 95
          <option>X Window System Programming
          <option>Object-oriented programming in C++
          <option>Visual C++ Developer's Guide
          <option>Borland C++ Developer's Guide
          <option>Turbo C++ Bible
          <option>Microsoft Macro Assembler Bible
        </select>

Special Instructions:
        <textarea name=instructions rows=2 cols=35></textarea>

Charge:  <input type=radio checked name=card value="Visa">Visa
         <input type=radio name=card value="MC">MasterCard
         <input type=radio name=card value="Amex">American Express

Acct No: <input type=text name=acct size=16>
Exp Date:<input type=text name=expire size=5>
```

```
<hr>
        <input type=submit value="Order">   <input type=reset>
</pre>
</form>
</body>
</html>
```

This is a good example of the typical HTML elements that you can use in interactive forms. You can also see how the **<form>** element associates a servlet URL with a form. Here are the key points to note in this HTML sample:

◆ The entire form is enclosed within **<form>** and **</form>** tags. The **action** attribute of the **<form>** tag specifies the URL of the servlet that processes this form's data. The **method** attribute specifies how the Web browser sends the form's data to the Web server.

◆ The **<input>** tag defines a number of common form elements, such as single-line text fields, password fields, radio buttons, and submit buttons.

◆ The **<select>** element defines menus. Each menu item is defined by an **<option>** tag.

◆ The **<textarea>** element allows the user to enter multiple lines of text.

◆ Most importantly, each of the tags—**<input>**, **<select>**, and **<textarea>**—has a **name** attribute that identifies that input parameter. In the servlet that handles this form's data, you have to use the value of the **name** attribute to indicate which input parameter's value you want to retrieve.

At the heart of an HTML form is a **<form>** element that starts with a **<form>** tag and ends with a **</form>** tag. The attributes of the **<form>** tag specify the servlet that processes this form's input and how the Web browser sends the user's input to the Web server. A typical **<form>** element definition has the following structure:

```
<form method="post" action="/servlet/servletName">
...(other form elements appear here)
</form>
```

The **<form>** tag's **action** attribute specifies a URL for the servlet that you have designed to handle the form's input. You can use an absolute URL that specifies the full server name as well as the path name for the servlet. Often, however, you'd use a relative URL that identifies the directory on your Web server where the servlets reside.

Sun's Java Web Server uses **/servlet** as the default location of servlets (this is essentially an alias for the actual directory where the servlet class files are stored). That's why you typically see **/servlet** in the **action** attribute of most forms designed to work with servlets.

The **method** attribute indicates how the Web browser sends form input back to the server. You can specify one of the following submission methods:

◆ The POST method causes the browser to send the data in a two-step process. First the browser contacts the server specified in the **action** attribute. Then, after a successful connection is established, the browser sends the form's data to the server, which in turn provides the data to the servlet.

◆ The GET method causes the browser to append the form's data to the URL specified in the **action** attribute and send everything to the Web server in a single step. A question mark (**?**) separates the data from the URL.

If you don't specify a method, the browser uses the GET method by default.

OrderBooks

A Servlet That Reads an HTML Form

The previous sections explain how servlets work, what you need to use and develop servlets, and how HTML forms are linked to servlets. This section shows you a simple Java servlet that retrieves the parameters that the user enters in the book order form shown in the section "How HTML Forms Relate to Servlets" (see Figure 13-6).

Note that the book order form uses a **<form>** tag that begins with the following:

```
<form action="/servlet/OrderBooks/" method=post>
```

This tells you that you need a servlet named **OrderBooks** to process the data sent by this form.

In the companion CD-ROM's **ch13\OrderBooks** directory, you'll find the files necessary to try out the **OrderBooks** servlet. If you are using Sun's Java Web Server, copy the **bkorder.html** file to the **c:\JavaWebServer1.1.3\public_html** directory, and copy the **OrderBooks.class** file to the **c:\JavaWebServer1.1.3\servlets** directory (assuming that you installed the Java Web Server in the default directory). Then load the **bkorder.html** file in a Web browser. (If everything is running on the same PC, use the URL **http://127.0.0.1:8080/bkorder.html**.) You should see a book order form similar to the one shown in Figure 13-6. Fill in the fields and click on the Submit button. Figure 13-7 shows the HTML document returned by **OrderBooks** if you were to click the Order button from the screen shown in Figure 13-6.

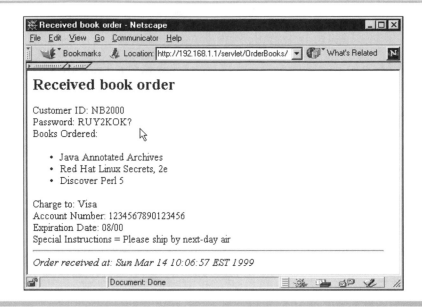

FIGURE 13-7. The **OrderBooks** servlet displays the parameters from the book order form.

Now that you have seen what the **OrderBooks** servlet does, here's the listing of the **OrderBooks.java** file that implements the servlet:

```
1  //-------------------------------------------------------------
2  // File: OrderBooks.java
3  // A servlet that demonstrates how to process data from
4  // a form.
5  //-------------------------------------------------------------
6  import java.util.*;
7  import java.io.*;
8  import javax.servlet.*;
9  import javax.servlet.http.*;
10 public class OrderBooks extends HttpServlet
11 {
12     public void doPost (HttpServletRequest request,
13                         HttpServletResponse response)
14                         throws ServletException, IOException
15     {
```

```
16        StringBuffer buffer = new StringBuffer();
17        String title = "Received book order";
18        // Set content type to HTML
19        response.setContentType("text/html");
20        // Write the response using HTML tags
21        PrintWriter out = response.getWriter();
22        buffer.append("<html><head><title>");
23        buffer.append(title);
24        buffer.append("</title></head><body bgcolor=\"#ffffff\">");
25        buffer.append("<h2>" + title + "</h2>");
26        buffer.append("Customer ID: ");
27        buffer.append(request.getParameter("id"));
28        buffer.append("<br>");
29        buffer.append("Password: ");
30        buffer.append(request.getParameter("passwd"));
31        buffer.append("<br>");
32        buffer.append("Books Ordered: ");
33        String books[] = request.getParameterValues("books");
34        if(books == null)
35            buffer.append("NONE<br>");
36        else
37      {
38            buffer.append("<ul>");
39            for(int i = 0; i < books.length; i++)
40            {
41                buffer.append("<li>");
42                buffer.append(books[i]);
43            }
44            buffer.append("</ul>");
45      }
46        buffer.append("Charge to: ");
47        buffer.append(request.getParameter("card"));
48        buffer.append("<br>");
49        buffer.append("Account Number: ");
50        buffer.append(request.getParameter("acct"));
51        buffer.append("<br>");
52        buffer.append("Expiration Date: ");
53        buffer.append(request.getParameter("expire"));
54        buffer.append("<br>");
```

```
55        buffer.append("Special Instructions = ");
56        buffer.append(request.getParameter("instructions"));
57        buffer.append("<hr>");
58        buffer.append("<em>Order received at: ");
59        buffer.append(new Date().toString());
60        buffer.append("</em>");
61        buffer.append("</body></html>");
62        out.println(buffer.toString());
63        out.close();
64    }
65 }
```

A real-life **OrderBooks** servlet would use the customer's ID and password to authenticate the customer and retrieve the customer record from a database. Then the servlet should probably display all of the information that will be used to process the order and allow the customer to confirm that information. Only then should the servlet actually record the order in the database. In this case, the **OrderBooks** servlet simply repeats back the parameters received from the order form.

To use the classes in the JSDK, you need to include the following **import** statements in a servlet:

```
8 import javax.servlet.*;
9 import javax.servlet.http.*;
```

Like everything else in Java, a servlet is also a class. Line 10 defines **OrderBooks** as a subclass of the **HttpServlet** class (from the **javax.servlet.http** package):

```
10 public class OrderBooks extends HttpServlet
```

This is how you would declare any servlet that is designed to work with the HTTP protocol (which is how the Web server communicates with the Web browser).

You would implement the servlet by overriding the appropriate methods of the **HttpServlet** class. If you are designing the servlet to handle HTML form data, the method of form data submission—GET or POST—determines the method you have to override. If the form's data is submitted using the GET method, you should override the **doGet()** method. On the other hand, if the **method** attribute of the **<form>** tag is POST, you should override the **doPost()** method.

The **OrderBooks** servlet expects the form data to be sent by the POST method, so it overrides the **doPost()** method, which starts on lines 12 through 14:

```
12    public void doPost (HttpServletRequest request,
13                        HttpServletResponse response)
14                          throws ServletException, IOException
```

The method receives two arguments: an **HttpServletRequest** and an **HttpServletResponse**. As line 14 shows, the **doPost()** method throws two exceptions: **ServletException** and **IOException**. Apart from declaring the function like this, there is no need to handle any exceptions in the method.

In the body of the **doPost()** method, you would use the **HttpServletRequest** interface to access HTTP-protocol-specified header information and any parameters sent by the Web browser. In particular, you would call this interface's **getParameter()** method to obtain the value of a parameter whose name matches the name assigned with the **name** attribute in the HTML tag. Recall from the discussion in the section "How HTML Forms Relate to Servlets" that the **name** attribute of the **<input>**, **<select>**, and **<textarea>** HTML tags identifies the input parameter. You have to use that name as an argument when retrieving the parameter value with the **getParameter()** method.

The **HttpServletResponse** interface is used to send data back to the Web browser. You would set the MIME type of the servlet response by calling a method of this interface. For example, line 19 sets the response type to **text/html** (this means that the servlet sends back a text file with HTML tags):

```
19          response.setContentType("text/html");
```

To actually send the response to the Web browser, you would get an output stream by calling a method of the **HttpServletResponse** interface, and then you would write the servlet's response to that output stream. For example, in the **OrderBooks** servlet, line 21 calls the **getWriter()** method of the **HttpServletResponse** interface named **response** to get a **PrintWriter** stream for formatted text output:

```
21          PrintWriter out = response.getWriter();
```

You can send HTML text to the Web browser client by calling the **println()** or **print()** method of this **PrintWriter**. However, instead of writing text a line at a time, it's better to accumulate the text in a **StringBuffer** and then send the accumulated text with a single call to the **println()** method. The **OrderBooks** servlet illustrates this approach. Line 16 initializes a **StringBuffer** named **buffer**:

```
16          StringBuffer buffer = new StringBuffer();
```

The servlet's response is then accumulated in this buffer through calls to the **append()** method of **StringBuffer**. For example, lines 22 through 24 append the HTML **<head>** and **<body>** tags to the buffer:

```
22          buffer.append("<html><head><title>");
23          buffer.append(title);
24          buffer.append("</title></head><body bgcolor=\"#ffffff\">");
```

Line 27 shows how to get the value of a parameter from the HTML form and append that parameter to the **StringBuffer**:

```
27          buffer.append(request.getParameter("id"));
```

In this case, the value of the parameter named **id** is obtained by calling the **getParameter()** method of the **HttpServletRequest** interface named **request**. The returned **String** is then appended to the **StringBuffer**.

If a parameter can have multiple values, you have to call the **getParameterValues()** method. In the book order form, the customer may select multiple books from the selection menu (in the HTML form that menu is assigned the name **books**). Lines 33 through 45 show how to get the values of the **books** parameter and format them in an unnumbered list enclosed in the HTML tags **<ul>** and **</ul>**:

```
33          String books[] = request.getParameterValues("books");
34          if(books == null)
35              buffer.append("NONE<br>");
36          else
37          {
38              buffer.append("<ul>");
39              for(int i = 0; i < books.length; i++)
40              {
41                  buffer.append("<li>");
42                  buffer.append(books[i]);
43              }
44              buffer.append("</ul>");
45          }
```

Line 33 calls **getParameterValues()** to get the values in a **String** array named **books[]**. If the return value is **null**, line 35 appends the string NONE. Otherwise, the **for** loop in lines 39 through 43 formats each value as an entry in an unnumbered list.

After everything has been appended to the **StringBuffer**, line 62 calls the **println()** method of the **PrintWriter** to send the response to the client:

```
62          out.println(buffer.toString());
```

After the response has been written to the **PrintWriter**, line 62 closes the stream:

```
63          out.close();
```

A Visit Counter Servlet

Chapter 6 presented a **VisitCount** applet that relies on a Perl CGI program to get and update a site visit counter. You can easily replace that CGI program with a servlet that maintains a site visit count in a file on the Web server. The **VCount** servlet shows you how to do this.

You should first test the **VCount** servlet using the **VisitCount** applet from Chapter 6. Then you can study the source code for the **VCount** servlet. By studying the **VCount** servlet, you'll learn how to read from and write to files on the server.

Using VCount

All of the files for the **VCount** servlet are in the **ch13\vcount** directory of the companion CD-ROM. I have also included the **VisitCount** applet and a sample HTML file named **Counter.html** that embeds appropriate parameters into the **VisitCount** applet so that it will work with the **VCount** servlet.

If you are testing with Sun's Java Web Server on a Windows 95/98 or NT PC, follow these steps to prepare for the testing (the steps assume that you have installed the Java Web Server in the **c:\JavaWebServer1.1.3** directory):

1. Copy the **Counter.html**, **VisitCount.class** (the applet), and **count.txt** files from the **ch13\vcount** directory of the CD-ROM to the **c:\JavaWebServer1.1.3\ public_html** directory. This is the directory from which the Java Web Server serves its documents. Note that any user must be able to write to the **count.txt** file (although this is not an issue on Windows 95 or 98 systems).

2. Copy the **VCount.class** file (the servlet) from the CD-ROM's **ch13\vcount** directory to the **c:\JavaWebServer1.1.3\servlets** directory. The Java Web Server uses this directory for its servlet classes.

PROGRAMMER'S NOTE *On the Apache HTTP server with Apache JServ, copy the **Counter.html**, **VisitCount.class**, and **count.txt** files to the document root directory (the directory from which the server serves documents). Copy the **VCount.class** file to the directory where servlet classes reside. Make sure that **count.txt** has write permissions for everyone (use the command **chmod 666 count.txt** to set the permission). Also, edit the **cgiurl** parameter in the **Counter.html** file to a URL that refers to the **VCount** servlet.*

Now open the **Counter.html** file in a Web browser, using an appropriate URL. If you are running the Java Web Server and the Web browser on the same PC, use **http://127.0.0.1:8080/Counter.html** as the URL. Figure 13-8 shows some typical output. Note that if you change the URL, you must also change the URL shown in the **Counter.html** file (see the listing following the next paragraph).

Although the **VisitCount** applet was originally written to get the visitor count from a CGI program, you can use it with the **VCount** servlet by specifying a URL that refers to the servlet. Here is a full listing of the **Counter.html** file, showing the parameters accepted by the **VisitCount** applet:

```html
<html>
<head>
<title>VisitCount applet</title>
</head>
<body>
<applet code=VisitCount.class width=400 height=60>
  <param name=message value="Visitor Number:">
  <param name=cgiurl value="http://127.0.0.1:8080/servlet/VCount/">
  <param name=msgfont value="Helvetica,BOLD,18">
  <param name=countfont value="Courier,BOLD,30">
  <param name=msgcolor value="0000ff">
  <param name=countcolor value="ff0000">
This is the VisitCount Java applet.
To run it you need a Java-capable browser.
</applet>
</body>
</html>
```

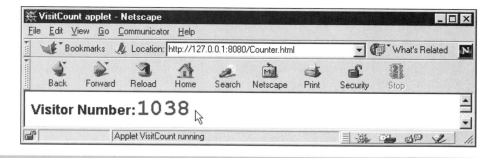

FIGURE 13-8. The **VisitCount** applet displaying a visitor count from the **VCount** servlet.

The **cgiurl** parameter specifies the URL of the CGI program that the **VisitCount** applet uses to get the visitor count. In this case, **cgiurl** specifies the URL of the **VCount** servlet. Because that servlet returns the visitor count in the expected format, everything works fine and the **VisitCount** applet can display the visitor count.

If you want to use the applet/servlet combination to display a visitor count on your Web page, embed the entire **<applet>** tag in the Web page at an appropriate location.

VCount

Understanding VCount

The following listing shows the **VCount.java** file that implements the **VCount** servlet. I explain the code in the section that follows the listing.

```
1  //-------------------------------------------------------------
2  // File: VCount.java
3  //
4  // A servlet that returns the visit count from a file and also
5  // increments the count stored in the file. The count is returned
6  // in the first line of a plain text document. You can use the
7  // VisitCount applet from Chapter 6 to test this servlet.
8  //-------------------------------------------------------------
9  import java.io.*;
10 import javax.servlet.*;
11 import javax.servlet.http.*;
12
13 public class VCount extends HttpServlet
14 {
15     public static BufferedReader inc = null;
16     public static PrintWriter outc = null;
17     public static String cfilename = "count.txt";
18     public void service(HttpServletRequest request,
19                         HttpServletResponse response)
20                 throws ServletException, IOException
21     {
22         PrintWriter out;
23         String docroot = request.getRealPath("/");
24         String cfname = docroot + cfilename;
25         int countnow = 0;
26         String line = "0";
27         synchronized(this)
```

```
28        { // Read line of text from file
29            inc = new BufferedReader(new FileReader(cfname));
30            line = inc.readLine();
31            inc.close();
32        }
33        try
34        {  // Convert to integer
35            countnow = Integer.parseInt(line);
36        }
37        catch(NumberFormatException e2){countnow = 0;}
38        int count = countnow + 1;
39        synchronized(this)
40        { // Save new count in file
41            outc = new PrintWriter(
42                new BufferedWriter(new FileWriter(cfname)));
43            if(outc != null) outc.println(""+count);
44            outc.close();
45        }
46        // Set content type to plain text
47        response.setContentType("text/plain");
48        // Then write a line with the value of the count
49        out = response.getWriter();
50        out.println(""+countnow);
51        out.close();
52    }
53 }
```

ANNOTATIONS

The **VisitCount** applet expects to receive a text response with the visitor count on a single line of text. The **VCount** servlet is designed to do exactly that. Lines 47 through 51 take care of sending the visitor count back to the client:

```
47        response.setContentType("text/plain");
48        // Then write a line with the value of the count
49        out = response.getWriter();
50        out.println(""+countnow);
51        out.close();
```

Line 47 sets the response type to plain text. Line 49 gets the **PrintWriter**. Line 50 then writes out the count (from a variable named **countnow**), and line 51 closes the **PrintWriter**.

The rest of the servlet deals with getting the visitor count from a file and saving an updated count in that file. The count is assumed to be in a text file named **count.txt** located in the Web server's document root (the directory from which the Web server serves all documents). Line 17 declares a **String cfilename** to hold the filename:

```
17      public static String cfilename = "count.txt";
```

Line 23 gets the document root by calling the **getRealPath()** method with a root directory ("/") as the argument:

```
23          String docroot = request.getRealPath("/");
```

The **getRealPath()** method returns the full path name of the directory where the Web server expects its documents. For example, on a UNIX system with the Apache HTTP server installed in the **/usr/local/apache** directory, the document root would be **/usr/local/apache/htdocs**.

Line 24 constructs a full path name for the visit count file by concatenating the document root with the **cfilename** string:

```
24          String cfname = docroot + cfilename;
```

Lines 27 through 32 show the code that reads the count from the file. The code is enclosed in a **synchronized** block to ensure that two threads do not access the count file at the same time:

```
27          synchronized(this)
28          { // Read line of text from file
29              inc = new BufferedReader(new FileReader(cfname));
30              line = inc.readLine();
31              inc.close();
32          }
```

Line 29 opens **BufferedReader** to read from that file. Line 30 reads a single line and line 31 closes the **BufferedReader**.

The **try** and **catch** blocks in lines 33 through 37 convert the line of text into an integer value stored in the **countnow** variable:

```
33          try
34          {  // Convert to integer
35              countnow = Integer.parseInt(line);
36          }
37          catch(NumberFormatException e2){countnow = 0;}
```

If there is any error, line 37 sets **countnow** to zero.

Line 38 increments the count:

```
38          int count = countnow + 1;
```

Lines 39 through 45 then use another **synchronized** block to open the count file and save the incremented count as a line of text:

```
39        synchronized(this)
40        { // Save new count in file
41            outc = new PrintWriter(
42                new BufferedWriter(new FileWriter(cfname)));
43            if(outc != null) outc.println(""+count);
44            outc.close();
45        }
```

A Wrapper for Your Home Page

I call this servlet **wrapper** because it essentially acts as a wrapper around the HTML file that constitutes your home page. The basic idea is to send the HTML file to the browser, but to append some useful information such as the time of last visit, the visitor number, and the current time at the server. The time of last visit is stored using a cookie, so you'll learn how to receive and send cookies by studying this servlet's code. You'll understand the idea when you try out the servlet and then read through the source code.

Using wrapper

All of the files you need to test the **wrapper** servlet are in the **ch13\wrapper** directory of this book's companion CD-ROM. To try out the servlet, follow these steps (I provide specific details for Java Web Server):

1. In the Web server's document directory, rename the HTML file for your home page (usually named **index.html**) to **home.html**. If you installed the Java Web Server in the default directory, the document directory is **c:\JavaWebServer1.1.3 \ public_html** and the home page file is **index.html**. Just to be safe, you may also want to make another copy of the original **index.html** file.

2. Open the **home.html** file in a text editor and add a **<base>** tag right after the **<head>** tag. The **<base>** tag should have the following form: **<base href="http://*your.server.com*/"></base>**, where *your.server.com* is the domain name of your server.

3. Create a new **index.html** file with the following lines in it (you'll find an **index.html** file in the **ch13\wrapper** directory; you can simply copy that file to your Web server):

```
<html>
<head>
```

```
<meta http-equiv="Refresh" content="0;
                  url=/servlet/wrapper?file=home.html">
</head>
</html>
```

4. Copy the **count.txt** file to the document root of your Web server. Everyone must be able to read from and write to this file. (This means that on UNIX systems, you have to change the file permission to allow read and write operations by everyone.)

5. Copy the **wrapper.class** file from the **ch13\wrapper** directory of the CD-ROM to the directory where servlet classes are kept. For a typical Java Web Server installation on a Windows PC, you should copy the **wrapper.class** file to the **c:\JavaWebServer1.1.3\servlets** directory.

After completing these steps, try loading your home page with the usual URL, such as **http://*your.server.com*/** or **http://*your.server.com*/index.html**, to see the result from the **wrapper** servlet. Figure 13-9 shows the output from the **wrapper** servlet when I followed these steps on my PC running the Java Web Server.

FIGURE 13-9. A home page from the **wrapper** servlet.

The Duke logo is a trademark or registered trademark of Sun Microsystems, Inc. in the United States and other countries.

Notice that the very end of the page shows the visitor number, the time of last visit, and the time at the server. These are the fields added by the **wrapper** servlet.

Understanding wrapper

wrapper

The following listing shows the **wrapper.java** file that implements the **wrapper** servlet. I explain the pertinent parts of the code in the section that follows the listing.

```
1  //--------------------------------------------------------------
2  // File: wrapper.java
3  //
4  // A servlet that echoes back a specified HTML file and appends
5  // additional information: visitor count, date of last visit,
6  // and current time at the server. The date of last visit is
7  // stored in a cookie. The visitor count is done the same way
8  // as in the VCount servlet.
9  //
10 // To use this as a wrapper for your home page, do the following:
11 //
12 // (1) Copy the home page HTML file (usually index.html) to
13 //     another file, say, home.html
14 // (2) Add a <base> tag to the home.html file (right after
15 //     <head>):
16 //             <base href="http://your.server.com/"></base>
17 // (3) Change index.html (or whatever your home page file
18 //     is called) to the following:
19 //     <html>
20 //     <head>
21 //         <meta http-equiv="Refresh"
22 //          content="0; url=/servlet/wrapper?file=home.html">
23 //     </head>
24 //     </html>
25 // (4) Place the count.txt file in the document root of
26 //     your Web server. Everyone must be able to read from
27 //     and write to this file.
28 // (5) Place the wrapper.class file in the servlet directory
29 //     of your Web server.
30 // (6) Now try loading your home page with the usual URL
31 //     such as http://your.server.com/ to see the result
32 //     from the wrapper servlet.
33 //--------------------------------------------------------------
```

```
34  import java.io.*;
35  import java.util.*;
36  import javax.servlet.*;
37  import javax.servlet.http.*;
38  public class wrapper extends HttpServlet
39  {
40      private static String domain;
41      private static BufferedReader inc = null;
42      private static PrintWriter outc = null;
43      private static String cfilename = "count.txt";
44      private static String hfilename = "main.html";
45      public void doGet(HttpServletRequest request,
46                          HttpServletResponse response)
47      throws ServletException, IOException
48      {
49          domain = request.getServerName();
50          String docroot = request.getRealPath("/");
51          String cfile = docroot + cfilename;
52          // URL can include filename as follows:
53          //     /servlet/wrapper?file=home.html
54          // Get the file parameter
55          String filep = request.getParameter("file");
56          if(filep != null) hfilename = filep;
57          String hfile = docroot + hfilename;
58          int countnow = 0;
59          String line = "0";
60          synchronized(this)
61        { // Read line of text from visit count file
62              inc = new BufferedReader(new FileReader(cfile));
63              line = inc.readLine();
64              inc.close();
65          }
66          try
67          {   // Convert to integer
68              countnow = Integer.parseInt(line);
69          }
70          catch(NumberFormatException e){countnow = 0;}
71          int count = countnow + 1;
72          synchronized(this)
73          { // Save new count in file
74              outc = new PrintWriter(
```

```
75              new BufferedWriter(new FileWriter(cfile)));
76          if(outc != null) outc.println(""+count);
77          outc.close();
78      }
79      // Open the HTML file being wrapped
80      inc = new BufferedReader(new FileReader(hfile));
81      StringBuffer buffer = new StringBuffer();
82      while(true)
83  {
84          line = inc.readLine();
85          if(line == null) break;
86          if(line.indexOf("</body>") != -1 ||
87              line.indexOf("</BODY>") != -1)
88        {
89              int indx = line.indexOf("</body>");
90              if(indx == -1) indx = line.indexOf("</BODY>");
91              String part = line.substring(0, indx);
92              buffer.append(part);
93              part = line.substring(indx); // rest of the line
94              buffer.append("<hr>");
95              buffer.append(
96                  "<font size=+1><em>Visitor number: </em><b>"+
97                  countnow+"</b></font><br>\n");
98              buffer.append("<em>Time of last visit: ");
99              buffer.append(lastVisitDate(request));
100             buffer.append("</em><br>\n");
101             buffer.append("<em>Current time at server: "+
102                             new Date().toString());
103             buffer.append("</em>\n");
104             buffer.append(part);
105             continue;
106         }
107         buffer.append(line+"\n");
108     }
109     // Set content type to HTML
110     response.setContentType("text/html");
111    // Set the lastvisit cookie
112     long time = new Date().getTime();
113     Cookie lastvisit = new Cookie("lastvisit", ""+time);
114     lastvisit.setDomain(domain);
115     lastvisit.setPath("/servlet/");
```

```
116         lastvisit.setMaxAge(31536000); // expire in one year
117         lastvisit.setComment("Time of last visit");
118         response.addCookie(lastvisit);
119         // You can set the content length, if you want:
120         // response.setContentLength(buffer.length());
121         // but it's not necessary.
122         PrintWriter out = response.getWriter();
123         out.println(buffer.toString());
124         out.close();
125         inc.close();
126     }
127     private String lastVisitDate(HttpServletRequest request)
128     {
129         // Get all the cookies in the request and
130         // look for the cookie named "lastvisit"
131         Cookie cookies[] = request.getCookies();
132         if(cookies == null) return "No cookies!";
133         for(int i=0; i<cookies.length; i++)
134         {
135             if(cookies[i].getName().equals("lastvisit"))
136             {
137                 long lvt = 0L;
138                 try
139                 {
140                     String s = cookies[i].getValue();
141                     lvt = Long.parseLong(s);
142                 }
143                 catch(NumberFormatException e){lvt = 0L;}
144                 if(lvt != 0L)
145                 {
146                     Date d = new Date(lvt);
147                     return d.toString();
148                 }
149             }
150         }
151         return("UNKNOWN");
152     }
153 }
```

As you found out in the previous section, the **wrapper** servlet sends a specified HTML file to the client, adding three items to the HTML text:

◆ The visitor count, obtained from a file named **count.txt**

◆ The time of last visit, obtained from a cookie

◆ The current time at the server

Lines 58 through 78 get the visitor count and save an updated count in the **count.txt** file. These steps are the same as in the **VCount** servlet described earlier in this chapter.

In addition to inserting extra HTML text, the **wrapper** servlet also sends back a cookie to the browser to save the time of the current visit. The next few sections describe how the extra text is inserted, how the time of last visit is obtained from a cookie, and how the current time is sent back in a cookie.

ADDING EXTRA HTML TEXT   The servlet stores the base filename for the HTML file in a **String** named **hfilename**:

```
44        private static String hfilename = "main.html";
```

The filename **main.html** is used if the servlet is invoked without any parameters. If the servlet URL includes a **file** parameter, the value of that parameter is used as the filename. Lines 55 and 56 take care of this step:

```
55        String filep = request.getParameter("file");
56        if(filep != null) hfilename = filep;
```

Line 55 gets the value of the **file** parameter by calling the **getParameter()** method of the **HttpServletRequest** interface. For example, if the servlet URL is **/servlet/wrapper?file=home.html**, the value of the **file** parameter is the string **home.html**. If the **file** parameter is present, line 56 places that filename in the **hfilename** string.

The document root directory is added to the front of **hfilename** to come up with the full path name of the HTML file that the servlet should send to the client. Line 50 gets the real path name corresponding to the document root directory, which is represented by a single forward slash (/) in a URL:

```
50        String docroot = request.getRealPath("/");
```

Line 57 adds the **docroot** string to the front of **hfilename** and comes up with the full path name:

```
57        String hfile = docroot + hfilename;
```

To send the file to the client, line 80 opens a **BufferedReader** to read from that HTML file:

```
80          inc = new BufferedReader(new FileReader(hfile));
```

Line 81 creates a **StringBuffer** where all of the HTML text will accumulate before being sent to the client:

```
81          StringBuffer buffer = new StringBuffer();
```

The **while** loop, shown in lines 82 through 108, reads a line at a time from the HTML file and keeps appending the lines to the **StringBuffer**.

Line 84 reads a line, and line 85 breaks the **while** loop if the line is **null** (meaning that the file has ended):

```
84              line = inc.readLine();
85              if(line == null) break;
```

The **wrapper** servlet is designed to insert the extra text just before the **</body>** tag, which marks the end of the HTML text's body. Lines 86 and 87 in the **while** loop check for the presence of the **</body>** tag (either all lowercase or all uppercase) in the **String** named **line** that contains the line just read from the file:

```
86              if(line.indexOf("</body>") != -1 ||
87                  line.indexOf("</BODY>") != -1)
```

If the **</body>** tag is found, lines 89 through 93 extract everything before the **</body>** tag, append that to the **StringBuffer**, and save the rest of the line for later use:

```
89                  int indx = line.indexOf("</body>");
90                  if(indx == -1) indx = line.indexOf("</BODY>");
91                  String part = line.substring(0, indx);
92                  buffer.append(part);
93                  part = line.substring(indx); // rest of the line
```

Lines 89 and 90 figure out where the tag starts. Line 91 extracts a substring containing everything before the tag, and line 92 appends that to the **StringBuffer**. Line 93 then saves the remainder of the line in a **String** named **part**.

Line 94 adds an **<hr>** tag to place a horizontal ruler in the HTML text:

```
94                  buffer.append("<hr>");
```

The extra text is placed after this horizontal ruler. Lines 95 through 97 add the visitor count with appropriate HTML formatting tags:

```
95                  buffer.append(
96                      "<font size=+1><em>Visitor number: </em><b>"+
97                      countnow+"</b></font><br>\n");
```

Specifically, the font size is increased with a **<font size=+1>** tag, and the visitor count is shown in boldface by enclosing it between **** and **** tags. The visitor count comes from the integer variable named **countnow**, which was set up on line 68.

Next, lines 98 through 100 insert the time of last visit:

```
98              buffer.append("<em>Time of last visit: ");
99              buffer.append(lastVisitDate(request));
100             buffer.append("</em><br>\n");
```

Line 98 adds the leading text. Line 99 calls the **lastVisitDate()** method (described later in the section "Getting the Time of Last Visit from a Cookie") to get the time of last visit and insert it into the HTML text. Line 100 adds some more HTML tags to break the line.

Lines 101 through 103 insert into the **StringBuffer** the current time at the server:

```
101             buffer.append("<em>Current time at server: "+
102                            new Date().toString());
103             buffer.append("</em>\n");
```

As you can see from line 102, the current time is obtained by creating a new **Date** object and then converting it to a **String** by calling the **toString()** method.

Finally, line 104 inserts into the **StringBuffer** the remainder of the line following the **</body>** tag:

```
104             buffer.append(part);
```

Line 107 of the **while** loop simply adds lines that do not contain the **</body>** tag to the **StringBuffer**:

```
107            buffer.append(line+"\n");
```

After the **while** loop finishes, lines 110 through 118 prepare the response header (including a cookie with the current time, as explained in the next section). Then lines 122 through 124 open a **PrintWriter** stream to the client, write out the contents of the **StringBuffer**, and close the stream:

```
122         PrintWriter out = response.getWriter();
123         out.println(buffer.toString());
124         out.close();
```

SENDING THE TIME OF LAST VISIT IN A COOKIE   The wrapper servlet uses a mechanism called *HTTP Cookie*, or simply *cookie*, to save the time of last visit on the client. A cookie is basically a small amount of data with a specified name that the Web server can send to the browser for storage at the client system. Later on, whenever the Web browser connects to the same server, it sends back the cookies that were set by that server.

Many Web sites use cookies to store user preferences to personalize the Web site for a specific user. Essentially, the Web server retrieves a previously set cookie and sends back a Web page based on the contents of that cookie. Web sites also use cookies to store other information such as user ID and password (usually encoded in some way).

While the Web browser is running, it maintains the cookies in memory, but when it exits, it saves the cookies in a text file. For example, on a Windows system running Netscape Communicator, the cookies are stored in a file named **cookies.txt** in your user directory (usually in **c:\Program Files\Netscape\Users**_yourname_, where _yourname_ is your Windows user name). You can open the file in a word processor or text editor and see the various types of cookies stored on your system. Each line starts with a domain name that identifies the server that stored the cookie. There is also a URL path fragment, usually **/cgi-bin/**, that represents the CGI program that set the cookie. The URL path can also be anything else, such as a single **/** or, for servlets, **/servlet/**.You'll also see a cookie's name and its value.

Each cookie has the following attributes:

◆ A name that identifies the cookie

◆ A value for the cookie (typically a bit of text that has some meaning to the server)

◆ A domain name (usually the full domain name of the server, but this can be a part of the domain name or even an IP address)

◆ A URL path fragment (usually the first part of the servlet or CGI program's URL that comes after the server's name)

◆ An optional keyword **secure** that, if present, causes the cookie to be sent to the server only if the communication channel is secure

The Web server sends the cookie to the browser by adding the following line to the HTTP header:

```
Set-Cookie: name=value; expires=DATE;\
path=URLpath; domain=DOMAIN_NAME [; secure]
```

The semicolon-separated fields represent the attributes of a cookie: the name and value, the URL path, the domain name, and the **secure** flag (which is optional).

For example, the **wrapper** servlet sets a cookie named **lastvisit** that has as its value the current time in binary format (a long integer with the number of milliseconds elapsed since January 1, 1970 00:00 GMT). Here is a sample HTTP header that sets the **lastvisit** cookie for a server in the **myserver.net** domain:

```
Set-Cookie: lastvisit=921547422413;\
 expires= Wednesday, 15-Mar-00 01:23:42 GMT;\
 domain=myserver.net; path=/servlet/
```

The Web browser then stores the cookie in its internal memory and, at the end of the session, saves the cookie in a text file. When that same Web browser accesses a URL with the **myserver.net** domain name and **/servlet/** in the path name (for example, with a URL such as **http://www.myserver.net/servlet/getCookie/**), the browser sends back the **lastvisit** cookie in a **Cookie:** header with the following format:

```
Cookie: lastvisit=921547422413
```

PROGRAMMER'S NOTE   *You can read Netscape's HTTP Cookie specification at **http://www.netscape.com/ newsref/std/cookie_spec.html**. You may also want to browse the Cookie Central Web site at http://www.cookiecentral.com/ for lots of useful information about cookies.*

If you want to send a cookie from a servlet, you do not have to actually prepare and send a **Set-Cookie:** header. Instead, all you need to do is create a **Cookie** (a class in the **javax.servlet.http** package), set its attributes, and add the cookie by calling the **addCookie()** method of the **HttpServletResponse** interface. Lines 112 through 118 show how the **wrapper** servlet sets the **lastvisit** cookie to the current time:

```
112        long time = new Date().getTime();
113        Cookie lastvisit = new Cookie("lastvisit", ""+time);
114        lastvisit.setDomain(domain);
115        lastvisit.setPath("/servlet/");
116        lastvisit.setMaxAge(31536000); // expire in one year
117        lastvisit.setComment("Time of last visit");
118        response.addCookie(lastvisit);
```

Line 112 gets the current time. Line 113 creates a new **Cookie** object with **lastvisit** as the name and the time as the value. Line 114 sets the cookie's domain attribute, and line 115 sets the path to **/servlet/** (because that path appears in the URL for the **wrapper** servlet). Line 116 sets the expiration date for the cookie. The **setMaxAge()** method requires the number of seconds after which the cookie will expire (the browser discards expired cookies). Line 118 calls **addCookie()** to add the **lastvisit** cookie to the header.

That's all there is to setting a cookie from a servlet. The next section describes how to get the cookies from the HTTP header.

GETTING THE TIME OF LAST VISIT FROM A COOKIE   The **lastVisitDate()** method, shown in lines 127 through 152, gets the cookies from the header, searches for the cookie named **lastvisit**, and converts the time into a human-readable representation.

Line 131 calls the **getCookies()** method of the **HttpServletRequest** interface to retrieve an array of cookies:

```
131        Cookie cookies[] = request.getCookies();
```

Because the browser sends back all cookies for a server, it may very well return many different cookies.

If the **cookies** array is **null**, line 132 returns a **String** saying that there are no cookies:

```
132         if(cookies == null) return "No cookies!";
```

The **for** loop in lines 133 through 150 goes through each entry in the **cookies** array. Line 135 looks for the cookie named **lastvisit**:

```
135             if(cookies[i].getName().equals("lastvisit"))
```

This line calls the **getName()** method to get a cookie's name and then calls the **equals()** method to check whether the name matches **lastvisit**.

If the cookie's name is **lastvisit**, lines 140 and 141 get the cookie's value and convert it into a long integer value:

```
140                 String s = cookies[i].getValue();
141                 lvt =  Long.parseLong(s);
```

Then line 146 creates a **Date** object with the long integer value of time, and line 147 returns a **String** representation of the **Date** object:

```
146                 Date d = new Date(lvt);
147                 return d.toString();
```

If the **lastvisit** cookie is not found, line 151 returns the UNKNOWN string as the last visit time:

```
151         return("UNKNOWN");
```

A Feedback Servlet

Often Web sites provide a form where visitors can provide feedback or request further information. Web sites call this a feedback form or a guest book. The **Feedback** servlet accepts the input from a feedback form and saves it in a text file.

Using Feedback

The files for the **Feedback** servlet are in the **ch13\Feedback** directory of this book's companion CD-ROM. Specifically, the **feedback.html** file contains the HTML form where the visitor enters information. The **Feedback.class** file is the servlet class. You have to copy these files to the appropriate directories of your Web server before you can try out the servlet. Perform the following steps to copy the files to the proper directories:

1. Copy the **Feedback.class** file to the directory where the servlet classes are stored. For the Java Web Server, copy that class file to the **c:\JavaWebServer1.1.3\servlets** directory.

2. Copy the **feedback.html** file to the Web server's document root directory where all other documents are kept. For the Java Web Server, copy the **feedback.html** file to the **c:\JavaWebServer1.1.3\public_html** directory.

3. Create an empty text file named **feedback.txt** in the document root directory. Make sure that all users can read from or write to this file. If you are using the Java Web Server, create the **feedback.txt** file in the **c:\JavaWebServer1.1.3\public_html** directory.

Now open the **feedback.html** file in a Web browser using the usual URL for your Web server. If you are testing with the Java Web Server on a PC, use the URL **http://127.0.0.1:8080/feedback.html** to view the HTML form. Figure 13-10 shows how the HTML form, filled out and ready for submission, typically appears.

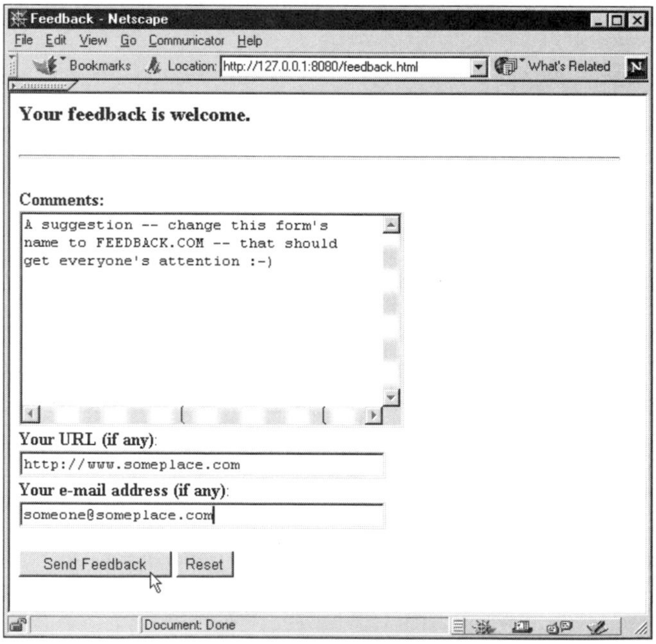

FIGURE 13-10. A feedback form with the fields filled in.

After filling out the fields in the form, the Web page visitor clicks on the Send Feedback button to submit the form. The **Feedback** servlet then gets the form's data and appends the data to the **feedback.txt** file. After that, the servlet sends back some HTML text with a thank-you message.

You can browse the **feedback.txt** file simply by entering your Web server's URL with the **feedback.txt** filename (for example, **http://127.0.0.1:8080/feedback.txt**).

Understanding Feedback

Feedback

The following listing shows the **Feedback.java** file that implements the **Feedback** servlet. I explain the code in the section that follows the listing.

```
1  import java.io.*;
2  import java.util.*;
3  import javax.servlet.*;
4  import javax.servlet.http.*;
5
6  public class Feedback extends HttpServlet
7  {
8      private static final String fbfilename = "feedback.txt";
9      public static PrintWriter outfb = null;
10     public void doPost (HttpServletRequest request,
11                         HttpServletResponse response)
12         throws ServletException, IOException
13         {
14             String remoteHost = request.getRemoteHost();
15             String remoteIP = request.getRemoteAddr();
16             String docroot = request.getRealPath("/");
17             String fbname = docroot + fbfilename;
18             String dateString = new Date().toString();
19             String comment = request.getParameter("comment");
20             String url = request.getParameter("url");
21             String email = request.getParameter("e-mail");
22             synchronized(this)
23             { // Save user feedback in file
24                 outfb = new PrintWriter(
25                             new BufferedWriter(
26                                 new FileWriter(fbname, true)));
27                 if(outfb != null)
28                 {
29                     outfb.println(dateString);
30                     outfb.print("From: ");
```

```
31              if(remoteHost != null)
32                  outfb.print(remoteHost+" : ");
33              else
34                  outfb.print("Uknown Host : ");
35              if(remoteIP != null)
36                  outfb.println(remoteIP);
37              else
38                  outfb.println("Unknown IP Address");
39              outfb.println("E-Mail: "+email);
40              outfb.println("URL: "+url);
41              outfb.println("Comment: "+comment);
42              outfb.println("---------------------------");
43              outfb.close();
44          }
45      }
46      // Send a response back to the client
47      String title = "Thank you for the feedback";
48      response.setContentType("text/html");
49      PrintWriter out = response.getWriter();
50      out.println("<html><head><title>");
51      out.println(title);
52      out.println(
53          "</title></head><body bgcolor=\"#ffffff\">");
54      out.println("<h3>" + title + "</h3>");
55      out.println(
56          "Thank you! Your feedback is appreciated.");
57      out.println("</body></html>");
58      out.close();
59  }
60 }
```

ANNOTATIONS

The **Feedback** servlet is implemented in a straightforward manner. It gets the values of all of the parameters in the form and then writes them out to the **feedback.txt** file. The only detail you may not have seen yet is how to open an output stream so that it appends to the **feedback.txt** file. You'll learn the details soon, but first let's go through the **feedback.html** file that displays the HTML form through which the user enters the feedback (see Figure 13-10).

```
<html>
<head>
<title>Feedback</title>
</head>
<body>
<h3>Your feedback is welcome.</h3>
<hr>
<form method="post" action="/servlet/Feedback/">
<b>Comments:</b><br>
<textarea name="comment" rows="10" cols="40">
</textarea><br>
<b>Your URL (if any)</b>:<br>
<input type="text" name="url" value="http://"
              size=40 maxlength=60><br>
<b>Your e-mail address (if any)</b>:<br>
<input type="text" name="e-mail" size=40 maxlength=60><br><br>
<input type=submit value="Send Feedback">  <input type=reset>
</form>
</body>
</html>
```

The **<form>** tag's **action** attribute specifies that this form's data is processed by the **Feedback** servlet (that's what the URL **/servlet/Feedback/** means). The **method** attribute says that the form's data is submitted by the POST method. This means that the **Feedback** servlet should override the **doPost()** method.

The form has three user input areas:

◆ A **<textarea>** element named **comment** where the visitor enters comments

◆ An **<input>** field named **e-mail** for the visitor's e-mail address

◆ An **<input>** field named **url** for the visitor's home page URL

This means that the **Feedback** servlet should call **getParameter()** with these three names to get the values of these fields.

Now let's look at the **Feedback** servlet's code. Like other servlets, **Feedback** is defined as a subclass of **HttpServlet**:

```
6 public class Feedback extends HttpServlet
```

It also overrides the **doPost()** method, as shown in lines 10 through 12:

```
10     public void doPost (HttpServletRequest request,
11                         HttpServletResponse response)
12         throws ServletException, IOException
```

The feedback filename is stored in the **String** named **fbfilename**:

```
8      private static final String fbfilename = "feedback.txt";
```

Because the feedback file will be in the document root directory of the Web server, lines 16 and 17 construct the full path name of the feedback file:

```
16             String docroot = request.getRealPath("/");
17             String fbname = docroot + fbfilename;
```

Line 16 gets the real path name (for example, **c:\JavaWebServer1.1.3\public_html**) corresponding to the root URL (/). Line 17 adds this path name to the front of the **feedback.txt** filename.

Before starting to write the feedback to the file, the servlet gathers all necessary information. This is done because the actual writing operation will be enclosed in a **synchronized** block to ensure that multiple threads can save comments in the same file and not get in one another's way.

Lines 14 and 15 get the host name and IP address of the client system where the Web browser is running:

```
14             String remoteHost = request.getRemoteHost();
15             String remoteIP = request.getRemoteAddr();
```

Line 18 gets the current date as a string (so the feedback entry can be timestamped):

```
18             String dateString = new Date().toString();
```

Lines 19 through 21 get the three parameters named **comment**, **url**, and **e-mail** from the request sent by the Web browser:

```
19             String comment = request.getParameter("comment");
20             String url = request.getParameter("url");
21             String email = request.getParameter("e-mail");
```

This is where the code refers to the names used for various fields in the HTML form.

After all of the information is ready, the servlet writes the feedback data to the feedback file in a **synchronized** block to protect against multiple threads writing to the same file. The skeleton of the **synchronized** block is as follows:

```
22             synchronized(this)
23             { // Save user feedback in file
24                 outfb = new PrintWriter(
25                             new BufferedWriter(
26                                 new FileWriter(fbname, true)));
27                 if(outfb != null)
28                 {
```

```
29                          outfb.println(dateString);
... print other lines to the feedback file...
43                          outfb.close();
44                  }
45              }
```

Lines 23 through 26 show a crucial step for the servlet—the creation of a **PrintWriter** that appends to the feedback file. The trick is to start with a **FileWriter** created with **new FileWriter(fbname, true)**, as shown on line 26. The **boolean** argument **true** indicates that you want to append to the file (instead of writing at the beginning of the file). Line 25 creates a **BufferedWriter** from that **FileWriter**. Then line 24 creates the **PrintWriter** named **outfb** with that **BufferedWriter**. The end result is that when you print anything to the **PrintWriter outfb**, the lines are appended to the current contents of the file. This is exactly what you want to do when saving feedback comments in a file—simply keep appending to a file to accumulate all comments.

After the **PrintWriter outfb** has been created successfully, lines 29 through 42 write out various fields to the file by calling the **print()** or **println()** method. The **println()** method adds a line-ending character and moves to the next line after printing the text, whereas **print()** doesn't.

The last step is to close the **PrintWriter** and end the **synchronized** block, which allows other threads to write to the feedback file:

```
43              outfb.close();
```

After saving the feedback, the servlet sends some HTML text with a thank-you message to the client. Lines 47 through 58 show these steps. As in other servlets, line 48 sets the content type to HTML and line 49 gets the **PrintWriter** for writing text to the client:

```
48              response.setContentType("text/html");
49              PrintWriter out = response.getWriter();
```

Then lines 50 through 57 print HTML text to the client. Finally, line 58 closes the **PrintWriter** used to write to the client:

```
58              out.close();
```

## CHAPTER 14

Three-Tiered Web Applications

Accessing a Database with a Three-Tier
   Web Application (dbaccess)

Chapter 13 provided an overview of servlet programming and showed you how to implement some simple servlets. This chapter turns to the general topic of Web-based applications in which servlets play an important role. In particular, it focuses on Web applications based on a three-tiered application architecture, with the Web server and Java servlets playing a prominent role in the middle tier, acting as intermediaries between the clients in the first tier and the database servers in the third tier.

The chapter starts with an overview of three-tiered architecture. The overview also briefly discusses application servers and Enterprise JavaBeans, which brings the JavaBeans component model to the server. (Chapters 7 and 8 cover Java beans.) The overview is followed by a simple three-tiered Web application that accesses a database through servlets running on a Java-capable Web server in the middle tier. The sample application illustrates how to retain state information using the session management facilities of the Java servlet API.

You will find the following Web application in this chapter:

◆ **dbaccess**—A sample three-tiered Web application that accesses a database

An Overview of the Three-Tiered Web Application Architecture

When the Web first became popular, companies began setting up Web sites simply to have a presence on the Internet. These corporate Web sites typically provided public relations and advertising information. Nowadays, however, more and more companies are starting to use the Web to conduct business or what is commonly referred to as electronic commerce (or e-commerce for short). A typical e-commerce Web site might allow the user to browse an online catalog of products, place an order by filling out a form, and check the status of an order. All of these actions require access to the corporate database. The Web server prepares the catalog by formatting data obtained from the company's products database. Placing an order involves entering information into the database, and checking order information requires querying the database to check the status. To conduct business, corporations need to make their existing data available to users over the Web. Web applications help corporations accomplish this goal.

Web applications are distributed applications that use the Web browser, the Web server, and standard Internet protocols to provide access to existing corporate data that often resides in older databases. The Web server acts as a gateway to corporate data, and the Web browser is turning into a universal client through which users access the corporate data. Java plays an important role. Java applets augment the Web browser by providing application-specific user interface and display data. On the server, Java servlets perform various computation and database access functions.

As corporations begin to rely on Web applications for e-commerce, the software industry is moving toward a standard Web application architecture and a well-defined Web application framework. The architecture defines how the components of a Web application are partitioned and how these parts interrelate. The partitioning allows an individual part (such as the user interface or the database structure) to be changed easily without affecting other parts. The application framework provides the APIs and conventions to create each part of the Web application, from the user interface to the database access components.

The next few sections explain a popular Web application architecture and describe Enterprise JavaBeans, which forms an important part of any Java-based Web application framework.

Problems with Two-Tiered Client/Server Applications

The traditional client/server architecture, described in Chapter 11, consists of two tiers—client and server—that communicate using a protocol. A common type of two-tiered client/server application is one in which the server is a database server and the client is a GUI application written in C++ or Visual Basic and designed to run on Windows. You have seen examples of this type of client/server application in Chapter 12 (except that there the client is a Java application that can run on any system that supports Java).

Traditional two-tiered client/server applications have several drawbacks:

- **Tight coupling between client and database.** The client application includes all of the logic needed to retrieve data from the database, apply any business logic to the data, and display the data in a user interface. In particular, the client's code includes detailed information about the data layout (table names and column names) of the database. This means that any change in the database tables affects the client application.

- **Fat client syndrome.** Because the client has a lot of functionality, it tends to be a large application. This is what is referred to as fat client syndrome, literally because the client's code size is large. The problem with fat clients is that you need a powerful system to run the client application.

- **Applications that are difficult to manage and upgrade.** By design, each user's system must have the client application installed. Essentially, the clients are distributed on systems throughout the network. This means that when the client application is upgraded (perhaps to handle a change in the database or to provide some new functionality), a copy of the upgraded client has to be installed at each client system. This can be a significant problem for organizations with thousands of networked users.

As you will see next, these problems can be avoided by inserting a middle tier that essentially insulates the client from the database server.

The Emergence of the Three-Tiered Web Application Architecture

With the advent of the Web server, the Web browser became a standard client application on each user's system. Initially, a rudimentary form of three-tiered architecture emerged, with the Web server as the middle tier between the Web browser and other servers such as databases. The Web server used CGI programs to get corporate data from databases and sent that data to the Web browser in the form of HTML documents. As Web browsers began supporting Java applets, Web servers also began to serve executable content in the form of Java applets. These applets run on Java-capable Web browsers and provide an application-specific user interface and enhanced display capabilities.

Many Web servers now incorporate Java Virtual Machine and run Java servlets on the server. These servlets take the place of CGI programs and perform tasks such as accessing a database and processing the data retrieved from the database server. APIs such as JDBC help the Java servlets access any database in a standard manner.

The three-tiered architecture has evolved, and a Java-capable Web browser has emerged as the universal client. The middle tier is usually a Java-capable Web server with servlets and possibly some CGI programs. The third tier is the database server. Figure 14-1 shows this three-tiered architecture for Web applications. Note that this architecture does not necessarily imply that the middle tier and the third tier are on two separate computers. Sometimes the middle-tier servers and the third-tier database run on the same computer. The three-tiered architecture is about the partitioning of a Web application's code, not the physical location of the partitioned code.

This three-tiered architecture overcomes the shortcomings of the two-tiered client/server applications as follows:

◆ **Loose coupling between client and database.** With the data access functionality moved to the middle tier, the client does not need any knowledge of the database structure. Even when applets are used, they provide the user interface and handle the presentation of information, but they do not directly access the database server. That step is performed by going through an object (such as a servlet) in the middle tier. This means that the database layout or database access methods can be changed without having to change the client.

◆ **Thin clients.** The client portion of a three-tiered Web application consists of dynamic HTML pages and Java applets that execute in a Java-capable Web browser. This results in a thin client compared to the client application in traditional client/server architecture. The Java-capable Web browser is the

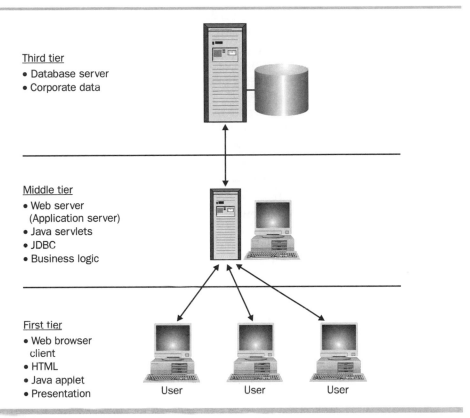

Third tier
- Database server
- Corporate data

Middle tier
- Web server
  (Application server)
- Java servlets
- JDBC
- Business logic

First tier
- Web browser
  client
- HTML
- Java applet
- Presentation

User   User   User

FIGURE 14-1. Three-tiered Web application architecture.

universal container in which all client applications run in the three-tiered architecture. The user accesses all three-tiered Web applications through a single Web browser.

◆ **Applications that are easy to manage and upgrade.** With the universal Java-capable Web browser as the client in a three-tiered architecture, there is nothing to manage or upgrade at the client systems. The applets, HTML content, servlets, and other Java objects are all managed at the middle-tier server. Upgrading a three-tiered Web application simply requires placing the new version of applets and servlets on the middle-tier server. The client browsers get the new version the next time the user accesses the server.

Although the three-tiered architecture has these advantages, you do need adequate network bandwidth to transfer data between the three tiers. For example, when Java applets are used, the applet code has to be downloaded to the browser before the applet can start. That can take some time over a slow network connection. This, however, is not a problem for corporate intranets using high-speed local area networks.

Another problem with the three-tiered model is the inherent lack of state information in the Web. The browser makes a separate HTTP request for each image embedded in an HTML document. Also, the server does not retain any information about the browser from one request to the next. This can be a problem for a Web application. For example, suppose that one screen shows an HTML form where the user enters a user name and password to log on to the application. The next screen shows a form where the user can enter a query for the application. A Web server does not provide any mechanism to remember the user's information from one screen to the next. However, developers have overcome this problem by using mechanisms such as cookies (see Chapter 13) to store information about a client. Additionally, the Java servlet API includes facilities for maintaining information about a session. (You can see an example of these servlet APIs in the section "A Simple Web Application for Database Access," later in this chapter.)

Web Application Servers

In the three-tiered Web application architecture, the first tier is a Web browser (capable of running Java applets) where the user views information. The middle tier includes the Web server and other helper software (CGI programs, servlets, and even other servers) that handle the data access and application logic (whatever has to happen to the data) and serve dynamically generated HTML pages to the first tier. The third tier is typically a database server or some other system that maintains the corporate data.

The Web browser at the first tier and the corporate database at the third tier perform well-defined roles and are fairly standardized. On the other hand, the role of the middle tier is not yet standardized. Yet the middle tier is crucial to a Web application because that's where everything happens.

This need for a comprehensive, standard middle tier has spawned a new product category called *Web application server* or simply *application server* that goes beyond Web servers and CGI programs used in older e-commerce Web sites. Whereas Web servers typically serve multimedia content (along with Java applets that constitute executable content), Web application servers provide a more complete environment for implementing Web applications. Web application servers typically provide many tools and utilities to run Java servlets, maintain session and state information, access databases, perform database transactions, process new content such as XML (extensible markup language), and generate dynamic HTML documents.

The capabilities of Web application servers vary from vendor to vendor, but the trend seems to be to include the following key features:

◆ **Session and state management.** An application server provides a standard way to maintain state information between successive requests to the server for the duration of a user's session. The session identifies the Web browser client, and the state information is usually some application-specific data stored using a session identifier as the key (this means that you can retrieve the state using the session identifier). This is one of the most important capabilities of an application server. If you have a Java-capable Web server (one that can run load and servlets), you can use the session management features of the servlet API.

◆ **HTML generation.** The application server has to process user input from the Web browser and return HTML (or XML) content back to the browser. A Java-capable Web browser provides this capability through servlets. You can write servlets that generate HTML based on user input sent through HTTP requests. Web application servers also include the ability to generate dynamic server pages (for example, Java Server Pages, GNU Server Pages, or Server Side Includes). This feature is typically supported by a Java-capable Web server.

◆ **Database access.** Application servers create and manage connections to databases. Java-capable Web servers can provide rudimentary database access through servlets that use the JDBC API. You can use the session and state management facilities of the servlet API to share a single database connection throughout a user's session. However, this approach is not efficient enough because it is not scalable. For example, if a thousand users were to run a Web application, there would be a thousand separate database connections. Sharing a pool of connections avoids this sort of problem. Advanced application servers include the ability to create a pool of database connections and manage that pool so that many servlets and other server components can share the same set of connections. (This avoids the inefficiency associated with each servlet creating a separate database connection.)

◆ **Transaction management.** Application servers also need to support connections to transaction processing systems such as IBM's Customer Information Control System (CICS), used by many corporations for online transaction processing that may involve multiple databases. Typically, transaction processing uses a two-phase commit model where changes are made to the databases only if all databases can successfully make the changes (*commit* refers to the act of permanently making a change in the database). The first phase polls all databases to check whether everyone is ready to commit. If all databases are ready, the second phase commits the database changes. A Java-based application server may use the Java Transaction API (JTA), which provides support for such two-phase commit protocols.

◆ **Business logic and processing.** This refers to code that performs the computations and applies the rules required by the business. For example, a step in a loan approval might be to add up all monthly payments and ensure that the total is less than a threshold, say 36 percent of the applicant's gross monthly income. That type of computation is usually performed by server-side components such as servlets. A Java-capable Web server can support business logic processing through servlets. Advanced application servers include more extensive support for standard component models such as Enterprise JavaBeans that allow packaging of business logic into standard objects.

◆ **User authentication and other security services.** Application servers need to provide a way to authenticate users before granting them access to Web applications. Most Web servers include a mechanism that can password-protect specific documents. Application servers may provide more advanced security through an X.509 digital certificate on the user's computer. Users can get digital certificates from a trusted certificate authority (CA) that verifies the user's identity and issues an X.509 certificate. For secure operations, the server also uses Secure Sockets Layer (SSL) along with HTTP. This protocol combination of HTTP with SSL is called HTTPS.

◆ **Standards-based distributed object services.** To allow developers to create business objects, application servers support a number of distributed object models such as Common Object Request Broker Architecture (CORBA), Java Remote Method Invocation (RMI), and Enterprise JavaBeans. (See Chapter 11 for examples of CORBA and RMI.) Other supporting services include APIs to create and process XML data. (XML provides a structured way to represent data just as HTML is meant for visual layout of text.)

You can have a rudimentary Web application server by adding Java servlet support to a plain Web server. For example, the Apache HTTP server with Apache JServ can run Java servlets. With the servlets you get the ability to save session and state information and also access many different databases with the JDBC API. Sun's Java Web Server is another such Java-capable Web server. Recently, IBM has released the WebSphere Application Server Advanced Edition, which uses an Apache-based HTTP server plus support for CORBA, Enterprise JavaBeans, and XML documents.

PROGRAMMER'S NOTE *Chapter 13 describes the Apache HTTP server, Apache JServ, and Sun's Java Web Server. You can learn more about IBM WebSphere (and download a 60-day trial version) from* **http://www.software.ibm.com/webservers/appserv/**. *Currently, IBM WebSphere supports Windows NT, Solaris, and AIX operating systems. IBM has announced that WebSphere will support Linux in the near future. Other prominent application server vendors include Oracle (***http://www.oracle.com/asd/oas/oas.html***), Sun NetDynamics (***http://www.netdynamics.com***), BEA WebLogic (***http://weblogic.beasys.com/***), Sybase (***http://www.sybase.com/products/application_servers***), Bluestone Software (***http://www.bluestone.com/***), Inprise (***http://www.inprise.com/appserver/***), SilverStream (***http://www.silverstream.com***), and Haht Software (***http://www.hahtsite.com***).*

Enterprise JavaBeans

Until recently, most application servers had their own APIs. To take advantage of a server's features, you had to use that server's API. Unfortunately, the use of a server-specific API meant that components built for one server would not work on another server without some changes. Server-specific APIs also hindered the development of reusable components that could be used with application servers from different vendors. The situation is changing with the newer Web application servers and the move toward a standard application framework consisting of standard APIs and conventions. For example, Java-capable Web servers support Java servlets that follow the standard servlet API. This means that a servlet that works with one vendor's server should work equally well with another vendor's product.

Enterprise JavaBeans (EJB) is a specification for three-tiered Web applications. EJB was developed by Sun, IBM, Oracle, and several other vendors to simplify development of three-tiered applications, and the middle-tier software in particular. Like JavaBeans (see Chapters 7 and 8), EJB is not a product; it's basically a model for Java software components (objects) for the server. You use a number of standard APIs to develop EJB components. Because all EJB components follow the same model, any EJB component will work with any EJB-compliant application server. This is expected to create a competitive market for EJB components and EJB-compliant application servers.

> **PROGRAMMER'S NOTE** *To learn more about EJB, visit Sun's EJB site at* ***http://java.sun.com/products/ejb/***. *In particular, this page provides links that you can follow to read an EJB FAQ (frequently asked questions) and download technical documents about the EJB specifications.*

A Simple Web Application for Database Access

As a programmer, you are probably anxious to see the innards of a three-tiered Web application. This section presents an application that illustrates the data access and session management features of the Java servlet API. Let's try the application first and then study the source code of its various parts. (As you'll see, a typical Web application consists of many parts—usually servlets—that work together.)

Trying Out dbaccess

All of the files for the **dbaccess** sample application are in the **ch14\dbaccess** directory of this book's companion CD-ROM. You will find an HTML file (**Main.html**), five servlet classes (**Login**, **Logout**, **dbaccess**, **dbsearch**, and **dbmore**), and a Microsoft Access database file (**Orders.mdb**). This sample database was generated by a database wizard in Access and contains sample data filled in by Microsoft Access. I added an extra **Password** table with user IDs and passwords that the application could use to check for valid users. The sample data is good enough to try out this application.

Even though this is a three-tiered application, you can try the application from a single PC, but you will need a Windows 95/98 or NT PC because you need an ODBC driver to connect to the sample Access database. You will also need a Web server that supports Java servlets. (After all, this is a Web application!) A good option is to download and install the trial version of Sun's Java Web Server (**http://www.sun.com/software/jwebserver/index.html**), because it runs on a Windows system. I will assume that you have already installed Sun's Java Web Server in the default directory, **c:\JavaWebServer1.1.3**. (See Chapter 13 for more information on downloading and installing the Java Web Server.)

To install the **dbaccess** application, perform the following steps:

1. Copy the **Main.html** file to the **c:\JavaWebServer1.1.3\public_html** directory.

2. Copy **Login.class**, **Logout.class**, **dbaccess.class**, **dbsearch.class**, and **dbmore.class** to the **c:\JavaWebServer1.1.3\servlets** directory.

3. Copy the **Orders.mdb** file to your system's hard disk.

4. Using the 32-bit ODBC icon in the Windows Control Panel, set up **Orders.mdb** as an ODBC data source with the name **Orders**. (See the "JDBC Programming" section of Chapter 12 for information on how to set up an ODBC data source.)

5. If it's not already running, start the Java Web Server by changing to the **c:\JavaWebServer1.1.3\bin** directory and typing **start httpd** in an MS-DOS prompt window.

Now you are ready to run the **dbaccess** application. Start a Java-capable Web browser (you can run it on the same PC as the one where you have started the Java Web Server), and use an appropriate URL, such as **http://127.0.0.1:8080/Main.html**, to open the **Main.html** file. Figure 14-2 shows the simple initial screen displayed by **Main.html**.

Click on the Login link. This activates the **Login** servlet, the entry point for the **dbaccess** application. Figure 14-3 shows an HTML form displayed by the **Login** servlet.

Enter **1** as the user ID and **001** as the password. (You can also try the user IDs 2, 3, and 4 with the passwords 002, 003, 004, and 005.) Then click on the Login button.

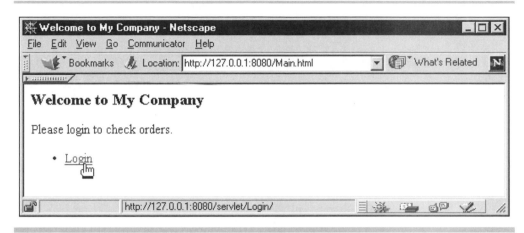

FIGURE 14-2. The initial screen of the **dbaccess** application.

The form's data is processed by the **dbaccess** servlet. That servlet checks the user ID against those in the database and returns another HTML document, as shown in Figure 14-4. Note that the screen welcomes the user and displays a session ID. Keep an eye on the session ID in the next two steps—it should remain the same.

The initial HTML document from **dbaccess** should offer links to all of the actions that the user might perform. In this example, the user can perform only one task: view the current list of orders. Click on the View Orders link. This invokes the **dbsearch** servlet, which queries the database and displays the list of orders for the current user, as shown in Figure 14-5.

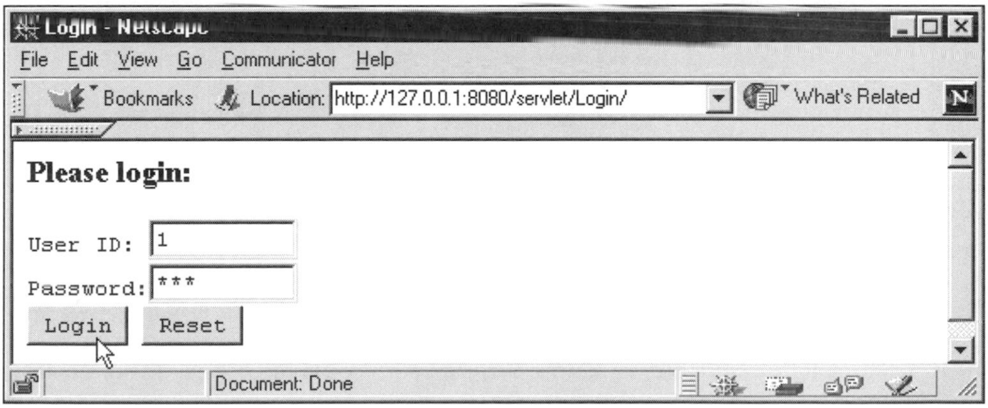

FIGURE 14-3. The login form displayed by the **Login** servlet.

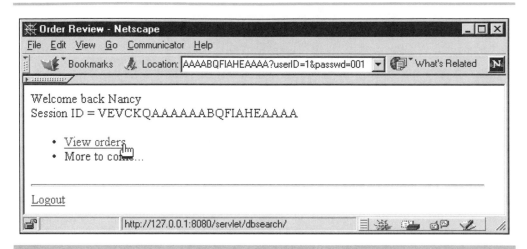

FIGURE 14-4. The HTML document returned by the **dbaccess** servlet after a successful login.

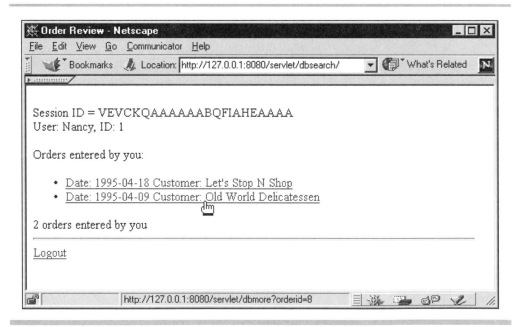

FIGURE 14-5. List of orders for the current user, displayed by the **dbsearch** servlet.

Note that this screen also shows the session ID and user name. These items are saved using the session management capabilities of the servlet API. From this list of orders, you can click on an order to view its details. When you click on an item, the **dbmore** servlet is invoked with the order number as a parameter. (Although Figure 14-5 does not show the order number, that number is retrieved from the database.) Figure 14-6 shows the result of clicking on an order to view more details.

When you are done reviewing an order, you can go back to the previous screen and select other orders to view. When you are finished with the Web application, you can click on the Logout link (at the bottom of the order details) to exit it. Logging out invalidates the current session and also performs any other cleanup, such as closing the database connection. (As you will learn later, the database connection is saved in the session.)

If at any time you click on a link and the servlet does not find a valid session, you'll be returned to the **Login** servlet, which displays the screen shown in Figure 14-3, and you'll have to log on again.

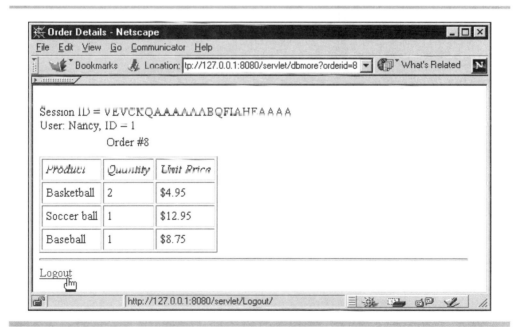

FIGURE 14-6. Order details returned by the **dbmore** servlet.

Understanding dbaccess

As you can see from trying out the **dbaccess** application, a three-tiered Web application is made up of many small parts—typically a mix of HTML files and servlets. In this case, the application consists of the **Main.html** file and the five Java servlets: **Login**, **dbaccess**, **dbsearch**, **dbmore**, and **Logout**. Figure 14-7 shows a storyboard illustrating how the application works. The remainder of this section goes through the code for each of the items in the storyboard, in the order in which they appear in Figure 14-7.

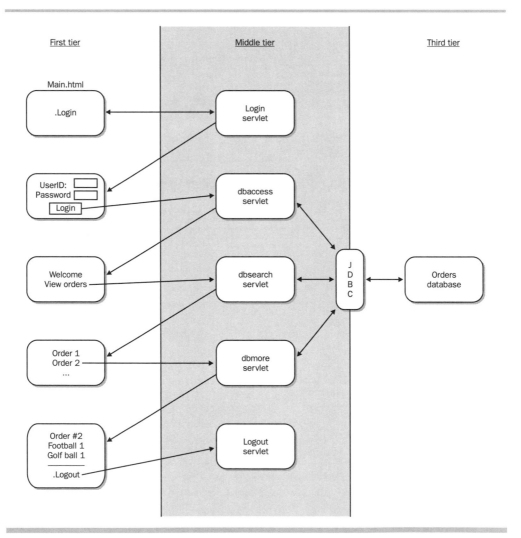

FIGURE 14-7. A storyboard for the **dbaccess** application.

To browse the application's code, start with the **Main.html** file, shown here:

```html
<html>
<head>
<title>Welcome to My Company</title>
</head>
<body>
<h3>Welcome to My Company</h3>
Please login to check orders.
<ul>
<li><a href="/servlet/Login/">Login</a>
</ul>
</body>
<html>
```

Note that the HTML tag **<a href="/servlet/Login/">Login</a>** refers to the **Login** servlet. This means that when the user clicks on the Login link, the browser sends back a request with the URL **/servlet/Login/**, and this causes the Web server to run the **Login** servlet.

The following listing shows the **Login.java** file that implements the **Login** servlet:

```
1  //-----------------------------------------------------------
2  // File: Login.java
3  //
4  // A servlet that display a login form and establishes a session.
5  //-----------------------------------------------------------
6  import java.io.*;
7  import java.util.*;
8  import java.sql.*;
9  import javax.servlet.*;
10 import javax.servlet.http.*;
11 public class Login extends HttpServlet
12 {
13     public void doGet(HttpServletRequest request,
14                       HttpServletResponse response)
15         throws ServletException, IOException
16     {
17         HttpSession session = request.getSession(true);
18         // Make sure a new session is started upon login
19         if(!session.isNew())
20         {
21             // Close database connection and then
22             // invalidate session
```

```
23          Connection theConnection =
24              (Connection)session.getValue("orders.connection");
25          try { theConnection.close();} catch(SQLException e){}
26          session.invalidate();
27      }
28      String msg = "Please login:";
29      StringBuffer buffer = new StringBuffer();
30      buffer.append("<html><head>");
31      buffer.append("<title>Login</title></head>\n");
32      buffer.append("<body><h3>"+msg);
33      buffer.append("</h3>\n<form method=get ");
34      buffer.append("action=\"");
35      buffer.append(response.encodeUrl("/servlet/dbaccess/"));
36      buffer.append("\">\n<pre>\n");
37      buffer.append(
38        "User ID: <input type=text name=userID size=10>\n");
39      buffer.append(
40        "Password:<input type=password name=passwd size=10>\n");
41      buffer.append("<input type=submit value=\"Login\"> ");
42      buffer.append("<input type=reset>\n");
43      buffer.append("</pre>\n");
44      buffer.append("</form></body></html>\n");
45      response.setContentType("text/html");
46      PrintWriter out = response.getWriter();
47      out.println(buffer.toString());
48      out.close();
49    }
50 }
```

The **Login** servlet follows the same conventions as the servlets shown in Chapter 13. **Login** is defined as a subclass of the **HttpServlet** class, and it overrides the **doGet()** method. This servlet illustrates how to use the session management features of the Java servlet API. Line 17 gets an **HttpSession** object by calling the **getSession()** method of the **HttpServletRequest** interface:

```
17          HttpSession session = request.getSession(true);
```

The **true** argument to the **getSession()** method specifies that a new session should be created if a session does not already exist. The servlet API usually places a cookie on the client browser to identify the session. (If cookies are not supported, another method known as URL rewriting is used.) From then on, whenever the same client sends any request to the server, it includes the cookie in the HTTP header. The **wrapper** servlet in Chapter 13 discusses cookies and how they are used. However, you don't have to know how the session is managed except to call the **getSession()** method and use the **HttpSession** object returned by that method.

If the session is not new, lines 19 through 27 of the **Login** servlet extract information about the database connection from the session and then close the database connection:

```
19          if(!session.isNew())
20          {
21              // Close database connection and then
22              // invalidate session
23              Connection theConnection =
24                  (Connection)session.getValue("orders.connection");
25              try { theConnection.close();} catch(SQLException e){}
26              session.invalidate();
27          }
```

Lines 23 and 24 call the **getValue()** method to get the **Connection** object. Line 25 closes the connection and line 26 invalidates the session. The reason for this is that the session stores the JDBC **Connection** object used to access the database, and this connection should be closed before the user is allowed to log on again.

The rest of the **doGet()** method—lines 28 through 48—prepares and sends back the login form. Note that lines 33 through 36 prepare the **<form>** tag with the **method** and **action** attributes:

```
33          buffer.append("</h3>\n<form method=get ");
34          buffer.append("action=\"");
35          buffer.append(response.encodeUrl("/servlet/dbaccess/"));
36          buffer.append("\">\n<pre>\n");
```

In particular, line 35 sets the value of the **action** attribute as the URL for the **dbaccess** servlet. Notice that line 35 calls the **encodeUrl()** method of the **HttpServletResponse** interface to encode the URL before sending it to the browser. This is a recommended step whenever you embed a URL in a dynamic HTML document such as this one.

After the user fills in the login form shown in Figure 14-3 and clicks on the Login button, the **dbaccess** servlet processes the form's data (the user ID and password). The following listing shows the **dbaccess.java** file that implements the **dbaccess** servlet:

```
1  //-----------------------------------------------------------
2  // File: dbaccess.java
3  //
4  // A servlet that accesses the password table in the Orders
5  // database and lets a valid user proceed to the next screen.
6  // Also saves state information in the session for use in
7  // other servlets servicing this session.
8  //-----------------------------------------------------------
9  import java.io.*;
10 import java.util.*;
11 import java.sql.*;
12 import javax.servlet.*;
13 import javax.servlet.http.*;
14 public class dbaccess extends HttpServlet
15 {
16     private static Connection theConnection;
17     private static final String driverName =
18                         "sun.jdbc.odbc.JdbcOdbcDriver";
19     private static final String dbName = "jdbc:odbc:Orders";
20     private static final String dbUser = "";
21     private static final String dbPass = "";
22     public void doGet(HttpServletRequest request,
23                       HttpServletResponse response)
24         throws ServletException, IOException
25     {
26         HttpSession session = request.getSession(false);
27         // Make sure a new session is started upon login
28         if(session == null)
29         {
30             response.sendRedirect(
31                 response.encodeRedirectUrl("/servlet/Login/"));
32         }
33         String userID = request.getParameter("userID");
34         String passwd = request.getParameter("passwd");
35         try
36         {
37             Class.forName(driverName);
38             theConnection = DriverManager.getConnection(dbName,
```

```
39                                                      dbUser, dbPass);
40          Statement select = theConnection.createStatement();
41          // Make the SQL query (you need to study the
42          // Orders.mdb database to formulate the query)
43          ResultSet result = select.executeQuery(
44              "SELECT Employees.FirstName, Employees.LastName"+
45              " FROM Employees, Password WHERE"+
46              " Password.EmployeeID = "+ userID +
47              " AND Employees.EmployeeID = Password.EmployeeID"+
48              " AND Password.Password = '"+ passwd +"'");
49          if(result.next())
50          {
51              String sessionID =
52                                request.getRequestedSessionId();
53              session.putValue("orders.userid", userID);
54              session.putValue("orders.connection",
55                                theConnection);
56              // There is at least one matching entry
57              // We'll assume it's a valid user
58              String name = result.getString(1);
59              session.putValue("orders.userfname", name);
60              StringBuffer buffer = new StringBuffer();
61              buffer.append("<html><head>");
62              buffer.append("<title>Order Review</title>");
63              buffer.append("</head><body>\n");
64              buffer.append("Welcome back "+name);
65              buffer.append("<br>Session ID = "+sessionID);
66              buffer.append("<ul><li><a href=\"");
67              buffer.append(
68                  response.encodeUrl("/servlet/dbsearch/"));
69              buffer.append("\">View orders</a>");
70              buffer.append("<li>More to come...</ul>");
71              buffer.append("<hr>");
72              buffer.append("<a href=\"");
73              buffer.append(response.encodeUrl("/servlet/Logout/"));
74              buffer.append("\">Logout</a>\n");
75              buffer.append("</body></html>\n");
76              buffer.append("</body></html>\n");
77              response.setContentType("text/html");
78              PrintWriter out = response.getWriter();
```

```
 79              out.println(buffer.toString());
 80              out.close();
 81          }
 82          else
 83          {
 84              response.sendRedirect(
 85                  response.encodeRedirectUrl("/servlet/Login/"));
 86
 87          }
 88          select.close();
 89      }
 90      catch(ClassNotFoundException e1)
 91      {
 92          StringBuffer buffer = new StringBuffer();
 93          buffer.append("<html><head><title>Error</title>");
 94          buffer.append("</head><body><h3>Database error</h3>");
 95          buffer.append(e1.toString());
 96          buffer.append("</body></html>");
 97          response.setContentType("text/html");
 98          PrintWriter out = response.getWriter();
 99          out.println(buffer.toString());
100          out.close();
101      }
102      catch(SQLException e2)
103      {
104          StringBuffer buffer = new StringBuffer();
105          buffer.append("<html><head><title>Error</title>");
106          buffer.append("</head><body><h3>Database error</h3>");
107          buffer.append(e2.toString());
108          buffer.append("</body></html>");
109          response.setContentType("text/html");
110          PrintWriter out = response.getWriter();
111          out.println(buffer.toString());
112          out.close();
113      }
114    }
115 }
```

The **dbaccess** servlet also overrides the **doGet()** method of the **HttpServlet** class. To use the session management capabilities, line 26 calls the **getSession()** method of the **HttpServletRequest** interface to get the current session:

```
 26          HttpSession session = request.getSession(false);
```

The **false** argument to the **getSession()** method indicates that the API should not create a new session if a session does not already exist.

If a session does not exist, it might have timed out (because the user was inactive for a long time), or no session may have been established. In either case, if there is no session, lines 28 through 32 redirect the browser to the **Login** servlet:

```
28          if(session == null)
29          {
30              response.sendRedirect(
31                  response.encodeRedirectUrl("/servlet/Login/"));
32          }
```

Note that the **sendRedirect()** method expects a URL to which the browser is redirected. (This means that the browser will immediately go to that URL.) However, the URL should be processed by the **encodeRedirectUrl()** method of the **HttpServletResponse** interface before it is passed to the **sendRedirect()** method. This is another common convention that you should follow whenever sending a URL for redirection.

Lines 33 and 34 extract the parameters entered by the user:

```
33          String userID = request.getParameter("userID");
34          String passwd = request.getParameter("passwd");
```

The **dbaccess** servlet then uses the JDBC API for database access. (See Chapter 12 for more information on the JDBC API.) The **try** block in lines 35 through 89 encloses the database code and anything else that depends on the success of the database access.

Lines 37 through 40 load the JDBC driver, get a JDBC **Connection**, and create a **Statement** to execute a SQL query:

```
37              Class.forName(driverName);
38              theConnection = DriverManager.getConnection(dbName,
39                                                  dbUser, dbPass);
40              Statement select = theConnection.createStatement();
```

The **driverName** string is set on lines 17 and 18 to **sun.jdbc.odbc.JdbcOdbcDriver** (this refers to the JDBC–ODBC driver). Also, line 19 specifies the **dbName** string as **jdbc:odbc:Orders**. (This should match the ODBC data source name for the database.)

Lines 43 through 48 execute a SQL query that extracts the employee's first and last name for the matching user ID and password:

```
43              ResultSet result = select.executeQuery(
44                  "SELECT Employees.FirstName, Employees.LastName"+
45                  " FROM Employees, Password WHERE"+
46                  " Password.EmployeeID = "+ userID +
47                  " AND Employees.EmployeeID = Password.EmployeeID"+
48                  " AND Password.Password = '"+ passwd +"'");
```

If the **ResultSet** has any rows, the servlet assumes that a valid user has been found. In this case, lines 51 through 80 send back the screen shown in Figure 14-4. Note that lines 51 and 52 get the session ID shown in that HTML document:

```
51              String sessionID =
52                              request.getRequestedSessionId();
```

Also, lines 53 through 55 store some state information in the session:

```
53              session.putValue("orders.userid", userID);
54              session.putValue("orders.connection",
55                              theConnection);
```

In this case, the state information includes the user ID (as a **String**) and the **Connection** object. Both of these items will be used in the **dbsearch** and **dbmore** servlets to access the database and to return information for the correct user. Note that these state variables are stored under the names **orders.userid** and **orders.connection**. You can pick a name that best suits your application. Later on, you have to use the same name to retrieve these states.

Additionally, lines 58 and 59 get and save the user name in the session:

```
58              String name = result.getString(1);
59              session.putValue("orders.userfname", name);
```

The name is used later on to display welcome messages to the user.

Note that in the case of errors, the **doGet()** method sends back HTML text with the errors. For example, the code in the **catch** block shown in lines 102 through 113 sends back the Web page shown in Figure 14-8. In this case the error occurred because the **Password** table has been locked by another user.

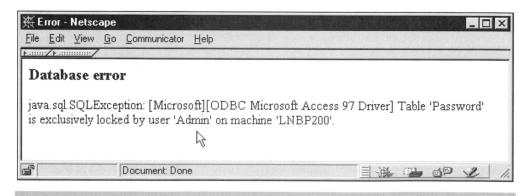

FIGURE 14-8.   Error message returned in a dynamic HTML document.

If all goes well, the **dbaccess** servlet sends back a dynamic HTML document with a link to the **dbsearch** applet, prepared by lines 66 through 69 of the **doGet()** method:

```
66              buffer.append("<ul><li><a href=\"");
67              buffer.append(
68                  response.encodeUrl("/servlet/dbsearch/"));
69              buffer.append("\">View orders</a>");
```

When the user clicks on that link, the browser sends a URL that requests the **dbsearch** servlet. The following listing shows the **dbsearch.java** file that implements the **dbsearch** servlet:

```
1  //-----------------------------------------------------------
2  // File: dbsearch.java
3  //
4  // A servlet that searches the Orders database for the current
5  // user's (a user is a company employee) orders. Gets the
6  // user ID and database connection from the session.
7  // Returns user to the login screen if the session has expired.
8  //-----------------------------------------------------------
9  import java.io.*;
10 import java.util.*;
11 import java.sql.*;
12 import javax.servlet.*;
13 import javax.servlet.http.*;
14 public class dbsearch extends HttpServlet
15 {
16     public void doGet(HttpServletRequest request,
17                       HttpServletResponse response)
18         throws ServletException, IOException
19     {
20         HttpSession session = request.getSession(false);
21         // Make sure a new session is started upon login
22         if(session == null)
23         {
24             response.sendRedirect(
25                 response.encodeRedirectUrl("/servlet/Login/"));
26         }
27         String sessionID = request.getRequestedSessionId();
28         String username = (String)session.getValue(
29                                         "orders.userfname");
30         String userID = (String)session.getValue("orders.userid");
```

```
31      Connection theConnection = (Connection)session.getValue(
32                                  "orders.connection");
33      try
34      {
35          Statement select = theConnection.createStatement();
36          // Make the SQL query
37          ResultSet result = select.executeQuery(
38              "SELECT Orders.OrderId, Customers.CompanyName,"+
39              " Orders.OrderDate"+
40              " FROM Orders, Customers WHERE"+
41              " Orders.CustomerID = Customers.CustomerID"+
42              " AND Orders.EmployeeID = "+userID);
43          StringBuffer buffer = new StringBuffer();
44          buffer.append("<html><head>");
45          buffer.append("<title>Order Review</title>");
46          buffer.append("</head><body>\n");
47          buffer.append("<br>Session ID = "+sessionID);
48          buffer.append("<br>User: "+username);
49          buffer.append(", ID: "+userID);
50          buffer.append("<br><br>Orders entered by you:");
51          buffer.append("<ul>");
52          int count = 0;
53          while(result.next())
54          {
55              int orderID = result.getInt(1);
56              String name = result.getString(2);
57              java.sql.Date date = result.getDate(3);
58              buffer.append("<li><a href=\"");
59              buffer.append(response.encodeUrl(
60                          "/servlet/dbmore?orderid="+orderID));
61              buffer.append("\">");
62              buffer.append("Date: ");
63              buffer.append(date+" Customer: ");
64              buffer.append(name+"</a>\n");
65              count++;
66          }
67          select.close();
68          buffer.append("</ul>\n");
69          if(count == 0)
70          {
71              buffer.append("<b>No orders entered by you.</b>");
```

```
72              }
73              else buffer.append(count+" orders entered by you");
74              buffer.append("<hr>");
75              buffer.append("<a href=\"");
76              buffer.append(response.encodeUrl("/servlet/Logout/"));
77              buffer.append("\">Logout</a>\n");
78              buffer.append("</body></html>\n");
79              response.setContentType("text/html");
80              PrintWriter out = response.getWriter();
81              out.println(buffer.toString());
82              out.close();
83          }
84      catch(SQLException e)
85      {
86          StringBuffer buffer = new StringBuffer();
87          buffer.append("<html><head><title>Error</title>");
88          buffer.append("</head><body><h3>Database error</h3>");
89          buffer.append(e.toString());
90          buffer.append("</body></html>");
91          response.setContentType("text/html");
92          PrintWriter out = response.getWriter();
93          out.println(buffer.toString());
94          out.close();
95      }
96   }
97 }
```

The **dbsearch** servlet returns all orders entered by the current user, as identified by the state information in the session. Like the **dbaccess** servlet, **dbsearch** starts by getting the current session. If the session is **null**, it redirects the browser to the **Login** servlet. (This forces the user to log on again.)

For a valid session, lines 27 through 32 of the **dbsearch** servlet retrieve the state information from the session:

```
27      String sessionID = request.getRequestedSessionId();
28      String username = (String)session.getValue(
29                                      "orders.userfname");
30      String userID = (String)session.getValue("orders.userid");
31      Connection theConnection = (Connection)session.getValue(
32                                      "orders.connection");
```

Line 27 gets the session ID. (This is not really needed for anything, but I wanted to show you that the session ID is the same during a session.) Lines 28 through 32 get the three state variables: the user name, the user ID, and, most importantly, the **Connection** object that represents the database connection (which was established in the **dbaccess** servlet).

Line 35 uses the **Connection** from the session and creates a **Statement**:

```
35              Statement select = theConnection.createStatement();
```

Lines 36 through 42 use that **Statement** to execute a SQL query and retrieve all of the orders entered by the user identified by the user ID in the session:

```
36              // Make the SQL query
37              ResultSet result = select.executeQuery(
38                  "SELECT Orders.OrderId, Customers.CompanyName,"+
39                  " Orders.OrderDate"+
40                  " FROM Orders, Customers WHERE"+
41                  " Orders.CustomerID = Customers.CustomerID"+
42                  " AND Orders.EmployeeID = "+userID);
```

After the query has executed, lines 43 through 82 format the result in an HTML document and return that to the browser. Note that lines 58 through 61 add a link to the **dbmore** servlet (with the order ID as a parameter) so that the user can click on the order to view more details:

```
58                  buffer.append("<li><a href=\"");
59                  buffer.append(response.encodeUrl(
60                          "/servlet/dbmore?orderid="+orderID));
61                  buffer.append("\">");
```

The following listing shows the **dbmore.java** file that implements the **dbmore** servlet:

```
1  //------------------------------------------------------------
2  // File: dbmore.java
3  //
4  // A servlet that retrieves and displays details of a specific
5  // order given an order ID. Gets user information from the
6  // HttpSession object for this session.
7  //------------------------------------------------------------
8  import java.io.*;
9  import java.util.*;
10 import java.sql.*;
11 import javax.servlet.*;
12 import javax.servlet.http.*;
13 public class dbmore extends HttpServlet
```

```
14  {
15      public void doGet(HttpServletRequest request,
16                      HttpServletResponse response)
17          throws ServletException, IOException
18      {
19          HttpSession session = request.getSession(false);
20          // If session is not valid, send the Login form
21          if(session == null)
22          {
23              response.sendRedirect(
24                      response.encodeRedirectUrl("/servlet/Login/"));
25          }
26          String orderID = request.getParameter("orderid");
27          String sessionID = request.getRequestedSessionId();
28          String userID = (String)session.getValue("orders.userid");
29          String username = (String)session.getValue(
30                                              "orders.userfname");
31          Connection theConnection = (Connection)session.getValue(
32                                      "orders.connection");
33          try
34          {
35              Statement select = theConnection.createStatement();
36              // Make the SQL query
37              ResultSet result = select.executeQuery(
38                  "SELECT Products.ProductName,"+
39                  " `Order Details`.`Quantity`,"+
40                  " `Order Details`.`UnitPrice`"+
41                  " FROM `Order Details`, Products WHERE"+
42                  " `Order Details`.`ProductID` ="+
43                  " Products.ProductID"+
44                  " AND `Order Details`.OrderID = "+orderID);
45              StringBuffer buffer = new StringBuffer();
46              buffer.append("<html><head>");
47              buffer.append("<title>Order Details</title>");
48              buffer.append("</head><body>\n");
49              buffer.append("<br>Session ID = "+sessionID);
50              buffer.append("<br>User: "+username);
51              buffer.append(", ID = "+userID);
52              buffer.append("<table border cellpadding=4>");
53              buffer.append("<caption>Order #"+orderID);
54              buffer.append("</caption><tr><td><em>Product</em>");
55              buffer.append("</td><td><em>Quantity</em></td>");
56              buffer.append("<td><em>Unit Price</em></td></tr>\n");
```

```
57          int count = 0;
58          while(result.next())
59          {
60              String productName = result.getString(1);
61              int quantity = result.getInt(2);
62              float unitPrice = result.getFloat(3);
63              buffer.append("<tr><td>"+productName);
64              buffer.append("</td><td>"+quantity);
65              buffer.append("</td><td>$"+unitPrice);
66              buffer.append("</td></tr>\n");
67              count++;
68          }
69          buffer.append("</table>\n");
70          select.close();
71          if(count == 0)
72          {
73              buffer.append("<b>No details available.</b>");
74          }
75          buffer.append("<hr>");
76          buffer.append("<a href=\"");
77          buffer.append(response.encodeUrl("/servlet/Logout/"));
78          buffer.append("\">Logout</a>\n");
79          buffer.append("</body></html>\n");
80          response.setContentType("text/html");
81          PrintWriter out = response.getWriter();
82          out.println(buffer.toString());
83          out.close();
84      }
85      catch(SQLException e)
86      {
87          StringBuffer buffer = new StringBuffer();
88          buffer.append("<html><head><title>Error</title>");
89          buffer.append("</head><body><h3>Database error</h3>");
90          buffer.append(e.toString());
91          buffer.append("</body></html>");
92          response.setContentType("text/html");
93          PrintWriter out = response.getWriter();
94          out.println(buffer.toString());
95          out.close();
96      }
97   }
98 }
```

The **dbmore** servlet returns detailed information about an order. The order is identified by an order ID passed as a parameter. The **dbmore** servlet is very similar to the **dbsearch** servlet, except that **dbmore** executes a different SQL query. Line 26 gets the order ID from the parameter passed in the HTTP request:

```
26          String orderID = request.getParameter("orderid");
```

Lines 37 through 44 use the order ID to get detailed information about the order from the table named **Order Details**:

```
37          ResultSet result = select.executeQuery(
38              "SELECT Products.ProductName,"+
39              " `Order Details`.`Quantity`,"+
40              " `Order Details`.`UnitPrice`"+
41              " FROM `Order Details`, Products WHERE"+
42              " `Order Details`.`ProductID` ="+
43              " Products.ProductID"+
44              " AND `Order Details`.OrderID = "+orderID);
```

In this case the table name includes an embedded space. Therefore, I had to enclose the table name and column name in backquotes (for example, `` `Order Details`.`Quantity` ``).

After the SQL query has executed successfully, lines 45 through 83 format the result in an HTML table.

You have not yet seen the **Logout** servlet, which is designed to close the database connection and invalidate the session. Each of the servlets—**dbaccess**, **dbsearch**, and **dbmore**—provide a link to **Logout**, in case the user wants to log out. The following listing shows the **Logout.java** file that implements the **Logout** servlet:

```
1  //---------------------------------------------------------------
2  // File: Logout.java
3  //
4  // A servlet that closes the database connection and ends
5  // the current session.
6  //---------------------------------------------------------------
7  import java.io.*;
8  import java.util.*;
9  import java.sql.*;
10 import javax.servlet.*;
11 import javax.servlet.http.*;
12 public class Logout extends HttpServlet
13 {
14     public void doGet(HttpServletRequest request,
15                       HttpServletResponse response)
```

```
16          throws ServletException, IOException
17    {
18          HttpSession session = request.getSession(true);
19          if(session.isNew())return;
20          String sessionID = request.getRequestedSessionId();
21          String username = (String)session.getValue(
22                                    "orders.userfname");
23          Connection theConnection = (Connection)session.getValue(
24                                    "orders.connection");
25          try { theConnection.close();} catch(SQLException e){}
26          session.invalidate();
27          StringBuffer buffer = new StringBuffer();
28          buffer.append("<html><head>");
29          buffer.append("<title>Logout</title></head>\n");
30          buffer.append("<body><h3>Thanks you, "+username);
31          buffer.append("</h3>Ending session "+sessionID);
32          buffer.append("<br><hr><a href=\"");
33          buffer.append(response.encodeUrl("/servlet/Login/"));
34          buffer.append("\">Login again</a></body></html>\n");
35          response.setContentType("text/html");
36          PrintWriter out = response.getWriter();
37          out.println(buffer.toString());
38          out.close();
39    }
40 }
```

The **doGet()** method of the **Logout** servlet starts by getting the session and returning if there is no existing session:

```
18          HttpSession session = request.getSession(true);
19          if(session.isNew())return;
```

If a valid session exists, lines 20 through 24 get the state information from the session:

```
20          String sessionID = request.getRequestedSessionId();
21          String username = (String)session.getValue(
22                                    "orders.userfname");
23          Connection theConnection = (Connection)session.getValue(
24                                    "orders.connection");
```

Line 25 uses the **Connection** object to close the database connection.

```
25        try { theConnection.close();} catch(SQLException e){}
```

Then line 26 invalidates the current session:

```
26        session.invalidate();
```

Finally, lines 27 through 38 send back a dynamic HTML document thanking the user by name. This is where the user name (from line 21) is used.

Java Resources

Throughout this book, I refer to many sources of information, programs, and utilities that can help you learn more about various aspects of Java programming. Most of these resources are located on the Internet, and you can access them from your Web browser. The best part is that most Web-based resources are updated frequently, so you can always get the latest information or the latest version of a program from the Web.

To use the Web-based resources, all you need is a starting point, a URL where you can begin your search. Once you have a good starting document, links within that document should lead you to other relevant resources. This appendix provides that starting point by listing some useful URLs, organized by subject. However, this appendix is by no means an exhaustive list of all Java resources on the Internet.

PROGRAMMER'S NOTE   *You will also find the following links in the HTML file named **JavaLink.html** located in the root directory of the companion CD-ROM. Simply open that file from your Web browser and click on the URL you want to visit.*

General Java Search Sites and Links

IBM jCentral Basic Search Page

`http://www.ibm.com/java/jcentral/basic-search.html`

IBM jCentral Power Search Page

`http://jcentral.alphaworks.ibm.com/Internet/power.htm`

Java Lobby

`http://www.javalobby.com/`

Links to Objects & Components (including Java)

`http://www.cetus-links.org/`

Java Source Code Downloads

JavaShareware.com

`http://www.javashareware.com/`

EarthWeb's JARS.COM Java Review Service

`http://www.jars.com/`

FreeCode, Free programming source code (C, C++, Java, Perl, and Visual Basic)

`http://www.freecode.com/`

Book Source—Focus on Java (links to source code from various Java books)

`http://java.miningco.com/msubbsrc.htm`

IBM alphaWorks (for Java code downloads)

`http://www.alphaWorks.ibm.com/Home/`

SOFTSEEK.COM (shareware, freeware, and evaluation software)

`http://babylontown.softseek.com/`

Gamelan Java directories

`http://www.developer.com/directories/pages/dir.java.html`

Java Boutique: The Java Source

`http://javaboutique.internet.com/javasource.html`

DaveCentral Java Software, Freeware, Demos and Betas

`http://www.davecentral.com/java.html`

Java APIs and Development Kits

All Java products and APIs from Sun Microsystems

`http://java.sun.com/products/`

Java® 2 SDK, Standard Edition, v 1.2 (formerly JDK™ 1.2)

`http://java.sun.com/products/jdk/1.2/`

JavaBeans Development Kit (BDK)

`http://java.sun.com/beans/software/bdk_download.html`

Java Servlet Development Kit (JSDK)

`http://java.sun.com/products/servlet/index.html`

Accessibility APIs to support people with disabilities

`http://java.sun.com/products/jfc/jaccess-1.2/doc/`

Java 2D API for two-dimensional (2D) graphics and imaging

`http://java.sun.com/products/java-media/2D/`

Java Media Framework (JMF)

`http://java.sun.com/products/java-media/jmf/`

List of JDBC drivers

`http://java.sun.com/products/jdbc/jdbc.drivers.html`

Enterprise JavaBeans

`http://java.sun.com/products/ejb/`

Java for various operating systems such as AIX, HP-UX, MacOS, OS/2, and OS/390

`http://java.sun.com/cgi-bin/java-ports.cgi`

Java for Linux

`http://java.blackdown.org/java-linux.html`

Mac OS Runtime for Java (MRJ)

`http://www.apple.com/java/`

Distributed Objects

Java Remote Method Invocation (RMI)

`http://java.sun.com/products/jdk/rmi/`

Java IDL

`http://java.sun.com/products/jdk/idl/index.html`

The **idltojava** compiler

`http://developer.javasoft.com/developer/earlyAccess/jdk12/idltojava.html`

Object Management Group (for information on CORBA, Common Object Request Broker Architecture)

`http://www.omg.org`

Java Web Servers

Sun's Java Web Server

`http://www.sun.com/software/jwebserver/index.html`

Trial version of Sun's Java Web Server

`http://www.sun.com/software/jwebserver/try/index.html`

Apache HTTP server (you also need Apache JServ)

`http://www.apache.org/`

Apache JServ

`http://java.apache.org/`

Netcraft Web Server Survey

`http://www.netcraft.com/survey/`

Application Servers

IBM WebSphere (60-day trial version available)

`http://www.software.ibm.com/webservers/appserv/`

Oracle

`http://www.oracle.com/asd/oas/oas.html`

Sun NetDynamics

`http://www.netdynamics.com`

BEA WebLogic

`http://weblogic.beasys.com/`

Sybase

`http://www.sybase.com/products/application_servers`

Bluestone Software

`http://www.bluestone.com/`

Inprise

`http://www.inprise.com/appserver/`

SilverStream

`http://www.silverstream.com`

Haht Software

`http://www.hahtsite.com`

Enhydra (Open Source, servlet-based Java Application Server)

`http://www.enhydra.org/`

Other Java Resources

Java frequently asked questions (FAQ) for Java programmers

`http://www.afu.com/javafaq.html`

IBM's Java FAQ for the JDK

`http://www.ibm.com/java/jdk/jdkfaq/`

Java Developer Connection

`http://developer.java.sun.com/developer/index.html`

Java Resource (a general-purpose Java site with source code samples)

`http://www.internethelpers.com/java/`

JavaWorld magazine

`http://www.javaworld.com/`

The Swing Connection online newsletter

`http://java.sun.com/products/jfc/tsc/`

Sun's online Java tutorial

`http://java.sun.com/docs/books/tutorial/`

Sun's online servlet book

`http://java.sun.com/docs/books/tutorial/servlets/TOC.html`

Inside Java (resource for Java programmers)

`http://www.inside-java.com/index.htm`

Digital Cat's Java Resource Center

`http://www.javacats.com/`

Internet Basics

Internet Network Information Center (InterNIC)

`http://www.networksolutions.com/`

Request for Comments (RFC)—the working papers of the Internet

`http://www.cis.ohio-state.edu/hypertext/information/rfc.html`

Internet Engineering Task Force (IETF)

`http://www.ietf.org/`

World Wide Web Consortium (W3C)

`http://www.w3.org/`

Internet network architecture

`http://nic.merit.edu/.internet.html`

Index

D

E

F

Q

R

S

Publisher Acknowledgment

Netscape Communications Corporation's ("Netscape") hereby grants permission to use the Netscape Browser Frame or GIF File in a book or book promotion ("Image"), or the most current non-beta version of the Netscape Communicator binary ("Binary") on electronic media under the following conditions:

1. This qualified permission extends only to the Image or the Binary, and does not extend to source code for any of Netscape's products including but not limited to the Netscape browser product;

2. The Image or binary may not be used for any purpose other than described above, without Netscape's prior written consent;

3. The title page, credit page, copyright page or other prominent location of the Work shall display the following statement:

   "Netscape Communications Corporation has not authorized, sponsored, or endorsed, or approved this publication and is not responsible for its content. Netscape and the Netscape Communications Corporate Logos, are trademarks and trade names of Netscape Communications Corporation. All other product names and/or logos are trademarks of their respective owners."

4. Publisher shall not modify or alter the Image or Binary in any manner;

5. At Netscape's request, Publisher will make available to Netscape a copy of any portions of the Work where the Image or Binary appears for the purpose of verification of usage in accordance with the terms set-forth herein;

6. Publisher shall not use the Image or Binary or any Netscape trademark, trade name, or logo in a manner which implies that Netscape is the source of, endorses, sponsors, or authorizes the Work; and

7. Publisher shall not use or display the Image or Binary or any Netscape trademark, logo, or trade name in conjunction with any offensive material or in any manner not suitable for all viewing audiences.

GNU GENERAL PUBLIC LICENSE

Version 2, June 1991

Copyright © 1989, 1991 Free Software Foundation, Inc.
675 Mass Ave, Cambridge, MA 02139, USA

Preamble

The licenses for most software are designed to take away your freedom to share and change it. By contrast, the GNU General Public License is intended to guarantee your freedom to share and change free software—to make sure the software is free for all its users. This General Public License applies to most of the Free Software Foundation's software and to any other program whose authors commit to using it. (Some other Free Software Foundation software is covered by the GNU Library General Public License instead.) You can apply it to your programs, too.

When we speak of free software, we are referring to freedom, not price. Our General Public Licenses are designed to make sure that you have the freedom to distribute copies of free software (and charge for this service if you wish), that you receive source code or can get it if you want it, that you can change the software or use pieces of it in new free programs; and that you know you can do these things.

To protect your rights, we need to make restrictions that forbid anyone to deny you these rights or to ask you to surrender the rights. These restrictions translate to certain responsibilities for you if you distribute copies of the software, or if you modify it.

For example, if you distribute copies of such a program, whether gratis or for a fee, you must give the recipients all the rights that you have. You must make sure that they, too, receive or can get the source code. And you must show them these terms so they know their rights.

We protect your rights with two steps: (1) copyright the software, and (2) offer you this license which gives you legal permission to copy, distribute and/or modify the software.

Also, for each author's protection and ours, we want to make certain that everyone understands that there is no warranty for this free software. If the software is modified by someone else and passed on, we want its recipients to know that what they have is not the original, so that any problems introduced by others will not reflect on the original authors' reputations.

Finally, any free program is threatened constantly by software patents. We wish to avoid the danger that redistributors of a free program will individually obtain patent licenses, in effect making the program proprietary. To prevent this, we have made it clear that any patent must be licensed for everyone's free use or not licensed at all.

The precise terms and conditions for copying, distribution and modification follow.

TERMS AND CONDITIONS FOR COPYING, DISTRIBUTION AND MODIFICATION

0. This License applies to any program or other work which contains a notice placed by the copyright holder saying it may be distributed under the terms of this General Public License. The "Program", below, refers to any such program or work, and a "work based on the Program" means either the Program or any derivative work under copyright law: that is to say, a work containing the Program or a portion of it, either verbatim or with modifications and/or translated into another language. (Hereinafter, translation is included without limitation in the term "modification".) Each licensee is addressed as "you".

   Activities other than copying, distribution and modification are not covered by this License; they are outside its scope. The act of running the Program is not restricted, and the output from the Program is covered only if its contents constitute a work based on the Program (independent of having been made by running the Program). Whether that is true depends on what the Program does.

1. You may copy and distribute verbatim copies of the Program's source code as you receive it, in any medium, provided that you conspicuously and appropriately publish on each copy an appropriate copyright notice and disclaimer of warranty; keep intact all the notices that refer to this License and to the absence of any warranty; and give any other recipients of the Program a copy of this License along with the Program.

   You may charge a fee for the physical act of transferring a copy, and you may at your option offer warranty protection in exchange for a fee.

2. You may modify your copy or copies of the Program or any portion of it, thus forming a work based on the Program, and copy and distribute such modifications or work under the terms of Section 1 above, provided that you also meet all of these conditions:

   a) You must cause the modified files to carry prominent notices stating that you changed the files and the date of any change.

b) You must cause any work that you distribute or publish, that in whole or in part contains or is derived from the Program or any part thereof, to be licensed as a whole at no charge to all third parties under the terms of this License.

c) If the modified program normally reads commands interactively when run, you must cause it, when started running for such interactive use in the most ordinary way, to print or display an announcement including an appropriate copyright notice and a notice that there is no warranty (or else, saying that you provide a warranty) and that users may redistribute the program under these conditions, and telling the user how to view a copy of this License. (Exception: if the Program itself is interactive but does not normally print such an announcement, your work based on the Program is not required to print an announcement.)

These requirements apply to the modified work as a whole. If identifiable sections of that work are not derived from the Program, and can be reasonably considered independent and separate works in themselves, then this License, and its terms, do not apply to those sections when you distribute them as separate works. But when you distribute the same sections as part of a whole which is a work based on the Program, the distribution of the whole must be on the terms of this License, whose permissions for other licensees extend to the entire whole, and thus to each and every part regardless of who wrote it.

Thus, it is not the intent of this section to claim rights or contest your rights to work written entirely by you; rather, the intent is to exercise the right to control the distribution of derivative or collective works based on the Program.

In addition, mere aggregation of another work not based on the Program with the Program (or with a work based on the Program) on a volume of a storage or distribution medium does not bring the other work under the scope of this License.

3. You may copy and distribute the Program (or a work based on it, under Section 2) in object code or executable form under the terms of Sections 1 and 2 above provided that you also do one of the following:

a) Accompany it with the complete corresponding machine-readable source code, which must be distributed under the terms of Sections 1 and 2 above on a medium customarily used for software interchange; or,

b) Accompany it with a written offer, valid for at least three years, to give any third party, for a charge no more than your cost of physically performing source distribution, a complete machine-readable copy of the corresponding source code, to be distributed under the terms of

Sections 1 and 2 above on a medium customarily used for software interchange; or,

c) Accompany it with the information you received as to the offer to distribute corresponding source code. (This alternative is allowed only for noncommercial distribution and only if you received the program in object code or executable form with such an offer, in accord with Subsection b above.)

The source code for a work means the preferred form of the work for making modifications to it. For an executable work, complete source code means all the source code for all modules it contains, plus any associated interface definition files, plus the scripts used to control compilation and installation of the executable. However, as a special exception, the source code distributed need not include anything that is normally distributed (in either source or binary form) with the major components (compiler, kernel, and so on) of the operating system on which the executable runs, unless that component itself accompanies the executable.

If distribution of executable or object code is made by offering access to copy from a designated place, then offering equivalent access to copy the source code from the same place counts as distribution of the source code, even though third parties are not compelled to copy the source along with the object code.

4. You may not copy, modify, sublicense, or distribute the Program except as expressly provided under this License. Any attempt otherwise to copy, modify, sublicense or distribute the Program is void, and will automatically terminate your rights under this License. However, parties who have received copies, or rights, from you under this License will not have their licenses terminated so long as such parties remain in full compliance.

5. You are not required to accept this License, since you have not signed it. However, nothing else grants you permission to modify or distribute the Program or its derivative works. These actions are prohibited by law if you do not accept this License. Therefore, by modifying or distributing the Program (or any work based on the Program), you indicate your acceptance of this License to do so, and all its terms and conditions for copying, distributing or modifying the Program or works based on it.

6. Each time you redistribute the Program (or any work based on the Program), the recipient automatically receives a license from the original licensor to copy, distribute or modify the Program subject to these terms and conditions. You may not impose any further restrictions on the recipients' exercise of the

rights granted herein. You are not responsible for enforcing compliance by third parties to this License.

7. If, as a consequence of a court judgment or allegation of patent infringement or for any other reason (not limited to patent issues), conditions are imposed on you (whether by court order, agreement or otherwise) that contradict the conditions of this License, they do not excuse you from the conditions of this License. If you cannot distribute so as to satisfy simultaneously your obligations under this License and any other pertinent obligations, then as a consequence you may not distribute the Program at all. For example, if a patent license would not permit royalty-free redistribution of the Program by all those who receive copies directly or indirectly through you, then the only way you could satisfy both it and this License would be to refrain entirely from distribution of the Program.

    If any portion of this section is held invalid or unenforceable under any particular circumstance, the balance of the section is intended to apply and the section as a whole is intended to apply in other circumstances.

    It is not the purpose of this section to induce you to infringe any patents or other property right claims or to contest validity of any such claims; this section has the sole purpose of protecting the integrity of the free software distribution system, which is implemented by public license practices. Many people have made generous contributions to the wide range of software distributed through that system in reliance on consistent application of that system; it is up to the author/donor to decide if he or she is willing to distribute software through any other system and a licensee cannot impose that choice.

    This section is intended to make thoroughly clear what is believed to be a consequence of the rest of this License.

8. If the distribution and/or use of the Program is restricted in certain countries either by patents or by copyrighted interfaces, the original copyright holder who places the Program under this License may add an explicit geographical distribution limitation excluding those countries, so that distribution is permitted only in or among countries not thus excluded. In such case, this License incorporates the limitation as if written in the body of this License.

9. The Free Software Foundation may publish revised and/or new versions of the General Public License from time to time. Such new versions will be similar in spirit to the present version, but may differ in detail to address new problems or concerns.

    Each version is given a distinguishing version number. If the Program specifies a version number of this License which applies to it and "any later version", you have the option of following the terms and conditions either of that version or of any later version published by the Free Software

Foundation. If the Program does not specify a version number of this License, you may choose any version ever published by the Free Software Foundation.

10. If you wish to incorporate parts of the Program into other free programs whose distribution conditions are different, write to the author to ask for permission. For software which is copyrighted by the Free Software Foundation, write to the Free Software Foundation; we sometimes make exceptions for this. Our decision will be guided by the two goals of preserving the free status of all derivatives of our free software and of promoting the sharing and reuse of software generally.

NO WARRANTY

11. BECAUSE THE PROGRAM IS LICENSED FREE OF CHARGE, THERE IS NO WARRANTY FOR THE PROGRAM, TO THE EXTENT PERMITTED BY APPLICABLE LAW. EXCEPT WHEN OTHERWISE STATED IN WRITING THE COPYRIGHT HOLDERS AND/OR OTHER PARTIES PROVIDE THE PROGRAM "AS IS" WITHOUT WARRANTY OF ANY KIND, EITHER EXPRESSED OR IMPLIED, INCLUDING, BUT NOT LIMITED TO, THE IMPLIED WARRANTIES OF MERCHANTABILITY AND FITNESS FOR A PARTICULAR PURPOSE. THE ENTIRE RISK AS TO THE QUALITY AND PERFORMANCE OF THE PROGRAM IS WITH YOU. SHOULD THE PROGRAM PROVE DEFECTIVE, YOU ASSUME THE COST OF ALL NECESSARY SERVICING, REPAIR OR CORRECTION.

12. IN NO EVENT UNLESS REQUIRED BY APPLICABLE LAW OR AGREED TO IN WRITING WILL ANY COPYRIGHT HOLDER, OR ANY OTHER PARTY WHO MAY MODIFY AND/OR REDISTRIBUTE THE PROGRAM AS PERMITTED ABOVE, BE LIABLE TO YOU FOR DAMAGES, INCLUDING ANY GENERAL, SPECIAL, INCIDENTAL OR CONSEQUENTIAL DAMAGES ARISING OUT OF THE USE OR INABILITY TO USE THE PROGRAM (INCLUDING BUT NOT LIMITED TO LOSS OF DATA OR DATA BEING RENDERED INACCURATE OR LOSSES SUSTAINED BY YOU OR THIRD PARTIES OR A FAILURE OF THE PROGRAM TO OPERATE WITH ANY OTHER PROGRAMS), EVEN IF SUCH HOLDER OR OTHER PARTY HAS BEEN ADVISED OF THE POSSIBILITY OF SUCH DAMAGES.

END OF TERMS AND CONDITIONS

Appendix: How to Apply These Terms to Your New Programs

If you develop a new program, and you want it to be of the greatest possible use to the public, the best way to achieve this is to make it free software which everyone can redistribute and change under these terms.

To do so, attach the following notices to the program. It is safest to attach them to the start of each source file to most effectively convey the exclusion of warranty; and each file should have at least the "copyright" line and a pointer to where the full notice is found.

```
<one line to give the program's name and a brief idea of what it does.>
Copyright (C) 19yy  <name of author>

This program is free software; you can redistribute it and/or modify
it under the terms of the GNU General Public License as published by
the Free Software Foundation; either version 2 of the License, or
(at your option) any later version.

This program is distributed in the hope that it will be useful,
but WITHOUT ANY WARRANTY; without even the implied warranty of
MERCHANTABILITY or FITNESS FOR A PARTICULAR PURPOSE.  See the
GNU General Public License for more details.

You should have received a copy of the GNU General Public License
along with this program; if not, write to the Free Software
Foundation, Inc., 675 Mass Ave, Cambridge, MA 02139, USA.
```

Also add information on how to contact you by electronic and paper mail.

If the program is interactive, make it output a short notice like this when it starts in an interactive mode:

```
Gnomovision version 69, Copyright (C) 19yy name of author
Gnomovision comes with ABSOLUTELY NO WARRANTY; for details type 'show w'.
This is free software, and you are welcome to redistribute it
under certain conditions; type 'show c' for details.
```

The hypothetical commands 'show w' and 'show c' should show the appropriate parts of the General Public License. Of course, the commands you use may be called something other than 'show w' and 'show c'; they could even be mouse-clicks or menu items—whatever suits your program.

You should also get your employer (if you work as a programmer) or your school, if any, to sign a "copyright disclaimer" for the program, if necessary. Here is a sample; alter the names:

Yoyodyne, Inc., hereby disclaims all copyright interest in the program 'Gnomovision' (which makes passes at compilers) written by James Hacker.

<signature of Ty Coon>, 1 April 1989
Ty Coon, President of Vice

This General Public License does not permit incorporating your program into proprietary programs. If your program is a subroutine library, you may consider it more useful to permit linking proprietary applications with the library. If this is what you want to do, use the GNU Library General Public License instead of this License.

ABOUT THE CD

All Java examples from the book are on the accompanying CD-ROM. You can browse the contents of the CD-ROM in Windows Explorer or open the **javaaa.html** file in your Web browser. The **javaaa.html** Web page also includes a link that allows you to try out the applets (from Chapters 1 through 6) directly from the CD-ROM.

The files are arranged by the chapter in the book. For example, the files for Chapter 2 are in the **ch02** directory. Each chapter's directory contains one or more program directories and each program directory contains the files for a specific example. You will find the programs directories organized as follows:

ch01	FTPapp	HTMLColr	**ch11**
AnimText	Telnet	Clock2	jPOP3
DDMenu			jChat
ImgBtn	**ch04**	**ch07**	rmi
FadeText	Viewer3D	hruler	corba
Ticker	SprAnim	calendar	
HRuler	SndPlay		**ch12**
	MPEGPlay	**ch08**	dbtst
ch02		timer	comcal
billbrd	**ch05**	speller	
calc	Mineswpr		**ch13**
calendar	mcii	**ch09**	vcount
chart	TicTacToe	ViewCal	wrapper
cconvert	Tetris	TextView	Feedback
mortgage			OrderBooks
	ch06	**ch10**	
ch03	VCount	lnum	**ch14**
GetHost	HPSearch	jprop	dbaccess
SMTPmail		rdate	
		rseq	